For Joan & Ted Hall —
This book is most important,
which shows how the US has
long & constantly acted to
destroy Cuba & Russia's
people and sovereignty, among
many peoples & nation.
Ted is the most important whistle blower ever.

Millions of people have struggled in a myriad of ways against oppression, exploitation, repression, racism, genocide, male and national chauvinism committed by the ruling classes since the beginning of their self-styled civilizations several millennia ago. I dedicate this book to all of them. In so doing, I use the words of Father Roy Bourgeois, initiator of the School of Americas Watch:

"It has always been about solidarity…to accompany, and to make another's struggle for justice and equality your struggle."

Ron Ridenour
Oct 21, 2022

Ron Ridenour

THE RUSSIAN PEACE THREAT

Pentagon on Alert

Punto Press

New York

THE RUSSIAN PEACE THREAT

Pentagon on Alert

First electronic and paperback editions published in the United States by
Punto Press Publishing
P.O. Box 943, Brewster, NY 10509 USA
Address all inquiries to admin@puntopress.com

•

ISBN-13: 978-0-9964870-6-1
Russia-United States-Europe-History-Current Events.
I. Title.
Cover illustration with Russian singer Yuliya Samoylova before kremlin, Russian trioka and American eagle and section illustrations by Jette Salling, the author, and Punto Press LLC.
Book cover and interior design by Sarah Edgar • Punto Press Publishing

•

First Edition

Print and eBook versions available at Amazon worldwide and at Ganxy.com

***

False Flag | Strategy of Tension | US Imperialism | Russian History | Fascism | War | Socialism

TABLE OF CONTENTS

INTRODUCTION

THE HOSTILITY the United States of America bears toward Russia must derive from something buried deep in the puritanical chromosomal-genetic make-up of Americans. In any case one wonders who these Russians are that the USA feels it has to encircle and contain, dictate and preach to, and look down on. It is not only fear of potential Russian competition for world domination. Maybe it is also jealousy. Envy for Russia's vast lands. For its great culture. For something Russia has that the USA lacks. The cynic would say, reductively, that it has to do with the great natural gas reserves in Siberia. However that may be, the true source of the perceived Russian Threat is a mystery.

The Cold War deformed immature minds in the West. Not only two generations or more of Americans were brainwashed; a whole world was hoodwinked by Western anti-Russian propaganda. Yet, despite the brainwash and the Cold War, despite what was instilled into the minds of Westerners about Stalin and Communism gone wrong, there were always many people who loved Russia. Russia would always be Russia.

In his beautiful book, *Dictionnaire Amoureux de la Russie* (editions Plon, Paris, 2007), Dominique Fernandez describes the dance as much more than a pastime in Russia. Speaking of the extraordinary ability of the world's greatest dancers, Nijinski and Nureyev, to levitate and hang majestically suspended in the air for several instants, Fernandez writes: "It is a necessity of the (Russian) soul, impatient to break away from the weight of matter, the battle of the spirit against the body." This French writer chose the dance as emblematic of the indomitable spirit of Russians to rise above normal human limitations, a national characteristic shown over and again throughout Russian history as in their wartime suffered victories over Nazi troops at Moscow, Stalingrad and Leningrad. The Italian Slavist and poet, the Communist Angelo Maria Ripellino, strove to compile a history of Russian letters based on the dance, a repetitious and obsessive theme in Russian literature: the dancing feet in Pushkin, the obscure leaps of Lermontov's characters, Blok's serpentine dances, Bely's mountebanks.

In a discussion of Russian values, Fernandez writes: "For the Russian, food, money, vacations are necessities, not values. Books, theater, music, hikes in forests, gathering mushrooms, family solidarity, hospitality, voilà Russian values." Far from undermining these basic values, the Soviet period enhanced them. An important achievement of the Soviet system, Fernandez notes, was low prices for culture enjoyment. Still today people with low incomes fill theaters and opera houses, concert halls and museums. The Soviet state lavished support on artists, a fact recognized by Nureyev, despite his ostensible defection to the West.

Paradoxically, this people of the far north are mentally a people of the South. Russians love Italy, and often resemble Italians, maybe because Russians also have a penchant for disorder, procrastination, inefficiency, qualities more than redeemed by their fantasy, poetry, nobility and confidence in life. In his book, *La Tregua* (The Truce. Abacus, London, 1987), Primo Levi, the great writer from Turin, describes his liberation from Auschwitz by Russian soldiers and the subsequent errant train voyage in the joyous chaos of Russian troops returning home from the war which first carried him north through Poland and Ukraine. Levi and the liberated Italians observed the Red Army soldiers homeward bound in a kind of "disorderly and multicolored biblical migration...." About the Russians' strength, Levi wrote: "It is an interior discipline born from the harmony, reciprocal love and love for their homeland; a discipline that triumphs—precisely because it is interior—over the mechanical and servile discipline of the Germans. It was easy to understand why they prevailed."

At the heart of Russian Communist Internationalism lies an age-old and traditional Russian idea: all-human brotherhood. Real understanding of Russia and Russian Communism is impossible without an awareness of that aspect. Actually Russians are also Europeans, albeit more cosmopolitan than most, much more so than inward-looking Americans. Dostoevsky was the embodiment of the Russian concept of all-human brotherhood. Until the great wars of the twentieth century even nationalism was largely foreign to Russian mentality. Nicolas Berdyaev, existentialist thinker and prolific writer, who broke with Marxism and Bolshevism and left Russia for West Europe in 1922, wrote that Russian Communism was the transformation and deformation of the Russian messianic idea of international brotherhood, in that sense a reflection of the Russian religious mind. Even though history demonstrates that universal brotherhood is utopian, Berdyaev insisted that Soviet Internationalism derived from that ancient, deep-seated Russian idea.

Both Fernandez and Levi mean that many characteristics of the seventy-year Soviet era did not represent a dramatic rupture with Tsarist Russia. Now that enough time has passed and some minds are free of Cold War brainwash, we can see that the Soviet Union was ALSO the continuation of former Russia to a more "modern" state, that is, to the Communist state. Fernandez writes that though the positive traits remaining from the Communist system are gradually being erased today—austerity and moral dignity are ceding to the vulgarity of imports from the West—nonetheless, degradation is slower than elsewhere because Russians have an exceptional force of passivity and resistance. Also because of the enormity of the country and the isolation of entire regions in the long winters thus far it has been saved from the fate of Prague, once one of the world's most beautiful cities, which the thirst for money has transformed into a tourist souk. The essence of today's new Russia is most visible in the big cities, especially in Moscow, a sensation of a kind of void remaining after the disappearance of the old eras.

The qualities and characteristics of Russians must account for their feeling of "differentness" and for the distinctive quality of Russian Communism. Communism elsewhere, Nicolas Berdyaev predicted, would be less integrated than in Russia, more secular and … and most likely it would be more bourgeois.

Bourgeois! The theme has run through Russian letters since the revolutionary period. The artistic work of the great poet Alexander Blok, the lyrical poem *The Twelve*, reflects the people's instinctive hate for the bourgeoisie. The Anglo-Saxon worship of bourgeois dissimulation is distant from Russian mentality. Reserve is considered a false social role. One reason for the initial success of the Bolsheviks around the world was their overt hate for the falsity of the bourgeoisie. Russians mistrust the surface of things. The raw and the crude are more likely to be free of deception. Form exhibits the lie while concealing the truth. Human greatness and a too well turned phrase are suspect. Systems and rules are departures from the human. Russians prefer living life to playing roles. So today, despite the threats, Western hostility and the temptations of capitalist values, this northern people with a southern mentality and a capacity for levitation has returned. The Russians are back, and how!

Ron Ridenour's book, *The Russian Peace Threat: Pentagon on Alert*, about these Russians is destined to endure and inform future readers, writers and researchers about both what has been reported and what truly took place in the one hundred years from the 1917 Russian Revolution until the eruption of the distinct harbingers of the collapse of the US empire in the early twenty-first century. Events often just seem to happen, caught up in the swirl of history. But still, we try to interpret them and to understand. And then, in many cases, take a stand for or against. Understanding is like discovering a new world, like converting to a new faith. Revolt invades your life and everything is different from what it once was. Ridenour's book helps us along the way to first remembering the historical facts so that we can then understand. His new work documents clearly facts about the early years of the Soviet Union's relations with the West, its difficult steps toward socio-political maturity and Communism, and its enormous sacrifices along the way: its defeat of Western intervention during the revolutionary and civil war period; its regulation of state economic planning and the reforms required for the industrialization of the nation; its defeat of the German Nazi military juggernaut at the gates of Russia's major cities and the coup de grace in the ferocious battle in Stalingrad, defeating German invaders and crushing Nazi Germany before the USA even entered the war; and finally the arduous salvation of Russia after the collapse of the USSR under US post-WWII economic firepower and the most treacherous anti-Russian policies which have marked US foreign policy since the early 1900s. Those Western policies continue to determine US-Russian relations today.

Throughout this long work Ridenour recalls and clarifies diverse significant historical details, obscured by time and by Western propaganda, facts that are so easily forgotten or that were never learned: such ignored truths as the importance of the USSR in the defeat of Japan in WWII and the timing of the US use of the atomic bomb in Japan. Not many people are aware of the extent of the destruction of many Japanese cities which the author details here. He points out that the Soviet Union kept its word to help the United States by its intervention against Japan, the decisive reason why Japan was defeated even before the atomic bombs fell. A stunning but little known fact is that in response Operation Unthinkable and Operation Pincher in which first Churchill and later Truman were prepared to launch a surprise war against Soviet forces in Europe, included the potential use of nuclear bombs.

Dealing with the more well-known US capitalist involvement with Fascist Italy and Nazi Germany, Ridenour reveals lurid details concerning the background to that involvement that are overwhelming. The story of the I.G. Farben Concern is a story in itself. Headquartered in its mammoth Frankfurt offices, once the biggest office building in Europe, it was "miraculously" spared by Allied bombing which leveled the city of Frankfurt. I.G. a chemical-pharmaceutical giant closely linked to Rockefeller's Standard Oil and its affiliates during the Nazi era, the war itself and in postwar. It was the producer of the insecticide Zyklon B, used then in the holocaust and was the notorious exploiter of tens of thousands of slave workers. The spared building became General Eisenhower's headquarters in the post-war and the CIA European headquarters and offices of related military intelligence agencies. In the 1990s it was returned to the German government to become the seat of the University of Frankfurt.

The Russian Peace Threat concentrates on revealing Yankee hypocrisy and double speak about Russia. Ridenour says that the degenerate Yeltsin period in the 1990s and the Putin bashing and Russiagate got him involved in this book in the first place: "I think that the main point of my approach to the Soviet Union and Stalin is my conviction based on my own experience and research that neither were ever a threat to world peace, nor to the United States. While the Kissinger approach included the ideology of good is bad and the domino theory, Stalin, on the other hand, kept his agreements with the Yanks and Brits from their three big wartime meetings."

Concerning the crucial 1930s, the author provides a rich chapter dedicated to Spain, almost a mere historical niche for educated people today, offering for example marvelous information about the numbers and fate of American volunteers to the Republican side in the Civil

War on their return home, a chapter in which he underlines George Orwell's important point that the Spanish Civil War was above all a class war.

Ron Ridenour who lived and worked for many years in Cuba presents a realistic view of the revolutionary island state that has exerted such wide influence in all of Latin America. Here his views are not those of the armchair analyst or superficial observer; his vision is more that of Cubans themselves caught up in the swirl of history. He writes of US Operation Mongoose against Cuba:

> *"The CIA was encouraging Cuban exile terrorist groups to be bolder in their sabotage. On August 24, 1962 José Basulto fired a 20mm cannon from the* Juanin *boat just 20 meters from the seaside Horneado de Rosita hotel in Havana. Basulto was best buddies with Che murderer Felix Rodriquez. Basulto would later say, 'I was trained as a terrorist by the United States, in the use of violence to attain goals.' He became all the more renowned in 1995-6 when he flew Brothers to the Rescue (BTTR) civilian aircraft from the CIA Opa-Locka Miami airport over Cuban territory. Cuba lodged complaints against the US government for allowing these aircraft to illegally fly over Cuba, trying to provoke a response. It came on February 24, 1996 when the Cuban Air Force, after several warnings, fired upon two of the three BTTR aircraft shooting them down. Four crewmen died. At the time, I was working in Cuba's international news agency* Prensa Latina, *which Che had started. I recall telling colleagues: 'It was about time Cuba reacted. The U.S. wouldn't have waited for a second to shoot down the first Cuban or Russian flying over its territory.'"*

The author today is impressed with the statesman-like qualities of Russian President Putin: his self-control in avoiding the trap of the US Deep State's provocations concerning Russiagate; his preventing war against Iran and total US war against Syria, while at the same time improving the social-economic lives of the Russian people.

The notes section at the end of some chapters of *The Russian Threat* is magnificent, covering many lesser known aspects of relations between Russia and the United States and, at the same time, the major events of the last century. The vast number of sources used in this work, all now available in one place, is most certainly a remarkable achievement. Thus, we have in our hands a guide, a trove, for anyone writing on these subjects. The author's research, tenacity for the discovery of little known details and his integrity make the book a reliable source for researchers and scholars, and most useful tool for anyone writing about the myriad aspects of US-Russian relations of our times.

—Gaither Stewart
Rome, Summer 2018

AUTHOR'S PREFACE

UNITED STATES' LEADERS HAVE THE GALL to accuse Russia, and the Soviet Union earlier, of being a threat to world peace, of annexing foreign territory, of meddling in the affairs of other nations even the greatest free country in the world, the United States of America. Vladimir Putin himself interfered in the 2016 election so that Hillary Clinton lost the presidency and his friend Donald Trump won.

This is truly Double Speak at its best. From the start of Russia's revolution, the U.S. has attempted to overthrow its governments, starting with an invasion (July 1918). Once defeated, the U.S. has done everything else to badger it, subvert it, surround it and overthrow it. Neither the Soviet Union, Russia, China, Cuba, Vietnam nor North Korea has ever invaded or subverted the United States.

After seeing the magnificent Oliver Stone interviews with Putin and reading the book (*Interviews with Putin*, Skyhorse, 2017), I decided to research just how much aggression the U.S. has committed against Russia over a century. The research included checking its aggression against scores of other countries, especially Cuba. That led to this book. It could be an encyclopedia. What I hope this effort will show is that the truth is the opposite of what the world's most effective governmental-military-intelligence liars tell us.

It is namely the Russians who have prevented world war and any use of nuclear weapons, while it is the leaders of the United States Government-Military-Industrial-Deep State-Media Complex that does all it can to rule the world by using war and threatening world war with nuclear weapons.

What the Wall Street/Deep State conspiracy is doing with Putin/Russiagate is what it did in the Cold War McCarthy period: demonize the peacemakers. I am proud to have known and worked with/for hundreds, thousands of radical/revolutionary activists in several countries in my lifetime. Some of them have been the Yankee Establishment's leading demons, among them: Fidel Castro, Evo Morales, Tomas Borge.

Incidentally, the true Russiagate was a "democratic" capitalist scandal in the late 1990s in which billions of dollars were illicitly "laundered" out of Russia with the assistance of several U.S. banks such as the Bank of New York, owned by the world's largest banking family, the Mellons. You'll read more about how the Mellons and company helped the Nazis become a powerful military force and how they tried to overthrow Franklin Delano Roosevelt dead or alive (chapter eight).

I am neither Leninist, Stalinist, Trotskyist or anarchist, and certainly not a liberal/progressive. I use Marx-Engels social scientific dialectical thinking and historical materialism as a basis for understanding human societies. I take what I see as wisdom and useful action strategies and tactics from all whose goal is to rid us from the inherent evils of capitalism and its imperialism. The main task in my life is to struggle for a truly humanitarian and effective permanent revolutionary course towards a socialist based society embracing Che's vision.

> *"At the risk of seeming ridiculous, let me say that the true revolutionary is guided by a great feeling of love. It is impossible to think of a genuine revolutionary lacking this quality."*

I wish to share a bit of the path I have taken to come to that view. I am reminded that I was asked when lecturing during a 1993 Cuba solidarity tour what motivated me to become an activist. This is what came to mind.

CONSCIENCE

A six year-old boy straddles a worn stuffed upholstered armchair.

"Giddy-up, giddy-up," the young cowboy orders his palomino as he rocks back and forth coaxingly, left hand gripping the reins. His leather chaps and felt Stetson flapping in the imaginary wind, he scoots across the wide range firing his six-shooter after the bad Indians. Just like his favorite star Roy Rogers and his horse Trigger, the fearless boy is protecting his people against the savages.

"BANG! BANG! Gotja. You're dead."

CRACK! CRACK!

The cowboy stops dead in his tracks.

"That sounds like real bullets", the boy, his big brown eyes blinking widely, says warily to himself.

He dismounts and walks hesitantly to the smudgy window facing a dirty Newark street. From the second-floor apartment, he sees a human figure on the sidewalk across the street. A boy is sprawled face down. A red liquid oozes from his back. An apple rolls slowly from his hand. A large man in blue uniform hurries up to the boy. He holds a pistol in his hand as he looks down upon the boy.

"Are they playing cowboys and Indians too", the little cowboy asks himself frightfully?

Later that day, Grandpa Tony came home and the boy heard him whispering to Grandmother Nana.

"Radio news reported that a policeman saw the boy steal an apple from Abe's store. The policeman says he yelled for the boy to stop but the kid ran. The policeman grabbed his pistol and shouted, 'Halt or I'll shoot.' The boy ran faster. The policeman fired a warning shot up in the air, then another. Apparently there was some sort of disturbance up in the air, which the bullet hit, and it ended in the boy's spine. He was just eight years old, not much bigger than Ronnie."

It was too difficult for me to comprehend, but I did understand that the boy would not play cowboys and Indians anymore. That frightened me. I could have been that boy. My young mind puzzled and my heart skipping, Grandma Nana told me to forget all about it. What happened to him couldn't happen to me. After all, I was not a thief nor, most significantly, was I black. I felt relief, yet shame. That day I learned I was privileged: I was white, never to be black.

Now, I think of what Nina Simone said when she left the United States behind her. She could not understand nor accept a destiny as a victim for something so absurd and misanthropic as racism. I was trapped in the color barrier too, despite the fact that I was born with the "dominating" color.

Before I understood what this meant, what the essence of United States racism and imperialism is all about, I joined the U.S. Air Force to fight the "commies". Posted to a radar site in Japan, I witnessed approved segregated barracks at the Yankee base, and the imposition of racism in Japanese establishments frequented by white G.I.s. I protested by entering a "black GI bar". The next day, I was tortured by my white "compatriots". Five of them held me down naked, sprayed DDT aflame over my pubic hairs, and then held me under snow. The base commander did nothing about this. He even allowed them to wear baseball caps, even when in uniform, with the letters "KKK" engraved. This was a major factor that led me to question American Morality.

RESPONSIBILITY

In shame and anger at what the U.S. does against peoples at home and around the globe, I took responsibility. My first demonstration was in Los Angeles, April 1961, against the Bay of Pigs invasion. The Cuban revolution, which sought equality and an end to racism, inspired me to become an activist. I helped build the budding student and anti-war movements just forming when I entered college, as well as participating in the civil rights movement and solidarity with Cuba. I joined the "Fair Play for Cuba" committee. I still carry the card.

I was on my way to Cuba with a buddy in a Volkswagen bug when we saw headlines in Managua that the Cuban Missile Crisis had begun. The streets were empty except for heavily armed troops. Huge black newspaper headlines blared: "**US Embargo of Russian Ships on Way to Cuba**".

We drove further from Nicaragua to our destiny, Costa Rica, from where we were to find a boat to take us to Cuba. We hoped to join the revolution in some romantic way and study at a university. Before long, however, there was an unusual national guard shooting at 5000 demonstrators in Cartago. Four demonstrators were killed and 30 wounded. Although we had not been there, we were soon arrested and jailed in isolation cells because we had come to the city the following day and spoken with survivors. The government needed a scapegoat and we were perfect. We had driven with a pistol for protection on Central American roads. We had some Marxist books, and I wore a black beard. We were on our way to Communist Cuba, and I had a loud mouth.

The U.S. embassy December 6, 1962 report to the Department of State explains the circumstances.

> *"Two American citizens and self-confessed communists were arrested on November 29 by Costa Rican authorities in the wake of the riot in Cartago on November 24...The two men had in their possession an automatic pistol, several knives, and a large amount of communist literature [in our rented room]. After several days of questioning by the local authorities, the two were deported to Miami on December 5. Their detention received widespread publicity in the Costa Rican press with Costa Rican officials charging them as being agents of international communism responsible in part at least for the blood affair in Cartago."*

This document led the FBI and CIA to classify me on Security Index with a concluding judgment at the end of their dossier reports, "RIDENOUR HAS HAD IN HIS POSSESSION IN THE PAST A .45 AUTOMATIC AND SHOULD BE CONSIDERED ARMED AND DANGEROUS."

I never used the pistol and eventually gave it away. Eighteen months later I was in Mississippi, one of nearly 1000 volunteer activists on the Freedom Summer campaign to force the state to allow black people the right simply to vote. I was arrested in Moss Point where I worked as the project's administrator and media person. This hit the local and national media. Senator James Eastland, Mississippi's chief racist and warring politician, seized the opportunity to use my arrest and membership in the Communist party to smear the entire campaign for equality. Only one other activist was a member of the C.P., my roommate.

"**Eastland Names Specific Communist Agents or Sympathizers Agitating in Mississippi: Senator Charges Heavy Infiltrations Throughout Nation; Man Arrested in Moss Point is revealed to have been kicked out of Costa Rica**" read the headlines in the "Mississippi Press Register", on July 23, 1964. Similar headlines ran around the country.

A phone call from one of the leading persons of the civil rights movement asking me if this were true, made me feel like a fool, a wrecker of our movement. While he was pissed off, he also said that I had every right to be with the movement despite being a communist. Non-exclusion was a major principle of the Students for Non-Violent Coordinating Committee (SNCC). Great, but I was a problem too. Nevertheless, when I came to our usual mass meeting that evening, I was greeted by a standing ovation not only from the young but from the elders as well. Nearly all at the meeting were local black people, many of whom housed us to their peril.

When the summer was over, I returned to Los Angeles and worked as SNCC's coordinator there for a time. I continued to act against the War in Vietnam, supported the Black Panther Party, and other liberation movements inside the monster as well as revolutionary movements throughout Latin America. One of those struggles was the retaking of the South Dakota Pine Ridge Indian Reservation led by the American Indian Movement (AIM).

This was where the Wounded Knee massacre had happened December 29, 1890 when government cavalry mowed down hundreds of Lakota Sioux with machine gun fire. Between 150 and 300 were murdered, over 50 wounded (mostly women and children). On February 27, 1973, AIM activists allied with their people on the reservation and occupied the reservation town for 71 days.

I drove to the encampment surrounded by U.S. Federal Marshals and FBI, and their Indian Uncle Tom lackeys led by tribal president Richard Wilson. As the political reporter for one of the best and widest circulating "underground" weeklies, "The Los Angeles Free Press", I wrote articles and helped the liberationists with their PR. I was beside one of the fighters when he got wounded. In all, three liberationists were killed and 13 wounded; one U.S. Marshall was shot and paralyzed.

The main objective demanding the government simply comply with its more than 100 treaties with Native Americans was not achieved, court cases were squashed. One of the three killed was Ray Robinson, an Alabaman civil rights worker who had been buried on the reservation, which the FBI confirmed in 2014. The other two were Native Americans whose names I cannot find.

This struggle received wide support, including Marlon Brando's refusal to accept the Oscar for best male actor in "The Godfather". He sent Apache Seechen Little Feather to speak for him at the Academy Awards. But conditions on Wounded Knee did not improve. Richard Wilson's "goon squad" murdered 60 fellow Native Americans on the reservation over the next three years.

The Watergate Affair was unfolding at this time, and at its conclusion the government made it easier to obtain one's dossiers from the dozen or so state security agencies through the Freedom of Information Act. I received about 1000 partially censored pages mainly from the FBI, but also the CIA and military intelligence agencies. They let me know there were more files but they were classified and would not be released.

I was listed in three categories, Rabble Rouser, Agitator Index, and Security Index. I felt pride in being one of those 4000 persons whom Richard Nixon had plans to round up and incarcerate in concentration camps. We dangerous persons were on the government's Security Index.

Secret agents followed me, noted the places and dates when I moved.

They noted my remarks at meetings where they had their spies; investigated my very loyal parents and my wife. The FBI visited at least two of my work places to speak with the owners or leaders. That got me fired from the "Riverside Press Enterprise" where I was an editor, and had just been promoted.

One of the Establishment's intelligence agencies, probably the Los Angeles Police Department's red squad, even fabricated my 1971 income tax return form, claiming I had been a spy for the Army. The Pentagon had supposedly paid me $17, 784.54 in wages and $8,634.21 for "other compensation", out of which I paid $3,201.21 in taxes. My job then, in fact, was at the "Los Angeles News Advocate".

Copies of this forgery were sent to the alternative media in Los Angeles area, I think there were four or five, and the anti-war and peace groups with a cover letter written by hand: "*I think you'll know what to do with this information about a pig agent. A concerned friend.*"

Had my colleagues, comrades, and other activists read this at a time when the various peoples movements were infiltrated by spies and agent provocateurs it could have ruined my reputation and effectiveness. Fortunately a reporter at another newspaper came to our office the night before his editor would have run an article about this "expose" with the cover letter. He asked me about the document. I was appalled and worried, but I always keep copies of important documents and writings. I retrieved my actual tax forms thus disproving the forgery. I was able to convince the social media and peace organizations who read the documents that it was a frame-up.

This occurred when the city and state were trying to put me in jail for something. I had two court cases running, one of them dealt with the beating of Ron Kovic, the Vietnam War veteran confined to a wheelchair who wrote the book *Born on the Fourth of July*, which is his real birth date. Oliver Stone made a film (1989) of the book, a biographical portrait of Kovic, which reveals how sick and criminal the Vietnam War was. Tom Cruise played Ron Kovic who had a cameo performance. I had participated in and reported on several days of picketing in front of the Nixon reelection campaign office in Los Angeles. Jane Fonda and Tom Hayden were well known activist participants as well. Two plainclothes cops (Joe Robinson and Mike Moran) came off the picket line after uniformed police declared our peaceful demonstration "illegal". They beat Kovic with blackjacks in his wheel chair as he shouted for us to continue picketing. This was a provocation to excite the crowd, causing some to rush the cops so they could declare us the aggressors—assaulting policemen in the line of duty, for which one can get a year or more in prison. And that's just what happened. Just short of throwing my body against the police I took photographs of the confrontation and at that moment another plainclothed undercover cop (Stanley Frugard) called out to uniformed police to arrest me. Of course, my film was destroyed and I was charged with interfering and assault. A defense organization was formed and even Establishment media supported me, including with editorials criticizing the police—something unimaginable today. Someone on our side spoke with Frugard's ex-wife who disliked the man. She said that he had told her I was a major target for him over a five year period. She later divorced him.

I lost the trial. The judge sentenced me to a year. The other activist case cost me six months, of which I served four and one-half. But media support helped me win the Kovic case on appeal.

I continued to fight for peace, equality and socialism in the United States until I met a Danish woman, Grethe, who inspired me to move to her country where we married. It was 1980 and the movements had died as Ronald Reagan took the warring reins. I hoped to continue the struggle for world peace from Denmark but eventually realized there was little chance since the vast majority would not lift a finger to risk such undertakings. Indifferent and too well fed, they look up to the U.S. for leadership and "protection". That has been my experience for 28 years of existence in Denmark. Whenever I told a Dane where I was born once asked, I was always met with a happy face and told how a relative lived there. I didn't want to hear about how glad they were for "god's own country", so I began answering thusly: "I was born in the devil's own land", or "the most war hungry country"—that put an end to that topic and maybe any other.

I have taken many trips abroad to participate in struggles and to write. I've spent months in Iceland, Nicaragua, Venezuela, Bolivia, Mexico, Spain, India, and eight years in Cuba.

Twenty-five years after trying to reach Cuba, I finally made it in 1988. My book in solidarity with the Nicaraguan Sandinista movement, *Yankee Sandinistas* [Curbstone Press, 1986], motivated the Cuban

Ministry of Culture to invite me to come and work for Cuba. I was overjoyed. My first task was to write a book about 26 Cubans and one Italian, who the CIA thought it had recruited to spy upon Cuba. The Cuban government had just brought them out to the public to show how the U.S. acts to subvert and destroy the country. It was foolish of the CIA to think that it could buy them, but racism is so deeply entrenched in the Establishment that they view any and all poor and especially dark-skinned humans as dollar corruptible.

I started working for the book publisher Editorial José Martí, and later for foreign news agency Prensa Latina. My work places and editors were so flexible that I was allowed to travel over and around the whole nation on all means of transportation from bicycle to ships. I did a lot of volunteer work in agriculture, a factory, a building brigade and on the decks and engine rooms of five tankers delivering oil around the country, and container ships, including a long journey to and from Europe.

My first of six books about Cuba, "*Backfire, The CIA's Biggest Burn*", came out in 1991. It portrays "the legitimate national security function performed by Cuba's state security". By infiltrating the CIA, Cuba was able to avert many planned terrorist actions—not all, however, as attested by the deaths of 158 victims to several CIA-induced chemical-biological warfare operations and two thousand others murdered outright or as bystanders in sabotage operations. "Backfire's" account of Cuba's double agents' "tenacious work is historical and political testimony of the United States government's arrogance and underestimation of the Cuban people."

"*Backfire*", I am proud to say, has been recognized by the CIA. Military counterintelligence officer Chris Simmons lists it as recommended reading. He classifies it under literature by "Cuban Intelligence Sympathizers" (http://cubanintelligence.com/?page_id=17). Chris Simmons currently has two websites, one of which is https://cubaconfidential.wordpress.com . Simmons posted a September 3, 2013 "Washington Post" article by David Fahrenthold, "Grounded TV Martí Plane A Monument to the Limits of American Austerity". An editor's note explains how Cuba's Communication Ministry mocked the subversive TV (and Radio) program. It declared, on March 27, 1990, that it would never be heard or seen by Cubans.

"To capitalize upon its espionage success [the ministry] invited domestic and foreign journalists to attend a ceremony marking Havana's jamming of TV Martí. Leftist US journalist Ron Ridenour attended the event and was actually selected to give the order to jam TV Martí. Within minutes of going on the air, Havana had neutralized TV Martí," reads the editor note.

Simmons also applauds himself for having been central in "identification, investigation, and debriefing of convicted Cuban spy, Ana Belen Montes". Ana is one of the bravest fighters for humanity. She worked 16 years for the Defense Intelligence Agency as a senior analyst, specialist in Cuba. She was, however, a double agent for Cuba. She was so good at her solidarity work that CIA director George Tenet personally awarded her with a certificate of distinction.

This brave woman was arrested for espionage in 2001. At her trial the next year, she told the sentencing judge: "*I obeyed my conscience rather than the law. I believe our government's policy towards Cuba is cruel and unfair, profoundly unneighborly, and I felt morally obligated to help the island defend itself from our efforts to impose our values and our political system on it.*"

Ana did not accept payment for her patriotic work for humanity. She followed Che's morality of the "power of example". For that, the amoral United States government considers her to be "the most dangerous spy you've never heard of". The U.S. government has her incarcerated in top-security isolation in Carswell Federal Medical Center, Fort Worth, Texas—a prison for mentally disturbed female criminals. She is in a torture chamber, and is not deranged. Here is a list of her conditions:

- Prohibited to inquire about her health or reasons for her detention in a center for the mentally ill.
- A prohibition on the receipt of packages.
- Letters sent to her are returned by registered post to the sender.
- She is not allowed to associate with other inmates.
- She is not allowed to make or receive phone calls.
- She is not allowed to read newspapers, magazines or watch TV.
- She is not allowed visits from friends.

Read Susan Babbitt's piece at: https://www.counterpunch.org/2017/05/23/the-most-dangerous-spy-youve-never-heard-of-ana-belen-montes/.

"Ana Belén Montes could have dismissed what she knew to be true about the US war on democracy. She is, in the end, a hero just because of what she believed, because she has believed it, and because she continues to do so."

"Years after she was caught spying for Cuba, Montes remains defiant. '***Prison is one of the last places I would have ever chosen to be in, but some things in life are worth going to prison for,***' Montes writes in a 14-page handwritten letter to a relative." She has no regrets.

"Montes spied for 17 years, patiently, methodically. She passed along so many secrets about her colleagues — and the advanced eavesdropping platforms that American spooks had covertly installed in Cuba — that intelligence experts consider her among *the most harmful spies in recent memory.*" http://www.washingtonpost.com/sf/feature/wp/2013/04/18/ana-montes-did-much-harm-spying-for-cuba-chances-are-you-havent-heard-of-her/?utm_term=.287df91fe25f

I am happy to say for the first time publicly that I also offered information to the Cuban security agency about so-called Cuban "dissidents" who worked for U.S. imperialism. I did so, however, without risking any of the severe punishment that Ana Montes could expect, and has suffered.

Me at helm of "Seaweed" tanker delivering oil at various ports.

During my years in Cuba, I met my first Russians and became friends with Veronica Spasskaya and her teenage son Andrei. Veronica worked as a translator at the publishing house where I worked for four years. She was an expert on the Russian poet Alexander Pushkin and a constant worrier. She told me that her country's long history of wars, class struggles, and famine affected all Russians, and was a major cause why the people, and most of their leaders, do not seek war but stand for world peace regardless of political or ideological attachment.

My book opens with astronaut Yuri Gagarin, comparing his peaceful path with that of the United States invading Cuba. The early chapters show how the U.S. tried to destroy the Cuban revolution—the Bay of Pigs, Cuban Missile Crisis, covert murder and sabotage operations. US-Soviet relations and near world war are involved tangentially through US-Cuban relations. Several chapters follow describing how the U.S. tried (eventually successfully) to destroy the Russian/Soviet revolution. I present some important internal events but I do not delve deeply into internal Soviet conflicts rather concentrate on the all important matter of world war or world peace.

The third part deals with what has been happening since the fall of the Soviet Union, beginning with U.S./Yeltsin's rape of the progress made before, followed by the sovereign leadership of Vladimir Putin. Chapter eighteen, albeit long, is but a summary of how much blood the United States has shed throughout much of the world in its rather brief tenure as the World's Military Empire. The conclusion—American Exceptionalism—touches on the possible end of the human species and much of planet IF ordinary people, the working classes, don't soon wake up and fight.

[This book has taken a year of trying months of research and writing—many tears, sweat sticking to my armpits, knots in my shoulders, gnawed fingernails, butterflies rumbling in my stomach—so many murders, so many tortured simply for the insatiable greed of a few men and a handful of women, and the many fools who the rich force or buy to commit the violence for them. During this process, I came to realize what have been the most important decisions I made that have guided me since my awakening in the early 60s: 1) seek the truth; 2) tell the truth; 3) do not be tied to any employer, media or otherwise, in which

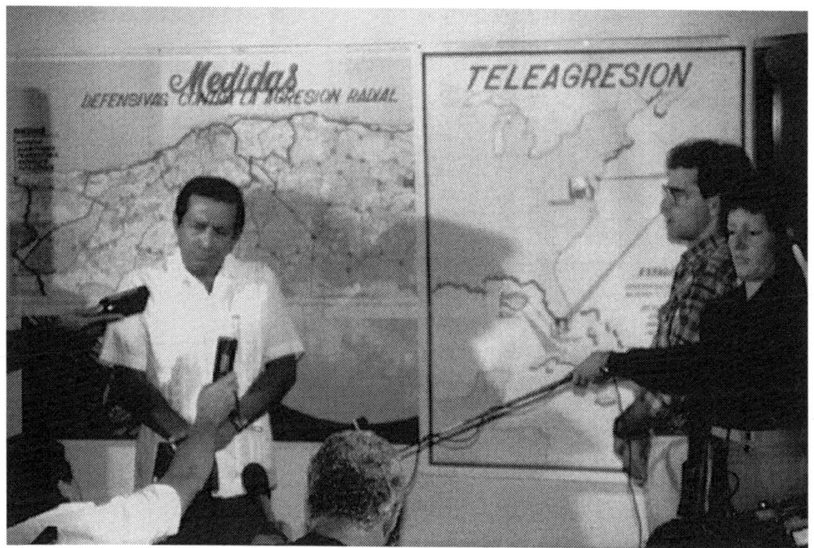

"Teleaggression" This is the night Simons speaks about. Here is Cuba's Communication Minister addressing journalists at the beginning and ending of TV Martí in Cuba. I was happily chosen to sound the jamming alarm, along with a Sandinista journalist.

I would be required to write or perform in any way against my own conscience and knowledge (something journalist Wilfred Burchett taught me—see chapters 10 and 12); 4) struggle for justice, equality and peace.]

To see all my books and many writings check out my website: http://ronridenour.com/index.htm http://ronridenour.com/books.htm); contact: ronrorama@gmail.com

—Ron Ridenour

HYMN TO FREEDOM

When every heart joins every heart and together yearns for liberty
That's when we'll be free

When every hand joins every hand and together molds our destiny
That's when we'll be free

Any hour any day, the time soon will come when men will live in dignity
That's when we'll be free, we will be

When every man joins in our song and together singing harmony
That's when we'll be free

—OSCAR PETERSON, 1962.
(Civil Rights Movement anthem;
it could well be an anti-war anthem too)

Ron Ridenour

THE RUSSIAN PEACE THREAT

RUSSIAN PEACE THREAT

Pentagon on Alert

Part I:
THE GREAT CAPITALIST-SOCIALIST DIVIDE

CHAPTER 1

Russia Sends Yuri Gagarin Around the World for Peace: US Invades Cuba

"WE SAW YURI as a national and world hero, a great human being. Yuri was very Russian. He was well received in Copenhagen during his long travels. We didn't know much about these travels with a peace message but we knew he wanted to protect the earth that he saw from above," Ambassador Mikjail Vanin told me during an interview in Copenhagen (2017).

The Russian ambassador to Denmark learned about Yuri's orbiting the earth and his humanitarian vision as a school boy.

***

Yuri with a peace dove on his world wide tour

Yuri Alexeyevich Gagarin was born in Klushino, a small village west of Moscow, in 1934. He was the third of four children and spent his childhood on a collective farm where his father, Alexey Ivanovich Gagarin, worked as a carpenter and bricklayer. His mother, Anna Timofeyevna Gagarina, was a milkmaid.

When Yuri was seven the Nazis invaded the Soviet Union. They confiscated the Gagarin's home and they "shipped his teenage siblings to slave labor camps and they did not return until 1945. Yuri and [brother] Boris sabotaged the German garrison in Klushino, scattering broken glass on roads, mixing chemicals in recharging tank batteries and pushing potatoes up exhaust pipes. One occupier tried to hang Boris from an apple tree with a woolen scarf, but his parents were able to rescue him," wrote Paul Rodgers, April 2, 2011 in *The Independent*. (http://www.independent.co.uk/news/science/yuri-gagarin-the-man-who-fell-to-earth-2257505.html)

> *"Amid the horrors, one event stood out for Yuri: a dogfight between two Soviet Yaks and a pair of Messerschmitts, ending in a one-all draw. The Soviet pilot landed near Klushino and the villagers rushed to help. Later, a rescue plane arrived to pick up the downed man and Gagarin scavenged fuel for it. The next morning, the airmen awoke to find him staring at them, entranced. He was still watching as they set fire to the wreck and took off in the rescue plane."*

Yuri excelled in mathematics and physics, and made aircraft models. After the war, he went to trade and industrial schools in Saratov where he joined a flying club. He made his first solo flight in 1955. After

The Yuri Gagarin Home-Museum in Klushino

Yuri with his daughters Yelena and Galina

school, he joined the Air Force and learned to fly MiGs. Upon graduating from flight school in November 1957, he married Valentina ("Valy") Ivanovna Goryacheva. They soon had two daughters: Yelena and Galina.

Gagarin was sent on fighter pilot missions, however he really wanted to become a cosmonaut. Along with 3,000 others, he made an application to be the first Soviet cosmonaut.

He made high marks in the extensive physical and psychological testing while maintaining a calm demeanor as well as his charming sense of humor. Yuri was chosen to be the first man into space because of these skills. His short stature helped too since the capsule of the space craft Vostok 1 was small. (https://www.thoughtco.com/yuri-gagarin-first-man-in-space-1779362)

"As the cold war reached freezing point, the USA and the Soviet Union entered the space race both hoping to be the first nation to conquer space. In 1957 the Soviets, led by the extraordinarily talented rocket scientist Korolyev, launched the first manmade satellite (sputnik) into orbit. This was soon followed by the first animal in orbit with Laika the dog. Laika sadly never returned to earth but in 1960 the heroic dogs Belka and Strelka successfully orbited the earth for a day and returned safely, laying the final grounds for the first human space flight" wrote Louise Whitworth. (https://www.inyourpocket.com/moscow/Yuri-Gagarin_72055f)

The 27-year old cosmonaut's space flight lasted just 108 minutes—enough time to orbit the earth once. He reached an orbital speed of 27,400 kilometers per hour. In his first message to mission control he exclaimed: "The Earth is blue...How wonderful. It is amazing…so beautiful."

Upon re-entering the earth's atmosphere he encountered serious technical problems that could have meant death had he not ejected himself from the capsule. From 7,000 meters above the earth Gagarin free-fell several kilometers before opening his parachute and floated down to the ground. Protected by his space suit he was able to withstand the air temperatures of -30c degrees.

English journalist Rodgers describe a strange encounter:

"Anna Takhtarova and her granddaughter, Rita, were weeding potatoes near the village of Smelovka on 12 April, 1961 when a man in a strange orange suit and a bulging white helmet approached across the field. The forest warden's wife crossed herself but the girl was intrigued. 'I'm a friend, comrades. A friend,' shouted the young man, removing his headgear. Takhtarova looked at him curiously. 'Can it be that you have come from outer space,' she asked. 'As a matter of fact, I have,' replied Yuri Gagarin.

"This story of Gagarin's return to Earth after orbiting the planet, the most important flight since the Wright brothers' at Kitty Hawk, was widely disseminated, not least because of its symbolism—a Soviet hero being welcomed home by his fellow peasants, a wise mother and a child of the future. It is probably true in essence, though the details changed with each retelling."

Back in Moscow, Yuri Gagarin was honored with a six-hour long parade on Red Square. Within days, he embarked on a trip around the world talking passionately about the wonders of the earth. These are excerpts from his key message in 30 countries over two years:

> *"Circling the earth in the orbital space, I marveled at the beauty of our planet. I saw clouds and their light shadows on the distant dear earth... I enjoyed the rich color spectrum of the earth. It is surrounded by a light blue halo that gradually darkens, becoming turquoise, dark blue, violet, and finally coal black. People of the world! Let us safeguard and enhance this beauty—not destroy it!"*

On the day that the Soviet Union ushered in a new world, the United States President John F. Kennedy held a news conference in which he flatly lied that his government was planning any violent action against Cuba. "First, I want to say that there will not be, under any conditions, an intervention in Cuba by the United States Armed Forces."

"The basic issue of Cuba is not one between the United States and Cuba. It is between the Cubans themselves. And I intend to see that we adhere to this principle."

The next day, April 13, CIA Operation 40 was launched from Guatemala. 1400 paramilitaries, mostly Cuban exiles and a handful of US Americans, sailed on U.S. boats to Cuba. The totally unprovoked invasion was underway. The same day, Secretary of State Dean Rusk (1961-9) told reporters, "The American people are entitled to know whether we are intervening in Cuba or intend to do so in the future. The answer to that question is no. What happens in Cuba is for the Cuban people themselves to decide." (1)

In July, Gagarin's worldwide peace mission tour found him in England for five days. His early experience as a steelworker stood him in good stead. Rodgers wrote about that visit:

Yuri "'received an invitation from the Amalgamated Union of Foundry Workers in Manchester,' says Gurbir Singh, an astronomy blogger who is writing a book on the spaceman's visit. [*Yuri Gagarin in London and Manchester: A Smile that Changed the World*]. The trip included the union hall, Marx's Highgate grave and an audience with the Queen."

Singh concluded that Gagarin's visit left an impression that thermonuclear war could be prevented.

A son of worker-peasants, Gagarin spread their message of environmentalism, of unity and peace while United States was invading and murdering Cubans, and politicians such as the Democratic Party congressman Victor Anfuso was telling people:

> *"I want to see our country mobilized to a wartime basis, because we are at war. I want to see our schedules cut in half. I want to see what NASA says it is going to do in ten years done in five. And I want to see some first coming out of NASA, such as the landing on the Moon."*

Anfuso had served in the Second World War in the CIA's predecessor intelligence service, the Office of Strategic Services. While his Sicilian-rooted language style was less elegant than the Camelot President John Kennedy, they were in agreement that the Russians' space achievement was a call to war for the Greatest Democratic Country in the World. To the battleships for winning the space race! Who comes first to the moon gets to build satellites for war. (2)

Fifty years later after Gagarin's orbiting, the cynicism towards Russia persists even among America's elite.

> *"Soviet leader Nikita Khrushchev seized on the propaganda value of Gagarin's coup in beating the United States into space, sending him on 'missions of peace' around the world, to meet figures including Britain's Queen. 'This achievement exemplifies the genius of the Soviet people and the strong force of socialism,' the Kremlin crowed in a statement at the time."* (https://phys.org/news/2011-04-russia-years-gagarin-triumph.html)

This sarcastic take on Gagarin's "peace missions" being "crowed" about by Kremlin leaders comes from *Science X* and its US-based website. *Science X* prides itself on being read monthly by 1.75 million well educated "sophisticated" readers, especially scientists and researchers. Even these Americans can't see through the jingoistic imperialist contempt for propagandizing for peace. Bear in mind that propaganda is not necessarily synonymous with lying, rather "to propagate", "to cause to increase the number" of supporters to the views presented. My writing here, and generally, is propaganda. I hope it is effective propaganda for a good cause: for peace and justice. That is what communist propaganda also was meant to be, not that communism has always been so practiced but that it has that vision. At the very least, it is a vision that humanity could and should embrace. Certainly more so than the vision of its counterpart, the imperialism and capitalism fostered by the United States and its vassal states in Europe and elsewhere. Their creed is greed: profit for profit's sake. As Wall Street stockbroker Gordon Gekko roared: "Greed is Good!" (3) And add to this the system's core foundation: selfish individualism.

When Gagarin had time, he participated as a member of the USSR Supreme Soviet (national legislature), kept training for flights, trained crews, visited plants, studied, and maintained a family life. Yuri was a religious man. He offered to rebuild the Church of Christ the Savior in Moscow, which had been blown up during the Stalin era. The church was rebuilt after the Soviet epoch. (http://yurigagarin50.org/history/gagarins-life and http://tass.com/science/868892.)

Due to his high profile, many were concerned that if Yuri traveled to space again he might die. So, Soviet authorities tried to prevent him from taking part in further space flights. Gagarin was forced to compromise and became the head of the cosmonaut's training center, and he re-trained as a fighter pilot. At the age of 34, he perished on March 27, 1968 in a fatal training flight outside of Moscow at Star City. His instructor, Vladimir Serugin, died with him. They might have saved themselves by bailing out, but seeing that their MiG-15 would crash right into a village, Yuri maneuvered the aircraft outside the village before it crashed.

Yuri Gagarin will be remembered for being the first man to orbit the earth, of course, but also for his many humanistic qualities. Maybe the peace tour Russia's leaders sent him on was propaganda, but isn't advocating for world peace good propaganda? Did the U.S. government send any of its astronauts on such missions?

US American artist Rockwell Kent beautifully expressed what Yuri was and what he stood for.

> *"Dear Soviet friends your Yuri is not only yours. He belongs to all mankind. The door to space which he opened, this door which the USSR and Socialism opened, is open for all of us. But*

for that, peace is necessary. Peace between nations. Peace between ourselves. Let the world celebrate the anniversary of Yuri's flight as a Universal Peace Day. Let that day be celebrated all over the world with music and dances, songs and laughter, as a worldwide holiday of happiness. Let that day be in every town and city square, where young and old gather and let their faces be illuminated with the same happiness that the photographs of people in the Soviet Union show how the Soviet people are happy and proud of the accomplishment of Yuri Gagarin." (http://www.northstarcompass.org/nsc9904/gagarin.htm)

Notes:

1. "The President's News Conference of April 12, 1961," John F. Kennedy, The Public Papers of the Presidents, 1961. (Washington: United States Government Printing Office, 1962, page 259). And "Text of Secretary Rusk's News Conference, Including Observations on Cuba," New York Times, 18 April 1961.

2. When the Russians were able to establish their major space station, February 20, 1986, and when Mikhail Gorbachev was General Secretary of the Communist Party of the Soviet Union, they named it MIR (meaning "Peace" and "World"). That was one month after Gorbachev proposed a 15-year abolition of nuclear weapons.

   MIR was the first modular space station and the longest lasting space station, 1986 to 2001. It had a greater mass than any previous spacecraft, 130,000 kilos. The station served as a laboratory in which crews conducted experiments in biology, physics, astronomy, meteorology and spacecraft systems with the goal of developing technologies required for permanent occupation of space.

   MIR was the first continuously inhabited long-term research station in orbit and held the record for the longest continuous human presence in space at 3,644 days. It holds the record for the longest single human spaceflight. Valeri Polyakov spent 437 days on the station between 1994 and 1995. MIR was occupied twelve and a half years out of its fifteen-year lifespan, having the capacity to support a resident crew of three, or larger crews for short visits. https://en.wikipedia.org/wiki/Mir; anhttps://en.wikipedia.org/wiki/List_of_space_stations

   Russia launched its first space station on April 19, 1971. Salyut reentered earth on October 11. NASA's first station, Skylab, was launched, May 14, 1973.

3. From Oliver Stone's great 1987 film "Wall Street". Stone directed and co-wrote the script, influenced by socialists Upton Sinclair, Sinclair Lewis and Victor Hugo. Ironically, according to Wikipedia, several people were inspired by the film to become Wall Street stockbrokers.

   Gordon Gekko's speech to stockholders concludes:

   "The point is, ladies and gentleman, that greed – for lack of a better word – is good. Greed is right. Greed works. Greed clarifies, cuts through, and captures the essence of the evolutionary spirit. Greed, in all of its forms – greed for life, for money, for love, knowledge – has marked the upward surge of mankind. And greed – you mark my words – will not only save Teldar Paper, but that other malfunctioning corporation called the USA."

CHAPTER 2
Bay of Pigs Invasion: Retake Cuba

VICE-PRESIDENT RICHARD NIXON met with Fidel Castro three months after the popular guerrilla forces overthrew the U.S. government-Mafia backed repressive regime of Fulgencio Batista. Nixon's April 19, 1959 assessment of the charismatic revolutionary leader led his government to attempt to murder him and to overthrow the people's government.

Nixon said: "Castro is incredibly naive about communism, or is under communist discipline." "It was this almost slavish subservience to prevail on majority opinion—the voice of the mob—rather than his naive attitude toward Communism…which concerned me most in evaluating what kind of a leader he might eventually turn out to be." (1)

A principal person involved in CIA efforts to be rid of Castro and retake Cuba was Air Force General and Deputy Director of the CIA (DDCI) Charles P. Cabell. He noted in November 1959 that while Castro was not a communist he allowed free opportunity to the Communist party in Cuba to grow and spread its message. By December plans were already being tossed around between high ranking officials that called for overthrowing the government, including assassinating Fidel, his brother Raul, and Che Guevara. Due to the United States' fear of repercussions from the United Nations, plans were kept at the highest level of secrecy. "Plausible deniability" was and is the key focal point in United States clandestine-covert practice.

The first known attempt on Fidel's life occurred just one month after he led the victory. On February 2, U.S. citizen Allen Mayer was arrested for that effort. He may not have been under U.S. control, which might have made its first murder attempt in July. One man who probably knew of the U.S.'s first attempt said it took place a bit later. "The Central Intelligence Agency flew a two-man assassination team into Cuba in an unsuccessful attempt to kill Premier Fidel Castro, a retired Air Force colonel said today," wrote *NYT* April 30, 1975. (http://www.nytimes.com/1975/04/30/archives/cia-plot-to-kill-castro-described-agency-flew-2-assassins-to-cuba.html?mcubz=1)

"The colonel, L.Fletcher Prouty, said that in 'late 1959 or early 1960', while he was serving in the Defense Department's Office of Special Operations, he handled a C.I.A. request for a small specially equipped Air Force plane that was used to land two Cuban exiles on a road near Havana."

"The two exiles were 'equipped with a high-powered rifle and telescopic sights' and 'knew how to get to a building in Havana which overlooked a building where Castro passed daily,' Colonel Prouty, now an official with Amtrak, said in a telephone interview.

"The plane, an L-28 "heliocourier," returned safely to Eglin Air Force Base in Florida, he said, but the 'Cuban exiles as far as I know were picked up between where they were left off and Havana.'" ...Prouty said one of them was Oscar Spijo, and the plane was flown by CIA 'mercenaries'".

In 1975, the Church Committee (US Select Senate Committee to Study Government Operations with Respect to International Activities) substantiated eight attempts by the CIA to assassinate Fidel. Colonel Prouty was a Committee witness. He asserted that the CIA also stood behind a coup d'état to stop President Kennedy from taking control of the agency after the Bay of Pigs.

No one in history comes close to surviving as many assassination attempts as did Fidel. The Cuban chief of counterintelligence General Fabián Escalante was responsible for protecting his president. Escalante estimated that between 1959 and 2000, the U.S. concocted 638 plots to murder Fidel. When Fidel died, England's Channel 4 ran a documentary on these attempts *638 Ways to Kill Castro*, and the "Daily News" (November 26, 2016) also used Escalante's estimates, listing the number of pursuits under each U.S. president:

> **Eisenhower, 38; Kennedy, 42; Johnson, 72; Nixon, 184; Carter, 64; Reagan, 197; Bush Sr., 16; Clinton, 21.**(http://www.nydailynews.com/news/world/fidel-castro-survived-600-assassination-attempts-article-1.2888111)

CHRONOLOGY OF CUBAN REVOLUTIONARY ACTIONS AND U.S. PRE-INVASION SUBVERSION

On January 21, 1959, Fidel Castro speaks to over a million workers and peasants: "When the People Rule". Castro explains that the U.S. has started "A campaign against the people of Cuba, because [we] want to be free not just politically, but economically as well—A campaign against the people of Cuba, because they have become a dangerous example for all America—A campaign against the people of Cuba because they know we are going to call for cancellation of the onerous concessions that have been made to foreign monopolies, because they know electric rates are going to be lowered here, because they know that all the onerous concessions made by the dictatorship are going to be reviewed and canceled." (https://www.marxists.org/history/cuba/archive/castro/1959/01/21.htm) (2)

March 3, the Cuban government nationalizes the Cuban Telephone Company, an affiliate of ITT, and drastically reduces its enormous telephone rates. Two days later, former Cuban President Ramon Grau San Martin (1933–1934, 1944–1948) demands the U.S. military leave its illegal occupation of Guantanomo Naval Base (116 sq. km). The U.S. refuses, instead blithely writes Cuba a check to forcefully "lease" the land for $2,000 a year. The Cuban government has never cashed them. Throughout the rest of the month, the price of medicine in Cuba is drastically reduced, while the Urban Reform Law lowers all rents by 30-50 percent. (3)

May 2, Nixon's negative assessment of Castro did not immediately change the great amount of positive encouragement for the Cuban revolution by a majority of citizens and liberal senators, so the government signs an agreement with Cuba offering technical cooperation in the development of agrarian reform—this was to be short lived.

May 17, Cuba enacts its Agrarian Reform Law: distributing all farmlands over 400 hectares to landless peasants and workers, and prohibiting foreign ownership of land, which was 75 percent of Cuba's most fertile land. The Cuban government begins nationalizing all foreign owned land with 20 year fixed-term bonds paying an annual interest rate of 4.5 percent (higher than most U.S. government bond rates then). Over 200,000 Cuban families own land for the first time in their lives as a result of the reform.

June 11, U.S. government officially protests the compensation terms offered U.S. companies for the Cuban land they had occupied. U.S.

landowners object that compensation is being granted in accordance to tax assessment rates, which did not depict the current value. For decades this had been of tremendous advantage to the foreign landowners. Not having tax rates updated meant paying taxes in terms of values 30 or 40 years old, which meant increasingly lower tax rates each year. Despite this protest, the Cuban government negotiates with other foreign landowners and reaches agreements with those from Britain, Canada, France, Italy, Mexico, Spain and Sweden.

The U.S. had no reason to complain about this mild agrarian reform, Fidel told his biographer Ignacio Ramonet, *My Life: Fidel Castro*, Penguin, 2006):

"I should even say that our agrarian reform was, at the time, less radical than the reform General MacArthur has instituted in Japan... MacArthur did away with large land holdings and parceled out the land and distributed it among the peasantry and the poor. But in Japan the large tracts of land hadn't belonged to big American companies, while in Cuba they had."

October 11- 21, three raids by U.S. military aircraft bomb Cuban sugar mills in Pinar del Rio and Camaguey provinces. Cuba begins efforts to purchase airplanes for its defense, looking first to Britain, which agrees to enter negotiations for sales but quickly withdraws once the U.S. objects.

Oct. 21, an aircraft raid on Havana kills two people and wounds 45 in the streets. The next day, in Las Villas province, a U.S. military aircraft strafes a train full of passengers. In response, Cubans form a popular militia.

October 28, Camilo Cienfuegos, popular charismatic leader of the Cuban revolutionary army, is killed in a mysterious plane crash.

In January 1960, Cuba expropriates 28,300 hectares held by U.S. sugar companies, which refuse to sell the land at any price. Cuba needed to make up for the lowered U.S. sugar quota that is damaging the nation's economy. This land includes 14,000 hectares held by United Fruit Co., which had attained more than 110,000 hectares of Cuban land over time.

United Fruit is known as "*El Pulpo*" (The Octopus) in Central America and the Caribbean for its monopoly of land in sugar and bananas (Chiquita). The disparaging term "Banana Republic" originates from the company, which owned 1.4 million hectares of land in those countries (1930s figures). The company's chief lawyer was Eisenhower's Secretary of State John Foster Dulles, who also owned stocks. His brother, CIA director Allen was once president of United Fruit.

January 12, revenging *El Pulpo* Eisenhower-Dulles government drops napalm on oil refineries and sugar cane fields. On the 21st, four 40-kilo bombs are dropped on Havana, causing extensive damage. On the 28th and 29th, U.S. military aircraft bombs wreck five sugar cane fields. These were U.S. military aircraft camouflaged as counterrevolutionary Cuban planes.

February 7, air attack by covert U.S. military aircraft burns 30 tons of sugar cane and several mills in the countryside. Sabotage operations of sugar production and terrorism in urban areas continue.

February 13, the Cuban and Soviet governments sign a trade agreement in which the Soviet Union agrees to purchase five million tons of sugar over a five-year period. In exchange, the S.U. agrees to export crude oil and petroleum products, as well as wheat, iron, fertilizers, and machinery. They also loan Cuba $100 million at a low 2.5 percent interest.

February 18, U.S. pilot Robert Ellis Frost is killed when his aircraft is shot down while attacking a sugar mill in Matanzas province. On the 23rd, several more air attacks bomb sugar mills in Las Villas and Matanzas provinces.

February 29, the Cuban government reaches out to the U.S. for peace negotiations on the condition that it stops bombing. Secretary of State John Foster Dulles refuses to negotiate for peace.

March 4, sabotage of a French ship, La Coubre, in Havana harbor. It is carrying arms for Cuba from Belgium. One hundred people are killed and 300 wounded. The following day at funerals for the victims Fidel Castro accuses the United States of responsibility for the action. (4)

The same month, Western European banks cancelled a planned $100 million loan to Cuba in response to U.S. threats.

March 17, President Eisenhower approves a covert action plan to overthrow the Cuban Republic, guided by CIA chief Allen Dulles, who is to report to Vice-President Nixon. The plan is a National Security Directive entitled, "***A Program of Covert Action Against the Castro Regime.***"

This "Cuba Project" laid the basis for the Bay of Pigs invasion. It grew out of a confidential memorandum Colonel J. C. King, chief of CIA's western hemisphere division, sent to Dulles, on December 11, 1959. King claimed that Cuba was now a "far-left dictatorship, which if allowed to remain will encourage similar actions against U.S. holdings in other Latin American countries." As a result of this memorandum, Dulles established a ZR/RIFLE unit aka Operation 40, which was the National Security Council "Group of 40" against Cuba.

ZR Rifle was an executive action codename for assassination of foreign leaders, which involved assessing the problems and requirements of assassination and developing a stand-by assassination capability. More specifically, it involved "spotting" potential agents and researching assassination techniques that might be used. (http://www.globalsecurity.org/intell/ops/zr-rifle.htm)

When Helms testified before congress in 1975 he denied the program was ever implemented. Helms lied. Two years later, he actually pleaded no contest in a federal court to misdemeanor charges for failing to testify fully before Congress about CIA subversive operations in Chile. No penalty was forthcoming.

Among the first 40 members of Operation 40 were key CIA figures and Cuban exiles, many of whom later figured in the murder of President Kennedy (see chapter six), and some in the Watergate break-in. From the CIA were: Tracy Barnes, operating officer of the Cuban Task Force; David Atlee Phillips, E. Howard Hunt, Frank Bender, Jacob Jake Esterline, David Sanchez Morales, Frank Sturgis, and Felix Rodriquez—the latter was the CIA officer in Bolivia involved in the summary execution of Che Guevara.

The *gusanos* ("worms" a Cuban term for those who betray their own people by sabotaging and murdering them) were: Luis Posada Carriles (also on CIA payroll) and Orlando Bosch (founder of Coordination of United Revolutionary Organizations, which organized the explosion of a civilian Cuban aircraft killing all 73 passengers and the murder of Chile's minister Orlando Letelier—both in 1976); Rafael 'Chi Chi' Quintero, Virgilio Paz Romero, Pedro Luis Diaz Lanz, Bernard Barker and Porter Goss. By 1961, Operation 40 had 86 employees, of which 37 were trained as case officers. Members took part in the Bay of Pigs invasion. It was officially disbanded in 1970 yet in reality continued.

Operation 40 concentrated on economic warfare: termination of all sugar trade with Cuba, the end of all oil deliveries, instructing all U.S.

companies in Cuba to refuse to cooperate with the Cuban Government, and conducting a campaign of terrorism against Cuban citizens and state institutions.

Also in March, Western European banks cancelled a planned $100 million loan to Cuba in response to U.S. threats. The CIA began training 300 guerrillas, initially in the U.S. and the Canal Zone. Following an agreement with President Miguel Ydígoras Fuentes, in June, training shifted to Guatemala. The CIA began work to install a powerful radio station on Greater Swan Island.

The reactionary Guatemalan government had been put in power by the CIA, in June 1954, after Guatemalan right-wing militarists under CIA control overthrew the elected government of Jacobo Arbenz Guzman. He was a social democrat, who sought to nationalize much of the nation's land, including vast tracks owned by the United Fruit Company.

Ydígoras later claimed that he had been introduced, in 1953, to two CIA agents by Walter Turnbull, an official of United Fruit Company. They offered him support to overthrow Árbenz. Ydígoras claimed to have refused their terms (5)

"New York Times" obituary of General Ydigoras, October 8, 1982, asserted that landowning military politicians "said he had allowed the C.I.A. to train the Cubans because the Eisenhower Administration had pledged to take a more friendly attitude toward his Government and to increase the United States import quota on Guatemalan sugar... [Ydigoras] expressed warm admiration for the United States and especially for its efforts to rid the hemisphere of Communism. But he was bitter over the failure of the Bay of Pigs invasion and blamed it for his downfall." (http://www.nytimes.com/1982/10/08/obituaries/general-ydigoras-of-guatemala-bay-of-pigs-figure-is-dead-at-86.html)

April 4, Cuba readies a plan to expropriate all Cuban land held by the United Fruit Company. On the same day a military aircraft flying from the U.S. naval base at Guantanamo drops napalm bombs in Oriente province.

May 7, The Cuban government establishes diplomatic relations with the Soviet Union, only *after* the Eisenhower administration had already ordered Fidel's murder and an invasion.

August 6, Cuba enacts its nationalization law number 851, which again offers compensation at the value stated by U.S. foreign companies for purposes of paying taxes. Among the properties nationalized for collective use were those with controlling interests by U.S. stockholders: Exxon, Texaco, Starwood Hotels & Resorts, Cuban Electric Company, North American Sugar Industries. (3) (http://scholarship.law.duke.edu/cgi/viewcontent.cgi?article=1848&context=dlj)

Nationalization of U.S. property was a key rationalization the U.S. used for invading Cuba. The Secretary of State in office at the time was Dean Rusk. Ironically, at a press release October 19, 1962 regarding a dispute between Brazil and Ceylon over property rights, he said:

> *"Any sovereign national has the right to expropriate property, whether owned by foreigners or nationals. In the United States we refer to this as the power of eminent domain. However, the owner should receive adequate and prompt compensation for this property."*

In September, Cuban civilian militia mobilizes cleanup operations, in the Escambray region of Las Villas Providence, against CIA-funded counterrevolutionary groups operating there. The CIA groups are crushed.

September 17, Cuba nationalizes all U.S. banks in Cuba (The First National Bank of Boston, First National City Bank of New York and Chase Manhattan).

October 7, United Nations is again informed by Foreign Minister Raul Roa Garcia that the CIA is training counterrevolutionaries in Guatemala for an invasion of his country. The United States vehemently denies this so the UN again dismisses the assertion.

October 8-10, weapons caches dropped from a U.S. military aircraft are seized in Escambray and over 100 counter-revolutionaries are arrested.

October 15, Cuba enacts a program of urban reform, guaranteeing every worker home ownership.

October 19, U.S. imposes a trade and economic embargo on Cuba excepting food and medicine.

By this time, the Cuban government has converted former army barracks into 10,000 new schools in cities and rural areas, a 200% increase in schools over the past 20 years.

November 8, the soon-to-be President Kennedy is briefed on the Cuba invasion plans.

November 13, nearly half of the entire Guatemalan army, led by over 120 officers, rebels against the government of Miguel Ydígoras Fuentes. The soldiers, partly in solidarity with Cuba's revolution, object to the U.S. government using their country for an invasion of Cuba. The Guatemalan government is not able to crush the rebellion, and appeals to the United States for assistance. The U.S. bombs the soldiers with B-26 bombers piloted by Cuban exiles it trained. To cover this action up, President Eisenhower orders the U.S. Navy to Nicaragua and Guatemala to protect these countries from "Cuban aggression".

January 1, 1961: Cuba launches a National Literacy Campaign. Within a year the rate of illiteracy in Cuba was reduced from 25 to 3.9 percent, setting an unprecedented standard throughout the underdeveloped world.

January 2, Soviet Premier Nikita Khrushchev tells a gathering at the Cuban embassy in Moscow: "Alarming news is coming from Cuba at present, news that the most aggressive American monopolists are preparing a direct attack on Cuba."

January 3, United States severs diplomatic and consular relations with Cuba. Castro banishes all but 11 of the U.S. Embassy's 300 employees—many CIA—from the country.

January 17, President Eisenhower delivers his farewell, double-speak "military-industrial complex speech" on television.

> *… "America's leadership and prestige depend, not merely upon our unmatched material progress, riches and military strength, but on how to use our power in the interests of world peace and human betterment."*
>
> *"In the councils of government, we must guard against the acquisition of unwarranted influence, whether sought or unsought, by the military-industrial complex. The potential for the disastrous rise of misplaced power exists and will persist."*
>
> *"Disarmament, with mutual honor and confidence, is a continuing imperative. Together we must learn how to compose differences, not with arms, but with intellect and decent*

purpose. Because this need is so sharp and apparent I confess that I lay down my official responsibilities in this field with a definite sense of disappointment. As one who has witnessed the horror and the lingering sadness of war—as one who knows that another war could utterly destroy this civilization which has been so slowly and painfully built over thousands of years—I wish I could say tonight that a lasting peace is in sight."

January 20, John F. Kennedy is inaugurated as president. He had defeated Richard Nixon, in part, by claiming that Nixon had not been tough enough on worldwide communism.

During the Eisenhower-Nixon regime (1953-61), they encouraged the Red Scare, purging hundreds of people from the government and imprisoning thousands suspected of being affiliated with the Communist Party. Eisenhower used the CIA to attack and overthrow the truly democratic Iranian government led by Mohammad Mosaddegh on August 19, 1953. Britain's MI6 was in partnership with the CIA, which admitted to its role, in 2013. (https://www.theguardian.com/world/2013/aug/19/cia-admits-role-1953-iranian-coup)

Operation Ajax was the coup's nomenclature and was deemed necessary because Mossadegh had the audacity to start progressive social and political reforms for his people, and he nationalized the country's oil, which Britain mainly controlled at that time. The Yanks-Brits brought back the Shah, Mohammad Reza Pahlavi, until he was overthrown in 1979. Mossadegh was imprisoned or held in house arrest until his death, March 5, 1967.

In 1954, the "soft-on-communism" Eisenhower-Nixon government took over Guatemala in a coup, and created the Southeast Asia Treaty Organization to ensure capitalism's stability in Southeast Asia.

In February-March 1961, just after the new hawk took office, the CIA made another attempt to assassinate Prime Minister Castro. The plan was to poison his Cuban cigars with botulism, a toxin so potent that its fumes are strong enough to kill. Various accounts maintain that either CIA's ZR/Rifle chief William Harvey or its Col. Sheffield Edwards delivered capsules containing the toxin to CIA's Mafia contact Johnny Roselli along with $10,000.

March 11, terrorists destroy electrical plants in Havana, leaving much of the city without electricity. Two days later, an oil refinery at the Santiago de Cuba port is attacked by terrorists.

April 3, U.S. State Department issues a White Paper on Cuba, explaining that Cuba is a Soviet satellite. It dictated that if Cuba breaks off ties with the Soviet Union the United States will be generous and aid such a "free" government. If Cuba refuses, the U.S. will view it as "a clear and present danger to the authentic and autonomous revolution of the Americas."

April 12, Soviet Union ushers the world into a new era when Yuri Gagarin becomes the first human being in space. The next day, the U.S. begins its invasion of Cuba.

INVASION

The invasion plan called for aerial attacks to destroy roads and bridges to prevent the Cuban army from reaching the Bay of Pigs before the counterrevolutionary mercenaries got a foothold. These raids would be extended by CIA operatives who had already penetrated Cuba. Once victory was achieved, a group of CIA picked Cuban leaders, which it was forcefully holding in a secret base at Florida's Opalocka airport, would be flown in as a proxy government.

April 13, CIA-chartered freighters *Atlántico, Caríbe, Houston and Rio Escondido* load 1,334 Cuban mercenaries along with tanks and other war vehicles. They sail from Guatemala (and Nicaragua) followed by USS Essex carrier and five destroyers. Operation Zapata is launched.

April 14, a squadron of U.S. B-26 bombers, camouflaged with Cuban insignias, begins bombarding airports in Cuba. These raids would last for two days, destroying a large portion of the Cuban Air Force. Kennedy's ambassador to the U.N., Adlai Stevenson, claims the raids are flown by Cuban dissident pilots in Cuban planes. On the 15th, Fidel declares to a huge cheering crowd that Cuba was now on a socialist path.

April 16, shortly before midnight, six U.S. frogmen, led by CIA's Grayston Lynch, land on Cuba's targeted beaches in a Landing Craft Infantry boat and set up lights to guide the invasion.

April 17, Brigade 2506 lands in Cuba. The men—now 1297, some had drowned—are led by Lynch and his operative William Robertson. They split into six battalions, landing at *Playa Girón* and *Playa Larga*,

Gusanos quickly captured as they invade their land of birth.

35 kilometers away. Coral reefs delay the landing several hours until boats could navigate around the coral. An additional 177 Cuban paratroopers land.

What the CIA failed to consider caused a rapid backfire. The vast majority of Cubans were happy with their revolutionary government, and they were prepared for a Yankee invasion.

Shortly before 3 a.m. on the day of attack, a civilian member of the Committee for the Defense of the Revolution spots the U.S. warships, just off the Cuban shores. Less than 20 minutes later, the entire Cuban government is informed about the invasion, and their response is immediate.

Fidel Castro coordinates the defense from the field. First the population is alerted. For months the Cuban government had been giving weapons to the entire population and training them in basic military defensive tactics. Militia men and women now confront the invaders. The remainder of the Cuban Air Force launches attacks and gains superiority over U.S. aircraft. Cuba's T33 jets shoot five of the brigade's 12 remaining aircraft out of the air, including the B-26 flown by Americans Pete Ray and Leo Francis Baker. They were killed on the ground when they tried to escape their crashed bomber. The Cuban Air Force then flies over the U.S. invasion fleet, bombarding and sinking the fleet command vessel "*Maropa*" and "*Houston*." The crews were rescued but artillery and heavy war munitions were lost. Cuban police hunt down and arrest CIA operatives before they can blow up any of their intended targets.

By midnight, Fidel and 20,000 soldiers trapped the invaders against the beaches, squeezing them into tight perimeters. Castro's tanks and infantry battered the brigade with artillery fire for 48 straight hours.

Diplomatic matters for the United States went poorly very quickly. U.S. involvement in the invasion of Cuba was a direct violation of Article 2 and Article 51 of the Charter of the United Nations, as well as Articles 18 and 25 of the Charter of the Organization of American States, and Article 1 of the Rio Treaty. (6)

This SU-100 tank stands before the Cuban Museum of the Revolution in Havana. It is said Fidel fired shots from it that hit and damaged a U.S. ship.

On the day of the invasion, U.S. Secretary of State Dean Rusk lies at a press conference. "The American people are entitled to know whether we are intervening in Cuba or intend to do so in the future," he said. "The answer to that question is no." U.S. ambassador to the United Nations Stevenson, now aware of U.S. involvement in the invasion, which he had been instructed to deny days earlier, publicly urges the United States to stop the attack.

Soviet ambassador to the UN Valerian Alexandrovich Zorin responds: "Cuba is not alone today. Among her most sincere friends the Soviet Union is to be found."

April 18, Kennedy receives a letter from Chairman Nikita Khrushchev:

> *"It is a secret to no one that the armed bands invading this country were trained, equipped and armed in the United States of America. The planes which are bombing Cuban cities belong to the United States of America; the bombs they are dropping are being supplied by the American Government....*
>
> *"All of this evokes here in the Soviet Union an understandable feeling of indignation on the part of the Soviet Government and the Soviet people.*
>
> *"Only recently, in exchanging opinions through our respective representatives, we talked with you about the mutual desire of both sides to put forward joint efforts directed toward improving relations between our countries and eliminating the danger of war.*
>
> *"Your statement a few days ago that the USA would not participate in military activities against Cuba created the impression that the top leaders of the United States were taking into account the consequences for general peace and for the USA itself which aggression against Cuba could have. How can what is being done by the United States in reality be understood when an attack on Cuba has now become a fact? ..."*
>
> *"As far as the Soviet Union is concerned, there should be no mistake about our position: We will render the Cuban people and their government all necessary help to repel armed attack on Cuba. We are sincerely interested in a relaxation of international tension, but if others proceed toward sharpening, we will answer them in full measure... I hope that the Government of the USA*

will consider our views as dictated by the sole concern not to allow steps which could lead the world to military catastrophe. (http://archives.chicagotribune.com/1961/04/19/page/4/article/nikita-tells-kennedy-halt-cuba-invasion)

KENNEDY BLINKS!

All support by the U.S. Air Force is called off. The battle was going poorly for the U.S. invaders, not able to gain an inch on the beach. In face of utter defeat, Kennedy continues to maintain that the U.S. is not involved in the invasion. Nevertheless, Kennedy momentarily reverses his previous decision, and orders the U.S. Air Force to assist the brigade in what way it can, but it was too late. At dawn on April 19, six unmarked U.S. fighter planes took off from Nicaragua to help defend the last of brigade's aircraft. They were shot down by the Cubans, and the invasion was crushed later that day. (7)

On the same day at 2:30 p.m., Brigade 2506 commander Perez San Roman transmits a final radio message: "We have nothing left to fight with."

One hundred and eighteen mercenaries were killed, 360 wounded in battle. Ten Cuban mercenary aircrew and four U.S. airmen were also killed. Some exiles escaped to the sea. Between 1,183 and 1,202, figures vary, were captured.

The Cuban people suffered greater losses. One hundred and seventy six soldiers were killed, while an estimated 2000 civilian militiamen and women were killed or wounded, and hundreds went unaccounted for.

The United States government had lied unconvincingly about the invasion. Its UN Ambassador Stevenson read President Kennedy's reply to Soviet Premier Khrushchev denying that the U.S. was intervening militarily in Cuba yet claimed "the right" to protect the hemisphere from "external aggression". Stevenson went on to claim that there is no evidence against the United States, and that it is "not true that the guerrillas have been brought by planes from the U.S. piloted by Americans." (http://nsarchive.gwu.edu/bayofpigs/chron.html)

(Khrushchev made one error. Most invaders had been brought to Cuba by U.S. sea vessels.)

Within 72 hours, Cuba had beaten the Yankees. The Cuban people had effectively protected their sovereignty and billions of folk the world over applauded.

The mercenary prisoners remained in captivity for 20 months as the United States negotiated a deal with Fidel Castro. Attorney General Robert F. Kennedy made personal pleas for contributions from pharmaceutical companies and baby food manufacturers. The Cuban government eventually settled on $53 million worth of baby food, other food and medicines in exchange for the prisoners.

The Cuban "Soviet puppets" took food and medicines from the aggressor war-makers—who should have been imprisoned under international law—so that Cuban children could be healthier and live longer than children still under the domination of U.S.-imposed Latin American dictators. Strange twist considering that Yankees tell us "Communists eat babies"! (8)

Notes:

1. See Appendix 1. pages 242-3 and Appendix F of the CIA's "Official History of the Bay of Pigs Operation". This report is in four volumes, seven parts plus attachments. 1,751 pgs. https://www.cia.gov/library/readingroom/collection/bay-pigs-release . The report by the Inspector General Lyman Kirkpatrick was declassified in 1998. The CIA's budget estimation for this covert operation was $13.1 million, but it would come to cost much more.

2. "Cuban History: U.S. Bay of Pigs Invasion" from the Marxist Internet Archive See also: https://www.marxists.org/history/cuba/subject/bay-of-pigs/

3. Several court cases were filed in the U.S. by wealthy Cuban owners of property nationalized and by U.S. corporation property owners.

   Some cases got tried, some in favor of Cuba, such as the Compania Azucarera Vertientes-Camaguey do Cuba, judged by N.Y. Supreme Court judge Baker. Most cases, however, came under the U.S. Supreme Court Act of State Doctrine determination: "the courts of one country will not sit in judgment on the acts of the government of another done within its own territory."

   Furthermore, the United Nations General Assembly resolved, on December 14, 1962, the Permanent Sovereignty Over Natural Resources, which permitted: "nationalization, expropriation or requisitioning shall be based on grounds or reasons of public utility, security or the national interests which are recognized as overriding purely individual or private interests, both domestic and foreign. In such cases the owner shall be paid appropriate compensations, in accordance with the rules in force in the State taking such measures in the exercise of its sovereignty and in accordance with international law."

   The vote for was 87, oddly including the U.S. France and South Africa voted against. Most ironically, the Communist block and Cuba abstained.

   A "Havana Times" article, "Seized US Properties in Cuba: Another Pending Issue for the Thaw"–June 18, 2015 by DPA journalist Beatriz Juez–described this history in contemporary politics. http://www.havanatimes.org/?p=112053

"The nationalization of US companies following the Cuban revolution, one of the measures that detonated the diplomatic break between Washington and Havana in 1961, is...[again] on the table...after the historic rapprochement between the two countries announced in December of last year.

"These demands could well be one of the thorniest issues to address in the long-term 'normalization' process the two countries aspire to, a process that also includes matters such as the return of the Guantanamo Naval Base territory to Cuba and the compensation the island's government demands for the damage caused by the embargo.

"According to the Foreign Claims Settlement Commission (FCSC), an independent agency of the US Department of Justice, "it is not yet clear what effect such changes will have on the status of the claims previously adjudicated by the Commission."

"The Commission has certified a total of ***5,913 claims made by US citizens or companies in connection with properties nationalized*** following Fidel Castro's arrival in power in 1959.

"According to the FCSC, tasked with arbitrating claims by US citizens against foreign governments, ***at the time of their nationalization, these US properties were valued at some 1.9 billion dollars. Today, this is equivalent to 7 billion dollars***," so estimated "The New York Times".

4. Informe Especial: 1960 http://nsarchive.gwu.edu/bayofpigs/chron.html. National Security Archives, George Washington University.

5. Gordon, Max "A Case History of U. S. Subversion: Guatemala, 1954". Science and Society, Summer 1971.

6. **UN Charter Article 2**

   Here are three of the seven points: 1. The Organization is based on the principle of the sovereign equality of all its Members. ***3. All Members shall settle their international disputes by peaceful means in such a manner that international peace and security, and justice, are not endangered. 4. All Members shall refrain in their international relations from the threat or use of force against the territorial integrity or political independence of any state, or in any other manner inconsistent with the Purposes of the United Nations.*** 7. Nothing contained in the present Charter shall authorize the United Nations to intervene in matters which are essentially within the domestic jurisdiction of any state or shall require the Members to submit such matters to settlement under the present Charter; but this principle shall not prejudice the application of enforcement measures under Chapter VII.

   Article 51

   Nothing in the present Charter shall impair the inherent right of individual or collective self-defence if an armed attack occurs against a Member of the United Nations, until the Security Council has taken measures necessary to maintain international peace and security. Measures taken by Members in the exercise of this right of self-defence shall be immediately reported to the Security Council and shall not in any way affect the authority and responsibility of the Security Council under the present Charter to take at any time such action as it deems necessary in order to maintain or restore international peace and security.

7. On July 19, 1979, the popular Sandinista guerrillas won their fight against the repressive Nicaraguan government. In 1980, with cowboy Ronald Reagan at the seat of power, a vicious counter-revolutionary force was financed, armed and trained to crush the people's government. The International Court of Justice ruled, on June 27, 1986, that U.S. support to the contras in Nicaragua is illegal, and mining the Managua harbor a war crime. It demanded that the US pay reparations to the Sandinistas. In a 16-point ruling on a complaint lodged by Nicaragua, the judges rejected U.S. claims of collective self-defense–the U.S. rejected the judgment because it said the Sandinista government was a "Soviet puppet"–and found it guilty of breaches of international law and the 1956 treaty of friendship between the two countries.

   The U.S. refused to participate and rejected the court as incompetent. Nevertheless, the invaders accepted its jurisdiction in other cases, such as the 1984 ruling on the Bay of Maine dispute with Canada.

   The United States warred against the Sandinistas, whose progressive social and political reforms were learned from the Cuban revolution, yet it had helped put in office and supported the three Somoza family dictators for nearly half-a-century. The first Somoza "president" was the wealthy coffee plantation owner, Anastasio Somoza Garcia (1937-47; 1956-63). President Franklin D. Roosevelt said of him: "Somoza may be a son-of-a-bitch, but he's our son-of-a-bitch." However, Somoza was merely one of many Latin American dictators that this was said of. Anastasio's son, Luis, was in office when the U.S. invaded Cuba with aircraft flown from Nicaragua.

8. See William Blum's "Killing Hope: U.S. Military and CIA Interventions Since World War II", Common Courage, 1987 edition.

   "Literally no story about the Bolsheviks was too contrived, too bizarre, too grotesque, or too perverted to be printed and widely believed – from women being nationalized to babies being eaten (as the early pagans believed the Christians guilty of devouring their children; the same was believed of the Jews in the Middle Ages). The story about women with all the lurid connotations of state property, compulsory marriage, 'free love', etc. 'was broadcasted over the country through a thousand channels,' wrote Schuman, 'and perhaps did more than anything else to stamp the Russian Communists in the minds of most American citizens as criminal perverts'". (See: Frederick L. Schuman, *American Policy Toward Russia Since 1917* (N.Y. 1928, p. 154)

CHAPTER 3

U.S. Subversion Leads to Cuban Missile Crisis

BAY OF PIGS invasion was the first United States failure of several hundred military interventions-wars throughout its history (Vietnam was next). President John F. Kennedy was indignant and sought revenge, not only by firing a few CIA heads but by launching other plans for sabotage and for a new government. In modern Establishment English: a regime change for human rights in support of democratic-seeking Cuban patriots—a la Syria and Libya.

"*In keeping with the spirit of the Presidential memorandum of 30 November 1961, the United States will help the people of Cuba overthrow the Communist regime from within Cuba and institute a new government with which the United States can live in peace,*" Gen. Edward Lansdale wrote.

Air Force Brigadier General Lansdale was placed on loan from the Defense Department to Attorney General Robert Kennedy as Chief of Operations for Operation Mongoose (aka "The Cuba Project") subversive plan. William King Harvey was Lansdale's main CIA liaison operator. (1)

The November 30 memorandum referred to did not contend that the Cuban government was attacking United States' peace—hardly something that one could expect seven million people to undertake—rather that the United State governments, including President Kennedy's, could not bear not being in charge of all of its Latin American "backyard". (https://history.state.gov/historicaldocuments/frus1961-63v10/d278)

Ironically, JFK had recently castigated the CIA for advising him that the population would back its Bay of Pigs invasion; yet now he approved another plan based upon another illusionary revolt.

The November memorandum's first of five decisions was: "We will use our available assets to go ahead with the discussed project in order to help Cuba overthrow the communist regime". (2)

Lansdale's February 20, 1962 Mongoose report (Appendix 11, nr. 2) called for "the open revolt and overthrow of the Communist regime" in October 1962, which was exactly when the U.S. started the "Cuban Missile Crisis" (CMC), by threatening to invade Cuba and perhaps the Soviet Union. (See the next chapters).

Mongoose called for "activating the necessary operations inside Cuba for revolution and concurrently applying the vital political, economic, and military-type support from outside Cuba."

That included "sabotage support plan" and psychological and intelligence support plans. This report, the earlier January 18, 1962 "program review" (Appendix 11, nr. 3). (https://history.state.gov/historicaldocuments/frus1961-63v10/d291)

All reports were sent to the Kennedy brothers, key CIA heads, General Lemnitzer, and other military heads.

The Program Review concludes: "*CIA has alerted Defense that it will require considerable military support (including two submarines, PT boats, Coast Guard type cutters, Special Forces trainers, C-54 aircraft, F-86 aircraft, amphibian aircraft, helio-couriers, Army leaflet battalion, and Guantanamo as a base for submarine operations). Also, CIA apparently believes that its role should be to create and expand a popular movement, illusory and actual, which will create a political climate which can provide a framework of plausible excuse for armed intervention. This is not in conformity with the Presidential directive now governing Project tasking. Actually, the role of creating the political climate and plausible excuse for armed intervention would be more properly that of State and Defense, if such an objective becomes desirable.*"

I have not found any document, however, that states President Kennedy rejected the idea of using "considerable military support". In fact, the July 25 memorandum stated there was a continuing planning and "essential preliminary actions for a decisive U.S. capability for intervention."

Operation Mongoose states that "such a plan would enable a logical build-up of incidents to be combined with other seemingly unrelated events to camouflage the ultimate objective and create the necessary impression of Cuban rashness and irresponsibility on a large scale, directed at other countries as well as the United States."

> *"The desired resultant from the execution of this plan would be to place the United States in the apparent position of suffering defensible grievances from a rash and irresponsible government of Cuba and to develop an international image of a Cuban threat to peace in the Western Hemisphere."*

Wow! Little Cuba was preparing to attack the mightiest nation in the world and other countries, too. Castro was one hell-of-a macho man, who could whip up enough of the seven million Cubans to do all that. But where would the internal uproar against such a ballsy idea come from?

Lansdale tried to be optimistic with the plan for an internal uproar. He said that there was a potential "sizeable guerrilla force" underway with an "estimated 250" recruits. "We brought in extra weapons, for which there were immediate recruits…" "Our best hope is that we will have viable teams in all the potential resistance areas by early October."

Lansdale was clearly uncertain that a potent enough internal revolt could succeed so he concluded this report with some alternative ideas:

> *"Commit U.S. to help Cubans overthrow the Castro-Communist regime, with a step-by-step phasing to ensure success, including the use of U.S. military force if required at the end, or use a provocation and overthrow the Castro-Communist regime by U.S. military force."*

At this time Cuba was not yet part of the Warsaw pact, and thus another U.S. military intervention in Cuba might not prompt Soviet Union involvement, or so hoped Kennedy. The generals were not worried about that. But before their Mongoose plan could be fully enacted, other events occurred: the United States discovered Cuba was about to have Soviet missiles for its legitimate defense.

OPERATIONS PATTY AND LIBORIO

Concurrent with Operation Mongoose, attempts to assassinate Fidel Castro continued. No direct mention of murdering Fidel Castro is in

Kennedy's Cuba Project plans but there were such efforts with Operation 40 in the previous administration, activities that did not cease under Kennedy. The most famous attempts to kill Castro in the early 1960s were the plots revealed by the Church Committee hearings of the 1970s. The Committee found evidence to support at least eight such schemes dreamed up by CIA spymasters William Harvey, David Morales and other CIA officers.

Regardless of whether JFK directly ordered the murder of Fidel, he had to know what was going down. Author Tim Weiner found 163 major covert operations against Cuba under JFK's reign and some of them were murder attempts. (*Legacy of Ashes*, Doubleday, 2007, p.180)

Operation Patty—murdering Raul and Fidel Castro, and taking over the government following a fake Cuban attack on the U.S. Guantanamo base—was to occur on July 24, 1961. There would be large celebrations on this eighth anniversary of the rebel attack (July 26) on Batista army's Santiago Moncado Garrison, which was hoped to spark a national revolution. Here is what Cuba's Radio Rebelde reported, on August 9, 2011, for the 50th anniversary:

> *"On August 11 the Cuban Ministry of Interior announced the capture of a contra-revolutionary group that tried to murder Commander Raul Castro and fake a retaliation attack by the Cuban Army against the Guantanamo Bay US naval base. These actions had been orchestrated by the US Central Intelligence Agency." (https://victoriafriendsofcuba.wordpress.com/2011/08/10/a-cia-cuba-episode-the-ill-fated-patty-operation/)*
>
> *"The CIA couldn't put to rest the sound defeat it had suffered barely four months before at the hands of the young Revolution when in less than 72 hours the 1600 men strong mercenary forces had surrendered in Bay of Pigs.*
>
> *"The new plan was known by the codename 'Patty', one of the most complex plans it had devised so far. The idea was to shoot Raul Castro using a 30 caliber machine gun from a house near the Santiago de Cuba baseball stadium where on July 24 the provincial main activity to mark the eighth anniversary of the attack of the Moncada Garrison was to be held. At the same time other team members were to throw hand grenades and shoot the tribune and the crowd.*

"In case the first attempt to kill Raul failed, they had set an ambush with six men armed with m3 rifles on the road to the airport, since they were expecting that the then Defense Minister will take that route to report the incident to Commander in Chief Fidel Castro.

"At the same time, the plan included a mortar attack on the Hermanos Diaz oil refinery in Santiago, and one hour later a similar action against the Guantanamo Bay base...Also, they were to bomb a Cuban artillery unit close to the border to fake a retaliation action.

"While the CIA was plotting to kill Raul, the Pentagon had organized a similar action against Fidel Castro in Havana city. The chief of the Guantanamo Bay had supplied another team, through the fence that surrounds the base, close to two tons of weaponry to shell the Jose Marti Revolution Square where Fidel would address the Cuban people.

"The Cuban State Security had managed to infiltrate both groups and its members had risen to important positions among them till the end, on July 22. On that date the mercenary forces were captured along with all the incriminating war material."

Researcher Bill Simpich wrote about Operations Patty and Liborio: "Operations Patty and Liborio, both staged during 1961, were not revealed during the 'limited hangout' conducted by the Agency during the 1970s. After Cuban intelligence chief Fabian Escalante wrote about these programs, the author took a look at how much supporting documentation existed in US intelligence files. The result of that research is that Patty and Liborio are important windows into the history of US covert operations in Cuba and the milieu that conceived the JFK assassination." (https://www.opednews.com/articles/1/The-Hidden-Castro-Assassin-by-Bill-Simpich-Assassinate_Assassination_Assassination-Attempt_Castro-Fidel-150610-653.html)

"New plans were brought into play after the collapse of Operation Patty. One network that tried to move assassination plans forward was AMBLOOD, run by former Cuban

government official Luis Toroella [under CIA JMWAVE control] in Miami. The exiles were trained by the CIA inside Guatanamo naval base itself. The network was rounded up on or before September 24, 1961.

"AMBLOOD's work seems to be tied to Operation Liborio, also run from Miami. CIA records show Anthony Veciana [Cuban leader of the exile terrorist group Alpha 66] had a meeting with Harry Real at the CIA's New York field office. He asked to speak to a senior CIA officer to discuss plans to assassinate Castro and requested CIA assistance. According to Veciana, he received a call from 'Maurice Bishop' months after the Bay of Pigs. Bishop was actually CIA covert action officer David Atlee Phillips. Phillips told Veciana that he had 'decided that the only thing left to be done was to have an attempt on Castro's life'. The plan was to kill Fidel with a bazooka from an apartment overlooking a public plaza on October 4, 1961."

"Things started going badly when a terrorist member, Dalia Jorge Diaz, was arrested while leaving a suitcase of explosives inside a Sears department store in Havana. Those known to her were also arrested. After Diaz' arrest, bombs and explosives were discovered planted in 15 stores. Diaz was released from jail and the plan was abandoned. Dalia may have been a double agent.

(Veciano wasn't dissuaded, though. He tried to murder Fidel three times.)

Operation Mongoose came soon thereafter. The key change here was that the U.S. would not invade directly after false flag operations, but indirectly following up a 'real or simulated' Cuban revolt. Kennedy's purported sensitivity could tolerate that nuance difference."

President Kennedy was also fulfilling what The Cuba Project called for economically—a complete embargo on Cuban trade, but not only for U.S.-Cuba relations. The mighty state believed that it could force other nations to end trade ties with the rebellious Cubans, and there was some success. The July 25, 1962 Mongoose memo stated: "Diplomatic means were used to frustrate Cuban trade negotiations in Israel, Jordan, Iran, Greece, and possible Japan." Soon, the Organization of American States cut trade. That meant all of Latin America except Mexico.

Yuri Gagarin at a Havana rally, July 27, 1961, just after Operation Patty called for the murder of Fidel.

TOTAL EMBARGO

Minutes after Kennedy's press secretary Pierre Salinger handed him 1200 Cuban Petit Upmann cigars, which his boss had ordered him to find and buy the day before, the glad Havana cigar smoker signed his Proclamation 3447—a total embargo of all trade between the United States and Cuba. As of February 3, 1961, no one in US America could any longer smoke the world's best cigars in their own country other than the President and his press secretary.

That boycott has cost Cuba an estimated $125 billion (2016. Its GDP was then $87 billon.) The Cuban government's estimates were reported by the U.S. government news agency, Voice of American News, on September 9, 2016: https://www.voanews.com/a/cuba-says-us-embargo-cost-it-four-point-six-billion-dollars-last-year/3501327.html

"The Cuban government has called on the United States to do more to ease economic pressure on the nation in light of improved relations between Washington and Havana, saying U.S. economic sanctions cost Cuba $4.6 billion in the last financial year...[in its full course] it had cost Cuba a total of $125.9 billion. The figure includes actual costs, such as fines on Cuba's business partners, and hypothetical figures, such as sales Cuban businesses could have been making in U.S. markets."

The United Nations General Assembly has condemned the embargo since 1991. The U.S. has rarely had more than Israel and one or two small States backing it while Cuba has had the backing of over 180 nations. 2016 was the first time that the vote was unanimously for Cuba (191) when the U.S. and Israel abstained.

Many companies and some banks in several nations have been fined by the U.S. for trading with Cuba. The losses take a toll on the U.S. economy too. The United States Chamber of Commerce maintains that the embargo hurts business to the tune of $1.2 billion annually, an estimate made during the Obama administration. The Chamber seeks a total end to the embargo.

OPERATION NORTHWOODS

"We could develop a Communist Cuban terror campaign in the Miami area, in other Florida cities and even in Washington. The terror campaign could be pointed at Cuban refugees seeking haven in the United States. We could sink a boatload of Cubans en-route to Florida (real or simulated)."

Operation Northwoods is the codename of this and other false flag terrorist plans aimed at casting blame on the Cuban government, thereby allowing for "pretexts which would provide justification for US military intervention in Cuba." So wrote the Commander of the Joint Chiefs of Staff, General L. L. Lemnitzer and approved by all chiefs of staff, on March 13, 1962. General Lansdale of Operation Mongoose had asked the JCS for such a plan. (See appendix 111) (3)

United States military and CIA terrorism would even include paying some Cubans to attack the U.S. Guantanamo military, kill a few American soldiers, and blow up the *USS Maine*—"Remember the Maine", referring to a U.S. ship which suddenly exploded, on February 15, 1898, in Havana Harbor. Most officers were on shore leave so only two died while most of the sailors, 251, were killed. It was an accident, the captain later constituted. Many believe it was set by a U.S. secret agent. The U.S. government wanted a war so media mogul William Randolph Hearst helped with his "yellow journalism" by blaming Spain.

Hearst sent illustrator Frederic Remington to cover the war. Remington telegrammed to say all was quiet. Hearst replied: "Please remain. You finish the pictures and I'll finish the war."

The U.S. declared war on Spain in April. By August, Spain was ready to surrender. Both countries agreed not to let Cubans have any say in terms. The U.S. forced conditions on the Cuban leadership, including what is still the Guantánamo naval base, used to torture people, and humiliate Cubans.

The Northwoods plan hoped for similar results, that "casualty lists in U.S. newspapers would cause a helpful wave of national indignation." (appendix 111) (https://nsarchive2.gwu.edu/news/20010430/northwoods.pdf)

"The plans were developed as ways to trick the American public and the international community into supporting a war to oust Cuba's then new leader, communist Fidel Castro," wrote ABC's David Ruppe, May 1, 2001, "U.S. Military Wanted to Provoke War With Cuba". (http://abcnews.go.com/US/story?id=92662)

"Details of the plans are described in *Body of Secrets* (Doubleday, 2001), a new book by investigative reporter James Bamford...but they apparently were rejected by the civilian leadership and have gone undisclosed for nearly 40 years."

These documents came to light, Bamford said, partly because of Oliver Stone's 1992 film *JFK*. The film caused massive interest in assassination efforts to kill Kennedy, and U.S. official endorsement of murdering Fidel Castro.

Kennedy apparently told the mad general that he would not authorize an obvious U.S. invasion plan. And he did not rename Lemnitzer to continue as JCS chief after he proposed the Northwood plan, but he did make him NATO's supreme allied commander.

Bill Simpich wrote in, "The Hidden Castro Assassination Plots":

> *"Although President Kennedy and Secretary of Defense Robert McNamara refused to consider Operation Northwoods, military chiefs and even Robert Kennedy lobbied for a 'Remember the Maine'-type incident, where the US allegedly sank its own ship in Cuba as a pretext to start the Spanish-American War. Robert Kennedy suggested at an early point of the Cuban missile crisis:*
>
> *"'We should also think of whether there is some other way we can get involved in this, through Guantanamo Bay or something. Or whether there's some ship that...you know, sink the Maine or something.'"*
>
> *"On RFK's advocacy of a 'Remember the Maine' pretext: See McCone memo, August 21, 1962, in 'CIA Documents on the Cuban missile crisis', CIA/CSI, 1992; RFK 'questioning the feasibility of provoking an action against Guantanamo which would permit us to retaliate', FRUS, Vol. X, document 383. Also see Tim Weiner,* Legacy of Ashes, *pp. 192-193."*

The Castro and Khrushchev governments could not avoid knowing that the Kennedy administration had not given up on retaking Cuba even after its defeat at the Bay of Pigs. As General Lansdale was preparing his July 25, 1962 "Review of Operation Mongoose" report, the two leaders agreed to construct sites inside Cuba to store defensive nuclear missiles hoping thereby to deter future U.S. invasions. Khrushchev, we can recall, had advised Kennedy, in his April 18, 1961 letter, that the Soviet Union would render Cuba "all necessary help to repel armed attack". He added that he hoped the U.S. would relax the "international tension". But Kennedy chose to ignore this plea.

Notes:

1. See Appendix 11, 25 July, 1962, nr. 1

   Edward Lansdale also asked the military to draft the Operation Northwoods invasion pretext proposal as part of Operation Mongoose. (See Appendix 111). Years later he said the idea had not been viable because it depended on recruiting Cuban exiles to generate an uprising in Cuba, and he had not formed that team, or rather could not.

Lansdale may have been Graham Greene's eponymous character in his novel about Vietnam, *The Quiet American* (Penguin, 1955). Lansdale was a key character in Eugene Burdick's and William Lederer's, *The Ugly American* (W. Norton, 1958). Oliver Stone tagged him as one of the "three tramps" seen near the Texas School Book Depository shortly after the assassination of John F. Kennedy in his film *JFK*. Stone was motivated by Col. L. Fletcher Prouty's testimony to the Church Committee about Lansdale being one of the those fake tramps (E. Howard Hunt and Frank Sturgis were also identified as "tramps", who played a role in the assassination.)

2. 278. Memorandum From President Kennedy (1)

https://history.state.gov/historicaldocuments/frus1961-63v10/d278

Washington, November 30, 1961.

MEMORANDUM TO: The Secretary of State, The Secretary of Defense, The Director of CIA, The Attorney General, General Taylor, General Lansdale, Richard Goodwin

The following is a summary of the major decisions which have been made in regard to the Cuba Operation.

1.) We will use our available assets to go ahead with the discussed project in order to help Cuba overthrow the communist regime.

2.) This program will be conducted under the general guidance of General Lansdale, acting as Chief of Operations. It will be conducted by him through the appropriate regular organizations and Departments of the government.

3.) The program will be reviewed in two weeks in order to determine whether General Lansdale will continue as Chief of Operations.

4.) The NSC 5412 group will be kept closely informed of activities and be available for advice and recommendation.

5.) The Secretary of State and the Secretary of Defense and the Director of the Central Intelligence Agency will appoint senior officers of their department as personal representatives to assist the Chief of Operations as required. These senior officers should be able to exercise–either themselves or through the Secretaries and Director–effective operational control over all aspects of their Department's operations dealing with Cuba.

Knowledge of the existence of this operation should be restricted to the recipients of this memorandum, members of the 5412 group and (Page 689) the representatives appointed by the Secretaries and the Director. Any further dissemination of this knowledge will be only with the authority of the Secretaries of State or Defense or the Chief of Operations.

(1)Source: Kennedy Library, President's Office Files, Countries Series, Cuba, Security, 1961. Top Secret; Eyes Only. Internal evidence indicates that the memorandum was apparently drafted by McGeorge Bundy. An earlier version of this memorandum was sent to the same seven people on November 22. (Department of State, Central Files, 737.00/11-2261) The most significant difference between the two memoranda was that the responsibilities assigned to General Lansdale under point 2 in the November 30 memorandum had been assigned to Attorney General Kennedy in the November 22 memorandum, with Lansdale in a subordinate role as the Attorney General's Chief of Operations. Point 4 in the November 22 memorandum reads "The NSC 5412 group will be informed of activities." The Attorney General was included under point 6 in the November 22 memorandum among those listed as controlling dissemination of knowledge of the operation.

3. General Lemnitzer was on Eisenhower's war staff during the Second World War. Lemnitzer ran the invasion of Sicily in 1944 in association with the regional Mafia. Once President, Eisenhower appointed Lemnitzer commander of the Joint Chiefs of Staff. During the Bay of Pigs invasion, Lemnitzer advocated that President Kennedy launch a total attack. Two months later, July 20, at a National Security Council meeting, Lemnitzer presented Kennedy with a military plan for a surprise nuclear attack on the Soviet Union. Kennedy refused. Then came Northwoods proposal, followed by the Cuban Missile Crisis, during which Lemnizter and Air Force chief General Curtis LeMay advocated nuclear war once again. Kennedy transferred him from JCS command to NATO's Supreme Allied Commander, in November 1962, just after the CMC. When Lemnizter died, he was not spoken of as the chief behind the nefarious plot to kill his own men in Operation Northwoods but as a "war hero".

CHAPTER 4
The Cuban Missile Crisis

"THE TWO MOST crucial questions about the missile crisis are: how did it begin, and how did it end?" asked Noam Chomsky in his 50 year commemorative article, "The Week the World Stood Still". (http://www.tomdispatch.com/post/175605/tomgram%3A_noam_chomsky,_%22the_most_dangerous_moment,%22_50_years_later/)

"It began with Kennedy's terrorist attack against Cuba, with a threat of invasion in October 1962. It ended with the president's rejection of Russian offers that would seem fair to a rational person, but were unthinkable because they would have undermined the fundamental principle that the U.S. has the unilateral right to deploy nuclear missiles anywhere, aimed at China or Russia or anyone else, and right on their borders; and the accompanying principle that Cuba had no right to have missiles for defense against what appeared to be an imminent U.S. invasion. To establish these principles firmly it was entirely proper to face a high risk of war of unimaginable destruction, and to reject simple and admittedly fair ways to end the threat."

Chomsky adds a question: "How should JFK's relative moderation in the management of the crisis be evaluated against the background of the broader considerations...But that question does not arise in a disciplined intellectual and moral culture, which accepts without question the basic principle that the U.S. effectively owns the world by right, and is by definition a force for good despite occasional errors and misunderstandings....[so] it is plainly entirely proper for the U.S. to deploy massive offensive force all over the world while it is an outrage for others (allies and clients apart) to make even the slightest gesture in that direction or even to think of deterring the threatened use of violence by the benign global hegemon."

What this leading linguist-political scientist describes above is what is often referred to as "American Exceptionalism". (see chapter nineteen)

CUBAN MISSILE CRISIS CHRONOLOGY

The hegemon's Operation Mongoose was directing constant sabotage against Cuba, which required the Cuban leadership to respond. A Soviet missile base was under construction in Cuba by July. It included nuclear-tipped missiles for defense, a regiment of MiG-21 fighters (60-80), four brigades of armored personnel carriers and tanks, and 42,000 Soviet soldiers alongside 300,000 Cuban military personnel.

The CIA was encouraging Cuban exile terrorist groups to be bolder in their sabotage, including attacking people other than Cubans if they did business with their country. There were even attacks on foreign ships sailing with cargo to Cuba.

On August 24, José Basulto fired a 20mm cannon from the Juanin boat just 20 meters from the seaside Horneado de Rosita hotel in the Miramar suburb of Havana. The group he was with, DRE (Revolutionary Student Directorate), had been tipped that Fidel Castro would be there with allies from Russia, Czechoslovakia and East Germany. Fidel had not yet arrived but there were many doctors and technicians from these Soviet countries waiting for him.

Luckily no one got killed but the boat sped away to safety in Miami. The next day, Basulto and DRE leader Juan Salvat adorned the front page of Miami and Washington newspapers. They were viewed as heroes rather than attempted murderers. (https://www.washingtonpost.com/archive/lifestyle/magazine/1997/05/25/shoot-down/294e3d0b-d5f0-48d8-ad3c-e72c68933ec8/?utm_term=.beeff4f36531)

The CIA was paying the DRE $20,000 a month at that time. Many of its members were involved in the Bay of Pigs invasion as was Basulto. He became best buddies with Che murderer Felix Rodriquez. Basulto would later say, "I was trained as a terrorist by the United States, in the use of violence to attain goals."

José Basulto became all the more renowned in 1995-6 when he flew Brothers to the Rescue (BTTR) civilian aircraft from the CIA Opa-Locka Miami airport over Cuban territory. Between August 1995 and February 1996, Cuba lodged complaints against the U.S. government for allowing these aircraft to illegally fly over Cuba, trying to provoke a response. It came on February 24, 1996 when the Cuban Air Force, after several warnings, fired upon two of the three BTTR aircraft shooting them down. Four crewmen died.

At the time, I was living in Cuba working for its international news agency *Prensa Latina*, which Che had started. I recall telling colleagues that, "it was about time Cuba reacted. The U.S. wouldn't have waited for a second to shoot down the first Cuban or Russia flying over its territory."

During the buildup to the missile crisis, scores of these dangerous and murderous raids were conducted by the Alpha 66 group. One can read on its "official history" website (http://cuban-exile.com/doc_351-375/doc0358.html) the following:

> *"The next attack followed on October 8, 1962, when commandos landed on the Cuban coast and attacked a Russian base at Isabella de Sagua, in Las Villas Province, capturing arms and flags, and killing 20 Russian soldiers."*

The Russians had every right to defend not only Cubans but themselves.

In Ignacio Ramonet's book with Fidel, *My Life: Fidel Castro*, the *comandante* said: "The world was on the verge of a thermonuclear war as a consequence of the United States' aggressive, brutal policy against Cuba. A plan [Operation Mongoose], approved about 10 months after the disastrous defeat they suffered in Girón and about eight months before the crisis broke out, to invade the island with the direct use of that country's naval, air and land forces." (p 271, in English version).

Fidel and other Cuban leaders discussed with key Soviet leaders what to do. The Cubans wanted to release a public statement that in the event of such an attack on Cuba, the Soviets would consider such to be an attack on it and respond accordingly. The Soviets declined and instead proposed placing defensive nuclear missiles, initially 42 medium-range rockets, on Cuban soil.

The Cuban leadership eventually accepted this proposal but initially Fidel's view was that the Soviets saw this situation as an opportunity "to obtain an improvement in the balance of power between the USSR and the United States. I confess I was none too happy about the presence of those weapons in Cuba, given our interest in avoiding the image of Cuba as a Soviet base." (p. 272)

In the Spanish edition of the biography, (pg. 249-50), Fidel said that an additional 192 strategic projectiles were installed in Cuba. While all the missiles were defensive, Fidel said, in the sense that they were to protect Cuba against an aggressive invasion from the U.S., strategic missiles could also be considered offensive. The terminology of defense-offense is important in the world of politics as the U.S. considers that no State it cannot like has the "right" to have offensive weapons that could be used against the U.S.—the exception of Russia and China had to be accepted, because they are big guys who might do as much damage to the U.S. as it could do against them.

An important US American expert on the matter of how these missiles were viewed by the Russian leadership is most relevant here. Sheldon Stern is a former historian at the John F. Kennedy Presidential Library He published a book based on his study of the extensive tapes of the EXCOMM (executive committee) meetings (declassified in the late 1990s) in which Kennedy and a circle of advisors debated what to do during those 13 days. (1)

"Khrushchev's original explanation for shipping missiles to Cuba had been fundamentally true: the Soviet leader had never intended these weapons as a threat to the security of the United States, but rather considered their deployment a defensive move to protect his Cuban allies from American attacks and as a desperate effort to give the U.S.S.R. the appearance of equality in the nuclear balance of power," Stern concluded from his study.

This American patriot and Kennedy supporter with actual proof in his hands makes the same observation of the Russians intentions as does Fidel Castro. Forty years after the crisis, Robert McNamara, Kennedy's defense secretary at the time of CMC, also conceded that Cubans were justified in fearing an attack from his government's military.

"If I were in Cuban or Soviet shoes, I would have thought so too." "We as a superpower did not look through to the ends of our actions. That was a real weakness." (2)

On October 15, 1962, a group of CIA analysts assigned to review aerial photographs of Cuba identify several newly established Soviet medium-range ballistic missile installations. These U.S. spy planes had been flying over Cuba at least since August. A Soviet colonel in information services, Oleg Penkovsky, had given the U.S. exact coordinates of the missiles.

President John F. Kennedy is briefed the next morning, setting in motion a crisis that brought the world frighteningly close to nuclear war. Over the next 13 tense days, the crisis deepened and people around the world feared the real possibility of a horrific worldwide conflict. In the U.S. people practice hiding in shelters at homes, work places and schools.

October 18, President Kennedy meets with Soviet Foreign Minister Andrei Gromyko and Ambassador Anatoly Dobrynin. He doesn't say he knows they are installing missiles. The Russians say their military assistance to Cuba is purely defensive.

October 22, President John F. Kennedy addresses the people over television and radio: the U.S. is setting up a naval quarantine (blockade) against Cuba. The president also says the U.S. would wreak "a full retaliatory response upon the Soviet Union" if any nuclear missile is fired on any nation in this hemisphere.

October 23, President Kennedy signs a proclamation enacting the U.S. arms quarantine against Cuba. U.S. Navy deploys an armada of 200 combat surface ships with 40,000 sailors in an arc 500 sea miles north of Havana, that is, in international water—that is, in itself, a violation of UN laws; the required approval of the UN never entered in EXCOMM talks. Eight of the ships were aircraft carriers with 50-60 aircraft. (This is Fidel's figures. The Soviet "After Action Report" states there were four aircraft carriers.)

In addition, 579 combat aircraft were on alert at Florida bases. The Yankees said they had the right to stop any ship, board it and check for "offensive weapons" that may be on their way to Cuba. They could then either confiscate the weapons or force the ship to turn back.

In response, Fidel Castro appears on television to alert and mobilize the people. He then commands anti-aircraft batteries to shoot down U.S. aircraft that overfly the country, fearing that they could be the vanguard of an invasion.

Fidel later told Ramonet: "We thought that conflict was inevitable. And we were determined to take that risk. It never occurred to us to give in to the adversary's threats."

The same day, Women Strike for Peace activists carry signs—"No

War" "Dead Men Can't Negotiate"—as they picket outside the United Nations headquarters in New York City where the U.N. Security Council considers the Cuban missile crisis.

Khrushchev's orders his missile-carrying ships to turn back. Sixteen to twenty missile-carrying ships did turn back. Khrushchev exempted those few ships already close to Cuba, mainly the four submarines in Brigade-69.

October 25, U.S. Ambassador to the United Nations, Adlai Stevenson, confronts Soviet delegate Valerian Zorin during an emergency session of the U. N. Security Council. He displays reconnaissance photographs and challenges Zorin to deny that the Soviet Union had introduced *offensive missiles* in Cuba. Zorin does not say "yes" or "no," but indicates to the other Council members that the charge was not to be believed. Zorin retorts, "'I am not in an American courtroom, sir, and therefore do not wish to answer a question that is put to me in the fashion in which a prosecutor puts questions. In due course, sir, you will have your reply."

Stating that Zorin was "in the courtroom of world opinion," Stevenson replies: "I am prepared to wait for my answer until hell freezes over, if that's your decision. And I am also prepared to present the evidence in this room."

October 26, Fidel sends a cable to Khrushchev. The interpretation of the exchange of cables between them is still being debated.

"I consider aggression to be almost imminent—within the next 24-72 hours." Fidel then presents two variants of attacks. The first is only an air attack to destroy the missiles. In the second variant, total invasion of Cuba with the intention of occupation. He stated:

"The dangers of this aggressive policy for humanity are so great that after such an event the Soviet Union must never allow circumstances in which the imperialists might carry out a nuclear first strike against it". If they invade Cuba, "that would be the moment to eliminate that danger for ever, in an act of the most legitimate self-defense. However hard and terrible the solution might be, there is no other."

In Khrushchev's October 30 reply, he interpreted Fidel's cable as proposing that the USSR "carry out a nuclear first strike against the enemy territory."

In Fidel's cable the next day, he wrote: "I was not unaware when I wrote that the words of my letter might be misinterpreted by you…I did not suggest to you, Comrade Khrushchev, that the USSR become the aggressor, because that would be worse than wrong, it would be immoral and unworthy of me…I did not suggest to you that the USSR attack in the midst of the crisis, as it seems from your letter you think, but rather that after the imperialist attack [against Cuba], the USSR act without hesitation and never commit the error of allowing the enemy to strike you first with nuclear weapons." (See Ramonet pgs. 278-84. See also footnote 3)

October 27, "**Black Saturday**", the day that the world came closest to a nuclear world war, started with Soviet-Cuban defense forces firing a surface-to-air missile at a USAF reconnaissance U-2 flying over Cuba. The plane crashed and the pilot died. The Joint Chiefs of Staff urge Kennedy to bomb the SAM missile site but the president fears it would escalate into a global war.

(When I was a U.S. Air Force radar operator in Japan (1956-7), we had orders that if any Soviet aircraft of any type flew over "our" territory in Japan, it was to be shot down. Because I was a flight tracker, I knew of at least two U.S. reconnaissance aircraft that flew from our area over Soviet territory daily. We airmen were told at weekly intelligence briefings that we flew many flights over Soviet territory. The Soviets never shot any down. I never heard anyone speak about the double morality of this. Finally, on May 1, 1960, the Soviets did shoot down one CIA spy plane, a U-2 piloted by Francis Gary Powers. At first President Eisenhower denied its military intention, but once the Soviets presented the unharmed captured pilot and spy technology equipment from the plane the embarrassed president admitted U.S. intentions.)

Later on October 27, another U-2 spy plane went missing off Alaska and strayed into Soviet territory. An intrusion into Soviet airspace at the height of a nuclear showdown between the two superpowers was a dangerously provocative act. The mission was to collect radioactive samples from the Soviet nuclear tests at Novaya Zemlya but, apparently, without entering Soviet space.

"As he crossed into Soviet airspace, [allegedly without knowing it] at least six Soviet interceptor jets took off from two different airfields in Chukotka. Their mission was to shoot the intruder down," wrote Michael Dobbs, "Washington Post" reporter and author of *One Minute to Midnight: Kennedy, Khrushchev, and Castro on the Brink of Nuclear War* (Knopf, N.Y, 2008).

"The Soviets had scrambled MiG fighters to intercept the missing U-2, and the U.S. Strategic Air Command (SAC) was scrambling American fighters in response. The Soviets might well perceive the U-2 incursion as a harbinger of an American nuclear attack."

The U-2 pilot realizing he was inside Soviet territory turned back to Alaska. By now SAC, General Curtis LeMay's favorite force, had scrambled two F-102 fighter-interceptors to provide protection. With the heightened alert, these aircraft were now loaded with nuclear-tipped Falcon air-to-air missiles. One F-102 could wipe out an entire fleet of incoming Soviet bombers. "In theory, nuclear weapons were to be used only on the authority of the president. In practice, an F-102 pilot had the physical ability to fire a missile by pushing a few buttons on his control panel. Because he was alone in the cockpit, no one could override such a decision," wrote Dobbs.

While the U-2 pilot was lost over the Chukotka Peninsula, Soviet troops were targeting their missiles on the U.S. naval base, waiting for an order from Moscow that fortunately never came. The pilot landed in Alaska with nearly no fuel.

On the same day, the *USS Randolph* aircraft carrier and 14 anti-submarine warfare (ASW) ships tracking the Soviet submarines fired upon three of the four—B-36, Captain Aleksei F. Dubivko; B-130, Captain Nikolai A. Shumkov; B-59, Captain Valentin S. Savitzky. The Brigade-69 chief commander, Captain Vasili Arkhipov, was on this ship. The B-4, captained by Ryurik Ketov, was not fired upon because it was not seen by U.S. forces when it surfaced to recharge its batteries. U.S. aviators did discover its existence at some point but it was able to evade pursuit and attack.

The other subs had been discovered days before because they had to surface to recharge their accumulator batteries, a technological necessity for these diesel vessels. On this fateful day, several ASW destroyers were dropping depth charges that hit three of the subs. Radio systems were damaged making communication impossible. The men in the sweltering hot subs felt that a war had begun. Their choices were to either fire their missiles or surface. They chose to surface and were fired upon by several aircraft flying 20-100 meters over them. Nevertheless, they were able to turn around and head home.

"Although firing live ammunition at a submarine was strictly prohibited, having been a member of an ASW squadron flight crew, I have no trouble believing Ketov's account" [referring to Captain Ryurik Ketov's subsequent report], wrote Martin Sherwin, who had been a junior officer attached to Patrol Squadron 31, an ASW squadron out of San Diego, California. (4)

The captains had averted a battle that could have resulted in a nuclear world war—the subject of the next chapter.

Despite this achievement the drama of nuclear war tension continued. That night, Robert Kennedy met with Russian Ambassador Dobrynin. He told him that Khrushchev had to conform to U.S. dictates, because if not, on Monday, (Oct. 29) the U.S. would bomb Cuba. RFK said that if his brother did not invade, the U.S. military might well overthrow him in a coup, take power and invade Cuba.

Robert Kennedy recalls: "We had to have a commitment by tomorrow that those bases would be removed...if they did not remove those bases, we would remove them."

In Dobrynin's cable to the Soviet Foreign Ministry he said that he asked RFK: "How would the USA have reacted if foreign planes appeared over its territory?"

RFK purportedly replied: "We have a resolution of the Organization of American States that gives us the right to such overflights."

Dobrynin replied: "I told him that the Soviet Union, like all peace-loving countries, resolutely rejects such a 'right' or, to be more exact, this kind of true lawlessness, when people who don't like the social-political situation in a country try to impose their will on it...The OAS resolution is a direct violation of the UN Charter...and you, as the Attorney general of the USA, the highest legal entity, should certainly know that." (5)

October 28 morning, Khrushchev announces the missiles would be withdrawn. In a private message to Kennedy he expressed alarm at the U.S. overflight: "One of your planes violates our frontier during this anxious time we are both experiencing when everything has been put into combat readiness. Is it not a fact that an intruding American plane could be easily taken for a nuclear bomber, which might push us to a fateful step?"

Khrushchev's "climb down averted the threat of nuclear exchange," Dobbs wrote.

Over the following weeks, U.S. forces monitored the departure of missiles aboard eight Soviet ships, and the crisis was averted.

AFTERMATH

On the same day Khrushchev announced that he would withdraw missiles from Cuba and shut down the Soviet base, he instructed Deputy Prime Minister Anastas Mikoyan to fly to Cuba and talk to his friend, Fidel Castro: to assure him that JFK promised not to invade his country; to smooth over his anger with Moscow's failure to consult him on the JFK negotiations; urge him not to shoot at U.S. spy planes flying over the country; settle the issue of tactical warheads and removal of the strategic weapons. Anastas took his son, Sergo, with him as his secretary.

Five decades later, Sergo Mikoyan wrote a book about this mission with the assistance of researcher/translator Svetlana Savranskaya—*The Soviet-Cuba Missile Crisis* (Woodrow Wilson Press-Stanford University Press, 2012. It is partly based upon Mikoyan's Russian language 2006 book, *Anatomy of the Cuban Missile Crisis*).

Juan O. Tamayo wrote a review of the book, *The untold story of the Cuban Missile Crisis*, in the Miami Herald, October 15, 2012. Excerpts:

"The Cuban Missile Crisis had just ended, with Soviet leader Nikita Khrushchev's promise to President John F. Kennedy on Oct. 28 1962 that he was withdrawing his strategic nuclear weapons from the island. But nearly 100 smaller Soviet nuclear warheads were also in Cuba, unknown to the U.S. government at the time and for decades into the future.

"Fidel Castro wanted desperately to keep them. Had Castro prevailed, Cuba would have become a nuclear power. And if Kennedy had known that Khrushchev had all but lied on Oct. 28, the hawks in Washington might have won their push for an all-out U.S. invasion of the island." (http://www.mcclatchydc.com/news/nation-world/world/article24738718.html)

Sergo Mikoyan's tale starts with the withdrawal from Cuba of what Kennedy called "offensive weapons"—Soviet R-14 and R-12 missiles with nuclear warheads and ranges of up to 1,550 miles, and medium-range IL-28 bombers, aged but still capable of carrying nuclear bombs."

"What Khrushchev did not reveal was that 98 tactical nuclear warheads also had been deployed in Cuba for the Luna and FKR-1 missiles, both coastal defense weapons deployed essentially to destroy a possible U.S. invasion armada."

In the July 1962 agreement between Khrushchev and Castro, "the deployment of all the nuclear weapons to the Caribbean island had included a promise that Cuban troops would control the tactical warheads after receiving training."

Although Mikoyan felt friendship and comradeship with Fidel, his judgment about Cuba keeping tactical nukes for self-defense under Fidel's hands changed. He now saw Fidel as too "hotheaded". Mikoyan reported to Khrushchev that he had never seen him "so distraught and irate."

When Mikoyan spoke of removing all the nuclear weapons, Castro shot back. "What do you think we are—a zero on the left, a dirty rag?"

"Mikoyan understood then that the Cuban tail was quite capable of wagging the Soviet dog," Savranskaya wrote in a postscript to the book. "What became clear to Mikoyan is that the Soviets could not really control their Cuban ally."

"The issue of the tactical warheads came to a boil on the night of Nov. 22, when Mikoyan met for more than three hours with Castro, Ernesto 'Che' Guevara and three other senior Cuban government officials at the Presidential Palace in Havana.

"'Is it true that all the tactical nuclear weapons are already removed?' Castro is quoted as asking Mikoyan…Mikoyan replies that Moscow 'has not given any promise regarding the removal' of the tactical weapons. 'The Americans do not have any information that they are in Cuba.'"

"Later in the notes, Castro returns to the tactical weapons, asking, 'Doesn't the Soviet Union transfer nuclear weapons to other countries?' Mikoyan replies that there is 'a law prohibiting the transfer of any nuclear weapons, including the tactical ones, to anybody. We never transferred it to anyone, and we did not intend to transfer it.'"

"Castro insists. 'Would it be possible to leave the tactical nuclear weapons in Cuba in Soviet hands, without transferring them to the Cubans?' Mikoyan says no, because the 42,000 Soviet troops in Cuba were technically only "advisers."

And there the matter was closed. Sergo is still uncertain if there was such a law as his father told Fidel, but he became determined not to leave any nuclear weapons in Cuban hands.

In my own view, it was not only a big power question of control over a small ally. It was the larger ethical concern of preserving world peace at all cost, taking precedence over justice and communist ideology! And here is one of many moments in Russian/Soviet history proving that Soviet/Russian leaders have opted for world peace at all costs.

The capitalists and their "democratic" governments do not think this way. We know that neither Kennedy nor any future U.S. president left Cuba in peace. Sabotage, assassination attempts, even chemical-biological warfare (chapter six) continued to challenge the Cuban people's existence and patience. The Kennedy administration allowed CIA-controlled exile groups to continue their murderous sabotage. One can read the following on Alpha 66's website. (http://cuban-exile.com/doc_351-375/doc0358.html)

"The next attack followed on October 8, 1962, when commandos landed on the Cuban coast and attacked a Russian base at Isabella de Sagua, in Las Villas Province, capturing arms and flags, and killing 20 Russian soldiers. On October 19, 1962, it was announced that Alpha 66 and II Frente Nacional del Escambray had united to further the war against Communism in Cuba. Under the command of Cmdte Eloy Gutierrez Menoyo, the next attack was carried out at Juan Francisco Beach in Las Villas Province December 4, 1962. The next and most important attack came on March 17, 1963, when the commandos entered the harbor of Isabella de Sagua and sank the Russian ship Lvov at the dock, by gunfire."

While Kennedy may not have known about these actions, at least in advance, he didn't rescind orders to subvert Cuba.

The 1,113 terrorists captured at the Bay of Pigs had been sentenced to up to 20 years in prison. Many of them were comrades with the terrorists who continued sabotaging Cuba, or themselves against took part after the CMC. Had the Cuban government been primarily motivated by revenge and punishment, it would have kept the captured terrorists in prison. But on December 24, just two months after the end of the missile crisis, they were flown to Miami, even before the full ransom of $53 million in food and medicines, and $2.9 million in cash had arrived in Cuba.

Chomsky wrote: "Kennedy officially renewed the terrorist operations after the crisis ebbed. Ten days before his assassination he approved a CIA plan for 'destruction operations' by U.S. proxy forces 'against a large oil refinery and storage facilities, a large electric plant, sugar refineries, railroad bridges, harbor facilities, and underwater demolition of docks and ships.'"

Nevertheless, Fidel had praise and respect for Kennedy, whom he saw as having to make concessions to madmen generals and CIA officials. (See Ramonet and my chapter six).

Thirteen Days, the 2000 film by Roger Donaldson is basically an homage to the Kennedy brothers for being the world's saviors in October. No wonder given that one of its sources was RFK's book published posthumously, in 1969, *Thirteen Days: A Memoir of the Cuban Missile Crisis.*

I know personally how the Cuban leadership still felt about Kennedy when I worked for government media in 1987-96. The chief editor of its main newspaper, "Granma", told me that they felt there would have been positive changes in U.S. relations towards Cuba, perhaps a lifting of the embargo and even the return of Guatánamo land where the U.S. naval base stands, had Kennedy lived and won a second term. That possible scenario was what mainly motivated his US American assassins to "take him out".

The record clearly proves, however, that it was Soviet leadership and a Russian submarine captain who were the world's saviors.

Notes:

1. See: *The Cuban Missile Crisis in American Memory: Myths vs. Reality* Stanford University Press, 2012.

2. As reported in the Boston Globe, October 13, 2002, "Soviets Close to Using A-Bomb in 1962 Crisis, Forum." The forum was organized by the Cuban government and the private National Security Archive at the George Washington University, Washington DC. Other participants at the forum, who had been involved in the crisis, included General Anatoly Gribkov, Sergo Mikoyan and an officer on submarine B-59, Vadim Orlov. Besides McNamara from the U.S. were JFK counsel Theodore Sorensen, JFK aide and historian Arthur Schlesinger, embassy political officer in Havana Wayne Smith, CIA officer Raymond L. Garthoff, watch commander on the USS Beale destroyer Captain John Peterson, and Navy pilot Captain William Ecker. Fidel Castro led a large delegation of Cuban leaders and participants in the crisis.

3. The Atlantic magazine's editor-in-chief, Jeffrey Goldberg, interviewed Fidel Castro in September 2010, "Castro: 'No one has been slandered more than the Jews" https://www.theatlantic.com/international/archive/2010/09/castro-no-one-has-been-slandered-more-than-the-jews/62566/)

As an aside, Goldberg asked Fidel: "At a certain point it seemed logical for you to recommend that the Soviets bomb the U.S. Does what you recommended still seem logical now?" He answered: "After I've seen what I've seen, and knowing what I know now, it wasn't worth it all."

4. See his article, "The Cuban Missile Crisis Revisited: Nuclear Deterrence? Good Luck!" (https://cornerstone.gmu.edu/articles/4198) Sherwin is now a university history professor.

5. See: Anatomy of a Controversy: The Cold War International History Project Bulletin. http://nsarchive2.gwu.edu/nsa/cuba_mis_cri/moment.htm

CHAPTER 5
Vasili Arkhipov: The Man Who Prevented World War Three

"THIS GUY CALLED Vasili Arkhipov saved the world." This is how the key United States organizer of the 2002 Havana conference on the Cuban Missile Crisis (CMC), Thomas Blanton, judged the part that Vasili Arkhipov played on **Black Saturday**, October 27, 1962.

Blanton is director of the private, non-profit, archival institution, National Security Archive (NS Archive). Founded in 1985 and located at George Washington University in Washington D.C., it is the largest repository of declassified U.S. documents outside of the federal government. It has the most extensive documentation on the CMC. (http://nsarchive.gwu.edu/project/cuba-project)

In correspondence with me (June-July 2017) Blanton wrote that while Arkhipov helped to calm down the situation, he had "overstated Arkhipov's role". This was said in reference to the 2012 British Bedlam film: "*Secrets of the Dead: The Man Who Saved the World*", which overdramatized a confrontation between Arkhipov and the B-59 submarine Captain Valentin Savitsky.

The exact details of what occurred deep down in the ocean aboard the Soviet submarine are not totally known since the official Soviet debriefing accounts are still secret. What can be pieced together indicates that there was a tense time in which the nuclear torpedo the sub carried could have been launched as the captain feared the U.S. Navy's grenade/depth charge attack on the sub indicated that the United States had begun warring against Russian and Cuba.

Regardless of the overdramatized Bedlam film, including some errors we come to later down, it resulted in mass media publications taking the matter up, and even giving credit to at least this one Russian

Captain Vasili Arkhipov

captain for saving the world from a possible apocalyptic catastrophe. I know of no other horrible event, war or possible war, in which anyone can assert that the United States leadership, or a single U.S. military person, has saved the world from such catastrophe. On the contrary, the only time nuclear bombs were used was the U.S atomic bombing of Hiroshima and Nagasaki, which, as we will see in chapter eleven, was totally unnecessary to win that war.

Like Yuri Gagarin, Vasili was born to a poor, peasant family in a small town near Moscow (Staraya Kupavna), on January 30, 1926. At the age of 16, he began his sailing education at the Pacific Higher Naval School. Vasili saw his first military action as a minesweeper in the Pacific Theater at the end of World War II. In 1947, he graduated from the Caspian Higher Naval School and served on submarines in the Soviet Black Sea, Northern, and Baltic fleets.

What follows is how close we all came to not being alive today. As National Geographic writer Robert Krulwich put it in his March 25, 2016 article: "You (and Almost Everyone You Know) Owe Your Life to This Man." (https://news.nationalgeographic.com/2016/03/you-and-almost-everyone-you-know-owe-your-life-to-this-man/)

Another writing with this theme worth mentioning is Edward Wilson's "Guardian" piece, October 27, 2012, "Thank you Vasili Arkhipov, The Man Who Stopped Nuclear War." (https://www.theguardian.com/commentisfree/2012/oct/27/vasili-arkhipov-stopped-nuclear-war)

The NS Archive October 24, 2012 briefing posted many relevant documents on the crisis, and a reference to the controversial British film: (http://nsarchive2.gwu.edu/NSAEBB/NSAEBB399/)

"The underwater Cuban Missile Crisis received new attention this week with two PBS Television shows, one of which re-enacts as 'overheated' docudrama (in the words of *The New York Times* reviewer) the confrontation between U.S. Navy sub-chasing units and the Soviet submarine B-59, commanded by Valentin Savitsky, on the most dangerous day of the Crisis, October 27, 1962." The PBS docudrama mentioned is the British film, which the U.S. TV channel showed.

The NS Archive posted short video excerpts from Vadim Orlov and Captain John Peterson presentations at the 2002 Havana conference. Orlov was signals intelligence officer on the B-59; Peterson was a lieutenant on one of the attacking subs, *USS Beale*.

Another posting was Orlov's account of sailing for weeks on B-59, according to Russian journalist Alexander Mozgovoi in his book, *The Cuban Samba of the Quartet of Foxtrots: Soviet Submarines in the Caribbean Crisis of 1962* (Moscow, Military Parade, 2002). It was translated Svetlana Savranskaya, a native of Russia.

The NS Archive was also able to reveal the Soviet "After Action Report" from the USSR Northern Fleet Headquarters, December 1962, and translated by Savranskaya. Extensive excerpts:

"1. The Navy carried out preparations for operation 'Anadyr' under the codename operation 'Kama.' Preparations for the operation started in March-April, 1962.

"2. For participation in the operation the 20th operative squadron of submarines was formed consisting of: the 69th brigade of diesel torpedo submarines "B-4," "B-36," "B-59," "B130" of project 641[known as Foxtrot according to NATO]...

[B-4 captained by Ryurik Ketov, B-36 Aleksei Dubivko, B-59 Valentin Savitsky, B-130 Nikolai Shumkov. The four made up the 69the brigade whose chief of staff was Vasili Arkhipov.]

"4. Preparations for the operation were completed on September 30, 1962 with loading 21torpedoes with conventional load and one torpedo with nuclear load onto each of the submarines.

"5. Instructions to the commanders of the submarines and ceremony of launch were conducted by first deputy of the Supreme Commander of the Navy Admiral Fokin V. A. and Chief of Staff of the Northern Fleet Vice Admiral Rassokho A. I.

"Admiral Fokin V. A. spoke to the personnel of the 69th submarine brigade and said that the brigade was given a special assignment of the Soviet government: to cross the ocean in secret and to arrive to a new basing point in one of fraternal countries. Several hours before the departure commanders of the submarines received 'top secret' envelopes, which they could open only after leaving the Kola Bay. They were instructed to inform the personnel of the submarines about the country of the new deployment only after the submarines reached the Atlantic Ocean…The shore submarine base of the 20th squadron was [to be] loaded onto the ships of the Merchant Marine Ministry, arrived in Cuba at Mariel harbor in October and remained there.

"6. Having overcome the obstacles of the Norwegian and the Faero-Icelandic submarine barriers, and the barrier between Newfoundland and the Azores islands, four submarines of the 69th brigade of the Northern Fleet arrived to the assigned positions in the Sargasso Sea, to the east of Cuba, in the week of the 20th of October.

"By the time of the submarines' arrival to the assigned positions, the Americans had discovered the deployment of the Soviet missiles in Cuba and Soviet-American relations reached the critical moment.

"Beginning from October 22, a naval blockade of the island went into effect. To carry it out and to search for our submarines, the U.S. Navy employed over 200 combat surface ships, up to 200 planes of the base patrol aviation, four aircraft carrier search and assault groups with 50-60 planes on board and destroyers charged with discovering and destroying our submarines at the start of the military action. For discovering the brigade submarines they also used the stationary hydroacoustic system of underwater reconnaissance and observation 'SOSUS', as well as the shore means of radio-electric resistance to create radio interference in the command and control systems of our submarines. Practically on every bandwidth, interference transmitters were turned on at the start of transmission of information from Moscow, which resulted in delays of reception of orders from the Headquarters of the Navy from several hours to a full day.

"Therefore, the *U.S. Navy concentrated forces, which were hundred times stronger than ours in their combat capabilities, to counter our four diesel submarines.* It is natural that in the situation of such concentration of anti-submarine forces in a small area of the ocean, discovering the diesel submarines that had to surface to recharge their accumulator batteries was just a question of time, which happened soon. [author emphasis, also other italicized sentences below]

"Submarine "B-130," which came to the surface for repairs of all three of its failed diesel engines (factory defects), was discovered by the anti-submarine aviation, and then also by the surface ships. When the fact of the presence of our submarines in the Sargasso Sea became obvious, the activity of anti-submarine warfare was stepped up even more.

"As a result, the following submarines were discovered, pursued for several days, and then came to the surface because of fully discharged accumulator batteries:—submarine "B-36" by the anti-submarine aviation and destroyer of the radiolocation patrol unit "Charles P. Cecil," ship No. 545.—submarine "B-59" by carrier aviation and destroyers "Berry," "Lowry," "Beale," "Beich," "Bill," "Eaton," "Cony," "Conway," "Murray," and the anti-submarine aircraft carrier "Randolph." —submarine "B-4" was discovered by anti-submarine aviation, but thanks to having fully charged accumulator batteries, was able to evade the pursuit and did not come to the surface.

"In the course of search and pursuit of the submarines by anti-submarine warfare forces, they actively used explosive sources [sic] of the location systems 'Julie-Jezebel', the blasts of which are impossible to distinguish from explosions of depth bombs. It is possible that depth bombs were actually used because three of the submarines suffered damage to the parts of radio systems antennas, which made reception and transmission of information substantially more difficult.

"During one of the pursuit episodes, the hydroacoustic systems of submarine "B-36" identified the noise of torpedo propellers launched against the submarine, and when the torpedo did not home on the target because the submarine was submerging very fast, *the destroyer attempted to ram [the submarine] and passed over the command room [rubka] and the conning tower of the boat. Luckily by that moment the boat already had submerged to the depth of 30 meters. When submarine "B-36" came up to the surface, the guns and the torpedo launchers of the destroyer were opened and aimed at the submarine.*

"When submarine "B-59" came up to the surface, airplanes and helicopters from the aircraft carrier "Randolph" flew over the submarine 12 times at the altitude of 20-100 meters. *With every over flight they fired their aviation cannons /there were about 300 shots altogether/, and in the course of the over flight above the boat, they turned on their search lights with the purpose of blinding the people on the bridge of the submarine.*

"Helicopters lowered floating hydroacoustic stations along the route of the submarine and dropped explosive devices, hovered over the conning tower of the submarine and demonstratively conducted filming. The destroyers maneuvered around the submarine at a distance of 20-50 meters *demonstratively aiming their guns at the submarine, dropped depth bombs and hydroacoustic buoys when they crossed the course of the submarine,* lifted flag signals and shouted in the loudspeaker demanding that the[sub] stops. Similar actions were undertaken in regard to submarine "B-130."

> "The fact that the submarines of the 69th brigade were not designed [neprisposobleny] to be used in tropical conditions also contributed to their discovery:—absence of air conditioning systems when the outside temperature was above 30 C—absence of cooling systems for charging accumulator batteries—high humidity in the sections and the salinity of the outside water—temperature at some combat positions /hydroacoustics, electricians, engine operators/ which reached 50-60 degrees.
>
> "All this led to failure of the equipment /decrease in resistance of the insulation of the antennas, salinization of water refrigerators, unsealing of hermetic hull openings [orifices] and cable openings and other issues/, and also to heat strokes and fainting among the sailors. *Limited reserves of fresh water did not permit us to give more than 250 grams of water per person per day—and that in the conditions of the strongest sweat production and dehydration of organism.* The impossibility to wash off sweat and dirt led to 100% of personnel developing rashes in the most serious, infected form. To alleviate these conditions, the captains were forced to partially surface to ventilate the submarine sections [otsek] and the accumulator battery, which [...] could lead to their discovery."

The NS Archive October 31, 2002 briefing summarizes some of the most important developments during this crisis relating to the Soviet submarines.

"During the missile crisis, U.S. naval officers did not know about Soviet plans for a submarine base or that the Foxtrot submarines were nuclear-armed. Nevertheless, the Navy high command worried that the submarines, which had already been detected in the north Atlantic, could endanger enforcement of the blockade. Therefore, under orders from the Pentagon, U.S. Naval forces carried out systematic efforts to track Soviet submarines in tandem with the plans to blockade, and possibly invade, Cuba." (http://nsarchive2.gwu.edu/NSAEBB/NSAEBB75/#1)

"While ordered not to attack the submarines, the Navy received instructions on 23 October from Secretary of Defense McNamara to signal Soviet submarines in order to induce them to surface and identify themselves. Soon messages conveying 'Submarine Surfacing and Identification Procedures' were transmitted to Moscow [Russia said it never received them] and other governments around the world.

"The next morning, on 24 October, President Kennedy and the National Security Council's Executive Committee (ExCom) discussed the submarine threat and the dangers of an incident. According to Attorney General Robert Kennedy, when Secretary of Defense Robert McNamara reviewed the use of practice depth charges (PDCs), the size of hand grenades, to signal the submarines, '*those few minutes were the time of greatest worry to the President. His hand went up to his face & he closed his fist*'".

"The U.S. effort to surface the Soviet submarines involved considerable risk; exhausted by weeks undersea in difficult circumstances and worried that the U.S. Navy's practice depth charges were dangerous explosives, senior officers on several of the submarines, notably B-59 and B-130, were rattled enough to talk about firing nuclear torpedoes, whose 15 kiloton explosive yields approximated the bomb that devastated Hiroshima in August 1945. Huchthausen includes a disquieting account of an incident aboard submarine B-130, when U.S. destroyers were pitching PDCs at it. In a move to impress the Communist Party political officer, Captain Nikolai Shumkov ordered the preparations of torpedoes, including the tube holding the nuclear torpedo; the special weapon security officer then warned Shumkov that the torpedo could not be armed without permission from headquarters. After hearing that the security officer had fainted, Shumkov told his subordinates that he had no intention to use the torpedo 'because we would go up with it if we did.' Peter Huchthausen, *October Fury* (New Jersey: John Wiley, 2002)."

U.S. Navy veteran Peter A. Huchthausen served on the *USS Blandy*, one of eight pursuing destroyers during the crisis. They surrounded the subs some 500 sea miles from Cuba. (Accounts differ on how many destroyers pursued the submarines, from 8 to 14 at various points over days.)

Huchthausen's book is an extensive study of Soviet ships involved in Operation Anadyr (the name for the delivery and deployment of modern weapons systems—nuclear—to Cuba) and the United States quarantine process to stop it. Operation Anadyr was devised in May

1962 by a high command army general, Anatoly Gribkov, with the mission to prevent a U.S. invasion

General Gribkov attended the 30 year commemoratory conference of the CMS in Havana, in 1992. Here he revealed to the world for the first time that Russia had deployed nine nuclear tipped Luna missiles in Cuba. Former Defense Secretary Robert MacNamara was shocked to hear this. The U.S. had no idea these advanced warheads had made it to Cuba. It was also unclear how much discretionary authority Soviet ground commanders in Cuba had to use those weapons.

By then, the U.S.-friendly Boris Yeltsin period had begun, and although Gribkov spoke on his own in Havana he was not punished for this revelation. On the contrary he co-authored a book, *Operation Anadyr: U.S. and Soviet General Recount the Cuban Missile Crisis* (Chicago, Edition q, 1994). His co-author was U.S. Air Force four-star General William Smith, who had served as chief of staff. Smith became a board member of NS Archive until his death, in 2016.

Svetlana Savranskaya wrote the preeminent article about the decision-making process concerning the use of the tactical nuclear weapons aboard the four submarines—"New Sources on the Role of Soviet Submarines in the Cuban Missile Crisis". http://www.belfercenter.org/sites/default/files/legacy/files/CMC50/SavranskayaJSSNewsourcesonroleofSovietsubmarinesinCMC.pdf

"Her research reveals how a chain of inadvertent developments at sea could have precipitated global nuclear war," wrote the publisher of The Journal of Strategic Studies, April 2005.

The submarine captains apparently were unclear themselves as to what authority they had to fire the nuclear missile, especially if there was no contact with Soviet command, which was the case some of the time. Some captains interviewed by Savranskaya meant that "no specific instructions were given about the use of the nuclear torpedoes."

B-4 Captain Ryurik Ketov's recollection during a 2001 Russian television interview was: "The only person who talked to us about those weapons was Vice-Admiral Rassokha. He said there were three scenarios: 'First, if you get a hole under the water. A hole in your hull. Second, a hole above the water. If you have to come to the surface, and they shoot at you, and you get a hole in your hull. And the third case, when Moscow orders you to use these weapons.'" (1)

The captains received packets with secret orders, which they could only open at sea. "The weapons on the boats were to be in a state of full combat readiness. Conventional weapons could be used on the orders of the Commander-in-Chief of the USSR Naval Forces, and the nuclear weapons could be used only on special orders from the Defense Minister," wrote Russian journalist Mozgovoi based on Ketov's account.

Communications officer Vadim Orlov believed the missiles could only be launched on orders from Moscow. Most accounts agree that if there were no contact from Moscow then the nuclear warhead on flagship B-59 could be fired if all three top officers agreed. But Orlov's greatest worry was that malfunctioning equipment or an accident could cause an unintentional nuclear explosion.

Savranskaya interviewed Orlov in Moscow, September 18, 2002. He confirmed the "crucial role played by brigade chief of staff Vasili Arkhipov in talking Captain Savitski out of any rash action." The men highly respected the even-keeled Arkhipov, a trait he was known for on the K-19 submarine the previous year when it experienced a leak in the coolant system that threatened a meltdown of a nuclear reactor.

Savranskaya relates in her 2005 article that Arkhipov's widow, Olga, stated, in 2004, that her husband had told her that officers on the B-59 "almost fired a nuclear torpedo at an American destroyer during the Cuban missile crisis." (2)

A National Security Archive briefing cites excerpts from Mozgovoi's book wherein he takes from Vadim Orlov's recollections that B-59 Captain Valentin Savisky "became furious" and "ordered the nuclear torpedo assembled for battle readiness".

Here is a larger account directly from the book.

> "The anti-submarine forces of the opponent, especially the aviation, were ready for an encounter with us from the very beginning of our sail to the Cuban shores... [Yet] we could not have expected this kind of counteraction...A naval forward searching aircraft carrier group headed the aircraft carrier "Randolf" confronted submarine B-59. According to our hydro-acoustic specialists, 14 surface units were following our boat....they surrounded us and started to

> tighten the circle, practicing attacks and dropping depth charges. They exploded right next to the hull. It felt like you were sitting in a metal barrel, which somebody is constantly blasting with a sledgehammer. The situation was quite unusually, if not to say shocking—for the crew.
>
> "...only emergency light was functioning. The temperature in the compartments was 45-50 C, up to 60C in the engine compartment. It was unbearably stuffy. The level of CO2 in the air reached a critical practically deadly for people mark. One of the duty officers fainted and fell down. Another followed, then the third one...They were falling like dominoes. But we were still holding on, trying to escape. We were suffering like this for about four hours. The Americans hit us with something stronger than grenades—apparently with a practical depth bomb. We thought—that's it—the end!
>
> "After this attack, the totally exhausted [Captain] Savitsky, who in addition to everything was not able to establish connection with the General Staff, became furious. He summoned the officer who was assigned to the nuclear torpedo, and ordered him to assemble it to battle readiness. (3)
>
> "'*Maybe the war has already started up there, while we are doing summersaults here*'—screamed Valentine Grigorievich, trying to justify his order. '*We're going to blast them now! We will die, but we will sink them all—we will not disgrace our Navy*'! [author emphasis]
>
> "But we did not fire the nuclear torpedo—Savitsky was able to rein in his wrath. After consulting with Second Captain Vasili Alexandrovich Arkhipov [deceased] and Deputy political officer Ivan Semenovich Maslennikov, he made the decision to come to the surface. We gave an echo locator signal, which in international navigation rules means that, 'the submarine is coming to the surface.' Our pursuers slowed down."

According to Lt. Peterson on *USS Blandy*, the U.S. ships stayed three kilometers away. After some strafing from aircraft, which did not hit anyone, the submarines sailed back to Russia.

ARKHIPOV AND THE K-19

Arkhipov was second in command on the K-19 when the leaking crisis occurred. He sided with the captain, Nikolai Zateeva, when some crewmen angrily demanded that he flood the ship and the crew would take life boats to nearby land. There was a danger that if a nuclear explosion happened, US Americans at a nearby NATO base could suspect that the Soviets had started a nuclear war and they might retaliate. The captain would not abandon ship. He thought it best to prevent the Soviet's most advanced submarine from being discovered with nuclear weapons, a military secret NATO could use, and he insisted on trying to repair the damage done.

Arkhipov supported that decision. He calmed the men down and convinced them to go back to work. Makeshift repairs were made by eight divers who managed to stop the leak. They were overexposed to radiation and died from the poisoning within three weeks. There were a score more such deaths within a few years. A U.S. destroyer stood nearby ready to "help". Fortunately a Soviet submarine arrived just in time and towed the damaged submarine back home.

In 2006, Mikhail Gorbachev nominated the crew for the Nobel Peace Prize.

The 2002 Hollywood film, *K-19: The Widow-Maker* is based on this episode. After the fall of the Soviet Union, the silence imposed upon the men about what occurred was lifted and Captain Zateeva wrote his memoirs. Herein he criticized Soviet leadership for rushing the submarine's construction, which meant some things were not adequately tested, and there was poor workmanship that could cause hazards. In fact, the inadequate installation of a cooling system burst. The tension Soviets felt from constant U.S. subversion and arms escalation led them to make unwise decisions in trying to keep up with the aggressors.

K-19 film-makers used Zateeva's memoirs as well as the book with the same title written by Captain Peter Huchthausen. K-19 experienced so many maladies that the crew nicknamed it "Hiroshima." But the filmmakers and the U.S. naval officer-author perhaps didn't want to use that name, which implied an association with the United States genocidal crime.

The Saint Petersburg Submarine and Naval Veterans Club took part in the film. The club is dedicated to the memory of perished crew

Olga and Vasili Arkhipov

members. Harrison Ford plays Captain Zateeva, and Liam Neeson plays Arkhipov. Of course, there is exaggerated drama and the scene of pistol-packing mutineers did not take place, but apparently this film has fewer errors than "*Secrets of the Dead: The Man Who Saved the World.*"

SECRETS OF THE DEAD: THE MAN WHO SAVED THE WORLD

This Bedlam Production film was released on the 50 year commemoration of the CMC, October 2012, and shown on the U.S. Public Broadcasting Service television channel. The synopsis reads:

"In October 1962, the world held its breath. On the edge of the Caribbean Sea, just a few miles from the Florida coast, the two great superpowers were at a stand-off. Surrounded by twelve US destroyers, which were depth-charging his submarine to drive it to the surface, Captain Vitali Grigorievitch Savitsky panicked. Unable to contact Moscow and fearing war had begun he ordered the launch of his submarine's nuclear torpedoes. As the two sides inched perilously close to nuclear war—far closer than we ever knew before—just one man stood between Captain Savitsky's order and mutually assured destruction."

What is quite interesting is the cooperation that Russians offered the film, which was shown in Russia. Even two of the actors were played by Russians who partook in the crisis: B-4 Captain Ryurik Ketov and Viktor Mikhailov, B-59 junior navigator. Olga Arkhipov also played herself.

On the U.S. side were Andy Bradick, an officer on one of the attacking destroyers, USS Cony and Gary Slaughter, communications officer on the same ship. NS Archive Director Thomas Blanton also played himself as archivist.

Another actual person who played himself was John G. Stoessinger, but falsely. He was cast as an alleged White House advisor.

Here are some of Blanton's 12 objections to the film, which he sent me after he had sent them to National Geographic when it was considering using the film.

1. In perhaps the greatest inaccuracy in the film— repeated over and over—John Stoessinger is described and quoted on camera as a White House aide, a Kennedy aide, giving eyewitness testimony to the reactions of the Kennedy White House. This is just not true. Stoessinger never worked in the Kennedy White House. He was a New York-based professor at the time and only in the Johnson administration did he have any position at the White House. The only record of him in the JFK Library files is an acknowledgement note from Mac Bundy for a copy of a book Stoessinger sent to Bundy. Stoessinger is quoting liberally from other sources but presenting himself as an eyewitness. With the availability of the White House tapes giving Kennedy's own voice and that of his real aides throughout the crisis, substituting a fake witness is inexcusable.

2. The subs had enough nuclear weapon power "to destroy the entire Atlantic fleet"—this statement is not true, a nuclear torpedo was enough to sink an aircraft carrier and close-by vessels, but even 4 of them would not be enough to take out the fleet. Unless it was all parked in the same harbor, say Pearl Harbor.

3. Captain Ketov's cut and spliced and translated quotes in the film directly misrepresent what Ketov actually said on camera in Russian: "Savitsky was an emotional man but he had his head on his shoulders. He made the right decision." The film presents this as Ketov saying Savitsky was right to arm the torpedo. In fact, Ketov means the opposite, that Savitsky was right not to launch the torpedo.

4. Vadim Orlov's translated and edited quotes from the 2002 Havana press conference footage directly misrepresent what Orlov said in Russian: "It is exactly the courage and reasonableness of the captain of the submarine and the chief of staff that prevented" launch of the torpedo. In other words, not Arkhipov alone overruling Savitsky, as the film's dramatization and falsification puts it, but calming the situation down so that Savitsky makes the right decision not to launch.

These criticisms make the film incredulous as far as they go. There were also accusations that some Soviet military leaders wished the submarine captains had used the nuclear missiles, and that the men should have drowned rather than surface. This is speculation and no evidence is offered.

The film, however, has some redeeming values. Statements made by Navy communications officer Gary Slaughter certainly are proof of how dangerous the Yankees were, especially in comparison to how cautious and responsible the Russians were.

"We were already prepared to use nuclear weapons. We had all our strategic aircraft ready to fly to Russia armed with nuclear weapons, and ready to drop nuclear bombs on key targets, and, and, and Russia.

So there was no doubt in my mind that we would have gone had this incident occurred and we would have nuclear exchange with the Russians if their nuclear ballistic missiles worked."

Slaughter also said that the way the destroyers were treating the submarines was "basically applying passive torture," making it hard for the men to breathe in the extreme heat. And it lasted for five hours before they finally surfaced.

Slaughter must have spoken his own words in the film. Here is what he said taken from my own notes and may not be verbatim: "The U.S. had invested billions, maybe trillions of dollars in beefing up its anti-submarine warfare capability and the only enemy that we were trying to suppress and confront and defeat was the Soviet Union."

BACK IN THE USSR

Once the Brigade 69 submarines made it back to Russia, the four captains and Arkhipov were debriefed at Main Navy Headquarters. The commission, headed by Rear Admiral P.K. Ivanov, was aimed at "uncovering violations of orders, documents, or instruction. The commanders were criticized for violating the conditions of secrecy by surfacing," recalled B-36 Captain Dubivko.

During these "acrimonious sessions" there was talk of the need or not to use nuclear weapons. The captains, including Chief of Staff Vasili Arkhipov "were asked to present oral reports to the Defense Minister."

No one was demoted or punished in any way. On the contrary, Arkhipov continued in the Navy with one promotion after another. He had been chief of staff of the 69th Brigade since December 1961 and in November 1964 he was made commander, and then commanded the 37th division of submarines. Next year he was promoted to Rear Admiral and made head of the Caspian Higher Naval School. In 1981, he was promoted to Vice-Admiral. Arkhipov was awarded the Order of the Red Banner, Red Star "For Service to Motherland in the USSR Armed Forces", and several medals for valor, including for "Victory over Japan," where he had served during the short-lived Soviet-Japanese War (August 9-September 2, 1945).

The man who, along with other Russians, saved the world from a nuclear war died August 19, 1998 due to kidney cancer developed from the radiation he got on the K-19. Its captain, Nikolai Zateeva, died from radiation contamination eight days later. They both lived to be 72.

CONCLUSION

"Soviet Foxtrot Submarines: The Cuban Missile Crisis" is the title of Air Force Lt. Colonel Edward Marek's detailed study. The SIGINT officer (Signals Intelligence Officer) published it, May 3, 2017, on his very patriotic American website: (http://www.talkingproud.us/Military/SovietFoxtrots/FoxtrotsCuba.html)

Here is one assessment he made: "I would like to comment that after reading as much as I have read about these four Foxtrot captains, the captains and crews were under a massive amount of pressure. They did not expect half the Atlantic fleet to be above them, they did not

---

Vasili was posthumously awarded a replica of this National Prize of Italy "Angels of Our Time" for steadfastness, courage, endurance manifested in extreme conditions. It was given to his wife Olga, 2005.

know what was happening in the outside world, they had these nuclear torpedoes aboard guarded by a non-submarine special officer, they knew almost nothing about those torpedoes, the captains had conflicting orders on how and when to employ them, and their boats had undergone a long and stormy voyage. The submarines were jam packed inside, they had to stay submerged for long periods of time, the crews were tiring, sweaty, and often on the verge of fainting. My guess would be tempers were short as well. The USN would not make life for them any easier, especially given the zest for chasing Soviet submarines among American sailors...and employing depth charges...couple that with the fact the Foxtrots had received no intelligences, you have four submarine captains who were really on their own. It is a wonder that something very grave did not occur."

In correspondence with me, he wrote his conclusion about **Black Saturday**: "Arkhipov certainly played a lead role. But I do not think we would have gone to nuclear war. Neither JFK nor Khrushchev wanted that. Nikita wanted to call his boats home fairly early in the game, but JFK kept hesitating. But my sense is Nikita did have a cooler head than the U.S. high officials."

Of the many sources Marek used to come to his conclusion is the captain of B-4. Here is one quote from Captain Ryurik Ketov: "Vasili Arkhipov was a submariner and a close friend of mine. He was a family friend. He stood out for being cool-headed. He was in control."

That assessment matches Arkhipov's wife, Olga: "My husband was shy, intelligent, very polite, always in touch with the modern world, kind and calm."

Olga understood how much the radiation leak on the K-19 could have escalated into a world-wide catastrophe from what her husband told her. "Vasili must have really felt it. It was a tragedy, a real tragedy. This tragedy was the reason that we could say no to nuclear war!" I think she meant the Russian people when referring to "we".

It is fair to say that a rational and moral person acts under pressure from attackers, like the ever hot-headed aggressive Yankees, to do what is necessary to maintain world peace. Vasili Arkhipov had these qualities and values. This is exactly what the current Russian leader, Vladmir Putin, possesses in face of the ever hot-headed aggressive Yankee leaders of today.

Notes:

1. Transcript of selections from Russian documentary program "How It Happened" (VID, 30 Jan. 2001) ORT (Russian Television Channel 1) with four submarine commanders who participated in Operation 'Anadyr'.

2. 37 Sobesednik: Obscherossiiskaya Yezhednevnaya Gazeta, No. 10 (1012), 17–23 March 2004, Moscow.

3. I had an hour-long telephone interview with Savranskaya, the Mozgovoi book translator of this account. She said she didn't think an actual "order" was given. The captain talked about it but the order never occurred, in part, because Arkhipov spoke against it and the three officers responsible for such an action agreed not to. She learned of this after having translated the book.

   Savranskaya also said that some Russian officers judged that the depth charges were part of the beginning of a war the U.S. had initiated and thus it might be necessary to fire their nuclear-tipped torpedoes at them. But in Arkhipov's judgment, the depth charges were aimed at their subs only to force them to surface and his argument ruled. Svetlana's study and interviews, including with the remaining three captains in 2003, proved to her that all the Russians involved in these actions were restrained. The men who knew Arkhipov did view him as wise and calm, and they respected him. Any unique role he played in those acute moments, however, was not publicized in Russia.

CHAPTER 6

CIA Complot murders JFK over Cuba

RUSSIANS GET BLAMED for everything since 2016, even the murder of President John F. Kennedy.

"Did Russia Kill a U.S. President? New CIA Documents Reveal Spy's Theory About JFK's Death," So read Newsweek's headline of July 27, 2017. The article cites just released CIA documents referring to Lt. Col. Yuri Nosenko, a KGB defector to the CIA, in 1964. (http://www.newsweek.com/cia-releases-secret-interviews-russian-spy-imprisoned-jfk-assassination-642486)

CIA's then Chief of Counter-Intelligence James Angleton imprisoned Nosenko in a secret jail between August 13, 1965 and October 27, 1967. There was only a cot in a small cell and never a visitor, other than interrogators. Angleton suspected Nosenko of knowing that Lee Harvey Oswald was connected with Soviet Union's KGB, though it maintained it had not recruited Oswald, because he was "mentally unstable."

Nosenko was exonerated in 1969. CIA Director Stansfield Turner (1972-4) said he had been mishandled by the CIA. Furthermore, the Newsweek story has nothing new, as the matter was in the public domain for many years. Nevertheless, Newsweek insinuates that Nosenko was a KGB mole sent to mislead the CIA from learning that it used Oswald to kill Kennedy. Newsweek claims that Oswald murdered Kennedy and therefore the Russian government was behind it.

Newsweek's main source for this assumption is an online news site, Muckrock. Newsweek writes:

> *"Intense debate exists to this day as to whether Nosenko was still working for Moscow under CIA captivity or not and*

> *whether he did successfully cover up some degree of Soviet involvement in Oswald's killing of Kennedy, a theory government transparency organization MuckRock determined could not be ruled out based on the CIA's investigation."*

Well, if that theory couldn't be "ruled out" are we to assume it is proof that Russia murdered America's charming president? Can one rule anything out about CIA's investigations and lies?

What is MuckRock? See https://www.muckrock.com/news/archives/2017/jul/10/cia-nosenko-logic/https://www.muckrock.com/about/

As a member of Global Investigative Journalism Network, it is associated with George Soros, who is the founder of one of its main financial sponsors, Open Society Foundations. Soros established his philanthropic enterprise—spending to date $11 billion—"to help countries make the transition from Communism." One of them is Ukraine where he is heavily involved to bring it into EU and NATO, laying the basis for war with Russia. We come to that in chapter sixteen. (https://www.opensocietyfoundations.org/about)

Nevertheless, it would be cheap to discredit MuckRock alone for that nefarious association. The main problem with its theory and Newsweek's article comes as the end of the magazine's story.

"*Despite Angleton's suspicions, the CIA and the FBI do not believe that the Soviet Union played a role in Kennedy's assassination and have concluded that Oswald acted alone.*" [My emphasis]

The damage was done, however, as many media picked up the Newsweek headline, thus spreading the message: Russia is the culprit. The mass media, in keeping with the CIA-led Deep State, systematically spread lies and "disinformation" to cover-up for what Noam Chomsky calls United States' *The Culture of Terrorism* (Boston: South End Press, 1988, pages 1 and 21).

"The central—and not very surprising—conclusion that emerges from the documentary and historical records is that U.S. international and security policy, rooted in the structure of power in the domestic society, has as its primary goal the preservation of what we might call the '*Fifth Freedom*', understood crudely but with a fair degree of accuracy as the freedom to rob, to exploit and to dominate, to undertake any course of action to ensure that existing privilege is protected and advanced."..."The doctrine of willful self-ignorance is so deeply rooted that it can efface [any facts that contradict] "that the U.S. is Good, its leaders are Good, the facts are irrelevant, no matter how prominently displayed."

The real murderers of their own president must be covered up to protect the Fifth Freedom (1).

Thousands of books have been written about the assassination; hundreds assert that the conspirators were top CIA officials and operators, Mafia bosses and their hit men, along with Cuban exiles (gusanos) under CIA control, some of whom were involved in the Bay of Pigs.

Even the House Select Committee on Assassinations, after a lengthy probe which included public hearings, determined in 1979 that JFK was "likely" killed as the result of a conspiracy.

President Richard Nixon's chief of staff H. R. Haldeman, who served 18 months in prison for his role with Nixon in Watergate, wrote in his autobiography, *The Haldeman Diaries: Inside the Nixon White House* (New York. G. P. Putnam's Sons, 1994):

"*In all those Nixon references to the Bay of Pigs he was actually referring to the Kennedy assassination.*" The President said he was most worried about E. Howard Hunt, because he had been arrested for leading the Watergate break-in. Hunt "*will uncover a lot of things—the whole Bay of Pigs thing,*" which included the assassination of Kennedy.

Rolling Stone writer Erik Hedegaard reported on April 5, 2007 about this in, "The Last Confession of E. Howard Hunt: The ultimate keeper of secrets regarding who killed JFK." (http://www.rollingstone.com/culture/features/the-last-confession-of-e-howard-hunt-20070405)

Hunt was a key CIA figure in the Bay of Pigs, and the 1954 coup against Guatemala's President Jacobo Arbenz. He was imprisoned 33 months for the Watergate break-in. In deathbed talks with his son, St. John Hunt, E. Hunt named several other CIA operatives involved: David Atlee Phillips, Frank Sturgis, Cord Meyer, David Morales, William Harvey, and Mafia hit man Lucien Sarti. He minimized his own involvement, and suggested Lyndon B. Johnson spearheaded the cover-up.

While dying in a hospital, Hunt wrote down who killed Kennedy and gave the paper to his son. (Hunt died January 23, 2007). Rolling Stone wrote about it this way:

"E. Howard scribbled the initials 'LBJ,' standing for Kennedy's ambitious vice president, Lyndon Johnson. Under 'LBJ,' connected by a line, he wrote the name Cord Meyer. Meyer was a CIA agent whose wife had an affair with JFK; later she was murdered, a case that's never been solved. Next his father connected to Meyer's name the name Bill Harvey, another CIA agent; also connected to Meyer's name was the name David Morales, yet another CIA man and a well-known, particularly vicious black-op specialist. And then his father connected to Morales' name, with a line, the framed words 'French Gunman Grassy Knoll.'

"So there it was, according to E. Howard Hunt. LBJ had Kennedy killed. It had long been speculated upon. But now E. Howard was saying that's the way it was. And that Lee Harvey Oswald wasn't the only shooter in Dallas. There was also, on the grassy knoll, a French gunman, presumably the Corsican Mafia assassin Lucien Sarti, who has figured prominently in other assassination theories."

"Later that week, E. Howard also gave Saint two sheets of paper that contained a fuller narrative. It starts out with LBJ again, connecting him to Cord Meyer, then goes on: "Cord Meyer discusses a plot with Phillips who brings in Wm. Harvey and Antonio Veciana. He meets with Oswald in Mexico City.... Then Veciana meets w/ Frank Sturgis in Miami and enlists David Morales in anticipation of killing JFK there. But LBJ changes itinerary to Dallas, citing personal reasons."

"In the next few paragraphs, E. Howard goes on to describe the extent of his own involvement. It revolves around a meeting he claims he attended, in 1963, with Morales and Sturgis. It takes place in a Miami hotel room. Here's what happens:

"Morales leaves the room at which point Sturgis makes reference to a 'Big Event', and asks E. Howard, 'Are you with us' [in] 'Killing JFK'. E. Howard, 'incredulous,' says to Sturgis, 'You seem to have everything you need. Why do you need me?' In the handwritten narrative, Sturgis' response is unclear, though what E. Howard says to Sturgis next isn't: He says he won't 'get involved in anything involving Bill Harvey, who is an alcoholic psycho.'"

Hedegaard adds that a few weeks after these talks, Hunt's son received in the mail, "a tape recording from his dad. E. Howard's voice on the cassette is weak and grasping, and he sometimes wanders down unrelated pathways. But he essentially remakes the same points he made in his handwritten narrative."

Among other sources I use concerning the murder of the president are:

Family Jewels https://www.cia.gov/library/readingroom/docs/DOC_0001451843.pdf This 702-page CIA report includes many of the Company's "skeletons", which were released on June 25, 2007 after a 15-year struggle by the National Security Archive. The report includes many assassination attempts on the life of Fidel Castro, and other mob-CIA-Cuban paramilitary connections. The CIA abuse of KGB defector Nosenko is there as well.

Double Cross: The explosive, inside story of the mobster who controlled America written by Chuck and Samuel M. Giancana (New York: Warner Books, March 1992, hardback). This book is an as-told-to account by Chicago Mafia Boss Sam (Salvatore) Giancana, aka "Mooney" and "Momo". Chuck is Mooney's brother, whose son Samuel is the Mobster's nephew, godson and namesake.

ZR Rifle: The Plot to Kill Kennedy and Castro by Claudia Furiati (Australia: Ocean Press, 1997). This book names the players, many of whom are those that Sam Giancana related. Furiati relies heavily on interviews with the former head of Cuba's State Security Department (DSE), General Fabian Escalante. The DSE knowledge is largely based on its double agents inside the CIA and several Cuban exile terrorist groups working within the CIA. My book, *Backfire: The CIA's Biggest Burn* (Havana: José Martí Publishing House, 1991) portrays what 27 of these double agents learned.

General Escalante says that operatives and plotters in the Kennedy assassination worked directly under Richard Helms, who directed Operation Mongoose and Operation 40 under President Eisenhower and Kennedy. For Helms' dedication to service, President Johnson later appointed him CIA chief. One of Helms' key CIA accomplices in the invasion and continued subversion against Cuba, and Kennedy assassination operator, was David Atlee Phillips, who considered Cuba's intelligence agency as one of the most efficient state security services in the world.

They Killed Our President by Jessie Ventura (New York: Skyhorse Publishing, 2013). Ventura is a former governor of Minnesota. He wrote: "John F. Kennedy was murdered by a conspiracy involving disgruntled CIA agents, anti-Castro Cubans, and members of the Mafia, all of whom were extremely angry at what they viewed as Kennedy's appeasement policies toward Communist Cuba and the Soviet Union."

Who Really Killed Kennedy by Jerome R. Corsi (WND books and Internet news daily, 2013). In its release of the book, WND wrote: "Was the JFK assassination a revenge killing masterminded by CIA Director Allen Dulles?"

> *"Corsi's extensive research shows JFK may have signed his death warrant the day he fired Dulles, accusing his spy chief of lying and manipulating him in the Bay of Pigs fiasco.*
>
> *"At a Jan. 22, 1961 meeting of Secretary of State Dean Rusk; Secretary of Defense Robert McNamara; Attorney General Robert Kennedy; Army General Lyman Lemnitzer, the chairman of the Joint Chiefs of Staff [also Operation Northwoods]; and various national security and foreign policy experts, Dulles stressed that the U.S. had only two months 'before something had to be done about' the Cubans being trained covertly by the CIA in Guatemala."*

The CIA knew it had Kennedy over a barrel, because of his aggressive election campaign statements claiming that Nixon was doing nothing about Communist Cuba and that he, Kennedy, would be a better anti-communist president. This virtually set him up to be blackmailed by Richard Bissell and Nixon, top proponents from the beginning of a Cuba invasion plan.

Bissell had been the Deputy Director of Plans in charge of the Bay of Pigs operation. The DDP was also involved in overthrowing and/or assassinating many heads of government: Guatemala President Jacobo

Arbenz Guzmán, Congo's Patrice Lumumba, Dominican Republic's Rafael Leonidas Trujillo, South Vietnam's Ngo Dinh Diem. Fidel was to be the star trophy.

After the invasion fiasco, Kennedy pushed Bissell to resign in February 1962. Kennedy had already fired the chief, D/CIA Allen Dulles on November 29, 1961. The number two CIA man, Air Force Lt. General Charles Cabell, was ousted two days later. He never forgave Kennedy for that.

Based upon congressional investigations, several articles and books, Wikipedia wrote that Bissell and Dulles met with Mafia men in September 1960:

> *[They] "initiated talks with two leading figures of the Mafia, Johnny Roselli and Sam Giancana. Later, other crime bosses such as Carlos Marcello, Santo Trafficante Jr. and Meyer Lansky became involved in this first plot against Castro. The strategy was managed by [Colonel] Sheffield Edwards and Robert Maheu"—a veteran of CIA counter-espionage activities who was instructed to offer the Mafia $150,000 to kill Fidel Castro. "The advantage of employing the Mafia for this work was that it provided CIA with a credible cover story. The Mafia was known to be angry with Castro for closing down their profitable brothels and casinos in Cuba. If the assassins were killed or captured the media would accept that the Mafia were working on their own. The Mafia played along in order to get protection from the FBI."*

Kennedy was narrowly elected to the presidency in November 1960 with Mafia financial and voting support; plus other big money interests. Although the Kennedys were rich every U.S. president must collaborate with big money else they would never have enough money to win an election.

What follows is taken from *Double Speak*. Background on JFK's father Joseph can be substantiated by many credible sources for readers who doubt a mobster and his family's account.

JFK's father was part of the organized crime cartel during alcohol prohibition days, in the 1920s. Joe Kennedy got rich running rum and raw sugar for alcohol production, much of which came from or through Cuba. He was indebted to the mob, and connected to Chicago capo Giancana in establishing the Chicago Merchandise Mart.

Besides the illegal money business, Joe Kennedy was indebted to Giancana for personal reasons. Joe enlisted his aid in getting the records annulled of his son John's first marriage. Mooney had his associate John Roselli take care of that. The woman was a socialite, Durie (Kerr) Malcolm, who had been married twice before marrying John Kennedy in 1947. The Kennedys deny this, and well known "Washington Post" editor Ben Bradlee debunked the notion. Nevertheless, Pulitzer Prize-winning investigative reporter Seymour M. Hersh gave credence to the marriage in his 1997 book, *The Dark Side of Camelot.*

The next favor Giancana performed was to get Joe out of a deal with New York capo Frank Costello, a payment for past favors. The elder Kennedy wanted out, because he feared these dealings would ruin his son's political career.

Giancana met with Joe, in May 1956, at Chicago's Ambassador East Hotel. Giancana agreed to help Joe for favors in return for something. Joe Kennedy told Sam Giancana: "*If my son is elected President he'll be your man. My son, the President of the United States, will owe you his father's life. He won't refuse you, ever. You have my word.*" (*Double Cross,* page 230)

We've all seen enough Mafia thriller films to know that the mob is very sticky about keeping personal promises. And Joe was now in Giancana's debt for life. Giancana kept his promise. He got capo Costello to drop his demand, and he pulled out the ropes for Kennedy's election. He forced his unionist partners to turn out for Kennedy in the 1959-60 campaign. He influenced his buddy, Chicago Mayor Richard Daley to back Kennedy. John Kennedy even went along with his father to some meetings with Giancana during the election campaign. Giancana arranged for dead persons to vote, arranged multiple voters, and applied muscle at the ballot boxes.

When Illinois went to Kennedy, Richard Nixon called for a recount. The first recount showed that Nixon had actually won Illinois by 4500 votes but, according to Giancana, the mob pressured Nixon to concede, and that stopped the electoral officialdom from going further with the recount. Nixon was already in debt to the mob, among other things for its attempts on Castro's life. The mob assured Nixon his time would come in the White House, a promise kept in 1968.

Giancana arranged through Frank Sinatra for one of his lovers, Judith Campbell, to become Kennedy's mistress. He later boasted to Campbell that he had put her boyfriend in office. The fact that the President of the United States was fucking one of the capo's mistresses irritated J. Edgar Hoover. The FBI boss had Campbell's and Kennedy's telephones and residences under surveillance, as well as her comings and goings in the White House. Hoover confronted Kennedy about this "illicit affair" and demanded he end it "for the sake of the nation". Kennedy obeyed.

Following the end of this affair, Mooney arranged for Marilyn Monroe to meet Kennedy. JKF went bananas for her and so did Bobby. Giancana also fucked Monroe, nevertheless he had her murdered, in order to force both Kennedys to stop prosecuting mobsters. Mooney even names the two hit men: "Needles" Gianola and "Mugsy" Tortorella. They came to her home shortly after Bobby Kennedy left her on the evening of August 4, 1962, and inserted a Nembutal suppository into her anus. Nembutal is an untraceable poisonous drug, making it appear that she overdosed herself. (*Double Cross*, pg. 313-5)

Despite this murder "warning", the Kennedys did not stop "badgering" the mobsters. Giancana felt personally betrayed by the Kennedys for using their powers to harass him and his co-capos, which was also hurting their lucrative businesses. The Kennedys were also costing other rich men, not only mobsters, too much money. So, the mob formed part of the triad that killed John Kennedy.

Giancana told his brother and nephew: "*On November 22, 1963, the United States had a coup; it's that simple. The government of this country was overthrown by a handful of guys who did their job so damned well... not one American even knew it happened. But I know. I know I've guaranteed the Outfit's future.*" (page 336).

THE ASSASSINS

New Orleans District Attorney James Garrison also believed the CIA and Mafia with Cuban exiles killed President Kennedy. He tried one of them, New Orleans businessman Clay Shaw, for his involvement but lost the case. Garrison wrote three books on the assassination and he is the main inspiration for Oliver Stone's 1991 film, "*JFK*".

Garrison believed that the conspiracy was discussed at a May 1963 meeting of the "Friends of Democratic Cuba", in New Orleans. Among those he named were: Carlos Prió (Cuba president from 1948 until deposed in a coup led by Batista in 1952), Orlando Bosch, Guillermo Novo Sampol, Eladio del Valle and Hermino Díaz García. Two of the conspirators, David Ferrie and Eladio del Valle, were murdered before they could testify in the New Orleans trial.

Giancana states that earlier, in March, he had John Roselli arrange a meeting for him with General Charles Cabell, former FBI agents Guy Banister and Bob Mahue to plan the assassination. After Kennedy fired Cabell, he went to work for Mahue, who was Howard Hughes detective and chief of Hughes Nevada operations.

Giancana named his own trigger men: Paul James, Lewis McWillie, Red Dorfman, Allen Dorfman, Chuck Nicoletti and Milwaukee Phil; plus New Orleans Mafia boss Carlos Marcello and his gunmen Jack Lawrence and Charles Harrelson. Miami capo Santos Trafficante was a key player too. He and Meyer Lansky were the main Havana casino owners, and they hated Castro and Kennedy equally. Giancana said the CIA put in policemen as actual gunmen: Roscoe White and J.D. Tippit, the latter was killed by somebody but not Oswald on the fateful day.

Frank Sturgis (Fiorini) and Richard Cain were with Giancana's men and the CIA. Giancana said the conspiracy went up to the top of the CIA and "half dozen fanatical right-wing Texans, Vice President Lyndon Johnson, and the Bay of Pigs Action Officer under Eisenhower, Richard Nixon." (*Double Cross*, pages 333-6).

Sturgis led a strange and dangerous life. He served in the Second World War as a Marine, then as a policeman. In 1954, he worked with the CIA in its Guatemalan coup d'état. He and Jack Youngblood arranged to free the imprisoned General Carlos Castillo Armas, who had been jailed for treason by the social democratic Arbenz government. The U.S. picked Armas as president after the coup. Sturgis is next heard about running guns to the Cuban guerrillas during the revolution and training guerrillas, then as a pilot under Fidel Castro's leadership. He was regarded as Fidel's "favorite Yankee". Not only did Fidel appoint him chief of air force security, but also in charge of security for the Havana casinos. They had been immediately closed down upon the revolutionary victory, but were reopened under government control until September 29, 1961 when all gambling was outlawed, and prostitutes and other casino employees were offered education and jobs.

For reasons unknown to me, Sturgis switched sides and joined forces with the CIA in plots to murder Castro. According to one of Fidel's lovers, German-born Marita Lorenz, Sturgis used her to put poison pills in Castro's food, in January 1960. She later testified that she had a change of heart and refused. Lorenza has also testified about knowing that Sturgis, Oswald and others were connected with JFK's murder. Sturgis was a close associate of E. Howard Hunt and he ran Oswald. Sturgis spent 14 months in prison for the Watergate break-in.

Three years after he was arrested as a Watergate burglar, Sturgis told Senate investigators he was a CIA agent who would do anything for the agency—even kill. He bragged that his reputation as a hit man led the FBI to grill him as a prime suspect in the JFK assassination. (https://www.maryferrell.org/showDoc.html?docId=111666&relPageId=1&search=Frank_Sturgis%20JFK%20assassin https://www.maryferrell.org/pages/Confession_of_Howard_Hunt.html?search=frank%20sturgis)

Most of these assassins mentioned by Garrison and Giancana were also on the list of Cuba's chief of security, General Fabian Escalante.

CIA: General Charles Cabell, Richard Helms, David Atlee Phillips, E. Howard Hunt, Frank Sturgis, Clay Shaw, Gerry Patrick Hemming(on contract), Guy Banister (FBI but also possibly tied to CIA), and Lee Harvey Oswald (provocateur and patsy, who also had ties with the FBI). Gen. Escalante added David Yaras and Lenny Patrick, and defected Cuban pilot Pedro Luis Díaz Lang as hit men.

Special mention about Phillips is appropriate. He ran Anthony Veciana of Alpha 66. Veciana was probably not directly involved in the JFK murder but he knew about it. Veciana confirmed to the House Select Committee on Assassinations that Bishop (code name for Phillips) was his case officer in the plot to murder Fidel in Chile, in October 1974, with a trick gun hidden inside a camera—one of his three attempts.

Jack Anderson quoted Veciana in a "San Francisco Chronicle" article, January 20, 1977: "It was a very similar plan to the assassination of

Kennedy because the person Bishop assigned to kill Castro was going to get planted with papers to make it appear he was a Moscow/Castro agent turned traitor, and then he himself would be killed."

Air Force generals Cabell and Curtis LeMay, and other key generals, were livid with Kennedy over the loss of retaking Cuba, no matter the risk of nuclear world war. After Kennedy refused to order second air attacks on Cuba during the April invasion, Cabell went around Washington calling the President "a traitor."

After Kennedy fired Cabell, the general was playing golf with his close friend, former Vice-President Nixon. They often played golf, and during one foursome they agreed to a scheme to flood Cuba with counterfeit peso currency, in order to "blow the Cuban economy off the face of the map," recounted engineer Robert D. Morrow. The engineer was employed at Comcor, a CIA proprietary. The counterfeit operation was his idea. Kennedy disapproved of the plan, so the CIA channeled their "private" money for the operation. Kennedy instructed his brother to apprehend all Cuban and US American personnel engaged in manufacturing bogus Cuban currency. Castro was informed and he ordered new currency printed in Czechoslovakia, thus averting the subversion. Secret Service agents arrested Morrow and two others on October 2, 1963 for conspiracy to counterfeit the currency of a foreign government.

Cabell was again furious with the "traitor" president. It was only six weeks before he would no longer be a problem. Cabell's brother, Earle, was a big help in the executive action cover up since he was the mayor of Dallas.

President Kennedy's attempt to shorten the Vietnam War without victory was the last straw for Cabell and other generals.

In the last months of Kennedy's life, he realized that the Vietnam War, which he also inherited from the Eisenhower-Nixon administration, was going badly and without the use of atomic weapons could not be won. As a political leader for big capital, he could not risk spending billions and billions on a war that would be lost, nor would he risk world annihilation in a nuclear war with the Soviet Union and China. He was willing to cool down international conflicts with the communist world, in order to avoid a nuclear holocaust. He was, of course, a supporter of capitalism against socialism, but he was also realistic. Unlike most presidents, he could study. This brought him into conflict with many capitalists and their military-intelligence representatives in government.

Kennedy initiated a double track policy toward Vietnam, as he had recently begun with Cuba. He enacted budget cuts for war machinery, which nearly bankrupt Bell Helicopter and General Dynamics. Napalm producer Dow Chemical, Lockheed and other aircraft companies were also anxious about war de-escalation and détente. Hughes Aircraft Corporation was servicing the CIA on a worldwide basis, its largest private contractor. Hughes' $6 billion non-competitive contract included supplying CIA spy satellites. Hughes' vast corporation was stocked with former CIA and Pentagon officials. He was also a major contractor for NASA satellites. Hughes instructed Maheu to tell Pentagon generals "to keep the Vietnam war going" so that he could sell more aircraft.

U.S. archives leaked in June 2005 show that Kennedy had his ambassador to India, John Kenneth Galbraith, contact the North Vietnamese government in April 1962. Peace negotiations were an issue. Another peace-seeking contact occurred in January 1963. Soon thereafter, Kennedy memo 263 calls for the beginning of troop withdrawal. At that time there were about 16,000 military "advisors" in Vietnam.

Quite ironically, Fidel Castro was conversing with the French director of "Le Nouvel Observateur", Jean Daniel, when a Castro assistant told them of Kennedy's murder. Fidel spontaneously said: "This is bad for Cuba." When told that Johnson had just been sworn in as President, Fidel asked: "What authority does he exercise over the CIA?"

In 2005, Fidel told Ignacio Ramonet (*Fidel Castro My Life*, the English 2006 Penguin edition) that Kennedy had sent a message to him through Daniel.

> *"In this way, a communication was being established that perhaps could have been favorable to improving our relations." "His death hurt me. He was an adversary but I felt his disappearance greatly...I experienced indignation, repudiation, pain..."*

That evening in Paris, the new CIA chief of Cuban Task Force W, Desmond Fitzgerald, and another CIA officer met with Rolando Cubela, a Castro official turned CIA agent. Earlier, on September 7, Fitzgerald had arranged with Cubela to prepare an "inside job". Cubela was assigned the code name AMLASH. Deputy Director Helms was in on the plan. The new Director John McCone was not told about it. He had assured Attorney General Kennedy that all Cuban assassination plans were off.

One year after JFK's murder, Cubela asked the CIA to give him a silencer for a FAL rifle to be used to kill Castro. Desmond Fitzgerald brought in Manuel Artime, Howard Hunt's man, and his amphibious team of saboteurs. Artime and Cubela boasted that they would share power in a new junta. The CIA furnished $100,000 for this plan. Artime provided Cubela with a silencer and explosives. The plot had to be postponed as there were too many loose ends and suspicions. On February 28, 1966, Havana security police arrested Cubela and six others for plotting to kill Castro. During their trial a Cuban double agent, Juan Feliafel, came out to reveal how he fooled the CIA, and was able to learn what the anti-Cuban paramilitaries were up to. He discovered the AMLASH plot. The conspirators were found guilty. Cubela shouted that he wanted to be executed, but Castro intervened. During the subsequent 25 year sentence, Castro sent Cubela books.

When President Johnson was informed of the AMLASH operation he is quoted as saying: "We were running a goddamn Murder, Inc. in the Caribbean."

In a lengthy "The Atlantic" magazine interview, "Last Days of the President: LBJ in Retirement", July 1973, author Leo Jones writes: "The talk turned to President Kennedy, and Johnson expressed his belief that the assassination in Dallas had been part of a conspiracy…"' I never believed that Oswald acted alone, although I can accept that he pulled the trigger.'" (https://www.theatlantic.com/magazine/archive/1973/07/the-last-days-of-the-president/376281/)

Johnson contradicted himself. He had appointed Chief of the Supreme Court Earl Warren to head the commission investigation into the JFK assassination with the singular purpose to conclude that it was Oswald alone who did the dirty deed and there was no conspiracy.

WITNESSES DROP LIKE FLIES

Many witnesses to the assassination reported that bullets came from various areas indicating more than one person did the shooting.

Eighteen material witnesses died within three years of the events. The actuarial odds of such a string of deaths to a single event in that amount of time was calculated by an actuarial firm hired by the London Sunday Times to be **100,000 trillion to one**.

Six were killed by gunfire, one's throat was slit with a knife, another was killed by a karate chop, three died in car accidents, two by supposed suicides, three by heart attack and two by other "natural causes".

These are some of the victims: Karyn Kupicinet, TV host's daughter who was overheard telling of JFK's murder to be before it happened; Rose Cheramie who knew in advance and told of Oswald riding to Dallas with Cuban exiles; *Gary Underhill, a CIA agent who claimed the Agency was involved*; Dorothy Kilgallen, a columnist who had a private interview with Jack Ruby, and pledged to "break" the JFK case; *Dallas police Captain Frank Martin*, who witnessed Oswald slaying and told the Warren Commission, "There's a lot to be said but probably be better if I don't say it"; and *Naval Lt. William Pitzer, JFK autopsy photographer*, whose film contradicted the official view. He described his duty as a "horrifying experience."

The House Select Committee on Assassinations was created, in 1979, in part, because of these deaths, and the Zapruder film (2). When this homemade film of Kennedy's motorcade was viewed on ABC, in 1975, there was an outcry against the Warren Commission's single-bullet, lone assassin conclusion. Although the House committee discredited the actuarial study of this unique phenomenon of dying witnesses, it was unable to come to any conclusion regarding the growing number of deaths. Moreover, the Committee said it could not make a valid actuarial study due to the broad number and types of dead persons.

How can it be that the mightiest State leader in the world is violently overthrown by about 30 men; that they had so much power and influence to cover up his murder; that they could stonewall scientific evidence and homicide investigative procedure? They could even manufacture an unscarred single bullet, and enough stealth to then "disappear" the president's brain so it could not be properly examined for bullet trajectory.

Then the murderers had enough "luck" that 18 material witnesses die. In all, 52 key people died within a few years: witnesses to the murder, or those overhearing telling information about the conspiracy to murder him, and players. Fourteen are verified murders, 12 died "suspiciously", two died in shooting "accidents", 15 in other accidents, one by drug overdose, and five by sudden heart attacks or cancer.

Among the 52 deaths were, of course, Lee Harvey Oswald and the man who killed him, Jack Ruby. Most revealing of all are the murders of two key Kennedy assassins: Sam Giancana and John Roselli. Sam had survived half-a-century of rugged Mafia infighting without getting himself harmed or killed. Yet he was murdered on June 19, 1975, the night before federal agents were to take him to Washington DC to testify before the Church Committee (US Select Senate Committee to Study Governmental Operations with Respect to International Activities), which focused on attempts to murder Fidel Castro and JFK.

At that time, Mooney was under police guard awaiting grand jury hearings regarding illegal gambling operations. Coincidentally, the two policemen were called off duty just hours before the target was murdered.

Giancana's family is certain no mobster would have done the deed rather that it was the CIA, which feared that he might talk about Kennedy. His family is certain that Mooney would never have betrayed confidence.

Next in turn was Mooney's main man, John Roselli. He had been called before the Church Committee on June 24 and September 22, 1975. According to Senator Frank Church, Roselli "gave us a good deal of detail." Roselli was to appear again in July 1976, shortly after his boss was murdered. Roselli disappeared. Next month, on August 9, his dissected body was found stuffed in a chain-weighted metal drum in Dumbfounding Bay near Miami.

Now, I ask you. Is anyone to believe that the Russians not only ran Lee Harvey Oswald to murder the most powerful president in the world, in his own country far from Moscow, but also arranged for the murders or "suspicious" murders or suicides of 26 of the 52 persons directly connected to the murder of the principle victim?

Not even *Newsweek* has come up with that theory, yet!

CIA CHEMICAL-BIOLOGICAL WARFARE

We've gone through several United States terror operations against the Cuban government and the Cuban people—Operations 40, Mongoose, Patty, Northwoods; The Bay of Pigs, the Cuban Missile Crisis, the murder of President Kennedy. Still Cuba stood strong, and still with Russian help. So, other medicine was needed. What about germ warfare? (3)

I cite the "Los Angeles Times", September 10, 1975: "*The Central Intelligence Agency violated a presidential order for five years by keeping quantities of deadly bacterial poison capable of killing 'many thousands of people'...CIA officials have told the [Senate investigating] committee that the poison was being held for laboratory tests, Church said. But the substances were unguarded, no tests were ever made and the poison was held in greater amounts than needed for testing.*"

Among the many uses of these poisons were capsules to murder Fidel Castro and Patrice Lumumba.

Warren Hinckle and William Turner (a former FBI agent) wrote *The Fish is Red* (New York: Harper & Row, 1981). They state that the chemical-biological warfare against Cuba probably began under Richard Nixon's presidential term. An early attempt to "destabilize" Cuban food crops and agricultural export income occurred in 1969-70 with deployment of futuristic weather modification technology. Planes from China Lake Naval Weapons Center, in a California desert, overflew Cuba, "seeding rain clouds with crystals that precipitated torrential rains over nonagricultural areas and left cane fields arid". Killer flash floods resulted and export income was lost.

The September 24, 1981 "New York Times" book review wrote: "genuinely useful...in its portrayal of the C.I.A.'s creation of a kind of permanent paramilitary subculture, trained to smuggle and kill."

Germ Warfare is the title of chapter four of my book, *Backfire: The CIA's Biggest Burn*. I cite the "San Francisco Chronicle" (January 10, 1977) and "Newsday" (January 9, 1977). They reported that in 1971 the CIA turned over to Cuban exiles a virus which causes the African swine fever. Six weeks later, an outbreak of the disease occurred, resulting in the loss of 500,000 meat-producing pigs. (*Backfire* page 80.)

Sudden outbreaks of the African swine fever, which Cuba had never experienced before, broke out in 1971 and 1979. Other CBW diseases occurred: sogata rice blight (1971), sugar cane rust and smut (1978-9), blue tobacco mold (1979), Newcastle disease (1982), and coffee smut (1983)—all causing serious damage to crops and animals and export income. Cane disease alone caused the loss of thousands of hectares, and blue mold losses amounted to $250 million.

Message 40XPossility of learning what types of dengue is known in CubaXDetails about what virus sicknesses affect the populationXMedicinesXCuba importsXCountriesXGreetingsXJulia

Dengue fever type 2 broke out in Cuba two months after this CIA message was sent, on February 16, 1981, to María Santiesteban Loureiro. She was agent *Regina* to the CIA. Unknown to the CIA their *Regina* was already agent *Any* to her country's security agency, DSE.

That attack and an earlier dengue fever, type 1, caused the deaths of 158 persons, including 101 children; 344,000 people fell sick.

(As CIA Note 2 shows, the U.S. government indirectly admits that it used chemical-biological warfare despite President Nixon claimed ban in 1969. The Deep State has its own rules. See also *Inside the Company: CIA Diary* by former CIA official Philip Agee.)

Among the many CIA murder programs was MK Naomi—poison and bacteria kept at the army's biological laboratory at Ft. Detrick, Maryland. The amount of shellfish toxin stored was capable of killing 14,000 persons. In all, they had 37 lethal or incapacitating substances. The CIA-Army was breeding mosquitoes to carry dengue fever. Much of this was revealed during congressional hearings. CIA chief William Colby testified at the Church Committee, but he could not explain why his Company had so many toxins and mosquitoes.

María Santiesteban received another CIA message asking about information concerning various infectious diseases, including hemorrhagic conjunctivitis. Before the disease could be controlled, one million people, one-tenth the population, had been affected. And because of the U.S. embargo against all trade, the medicine needed had to be bought elsewhere at higher prices.

When I conducted research for *Backfire* in Cuba (1987-9), I was privileged to have lengthy interviews with several of the 27 double agents, and see some material evidence of CIA subversion and terrorism. Some CIA messages, such as those sent to María Santiesteban, were included in photos and videos I saw. The DSE caught CIA official working out of the U.S. Interest Section in Havana on film as they handed spy equipment to what the Yankees thought were its Cuba agents.

(Photos and materials of CIA spies can be seen in the Cuban

intelligence museum in Havana (http://www.latinamericanstudies.org/espionage/spy-museum.htm))

A great deal of this material was shown on Cuban television in the July 1987 11-part series, "The CIA War Against Cuba." The DSE had identified 179 CIA officers using false diplomatic covers working in Cuba or passing through on special missions. Cuba discovered 27 lie detector technicians, 28 communication workers and 18 collaborator "assets".

Cuba possesses some of their apparatuses, such as coding machines CDS-501 and RS-804. The latter is designed for agent-main center communication via satellite, known as FLATSATCOM, which has a range of 30,000 kilometers.

I became close to one of those double agents, the DSE's dean of infiltrators, Ignacio Rodríguez-Mena Castrillón. He was dean because he was a double agent the longest, 1966-87. Ignacio, like the vast majority of infiltrators, was not a professional spy but held a civilian job as a flight steward. The CIA gave him the code name *Julio*. He was *Isidro* for Cuba.

He told me that the CIA asked him to help with these germ plagues.

"The CIA was often interested in crop plagues and domestic animal sicknesses. My handler, Nicolás, asked me in the Madrid Hotel Sideral to get close to places where I could plant a virus. They asked me if we carried pesticides or other chemicals on our flights, which could combat the germ carrying mosquitoes. They wanted to know how we combated African swine fever. They wanted to know who sold us chemicals and what make they were. They wanted whatever I could give them so that they could trace the producer seller of these products, in order to stop them from selling to us, or to sabotage them." (*Backfire*, page 77)

Ignacio also told me, "Yeah, they worked us as a team to try to kill our Commander. When I was in Madrid, in April 1985, CIA officer Martin [actually Allen Cooper] told me: "'You have to try and find out, with your wife's help, what preparations are taken when it's known that the Commander is expected at the airport, what security measures are taken, the license the plane has, what route they'll take, what stopovers they'll make, and the day and time. That's your most important task right now. When your get this information, send me a message right away with the set [RS-804] you were given." [*Backfire*, pages 58-61]

The CIA was especially keen on Ignacio. He had played on a Washington Senator's minor league professional baseball team in Florida. Ignacio was "Americanized", so they thought. They let him recruit his wife, Mercedes. She then worked for the DSE, too. He was most useful especially because he was a Cuban civilian aircraft crew member. But they neglected to let him know that on one flight he and his wife were scheduled to take, the plane was to be exploded. Ignacio explained:

"The worst event through all those years was the brutal sabotage of *Cubana Aviación* CUT-1201, on October 6, 1976, in Barbados. Seventy-three people died: 57 Cubans; the rest were Koreans and Guyanese. Cuba's entire junior fencing team died on Flight 455. Mercedes and I [would have been] among the dead."

The couple was coming from separate flights to take Flight 455 from Barbados. But because Mercedes got sick, she wasn't on that flight.

"My best buddy told me he'd take my place. I protested but he insisted. His last words to me were, 'Your woman didn't come. Let me take your flight.'

"That was my great friend, Ramón Ferrándiz."

"The DC-8 took off at 17:15. The pilot radioed the tower at 17:23 for emergency landing clearing because of an explosion and fire on the plane. He turned his wings and a second blast occurred at 17:28. The plane went out of control and went down into the sea just short of land."

"Just imagine this dirty deed! Everybody dead! All my *compañeros*; at least 20 colleagues were murdered. The CIA was involved in this atrocity, and here I was working with them."

When Ignacio saw his CIA handler Nicolás again, he was livid. Nicolás protested: "'I didn't participate in this. I didn't know anything about it...For your peace of mind, I assure you, and headquarters told me to assure you, that from now on we will take special precautions so that you, and your wife, will not be aboard any aircraft that may be subject to an act like that.'"

To Ignacio's outburst of indignation, the CIA man added: "'Yes, it's true. We trained these people in explosives. We even gave them the explosives they used... [but] Listen, I didn't have anything to do with this.'"

Ignacio grabbed a chair and hit him on the head, and slapped him in the face. But the dedicated patriot of his sovereign land bit the grit for the next 11 years until his government called him, and 26 other double agents, out of the cold.

It wasn't Afghanistan, Libya, Iraq or any other Arab country that first blew up a commercial airplane, not even al Qaida or the Islamic State, and certainly not Russia. It was self-exiled Cuban mercenaries backed and covered up by the United States government.

Former CIA terrorist operative Luis Posada Carriles provides many details of the sabotage in his book *Caminos del Guerrero* (Ways of the Warrior). The CIA-backed terrorist group Coordination of United Revolutionary Organizations, of which Carriles was a member, is widely viewed as directly responsible for the bombings.

Four men were arrested in connection with the bombing, and a trial was held in Venezuela, long before Hugo Chavez. Venezuelans Freddy Lugo and Hernán Ricardo Lozano said they worked for Carriles to bomb the plane. They were sentenced to 20-year prison terms. Cuban-born Dr. Orlando Bosch was acquitted and later moved to Miami where he was treated as a hero until his death, in 2011. Carriles was imprisoned in Venezuela for eight years but escaped, presumably with CIA aid. He later entered the US and was held on charges of entering the country illegally but was released, and took on hero status in Miami despite the fact that he was on the FBI list as a terrorist. (http://nsarchive2.gwu.edu/NSAEBB/NSAEBB153/)

The U.S. Justice Department maintained that Dr. Bosch was responsible for at least 30 acts of sabotage inside the United States, in Cuba, Puerto Rico and Panama. It didn't seek to imprison him, only to deport him. But the first Bush president overruled his law enforcement department.

On the day of the massacre of the passengers on the Cuban civilian aircraft Bosch and Carriles ultimate boss was CIA chief George H.W. Bush. His "dirty deeds" stood him in good enough stead to actually be voted in as the President of the United States of America.

The death-reach of USA Murder Incorporated is endless. Mexicans know this. That is why they call the U.S. embassy in their country: "*La embajada de muerte*"—the embassy of death.

Neither Russia or Cuba has ever attacked the US—no assassinations of presidents, no chemical-biological warfare, no sabotage of civilian aircraft and murder of passengers, no blowing up of schools or anything else inside the greatest democratic country on earth, nor have they conducted genocide against an entire people, or enslaved another entire people.

Notes:

1. The first four freedoms are those in Article 1 of the first 10 amendments of the Constitution of the United States (1787), ratified in 1791.

   "Congress shall make no law respecting an establishment of religion, or prohibiting the free exercise thereof; or abridging the freedom of speech, or of the press; or the right of the people to peaceably to assemble and to petition the Government for a redress of grievances."

2. The **Zapruder film** is a silent, color motion picture sequence shot by private citizen Abraham Zapruder with a home-movie camera. He unexpectedly captured the assassination as the motorcade passed through Dealey Plaza in Dallas, Texas, on November 22, 1963. (Wikipedia summary).

   It has been called the most complete film, giving a relatively clear view from a somewhat elevated position on the side from which the president's head wound is visible. It was an important part of the Warren Commission hearings and all subsequent investigations of the assassination, and is one of the most studied pieces of film in history. Of greatest notoriety is the film's capture of the fatal shot to Kennedy's head when his limousine was almost in front of, and slightly below, Zapruder's position.

   On March 6, 1975, on the ABC late-night television show *Good Night America* (hosted by Geraldo Rivera), assassination researchers Robert Groden and Dick Gregory presented the first-ever network television showing of the Zapruder home movie. The public's response and outrage to showing led to the forming of the Hart-Schweiker investigation, and contributed to the Church Committee Investigation on Intelligence Activities by the United States, and resulted in the 1979 House Select Committee on Assassinations investigation.

   In October 1964, the U.S. Government Printing Office released 26 volumes of testimony and evidence compiled by the Warren Commission. Volume 18 of the commission's hearings reproduced 158 frames of the Zapruder film in black and white. However, frames 208–211 were missing, a splice was visible in frames 207 and 212, frames 314 and 315 were switched, and frame 284 was a repeat of 283. In reply to an inquiry, the FBI's J. Edgar Hoover wrote in 1965 that 314 and 315 were switched due to a printing error, and that the error did not exist in the original Warren Commission exhibits. In early 1967, *Life* released a statement that four frames of the camera original (208–211) had been accidentally destroyed, and the adjacent frames damaged by a *Life* photo lab technician on November 23, 1963. *Life* released the missing frames from the first-generation copy it had received from Zapruder with the original.(Of the Zapruder frames outside the section used in the commission's exhibits, frames 155–157 and 341 were also damaged and spliced out of the camera original, but are present in the first-generation copies.)

   The **single-bullet theory** (or **magic-bullet theory**, as it is commonly called by its critics) was introduced by the Warren Commission in its investigation of the assassination of

President John F. Kennedy to explain what happened to the bullet that struck Kennedy in the back and exited through his throat. Given the lack of damage to the presidential limousine consistent with it having been struck by a high-velocity bullet and the fact that Texas Governor John Connally was wounded and was seated on a jumper seat half a meter in front of and slightly to the left of the president, the Commission concluded they were likely struck by the same bullet.

The theory, generally credited to Warren Commission staffer Arlen Specter (later a senator) posits that a single bullet, "Warren **C**ommission **E**xhibit **399**" (also known as "**CE 399**"), caused all the wounds to the governor and the non-fatal wounds to the president (seven entry/exit wounds in total).

According to the single-bullet theory, a three-centimeter-long copper-jacketed lead-core 6.5×52mm Mannlicher–Carcanorifle bullet fired from the sixth floor of the Texas School Book Depository passed through President Kennedy's neck and Governor Connally's chest and wrist and embedded itself in the Governor's thigh. If so, this bullet traversed 15 layers of clothing, 7 layers of skin, and approximately 15 inches of tissue, struck a necktie knot, removed 4 inches of rib, and shattered a radius bone. The bullet was found on a gurney in the corridor at the Parkland Memorial Hospital, in Dallas, after the assassination. The Warren Commission found that this gurney was the one that had borne Governor Connally. This bullet became a key Commission exhibit. ***Its copper jacket was completely intact.*** While the bullet's nose appeared normal, the tail was compressed laterally on one side.

In its conclusion, the Warren Commission found "persuasive evidence from the experts" that a single bullet caused the President's neck wound and all the wounds in Governor Connally. It acknowledged that there was a "difference of opinion" among members of the Commission "as to this probability", but stated that the theory was not essential to its conclusions and that all members had no doubt that all shots were fired from the sixth floor window of the Depository building.

Most pro- and anti-conspiracy theorists believe the single-bullet theory is essential to the Warren Commission's conclusion that Oswald acted alone [because] of the timing: if, as the Warren Commission found, President Kennedy was wounded sometime between frame 210 and 225 of the Zapruder film and Governor Connally was wounded in the back/chest no later than frame 240, there would not have been enough time between the wounding of the two men for Oswald to have fired two shots from his bolt-action rifle. FBI marksmen, who test-fired the rifle…concluded that the "minimum time for getting off two successive well-aimed shots on the rifle is approximately 2 and a quarter seconds" or 41 to 42 Zapruder frames.

The first preliminary report on the assassination, issued by the FBI on December 9, 1963, said: "Three shots rang out. Two bullets struck President Kennedy, and one wounded Governor Connally." After the report was written, the FBI received the official autopsy report which indicated that the bullet that struck the president in the back had exited through his throat. The FBI had written their report partly based on an initial autopsy report written by their agents, which reflected the early presumption that that bullet had only penetrated several inches into the president's back and had likely fallen out. The FBI concluded, therefore, that the governor had been struck by a separate bullet.

[By the time the Warren Commission commenced study of the Zapruder film] the FBI had determined that the running speed of Abraham Zapruder's camera was 18.3 frames per second, and that the Mannlicher–Carcano rifle found at the Texas School Book

Depository, the presumed murder weapon, could not be fired twice in less than 2.3 seconds, or 42 frames of the Zapruder film.

When the Commission...received after February 25 higher-resolution images of the Zapruder film from Life magazine (who had purchased the film from Zapruder), it was immediately apparent that there was a timing problem with the FBI's conclusion that three bullets had found their mark. Kennedy was observed by the Commission to be waving to the crowd to frame 205 of the Zapruder film as he disappears behind the Stemmons Freeway sign, and seems to be reacting to a shot as he emerges from behind the sign at frames 225-226, a little more than a second later. In their initial viewing of the film, Connally seemed to be reacting to being struck between frames 235 and 240.

Given the earliest possible frame at which Kennedy could have been struck (frame 205), and the minimum 42 frames (2.3 seconds) required between shots, there seemed to be insufficient time for separate bullets to be fired from the rifle. Several assistant counsels, upon viewing the film for the first time, concluded there had to be two assassins.

3. Here is a former secret document revealing that the CIA and military did develop and use CBW. While Nixon was supposed to have stopped this, there is evidence that the Deep State ignored his decision.

   THE NIXON ADMINISTRATION'S DECISION TO END U.S. BIOLOGICAL WARFARE PROGRAMS Volumne III: BIOWAR (http://nsarchive2.gwu.edu/NSAEBB/NSAEBB58/)

   The documents included in this briefing book shed light upon the decision made by President Richard M. Nixon in 1969 to end all U.S. offensive biological (and chemical) weapons programs, as well as upon the history of the U.S. program. Remarkably, neither Nixon nor Henry A. Kissinger, his National Security Advisor at the time, makes any mention of this decision in their memoirs.

   As subsequent revelations made clear, continued classified biological warfare programs did continue, and the ordered destruction of biological and toxin agents was not as thorough as first believed. Judith Miller, Stephen Engelberg and William Broad book, *Germs: Biological Weapons and America's Secret War*, Simon & Schuster, 2001, details the subsequent history of U.S. classified research on biological warfare agents. One critical piece was provided by the Church Committee investigations into the activities of the CIA in 1975. As detailed in the committee hearings (see Document 25) and discussed in *Germs*, these hearings revealed that the CIA had long been involved in stockpiling biological agents for use in assassination attempts on foreign leaders, most notably Cuba's Fidel Castro, and had worked closely with Ft. Detrick in this program between 1952 and 1970. Equally troubling was the evidence that the CIA had maintained a small stockpile of biological agents and toxins in violation of Nixon's ban that were capable of sickening or killing millions of people. Among this stockpile was 100 grams of anthrax, as well as smallpox, Venezuelan equine encephalomyelitis virus, salmonella, and clostridium botulinum, or botulism germs.

   Miller-Engelberg-Broad's article "U.S. Germ Warfare Research Pushes Treaty Limits" in the Times on September 4, 2001, described a series of secret U.S. biological warfare experiments and programs conducted under the Clinton and Bush administrations, including a Pentagon plan to engineer genetically a potentially more deadly version of anthrax, and concerns that these programs might violate the 1972 treaty banning the development or acquisition of biological weapons.

Part II:
PEACE, LAND, BREAD

PEACE, LAND, BREAD

This part of the book describes international relations mainly between the United States and the Soviet Union-Russia for nearly a century, 1917-1991. It is not my intent to delve into or analyze Russia's internal developments, socialism's growth and failures, its leaders' wisdom or lack thereof. I will present a few facts of some importance inside Russia-Soviet Union but to find definitive reasons and theories look in other books. I concentrate on war and peace—what motivations are at work between the two systems: western capitalism and Russia's socialism or the nationalism of today.

CHAPTER 7

October Revolution: the West Prohibits Socialism's Natural Course

> *"Were they (Allies) at war with Soviet Russia? Certainly not; but they shot Soviet Russians at sight. They stood as invaders on Russian soil. They armed the enemies of the Soviet Government. They blockaded its ports, and sunk its battleships. They earnestly desired and schemed its downfall. But war – shocking! Interference – shame! It was, they repeated, a matter of indifference to them how Russians settled their own internal affairs. They were impartial – Bang!"*
>
> (Winston Churchill) (1)

THE 1917 OCTOBER Revolution culminated the short-lived February Revolution of 1917, which overthrew the Tsarist autocracy and resulted in a provisional government. It began in Petrograd, Russian Empire's capital (Saint Petersburg), on February 23 (old calendar, March 8 new calendar). This was International Women's Day, which started in Germany on March 8, 1914. The 90,000-strong Petrograd march was led by women textile workers seeking the right to vote, and protesting the lack of bread, food shortages generally, largely due to World War I. The Bolsheviks were not in the vanguard this time.

Seven days later, the last Emperor of Russia, Nicholas II, abdicated and the new Provisional Government granted women the right to vote. March 8 was declared a national holiday later in Soviet-led Russia.

When Russian workers struggled for reforms during the February Revolution, they had already created a history of revolutionary struggle to guide them. It was built upon the gains and abortions of the revolution of 1905, prompted by poverty, poor working conditions, and Russian losses in the war with Japan (1904-5). Widespread dissatisfaction with the government created conditions for a liberal opposition movement that demanded a legislative parliament. Nicolas 11 response was paternalistic. Reform, he explained, would be "harmful to the people God has entrusted to me".

Workers had hoped that the Tsar would hear their petition for, "an eight-hour day, a minimum daily wage of one ruble (fifty cents), a repudiation of bungling bureaucrats, and a democratically elected constitutional assembly to introduce representative government into the empire." (2)

Controversial Orthodox priest Georgy Gapon, who headed a police-sponsored workers' association, led a huge workers' procession to the Winter Palace to deliver the petition to the Tsar on Sunday, January 9, 1905. Troops guarding the Palace were ordered not to let demonstrators pass a certain point. Without warning, the Tsar's men opened fire on the people, killing between 300 and 1000 and wounding hundreds more. "Bloody Sunday" signaled the start of the three-stage revolution until victory on October 26, 1917.

The massacre provoked great indignation, and a series of massive strikes spread quickly throughout the industrial centers of the Russian Empire. By the end of January 1905, over 400,000 workers in Russian Poland were on strike, and it grew to 90% of all workers there. In Riga, Latvia, 130 protesters were killed on January 13. A few days later, in Warsaw, over 100 strikers were shot on the streets. Half of European Russia's industrial workers went on strike. There were also strikes in Finland and the Baltic coast. There were strikes in the Caucasus in February, and by April in the Urals and beyond. In March, all higher academic institutions were forcibly closed for the rest of the year. A strike by railway workers on October 21quickly developed into a general strike in Petrograd and Moscow. Two million workers were on strike and most railways were shut down.

Students also organized protests. In the countryside, peasants refused to pay rent. They seized land and burned down some 3,000 manor houses. The regime used the army to put down rural rebellions but by June the unrest had spread to the navy. There was a mutiny among sailors on the Battleship *Potemkin*, an event later made famous by film director Sergei Eisenstein.

While workers, peasants and students rebelled, Russians soldiers were being killed in the spurious war between its government and Japan, fought between February 4, 1904 and September 5, 1905 over which elitist leaders should control Manchuria and Korea. Surprisingly, Japan won.

During the war, Japan was able to invade and briefly occupy the entire Sakhalin Island, which had been a land border between the two nations. By the Treaty of Portsmouth, which concluded the war, Russia ceded the southern half of Sakhalin to Japan, while Japanese troops withdrew from its northern half. Thus for the first time, they shared a land border, which ran along the 50th parallel north across the entire island of Sakhalin, from the Strait of Tartary to the Sea of Okhotsk. The short Korea–Russia border also became part of the border between the Japanese and Russian Empires, and later (until 1945) between the Japanese Empire and the USSR. (3)

There was no other exchange of territory at the end of the war, but Russians were angry, and many anti-war protests took place, including unrest in army reserve units, and among sailors. As many as two thousand sailors were killed in the ensuing suppression.

Faced with the sustained movement of strikes and protests, the Tsar was forced to acknowledge reforms. His advisors drew up plans for a *consultative* parliament. In the early days of 1905 this concession may have been enough, but with the following months of militant action it was too little too late. In September, with the end of the Japanese war, the revolution culminated in a massive general strike. Printers struck in Moscow, and were joined by rail workers and then by millions more in cities across Russia.

The Tsar was forced to sign the October Manifesto, which established a slightly real parliament called the Duma. While there was general jubilation, the October Manifesto mainly satisfied the middle classes and the liberals. Workers and peasants soon sought more fundamental change.

The Council of United Nobility was created by the largest estate owners, a "gentry reaction" to "their" upstart serfs and peasants. They had one-third of Duma membership and could curtail or stop liberal reforms. The Tsar's court backed them. Since the time of Ivan the Terrible (the Tsar of all the Russias in 1500s), the tsars had centralized their power while granting the nobility dominion over land and peasants—a system known as feudalism or serfdom. The combined imperial forces were able to disband the first Duma, claiming it was "too liberal". Election rules were amended to prevent representation from the most threatening parts of society. The Duma became transformed from its original intent into a pillar of autocracy.

Emboldened, the Council of United Nobility established the Black Hundreds, which drew support from rich land owners, merchants, clergymen and policemen. They whipped up monarchist fervor and conducted anti-Semitic pogroms and violence against socialists and trade unionists. The Black Hundreds assisted the Tsarist regime maintain its rule, especially from 1906 until 1914, and lay the way for the future White Army.

The Black Hundreds lay low when Russia engaged in World War I. The trigger for war came on June 28, 1914 with the assassination of Archduke Franz Ferdinand of Austria, heir to the throne of Austria-Hungary, and his wife Sophie. They were shot by Yugoslav nationalist Gavrilo Princip, in Sarajevo. (4) This set off a diplomatic crisis. Austria-Hungary inanely declared war on Serbia, on July 28, over the act of this one man, and Germany joined in. Russia's monarchy started mobilizing an army. Germany presented an ultimatum to Russia to demobilize. Russia refused and Germany declared war against it, on August 1. Eventually the Central Powers included Bulgaria and the Ottoman Empire (Turkey).

Russia entered the war with the largest army in the world, standing at 1,400,000 soldiers. At its peak there were five million soldiers with a supply of only 4.6 million rifles. By March 1917, ten million men, mostly poor peasants, had been forced into military service. Many of their wives were forced off the land and into factories to support the war effort.

The war wore upon Russians' spirits and stomachs. By the time the Bolshevik leadership could end Russia's participation, two percent of the 175 million-population was dead or wounded: about two million soldiers and 410,000 civilians killed; 730,000 deaths due to starvation and war-related diseases; 3.7-5 million wounded. (5)

OCTOBER REVOLUTION

Two wars and a revolution within 13 years time did not improve conditions for the people. The momentous year of 1917 was only eight days old when Russian activists took to the streets. On January 9, around 160,000 marched through St Petersburg in freezing temperatures to commemorate the Bloody Sunday massacre. In the coming weeks, workers and police clashed as World War I raged on under both the monarchy, and after its abdication in February with the bourgeoisie provisional government.

In April 1917, Germany allowed Bolshevik leader Vladimir Lenin to pass through its territory from his exile in Switzerland so that he could return to Russia. Germany sought to assist Lenin as he wished to end the war, in order to start a new Russia, as Germany wanted to concentrate on the other allied armies on the Western Front. Upon his arrival in Petrograd, Lenin proclaimed the April Theses, which included a call for ending the war, and turning all political power over to workers and soldiers.

Also in April, the new Provisional Government minister of foreign affairs, Pavel Milyukov, announced the government's desire to continue the war "to a victorious conclusion".

This aroused broad indignation and more protests and strikes. On May 1-4, Bolsheviks in Petrograd led about 100,000 workers and soldiers in protests, followed by more cities joining in under banners reading, "down with the war!" and "all power to the soviets!" The mass demonstrations resulted in a governmental crisis. Throughout July even more millions of workers and soldiers marched against the war, and "down with the ten capitalist ministers".

Yet the government defied the people by opening an offensive against the Central Powers, which soon collapsed. On July 16, spontaneous demonstrations of workers and soldiers in Petrograd added the demand that power be turned over to the soviets—factory workers, sailors, soldiers, and local councils, initially set up during the 1905 revolution and now reconstituted. The Central Committee of the Russian Social Democratic Labor Party provided leadership to these movements.

On July 17, 500,000 people participated in what was intended to be a peaceful demonstration in Petrograd. The government, with the support of Socialist-Revolutionary Party-Menshevik (minority) leaders of the All-Russian Executive Committee of the Soviets, ordered an armed attack against the demonstrators, killing hundreds.

A pause in street activities ensued while soviet councils and Bolsheviks discussed what to do next. Lenin fled to Finland under threat of arrest while Leon Trotsky, among other prominent Bolsheviks, was arrested. The July Days confirmed the popularity of the anti-war movement and the radical Bolsheviks, but their failure to capitalize on July actions temporarily lost them some support.

During the February Revolution, Bolsheviks had 24,000 members but by September there were 200,000. In early September, the Petrograd Soviet freed all jailed Bolsheviks and Trotsky became chairman of the capital's Soviet. Lenin returned within days.

The moment to revolt seemed right in October. On the 23rd, the Bolsheviks' Central Committee voted 10–2 for a resolution stating that, "an armed uprising is inevitable, and the time for it is fully ripe". A revolutionary military committee was established led by Trotsky. It included armed workers, sailors and soldiers, which assured the support or neutrality of the capital's garrison. The committee planned to occupy strategic locations.

The "ten days that shook the world" actually entailed only two days of fighting, but there were no formal battles.

["The Revolution" a Russian produced rather objective and sympathetic documentary by Masterskaya Movie Company, 2017, characterizes the October revolution as a "coup" in which the masses did not participate at first. BBC's take "Russia with Simon Reeve" was surprisingly quite favorable. It even praised the current Russian President Vladimir Putin as most popular and effective, much more so than Western leaders, and stated that he "made Russians proud to be Russians again" following the Yeltsin-Clinton period. More on that in chapters 13-14.]

On October 25, Bolsheviks led their forces in the Petrograd uprising against the Alexander Kerensky-led Provisional Government. They quickly took over communication centers, electric plants, banks and rail stations. This coincided with the arrival of a flotilla of pro-Bolshevik Kronstadt marines.

The next day, government buildings were occupied. The Winter Palace (the seat of the Provisional Government) was captured with the loss of only two persons.

A new government, the Council of People's Commissars, was set up: Vladimir I. Lenin, chairman; Leon Trotsky, foreign commissar; Aleksey Ivanovich Rykov, interior commissar; Joseph Stalin, commissar of nationalities.

PEACE LAND BREAD

Bolsheviks promised the people Peace, Land, Bread. This core program embraced soldiers, factory workers and peasants, that is, most of the Russian people.

Peace: Withdraw Russia from World War I especially appealed to soldiers and sailors.

Land: A burning issue for peasants who had worked the land for centuries either as serfs or as peasants but owing rent to their masters. The peasants wanted to own their own land.

Bread: People everywhere especially in the cities and the army were hungry and even starving. This was because too many young peasant men were conscripted into the army, which left the lands fallow. Bolsheviks prioritized feeding the people.

Immediately upon victory, the Decree on Peace, the Decree on Land and the Decree on an eight-hour work day, all written by Vladimir Lenin, were passed by the Second Congress of the Soviet of Workers', Soldiers', and Peasants' Deputies on October 26 (old calendar, November 8 on the new).

Several other Soviet decrees were made during November:

- All Russian banks were nationalized.
- Private bank accounts were expropriated, hardly affecting most people who had no accounts.
- The properties of the church (including bank accounts) were expropriated.
- All foreign debts were repudiated.
- Control of the factories was turned over to the soviets.
- Wages were fixed at higher rates, and an eight-hour working day was introduced.

As Russia started negotiating with Germany for peace, and the people's decrees were being passed by the Soviet councils, the pro-monarchy nobility and its defeated Imperial army generals launched a counter-revolution, which the official church backed as did Western "allies".

RUSSIAN CIVIL WAR

The Russian Civil War was forced upon the war weary people by the aristocracy's White Army. In the Russian context after the 1917 revolution, "White" had three main connotations:

(1) Political contra-distinction to the revolutionary *Reds* whose Red Army supported the Bolshevik government.
(2) Historical reference to absolute monarchy, specifically recalling Russia's first Tsar, Ivan III (1462–1505) when some called the ruler of Muscovy *Albus Rex* ("the White King").
(3) The white uniforms of Imperial Russia worn by some White Army soldiers

Alexander Kerensky, the deposed head of the provisional government and commander of the Imperial Army, had managed to escape arrest. He assembled his loyal troops from the Northern Front. Pro-revolutionary troops soon defeated them at Pulkova. By December, central Russia and Siberia were under control by the revolutionary government.

On December 15, 1917, an armistice between Russia and the Central Powers was made and fighting stopped. December 22, peace negotiations began at Brest-Litovsk, Poland.

The Russian government demobilized the old army, and in January 1918, the government ordered the formation of the Red Army of Workers and Peasants. Leon Trotsky was made commissar of war and headed the Red Army from March 13 until displaced by Stalin. In addition to Russians, there were some foreigners fighting alongside and even in the Red Army. These included several thousand Chinese, who had been construction workers in Novgorod and near the Gulf of Finland. Most were not political but they became soldiers, in order to gain rights and perhaps citizenship. There were also some Hungarian Jews, Czech and Slovak nationals, and a few Red Latvian Riflemen while White Latvian Riflemen sided with the White Army.

As the new army was forming, General Lavr Kornilov organized the Volunteer Army numbering 3,000 men. Others who opposed the Bolshevik government soon joined. The Kuban Cossacks aligned with the White Army. Cossacks are a group of predominantly East Slavic-speaking people, mainly located in the Ukraine and Russia's Kuban region in Northwest Caucasus.

In late February 1918, 4,000 soldiers under the command of General Aleksei Kaledin were forced to retreat from Rostov-on-Don by the advancing Red Army. In what became known as the Ice March, they traveled to Kuban in order to unite with the Cossacks. In March, 3,000 men under the command of General Viktor Pokrovsky joined the Volunteer Army, increasing its membership to 6,000, and by June to 9,000.

By February, Trotsky was frustrated with growing German demands for cessions of territory and he announced a new policy on the 10th. Russia unilaterally declared an end of hostilities against the Central Powers, and withdrew from peace negotiations—a position summed up as "no war – no peace". The consequences for the Bolsheviks were worse than what they had feared. The Central Powers repudiated the armistice, and soon seized most of Ukraine, Belarus, and the Baltic countries. A German fleet approached the Gulf of Finland and Petrograd. On February 19, the Bolsheviks sent a radio message to the Germans agreeing to the original peace treaty, but the Central Powers sent new terms requiring greater territorial concessions.

Russia sent a new delegation headed by Georgy Chicherin and Lev Karakhan with instructions to accept their demands. On March 3, 1918, Russia agreed to terms worse than those they had previously rejected. This amounted to surrendering over 25% of Russia's population so that the rest could begin to rebuild the devastation the wars were causing. Immediately after signing the treaty, Lenin moved the Russian government from Petrograd to Moscow.

The end of hostilities with the Central Powers did provide some relief to the people and the Red Army. There was one less enemy to fight—one down, two to go: one internal and another foreign. The initially volunteer red army suffered so many loses and had so many enemies that the government was forced to introduce conscription in June.

WEST INTERVENES IN RUSSIA

Allied intervention entailed a multi-national military expedition launched in summer 1918. The first to intervene were Britain and France, followed by the U.S., Canada, Italy, Romania, Greece, Poland, and Japan. The West sent over 100,000 troops to assist another 100,000 Czechs and Slavs (the Czechoslovak Legion) backing the anti-revolutionary White Army. At times, the Czechoslovak Legion controlled the entire Trans-Siberian railway and several Siberian cities.

The Western allies armed and supported Bolshevik opponents. They were worried about:

(1) A possible Russo-German alliance or, at least, greater numbers of German troops to fight.
(2) The prospect of the Bolsheviks defaulting on Imperial Russia's massive foreign loans.
(3) Fear that revolutionary ideas would spread. It was imperative to prevent success of the new government's socialist agenda—one

> that if not quelled could lead the world into a unique era of peace-land-bread for all. The U.S. strategy later became known as, "the domino theory".

Winston Churchill declared that Bolshevism must be "strangled in its cradle".

Besides aiding the Czechoslovak Legion, the West secured supplies of munitions and armaments in some Russian ports, and re-established the Eastern Front hoping to reverse the revolutionary victory. Allied efforts were hampered by their troops' war-weariness after they had just finished the greater conflict, and a lack of domestic support. Most Russian troops in the Imperial Russian Army had given up the World War, shook hands with German troops and went home. Many of them now supported the revolution.

The Japanese sent the largest military force, about 70,000. The Imperial Japanese Army General Staff viewed the situation in Russia as an opportunity for settling Japan's "northern problem"; they sought a buffer state in Siberia. The Japanese government was also hostile to communism.

The U.S. had come into the world war late, April 2, 1917. Upon the revolutionary victory in Russia half a year later, the government and the mass media immediately started a hysteria campaign against Bolshevikism/Communism, which lasted until 1991 with the end of the Soviet Union. Westerners were to learn to fear Communists, those cannibal monsters who even eat children.

> *"Literally no story about the Bolsheviks was too contrived, too bizarre, too grotesque, or too perverted to be printed and widely believed – from women being nationalized to babies being eaten (as the early pagans believed the Christians guilty of devouring their children; the same was believed of the Jews in the Middle Ages). The story about women with all the lurid connotations of state property, compulsory marriage, 'free love', etc. 'was broadcasted over the country through a thousand channels," wrote Frederick Schuman, "and perhaps did more than anything else to stamp the Russian Communists in the minds of most American citizens as criminal perverts".* (6)

In July 1918, President Woodrow Wilson sent 5,000 United States Army troops to northern European Russia at Arkhangelsk and seized the White Sea port. They became known as the "American North Russia Expeditionary Force". In August, 8,000 soldiers from occupied Philippines (and from California) were shipped to Vladivostok, a major Pacific port city near the borders with China and North Korea.

The State Department told Congress: "All these operations were to offset effects of the Bolshevik revolution in Russia."

The capitalist states of the U.S. and allies would rather war, in order to maintain and extend private property and wealth, than establish a peaceful world. Their slogans could have been: *War, Land and Lobsters for the Rich.*

Gaither Stewart, a novelist with three books concerning Russia, and an editor for The Greanville Post explains what the West's interest in Russia was, and still is:

> *"The West in general and the USA in particular envy Russia for: its natural wealth much of which is still buried under the soil beyond the Ural Mountains. Why should they have all that wealth is the U.S. attitude, part of the justification for its great plot to subjugate Russia and split it up into small states [also a contemporary vision]."* (http://www.greanvillepost.com/2017/08/09/the-character-of-russian-communism/)

Yet the West did not achieve its will. Russia is the world's largest country, and Russians far outnumbered the combined armies they sent. Conditions for their troops were also miserable, and many Western soldiers, including US Americans, were tired of war and reluctant to fight. The last U.S. troops left Russia on April 1, 1920. Four hundred and twenty-four had died of various causes, most from battle.

Major General William Graves, who commanded the American Expeditionary Force, wrote in his memoirs: "I do not know what the United States was trying to accomplish by military intervention."

General Graves said he had conflicting orders: help the counter-revolutionaries but don't interfere in internal affairs. Yet his soldiers destroyed 25 villages in the eastern Russian Amur district alone, wrote the Red Star, the Russian army's official publication. "In March 1919…

they attacked the totally peaceful village of Ivanovka, burned it down and killed 1,300 inhabitants." (7)

THE CIVIL WAR CONTINUES WITHOUT THE WEST

Between May and October 1919, the White Army grew from 64,000 to 150,000 soldiers. Thanks to nobility wealth and Western financing, they were better supplied than the Red Army. Nevertheless, they met defeat after defeat by soldiers fighting for their own land and bread. The Red Army defeated the White forces in the Ukraine, and the army led by Admiral Aleksandr Kolchak in Siberia, in 1919. The remains of the White forces commanded by Pyotr Nikolayevich Wrangel were beaten in Crimea and survivors left Russia in late 1920.

The Polish–Soviet War (February 1919-March 1921) was particularly bitter. It was fought within the context of the Russian Civil War but also over border lines, the current foreign invasion and potential ones in the future. Both sides lost nearly equal numbers of soldiers, about 100,000 killed and 200,000 wounded.

The war ended with the Treaty of Riga, March 18, 1921. The Soviet-Polish borders established by the treaty remained in force until the Second World War. They were later redrawn during the conferences at Yalta and Potsdam.

Although most of Ukraine fell under Bolshevik control and eventually became one of the constituent republics of the Soviet Union, other parts of the Russian Empire—the Baltic States and Finland—emerged as independent countries. They could now have their own civil wars.

The rest of the former Russian Empire was consolidated into the Soviet Union, December 28, 1922. A conference of delegations from Russia, the Ukraine and Byelorussia approved a treaty, which created the Soviet Union, formally named the Union of Soviet Socialist Republics (USSR).

The war officially was now ended, although lesser battles continued on the periphery in the Far East until late 1923. National resistance in Central Asia was not completely crushed until 1934.

Japan had occupied the northern part of Sakhalin in 1920-1925. Soviet control of northern Sakhalin was established in 1925, and the 50th parallel became the Japan-USSR border. The last Japanese troops then left Russia.

The Red Army now had five million men. Most were demobilized; 600,000 were retained to form a regular army. The Russian Civil War caused an estimated 7,000,000–12,000,000 casualties, mostly civilians. As many as three-five million died of starvation and war-related diseases. This was the greatest national catastrophe ever seen in one country in Europe.

Russia finally was at peace, land was being used by and for the people, and gradually more people were eating more bread. But peacetime was short lived due to more Western capitalist interventions.

Notes:

1. Winston Churchill, *The World Crisis: The Aftermath*, London, 1929, p. 235. Churchill was Britain's Minister of War. As such he sent allied troops to battle on the side of the "White Army".

2. R.R. Palmer, *A History of the Modern World*, Alfred A. Knopf, New York, 1960, p. 715. See also: http://www.revolution-1917.org/2016/12/21/1905-prelude-to-revolution/ https://www.thoughtco.com/prelude-to-the-russian-revolution-1779472

3. The war caused both sides around 300,000 casualties. Russians killed range from 40,000 to 70,000, with 150,000 wounded and 75,000 captured. Japanese killed in combat was put at about 47,000, between 6,000 and 12,000 wounded, and around 27,000 additional casualties from disease. China suffered 20,000 civilian deaths.

4. Princip was associated with the movement Mlada Bosna (Young Bosnia) which consisted of Serbs, and some Bosniaks and Croats. On trial, he stated: "I am a Yugoslav nationalist, aiming for the unification of all Yugoslavs. I do not care what form of state, but it must be freed from Austria." Princip died on April 28, 1918 from tuberculosis caused by poor prison conditions.

5. Total deaths on all sides were about 18 million; 23 million wounded. Eleven million soldiers and seven million civilians died–three million from typhus alone. The Central Powers (Austria-Hungary, Germany, Bulgaria, Ottoman Empire/ Turkey) suffered casualties of between 5 and 8 percent of their populations: 3-4.5 million military killed; 1.6 million civilians killed plus 2-2.3 million deaths due to starvation and war-related diseases. The entente-allies' populations collectively suffered 1 percent casualties: 5 to 6.5 million military deaths; 630,000 civilians killed plus 3.4-3.8 million deaths due to starvation and war-related diseases. Of these, US Americans suffered only 0.13 percent casualties of its 92 million people: 53,000 soldiers killed, 116,000 died from all causes; 757 civilians died. 204,000 military wounded.

6. Citing Frederick L. Schuman, *American Policy Toward Russia Since 1917* (New York, 1928), p. 154.

7. "1918 Occupation Force: Forgotten War: Yanks in Russia," wrote William Eaton, reporter for the "Los Angeles Times", March 10, 1987.

CHAPTER 8

U.S. Capital Plans Fascist FDR Coup; Finances Hitler-Mussolini

Henry Ford received the highest medal Nazi Germany could award a foreigner: the Grand Cross of the German Eagle, July 30, 1938. "I regard Henry Ford as my inspiration," declared Hitler.

IBM founder Thomas John Watson received the Order of the German Eagle (2nd class), June 1937.

General Motor's chief executive for overseas operations James Mooney was awarded the Order of the German Eagle (1st class) by Adolf Hitler, in 1938.

J.P. Morgan agent Grayson Murphy was decorated by Mussolini with the "Order of the Crown of Italy," Commander Class, for his role in syndicating Morgan loans to fascist Italy

NEARLY A YEAR after Russia and Germany signed the armistice, December 15, 1917, the remaining Allied Powers agreed with the Central Powers to an armistice, on November 11, 1918. Half a year later, June 28, 1919, the Treaty of Versailles put an end to the state of war between Germany and the Allied Powers. The other Central Powers made separate treaties.

Article 231 was the most difficult and controversial of many provisions. It became known as the War Guilt clause, because it required "Germany [to] accept the responsibility of Germany and her allies for causing all the loss and damage" during the war. The other Central Powers treaties

Henry Ford receiving Grand Cross of the German Eagle from Hitler's U.S. consuls. The occasion was Ford's 75th birthday, July 30, 1938, in Dearborn, Michigan where his auto plants were, and where his museum is today.

contained similar articles. The total cost of these reparations was assessed at 132 billion marks. (Then $31.4 billion, roughly equivalent to US $442 billion, in 2017).

The treaty also forced Germany to disarm much of its arsenal and troops, and make substantial territorial concessions. Problems of payment would lead to the Locarno Treaties, followed by Dawes and Young re-negotiations, which improved relations between Germany and other European powers. Indefinite postponement of reparations was agreed at the 1932 Lausanne Conference.

The original treaty stripped Germany of 65,000 km2 of territory and 7 million people. It also required Germany to give up the gains made via the Treaty of Brest-Litovsk and grant independence to the protectorates that had been established.

Germany had to recognize the independence of Czechoslovakia and cede parts of the province of Upper Silesia. Germany also had to recognize the independence of Poland.

The provisions were intended to make the Reichswehr (military forces) incapable of offensive action and to encourage international disarmament.

Germany was to demobilize soldiers by March 21, 1920, leaving an army of no more than 100,000 men.

Germany was prohibited from the arms trade; limits were imposed on the type and quantity of weapons; and it was prohibited from the manufacture or stockpile of chemical weapons, armored cars, tanks and military aircraft.

Germany was also required to join the League of Nations. This inter-governmental organization started on January 10, 1920. The main goal was to prevent future wars, while relying on collective security and disarmament.

The United States Senate refused to sign the Treaty of Versailles as it opposed joining the League of Nations. There was much too much money to be made in armament. Without the U.S. the organization never became effective.

Instead, the senate agreed to a separate document, on August 25, 1921, the *United States-German Peace Treaty.*

Article 1 obliged the German government to grant to the U.S. government all rights and privileges enjoyed by the other allied powers which had ratified the Versailles peace treaty. The provisions limiting Germany's militarization and prohibiting arms trade should also apply. This treaty laid the foundations for a U.S.-German cooperation, which otherwise would have been more limited under the supervision of the League of Nations. The U.S. government could more easily assist the new Weimar Republic ease the burden of war reparations imposed in the Treaty of Versailles.

Weimar Republic was an unofficial, historical designation for the German state between 1919 and 1933. The name derives from the city of Weimar, where its constitutional assembly first took place. Weimar Germany fulfilled most of the requirements of the Treaty of Versailles although it never met its disarmament requirements, and eventually paid only a small portion of reparations. Even this payment placed a significant burden on its economy, which disquieted the majority.

ADOLF HITLER

Like many Germans of the period, Adolf Hitler believed that the treaty was a betrayal. He said his country had been backstabbed " by its own government and by Marxists".

Hitler joined the Nazi party (National Socialist German Worker's Party/NSDAP) in 1920, a year after its founding in a Munich hotel. Nazism stood for the collective good of the "Aryan Master Race", which required suppression of many individual rights. Its basis was German nationalism with "*Lebensraum*"/international expansion as a goal. Inferior peoples, first and foremost Jews, but also Gypsies and handicapped people, were to be suppressed and/or eliminated. (1)

In 1921, Hitler's bellicose oratorical style appealed so much to Nazi members that they made him their leader. On November 8, 1923, Hitler led 2000 members in Munich to seize state power. The Beer Hall Putsch resulted in the death of 16 Nazis and four police officers. He was sentenced to five years in prison for treason but was released after only nine months. Authorities feared his rising popularity. While in prison, the relatively easy conditions allowed him to write Mein Kampf, an imperialist, racist and anti-Semitic diatribe.

Nazis, Social Democrats (SPD) and Communist (KPD) engaged in heated conflicts during the 1920s. Nazis were brutal, beating to death many Jews and Communists.

Black Tuesday—October 29, 1929—the Wall Street Crash heralded worldwide economic disaster. As a result, Nazis and Communists (KPD) made great gains during the September 1930 election. The NSDAP leapt forward from 2.6%, in May 1928 (gaining only 12 seats), to 18% for 107 seats. The KPD got 13% for 77 seats, an increase of 23 seats. The SPD took 24.5% of the vote for 143 seats, a loss of ten, but it was still the largest party.

The conservative-rightest Paul von Hindenburg government imposed emergency powers to back his three Chancellors Heinrich Brüning, Franz von Papen and General Kurt von Schleicher. The Great Depression, exacerbated by Brüning's policy of deflation, doubled unemployment to 30%.

In July 1932 elections, a majority of voters placed their mark on the Nazis. They doubled their percentage (37%) and took 230 seats. Again the SPD fell back, losing ten more seats to 123, while the KPD made a modest advance winning 89 seats with 14% votes.

With widespread dissatisfaction, greater unemployment and poverty, and more violence, President Hindenburg felt obliged to appoint Adolf Hitler as the Chancellor, on January 31, 1933. Von Papen as Vice Chancellor was intended to be the "éminence grise", who should keep Hitler under control. But four days later, Hitler announced his aggressive foreign policy, Lebensraum for the German master race, and damn the Treaty of Versailles.

Quite conveniently for Hitler, an angry Dutchman, perhaps a communist, set fire to the government Reichstag gutting several buildings, on February 27. The fire has been widely suspected of having been set by the Nazis themselves, a bold false flag to smooth the road to authoritarianism. The next day, Hitler-Hindenburg made the Decree for the Protection of the People and the State. Popularly known as the Reichstag Fire Decree, the regulations suspended the right to assembly, freedom of speech, freedom of the press, and other constitutional protections, including all restraints on police investigations.

Neither the KPD, nor the Comintern, as was claimed, had anything to do with the fire. Nevertheless, Communists were prohibited from voting and sitting in the Parliament, on the pretext that they were planning an uprising to overthrow the state.

Hitler took full plenary powers, on March 24, with his Enabling Act. In less than two months, Hitler had come into a democratic government as chancellor and become a legal dictator. His seizure of power (*Machtergreifung*) permitted government-by-decree. These events brought the republic effectively to an end.

GERMANY VIOLATES TREATY OF VERSAILLES

- At the time of signing in 1919, the dissolution of the army General Staff (*Heer*), according to Article 160, appeared to happen, however its core was reestablished and hidden in the *Truppenamt* (Troop Office). The cover organization functioned until March 1935 when the general staff was re-created. Hitler also violated part V of the Treaty of Versailles by introducing compulsory military conscription and rebuilding the armed forces.
- March 7, 1936, Germany violated article 43 of the treaty by reoccupying the demilitarized zone in the Rhineland. The remilitarization of the Rhineland changed the balance of power in Europe from France towards Germany, and made it possible for the latter to pursue a policy of aggression

in Eastern Europe. Even so two-time former Labour Party Prime Minister Ramsay MacDonald said he was pleased that the Treaty of Versailles was vanishing.

- March 1938, Germany violated article 80 of the treaty by annexing Austria in the *Anschluss*.

This idea of a united Austria-Germany that would form a "Greater Germany" stems from 1871.

As the tepid reaction to the German *Anschluss* with Austria had shown, the governments of France, the United Kingdom and Czechoslovakia were set on avoiding war at any cost. The French government did not wish to face Germany alone and took its lead from the British Prime Minister Neville Chamberlain. When Hitler threatened to intervene in Sudeten, Chamberlain contended that Sudeten German grievances were justified and believed that Hitler's intentions were limited. Most inhabitants in Sudeten were of German descent but had been incorporated into Czechoslovakia as part of the treaties ending WWI.

On September 28, 1938, Chamberlain appealed to Hitler for a conference. They met in Munich with the government leaders of France and Italy. The Czechoslovak government was neither invited nor consulted. On September 29, the Munich Agreement was signed by Germany, Italy, France, and Britain. The agreement allowed Hitler to annex what became known as Sudetenland, that part of Czechoslovakia where most industry and banks were located and borders as well.

The Czechoslovak government capitulated the next day. The incorporation of the Sudetenland into Germany began on October 1, 1938. This weakened Czechoslovakia, and it became powerless to resist subsequent occupation. On October 5, Edvard Beneš resigned as President of Czechoslovakia and went into exile.

On March 15, 1939, the German *Wehrmacht* took over the rest of Czechoslovakia, and Hitler proclaimed Bohemia and Moravia the Protectorate of Bohemia and Moravia.

ITALIAN FASCISM

Born to a leftist father, Benito Amilcare Andrea Mussolini was a journalist and ardent socialist before he became a politician and leader of the National Fascist Party (*Partito Nazionale Fascista*; PNF). He ruled the country as prime minister from 1922 to 1943. Mussolini ruled constitutionally from 1922 to 1925 when he dropped all pretense of democracy and set up a legal dictatorship.

Known as *Il Duce* ("The Leader"), Mussolini was the founder of Italian Fascism, in 1915. Known simply as Fascism (*fascismo*), it is the original Fascist ideology, rooted in nationalism, national syndicalism, and the desire to restore and expand Italian territories, deemed necessary to assert national superiority, and to avoid succumbing into "bourgeois decadence." Mussolini and Hitler were not united when the Spanish Civil War broke out but Franco made separate deals with them. So Germany and Italy fought separately and together for Franco, and to prepare for the greater European war. (See chapter nine)

In September 1937, Mussolini visited Germany. Hitler put on a big display of military power for Mussolini, which convinced *Il Duce* that Germany was the power he should ally with. In May 1939, Germans and Italians cemented their alliance with the *Pact of Steel*. This committed both countries to support the other if one of them became involved in a war.

Given the "neutrality" of the West towards Hitler's aggression, until his entering Poland, and the illegal rearmament of his military with Western aid, Soviet leaders thought it best to make a neutrality pact with Hitler. Joseph Stalin hoped either that Hitler would not invade their huge country or, at least, give it time to prepare for war. In August 1939, Germany and the Soviet Union signed a non-aggression treaty in Moscow known as the Molotov–Ribbentrop Pact. A protocol outlined dividing the eastern European border states between their respective "spheres of influence". The Soviet Union and Germany would partition Poland in the event of an invasion by Germany, and the Soviets would be allowed to overrun the Baltic States and Finland.

On August 23, 1939, the rest of the world learned of this pact but were unaware of the Poland provisions. World leaders were caught by surprise, because of Germany and Soviet mutual hostility and conflicting ideologies. Communist parties throughout the world had been following the Moscow line and were preparing for war against Nazi Germany. They suddenly had to change their tune, which cost them members and general sympathy.

Hitler was an impatient man. One week later, September 1, following another false flag ("the Poles have fired on German territory and citizens!") Germany invaded Poland, triggering the outbreak of World War II in Europe. The Soviet Union quickly annexed the eastern part of the country. The two governments maintained reasonably strong diplomatic relations for two years. They made a trade pact in 1940 by which the Soviets received German military equipment and trade goods in exchange for oil and wheat, thereby helping Germany to circumvent a British blockade.

Mussolini considered that the non-aggression pact somehow involved Italy, but he had not been advised about it nor did he sign the treaty.

British and French leaders finally woke up to the true *Lebensraum* plan. They declared war two days after Germany invaded Poland. The first war casualty was the British ocean liner, *Athenia*, which was sunk by a German submarine. Of the 1,100 passengers on board, 112 lost their lives. Of those, 28 were Americans, but President Franklin Roosevelt declared there would be no talk of "America sending its armies to European fields." The United States would remain neutral.

Germany opened The Battle of France alone on May 10. Italy joined in on June 10 in southern France. It took but six weeks to defeat France, conquering Belgium, Luxembourg and the Netherlands along the way. A much smaller German force had occupied Denmark the month before, April 9, in three hours, and went on to Norway. It took the Nazis two months to beat a determined resistance. Norway surrendered on June 10.

Vidkun Quisling founded Norway's fascist party, in 1933, was made prime minister under the Nazis, 1942-5. He was tried for high treason and murder after the war and executed on October 24, 1945. His surname is synonymous with collaborator and traitor.

Western Front fascist troops and war materials matched the strength of the combined allied forces—France, UK, Belgium, Netherlands, Luxembourg, Canada, and the unoccupied parts of Poland and Czechoslovakia, but in this short period the allies suffered far greater casualties: 2.2 million killed and wounded compared to 163,000 Germans and Italians. German tactics and high morale were paying off.

On June 22, the Second Armistice was signed by France and Germany, which resulted in a division of France. The anti-Semitic Vichy government, led by World War I hero Marshal Philippe Pétain, was allowed to control a small zone in the south known as *zone libre*. Germany occupied the north and west. Italy took a small zone in the south-east. The *de facto* Vichy client state ended the Third Republic.

Such a quick victory over so much European territory encouraged Hitler to focus on bombing London, and the ensuing *Blitzkrieg* against several cities—July 1, 1940-May 1941.

WALL STREET COUP ATTEMPT: OUT WITH FDR, IN WITH FRANCO, MUSSOLINI AND HITLER

President Herbert Hoover lost his re-election bid on November 8, 1932. His government had not recuperated from *Black Tuesday*. Unemployment at the time of the crash stood at 3%. By 1932, it had risen to 24% (12 million of the 51 million labor force; total population 91 million).

Democrat Franklin Delano Roosevelt won 57% of the vote. He took office on March 4, 1933, just as Hitler was consolidating his Nazi regime. Roosevelt quickly launched his New Deal program to provide state-supported jobs and greater social welfare. Roosevelt also had to face poor war veterans demanding bonuses promised them.

Hoover's administration had been confronted by 43,000 *Bonus* marchers during July 1932—17,000 World War I veterans, their families, and affiliated groups. They camped out in Washington, D.C. Many had been out of work since the beginning of the Great Depression. The World War Adjusted Compensation Act of 1924 had awarded them bonuses in the form of certificates but they could not redeem them until 1945.

On July 28, 1932 U.S. Attorney General William D. Mitchell ordered the veterans removed from all government property. Washington police met with resistance. Two veterans were shot and later died. Hoover then ordered the army to clear the veterans' campsite. Army Chief of Staff General Douglas MacArthur commanded infantry and cavalry supported by six tanks. The Bonus Army marchers were driven out, and their shelters and belongings burned.

A second, smaller Bonus March took place in May 1933. The new president's wife Eleanor Roosevelt met with them cordially on May 18. There was no money for bonuses but the Civilian Conservation Corps offered them jobs, which most accepted. Those who chose not to work for the CCC were given transportation home. (Congress overrode

President Roosevelt's veto in 1936, and paid the bonuses nine years early.)

Most capitalists hated Roosevelt for his New Deal, and for providing jobs, social and cultural benefits for all people regardless of color. Major businessmen were racists and favored fascist solutions. They thought they could use unemployed white war veterans to their advantage.

The Business Plot (aka The White House Coup Plot) was a political conspiracy in 1933-4. Retired General Smedley Darlington Butler was approached by Gerald MacGuire, representing the wealthiest businessmen seeking to use the popular general in a coup d'état to overthrow President Roosevelt. Smedley Butler was a Marine Corps major general, the highest rank authorized then. When he died (June 21, 1940), he was the most decorated Marine in U.S. history.

Butler pretended to go along with the idea before revealing its insidious nature. When he went public, he explained what he had done during his military career:

> *"I spent 33 years and four months in active military service and during that period I spent most of my time as a high class muscle man for Big Business, for Wall Street and the bankers. In short, I was a racketeer, a gangster for capitalism. I helped make Mexico and especially Tampico safe for American oil interests in 1914. I helped make Haiti and Cuba a decent place for the National City Bank boys to collect revenues in. I helped in the raping of half a dozen Central American republics for the benefit of Wall Street. I helped purify Nicaragua for the International Banking House of Brown Brothers in 1902-1912. I brought light to*

General Smedley Butler

the Dominican Republic for the American sugar interests in 1916. I helped make Honduras right for the American fruit companies in 1903. In China, in 1927, I helped see to it that Standard Oil went on its way unmolested. Looking back on it, I might have given Al Capone a few hints. The best he could do was to operate his racket in three districts. I operated on three continents."

When the plotters approached Butler, they did not know he had changed his mind about business.

"In the summer of 1934, Gerald MacGuire, a lawyer in the Morgan brokerage office of Grayson M. -P. Murphy and an official of the American Legion, visited General Smedley Butler at his home in Newton Square, Pennsylvania. [Butler's military career had ended three years earlier] amid a storm of diplomatic protest over his public description of Italian dictator Benito Mussolini as 'a mad dog about to break loose in Europe.'" wrote Gerard Colby, "The MacGuire Affair", an excerpt from DuPont Dynasty *(Secaucus, NJ: Lyle Stuart, Inc.), pp. 324-330.* (http://coat.ncf.ca/our_magazine/links/53/dupont-by_colby.html)

"The General had stubbornly rejected Hoover's demand for a retraction and had retired from the service a proud but bitter man. But he was also probably the most popular soldier in America. As such, he was an attractive prize for any movement, and it was for this reason that MacGuire, mistakenly banking on the General's personal bitterness and the then frequent brandings of Roosevelt as a 'dictator,' paid the old soldier a call."

MacGuire was himself rich and he represented the elite of the elite. Here is a glimpse of his Big Capital America. The brokerage firm he worked for, Grayson Mallet-Prevost Murphy, led N.Y. trading in stocks and international bonds. MacGuire was also a director of Morgan's Guaranty Trust and New York Trust banks, and worked with several Morgan-connected corporations, including: Du Pont, Bethlehem Steel

Corp., U.S. Steel Corp., together with copper, oil, electric appliances, locomotive, telephone and telegraph interests (AT&T). These were tied to other great banks: National City, Corn Exchange, Chase National.

Murphy's boss also controlled General Motors, General Electric and New York Central Railroad.

These were tied to other great banks: National City, Corn Exchange, Chase National. The House of Morgan catered to the Astors, DuPonts, Guggenheims, Vanderbilts and Rockefellers. He gave preferential shipping rates to John D. Rockefeller's Standard Oil monopoly, cementing their markets. The Morgan Group dominated United States arms industry. (See, H.C. Engelbrect's *Merchants of Death: A Study of the International Arms Industry*, Dodd, Mead &Co., 1934)

Grayson Murphy played an important role in syndicating Morgan loans to fascist Italy, for which he was decorated by Mussolini. [The "*Order of the Crown of Italy*," *Commander* class.] He met with Mussolini on assignment from Morgan.

Grayson Murphy was the first treasurer of the American Liberty League just launched by rich magnates to "combat radicalism, to teach…respect for the rights of persons and property, and generally to foster free private enterprise." It was designated to organize the fascist coup. (2)

One of the League's founders was Senator Prescott Bush, a partner in the Brown Brothers Harriman bank, which General Butler had fought for in Nicaragua. He had business ties with Hitler.

Prescott Bush fathered two future presidents. He was one of seven directors of Union Banking Corporation, an investment bank that operated as a clearing house for assets and enterprises held by German steel magnate Fritz Thyssen. In October 1942, the U.S. seized the fascist war-profiteering bank under the Trading with the Enemy Act, but only held its assets until the war ended.

Bush's American Liberty League buddy, Murphy, had been one of 20 elite U.S. military intelligence officers (Office of Strategic Services, precursor to CIA), who met with other businessmen in Paris to found the American Legion. In the 1920s and 1930s, these super patriots were a reactionary outfit that used baseball bats to break up strikers and civil rights demonstrations. Colonel William F. Easterwood, national vice-commander of the Legion, pinned a Legion button on Mussolini, in 1935, making him an "honorary member."

Many of America's rich and famous were directly involved in fascism and murder:

Besides J.P. Morgan, jr. other FDR coup conspirators included: Irenee du Pont, American Liberty League and Black Legion founder; William Doyle, former state commander of the American Legion; John Davis, former Democratic presidential candidate and a senior attorney for J.P. Morgan; Al Smith, Roosevelt's bitter political foe, a former governor of New York and a co-director of the American Liberty League; Robert Clark, one of Wall Street's richest bankers and stockbrokers; John J. Raskob, a high-ranking Du Pont officer and a former chairman of the Democratic Party. Later, Raskob would become a "Knight of Malta," a Roman Catholic Religious Order with a high percentage of CIA spies, including CIA Directors William Casey, William Colby and John McCone.

In 2012, the A&E Television Networks released the series, "The Men Who Built America". The "entertainment media company" chose Henry Ford, Nelson Rockefeller, Andrew Carnegie, J.P. Morgan and Cornelius Vanderbilt as THE builders. (http://www.history.com)

The documentary blurb invites viewers to: "Meet the titans who forged the foundation of modern America and created the American Dream."

Well, at least two of these titans, Morgan and Rockefeller, conspired to overthrow, even murder President Roosevelt. They, along with Henry Ford, gladly financed Hitler and Mussolini's rise to power, and thus encouraged them to murder fellow American citizens while endeavoring to rule the world with fascism's might.

"Along with friends of the Morgan Bank and General Motors," wrote Charles Higham, *Trading with the Enemy: An exposé of the Nazi American Money Plot 1933-1949* (Delacorte Press, 1983), "Du Pont backers financed a coup d'état that would overthrow the President with the aid of a $3 million-funded army of terrorists". They would force Roosevelt "*to take orders from businessmen as part of a fascist government or face the alternative of imprisonment and execution*".

If these "American Dreamers" had had their way the dream would have embraced fascism. Historian James Truslow Adams was the first to publicly define the "American Dream" in his 1931 book, *Epic of America*. "The American Dream is that dream of a land in which life should be better and richer and fuller for everyone, with opportunity for each according to ability or achievement."

GENERAL BUTLER AND THE FASCIST AMERICAN DREAM

America, Gerald MacGuire told Butler that 1934 summer, was in great danger from a "communist menace," and needed a complete change of government. MacGuire explained that a, "militantly patriotic" veterans' organization, like the fascist Croix de Feu operating in France, was the only kind of organization that could force a change in Washington. He suggested that Butler lead such an organization in "a march on Washington." "We have three million dollars to start with on the line," he told Butler, "and we can get three million more if we need it." (3)

Butler was amazed at this plan, and played along to uncover details. "Is there anything stirring yet?" he asked MacGuire.

"Yes, you watch," the broker replied. "In two or three weeks, you will see it come out in the papers. There will be big fellows in it. This is to be the background of it."

Exactly two weeks later, on August 23, the American Liberty League publicly announced its existence with MacGuire's employer, Grayson M. P. Murphy, as its treasurer.

Butler knew that MacGuire worked for Morgan and Murphy. In a second meeting, MacGuire told Butler that nine very wealthy men were doing the financial backing, one being Murphy.

"I work for him," MacGuire assured the General, "I'm in his office."

Appalled by MacGuire's proposal, Butler contacted a crusading reporter for the *Philadelphia Record*, Paul Comly French. "The whole affair smacked of treason to me", Butler remarked. On September 13, 1934 French visited Gerald MacGuire at the brokerage firm of Grayson M.-P. Murphy Company and, posing as a sympathizer trusted by Butler, won MacGuire's confidence.

"The whole movement is patriotic because the Communists will wreck the nation unless the soldiers save it through fascism," MacGuire reportedly told French. "All General Butler would have to do to get a million men would be to announce the formation of the organization and tell them it would cost a dollar a year to join."

On November 20, 1934, General Butler revealed the whole scheme by testifying before a private session of the Special House Committee on Un-American Activities. He suggested that if the Committee wanted to get to the bottom of this, they question the biggest interests involved:

Grayson M. P. Murphy, General Douglas MacArthur, Hanford MacNider—ex National Commander of the American Legion—and leaders of the American Liberty League.

News media at first reported earnestly on the plot, then quickly changed course and dismissed it. The *New York Times* newsroom, for instance, gave the plot front page coverage until an editorial characterized it as a "gigantic hoax". But the fact that much of the Congressional records of the hearings were destroyed is good evidence that powerful people did not want the truth known.

"It was four years," wrote Charles Higham, "before the committee dared to publish its report in a white paper that was marked for 'restricted circulation'. They were forced to admit that 'certain persons made an attempt to establish a fascist organization in this country … [The] committee was able to verify all the pertinent statements made by General Butler.' This admission that the entire plan was deadly in intent was not accompanied by the imprisonment of anybody. Further investigations disclosed that over a million people had been guaranteed to join the scheme and that the arms and munitions necessary would have been supplied by Remington, a Du Pont subsidiary."

Copyright, 1934, by The New York Times Company.

NEW YORK, WEDNESDAY, NOVEMBER 21, 1934.

Gen. Butler Bares 'Fascist Plot' To Seize Government by Force

Says Bond Salesman, as Representative of Wall St. Group, Asked Him to Lead Army of 500,000 in March on Capital—Principals in Angry Denials—Dickstein Gets Charge.

"FDR's main interest was getting the New Deal passed, and so he struck a deal in which it was agreed that the plotters would walk free if Wall Street would back off of their opposition to the New Deal and let FDR do what he wanted". Had the plotters been tried for the treason they committed, they could have been executed. Instead they continued to rule America.

WASHINGTON Major General Smedley D. Butler, U.S.M.C., retired, caused a sensation here today [Nov. 20] by testifying before the House committee investigating un-American activities... (http://www.nytimes.com/2009/11/21/opinion/21iht-oldnov21.html?mcubz=1)

In 1935, Butler wrote a little book, *War Is a Racket*, in which he described and criticized the workings of the United States in its foreign actions and wars. It is THE anti-war classic, especially since it is written by the most decorated U.S. Marine. Excerpts:

> *"War is possibly the oldest, easily the most profitable, surely the most vicious racket. It is the only one international in scope. It is the only one in which the profits are reckoned in dollars and the losses in lives. A racket is best described, I believe, as something that is not what it seems to the majority of the people. Only a small 'inside' group knows what it is about. It is conducted for the benefit of the very few, at the expense of the very many. Out of war a few people make huge fortunes. In the World War [I] a mere handful garnered the profits of the conflict. At least 21,000 new millionaires and billionaires were made...That many admitted their huge blood gains in their income tax returns. How many other war millionaires falsified their tax returns no one knows."*

> *"Three steps must be taken to smash the war racket.*
> 1. *We must take the profit out of war.*
> 2. *We must permit the youth...who would bear arms to decide whether or not there should be war.*
> 3. *We must limit our military forces to home defense purposes."*

UNITED STATES BUSINESS ARMS AND FINANCES MUSSOLINI AND HITLER

Many of the plotters exposed by General Butler had been boosting their fortunes by investing in the fascist movements of Mussolini and Hitler.

Some of them amassed great fortunes by arming fascists before and during WWII.

William Dodd, the U.S. Ambassador to Germany, wrote to his president, Roosevelt, about this:

"'A clique of U.S. industrialists is hell-bent to bring a fascist state to supplant our democratic government and is working closely with the fascist regime in Germany and Italy. I have had plenty of opportunity in my post in Berlin to witness how close some of our American ruling families are to the Nazi regime.... A prominent executive of one of the largest corporations told me point blank that he would be ready to take definite action to bring fascism into America if President Roosevelt continued his progressive policies. Certain American industrialists had a great deal to do with bringing fascist regimes into being in both Germany and Italy. They extended aid to help Fascism occupy the seat of power, and they are helping to keep it there. Propagandists for fascist groups try to dismiss the fascist scare. We should be aware of the symptoms. When industrialists ignore laws designed for social and economic progress they will seek recourse to a fascist state when the institutions of our government compel them to comply with the provisions.'" (http://coat.ncf.ca/our¬_magazine/links/53/53-index.html)

J.P. Morgan funded the rise of Italian Fascism. His company was Mussolini's main overseas bank. "In 1926, Morgan partner, Thomas Lamont, who was later the chair of J.P. Morgan Co., secured a $100 million loan for Mussolini. As Noam Chomsky put it, Morgan's man described himself as 'something like a missionary' for Italian Fascism, expressing his admiration for Il Duce, 'a very upstanding chap' who had 'done a great job in Italy' and for the 'sound ideas' that guide him in governing the country." (*Deterring Democracy*, 1991). (http://coat.ncf.ca/our_magazine/links/53/morgan.html and http://coat.ncf.ca/)

As for Morgan's own bank, it kept a branch open for business in Nazi-occupied France to serve German interests throughout the war. As we were told about Wall Street by the Barak Obama government in 2008-9, these capitalists are too big to fail. Morgan was too big to be held accountable to the Trading with the Enemy Act. Instead of being executed for treason he got richer.

Irish journalist Finian Cunningham writings about the West's rearming Hitler and Mussolini is quoted extensively by Jay Jason in his article, "Buried History: 27 million died in Russia because Wall Street built up Hitler's Wehrmacht to knock out Soviet Union". (http://www.greanvillepost.com/2017/08/08/buried-history-27-million-died-in-russia-because-wall-street-built-up-hitlers-wehrmacht-to-knock-out-soviet-union/)

> *"The Western public, inculcated with decades of brainwashing versions of history, have a particular disadvantage in coming to a proper understanding of the world wars…European fascism headed up by Nazi Germany, along with Mussolini in Italy, Franco in Spain and Salazar in Portugal, was not some aberrant force that sprang from nowhere during the 1920s-1930s. The movement was a deliberate cultivation by the rulers of Anglo-American capitalism. European fascism may have been labeled 'national socialism' but its root ideology was very much one opposed to overturning the fundamental capitalist order. It was an authoritarian drive to safeguard the capitalist order, which viewed genuine worker-based socialism as an enemy to be ruthlessly crushed."*

> *"This is what made European fascism so appealing to the Western capitalist ruling class in those times. In particular, Nazi Germany was viewed by the Western elite as a bulwark against possible socialist revolution inspired by the Russian revolution of 1917."*

Edwin Black's, *IBM and the Holocaust* (Crown Books, 2001), shows how IBM helped the genocide of Jews. "The major software company IBM was the company which provided Hitler with the technical means to catalogue Jews population and organize the 'Final Solution', i.e. the killing of millions of people." (http://news.cnet.com/2009-1082-269157.html)

> *"Why Allies claimed complete ignorance on what happened to the millions of Jews in Europe during the War, or why they were 'astounded' to discover the death camps after the war was over is a 'mystery' never to be solved."*

GM and Ford automobile companies had subsidiaries and conducted business with the Third Reich. GM supplied the Wehrmact with Opel "Blitz" trucks from its Brandenburg complex. For these and other contributions to wartime preparations, James Mooney, GM's chief executive for overseas operations was awarded the Order of the German Eagle (first class), in 1938, by Adolf Hitler.

Texaco's CEO Torkild Rieber was a friend of Francisco Franco (chapter nine), and once his forces defeated the democratic Spanish Republic, Rieber offered his aid to Hitler.

"After the Spanish war ended, Texaco continued to make its own foreign policy. Even after Germany went to war with Britain and France in September 1939, Rieber made no secret of his enthusiasm for Hitler. He sometimes joked with friends that the Führer's anti-Semitism might be a touch excessive, but he was just the sort of strong, anti-communist leader with whom one could do business. This Rieber did, with gusto, selling Texaco oil to the Nazis, ordering tankers built in Hamburg shipyards, and traveling to Germany after the Polish Blitzkrieg *so that Hermann Göring could take him on a tour by air of key industrial sites. On that trip he spent a weekend at the* Luftwaffe *commander's country estate, Carinhall, soon to be extravagantly decorated with art treasures looted from across Europe,"* wrote Adam Hochschild, *Spain in Our Hearts: Americans in the Spanish Civil War*, 1936-1939 (Houghton Mifflin Harcourt, 2016].

Rieber's rival, John Rockeller's Standard Oil of Jersey was also a fan of fascism. He transferred hydrogenation patents and technology to I.G. Farben chemical industry enabling it to produce 6.5 million tons of oil for war aircraft. This was 20 times what it had been producing using only its own natural petroleum products.

"GM and Standard Oil of New Jersey formed a joint subsidiary with the giant Nazi chemical cartel, I.G. Farben, named Ethyl G.m.b.H. [now Ethyl, Inc.] which provided the mechanized German armies with synthetic tetraethyl fuel [leaded gas]. During 1936-39, at the urgent request of Nazi officials who realized that Germany's scarce petroleum reserves would not satisfy war demands, GM and Exxon joined with German chemical interests in the erection of the lead-tetraethyl plants. According to captured German records, these facilities contributed substantially to the German war effort: 'The fact that since the beginning of the war we could produce lead-tetraethyl is entirely due to the circumstances that, shortly before, the Americans [Du Pont, GM, Standard Oil] had presented us with the production plants complete with experimental knowledge. Without lead-tetraethyl the present method of warfare would be unthinkable," wrote George Seldes, Facts and Fascism, 1943.

I.G.'s industrial complex built at Auschwitz to exploit the supply of death camp labor for the production of synthetic rubber and oil was so enormous that the complex used as much electricity as the city of Berlin. I.G. also made money from the sale of Zyklon B used in the gas chambers.

The Nuremberg trial of industrial war criminals held by the United States (May 1947 to May 1948) indicted 24 I.G. Farben executives, and charged them with five counts including "slavery and mass murder". They received sentences "light enough to please a chicken thief", decried dissenting Judge Paul Herbert. Half of them were let off. The other 12 got 18 months to eight years imprisonment for crimes of slavery, mass murder, torture, and what amounted to genocide.

While a few German capitalists were convicted, none of their American partners served any time.

Irenee du Pont, for instance, was "the most imposing and powerful member of the clan," according to biographer and historian Charles Higham. He "was obsessed with Hitler's principles. He supported the superman race 'theory.'"

"The Du Ponts' fascistic behavior was seen in 1936, when Irenee du Pont used General Motors money to finance the notorious Black Legion. This terrorist organization had as its purpose the prevention of automobile workers from unionizing. The members wore hoods and black robes, with skulls and crossbones. They fire-bombed union meetings, murdered union organizers, often by beating them to death, and dedicated their lives to destroying Jews and communists. They linked to the Ku Klux Klan... at least fifty people, many of them blacks, had been butchered by the Legion."

"Between 1932 and 1939, bosses of General Motors poured $30 million into I.G. Farben plants." Furthermore, Charles Higham wrote, by "the mid-1930s, General Motors was committed to full-scale production of trucks, armored cars, and tanks in Nazi Germany."

Seldes wrote, "Most notorious of all [capitalists] was Alcoa, the Mellon-Davis-Duke monopoly, which is largely responsible for the fact America did not have the aluminum with which to build airplanes before and after Pearl Harbor, while Germany had an unlimited supply."

Alcoa sabotage of American war production had already cost the U.S., "10,000 fighters or 1,665 bombers," according to Congressman Pierce of Oregon, speaking in May 1941, because of "the effort to protect Alcoa's monopolistic position. . ." "If America loses this war," said Secretary of the Interior [Harold] Ickes, June 26, 1941, "it can thank the Aluminum Corporation of America".

"By its cartel agreement with I.G. Farben, controlled by Hitler," Seldes wrote, "Alcoa sabotaged the aluminum program of the U.S. air force. The Truman Committee [on National Defense, chaired by then-Senator Harry S. Truman in 1942] heard testimony that Alcoa's representative, A.H. Bunker, $1-a-year head of the aluminum section of O.P.M., prevented work on our $600,000,000 aluminum expansion program."

The Truman Committee must have known that American capitalists had at least $475 million investments in Nazi Germany at the time of the Japanese attack on Pearl Harbor. Higham wrote:

> *"Standard Oil of New Jersey had $120 million invested there; General Motors had $35 million; ITT had $30 million; and Ford had $17.5 million. Though it would have been more patriotic to have allowed Nazi Germany to confiscate these companies for the duration—to nationalize them or to absorb them into Hermann Göring's industrial empire—it was clearly more practical to insure them protection from seizure by allowing them to remain in special holding companies, the money accumulating until war's end. It is interesting that whereas there is no evidence of any serious attempt by Roosevelt to impeach the guilty in the United States, there is evidence that Hitler strove to punish certain German Fraternity associates on the grounds of treason to the Nazi state. Indeed, in the case of ITT, perhaps the most flagrant of the corporations in its outright dealings with the enemy, Hitler and his postmaster general, the venerable Wilhelm Ohnesorge, strove to impound the German end of the business. But even they were powerless in*

> *such a situation:* the Gestapo leader of counterintelligence, Walter Schellenberg, was a prominent director and shareholder of ITT by arrangement with New York—and even Hitler dared not cross the Gestapo."

Capitalism, though, isn't all strictly business. Henry Ford, a notorious anti-Semite, formed a mutual admiration society with Adolf Hitler. The German dictator enthusiastically applauded American mass-production techniques. Hitler regarded Ford as his inspiration and kept a life-size portrait of the industrialist next to his desk. Ford was awarded the highest medal that Nazi Germany could award a foreigner when his truck assembly opened in Berlin, in 1938. This was a great aid for Nazi Germany's military buildup, a U.S. Army Intelligence reported. (http://www.ranknfile-ue.org/uen_nastybiz.html)

In 1940, with Europe at war, the Krupp AG 400-year old family firm, Europe's largest armament firm, arranged to have its royalties from General Electric collected by a Swiss go-between.

In September 1940, the *UE NEWS*, a medium of the independent union of electrical workers, reported that two federal anti-trust indictments had been returned against GE and the Krupp company charging them with conspiring to maintain a world monopoly in the production and sale of tungsten carbide. U.S. entry into World War II interrupted the proceedings, however.

"In the meantime, a subcommittee of the Senate Committee on Military Affairs took an understandably dim view of how international cartels had hindered the anti-fascist war effort. The Senate subcommittee charged that the GE-Krupp arrangement had created a bottleneck in production of tungsten carbide. 'In contrast with the situation in Germany, the present drastic shortage of this essential material in this country is notorious,' stated John Henry Lewin, special assistant to the Attorney General. 'The need to produce it, to retool our manufacturing plants with it, and to instruct workmen in the use of such tools, has constituted one of the principal bottlenecks in our production program,'" wrote *UE NEWS*.

In a New York anti-trust trial against General Electric, 1946-7, GE and subsidiaries, with named company officials were found guilty on five counts of criminal conspiracy with Friedrich Krupp A.G. of Essen,

Germany—not for murder or genocide but for violating a law against monopolizing a market, for raising prices by driving competitors out of the business of mass murder.

Summing up his opinion on one count, Judge John C. Knox declared, "Competitors were excluded by purchase and by boycott; prices on unpatented products were fixed, future patent rights were forced into the pool, world markets were divided, and on occasion prices were fixed beyond the scope of any asserted patent protection…Defendants did unlawfully monopolize."

No jail time. Defendants were fined between $2,500 and $20,000. Profits GE made through Krupp's murder of millions of Jews and other human beings amounted to millions of dollars. And the mass media didn't even report on the trial or buried information inside the press.

Of the many important "bits" of information that this trial did not take up was the involvement of the Dulles brothers in Krupp company crimes against humanity. Dulles fascist connection did not bother General Dwight Eisenhower, because he appointed him Secretary of State when he became president, and Eisenhower appointed brother Allen head of the CIA.

Stephen Kinzer, former "N.Y. Times" foreign correspondent, wrote, *The Brothers: John Foster Dulles, Allen Dulles and their secret World War* (Times Books, 2013).

A *NewYork Times* review summarized John Foster Dulles friendship with Hjalmar Schacht, the Reichsbank president and Hitler's minister of economics. John and Allen Foster were partners in the international law firm Sullivan & Cromwell. The New York-based firm floated bonds for Krupp A. G., the arms manufacturer, and also worked for I. G. Farben. (http://www.nytimes.com/2013/11/10/books/review/the-brothers-by-stephen-kinzer.html)

Kinzer lists what he calls the "six monsters" that the Dulles brothers believed had to be brought down when they were in government: Mohammed Mossadegh in Iran, Jacobo Arbenz in Guatemala, Ho Chi Minh in Vietnam, Sukarno in Indonesia, Patrice Lumumba in the Congo and Fidel Castro in Cuba. The Dulles' succeeded in bringing down Mossadegh, Arbenz and Lumumba.

As dedicated civil servants for "American Philanthropists", the Dulles extolled "American Exceptionalism", which President Roosevelt wrote about to his confidant, Colonel Edward House, on November 22, 1933.

"As you and I know, this government has been owned by a financial element in the centers of power since the days of Andrew Jackson" (president 1829-37). (4)

"It is to be regretted," Jackson said, "that the rich and powerful bend the acts of the government to their own purposes." He said the Bank of the United States was dangerous to the liberty of the people; that the bank could build up or pull down political parties through loans to politicians.

Most of the U.S. companies mentioned in this chapter continue flourishing as they were, under different names or as part of greater corporation groups: ***Krupp is now part of ThyssenKrupp, Standard Oil is Exxon; Du Pont, GM, Ford, Alcoa and IBM have the same names.***

Notes:

1. The Holocaust caused the murder of approximately six million Jews and five million other targeted groups, such as gypsies and handicapped people of various nationalities, including Aryans, not to mention socialists and communists and homosexuals. There were about nine million Jews in pre-war Europe.

2. American Liberty Legion attacked government funding for poverty relief and social services and opposed all "burdensome taxes imposed upon industry for unemployment insurance and old age pension." On Jan. 3, 1936, in an unprecedented joint session of Congress when President Roosevelt announced a ban on military exports to fascist Italy, he blasted the American Liberty League: "They steal the livery of great national ideals to serve discredited special interests.... This minority in business and industry... engage in vast propaganda to spread fear and discord among the people."

3. Dickstein-McCormick Special Committee on Un-American Activities, House of Representatives, 73rd Congress, 2nd Session, Testimony of Major General Smedley D. Butler, November 20, 1934, pp. 8-114, DC.

4. Morgan would have been one of the bankers that President Jackson would have been talking about had he lived then. In May 1933, J.P. "Jack" Morgan, Jr., as well as several of his partners and other major bank executives, testified at hearings held by the Senate Committee on Banking and Currency investigating the causes of the 1929 stock market crash and the subsequent banking crisis. The hearings raised the question of the role banks played in the speculative fever leading up to the crash.

   In the 1930's populism resurfaced in America after Goldman Sachs, Lehman Bank and others profited from the Crash of 1929. House Banking Committee Chairman Louis McFadden (D-NY) said of the Great Depression, "It was no accident. It was a carefully contrived occurrence...The international bankers sought to bring about a condition of despair here so they might emerge as rulers of us all". (https://www.globalresearch.ca/the-federal-reserve-cartel-the-eight-families/25080)

CHAPTER 9

Soviet Sides with Democratic Spanish Republic: U.S. Helps Fascist Victory

Franco honored Texaco CEO Torkild Rieber with a "Knight of the Grand Cross of Isabella the Catholic" one of the most prestigious Spanish honors.

"Without American petroleum and American trucks, and American credit, we could never have won the Civil War," said Franco foreign ministry foreign policy director, José Maria Doussinague. (1)

GENERAL PRIMO DE Rivera ruled Spain as a military dictatorship (1923-30). King Alfonso XIII approved his rule and he absolved him when it fell in 1930, and elections were held.

The Second Republic was established in June 1931 after democratically held municipal and general elections, in which the overwhelming majority rejected a monarchy for a republic form of government. (2)

During the Second Republic, there were many political parties and contradictory approaches about how to rule. Intolerant to democracy and collectivism, the fascists launched a civil war in July 1936. The fascists viewed the conflict as Christian Civilization vs. godless atheism, communism and anarchy. Republicans viewed the conflict as one of freedom vs. tyranny. Most Catalonians supported the Republic, as did Basques. Although most Basques were conservative Catholics, the progressive Republican government promised them self-government.

Of the 25 million-population at the time around one million fought for the Republic and another million fought for the fascists, the aristocracy and the official Catholic Church. General Franco had mercenaries from

Morocco, the feared Army of Africa, comprised of "moors", plus the German, Italian, and Portuguese governments and military on his side. Franco, Mola, Sanjurjo, Millán Astray (founder of the Spanish Legion), and Yague, were all prominent "Africanist" officers, accustomed to brutal warfare in Spain's North African colony. (3)

The Republic only had significant aid from Russia. (4) Moreover, Spain welcomed between 30-40,000 volunteers from 52 countries organized in the Communist-led International Brigades. About three thousand volunteers fought with the left-wing socialists and Trotskyists in POUM (Unified Workers Marxist Party), and the anarcho-sindicalist CNT union. CNT-anarchists were the strongest leftist force among Catalonians partly because they had won an 8-hour work day already in 1919.

Conscientious US Americans were among many nationalities to fight in solidarity with Spaniards. The first volunteers in the Abraham Lincoln Battalion (ALB) sailed from New York City on Christmas Day, 1936, and joined the other International Brigades at Albacete. An estimated 3,000 men fought in this 15th battalion. Of these, over 1,000 were industrial workers. Another 500 were students or teachers. Around 30% were Jewish. There were also a large number of African-Americans. Most were members of the Communist party, but some were with the Socialist Party and the Socialist Labor Party.

Of all the gruesome battles during the war, the most infamous was the bombing of Guernica. When Franco organized the takeover of the Basque Country, he sought air raids from Germany and Italy. They were glad to assist—good training for terror bombings in the upcoming world war. Hitler and Mussolini's planes made their entre in Guernica on April 26, 1937.

Three-fourths of the defenseless village was destroyed by 6000 bombs in three hours of constant bombings. Most of the rest of the city was damaged, all but wealthy areas, the town assembly hall and its revered Guernica Tree, and the two weapons factories, which Franco would use in three days when his troops took over. The fascists knew where not to bomb thanks to rich Basque informants.

The Spanish Republic commissioned Pablo Picasso (without pay) to make what became the most famous of paintings, the 8-meter long Guernica, which was displayed first at the World Fair in Paris, July 1937. The New York Museum of Modern Art kept it safe throughout the war and turned it over to the Reina Sofía Museum in Madrid, in 1981.

In 2017, Jette and I stood before "Guernica", in Madrid, alongside people from around the world. My emotions were strong and mixed: joy for the symbolism of solidarity it represents, and tears of sorrow for the tragedy and excruciating pain people felt, the wanton murder simply for the boundlessly inane desire for power and material wealth. And it continues. Today the "democratic" states commit their terror bombings for endless material wealth.

September 23, 1938, Juan Negrin, head of the Republican government, announced that the International Brigades would be unilaterally withdrawn from Spain. The Republican government foresaw defeat and did not want foreign friends to needlessly die.

Catalonia and Madrid were the Republic's last holdouts. They fought bravely to the end well knowing they had no chance against Europe's most modern military. Franco's forces attacked Catalonia for weeks on end until they took Barcelona on January 21, 1939. Madrid was still holding out but England and France couldn't wait to butter up to Franco. On February 27, they recognized his government, a month before the Republic fell when the fascists occupied Madrid, March 28.

Upon returning to their homeland, Abraham Lincoln brigade volunteers faced scrutiny and persecution from the U.S. Government, just as did many internationalists elsewhere.

During World War II, the U.S. government considered former members of the brigade to be security risks. FBI Director J. Edgar Hoover requested that President Roosevelt ensure that former ALB members fighting in World War II not be allowed to be officers. In 1947, the Veterans of the Abraham Lincoln Brigade were placed on the Attorney General's List of Subversive Organizations.

The House Un-American Activities Committee also blacklisted all veterans of the Lincoln Battalion. Many veterans were fired, denied housing and were refused passports for decades.

The numbers of people killed during the war are contested, but at least half-a-million were killed on both sides. General estimates are that ca. 110,000 Republic forces died in combat, and about 90,000 nationalist-fascists. The so-called "red terror" executions of nationalist soldiers and civilians are estimated at 30,000 to 38,000. Fifteen thousand brigade volunteers also died. Of the approximately 3,015 US American volunteers, 681 were killed in action or died of wounds or sickness.

Hundreds of Republicans and internationalist supporters were also killed in internal battles. Communist party soldiers and volunteers, Trotskyists and anarchists clashed over end goals. Was the struggle one of maintaining the democratic republic and fighting only fascism, or was it also a revolutionary struggle for socialism, which the more pragmatic communists considered impossibly utopian given the circumstances?

Fascists were by far the most brutal and indiscriminate in their violence. Franco's "white terror" eliminated between 150,000 and 200,000 people through executions and "cleansings". There were massacres of mainly civilians when the fascists took towns—22,000 in Basque towns, 10,000 in Cordoba, 8,000 in Seville, 6-12,000 in Badajoz, 7,000 in Malaga, 2000 in Granada.

After the end of the Spanish war, on April 1, 1939, the new government established a central-state monarchy, and continued harsh reprisals. Thousands of Republicans were imprisoned and perhaps as many as 200,000 more were executed. Many more thousands died during forced labor—building railways, drying out swamps, and digging canals. Perhaps 35,000 died in concentration camps.

Hundreds of thousands of Republicans fled abroad; at least half-a-million to France. Refugees were confined in internment camps of the

French Third Republic. Some who fled to France, even before the end of the war, engaged in guerrilla warfare, and they continued following the fascist victory. The Spanish *Maquis* exiled in France fought Franco's regime until the early 1960s. They carried out sabotage and robberies to help fund guerrilla activity. They occupied the Spanish Embassy in France and assassinated *Francoists*. They also fought against Nazi Germany and the French Vichy regime during the Second World War.

The term "*Maquis*" is French and refers to scrub-bush country. These Spanish and French peasants who fought guerrilla style saw themselves as "bush hardened". Their numbers ranged from 20,000 to 150,000 during WWII. They sought an anarchistic or pure communist society.

Reporter and novelist Martha Gellhorn covered the Spanish Civil War alongside and separate from Ernest Hemingway, whom she married (1940-5). She also covered World War II and wrote a book about it, The Undefeated (1945). Here is an excerpt about the audacious "*Maquis*":

> *"During the German occupation of France, the Spanish Maquis engineered more than four hundred railway sabotages, destroyed fifty-eight locomotives, dynamited thirty-five railway bridges, cut one hundred and fifty telephone lines, attacked twenty factories, destroying some factories totally, and sabotaged fifteen coal mines. They took several thousand German prisoners and—most miraculous considering their arms—they captured three tanks. In the south-west part of France where no Allied armies have ever fought, they liberated more than seventeen towns."*

I also quote from *Homage to Catalonia* by George Orwell (1938). He was severely wounded in the throat while fighting with POUM.

> *"The war was actually won for Franco by the Germans and Italians... The outcome of the Spanish war was settled in London, Paris, Rome, Berlin..."*
>
> *"The common people knew in their bones that the Republic was their friend and Franco was their enemy. They knew that they were in the right, because they were fighting for something which the world owed them and was able to give them."*

> *"In practice, however, one cannot be neutral, and there is hardly such a thing as a war in which it makes no difference who wins...In essence it was a class war. If it had been won, the cause of the common people everywhere would have been strengthened. It was lost, and the dividend-drawers all over the world rubbed their hands. That was the real issue; all else was froth on its surface."*

US AMERICAN CAPITALISTS HELPED FRANCO WIN THE WAR

What Orwell meant by the outcome being settled in Western European cities was that some directly assisted Franco while others aided by being allegedly "neutral". I add that fascist capitalists in the United States did much more than remain neutral. They did their utmost to bring victory to the European fascists, as the previous chapter shows. One of them, Texaco, was especially dear to Franco. Texaco's fuel provided Franco (and his partner Hitler) with the resources necessary to run his war machinery, and most of it was sold on credit and paid for upon their victory.

Journalist-author Adam Hochschild, a founder-editor-writer for the magazine *Mother Jones*, has just written a book, *Spain in Our Hearts: Americans in the Spanish Civil War, 1939-1939* (Houghton Mifflin Harcourt, 2016). Herein are excerpts from his March 29, 2016 piece in *Mother Jones*, "How Texaco Helped Franco Win the Spanish Civil War: The lost history of a dictator-loving, Nationalist-supporting American oilman". (http://www.motherjones.com/politics/2016/03/texaco-franco-spanish-civil-war-rieber/)

"No corporations have been more aggressive in forging their own foreign policies than the big oil companies. With operations spanning the world, they—and not the governments who weakly try to tax or regulate them—largely decide whom they do business with and how."

Hochschild wrote that Texaco's CEO Torkild Rieber, a Norwegian-born US citizen, was "the best American friend a Fascist dictator could have. He would provide the Nationalists not only with oil, but with an astonishing hidden subsidy of money, a generous and elastic line of credit, and a stream of strategic intelligence."

"In 1935, the Spanish Republic signed a contract with Rieber's Texaco, turning the company into its major oil supplier. The next year, after Franco and his allies made their grab for power, however, Rieber suddenly changed course and bet on them. Knowing that military trucks, tanks, and aircraft need not just fuel, but a range of engine oils and other lubricants, the Texaco CEO quickly ordered a supply at the French port of Bordeaux to be loaded into a company tanker and shipped to the hard-pressed Nationalists. It was a gesture that Franco would never forget.

"FBI agents questioned Rieber about his tankers in Texas filled with oil for European destinations. They suspected he was breaking the neutrality laws of the 1930s prohibiting the sale of arms or providing finances to warring parties, regardless of whether aggressor or victim.

"But President Franklin D. Roosevelt was leery of getting drawn into the Spanish Civil War in any way, even by prosecuting such a conspicuous violation of American law. Instead, Texaco received no more than a slap on the wrist, eventually paying a fine of $22,000 for extending credit to a belligerent government. Years later, when oil companies began issuing credit cards to consumers, a joke began making the rounds among industry insiders: Who did Texaco give its first credit card to? Francisco Franco."

The meager fine did not stop Texaco from continuing to extend credit until the end of the war.

Franco had vessels and planes looking for and attacking ships carrying goods to Republican Spain. Hochschild wrote, "Commanders directing these submarines, bombers, and surface ships were always remarkably well informed on the travels of tankers bound for the Spanish Republic. These were, of course, a prime target for the Nationalists and during the war at least 29 of them were either damaged, sunk, or captured...One reason those waters became so dangerous: the Nationalists had access to Texaco's international maritime intelligence network."

Texaco also relayed information on tankers sailing to the Republic to fascist submarine captains and pilots. This spy company helped the fascists win the war to the tune of $20 million in oil revenues—worth $325 million today. Rieber's tankers made 225 trips to Spain, and another 156 trips made by ships that Texaco chartered. Franco made his spy friend Rieber a "Knight of the Grand Cross of Isabella the Catholic".

"Eventually, Rieber's love of dictators got him in trouble. In 1940, it was revealed, among other things, that several Germans he had hired were Nazi spies using Texaco's internal communications to transmit intelligence information to Berlin. Rieber lost his job, but thanks to a grateful Franco the deposed tycoon landed on his feet: the dictator made him chief American buyer for the Spanish government's oil company."

While Texaco was the greatest and most vigorous of Franco's American capitalist-fascist supporters, other giants assisted as well, many who came to Hitler's aid soon thereafter. Among them were: Ford, Studebaker and General Motors. They sold 12,000 trucks to the fascists.

Shortly after U.S. businessmen had made tons of money supplying armaments, oil and other war necessities to both the fascists and the defending Allies, and had just started the Cold War against socialist Soviets, Picasso created the peace dove. Luis Aragon, a leading French Communist, poet and author, had fought in the resistance and in Spain. He asked Picasso, who was also a Communist party member, to

contribute a work for the World Conference for Peace, to be held in Paris, April 1949. Aragon thought of using a dove as a symbol for justice, a bearer of messages for peace as a poster. Matisse had recently given his friend a few Milanese pigeons, and Picasso made a lithograph of one. Aragon came across it when browsing through sketches, so wrote Francoise Gilot in her 1964 book, *Life with Picasso*. She was one of Picasso's lovers and "muse", as well as an artist. At this writing, she is still alive at age 95, and the pigeon is still the world's peace dove.

I am only a human
but I shall one day
raise earth's mountains
and let them shake
in the ears of those who sleep

I am only a human
but I shall one day
take the sun down from heaven
and light up all the dark holes
with merciless white light

I am only a human
but I shall one day
steal the gods lightning
and sweep the earth clean of dust (5)

Notes:

1. See Antony Beevor's *The Battle for Spain: The Spanish Civil War 1936-1939*, (Weidenfeld & NIcolson, 2006)

2. In April municipal elections pro- monarchists received 25.6% of the vote; the rest were for a republic. In general elections, 70% of those eligible voted, considered high. At that time, however, women were denied the vote, although ironically they could run for office. The republican constitution of December 1931 granted women the right to vote, and many other equal rights. Of the 34 political parties that won over 1% of the vote and thereby a seat in the 473-seat parliament, outright monarchist parties received only 10 seats; and rightist parties won 20 seats. The republican and socialist coalition won a huge victory with 34% of votes (193 seats), while the social democratic PSOE took 14% (80 seats).

3. Germany provided Franco forces with 600 war planes, 200 tanks, and 16,000 soldiers. Italy added 660 warplanes, 150 tanks, 800 artillery pieces, 10,000 machine guns, 140,000 rifles, and 50,000 troops. Portugal sent 20,000 "volunteer" soldiers.

4. The Soviet Union provided military assistance at the cost of most of the Republic's gold reserves, some $500 million worth. The equipment it sent was no match for the more modern Axis weapons: 700-1000 artillery pieces, 500,000 mostly out-dated rifles, 730 tanks, 45,000 heavy machine guns and sub-machine guns and 600-800 planes. Their 2000-3000 soldiers were mostly volunteers, advisors and secret service personnel. Half of Soviet arms production went to Spain, and some went to Mao's forces in China fighting a civil war. Some arms were provided by Poland, Czehoslovakis and Estonia.

   Mexico was the only other country to help the Republic. It provided about $2 million in aid, which included 20,000 rifles. It also offered sanctuary for about 50,000 refugees after the Republic fell. The European democracies and the U.S. declared "neutrality" and didn't even offer returning internationalists safety. Some were imprisoned in their home countries in Europe and the U.S.

5. "The naked human" poem written by Gustav Munch-Petersen at age 20 before he went to Spain. He was one of 550 Danish solidarity fighters, and one of 220 who was killed on the battlefield, or tortured to death in prison, or died of a war-related disease. I translated the poem.

CHAPTER 10

World War II and Soviet Union pre-war internal developments

EARLY SPRING MARCH winds brought the most critical crisis the Bolshevik revolution had had to face and with it a significant shift in economic policy. By 1921, it was hard enough fighting the internal class enemy, which started the Russian Civil War, and their foreign allies—the mightiest Western powers with Japan—and to do so without having time to recover the damages caused by World War I. But to fight one's own too, that must have been devastating for most souls.

The civil war caused the Bolsheviks to adopt what they called War Communism—breakup of landed estates and forcible seizures of other agricultural lands and products. This forced peasants to sell food without profits to city dwellers. There were food shortages and a breakdown in the money system. Even small scale capitalist production was suppressed. Many city workers fled to the countryside in search of food. In February, many peasants had stopped working, and many factory workers went on strike. The war with Poland was still on, and the last foreign armies had not left. The Red Army and police used force to break up protests and strikes.

Then came the Kronstadt rebellion! Several thousand revolutionary sailors, soldiers and workers guarded a huge naval fortress on Kotlin Island just 55 kilometers from the capital. They held a conference at the end of February. A Provisional Revolutionary Committee was constituted and proposed 15 demands to the Bolshevik government. Here are the most poignant points:

1. Immediate secret elections to the Soviets.
2. Freedom of speech and of the press.

3. The right to assemble, and freedom for trade union and peasant associations.
4. The liberation of all political prisoners of the Socialist parties, and of all imprisoned workers and peasants, soldiers and sailors belonging to working class and peasant organizations.
5. The abolition of all political sections in the armed forces; no political party should have privileges for the propagation of its ideas.
6. Equalization of rations for all workers, except those engaged in dangerous or unhealthy jobs.
7. Granting peasants freedom of action on their own soil, and the right to own cattle provided they look after them themselves and do not employ hired labor.
8. Handicraft production allowed provided it does not utilize wage labor.

On March 7, 60,000 Red Army soldiers crossed over the frozen Baltic Sea and attacked the fortress. The next day, the Tenth Bolshevik Party Congress met. By its conclusion, on March 16, it decided to end War Communism and begin the New Economic Policy (NEP). On March 18, the Treaty of Riga was signed ending the Polish-Soviet War. The next day, the Kronstadt rebellion was put down. Several thousand revolutionaries differing over policies had killed one another, between 500 and 2,000 rebels were executed, and thousands imprisoned. It is still debated whether the rebellion was purely an internal one or was part of an international conspiracy hatched in France. Regardless, comrade killed comrade.

With NEP, Lenin was admitting that a worldwide revolution was not around the corner; the proletariat also had to embrace the peasantry as partners; and socialism could not be truly shaped so soon. NEP allowed a limited market, small private businesses, and eased restrictions on some political activities.

The key shift involved the status of agricultural products. Rather than simply requisitioning agricultural surpluses in order to feed the urban population, NEP allowed peasants to sell their surplus yields on the open market. The state still maintained ownership of what Lenin deemed the "commanding heights": heavy industry (coal, iron, and other metallurgical sectors) along with banking and financial components. State industries would have flexibility in making decisions.

The economy expanded. Much trade was taken over by full-time merchants, who were denounced as "speculators" by leftists, and resented by the public. The growth in trade, though, did generally coincide with rising living standards in the city, and the countryside where 80% lived.

The Soviet NEP was essentially a period of "market socialism" and lasted until 1929. Agricultural yields recovered and improved. The break-up of the landed estates gave peasants their greatest incentives ever to maximize production, and peasant spending gave a boost to the manufacturing sectors. As a result, the Soviet Union became the world's greatest producer of grain.

Factories did not recover as rapidly having been badly damaged by wars and capital depreciation. Some enterprises were organized into trusts or syndicates representing one sector of the economy, which contributed to imbalances between supply and demand. With little state control, trusts sold products at higher prices.

The slower recovery of industry posed problems for the peasantry since price indexes for industrial goods were higher than those for agricultural products. Peasants had to produce more grain to purchase consumer goods. As a result, some peasants withheld agricultural surpluses in anticipation of higher prices, thereby contributing to shortages in the cities. The Communists attempted to bring prices down for manufactured goods, stabilize inflation by imposing price controls on essential industrial goods, and break-up the trusts to increase economic efficiency.

LENIN DIES

Lenin was shot on August 30, 1918 at a Moscow factory by Feiga Kaplan. She was an angry young Socialist Revolutionary, who believed Lenin had betrayed the revolution when he banned her party. Kaplan used a pistol to shoot him in a shoulder and the neck, which punctured a lung. She said she acted alone. She was executed three days later, and many fellow members were shot without trials.

Lenin never fully recovered and had three strokes between May 1922 and March 1923, which impaired his speech to the point where he could not speak. Following his last stroke, a troika—Joseph Stalin, Grigory Zinoviev, and Lev Kamenev—took over party and state leadership. These three, along with Lenin, Trotsky, Grigori Sokolnikov and Andrei Bubnov made up the first Politburo from the start of the revolution.

Before Lenin died, on January 21, 1924, he presumably dictated two letters in December 1922, which became known as Lenin's Testament. Many who supported Stalin then and now cast aspersions on its veracity. If there was a testament, Lenin apparently dictated it to his secretary. Lenin criticized Stalin's leadership and urged his removal as general secretary. In May 1924, the Central Committee discussed the testament but no action was taken nor was it published. (1)

During Lenin's sickness, serious differences arose between Stalin and Trotsky. Among them were whether socialism could be built only in one country (Russia), Stalin's view; or if it was necessary to make a permanent revolution both internally and by actively encouraging a worldwide revolution, professed by Trotsky. By the end of 1924, Stalin was able to maneuver Trotsky out as commissar of war. Trotsky was dismissed, in part, for heading the Left Opposition faction, 1923-7.

Trotsky was dropped from the politburo entirely in 1926 when he formed the United Opposition with Zinoviev and Kamenev. They opposed some policies of Stalin and Nikolai Bukharin, editor of the party newspaper *Pravda* and general secretary of the international Comintern. But the three lost influence as a result of party disputes. In October 1927, they were expelled from the Central Committee and expelled from the Communist Party in December. In early 1928, Trotsky and other leading members of the Left Opposition were sentenced to internal exile. Zinoviev and Kamenev admitted mistakes and were readmitted. In February 1929, Trotsky was exiled to Turkey. He was eventually murdered in Mexico, August 20, 1940. Ramón Mercader, a Spanish-born NKVD agent, had infiltrated Trotsky's inner circle. He killed Trotsky with an ice axe. Mercader served 20 years in a Mexican prison. Stalin presented him with an Order of Lenin in absentia.

DIFFERENT IDEAS, WESTERN SUBVERSION AND PARANOIA

In every revolution, or transformational economic upheaval leading from one system to another, there is always counter-revolution. Internal conflicts and transformations are often utilized by foreign powers to their advantage. We've witnessed this for millenniums, and the Russian movement to transform from the feudal-capitalist system to a socialist one was no different or, perhaps, it was the most threatening one.

No one had attempted to interfere with United States' sovereignty and its imperialism between 1812 and 1941, but it did not reciprocate—its interventionist policy in other States is classic in scope. So, by 1917, it was already routine to stop changes in countries that it regarded as unprofitable for Wall Street. Certainly a Russia, and then Soviet Union, that would rule its own resources and make its own economy distinct from that of the U.S. (U.K, Europe generally, along with Japan) could not be tolerated. Subversion and military intervention started from the first, as we have already seen. And when the great bear of the nation was nearly on its knees from so much violence and lack of food, its leaders naturally could see enemies where there were none—paranoia sets in, and causes mistakes and even immoral actions. The reality of subversion, of infiltration by mighty enemies is so omnipotent and omnipresent, that this can cause one to oversee that actions chosen could also be caused by one's paranoia.

As I wrote at the beginning of chapter seven, "it is not my intent to delve into or analyze Russia's internal developments, socialism's growth and failure, its leaders' wisdom or lack thereof…." but I do present some pertinent facts, as much as I can discern, about some of the purges and internal violence that took place in Russia. This is relevant to the overall theme of this book.

With the end of Communist party factions, Stalin had a free hand for a while. In 1929, he launched the first Five-year plan with near total collectivization of agricultural and industry. There was a famine in 1932-3, and resistance to some measures propped up among some party members, much of the peasantry, and some military leaders. The term "purge" in Soviet political slang was an abbreviation of the expression *purge of the Party ranks*. In 1933, the party expelled about 400,000 people, 18% of its membership. An equal number had already been purged since 1921.

The "Great Purge", or "Great Terror", or the "Yezhov doings" occurred from 1936 to 1938. Nikolai Yezhov was head of the Soviet secret police (NKVD), formed in 1934. This campaign included three major trials and a large-scale "cleansing" of Communist party leaders and other members, government civil servants, Red Army leaders, artists and intellectuals, and repression of peasants.

In these "Moscow Trials" confessions of betrayal to the revolution were voiced and hundreds of defendants were executed, even Politburo members and two NKVD leaders, including Yezho and his predecessor Genrikh Yagoda. Of the original seven Politiburo leaders, whom Lenin had picked, only Stalin remained. Lenin had died; Trotsky was exiled; Zinoviev, Kamenev and Bubnov were executed (1936-7), and Sokolnikov was killed in prison (1939). Even Stalin's closest ally, Bukharin, was arrested in February 1937 on suspicion of trying to overthrow him. Bukharin was executed in March 1938.

Figures vary according to sources, but hundreds of thousands up to one or two million of what was called "fifth column of wreckers, terrorists and spies" were killed or imprisoned in Corrective Labor Camps, what some call the Gulag. The term "repression" was officially used to describe the prosecution of people considered to be counter-revolutionaries and enemies of the people.

These internal trials and tribulations took place during the Spanish Civil War in which the Soviet Union was the only active supporter of the Spanish Republic. One wonders what the Soviet soldiers fighting in Spain thought about the purge underway when it hit their officers too. Stalin suspected many of his officers of conspiring with Germany. Of the top 29 marshals, admirals and generals, 24 were purged—imprisoned or executed. Hundreds of division commanders were purged as well. Twenty to thirty thousand members of the armed forces were executed. Thirty percent of officers dismissed were allowed to return to service when World War II broke out.

The most prominent general executed was Mikhail Nikolayevich Tukhachevsky. He had commanded the Soviet Western Front in the Soviet-Polish War, was the Red Army chief of staff (1925-8), and performed other important military and theoretical duties until Stalin accused him of treason. It was claimed that he had engaged in correspondence with some persons in the German high command. He was executed on June 12, 1937. His reputation was rehabilitated in the 1960s.

These purges were taking place as Adolf Hitler was remilitarizing the German Army. On the one hand, Stalin was "cleansing" his army, while increasing the number of soldiers to 1,300,000 men, more tanks (10,000) and more front line planes (5,000).

The so-called Kulak Operation—or the campaign to eliminate anti-Soviet elements—occurred during the trials. Kulaks were originally affluent peasants in the Ukraine. The term took on general reference to any independent peasant owning a couple hectares or more, and included those who resisted delivering products to the city. Lenin had called them "bloodsuckers" fattened by famines. Orthodox Church clergymen were also caught in this sweep. Most of the 35,000 Kulaks were arrested. Poles suspected of "diversion-ism" were also arrested and many executed in this period.

At the same time, Soviet troops were engaged in military conflict with Japan once again, known as the *Soviet-Japanese border conflicts.* This was a series of battles and skirmishes over borders, and included the puppet states of Mongolia (Soviet) and Manchukuo (Japan). These conflicts flashed on and off between 1932 and 1939. In May 1939, the Soviets finally inflicted a decisive defeat. During this mini-war, the Russians lost another 32,000 troops; the Japanese 20,000. On April 13, 1941, the two nations signed the *Japanese–Soviet Non-aggression Pact*, assuring neutrality during World War II, which was about to begin for the Soviets.

This agreement, aka the *Soviet-Japanese Neutrality Pact*, followed another pact that Japan had made with Germany and Italy, the *Tripartite* or *Berlin Pact*, signed on September 27, 1940. But rather than stressing neutrality, it called for a joint military alliance in the event of an attack. Japan recognized the leadership of Germany and Italy in establishing "a new order in Europe". They, in turn, recognized Japan in establishing "a new order in Greater East Asia".

The *Berlin Pact* was directed mainly at the U.S. Within months, several East European countries signed on: Hungary, Romania, Bulgaria, Yugoslavia and Croatia.

Shortly after the Soviet victory against the Japanese, NKVD operatives were set up in the Mongolian People's Republic. Many thousands of people accused of being "pro-Japanese spies" were executed. Buddhist lamas were among them. (Contrary to image disseminated in the West, the Lamas constituted a brutal feudal upper class. See Michael Parenti, Friendly Feudalism: The Tibet Myth [http://

www.michaelparenti.org/Tibet.html] Within months after these violent processes took place, the Soviet Union invaded Finland, on November 30, 1939. Russia was worried that Germany would come there first, and Leningrad was just 32 kilometers from a Finland-Russian border. Stalin first offered an exchange of territory that would allow a buffer zone for Russia, especially to protect Leningrad. But Finland refused. The war was short-lived, but extremely costly for the Red Army now run by new and inexperienced officers.

Soviet casualties amounted to roughly 300,000 about half killed, while Finland suffered one fourth that. Finland lost 20-30 tanks and 60 aircraft. Soviets lost 1,200 to 3,500 tanks and 250 to 500 aircraft. But Russia got what it wanted in the Moscow Peace Treaty, March 13, 1940, a buffer zone.

Many Russians not caught up directly in internal conflicts looked up to Stalin as their strong leader. Others feared him as a brutal cultist of his own personality. With Hitler advancing closer to the Soviet Union, having easily taken the Western front, and the Soviet military weakened by purges and the Finnish and Japanese mini-wars, a socialist future looked grim. Stalin, however, thought the purges strengthened his hand in the eventuality of a Nazi invasion.

Operation Barbarossa was the Axis code name for Germany's invasion of the Soviet Union, on June 22, 1941, 22 months after signing the non-aggression pact. Germany first sought to conquer western Soviet Union so that it could seize Caucasus oil and agricultural resources. It planned to repopulate the territory with Arian Germans, who would use Slavs as a slave-labor force for the Axis war-effort. (2)

It should not have been any wonder that Nazi Germany would invade the Soviet Union. Adolf Hitler wrote his intention as early as 1925 in *Mein Kampf*, in which he asserted that the German people needed to secure *Lebensraum* to "ensure the survival of Germany".

In the two years of détente leading up to the invasion, Germany and the Soviet Union signed political and economic pacts for strategic purposes. Simultaneously, Germany's military was planning an invasion of the Soviet Union.

Over the course of three years of war inside the Soviet Union, Germany sent about four million troops along the 2,900 kilometer western front, which was the largest invasion force in the history of warfare. Germany deployed some 600,000 motor vehicles, about 5000 aircraft, and between 600,000 and 700,000 horses for non-combat operations.

German forces achieved major victories and occupied some of the most important economic areas, especially in the Ukrainian Soviet Socialist Republic. Despite these successes, the German offensive stalled in the battles of Leningrad and Moscow, and subsequently the Soviet winter counteroffensive pushed German troops back. The Red Army repelled the Wehrmacht's strongest blows and forced the Germans into a war of attrition.

The failure of Operation Barbarossa proved a turning point in the fortunes of the Third Reich. Now the Eastern Front was open, and more forces were committed there than in any other theater of war in world history. The Eastern Front became the site of some of the largest battles, most horrific atrocities, and highest casualties for Soviet and Axis forces.

The German armies captured 5,000,000 Red Army troops, who were denied the protection guaranteed by Geneva Conventions. The Nazis deliberately starved to death, or otherwise killed 3.3 million military prisoners, as well as huge numbers of civilians through the "Hunger Plan" to starve Slavs. Nazi death squads (*Einsatzgruppen*) and gassing operations murdered 1.4 million Soviet Jews as part of the Holocaust. That was over half the Jews then living in the Soviet Union.

Just in the first six months of the war several million Russian civilians were murdered, starved to death or died of war-related diseases. Five million Soviet troops were killed or seriously wounded—some died of starvation and diseases. 1,710 towns and 70,000 villages were razed. 21,200 of 23,000 Soviet aircraft were destroyed—2,000 on the first day of the invasion. 20,500 of its 23,000 tanks were destroyed.

The Soviet people had to die in the multi millions before Westerners could see that the Soviet people would eventually beat the Germans, and then decided to back them. This truth was corroborated by the United States second ambassador to the Soviet Union, Joseph Davies.

The U.S. had withdrawn its ambassador to Russia in November 1917 after refusing to recognize the revolutionary government. Under FDR, diplomatic relations were reestablished in 1933. William Christian Bullet was the first ambassador (November 1933-May 1936).

Davies represented the U.S. from November 1936 to June 1938, about which he wrote a book. *Mission to Moscow* (Simon & Schuster, N.Y., 1941) was made into a film in 1943. Davies portrayed how desperate Russians had felt about an eventual war with Germany even before the invasion, given that England and France, and isolationist U.S. refused to make a defensive alliance. Davies wrote that the Soviets knew that the West's illegal but profitable aid in rearming Hitler was not meant to be a "bulwark" but meant to war on them. The August 1939 non-aggression pact was therefore necessary, in order to derail that invasion for a time. Davies also took Stalin's part in the need for the internal purges.

Half a year after the Nazis invaded the Soviet Union, its Asiatic ally attacked the United States at Pearl Harbor naval base on the Hawaii colony. The Empire of Japan declaration of war on the United States and the British Empire was published on December 8, 1941, shortly after Japanese forces had pounded both Pearl Harbor and British forces in Malaya, Singapore, and Hong Kong.

In response, the United States Congress declared war on the Empire of Japan the same day, just nine hours after the UK declared war on Japan.

Pear Harbor was attacked by 353 Imperial Japanese aircraft launched from six aircraft carriers. All eight U.S. Navy battleships at anchor were damaged, four sank. The Japanese also sank or damaged three cruisers, three destroyers, an anti-aircraft training ship, and one minelayer. 188 U.S. aircraft were destroyed. 2,403 Americans were killed and 1,178 others wounded. Japanese losses were light: 64 servicemen killed; 29 aircraft and five U-boats lost. One Japanese sailor was captured.

Three days later, Germany and Italy declared war on the U.S. The U.S. responded with a declaration of war against them.

Two years after the U.S. entered the war, and two and one-half years after the Nazis had invaded the Soviet Union, the U.S. and U.K. welcomed the hated Communists to a conference in Iran, in order to forge a joint strategy.

The **Tehran Conference** was a strategy meeting of Joseph Stalin, Franklin D. Roosevelt, and Winston Churchill from November 28, to December 1, 1943. The first West-USSR war cooperation had just taken place—the Anglo-Soviet Invasion of Iran, August 25-September 17, 1941. This operation assured oil supplies for the Allies, especially Russia on the Eastern Front. The conference was held in the Soviet Union's embassy in Tehran, the first of the "Big Three" World War II conferences, and followed on the heels of the Cairo Conference without Stalin.

The **Cairo Conference** of November 22–26, 1943, held in Egypt, outlined the Allied position against Japan and made decisions about postwar Asia. The meeting was attended by Franklin Roosevelt, Winston Churchill and Generalissimo Chiang Kai-shek of the Republic of China. Joseph Stalin did not attend because his meeting with Chiang could have caused friction between the Soviet Union and Japan. Due to the Soviet-Japanese Neutrality Pact, the Soviet Union was not at war with Japan, whereas China, the U.K. and the U.S. were.

The main agreement at Cairo was to continue deploying military force until Japan's unconditional surrender. The allies sought to restrain and punish Japan's aggression without involving themselves in territorial expansion after the conflict. Japan would be stripped of all the islands in the Pacific, which she had seized or occupied since the beginning of the First World War. All the territories Japan had seized from the Chinese would return to China—Manchuria, Formosa and the Pescadores. Korea must also be returned and, "in due course shall become free and independent".

At **Tehran**, the main outcome was the Western Allies' commitment to open a second front against Nazi Germany, which would bring relief to Russia.

A prelude to a second front began as soon as the German-Soviet war broke out in June 1941. Churchill voiced assistance to the Soviets and an agreement to this effect was signed on July 12, 1941. When the United States joined the war in December, a combined chiefs of staff committee was created to coordinate British and US American operations as well as their support to the Soviet Union. There was the question of opening a second front to alleviate the German pressure on the Red Army on the Eastern Front. It was also agreed that the U.S. would aid Britain and the Soviet Union with credit and material support.

Nevertheless, it took three years after Churchill's original promise, and seven months after the Tehran agreement before the second front opened. Large-scale combat forces landed at Normandy in June 1944, and fought until Germany's defeat in May 1945, with the Soviet armies squeezing the Germans from the East, and eventually—at great cost—taking Berlin.

The **Yalta Conference**, also known as the *Crimea* conference, was held from February 4 to 11, 1945. The three States were again represented by Roosevelt, Churchill and Stalin. The conference convened in the Livadia Palace near Yalta in Crimea, Soviet Union. Its aim was to shape the liberation of Europeans, a post-war peace and collective security. (By then, Red Army Marshal Georgy Zhukov's forces were 65 km from Berlin.)

The Red Army had occupied all of Poland, and held much of Eastern Europe with three times the force than the other Allied forces had in the West.

Stalin's position at the conference was the strongest. Roosevelt wanted Soviet support in the U.S. Pacific War against Japan, specifically for the planned invasion, Operation August Storm, and he wanted Soviet participation in what became the United Nations. Churchill pressed for free elections and democratic governments in Eastern and Central Europe, namely Poland. Stalin demanded a Soviet sphere of political influence in Eastern and Central Europe as an essential aspect of the USSR's national security strategy. He agreed to join the UN, given the understanding of veto power for permanent members of the Security Council, which would ensure that each country could block undesired decisions.

Stalin agreed that the Soviet Union would *enter the Pacific War three months after the defeat of Germany—a pledge he fulfilled.* All three leaders agreed that, in exchange for potentially crucial Soviet participation, the Soviets would be granted a sphere of influence in Manchuria following Japan's surrender. Stalin also agreed to keep the nationality of the Korean Peninsula intact as it entered the war against Japan.

The key points of the meeting are as follows:

- Agreement to the priority of the unconditional surrender of Nazi Germany. After the war, Germany and Berlin would be split into four occupied zones. Stalin agreed that France would have a fourth occupation zone in Germany, but it would have to be formed out of the U.S. and British zones.
- Germany would undergo demilitarization and de-Nazification.

- German reparations were partly to be in the form of forced labor to repair damage that Germany had inflicted on its victims.
- Creation of a reparation council to be located in the Soviet Union.
- It was agreed to reorganize the communist Provisional Government of the Republic of Poland, which had been installed by the Soviet Union "on a broader democratic basis," with elections. The Polish eastern border would follow the Curzon Line, and Poland would receive territorial compensation in the west from Germany.
- Stalin agreed to participate in the UN. Stalin requested that all of the 16 Soviet Socialist Republics would be granted UN membership. This was taken into consideration, but the two Allies denied membership to 14 republics. After Roosevelt's death, Truman agreed to membership for Ukraine and Byelorussia while reserving the right, which was never exercised, to seek two more votes for the United States.
- As a result of Stalin's agreement to fight the Japan Empire, the Soviets would take possession of Southern Sakhalin and the Kuril Islands, the port of Dalian would be internationalized, and the Soviet lease of Port Arthur would be restored.
- Nazi war criminals were to be found and put on trial.
- A "Committee on Dismemberment of Germany" was to be set up.

Potsdam Conference aka **Berlin Conference of the Three Heads of Government of the USSR, USA and UK** was held July 17-August 2, 1945, five months after Yalta and two months after Germany surrendered. It took place in Potsdam, Germany. The powers were represented by Stalin and Winston Churchill, and later by Clement Attlee, and President Harry S. Truman. Roosevelt had died on April 12.

They were to decide how to administer defeated Nazi Germany, which had agreed to unconditional surrender on May 8. Goals also included the establishment of post-war order, peace treaty issues, and countering the effects of the war.

In the time since the Yalta Conference, a number of changes had taken place which would affect their relationships and the world's future. Stalin insisted that Soviet control of some Central and Eastern Europe was a defensive measure against possible future attacks, asserting that it was a legitimate sphere of Soviet influence. Truman's abrupt entrance into the theatre was most unfortunate for a future peace with the Soviets due to his unrepentant anti-communist ideology, and with his soon-to-be creation of the Central Intelligence Agency, whose mission would be world domination. And Labour Party leader Clement Attlee had unexpectedly beaten Churchill in the election, July 26 mid in the Postdam Conference.

The Potsdam Conference resulted in: (1) details for Japan's unconditional surrender; (2) an agreement regarding Soviet annexation of former Polish territory east of the Curzon Line; (3) provisions to be addressed in an eventual Final Treaty ending World War II for the annexation of parts of Germany east of the Oder-Neisse line into Poland, and northern East Prussia into the Soviet Union; (4) German industrial war-potential was to be eliminated by the destruction or control of all industry with military potential.

Most other issues were reconfirmation of Yalta agreements. This included dealing with Japan's occupation of Korea, in which a temporary division was made. This soon happened at the infamous 38th parallel. Korea was to eventually become "free and independent", "mindful of the enslavement of the people of Korea" by Japan, as had been established at the Cairo Conference.

Truman mentioned an unspecified "powerful new weapon" to Stalin during the conference without mentioning its atomic nature. While still at the conference, Truman gave Japan an ultimatum to surrender (in the name of the United States, Great Britain and China), or meet "prompt and utter destruction". Prime Minister Kantarō Suzuki did not immediately respond. Truman then dropped the bombs on Hiroshima, August 6, and Nagasaki, August 9, murdering nearly 200,000 people, mostly civilians, and many more from radiation poisoning in years to come.

The justification was: preserving American lives by ending the war swiftly, and both cities were legitimate military targets. According to Truman's diary notes of July 25, 1945, he told Secretary of War Henry

Stimson to use the bombs so that "military objectives and soldiers and sailors are the target and not women and children. Even if the Japs are savages, ruthless, merciless and fanatic, we as the leader of the world for the common welfare cannot drop that terrible bomb on the old capital or the new."

However, Japan was already smashed and ready to surrender, especially when the Soviet Union invaded just hours before the A-bomb was dropped on Nagasaki. Japan surrendered to the Soviet Union on September 2, after surrendering to the U.S. on August 15. The surrender ceremony took place on September 2 on the USS Missouri flying the flags of the United States, Britain, and China, alongside the Soviet Union.

The timing of using the A-bomb suggests that Truman did not want Stalin involved in the terms of Japan's surrender, contrary to the Tehran agreement. Truman even delayed the Potsdam Conference in order to be sure of the functionality of this "powerful new weapon". The Trinity test on July 16 was the first-ever test of a nuclear weapon (yield of 20 kilotons).

A-BOMBING JAPAN: IMMORAL GENOCIDE AND UNNCESSARY

Major General Curtis LeMay opposed using the A-bomb in Japan not out of moral concerns. He was ready to use it against Russia and perhaps Cuba and China during the Cuban Missile Crisis. But LeMay knew it was unnecessary, and he wanted credit for having destroyed the country. He had designed and implemented the systematic strategic bombing campaign in the Pacific Theater, and pioneered low-altitude nighttime firebombing raids. On March 10, 1945, more than 300 B-29s dropped incendiary bombs over Tokyo. Over 100,000 people died. LeMay then directed similar raids at every major industrial city in Japan. Hundreds of thousands of civilians were burned alive. The U.S. knew the war was ending. Japan could not last much longer. Sustained, massive destruction was routine by August 1945. Dropping "Little Boy" and "Fat Man"—cute nick-names for genocidal atomic bombings on Hiroshima and Nagasaki—was thoroughly unnecessary.

"On September 20, 1945 the famous 'hawk' who commanded the Twenty-First Bomber Command, Major General Curtis E. LeMay (as reported in The New York Herald Tribune) publicly said flatly at one press conference that the atomic bomb 'had nothing to do with the end of the war.'" "He said the war would have been over in two weeks without the use of the atomic bomb or the Russian entry into the war." (http://www.colorado.edu/AmStudies/lewis/2010/atomicdec.htm)

"Soviet offensive, key to Japan's WWII surrender, was eclipsed by A-bombs"

This was Fox News headline, August 14, 2010.

"As the United States dropped its atomic bombs on Hiroshima and Nagasaki in August 1945, 1.6 million Soviet troops launched a surprise attack on the Japanese army occupying eastern Asia. Within days, Emperor Hirohito's million-man army in the region had collapsed.

"Following the German surrender on May 8, 1945, and having suffered a string of defeats in the Philippines, Okinawa and Iwo Jima, Japan turned to Moscow to mediate an end to the Pacific war…Joseph Stalin had already secretly promised Washington and London that he would attack Japan within three months of Germany's defeat. He thus ignored Tokyo's plea, and mobilized more than a million troops along Manchuria's border. Operation August Storm was launched Aug. 9, 1945, as the Nagasaki bomb was dropped, and would claim the lives of 84,000 Japanese and 12,000 Soviet soldiers in two weeks of fighting." (http://www.foxnews.com/world/2010/08/14/historians-soviet-offensive-key-japans-wwii-surrender-eclipsed-bombs.html)

"*The Bomb Didn't Beat Japan, Stalin Did*" was Foreign Policy journal writer Ward Wilson's headline, May 30, 2013. (http://foreignpolicy.com/2013/05/30/the-bomb-didnt-beat-japan-stalin-did/)

> *"In the summer of 1945, the U.S. Army Air Force carried out one of the most intense campaigns of city destruction in the history of the world. Sixty-eight cities in Japan were attacked and all of them were either partially or completely destroyed. An estimated 1.7 million people were made homeless, 300,000 were killed, and 750,000 were wounded. Sixty-six of these raids were carried out with conventional bombs, two with atomic bombs. The destruction caused by conventional attacks was huge. Night after night, all summer long, cities would go up in smoke."*
>
> *"If the Japanese were not concerned with city bombing in general or the atomic bombing of Hiroshima in particular, what were they concerned with? The answer is simple: the Soviet Union.*

"...Foreign Minister Togo Shigenori hoped that Stalin might be convinced to mediate a settlement between the United States and its allies on the one hand, and Japan on the other...The destruction of Hiroshima had done nothing to reduce the preparedness of the troops dug in on the beaches of Japan's home islands...they were still dug in, they still had ammunition, and their military strength had not been diminished in any important way. Bombing Hiroshima did not foreclose either of Japan's strategic options [diplomacy or continuing the war].

"The impact of the Soviet declaration of war and invasion of Manchuria and Sakhalin Island was quite different, however. Once the Soviet Union had declared war, Stalin could no longer act as a mediator—he was now a belligerent. So the diplomatic option was wiped out by the Soviet move. The effect on the military situation was equally dramatic. Most of Japan's best troops had been shifted to the southern part of the home islands...When the Russians invaded Manchuria, they sliced through what had once been an elite army...The Soviet 16th Army—100,000 strong—launched an invasion of the southern half of Sakhalin Island. Their orders were to mop up Japanese resistance there, and then—within 10 to 14 days—be prepared to invade Hokkaido..."

"The Soviet invasion made a decision on ending the war extremely time sensitive. And Japan's leaders had reached this conclusion some months earlier. In a meeting of the Supreme Council in June 1945, they said that Soviet entry into the war 'would determine the fate of the Empire.' Army Deputy Chief of Staff Kawabe said, in that same meeting, 'The absolute maintenance of peace in our relations with the Soviet Union is imperative for the continuation of the war.'"

"When Truman famously threatened to visit a 'rain of ruin' on Japanese cities if Japan did not surrender, few people in the United States realized that there was very little left to destroy. By Aug. 7, when Truman's threat was made, only 10 cities larger than 100,000 people remained that had not already been bombed. Once Nagasaki was attacked on Aug. 9, only nine cities were left."

Ward Wilson's conclusion: *"Attributing the end of the war to the atomic bomb served Japan's interests in multiple ways. But it also served U.S. interests. If the Bomb won the war, then the perception of U.S. military power would be enhanced, U.S. diplomatic influence in Asia and around the world would increase, and U.S. security would be strengthened. The $2 billion spent to build it would not have been wasted. If, on the other hand, the Soviet entry into the war was what caused Japan to surrender, then the Soviets could claim that they were able to do in four days what the United States was unable to do in four years, and the perception of Soviet military power and Soviet diplomatic influence would be enhanced. And once the Cold War was underway, asserting that the Soviet entry had been the decisive factor would have been tantamount to giving aid and comfort to the enemy."*

Translation: The main reason to drop nuclear weapons on defenseless civilians was to threaten the Soviet Union, to show the bear that it must buckle under to the eagle's worldwide domination. Another reason was to show the whole world how ruthless the United States can be if any people resist its wishes, or try to overthrow it.

Nevertheless, the U.S. Army did not want the world to know what it had done to human beings. It was left to an Australian war correspondent Wilfred Burchett of UK's *Daily Express* to tell the wider world that the residents of Hiroshima were suffering. The following comes from, "The Fallout: the medical aftermath of the day that changed the world," published here: http://hiroshima.australiandoctor.com.au/

Burchett story was headlined "The Atomic Plague".

"I write this as a warning to the world.

In Hiroshima, 30 days after the first atomic bomb destroyed the city and shook the world, people are still dying, mysteriously and horribly—people who were uninjured by the cataclysm—from an unknown something which I can only describe as atomic plague.

Hiroshima does not look like a bombed city. It looks as if a monster steamroller had passed over it and squashed it out of existence. I write these facts as dispassionately as I can in the hope that they will act as a warning to the world. In this first testing ground of the atomic bomb I have seen the most terrible and frightening desolation in four years of war. It makes a blitzed Pacific island seem like an Eden."

"Burchett had covered the US war against the Japanese from Burma through the island-hopping campaigns of the Pacific and had arrived in Japan on a ship with US Marines," wrote an unnamed person on this website.

"He quickly shrugged off the restrictions of US military control in Tokyo and beat the official press delegation to Hiroshima by jumping on a local train.

"After a hazardous 21-hour journey surrounded by resentful Japanese soldiers, Burchett hopped off the train in Hiroshima. It was 3 September. What he saw there shocked him and transformed his views forever.

"He walked three miles to the centre of the blast and saw only piles of rubble—the only things standing were a few shells of concrete buildings. It soon became clear that tens of thousands of Hiroshima residents had been killed by the blast and heat wave of the bomb.

"With the help of the Japanese Domei press agency, Burchett visited one of the few hospitals still functioning." Burchett wrote:

"In these hospitals I found people who, when the bomb fell, suffered absolutely no injuries, but now are dying from the uncanny after-effect. For no apparent reason their health began to fail. They lost appetite. Their hair fell out. Bluish spots appeared on their bodies.

And the bleeding began from the ears, nose and mouth. At first the doctors told me they thought these were the symptoms of general debility. They gave their patients vitamin A injections. The results were horrible. The flesh started rotting away from the hole caused by the injection of the needle. And in every case the victim died.'"

"Burchett spoke to Japanese doctors who said that 100 patients a day were dying of this mysterious illness, which they believed was caused by radioactivity released from the atomic bomb that had permeated into the ground, dust and water supply.

"Burchett reported that visitors to the city—including the first teams of Japanese scientists—also experienced strange symptoms such as wounds that would not heal and susceptibility to infections."

I met Wilfred Burchett at the Assembly for Peace and Independence of the People of Indochina held at Versailles, France, February 1972. I was there as both an "underground media" reporter for the *Los Angeles Free Press*, and as an anti-war activist. He struck me as a modest and honest man, one whose copy could be relied upon. We spoke of doing some work together in Cuba but it never came off.

Another Australian reporter, John Pilger, whom I also read for understanding, conducted a film interview with him, in 1983, shortly before Burchett died. See it here: http://johnpilger.com/videos/vietnam-the-quiet-mutiny.

POST-WAR 1945

While Allied leaders were meeting at Potsdam to decide how to divide up Europe in a new era of peace, and while Russia organized its promised invasion of Japan to help its ally, the United States of America, Britain's prime minister was preparing to invade Soviet troops in Europe to prevent a new world in peace.

Operation Unthinkable was the code name of a plan to basically break-up the Soviet Union, which Prime Minister Winston Churchill ordered. The British Armed Forces' Joint Planning Staff presented Churchill with a plan on June 8, just before the Potsdam Conference. It called for a surprise attack on Soviet forces stationed in Germany, to "impose the will of the Western Allies" on the Soviets. "The will" was ostensibly meant to be "a square deal for Poland". (http://www.historylearningsite.co.uk/world-war-two/world-war-two-in-western-europe/operation-unthinkable/

This plan set the stage for the Cold War with the Soviet Union. It was kept secret until 1998. You can see more about it on this alternate history hub video: https://www.youtube.com/watch?v=epW5ktfYt9Q

The hypothetical date for the start of a UK-US invasion of Soviet-held Europe was scheduled for July 1, 1945, four days before the originally set UK general election. There would be a surprise attack by 47 British and U.S. divisions in the area of Dresden, in the middle of Soviet lines. This was half the British, U.S. and Canadian troops in Europe at that time. But since the Soviet Union still had 11 million combat ready troops, 6.5 million of whom were on the German front, the two Western powers would be outnumbered 2.5 to 1. So Churchill planned to rearm 100,000 enemy German troops to fight alongside their victors.

Churchill was so livid that the Soviets had not been defeated by the Nazis, and instead had expanded their might into Eastern Europe that he was willing to use the new nuclear weapons that he knew Truman had. Churchill had been informed about Operation Manhattan, and he considered using the big bombs on Moscow, Stalingrad and Kiev. His Field Marshall Bernard Montgomery was stockpiling captured German weapons "for future use", and Stalin's counter-intelligence found out about the plan.

The Soviet Union had yet to launch its attack on Japanese forces, which was to occur within five weeks. Some Western planners were worried that if attacked the Soviet Union would instead ally with Japan. Truman didn't like Churchill's plan and then with a Labour Prime Minister the plan was dropped as unfeasible—until another day.

RUSSIAN DEAD REMEMBERED

By the end of the war, the Soviets had lost 13% of their population of 190 million. In contrast, the U.K. lost 1% of its 48 million people—67,000 civilians, 383,000 military; US Americans lost 0.32% of its 131 million people—12,000 civilians, 407,300 military. (3)

Statistics can seem blurry. I can't avoid, however, arithmetically showing how much the Russian people suffered, at least in numbers of casualties in the first four decades of the 20th century.

1. Japan war, 1904-5=40,000-70,000 dead; 150,000 wounded.
2. World War I, 1914-17=ca.3.2 million soldiers & civilians dead; 3.7-5 million wounded.
3. Russian Civil War, 1917-21+=ca. 9 million soldiers & civilians dead; at least 3 million wounded (the greatest casualty rate of any single European country in war to date).
4. Japanese and Finnish mini-wars, 1939-40=ca. 180,000 soldiers dead; ca. 200,000 wounded.
5. World War II, 1941-45=27 million dead, between 16-18 million civilians, 9-11 million soldiers; at least 22.6 million wounded.

Not attempting to calculate how many millions of Soviet people perished due to purges and famines in the 1920s-30s, I surmise that the declared wars with foreign forces (and the White Army) caused at least ***40 million dead and 30 million wounded*** (the wounded figures are quite low and not well corroborated). At this low calculation that would mean the number of casualties would represent 40% of Soviets who survived WWII, and half the number of Russians living today.

A people do not forget so many dead and handicapped countrymen whilst it is easier for US Americans and Brits who lost so few, in comparison. Western leaders continue those wars they began years ago in the Middle East; and are ripe for more wars, for demonizing President Vladimir Putin, hoping still to take over Russia's vast territory with so many resources. So much more money! Hopefully, not so many of the West's people are willing to murder others and to risk their lives for the few super wealthy warmongers.

Notes:

1. Excerpts from December 24, 1922 letter: "Our Party relies on two classes and therefore its instability would be possible and its downfall inevitable...the prime factors in the question of stability are such members of the C.C. [Central Committee] as Stalin and Trotsky. I think relations between them make up the greater part of the danger of a split, which could be avoided, and this purpose, in my opinion, would be served, among other things, by increasing the number of C.C. members to 50 or 100."

   "Comrade Stalin, having become Secretary-General, has unlimited authority concentrated in his hands, and I am not sure whether he will always be capable of using that authority with sufficient caution. Comrade Trotsky, on the other hand...is distinguished not only by outstanding ability. He is personally perhaps the most capable man in the present C.C., but he has displayed excessive self-assurance and shown excessive preoccupation with the purely administrative side of the work..."

   Excerpt from December 25, 1922 letter:

   "Stalin is too rude and this defect, although quite tolerable in our midst and in dealing among us Communists, becomes intolerable in a Secretary-General. That is why I suggest the comrades think about a way of removing Stalin from that post and appointing another man in his stead who in all other respects differs from Comrade Stalin in having only one advantage, namely, that of being more tolerant, more loyal, more polite, and more considerate to the comrades, less capricious, etc." (http://www.historyguide.org/europe/testament.html)

2. See Norman Rich's *Hitler's War Aims Ideology: The Nazi State and the Course of Expansion*. W.W. Norton, 1973, and Wikipedia.

3. Estimates of total deaths during the war vary from 50 to 80 million; between 50-55 million civilians, and 20-25 million military. 17% of 35 million Poles: 5.6/5.8 million civilians, 240,000

military. 10% of 69 million Germans: 1.5-3 million civilians, 4.4-5.3 million military. 4% of 71 million Japanese: 550-800,000 civilians, 2.1-2.3 million military. 3% of China's 520 million population: between 12 and 18 million civilians, over half from starvation and diseases; 3-3.7 million military. 1% of 44 million Italians: 153,000 civilians, 320-340,000 military plus 20,000 conscripted Africans. Many more millions in other nations, including gypsies.

The total numbers of Chinese dead is second to the numbers of Russians. Both countries were victims of the Axis powers, and are now considered enemies of the current Allies, who during the world war lost far fewer people. The allies, except for Poland, lost less than 1% of its peoples compared to 13% Russians. In fact, the greatest percentage of deaths to a population occurred in Poland.

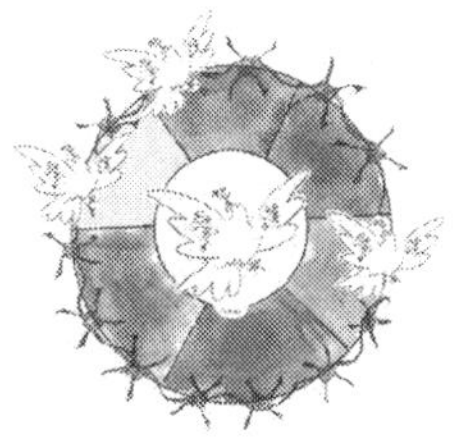

CHAPTER 11
Cold War (A)

PRESIDENT HARRY TRUMAN invited his mentor Winston Churchill to the United States to visit him and offer strategic advice on how to "contain the Communist Soviets".

Churchill delivered an historic oration at Westminster College in Fulton, Missouri, on March 5, 1946. He called for closer Anglo-American cooperation in the post-war world. Best remembered for thunderous warnings of the "threat of Soviet expansionism", cemented in the phrase "Iron Curtain".

Churchill's speech sounded the start of the Cold War in contradiction to the fake news propaganda propagated by Wall Street and Washington DC that it was the Russian bear that started it all.

Churchill sought to divide the good West from the bad East: "From Stettin in the Baltic to Trieste in the Adriatic, *an iron curtain* has descended across the Continent." "The United States stands at this time at the pinnacle of world power. It is a solemn moment for the American Democracy. For with primacy in power is also joined an awe-inspiring accountability to the future…" "If now the Soviet Government tries, by separate action, to build up a pro-Communist Germany in their areas, this will cause new serious difficulties in the British and American zones."

"From what I have seen of our Russian friends [sic] and Allies during the war, I am convinced that there is nothing they admire so much as strength, and there is nothing for which they have less respect than for weakness, especially military weakness. For that reason the old doctrine of a balance of power is unsound. We cannot afford, if we can help it, to work on narrow margins, offering temptations to a trial of strength."

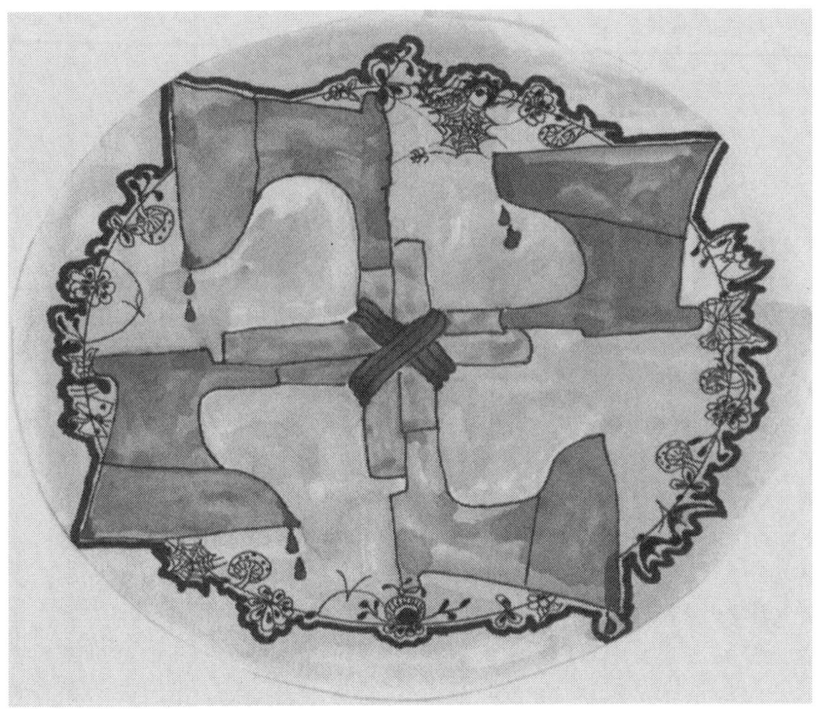

Jette Salling's paraphrase art of John Heartfield's iron and blood ax swastika

Although Harry Truman had not jumped onto Churchill's nuclear war plan against the Soviet Union in July 1945—too busy was Truman then with preparing to "nuke" Japan—he now let his generals consider the idea since his aristocratic friend had declared the Cold War.

In anticipation, the U.S. Joint War Plans Committee (JWPC) produced a draft for Operation Pincher, on March 2, 1946—an equivalent to Churchill's Operation Unthinkable. It was assumed that the Soviet Union had already set up its ring of satellite states to protect its borders, and a worldwide conflict would arise as the Soviets infiltrated more countries beyond that ring. Operation Pincher singled out the Middle East as a flashpoint where U.S. and British interests could be undermined. There might also be incidents in Turkey or Iran, which would compel the Western Allies to retaliate with military force, thereby sparking a Third World War. The original plan envisaged a war sometime between 1946 and 1949.

Something like Operation Pincher had already been put on the drawing board in the autumn of 1945 when the military command "concluded that Soviet forces could easily overrun Western Europe and the Middle East any time before 1948; such an alarming prospect made the US Joint Intelligence Committee calculate the effect of 'blocking' that advance by *unleashing nuclear weapons.*" (1)

So even before Churchill's Iron Curtain-Cold War speech, U.S. jingoists were connecting with him. In February 1946, just a month before Churchill's six-week United States tour, George Kennan had sent his famous "Long Telegram" from the U.S. Mission in Moscow to Washington. The 8,000-word telegram detailed his views on the Soviet Union, and U.S. policy toward it. Like Churchill, Kennan believed the Soviets would do all they could to "weaken power and influence of Western Powers on colonial backward, or dependent peoples." Although the Soviet Union was "impervious to logic of reason," it was "highly sensitive to logic of force." Therefore, it would back down "when strong resistance is encountered at any point." The United States and its allies, Kennan concluded, would have to offer that resistance. His opinion that Soviet expansionism needed to be contained through a policy of "strong resistance" provided the basis for Cold War diplomacy for decades, and Kennan was named U.S. ambassador to the Soviet Union in 1952.

TRUMAN DOCTRINE

Truman delivered this doctrinal speech to Congress on March 12, 1947.

With the "Truman Doctrine", President Harry S. Truman established that the United States would provide political, military and economic assistance to all democratic nations under threat from external or internal authoritarian forces. The Truman Doctrine effectively reoriented U.S. foreign policy, away from its usual stance of withdrawal from regional conflicts not directly involving the United States, to one of possible intervention in far away conflicts. (https://history.state.gov/milestones/1945-1952/truman-doctrine)

The immediate cause for the speech was a recent announcement by the British Government that, as of March 31, it would no longer provide military and economic assistance to the Greek Government in its civil war against the Greek Communist Party. Truman asked Congress to support the Greek Government against the Communists. He also asked Congress to provide assistance for Turkey, since that nation, too, had previously been dependent on British aid.

In fact, Soviet leader Joseph Stalin had deliberately refrained from providing any support to the Greek Communists and had forced Yugoslav Prime Minister Josip Tito to follow suit, much to the detriment of Soviet-Yugoslav relations. [my emphasis]

President Truman requested that Congress provide $400,000,000 worth of aid to both the Greek and Turkish Governments and support the dispatch of American civilian and military personnel and equipment to the region.

Truman's doctrine was guided by his main foreign policy adviser, the self-styled "liberal" George Kennan. The basis for Truman's thinking was fully expressed in Kennan's February 24, 1948 State Department brief, "Review of Current Trends in U.S. Foreign Policy":

> *"Occasionally, it [the United Nations] has served a useful purpose. But by and large it has created more problems than it has solved, and has led to a considerable dispersal of our diplomatic effort. And in our efforts to use the UN majority for major political purposes we are playing with a dangerous weapon which may someday turn against us. This is a situation which warrants most careful study and foresight on our part."*

What this conveys is an escalation in U.S. foreign policy, from "containment" to "pre-emptive" war. It states in subtle terms that God's chosen people should seek economic and strategic world dominance through military means. Henceforth, it would be the United States of America that would determine war policy not the peace-oriented United Nations.

An essential aspect of the Truman Doctrine was the National Security Act signed on September 18, 1947, which created the Central Intelligence Agency (CIA) to gather information and commit covert actions abroad. It is the offspring of the Office of Strategic Services from 1942-45, and many of the first CIA officials came from OSS. To Truman's later regret, the CIA has since gone beyond its origins. Covert actions have become any political and military operation that the agency and the entire government can deny—from fake propaganda to assassinations and paramilitary actions, overthrowing governments and engaging in undeclared wars. (More on this on chapter 18. Read any and all of William Blum's books.)

In 1974, Truman told his biographer, Merle Miller, that the CIA "doesn't just report on wars and the like, they go out and make their own, and there's nobody to keep track of what they're up to. They spend billions of dollars on stirring up trouble so they'll have something to report on. They've become ... it's become a government all of its own and all secret. They don't have to account to anybody." (2)

Despite Truman's disclaimer while in office he allowed CIA agents, including Russian émigrés, to infiltrate the Soviet Union to commit assassinations; sabotage trains, bridges, power plants, arms factories; obtain documents; assist Western agents to escape; promote political struggles within the Communist party and government. Truman had, in effect, created what soon became the Deep State, and *this subversion continues as you read this book.*

But for big business the Truman Doctrine has been a stunning success. The United Nations is but a rubber stamp on all the wars that the United States Military Empire desires as promulgated by what Wall Street deems profitably expedient and necessary. Oh, and serendipity added, they can sell the bloody profitable wars on their video games, in all entertainment, and their news media.

At the end of WWII, the U.S. re-colonized Japan's colonies: South Korea by dividing Korea, which Japan had annexed in 1910; the Philippines, a U.S. possession taken over from Spain in 1898 and occupied by Japan during World War II; and Thailand, a Japanese protectorate during the war.

This U.S. sphere of influence in Asia extended its grip into France's former colonial possessions in Indochina, including Vietnam, Laos and Cambodia, which were under Japanese military occupation during World War II. Indonesia became a U.S. proxy following the establishment of the Hajji Suharto military dictatorship. (3)

The **Greek Civil War** was fought from March 30, 1946 to October 16, 1949 between the government army, and the Democratic Army of Greece (DSE, the military branch of the Greek Communist Party/KKE. Communists had fought as partisans against German and Italian occupation forces. The civil war resulted from a struggle between left and right ideologies that started in 1943. This was the first proxy hot war of the Cold War.

The insurgents were demoralized by the bitter split between Stalin and Tito. In June 1948, the Soviet Union and its satellites broke off relations with Tito. Stalin explained to a Yugoslav delegation that the situation in Greece has always been different from the one in Yugoslavia because the U.S. and Britain would "never permit [Greece] to break off their lines of communication in the Mediterranean".

U.S. aid to Greek fascists, the failure of the DSE to attract sufficient recruits, and the side-effects of the Tito–Stalin split led to victory for government troops. The communist party and other leftist parties and organizations were outlawed and tens of thousands were imprisoned, tortured, murdered, and thousands more fled in exile.

Around 80,000 Greek combatants on both sides were killed, and 200 Brits. There were more Greek casualties than in WWII.

The civil war left Greece with a vehemently anti-communist security establishment, which the Truman Doctrine and the Marshall Plan funded. After the monarchy joined NATO, in 1952, the CIA worked closely with its repressive forces. Gust Avrakotos and Clair George were among the CIA officers. Avrakotos maintained a close relationship with the colonels who would figure in the later coup, and the military juntas (1967-74).

The CIA learned quickly how to prop up rightist and fascistic forces around the world. Next it would be Iran and Guatemala. (See chapter two and William Blum books). The most popular and democratic election in Guatemala's history brought Jacobo Arbenz into power as president, March 15, 1951. He, too, made land reforms for small farmers' benefit, and he did not ban communist and other leftists associations. The United Fruit Company was furious so its CIA organized a coup and put in one of the most ruthless of generals, Castillo Armas, on June 27, 1954.

PALESTINE-ISRAEL

Soviet interests were judged as best protected by a transfer of Palestine "to the collective trusteeship of the three states—the USSR, the US and Great Britain". But the U.S. and Britain opposed this. Britain did not wish to abandon Palestine as basically a colony, because it was needed to guard UK's strategic assets, particularly the approaches to the Suez Canal.

Many Soviets felt connected to Jews because of the Nazi war and the fact that half of Russia's Jews were killed by Nazis. Furthermore, Stalin was dead set on not antagonizing the United States and keeping to the agreements made at the three Big Conferences.

On November 29, 1947 all five Soviet and Eastern European States voted for the creation of the State of Israel. A partition map had been drawn dividing Jews and Palestinians physically but there was to be economic union. Great Britain had been opposed but the U.S. convinced it to change its vote. The U.K. was one of 10 abstaining countries. There were 33 for and 13 against. All Arab and Middle Eastern States opposed partition. The day after the vote, many Palestinians rebelled and the endless war for and against liberation began.

CZECHOSLOVAKIA 1948

The Red Army liberated Czechoslovakia in the autumn of 1944. A National Front of Czechs and Slavs in six political parties formed a government in March 1945. The former president, Edvard Benes returned as president April 2. He was a moderate socialist in the National Social Party and had been president in 1935-8 and president-in-exile thereafter.

On February 25, 1948, Benes, fearful of civil war and possible Soviet intervention, accepted the resignations of the non-Communist ministers and appointed a new government in accordance with the Czechoslovakia Communist Party (KSC). Its leader, Klement Gottwald, continued as prime minister in the government led by Communists and pro-Moscow Social Democrats. The Social Democrats' leader, Zdenek Fierlinger, was a proponent of closer ties with the Communists. The People's National Socialist and Slovak Democratic parties still participated in a coalition, and the National Assembly gave Gottwald's changed government a vote of confidence.

On May 9, parliament approved a new constitution, which declared Czechoslovakia a "people's democracy" under the leadership of the KSC. The constitution was not entirely communist but Benes refused to sign it. At the May 30 elections, voters were presented with a single list from the National Front, which officially won 89% of the vote.

Communists held an absolute majority of seats within the National Front list. This majority grew even larger when the Social Democrats merged with the Communists later in the year. Benes resigned on June 2, and was succeeded by Klement on June 14.

ITALIAN ELECTIONS 1948

The capitalist States had now lost Czechoslovakia. The year before, they had lost any chance of retaking Poland, which held its first post-war election on January 19, 1947. Pro-fascists and other rightist parties were not allowed, and the Democratic Bloc of four socialist, social democratic and Communist parties won a large majority over the three opposition parties. The opposition claimed that the election was stacked against them.

Then came the Italian election, April 18, 1948. It was acrimonious and fanatical. It seemed certain that communists and socialists would win but the newly created CIA performed one of its first of thousands of covert actions for the benefit of big capital.

The election was between two competing visions. On the one hand, a Roman Catholic, conservative and capitalist Italy, represented by the governing Christian Democrats and U.S. imperial interests; on the other hand, a secular, revolutionary and socialist society, represented by the Popular Front, a coalition of the Communist and Socialist parties.

The CD surprisingly got 48% (12 million votes) for 305 seats; Popular Front got 31% (8 million) for 183 seats; other socialists got 7% (1.8 million) for 33 seats.

The Christian Democrats frightened many by claiming that in communist countries, "children send parents to jail", "children are owned by the state", "people eat their own children", and assured voters that disaster would strike Italy if the Left were to take power. Another slogan was, "In the secrecy of the polling booth, God sees you—Stalin doesn't."

Many historians believe that if the U.S./CIA had not intervened the left would have won.

The CIA later admitted giving $1 million to Italian "center parties", and published forged letters in order to discredit the leaders of the Italian Communist Party. "We had bags of money that we delivered to selected politicians, to defray their political expenses, their campaign expenses, for posters, for pamphlets," according to CIA operative F. Mark Wyatt.

"F. Mark Wyatt, a career Central Intelligence Agency officer who played a significant role in the agency's first major cold war covert action, an operation to swing the Italian elections of 1948, died on Thursday in Washington," wrote *The New York Times*, July 6, 2006.

The CIA's continued influencing the political situation in every Italian election for decades. A leftist coalition would not win a general election until 1996. (4)

BERLIN CRISIS 1948-9

In March 1948, the U.S. planned to make only one currency in West Berlin, which the Soviets saw as a threat to economic stability.

Running one city inside the eastern part of Germany with four big powers was bound to create tensions, confusion, and fear among its population. Stalin suggested that a unified, but demilitarized German state be established. He hoped that it would either come under Soviet influence or remain neutral. The U.S. and UK opposed this. Stalin then blockaded Berlin on June 24. The next day, the West introduced the Deutsche mark as the official currency in the western sectors, and started airlifting supplies into West Berlin. The Soviets meant that the single currency violated the Potsdam Agreement. They responded with the *Reichsmark* "sticker", so named because there was a sticker attached. This would henceforth be the legal tender in the eastern sector and the Soviet occupation zone generally. The battle of currencies created a black market that damaged the economy in the east more than in the west.

Both sides escalated their military units. On May 12, 1949, Stalin ended the blockade. In September 1949, the Western powers transformed Western Germany into the independent Federal Republic of Germany. In response the Soviets formed East Germany into the German Democratic Republic, in October, which the U.S. refused to recognize.

After the blockade was lifted, the four occupying States maintained the status quo, whereby each of the former World War II allies governed its own sector and had free access to all other sectors.

NATO 1949

Great Britain, France, Belgium, the Netherlands and Luxembourg signed the Brussels Treaty on March 17, 1948. The treaty provided for collective defense. If any one of these nations was attacked, the others were bound to help defend it. At the same time, Truman instituted a peacetime military draft and increased military spending.

The Marshall Plan was initiated on June 3, using $13 billion (equivalent to $132 billion today) to rebuild Western Europe conditioned on accepting U.S. domination in world policy and cultural imperialism.

On April 4, 1949, the North Atlantic Treaty was signed, creating the NATO military alliance under U.S. leadership. The first of the current 29 members were: United Kingdom, Canada, Belgium, Denmark, France, Iceland, Italy, Luxemburg, the Netherlands, Norway, and Portugal. They agreed to consider any attack against one as an attack against all. After the treaty was signed, many signatories made requests to the United States for military aid. Later in 1949, President Truman proposed a military assistance program, and the Mutual Defense Assistance Program passed the U.S. Congress in October, appropriating $1.4 billion dollars for the purpose of building Western European military forces.

I think it appropriate here to cite part of a 2017 article by retired journalist and author Gaither Stewart. He reminds us of what the European conflict was all about—pre-war, during the war and post-war. From "Definitions: The Bourgeoisie" published here: http://www.greanvillepost.com/2017/10/02/definitions-the-bourgeoisie/

> *"One doesn't forget easily that the bourgeoisie was guilty of creating Fascism. The European and American bourgeoisie propped up Fascism in order to preserve its own social rule. For the basis of its rule, private property and capitalism was threatened by the proletarian revolution that Western Socialists (largely emerging from the same bourgeoisie), still in the throes of nationalism, were never able to pull off. For the European upper bourgeoisie, Fascism was little more than an annoyance that saved their system. World War II was preferable to proletarian revolution. We are witnessing a repetition of that history in the USA today."*
>
> *"The close collaboration of American and European capitalism up until World War II was a confirmation of their secret alliance sans frontières. In the immediate post-war, America's renewed alliance with the residue of Nazi Germany*

against Communist Russia was a resumption of the pre-war Fascist-Capitalist bond against Soviet Russia. In that sense the Fascist-Capitalist blood alliance created by the bourgeoisie of Europe and the USA controlled and protected each other against the working class."

USSR A BOMB

As the Greek civil war was ending, the Soviet Union was able to secretly test its first atomic bomb on August 29, 1949. The U.S. government found out about this to their surprise and dismay. Truman announced the fact publicly on September 23.

Now, there could be a military balance between the two superpowers. Many people, including some scientists and technicians working on the Manhattan Project, felt that the world could be safer if both had the same weapons that could destroy one another and the entire world.

The Soviet Union had begun building this "super-weapon" in 1942, and stepped up the process once the United States dropped its atomic bombs in Japan. Captured German scientists helped both the Soviets and the Yankees with their knowledge, but it was concerned U.S. scientists and peace advocates who were most helpful in passing on to the Soviets important information acquired from the Manhattan Project.

Harry Gold, a chemist and Soviet spy, passed on information he received from at least two persons working on Project: Klaus Fuchs, an Englishman, and David Greenglass, a US American whose parents had been born in Russia. Greenglass was aided by his wife, Ruth, and his brother-in-law Julius Rosenberg. Julius had married Ethel, and it was her brother David who snitched to U.S. authorities. Tried in a lynchmob atmosphere the Rosenbergs were executed on June 19, 1953. The massive solidarity campaign in the United States and around the world did not convince the government to not murder them. Many people viewed them as international heroes, but some on the left betrayed them. (5)

CHINA REVOLUTION

On October 1, 1949, Chinese Communist leader Mao Zedong declared the start of the People's Republic of China (PRC). The announcement ended the full-scale civil war between the Chinese Communist Party

(CCP) and the Nationalist Party, or Kuomintang (KMT), which broke out immediately following World War II. They had fought each other off and on since the CCP began in 1921. At one point, 1926-7, they joined forces to rid the country of warlords, and to shape one untied nation. Suddenly, the KMT turned on the communists and slaughtered thousands.

After the 1927 slaughter, communist forces regrouped and the conflicts continued, leading to the October 1934 Long March when 86,000 communists and families trekked 10,000 kilometers from southeast China to the northwest. Upon arriving at their destiny, in October 1935, only 8,000 had survived. They united with the local communists. CCP-KMT conflicts continued until the Sino-Japanese War, 1937-45. During the civil war, the U.S. provided assistance to their ally Chiang Kai-Shek. It didn't matter that the CCP had been a much better ally against the Japanese enemy—they were communists after all. Gen. MacArthur ordered all Japanese forces in China proper to surrender their arms only to forces of the Nationalist government. They were then forced to fight against Chinese communist forces.

Nevertheless, the better organized and disciplined communists won, not the least because of land reforms in their areas that brought peasants to support them. As the communists were winning, Chiang Kai-Shek fled to Taiwan with 600,000 soldiers and two million sympathizers. Some soldiers went to Burma.

The creation of the PRC completed the long process of governmental upheaval in China begun in October 1911 with the Chinese Revolution. In February 1912, the last imperial dynasty was overthrown and a republic established. Now with communists in power, the United States suspended diplomatic ties with China. Not only did the U.S. support the Nationalist Chinese on Taiwan with money, supplies and weaponry it sent in "China Hands". These were old OSS types and new CIA warriors, some of whom were killed fighting communists. For several years, CIA officials organized thousands of Chinese nationalists brought in from Burma to sabotage economic and military targets, and murder Communist Chinese.

The death toll of the civil war in two stages (1927-37; 1945-9) was at least 17-18 million people, more than half of them non-combatants. And the death toll during the Japanese invasion-occupation 1937-45 was at least 14 million. It was not possible to find the numbers of wounded, or those who died from malnutrition and sicknesses caused by the wars. So many deaths, so much suffering in just 22 years cannot be forgotten. These people do not want more war.

In the 1950s and the 1960s, the Sino-Soviet Dispute broke out, ending the initial communist unity between Red China and Red Russia. An ideological debate between the communist parties made them increasing hostile to one another, and communist parties throughout the world broke up into two: one pro-Soviet, another pro-Maoist. There were also other groupings of New Leftists and non-aligned communists, and several Trotskyist groups.

The key Sino-Soviet debate started over the possibility and worthiness of peaceful coexistence with the capitalist West. Mao Zedong rejected peaceful coexistence as impossible and undesirable to have with belligerent capitalist countries. Ironically, China sided with the U.S. and the rightist Islamic fundamentalists when the Soviet Union sided with the communists and socialists in Afghanistan many years later, and later China sided with racist apartheid South Africa.

In 1961, the CCP formally denounced the Soviet variety of communism as a product of "Revisionist Traitors". Professor of History at Montreal University, Lorenz M. Lüthi, argues:

"The Sino-Soviet split was one of the key events of the Cold War, equal in importance to the construction of the Berlin Wall, the Cuban Missile Crisis, the Second Vietnam War, and Sino-American Rapprochement. The split helped to determine the framework of the second half of the Cold War in general, and influenced the course of the Second Vietnam War in particular. Like a nasty divorce, it left bad memories and produced myths of innocence on both sides." (*The Sino-Soviet Split: Cold War in the Communist World.* Princeton UP, 2010)

But the Korean War came before the split. In the 1950s, the USSR assisted the Chinese communists in their support of the Democratic People's Republic of Korea (DPRK).

KOREAN WAR 1950-3

The Korean War was the first major, direct military operation undertaken by the U.S. in the wake of World War II, a key part in what is euphemistically called "The Cold War". In many respects it was a continuation of the

Second World War whereby Korean lands under Japanese colonial occupation were simply handed over to a new colonial power, the United States of America.

When Japan surrendered, the 38th parallel was established as a temporary boundary between Soviet and U.S. occupation zones. This parallel divided the Korean peninsula roughly in the middle.

After the official ceremonial surrender, September 2, General Douglas MacArthur flew Syngman Rhee to Seoul in his personal airplane, *The Bataan*. Rhee had lived in the U.S. for two decades. He was a right-wing Christian and fanatic anti-communist. The U.S. Army placed him under it as president of the Provisional Government over the objections of the State Department. It was the MacArthur-led military government that provided Rhee with a passport after the State Department refused him one. British historian Max Hastings wrote in *The Korean War* (Simon & Schuster, 1988) that there was "at least a measure of corruption in the transaction", because OSS agent Preston Goodfellow, who provided Rhee with the passport, was apparently promised that if Rhee came to power Goodfellow would be awarded commercial concessions.

From the start of the temporary division of Korea, the United States provoked conflict, which led to the Korean War. Stalin wanted to avoid direct Soviet conflict with the U.S. and did not send troops.

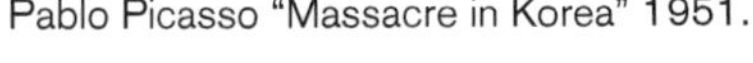

Pablo Picasso "Massacre in Korea" 1951.

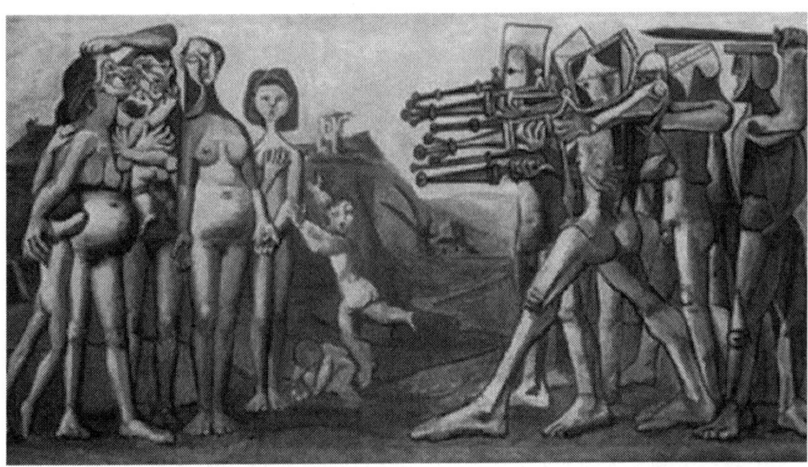

On September 7, 1945, General MacArthur announced that General John R. Hodge was to administer Korean affairs. The Provisional Government of the Republic of Korea, which had operated from China, sent a delegation to Hodge but he refused to meet with them. Hodge also refused to recognize the newly formed People's Republic of Korea (PRK) and its People's Committees, and outlawed it on December 12.

The PRK had an anti-colonial mandate and was at first non-aligned. It proposed the establishment of close relations with the United States, USSR, England, and China. It was opposed to any foreign interference. The PRK started major social reforms: land distribution, laws protecting the rights of workers with minimum wage legislation, and sought the reunification of North and South Korea.

After a millennium of unity, the division of Korea was not welcomed by most Koreans. In September 1946, thousands of laborers and peasants rose up against the U.S.-Rhee Military government. The rebels hoped to stop the scheduled October elections for the South Korean Interim Legislative Assembly. The uprising was quickly crushed. The Rhee government then conducted several military campaigns against left-wing insurgents. Over the course of the next few years, between 30,000 and 100,000 people were killed.

In 1948, the 38th parallel was made a fixed boundary between the Democratic People's Republic of Korea (North Korea) and the Republic of Korea (South Korea), both of which claimed to be the government of the whole of Korea. Bloody border clashes occurred from that point onward until the start of the civil war on June 25, 1950.

According to Bruce Cumings' *The Korean War: A History* (Modern Library, 2010), it is unclear who first crossed the 38th parallel. By June 25, both sides were skirmishing daily. Since there were no impartial observers on hand, the absolute truth is not known. Two days later, without consulting Congress, Truman illegally ordered U.S. ground troops to engage in combat. On the same day, the U.S. convinced the UN to adopt Security Council Resolution 83 for authority to conduct a UN condoned war, euphemistically called a "police action". MacArthur was made head of the UN Command (UNCOM).

The Soviet Union challenged the legitimacy of the war. Its reason: the intelligence upon which Resolution 83 was based was partial as it came from the U.S.; North Korea was not invited as a sitting temporary member of the UN (until 1991), which violated Charter Article 32; and the fighting was beyond the Charter's scope, because initial north-south border fighting was classed as a civil war.

The Soviet Union was boycotting the Security Council at the time, as an act of solidarity with the Chinese government, which demanded it replace the Nationalist Chinese at the UN. Several legal scholars posited that deciding upon an action of this type required the unanimous vote of all permanent members including the S.U.

Bruce Cumings books on Korea dispute what the Western public has been fed since the war. Cumings is a well reputed chairman of the University of Chicago's history department, and author of the two-volume, *The Origins of the Korean War* (Princeton University Press, 1981).

The July 22, 2010 *New York Times* review of Cumings latest Korea book states:

> *"[It] is a squirm-inducing assault on America's moral behavior during the Korean War, a conflict that he says is misremembered when it is remembered at all. It's a book that puts the reflexive anti-Americanism of North Korea's leaders into sympathetic historical context."* (http://www.nytimes.com/2010/07/22/books/22book.html)

The war had "long, tangled historical roots, one in which America had little business meddling." Cumings notes how "appallingly dirty" the war was. It was the Rhee government, and U.S. soldiers and air force that were the worst offenders, contrary to the "American image of the North Koreans as fiendish terrorists."

"The most eye-opening sections of *The Korean War* detail America's saturation bombing of Korea's north. 'What hardly any Americans know or remember,' Mr. Cumings writes, 'is that we carpet-bombed the north for three years with next to no concern for civilian casualties.' The United States dropped more bombs in Korea (635,000 tons, as well as 32,557 tons of napalm) than in the entire Pacific theater during World War II. Our logic seemed to be, he says, that 'they are savages, so that gives us the right to shower napalm on innocents.'"

According to Bruce Cumings, the Korean War "bore a strong resemblance to the air war against Imperial Japan in the second world war, and was often directed by the same US military leaders", including generals Douglas MacArthur and Curtis Lemay.

Although nuclear weapons were not used, what prevailed was the strategy of "mass killings of civilians". In a bitter irony, military targets were safeguarded.

On August 12, 1950, the USAF dropped 625 tons of bombs on North Korea. Two weeks later, the daily tonnage increased to 800 tons, causing the destruction of 78 cities and thousands of villages, as well as crushing huge dams in the final stages of the war, which unleashed massive amounts of water destroying people and buildings. Almost every northern city was wiped out.

The U.S. was not satisfied with saturation bombing of every North Korea city, dropping ten times the firepower of their A-bombs over Japan. The army also dropped canisters filed with disease-infected insects over both North Korea and China. They hoped to wipe out large numbers of people with deadly bacteria and viruses, which they had taken from Japanese experimentations during the Second World War. The Japanese used several thousand captured and abducted Chinese and Russians as guinea pigs. Cholera and anthrax were among the diseases.

The U.S. military granted amnesty to Japanese scientists so they could utilize their knowledge to set up their own similar laboratories. The most well know is at Fort Detrick in Maryland. Chemical-biological warfare has been used by the U.S. over many decades and in many countries. This subject was introduced in chapter six.

Thomas Powell has researched and documented this U.S. genocide. He has many sources, including a British-led scientific commission that interviewed subjects and perpetrators. Read his piece, *Biological Warfare in the Korean War: Allegations and Cover-up, Socialism and Democracy* Vol. 31, No1 March 2017 (http://www.tandfonline.com/doi/full/10.1080/08854300.2016.1265859). Hear an interview with him by Jeff J. Brown. http://chinarising.puntopress.com/2017/07/29/americas-big-lie-about-bioweapon-crimes-in-korea-tom-powell-on-china-rising-radio-sinoland-170729/

"The winter 1950–51 BW [biological warfare] deployment…as spreading infectious disease now enters the repertoire of scorched earth tactics of retreating armies which historically include plundering goods, abducting women and girls, slaughtering civilians and livestock, burning towns, setting forest fires, poisoning wells, and sowing salt."

During a 1952 offensive, "US planes [dropped] bombs of diseased insects and rodents as an offensive tactic to spread panic and cause massive disease outbreaks in military and civilian populations in North Korea and China. Outbreaks of hemorrhagic fever and plague were reported. Both military and civilian populations were infected," wrote Thomas Powell.

Michael Chossudovsky, professor of economics and founder of Global Research delivered a speech, August 1, 2013, on the subject. His speech, "America's War against the People of Korea: The Historical Record of US War Crimes" was made at Tokyo's foreign correspondent's club.

"It is important to understand that these US sponsored crimes against humanity committed in the 1950s have, over the years, contributed to setting 'a pattern of killings' and US human rights violations in different parts of the World. The Korean War was also characterized by a practice of targeted assassinations of political dissidents, which was subsequently implemented by the CIA in numerous countries, including Indonesia, Vietnam, Argentina, Guatemala, El Salvador, Afghanistan, Iraq…More recently, targeted assassinations of civilians, 'legalized' by the US Congress have become, so to speak, the 'New Normal'". (http://www.greanvillepost.com/2017/08/24/americas-war-against-the-people-of-korea-the-historical-record-of-us-war-crimes/)

Chossudovsky said that the "US deliberately sought a pretext, an act of deception, which incited the North to cross the 38th parallel ultimately leading to all out war", and General MacArthur did everything possible to avoid peace.

"This pattern of inciting the enemy 'to fire the first shot' is well established in US military doctrine. It pertains to creating a 'War Pretext Incident' which provides the aggressor a pretext to intervene on the grounds of 'Self- Defense'. It characterized the Japanese attack on Pearl Harbor, Hawaii in 1941, triggered by deception and provocation of which US officials had advanced knowledge. Pearl Harbor was the justification for America's entry into World War II."

The U.S. likes to say that the North Korean attack was a surprise. "But was it a surprise? Could an attack by 70,000 men using at least

70 tanks launched simultaneously at four different points have been a surprise?" Chossudovsky asks.

Stalin convinced the new Communist government to help hold the 38th Parallel. Yet China couldn't sit back and let the U.S. and its allies destroy the entire northern half of Korea and much of its population. Its leaders agreed to counter U.S./UN forces crossing the 38th parallel. At the end of August, the Soviet Union agreed to support Chinese forces with air cover, and China deployed 260,000 soldiers along the Korean border. On September 30, Premier Zhou Enlai warned the U.S. that China was prepared to intervene in Korea if it crossed the 38th parallel. The U.S. ignored his advice. Two hundred thousand Chinese troops entered North Korea on October 25. China's well trained troops became the main challenge.

At a November 30, 1950 news conference, Truman said the use of The Bomb in Korea had always been under "active consideration." But on April 11, 1951 Truman fired MacArthur as supreme commander, because he wanted to go into China and destroy the communist government and army with nuclear weapons. He also believed that he and not the president should be the one to decide when and where to use nuclear bombs. In fact, other U.S. military leaders also proposed using the A-bomb in Korea.

MacArthur's replacement, General Matthew B. Ridgway, requested thirty-eight atom bombs in May 1951.The Joint Chiefs again contemplated use of the bomb in June 1951. In September and October, Operation Hudson Harbor made simulated bombing runs on the North which dropped dummy atomic bombs. In 1953, the Pentagon recommended using A-bombs in memos issued in February, May, June, and July. But by then the Soviet Union also had the bomb.

War casualties were horrendous. Chossudovsky refers to Brian Willson's article, "Korea and the Axis of Evil" (Global Research, October 2006). He wrote that nearly one-third of the 8-9 million- population north of the imposed 38th Parallel was killed during the 37-month long war, perhaps an unprecedented percentage of mortality suffered by one nation due to the belligerence of another. (6)

Extensive war crimes were also committed by U.S. forces against South Koreans as documented by the Korea Truth and Reconciliation Commission (ROK). According to ROK sources, almost one million civilians were killed in South Korea:

"In the early days of the Korean War, other American officers observed, photographed and confidentially reported on such wholesale executions by their South Korean ally, a secretive slaughter believed to have killed 100,000 or more leftists and supposed sympathizers, usually without charge or trial, in a few weeks in mid-1950," taken from Associated Press, July 6, 2008.

Somewhere around five million people were killed in this war.

U.S. sources acknowledge 1.55 million civilian deaths in North Korea, and 215,000 combat deaths. MIA/POW 120,000, 300,000 combat troops wounded. North Koreans figure twice that.

South Korean military sources estimate the number of civilian deaths/wounded/missing at 2.5 million, of which some 990,900 were South Korean.

China acknowledged 114,000 battle deaths, and 34,000 non-battle deaths, plus 340,000 wounded. Some sources indicate that as many as 600,000 Chinese died directly or indirectly from the war.

The U.S. had 33,000 casualties—8,500 battle deaths, 3,000 non-battle deaths, and wounded.

After the Korean Armistice agreement was signed by the new Dwight Eisenhower government and Koreans, on July 27, 1953, a new line was established to separate North and South Korea. This Military Demarcation Line is surrounded by a demilitarized zone. The United States refused to make a peace treaty and is still officially at war with the People's Republic of Korea, which it still refuses to recognize. Even after hostilities ended, the Eisenhower Administration was planning to use the A bomb should China and North Korea violate the armistice.

United States Forces Korea (USFK) was established in 1957. It is described as "a subordinate-unified command of U.S. Pacific Command (USPACOM)", which could be deployed to attack third countries in the region, that is, Russia and China. Department of Defense figures (2013) state there are 37,000 US troops under USFK.

South Korea is a multibillion bonanza for U.S. weapons industry. For the last four years the ROK ranks as the world's fourth largest arms importer. The U.S. accounts for 77% of its arms purchases.

Shortly after the war, the U.S. sent nuclear warheads to South Korea, again in violation of treaties/agreements U.S. governments blithely sign—in this case paragraph 13(d) of the Armistice Agreement, which prohibited the warring factions from introducing new weapons into Korea. These nuclear weapons were withdrawn in 1991, but since then North Korean cities have been targeted with nuclear warheads from U.S. continental locations and from strategic submarines (SSBN).

POST-WAR RUSSIA; STALIN DIES; HUNGARY REBELS

Post-world war Soviet society was calmer than its pre-war phase in various respects. Stalin was seen as the heroic leader of the war, and he was unchallenged. Stalin allowed the Russian Orthodox Church to retain the churches it had opened during the war. Academia and the arts were also allowed greater freedom than they had prior to 1941. In order to promote economic recovery, the government devalued the ruble and abolished the ration-book system. Nevertheless, the USSR experienced a major famine from 1946 to 1947 caused by drought and war devastation.

Ecstatic U.S. political leaders now pushed its power interests onto every continent, acquiring air force bases in Africa and Asia and ensuring pro-U.S. regimes took power throughout Latin America. The U.S. demanded that Stalin withdraw his army from northern Iran; he did so in April 1947.

Despite Stalin's willingness to cooperate with the West, the U.S. infiltrated hundreds of Russian émigrés into the Soviet Union. They committed assassinations, sabotaged trains, bridges, arms and power plants. They gathered information about military and technological installations for the CIA, which ran the infiltrators and created a massive world-wide anti-Soviet propaganda campaign in several languages. They painted Stalin as Hitler, the "most evil dictator alive."

Stalin's health declined in the early 1950s. He brought Nikita Khrushchev to Moscow and made him part of his inner circle. Khrushchev was born in 1894 in the village of Kalinovka, which is close to the present-day border between Russia and Ukraine. He was a metal worker during his youth before Stalin made him a political commissar in Ukraine, in charge of political education and civilian control by the military. In 1937, he headed Ukraine's CCP. He was a political commissar during World War II at Stalingrad (now Volgograd) and elsewhere.

Upon Stalin's death, March 5, 1953, Khrushchev emerged as General Secretary of the Central Committee after an internal power struggle, on September 14, 1953. He was made Chairman of the Council of Ministers (Premier) from March 27, 1958 until succeeded by Leonid Brezhnev as First Secretary and Alexei Kosygin as Premier, on October 14, 1964.

Hoping to eventually rely on missiles for national defense, Khrushchev ordered major cuts in conventional military forces. Khrushchev was responsible for backing the early space program and for several liberal reforms in domestic policy. He has also been characterized for what is called the "de-Stalinization" of the Soviet Union.

On February 25, 1956 he made his famous "secret speech" at the 20th Party Congress. He denounced "Stalin's Purges", of which he had been a part, and forced confessions at trials.

"Khrushchev charged Stalin with having fostered a leadership personality cult despite ostensibly maintaining support for the ideals of communism…As a whole the speech was an attempt to draw the Soviet Communist Party closer to Leninism. However it possibly served Khrushchev's ulterior motives to legitimize and consolidate his control of the Communist party and government, after political struggles with Georgy Malenkov and firm Stalin loyalists such as Vyacheslav Molotov, who were involved to varying degrees in the purges." (https://en.wikipedia.org/wiki/On_the_Cult_of_Personality_and_Its_Consequences)

"The Secret Speech, while it did not fundamentally change Soviet society, had wide-ranging effects. The speech was a factor in unrest in Poland and revolution in Hungary later in 1956, and Stalin defenders led four days of rioting in his native Georgia in June, calling for Khrushchev to resign and Molotov to take over…However, Stalin was not publicly denounced, and his portrait remained widespread through the USSR", even in Khrushchev's office. (See William Taubman *Khrushchev: The Man and His Era*, W.W. Norton, 2003. (https://en.wikipedia.org/wiki/Nikita_Khrushchev)

Mikhail Gorbachev, then a Komsomol official, recalled that young and well-educated Soviets in his district were excited by the speech, while many others decried it, either defending Stalin or seeing little point in digging up the past. Forty years later, after the fall of the Soviet Union, Gorbachev applauded Khrushchev for his courage in taking a huge political risk and showing himself to be "a moral man after all". (https://sourcebooks.fordham.edu/halsall/mod/1956khrushchev-secret1.html)

Khrushchev's speech was a prelude to the Warsaw Pact on May 14, 1955. All Soviet States formed a political and military alliance, which called for non-interference in internal sovereign affairs. Another consequence of the "secret speech", in part, was the uproar in Hungary. The CIA's Radio Free Europe broadcast it, and pro-capitalist, anti-socialist propaganda inside Eastern Europe aimed to encourage revolts. Many students wanted more say in their educational institutions and some workers went on strike. Some Hungarians sought a multi-party electoral system. On October 23, a massive march was met by State Security forces, and an armed rebellion broke out. Soviet soldiers fought with Hungarian government forces and the rebellion ended on November 10. Hundreds of Soviet and Hungarian military-security personnel were killed and a couple thousand wounded. Two to three thousand rebels were killed and 13-15,000 wounded.

Besides the Hungarian rebellion, Khrushchev weathered two potentially doomsday international storms: the Cuban Missile Crisis, and the Berlin Crisis. He helped prevent a world war on both occasions, and he held the Soviet Union together despite sharp differences within party leadership.

BERLIN CRISIS 1958-61

Konrad Adenauer, chancellor (1946-63) of the Federal Republic of Germany (FRG), often made public appeals for German reunification on Western terms. This antagonized Moscow, especially his insistence on the return of German lands annexed after the Second World War by the Soviet Union, Poland and Czechoslovakia.

This '*revanchism*'—combined with West Berlin and the West's general rearmament, capitalism's propaganda to come to the land of freedom, and the economic and demographic drain of some three million citizens—could not be ignored by the Soviets or Eastern Germans.

An expert on the Cold War from both Soviet and Western views, the Russian born and educated Vladislav Zubok is now a professor in the U.S. and England. He is an international history professor at the London School of Economics, and a fellow at the National Security Archives.

I believe him to be a liberal yet generally objective in his understanding and analysis of historical events. I excerpt from his May 1993 piece, "Khrushchev and the Berlin Crisis (1958-1962)".

> *"Unlike the West, which refused to recognize the GDR, Khrushchev had to deal with two German states, Walter Ulbricht's German Democratic Republic and the Federal Republic of Germany. His German policy therefore had always been two-pronged: propping up the East German regime (sic) and containing the FRG."* (https://www.wilsoncenter.org/sites/default/files/ACFB7D.pdf)
>
> *"Khrushchev felt special affinity for the first German state of 'workers and peasants' because he believed it was bought at the price of millions of Soviet lives during the war with the Nazis."*
>
> *"Khrushchev bitterly complained that the United States encouraged West German remilitarization, warning that 'Americans seem not to realize the dangers which their present politics may well bring them.' At present, he said, there was no country in Europe as strong as West Germany."*
>
> *"The Soviet ambassador in Bonn, Smirnov, informed Ulbricht on 5 October 1958 that 'since April ... the situation in West Germany seriously deteriorated and took an unwelcome direction ... The formation of* Bundeswehr *[Germany's armed forces] goes on, atomic armament is now legalized.'"*
>
> *"The menacing rise of West Germany coincided with an aggravation of the economic situation in the GDR. The disparity in living standards...produced an ever growing flight of skilled workers and professionals from the GDR to the FRG through the open border in Berlin."..."Two weeks later [November 1958] Khrushchev in two speeches presented the West with a choice: either the German peace treaty would be signed by all former Allies with occupation rights in Germany, or the Soviet Union would do it alone by reaching a separate treaty with the GDR."*
>
> *"In January 1959 Deputy Prime Minister Anastas Mikoyan arrived in Washington and, during a conversation with Eisenhower, said that he was instructed by Khrushchev to propose to the president '**to end the cold war**.'* [My emphases]

> "'We do not want to fight over Berlin,' *he continued, 'and we hope you don't want to, either.' He had instructions from Khrushchev to propose U.S.-Soviet talks on Germany as a whole and to keep Adenauer out of these talks as a major opponent of the peace treaty. Perhaps Adenauer thought that by delaying a peace treaty he might become stronger, exploit the differences between us and base his position upon force.'"*
>
> *"Khrushchev clearly expected that, with Dulles bedridden and dying from cancer, the U.S. president would be more flexible. But Mikoyan came back convinced that 'the U.S. government still clings to its old position and expresses no wish to undertake any steps' toward a compromise."*

There was to be an east-west summit in Paris on the crisis when the Soviets finally decided to shoot down a U-2 spy plane over their territory. This was the first of thousands of spy planes the Pentagon and CIA routinely flew illegally over Soviet territory that the Soviets decided to shoot down.

The aircraft, flown by Central Intelligence Agency pilot Francis Gary Powers on Mayday 1960, was performing photographic aerial reconnaissance when it was hit by an S-75 Dvina surface-to-air missile and crashed near Sverdlovsk. Powers parachuted safely and was soon captured.

The Eisenhower administration tried to cover up the plane's purpose and mission, but was forced to admit its military nature when the Soviet government came forward with the captured pilot and remains of the U-2 including spying technology, as well as photos of military bases in the Soviet Union taken by the aircraft.

Caught with its pants down, the incident was a great embarrassment to the United States, and prompted a marked deterioration in its relations with the Soviet Union. Powers was convicted of espionage and sentenced to three years imprisonment plus seven years of hard labor. He was released two years later in a prisoner exchange for Soviet officer Rudolf Abel.

In an effort to present a less hostile, more cordial Soviet Union, Khrushchev publicly advocated a policy of "*peaceful coexistence with the United States.*" May Day celebrations in Russia were marked by this newfound cooperative spirit. Absent were the militarized symbols of previous parades. Instead there were children, white doves, and athletes.

Although the U.S. rejected Khrushchev's "peaceful coexistence"—each with its own sphere of influence and territories and don't mess with one another—the Soviets and communist parties the world over operated as if this were world policy. I know this first hand having been a CP member both in the U.S. and in Denmark, six years in all.

Zubok also wrote that Khrushchev did not abandon hopes of reaching out to the U.S.

"In his [April 10, 1961] conversation with [Walter] Lippmann, Khrushchev made it clear that he dreaded the tension over Berlin but could not live with a stalemate on the German question. He acknowledged that here the United States and the Soviet Union had opposite positions, largely because the Americans supported Adenauer and viewed the FRG as a cornerstone of NATO. But, he suggested, if the United States wanted to avoid a showdown, a compromise could be within reach. If the Americans sought guarantees of their interest and prestige in West Berlin they should stop promoting West German interests there. '*We are ready to take any actions that could guarantee [the] freedom and independence of West Berlin and non-interference in its affairs.*'"

"On July 25, Kennedy came up with an ultimatum of his own. He stressed that any unilateral Soviet action against West Berlin would mean war with the United States and announced a panoply of military preparations to make this linkage look credible."

"Khrushchev asked [U.S disarmament negotiator, John] McCloy to tell Kennedy that if he starts a war then he would probably become the last president of the United States of America."

"*The danger of nuclear war made Khrushchev prudent.* However, it was the danger of spontaneous or accidental conflict, as the previous quotation suggests, not U.S. or Soviet nuclear superiority that bothered Khrushchev most. Unlike Ulbricht, he did not even talk about the nuclear balance. Leaders and forces who could unleash a war seemed in his eyes to be more important factors than the number of nuclear missiles or warheads."

"It seems, although Khrushchev does not mention it, that he decided to leave his personal imprint on Ulbricht's idea. Instead of just barbed-wire installations between East and West Berlin he proposed a concrete wall. The construction of the Wall began on 13 August 1961. The failure of the West to react to it other than verbally meant that Khrushchev's plan succeeded. From Soviet diplomats and intelligence Khrushchev learned that the idea of 'something like a Wall' had indeed been afloat in political Washington, especially among people close to or part of the Kennedy Administration, among them Sen. William Fulbright and Arthur M. Schlesinger, Jr. Khrushchev also studied a KGB report on a conference of Western powers in Paris on August 5-7. Soviet intelligence found out that Western powers were not ready to risk a war over West Berlin."

"Conclusion—The Berlin Crisis was not a product of Khrushchev's bad temper. He started the Crisis because he was genuinely concerned by West German designs against the GDR and for nuclear armament. Even the threat of the 'loss' of the GDR was intolerable in those times for the Soviet leadership. Inspired in all likelihood by the crisis in the Far East, *Khrushchev hoped to force the United States to acquiesce to the existence of 'two Germanys' just as they had acquiesced in, indeed supported the existence of, 'two Chinas' in the Far East. Khrushchev always expected to manage the Crisis without resorting to brinkmanship with the United States.*

"As Sino-Soviet relations deteriorated, many in the Kremlin, including Khrushchev himself, began to wonder if it would not be better to ally the Soviet foreign policy with a militant Chinese line rather than to continue to play diplomatic games with the West. The pressures from Ulbricht certainly contributed to this dilemma. These pressures on Khrushchev explain why he quickly turned to brinkmanship in the summer of 1961, when a new U.S. president, John Kennedy, rejected his proposals to negotiate a compromise on Germany. But even then Khrushchev did not succumb to the idea of annexing West Berlin: he preferred to keep it as a 'free city' in order to leave open the chances of a compromise on Germany with the West [Thus the Wall was built]. ...Soviet assistance and the closed border in Berlin helped Ulbricht consolidate communist control in the GDR. The negotiations with the United States on Germany began. *With these achievements at hand, Khrushchev could bring the Crisis to its conclusion.*"

SOVIET SOLIDARITY WITH AFRICAN LIBERATION MOVEMENTS

To introduce this subject, I checked on the internet for information I felt I could trust. When I found the following report, I felt I could trust its contents as an accurate portrayal of much of what the Soviet Union did to aid African liberation movements. I believe this, in part, because my eight years in Cuba allowed me to learn from Cubans what they experienced fighting for African liberation in Angola, and what they told me about the Soviets at that time. My two best Cuban friends had served in Angola.

I have excerpted extensively from this long work, "Cold War History", published first on May 2, 2007. I found it on the Sons of Malcolm blogspot. The author is Vladimir Shubin, deputy director of the Institute for African Studies at the Russian Academy of Sciences. He is also a professor of history and politics. Shubin served in the Soviet Armed Forces (1962-69). For many years he was an active supporter of liberation movements in Southern Africa, in particular as secretary of the Soviet Afro-Asian Solidarity Committee and head of the African Section in the international department of the CPSU. (http://sonsofmalcolm.blogspot.dk/2015/06/soviet-role-in-african-liberation.html)

Unsung Heroes: The Soviet Military and the Liberation of Southern Africa

"This paper attempts to present a 'factual version of history'. It addresses in particular the issues of training the African combatants in the USSR, and the activities of the Soviet teams attached to the ANC, SWAPO and ZAPU as well as to the armed forces of the independent African countries. While most of the Russian archives are still 'sealed off', the author has used oral history sources and memoirs as an invaluable means of painting a picture of the Soviet involvement from the early1960s to 1991.

"It was only in 1970, almost ten years after the co-operation had commenced that, in an interview given for Pravda, the head of the Soviet delegation to the international conference in solidarity with the peoples of the Portuguese colonies, Professor Vassily Solodovnikov, clearly stated for the first time that Moscow was supplying the liberation movements with 'arms, means of transport and communications, clothes and other goods needed for successful struggle' and that 'military and civilian specialists [were] being trained in the USSR'."

"The question of military co-operation between the USSR and the South African liberation movement was raised for the first time when two prominent leaders of the Congress movement and South African Communist Party (SACP), Moses Kotane and Yusuf Dadoo, visited Moscow in late 1961..."

"The Soviet military co-operation with the ANC continued in various forms until the radical political changes took place in Moscow in August 1991 followed by the 'dissolution' of the USSR in December of that year. The Russian press has calculated that between 1963 and 1991, 1,501 ANC activists were trained in Soviet military institutions. However…the total number was well above 2,000. The most striking example of co-operation and mutual trust was Soviet involvement in Operation Vula, aimed at the creation of the armed underground network inside South Africa which began in 1987-88 and extended into the post February-1990 period."

"Moscow's military co-operation with the South West African People's Organisation (SWAPO) and its military wing-the People's Liberation Army of Namibia (PLAN)-developed in a similar way. Most of the top commanders of the PLAN studied in the USSR, including Charles Namoloh (his nom de guerre was 'Ho Chi Minh'), the recently appointed Namibian Minister of Defence. Many hundreds of PLAN fighters were trained in the USSR (including three sons of Sam Nujoma)."

"Apart from military training in the USSR, from 1977 a group of the Soviet military specialists stayed with PLAN in Lubango, in the south of Angola. Its most popular chief (in 1979-83) was 'Colonel Nikolay' (Nikolay Kurushkin, later Major-General and head of the 'Northern Centre'). The mission of the Soviet specialists and advisors was primarily training of the PLAN personnel. However, it appears that their duties in the field sometimes went far beyond this…"

"In the final stage of the liberation struggle in Zimbabwe, a similar group, headed by the late Colonel Lev Kononov, was stationed in Zambia. In addition, hundreds of fighters of the ZAPU wing of the Patriotic Front underwent training with the Soviet specialists in Angola in the late 1970s. They were in the Zimbabwe African People's Union (ZAPU) camp when it was bombed by the Rhodesian Air Force in 1979 and one of them, Warrant Officer Grigory Skakun, died after being hit by a cluster bomb containing ball bearings. Military training of Zimbabweans took place in various areas of the USSR as well."

"In all three cases, for MK, PLAN and the Zimbabwe People's Revolutionary Army (ZIPRA), it was Angola which served as a reliable rear base."

"The Soviet involvement in Angola produced many 'unsung heroes'. The name of the Deputy Commander of Air Transport Wing from the

town of Ivanovo, who risked his life and the lives of his crew to airlift two Katyusha rocket launchers from Brazzaville to Point-Noir, where the runway was unfit for the heavy Antonov transport aircraft, has yet to be revealed. These same rocket launchers were further moved by a Cuban ship to Luanda and played a critical role in rebuffing the attack of Mobutu/FNLA troops against Luanda at the time. According to General Roberto Monteiro 'Ngongo' (the former Angolan Ambassador in Moscow and now Minister of the Interior), all in all, over 6,000 Soviets came to Angola 'to teach in military schools and academies and to train our regular units', and over 1,000 Soviet military visited it for 'shorter periods of time', while 6,965 Angolans underwent military training in the Soviet Union."

"The Soviets suffered casualties in Southern Africa, especially in Angola. According to General 'Ngongo', Soviet military (including aircraft crew members) had been killed in Angola in the period up to 1991. Russian military historians state that by the same date 51 persons were killed or died and 10 were wounded. The 'battle of Cuito-Cuanavale' in 1987-88 was particularly grueling. Two Soviet officers—Colonel Gorb and Lieutenant Snitko—sacrificed their lives while assisting Angolan government forces to rebuff Pretoria's troops.

"The defeat of South Africa and UNITA at Cuito-Cuanavale and the advance of Cuban, Angolan and SWAPO forces towards the Namibian border was possible to a large extent due to supplies of modern Soviet equipment. An extensive Air Defence system based on the Soviet-made anti-aircraft missiles was created in Southern Angola and MIG-23 and SU-22 aircraft proved to be superior to South African weaponry. These developments created favourable conditions for the completion of talks on the settlement in South-Western Africa which opened the way for the independence of Namibia in 1989 and, in the long run, for the abolition of apartheid in South Africa itself in 1994."

Angolan Africans fought a war of liberation against Portugal, backed by South Africa, from 1961 until April 1974 when the green revolutionaries stopped fighting in Portugal's three African colonies. There were three guerrilla movements: MPLA (Marxist Leninist People's Movement for Liberation of Angola), and its sometimes partners and rivals, UNITA and FNLA. They signed an agreement in January 1975 to rule in a coalition but it never worked. They often fought each other. MPLA took the capital, Luanda, and the others held territory in the south. On October 23, 1975, two thousand South African troops crossed into south Angola to support UNITA and FNLA.

On December 3, 1975, China's Vice Premier Deng Xiaoping and Foreign Minister Chiao Kuan-hua met with President Gerald Ford, Secretary of State Henry Kisssinger, and George H.W. Bush, then chief of U.S. liaison in China, to discuss supporting Angolan opponents to the liberation government. Although China had supported MPLA in the past, it switched sides to UNITA and FNLA and therewith became an ally of the United States and the invading apartheid South Africa. UNITA's leader, Jonas Savimbi, got direct support from the CIA and was the darling of the reactionary Heritage Foundation think tank.

From that point forward to May 1991, Cuba was the main on hands supporter of MPLA and its government led by Agostinho Neto. In late

Pablo Picasso's War and Peace, 1951

December, the island-nation sent 25,000 troops, pilots and engineers, and at one point as many as 50,000 military personnel were in Angola. Cuba also sent thousands of medical and educational staff, technicians and construction workers. It lost about 3000 men and women in the solidarity war.

Fidel was overall responsible for leading the decisive battle at Cuito Cuanavale, August 1987-March 1988. This led to a peace agreement, in which Cuba was a major participant.

I was a proud observer when the last Cuban troops arrived in Havana, and reported on that and Nelson Mandela's subsequent trip to Cuba. On the occasion of the 38th anniversary of the start of the Cuban Revolution, July 26, 1991, Nelson Mandela delivered a speech in Matanzas province to praise Cuba for its solidarity:

> *"The Cuban people hold a special place in the hearts of the people of Africa. The Cuban internationalists have made a contribution to African independence, freedom and justice unparalleled for its principled and selfless character."*
>
> *"We in Africa are used to being victims of countries wanting to carve up our territory or subvert our sovereignty. It is unparalleled in African history to have another people rise to the defence of one of us. The defeat of the apartheid army was an inspiration to the struggling people in South Africa! Without the defeat of Cuito Cuanavale our organizations would not have been unbanned! The defeat of the racist army at Cuito Cuanavale has made it possible for me to be here today! Cuito Cuanavale was a milestone in the history of the struggle for southern African liberation!"*

Notes:

1. See the pro-Churchill World Press blog https://weaponsandwarfare.com/2016/10/17/plan-for-wwiii/ ; See also Max Hastings piece, "Operation Unthinkable. How Churchill wanted to recruit defeated Nazi troops and drive Russia out of Eastern Europe." (http://www.dailymail.co.uk/debate/article-1209041/Operation-unthinkable-How-Churchill-wanted-recruit-defeated-Nazi-troops-drive-Russia-Eastern-Europe.html#ixzz4v0YfarN0.) See also Jonathan Walker's *Operation Unthinkable: The Third World War* (History Press, 2013) https://searchworks.stanford.edu/view/10256386

2. Excerpts from Merle Miller's 1974 book, *Plain Speaking: an oral biography of Harry S. Truman*, published after Truman's death.

"Mr. President, I know that you were responsible as President for setting up the CIA. How do you feel about it now?

"Truman: I think it was a mistake. And if I'd know what was going to happen, I never would have done it...Now, as nearly as I can make out, those fellows in the CIA don't just report on wars and the like, they go out and make their own, and there's nobody to keep track of what they're up to. They spend billions of dollars on stirring up trouble so they'll have something to report on. They've become ... it's become a government all of its own and all secret. They don't have to account to anybody.

"That's a very dangerous thing in a democratic society, and it's got to be put a stop to. The people have got a right to know what those birds are up to. And if I was back in the White House, people would know. You see, the way a free government works, there's got to be a housecleaning every now and again, and I don't care what branch of the government is involved. Somebody has to keep an eye on things.

"And when you can't do any housecleaning because everything that goes on is a damn secret, why, then we're on our way to something the Founding Fathers didn't have in mind. Secrecy and a free, democratic government don't mix. And if what happened at the Bay of Pigs doesn't prove that, I don't know what does. You have got to keep an eye on the military at all times, and it doesn't matter whether it's the birds in the Pentagon or the birds in the CIA."

Truman wrote an article, "Limit the CIA Role to Intelligence," published in the *Washington Post*, December 22, 1963: "For some time I have been disturbed by the way CIA has been diverted from its original assignment. It has become an operational and at times a policy-making arm of the Government. This has led to trouble and may have compounded our difficulties in several explosive areas,"

The former head of the OSS, General William (Wild Bill) Donovan, who played a leading role in the new CIA, believed differently: "In a global and totalitarian war, intelligence must be global and totalitarian." http://www.nytimes.com/2007/07/22/books/chapters/0722-1st-wein.html

The CIA didn't like what Truman said about it. https://www.cia.gov/library/center-for-the-study-of-intelligence/kent-csi/vol20no1/html/v20i1a02p_0001.htm

3. Indonesia became independent from the Netherlands at the end of WWII and the nationalist liberation leader Kusno Suharno became president from August 1945 to March 1967. Suharno was able to unite all ethnic and religious groups without bloodshed. Soon he embraced world peace and friendship with the Soviet Union. But one of his generals, Hajji Suharto, launched an internal war against all leftists (1965-1966). Military massacres eliminated the entire Communist party (PKI) membership, other leftist and unionist opposition, and ethnic Chinese. Between one and three million people were killed. Suharto ruled from then on, removing Suharno officially in March 1967. He died under house arrest in 1970. The U.S. backed the army and Muslim groups, who slaughtered and tortured countless numbers of people. Decapitated heads were paraded through the streets as if in a carnival. (https://www.wsws.org/en/articles/1999/07/indo1-j19.html)

4. See: "NATO's Secret Armies. Operation Gladio and Terrorism in Western Europe", by Daniele Ganser. October 2005.

5. One of those who betrayed the brave Rosenbergs was the founder and chief editor of "In These Times", James Weinstein. He wrote an exuberant and cathartic review of Ronald Radosh's just released book, *The Rosenberg File: A Search for the Truth* (Henry Hold, 1983). Weinstein had believed in the Rosenbergs' guilt but supported them despite his opposition to collaboration, and now he was relieved to see that the truth was corroborated and by a fellow leftist. I was appalled. The book was largely based on FBI files with the aim of proving that both Rosenbergs were guilty of espionage and therefore their sentence justified.

   At the time, I was "ITT" Denmark correspondent. I immediately wrote a scathing resignation. Had the Rosenbergs helped the world balance of weapons in any way, they were heroes. The traitor was Radosh, and now this so-called progressive editor Weinstein. Radosh had been in the Communist Party and, like Weinstein, had demonstrated for the Rosenbergs. I foresaw that Radosh would sell completely out and side with humanity's enemy. He has since written against the left and praises capitalism. Today, Radosh is "adjunct fellow" at the Herman Kahn-founded reactionary Hudson Institute think tank. Kahn was a nuclear weapons militarist spokesman, a "Dr. Strangelove" type. Rosdosh is still listed as a founding sponsor of "In These Times".

6. S. Brian Willson is a Vietnam veteran, peace activist, and writer. His essays are posted on his website, www.brianwillson.com. He published a small autobiography, *On Third World Legs* (Charles Kerr, 1992), which describes how he was intentionally run over by a U.S. Government munitions train accelerating to over three times the 5 mph legal speed limit during a peaceful protest in California in 1987. He walks on two prostheses since losing each leg below the knee.

CHAPTER 12
Cold War (B)
Vietnam War 1961-75: US-VN-Soviet-China

He's 5 foot 2 and he's 6 feet 4
He fights with missiles and with spears
He's all of 31 and he's only 17.
He's been a soldier for a thousand years

He's a Catholic, a Hindu, an atheist, a Jain
A Buddhist, and a Baptist and a Jew.
And he knows he shouldn't kill
And he knows he always will kill
You for me my friend and me for you

And He's fighting for Canada.
He's fighting for France.
He's fighting for thc USA.
And he's fighting for the Russians.
And he's fighting for Japan
And he thinks we'll put an end to war this way.
And he's fighting for democracy,
He's fighting for the reds
He says it's for the peace of all.
He's the one, who must decide,
who's to live and who's to die.
And he never sees the writing on the wall.
But without him,

how would Hitler have condemned him at Dachau?
Without him Caesar would have stood alone
He's the one who gives his body
as a weapon of the war.
And without him all this killing can't go on

He's the universal soldier
And he really is to blame
His orders comes from
far away no more.

They come from him.
And you and me.
And brothers can't you see.
This is not the way we put an end to war
(Buffy St. Marie's Universal Soldier)

ON THE DAY that the Vietnamese people kicked out the invading Yankees—and that was the international working class day, May I, in 1975—I listened to a promotional recording I had kept for years without playing it. It was a song about the "War is Over" given to me by the producer. The idea was for the anti-war/peace movement in Los Angeles where I was an activist and organizer to use it. The song meant to inspire the end of the Vietnam War but I thought it too subtle and optimistic so I did not promote it but promised him I would use it once the Vietnamese won. After 15 years of anti-war activism, Vietnam won so now I could play it and I did repeatedly, crying on and off for hours—*Just reading these sentences out loud I break out in tears and heartache.*

France began milking Southeast Asia in the mid-1800s. It officially occupied and colonized Vietnam, Laos, Cambodia and Thailand into French Indochina from 1887 to 1954 when it was defeated, and signed peace and independence accords at the Geneva Conference (April 26-July 20).

During World War II, Vichy France had allowed Japan to occupy French Indochina. In 1941, the League for the Independence of Vietnam was formed under the leadership of Ho Chi Minh. This national liberation front fought the Japanese and did so with the blessing and some material assistance from the United States.

Upon Japan's peace signing ceremony, September 2, 1945, the Vietnamese liberation forces declared their independence in Hanoi and established the Democratic Republic of Vietnam (DRV) with Ho Chi Minh as president. U.S. warplanes flew overhead in a salute to Ho's inauguration.

Ho Chi Minh thought highly of many aspects of the United States and used its Declaration of Independence in Vietnam's new constitution, and France's rights of men as well:

> *"All men are created equal. They are endowed by their Creator with certain inalienable rights, among them are Life, Liberty, and the pursuit of Happiness." The Declaration of the French Revolution made in 1791 on the Rights of Man and the Citizen states: "All men are born free and with equal rights, and must always remain free and have equal rights." "In a broader sense, this means: All the peoples on the earth are equal from birth, all the peoples have a right to live, to be happy and free."*

But France would not abide such impudence. It started the First Indochina War, supported by British soldiers and recently captured Japanese soldiers.

Ho Chi Minh wrote numerous letters to President Harry Truman and the State Department asking for help in finding a peaceful solution for his country in its independence from France. He was ignored. President Roosevelt had not wanted France to retake Indochina once the Allies would win the war but cold warrior Truman switched sides and supported the colonialists.

The United States provided aid to the French from early 1950s, including some weapons and mechanics. The most significant aid came from the CIA through one of its first proprietaries, Civil Air Transport (CAT). During the Second Indochina War, CAT changed its name to Air America. The airline had originally belonged to the rogue General Claire Chennault, which he used to aid Chiang Kai-shek forces.

Proprietaries "are corporations secretly owned by an intelligence agency that do business as private companies, or appear to. They provide useful cover for agents and launder money for covert operations. They also provide contacts with bona fide businesses to gather intelligence and facilitate covert operations. But they are open to abuse and are very difficult to police." (1)

Tad Szulc, an investigative journalist expert on "the intelligence community" wrote about CIA front corporations for the "New York Magazine", January 20, 1975.

"The holding company for the CIA's corporate empire is the Pacific Corporation located in Washington. Pacific, whose subsidiaries are said to employ some 20,000 people worldwide, was incorporated in Dover, Delaware, on July 10, 1950… [It had $200 million in "sales" in 1972.]

"The Pacific Corporation owns such operational CIA companies as Air America…C.A.T.…a Taiwan-based airline often used by the CIA…"

CAT aircraft were flown by CIA "civilian pilots" without the U.S. flag emblem. Two U.S. pilots were shot down towards the end of the First Indochina war: James McGovern Jr. and Wallace Buford. Once McGovern's skeleton was found, President Jacques Chirac awarded him the Legion of Honour (2005).

U.S. Chairman of Joint Chiefs of Staff at the time, Admiral Arthur W. Radford, offered France nuclear weapons to win its last battle at Dien Bien Phu. But France rejected the gift. (2)

After France's attempted re-colonization of Indochina failed, an agreement to temporarily partition the country in two with a demilitarized zone at the 17th parallel was reached at the Geneva Conference, April 27, 1954.

The Second Indochina War, best known as the Vietnam War, began once the United States took over from France. North Vietnam's government sought unity of the whole country but the U.S. put in Dinh Diem, October 1955, as its preferred president for South Vietnam, or the Republic of Vietnam (RVN). The Geneva Conference treaty called for elections for all of Vietnam in two years. Neither Diem nor President Dwight D. Eisenhower allowed this election because, as Eisenhower wrote in his memoirs, perhaps 80% of all Vietnamese would have voted for the DRV with Ho Chi Minh as president. (3)

So, a new war was launched to prevent Vietnamese sovereignty. The United States began its involvement officially—"Vietnam Conflict"—on November 1, 1955 when President Truman deployed the Military

Assistance Advisory Group (MAAG) to Southeast Asia. The first official fighting between the National Liberation Front (NLF) and the South Vietnam army (RVN) took place on September 29, 1959 but there had been a growing insurgency since December 1956. The Vietnam War Memorial reports U.S. casualties as early as 1957.

While the NLF mainly fought a guerrilla war, its northern ally, The People's Army of Vietnam (NVA) engaged in conventional warfare, some times with large forces. U.S. and its South Vietnamese forces relied on air superiority and overwhelming firepower to conduct search and destroy operations, massive artillery weaponry, and ground forces. The U.S. conducted large-scale strategic bombing campaigns against North Vietnam, also in Laos and Cambodia later on.

The North Vietnamese army was supported by the Soviet Union, China and other communist allies. U.S.—South Vietnam was supported by South Korea, Canada, Australia, New Zealand, Thailand and other anti-communist allies. This conflict is therefore considered a Cold War-era proxy war.

The North Vietnamese government and the NLF fought to implement the Geneva Conference: to reunify Vietnam. They viewed the conflict as a colonial war and a continuation of the First Indochina War. The U.S. government viewed its involvement as part of the "domino theory", a wider containment policy, with the stated aim of stopping the spread of communism. Incidentally, Vietnam also has many billions of tons of several minerals, including titanium most useful for aerospace and military purposes.

President Lyndon B. Johnson came to the same conclusion as his murdered predecessor: you can't beat a people determined to control its own destiny. The liberation movement could not be crushed by a proxy army only interested in fighting because of a salary and under forced conscription. Short of nuclear war, an all-out conventional war was necessary. But a convenient excuse to invade North Vietnam was necessary. Enter the Gulf of Tonkin.

THE GULF OF TONKIN LIE

"Lyndon Johnson interrupted TV broadcasts shortly before midnight to announce that two US ships in the Gulf of Tonkin had come under fire in international waters, and that in response to what the president described as this 'unprovoked' attack, "air action is now in execution" against "facilities in North Vietnam which have been used in these hostile operations", so wrote DD Guttenplan for *The Guardian*, August 2, 2014. (https://www.theguardian.com/commentisfree/2014/aug/02/vietnam-presidents-lie-to-wage-war-iraq)

This alleged attack, on August 4, 1964, would have been perfectly legitimate against an intruding warship. But it never happened. Once LBJ announced the lie, he sent 64 bombing sorties. They destroyed an oil depot, a coal mine and a significant part of the North's navy. Three days later, Congress passed a resolution authorizing "the president, as commander-in-chief, to take all necessary measures to repel any armed attack against the forces of the US and to prevent further aggression".

Daniel Ellsberg had just started work at the Pentagon. He was a young mathematician who had served as a captain in the marines, and became an analyst at the war think tank Rand Corporation. Ellsberg was among the first to receive the classified "flash" signal from the *USS Turner Joy*, the destroyer that was supposedly attacked. He knew that LBJ lied and disillusionment set in. This led him to leak the top secret Pentagon Papers seven years later, with the help of Anthony Russo.

Secretary of Defense Robert McNamara created the Vietnam Study Task Force, June 17, 1967, in order to write an "encyclopedia of the Vietnam War". Although LBJ stated the war was aimed to secure an "independent, non-Communist South Vietnam", a January 1965 memo by McNamara stated the purpose was not that but rather to "contain China".

Ellsberg was close to the task force and was able to photocopy thousands of pages of its report. In March 1971, Ellsberg gave *New York Times* reporter Neil Sheehan 43 volumes. The newspaper announced it would publish, and the government sought and was granted a prior restraint injunction. The *Washington Post* then received some pages and reported on them in defiance of the court order and to support the *NYT* and free press. On June 30, 1971, the Supreme Court voted 6-3 against the government, and the papers were published. Immediately, opposition to the war flourished as the lies and brutality were revealed.

In the 2003 documentary *The Fog of War*, Robert McNamara admitted that the August 4 Gulf of Tonkin attack never happened. In 2005, an internal National Security Agency historical study was declassified. It concluded that *USS Maddox* had briefly engaged the

North Vietnamese Navy on August 2, but that there were no North Vietnamese naval vessels present during the incident of August 4. The report stated that in the August 2 incident, Captain Herrick ordered gun crews to open fire if the "enemy" ships approached within ten thousand yards. *Maddox* fired three rounds to warn off the N.V. ships. This initial action was never reported by the Johnson administration.

Coincidental to my final edit of this manuscript, I saw the film, *The Post*. I was impressed by its accuracy and truthfulness including how close the newspapers *Post* and *NYT* were to the government and specific personages, such as the relationship between *The Post* owner Katherine Graham and Robert McNamara, and its chief editor Ben Bradlee and the Kennedy family. One moving scene that surprised me was when Graham confronts her friend McNamara for lying, for knowingly sending American boys to kill and get killed when he and the government leaders knew they could not win the war; that prolonging the war was only to "save face".

Of course, movie producer Steven Spielberg wants us to feel good about the main characters, to trust them as persons and their media work, especialy in an age when the US and western media have become almost openly an Orwellian machine of disinformation at the service of the global capitalist empire, "stenographers to power," and the Washington Post, in particular, now with deep commercial and organizational ties to the CIA, has spearheaded campaigns to stifle and criminalise dissent. I go more into what has happened to these and other mass media in chapter 17.

Today, as evidenced by the appalling accumulating lies underscoring the "Russiagate" media obsession, the media would not be as daring as some were then; nevertheless reporters and editors had to know what they could and could not report. In my own life at the time of the Pentagon Papers and Watergate, I was a freelance reporter as well as a determined anti-war activist. I was even a stringer for *The Post* during the Watergate coverage and was offered a chance to take its training course for a full time job. I had to turn it down as I knew working for the paper on staff would require self-censorship.

CHEMICAL-BIOLOGICAL WARFARE

One of the most horrendous aspects of U.S. military behavior was (and continues to be) the widespread use of chemical-biological warfare. The Kennedy administration authorized the use of chemical weapons in 1961-2 to destroy rice crops. After Kennedy's murder, the Lyndon Johnson government escalated the use of chemicals in large parts of the countryside, in order to prevent the NLF from being able to hide their weapons and encampments under the foliage.

Operation Ranch Hand used herbicides produced by Dow Chemical Company and Monsanto, and other war-profiteering companies. Napalm was also produced to burn plants and human skin. The defoliants were distributed in drums marked with color-coded bands. They included the "Rainbow Herbicides"—Agent Pink, Agent Green, Agent Purple, Agent Blue, Agent White, and most famously, Agent Orange, which included dioxin as a by-product of its manufacture. The U.S. Veterans Administration lists prostate cancer, respiratory cancers, multiple myeloma, Diabetes mellitus type 2, B-cell lymphomas, soft-tissue sarcoma, chloracne, porphyria cutanea tarda, peripheral neuropathy, and spina bifida in children of veterans exposed to Agent Orange.

Between 1961 and 1967, the U.S. Air Force sprayed 20 million U.S. gallons (75,700,000 liters) of concentrated herbicides over 6 million acres/24,000 km of crops and trees. In 1965, *42% of all herbicides were sprayed over food crops.* Another purpose of herbicide use was to drive civilian populations into RVN-controlled areas.

Once the war ended, the UN reported that 13% of Vietnam land would never be fertile again. Chemicals continue to change the landscape, cause diseases and birth defects, and poison the food chain. As of 2006, the Vietnamese government estimated that there were over 4,000,000 victims of dioxin poisoning in Vietnam. In some areas of southern Vietnam, dioxin levels remain at over 100 times the accepted international standard. (http://www.history.com/topics/vietnam-war/agent-orange; https://www.theguardian.com/world/2003/mar/29/usa.adrianlevy)

AMERICAN ASSASSINATIONS, TORTURE, RAPE, DRUG SMUGGLING

Germ warfare was just one of many methods employed to "eliminate the enemy." The CIA's Phoenix Program aimed directly at the cadre of the Vietnamese insurgency. Picking off one at a time, the CIA assassinated about 40,000 Vietnamese defenders and their families between 1965 and 1972. They otherwise "neutralized" another 40,000 people by purposefully inflicting excruciating pain through torture and rape. They also incarcerated half-a-million others in "pacification" concentration camps. (4)

When Nixon extended the war into Laos and Cambodia, the CIA increased its business with narcotics (mainly opium later converted to heroin) by using its local contacts there and in Burma and Thailand to create a triangular drug route. Some drugs were even transported on its private Air America company planes, and some on military planes. So crass were these patriotic spooks that they used dead American soldiers to hide their drugs sewn inside their carcasses when transporting them to the U.S. In its own homeland, the CIA would sell these drugs through contacts, making money while keeping the natives down.

Here are just a few examples of material that can be found about this patriotic activity.

"Other C.I.A. proprietaries have spawned criminal activities. Air America operated a substantial air transport business. It also helped conduct the covert war in Laos. Local 'assets' -- Laotians employed by C.I.A. agents—were soon transporting narcotics on the airline." (1)

"*Drug feared sent in bodies of G.I.'s*", headlined the *NYT* December 17, 1972. "An eight-year smuggling conspiracy brought heroin into the United States inside the bodies of soldiers killed in Vietnam, according to testimony from military and customs men in Federal court here."

"During the Vietnam War, the amount of heroin, which was exported to the United States, became so immense that the operations could not remain clandestine. Consequently, in the 1960s, it became prudent for CIA operatives to stash heroin in caskets of dead Americans as well as in body bags, areas, which would be least, searched. When the bodies of American GIs were flown to military bases on the West coast, the heroin could be easily removed. In addition, boxes and crates, which were sent back to the states, carried heroin and coded labels alerted CIA operatives as to where to look." (5)

"On the government side, the two main Golden Triangle runners were Ted Schackley and Thomas Clines—the same two men who ran Operation Mongoose (the plot to take out Fidel Castro). Thus, from 1960-1975, the CIA deployed a secret force of 30,000 Hmong tribesmen to fight the Laotian Communists. They also created heroin labs in this area; then brought it out via their own private airline—Air America."

Drug Enforcement Director Robert Bonner told CBS News in 1993 that the CIA was also shipping cocaine from Venezuela. (https://www.scribd.com/document/131231070/60-MINUTES-Head-of-DEA-Robert-Bonner-Says-CIA-Smuggled-Drugs)

Muckraker Douglas Valentine told Lars Schall, September 22, 2017: https://www.counterpunch.org/2017/09/22/the-cia-70-years-of-organized-crime/

"Everything the CIA does is illegal, which is why the government provides it with an impenetrable cloak of secrecy. While mythographers in the information industry portray America as a bastion of peace and democracy, CIA officers manage criminal organizations around the world. For example, the CIA hired one of America's premier drug traffickers in the 1950s and 1960s, Santo Trafficante, to murder Fidel Castro. In exchange, the CIA allowed Trafficante to import tons of narcotics into America. The CIA sets up proprietary arms, shipping, and banking companies to facilitate the criminal drug trafficking organizations that do its dirty work. Mafia money gets mixed up in offshore banks with CIA money, until the two are indistinguishable."

"The CIA officer who created the Phoenix program, Nelson Brickham, told me this about his colleagues: 'I have described the intelligence service as a socially acceptable way of expressing criminal tendencies.'"

"The US military resisted being involved in this repugnant form of warfare (modeled on SS Einsatzgruppen-style special forces and Gestapo-style secret police)...but got hooked into providing soldiers to flesh out Phoenix. That's when the CIA started infiltrating the military's junior officer corps. CIA officers Donald Gregg (featured by the revisionist war monger Ken Burns in his Vietnam War series) and Rudy Enders (both of whom I interviewed for my book *The Phoenix Program*), exported Phoenix to El Salvador and Central America in 1980, at the same time the CIA and military were joining forces to create Delta Force and the Joint Special Operations Command to combat 'terrorism' worldwide using the Phoenix model. There are no more conventional wars, so the military, for economic and political reasons, has become...the de-facto police force for the American empire, operating out of 700 + bases around the world."

(This lucrative drug business continues today in Afghanistan, which is a main reason why that long-lost war exists. Chapter 18)

Besides using Laos for its drug operation, the CIA and U.S. military destroyed much of the country with bombings between 1964 and 1973. It was the *most bombed country in the history of warfare*, even more bombs than during the entire Second World War—some 260 million bombs, of which it is estimated that 80 million did not explode. This figures out to be *eight bombs per minute over a nine year period* in 580,000 bombing raids. Many were the dreaded clusters, which still kill and injure people, around 50,000 since the war. A similar number of people were killed and wounded during the bombings. (http://legaciesofwar.org/about-laos/secret-war-laos/)

In Cambodia, bombs and tanks killed 300,000 people between 1967 and 1975. Operations Freedom Deal—note the sardonic Orwellian name—and Operation Menu dropped more than 540,000 tons of bombs and killed upwards to 150,000 people. (https://en.wikipedia.org/wiki/Operation_Freedom_Deal)

TET OFFENSIVE

The Tet Offensive was a coordinated series of North Vietnamese and NLF attacks on more than 100 cities and towns, and outposts in South Vietnam, conducted in 1968 in three phases—January-March, May-June, August-September.

The offensive aimed to break the military stalemate, to foment more rebellion among the South Vietnamese population, and to encourage the United States to begin to withdraw. It was audacious, costly in lives lost, but successful. News coverage of the massive offensive, which included an unsuccessful attack on the U.S. embassy, shocked the U.S. population, and encouraged greater anti-war protests throughout the society, also in Europe, and parts of Asia.

The liberation forces of north and south suffered 112,000 casualties, 45,000 killed. U.S.-South Vietnam forces suffered 50,000 casualties, 10,000 killed. Another U.S. casualty was the demoralization that set in amongst its soldiers.

GIs began smoking marijuana and hashish already early on in the war. The plant grew profusely throughout Southeast Asia. After the Tet Offensive LSD was used too, but heroin became the drug of choice—from mellow yellow to just flaking out, ignoring the pain and bloodshed. The Army estimated that in the early 1970s, 15% of its soldiers were taking heroin. While some tried to mellow out, others took their war frustrations out on their officers.

The term *fragging* is used to describe the deliberate killing or attempt by a soldier of another, usually officers and sergeants. The word was coined in Vietnam by U.S. military personnel by killing officers who were deemed incompetent, aggressive or otherwise considered a danger with untraceable fragmentation grenades.

The high number of *fragging* incidents was symptomatic of the unpopularity of the war and the breakdown of discipline in the U.S. armed forces. Documented and suspected fragging incidents totaled around nine hundred from 1969 to 1972.

One of the best Western mass media journalists working in Vietnam was John Pilger. His first film documentary, *The Quiet Mutiny*, 1970, describes the *fragging* phenomenon. His motto is also one of mine: *"It is not enough for journalists to see themselves as mere messengers without understanding the hidden agenda and the message of myths that surround."* (http://johnpilger.com/videos/vietnam-the-quiet-mutiny)

A combination of the Tet Offensive, the growing unpopularity and protests against the war at home, and demoralization among the troops caused President Johnson to stop escalating the war.

PEOPLE'S REPUBLIC OF CHINA SUPPORTS VIETNAM

In 1950, the People's Republic of China extended diplomatic recognition to the Viet Minh's Democratic Republic of Vietnam and sent weapons, as well as military advisers to assist them in its resistance war against French invaders. The first draft of the 1954 Geneva Accords was negotiated by French Prime Minister Pierre Mendès France and Chinese Premier Zhou Enlai who, fearing U.S. intervention, urged the Viet Minh to accept a partition at the 17th parallel.

China subsequently supported North Vietnam when the U.S. took over the colonialist war. This aid included finances and the deployment of military personnel in support roles. In the summer of 1962, Mao Zedong agreed to supply Hanoi with 90,000 rifles and guns free of charge. Starting in 1965, China sent anti-aircraft batteries and engineering battalions to North Vietnam to repair the damage caused by U.S bombing. It helped rebuild roads and railroads, transport supplies, and performed other civilian works. This freed North Vietnamese army units for combat in the South.

China sent a total of 320,000 troops (25-45,000 combat troops), 1,000 of whom were killed. The Chinese military claims to have caused 38% of U.S. air losses in the war, 1,707 aircraft. China asserted that its military and economic aid to North Vietnam and the NLF totaled $20 billion (approx. $143 billion in 2015). Included in that aid were donations of five million tons of food to North Vietnam—equivalent to NV yearly food production in a single year. From 1964 to 1975, China provided North Vietnam with two million guns, 65,000 artillery pieces, 560 tanks, 164 planes and 15,700 automobiles. (Wikipedia gathered statistics)

SOVIET UNION CLASPS VIETNAM

Soviet ships in the South China Sea gave vital early warnings of B-52 bombers advancing on NLF forces. The Soviet Union supplied North Vietnam with medical supplies, arms, tanks, planes, helicopters, artillery, anti-aircraft missiles and other military equipment. Soviet crews fired Soviet-made surface-to-air missiles at U.S. F-4 Phantoms.

Some Russian sources indicate that between 1953 and 1991, the hardware donated by the Soviet Union included 2,000 tanks, 1,700 APCs, 7,000 artillery guns, over 5,000 anti-aircraft guns, 158 surface-to-air missile launchers, 120 helicopters. The Soviets sent North Vietnam annual arms shipments worth $450 million. Soviet military schools and academies trained 10,000 Vietnamese soldiers. Following the collapse of the Soviet Union in 1991, Russian officials acknowledged that the Soviet Union had stationed up to 3,000 troops in Vietnam during the war, and 6,500 officer and 4,500 soldier observers. Over a dozen Soviet citizens lost their lives in the conflict. (Wikipedia)

NORTH KOREA JOINS IN

In early 1967, North Korea sent a fighter squadron to North Vietnam to back up the defense of Hanoi. They stayed through 1968; 200 pilots served. In addition, at least two anti-aircraft artillery regiments were sent. North Korea also sent weapons, ammunition and two million sets of uniforms.

CUBA A BROTHER INDEED

The contribution to North Vietnam by the Republic of Cuba has been recognized several times by representatives of the Democratic Republic of Vietnam. Fidel Castro mentioned in his discourses the Batallón Girón (Giron Battalion), the engineering contingent and military advisors. Fidel showed his personal support by visiting North Vietnam.

U.S. AND ALLY TROOPS, HARDWARE AND CASUALTIES

The United States sent 8.6 million military personnel to Vietnam/ Southeast Asia over the war years; 2.2 million served in combat zones. At the peak, in 1968, there were 536,000 U.S. soldiers in Vietnam.

U.S. Casualties: Killed 58,300 (47,424 in combat), wounded 153,000, missing 1,600. Between 70,000 and 300,000 soldiers/veterans committed suicide; 700,000 suffered psychological trauma. This is an extraordinary statistic.

Over 100,000 deserted the battlefield. Many ended in Canada where they were generally protected. 210,000 draftees escaped service as war resisters. 30-40,000 went to Canada where they were largely appreciated. The day after President Jimmy Carter was inaugurated, January 21, 1977, he offered pardons to all draft resisters. Half of those in Canada stayed. The Pentagon learned from the resistance movement and abolished the draft at the end of the war.

The amount of military equipment used: weapons, vehicles, aircraft and helicopters, and ships is incalculable. Research shows, however, that tens of thousands of U.S. aircraft and helicopters flew five million sorties, and 10,000 were shot down. The South Vietnamese air force lost 2,500 of its aircraft, all of which came from the U.S. In contrast, the North Vietnamese had few aircraft and lost between 150 and 200.

The U.S. built 165 military bases and other war installations. Official war costs amounted to $173 billion (one trillion dollars in 2013 figures). In addition, war veteran benefits and interests have run upwards to one trillion dollars.

Australia provided 60,000 soldiers; 500 killed. Canada sent 30,000 volunteer soldiers; 110 killed.

Philippines sent 10,000 medical and engineer personnel with few deaths. New Zealand sent 3,500 troops; 37 deaths. CIA used many Thais as spies.

VIETNAMESE CASUALTIES

Estimates of Vietnam casualties vary from three to five million violent deaths.

Estimates of civilian deaths caused by U.S. bombings of North Vietnam just during Operation Rolling Thunder (March 1965-November 1968) range from 52,000 to 182,000. In that period, 300,000 bombing raids dropped 864,000 tons of explosives. 922 aircraft were destroyed. The Vietnamese lost 122 aircraft. Four years later, Christmas 1972, the U.S. launched its biggest B-52 bombing campaign in history, Operation Linebacker II. In just a few days 129 bombers dropped 20,000 tons of explosives, killing around 1,000 people in Hanoi.

In the South, between 300,000 and half-a-million civilians died during the war. Most South Vietnamese civilians were simply murdered for no reason other than because U.S. and South Vietnamese soldiers could kill with impunity. The Pentagon established a secret task force, the Vietnam War Crimes Working Group, to look into possible war crimes. It produced a 9000 page report that was partially declassified in 1994. The report was held at the National Archives in College Park, Maryland for a time but the government removed it. The task force reported on hundreds of verified mass murder atrocities and many hundreds more not investigated. Other than the My Lai massacre, no punishments were forthcoming. (5)

My Lai village lost a large part of its population, around 500 unarmed civilians, when U.S. soldiers went amok. Ron Ridenhour (no relation to this author), a soldier in another area, heard of this massacre and got information out to *New York Times* reporter Seymour Hersh (See his book, *My Lai 4*, Random House, 1970). Because of the public exposé, someone had to be punished. Lt. William Calley was the only soldier punished. President Nixon intervened so that he could spend his sentence of three years under house arrest.

The military forces of South Vietnam suffered an estimated 254,256 killed between 1960 and 1974 and additional deaths from 1954 to 1959, and in 1975. The US Department of Defense figured 950,765 Vietnamese communist forces were killed from 1965 to 1974. Guenter Lewy assumes that one-third of the reported enemy killed may have been civilians, concluding that the actual number of deaths of communist military forces was probably closer to 444,000. (6)

According to figures released by the Vietnamese government in 1995, there were 1,100,000 North Vietnamese Army and National Liberation Front military deaths, missing included.

Unexploded ordnance, mainly U.S. bombs continue to detonate and kill people and animals today. According to recent Vietnamese government statistics, such ordnance has killed about 42,000 people since the war officially ended. According to recent Laotian government statistics, unexploded ordnance has killed or injured over 20,000 Laotians since the end of the war.

After fifteen years of protracted fighting major direct U.S. involvement ended with the signing of the Paris Peace Accords, January 27, 1973. Fighting between ARV, still supported by U.S. war materials, against the People's Army of Vietnam and NLF forces would bring an end to the Republic of Vietnam and the war on April 30, 1975. With the Northern victory, the country was reunified as the Socialist Republic of Vietnam (SRV) with a communist party-controlled government based in Hanoi.

POST-WAR COMMUNIST CONFLICTS

Sino-Soviet relations had soured after the Soviets invaded Czechoslovakia in August 1968. In October, the Chinese demanded North Vietnam cut relations with Moscow but Hanoi refused. The Chinese began offering less support to Vietnam in November 1968 in preparation for a clash with the Soviets, which occurred at Zhenbao Island where Soviet-China has a border. During the seven-month conflict in 1969 between 50 and 100 Chinese died, and 80-200 Soviet forces were killed. Although neither side won the battle, the dispute continued without warfare and was resolved in a border agreement between China and the new Russia, October 14, 2004.

At the same time of the Sino-Soviet conflict, the Chinese began financing the Khmer Rouge as a counterweight to the Vietnamese communists. China armed and trained the Khmer Rouge during the Cambodian civil war and continued to aid them for years afterward. The U.S. also secretly gave material aid to the Cambodian Communists after the war. The Khmer Rouge launched ferocious border raids into Vietnam immediately after the Second Indochina War forward to the end of 1978. The Vietnamese finally tired of these encroachments and sent 150,000 troops to remove the brutal and aggressive Khmer Rouge Pol Pot regime, which succeeded in just two weeks. But the casualties over this three year period were great: between 15- 25,000 Cambodians died, 30,000 wounded; and a similar number or more of Vietnamese.

Following Vietnam's military response in Cambodia, China launched a brief, punitive invasion of Vietnam in February-March 1979. Within the three weeks before China withdrew, tens of thousands on both sides were killed or wounded.

China and Vietnam have had running disputes and battles over 2300 years. Ethnographically, the Vietnamese are close to the Han Chinese.

During the entire post World War II period, the destruction of Vietnam was overwhelming. At the Paris Peace talks, the aggressors had promised to pay reparations but never did. The Vietnamese faced monumental rebuilding tasks with nearly no money. They slowly did rebuild their nation but the United States returned, which is another sad story for another time.

The unwarranted invasion murdering was not limited to US imperialism, however, Pol Pot's forces did the same against Vietnamese and were aided by Communist China. In Burchett's *The Memoirs of a Rebel Journalist* (Quartet Books, London, 1980) he defines what journalism means to him, and in the context of the struggle for a better world, a socialist one. This excerpt is also my own understanding of what we journalists-activists on the left should be about.

"Now my Asian friends were at each other's throats—each waving the banner of socialism and revolution—and I was again in the thick of it. It was a shattering blow to a vision of things acquired during the previous four decades, including my certainty as to the superior wisdom and morality of Asian revolutionaries.

"Back in Paris, despondency was compounded by frustration. The Guardian (formerly National Guardian) of New York, the newsweekly in which my reports had regularly appeared for many years, had not published my reports from Vietnam, nor was the editor interested in any material about the situation in Kampuchea [Pol Pot's purges]."

Burchett then refers to his readers left ignorant that he had "spent the whole of that fateful month of December 1978 along Vietnam's frontiers with Kampuchea and China—the only Western journalist in the world to have done so."

"On January 23, 1979, The New York Times published an op-ed page article in which I gave my impressions of the impending Vietnam-China crisis. It was one of the rare warnings of what was to happen twenty-five days later, when China invaded Vietnam..."

Burchett's first hand reportage was again censored so he resigned after 22 years of association with The Guardian, whose "abdication of editorial responsibility [was] an unacceptable violation of my own perhaps unorthodox concepts of journalistic ethics."

These ethics Burchett writes about on page 59, which follows logically the citation above from pages 12-13. These four points I have taken as my own journalistic morality as well my political viewpoint: we radical/ revolutionaries must not ignore or negate our own flaws, errors and "sins".

Burchett:

1. *It is not a bad thing to become a journalist because you have something to say and are burning to say it.*
2. *There is no substitute for looking into things on the spot, especially if you are going to write on burning international issues of the day.*
3. *Make every possible effort to get the facts across to at least some section of the public.*
4. *Do not be tied to a news organization in which you would be required to write against your own conscience and knowledge.*

The war influenced musicians and songwriters in Vietnam, the United States and Europe. Country Joe and the Fish recorded "I-Feel-Like-I'm-Fixin'-To-Die Rag" / The "Fish" Cheer, and it became one of the influential anti-Vietnam protest anthems. Here is a selection of the many songwriters and musicians that the U.S. anti-war movement inspired: Pete Seeger, Peggy Seeger, Joan Baez, Buffy St. Marie, Ewan MacColl, Barbara Dane, The Critics Group, Phil Ochs, John Lennon, Nina Simone, Neil Young, Tom Paxton, Jimmy Cliff, Arlo Guthrie. Here is one contribution by Pete Seeger made popular by Joan Baez.

Where have all the flowers gone? Long time passing
Where have all the flowers gone? Long time ago
Where have all the flowers gone?
Girls have picked them every one
When will they ever learn? When will they ever learn?

Where have all the young girls gone? Long time passing
Where have all the young girls gone? Long time ago

Where have all the young girls gone?
Gone to young men every one
When will they ever learn? When will they ever learn?

Where have all the young men gone? Long time passing
Where have all the young men gone? Long time ago
Where have all the young men gone?
Gone for soldiers every one
When will they ever learn? When will they ever learn?

Where have all the soldiers gone, long time passing?
Where have all the soldiers gone, long time ago,
Where have all the soldiers gone,
gone to graveyards every one
When will they ever learn, when will they ever learn?

Where have all the graveyards gone,
covered with flowers every one
When will they ever learn, when will they ever learn?

1968 A YEAR OF WORLDWIDE UPHEAVAL

The Vietnam War and the Tet Offensive sparked greater interest in radical political and anti-war movements in the United States and Europe. U.S. anti-war protests varied in strategies and tactics. Some campuses were shut down, most notably Columbia University. We shut down California State University at Los Angeles for a day where I was a radical student activist. The Black Panther Party opposed the war and the draft, which affected blacks more than whites. White radical groups, such as the Students for Democratic Society, held actions in conjunction with the BPP. Several "Panthers" and other black radical-revolutionaries were killed in this period by police and FBI.

Mexican-American/*Chicano* groups in California and the southwest, and Puerto Rican "Young Lords" rebelled for equal rights and against the war.

Martin Luther King came out against the war. He was gunned down on April 4, 1968, and uprisings followed in 115 cities. Robert Kennedy was criticizing the war and if elected to the presidency, he would have reopened an investigation into his brother's murder. Bobby Kennedy was assassinated on June 6 at the Ambassador Hotel, a site of many Los Angeles anti-war protests.

GIs returning home were angry at the war's brutality and meaninglessness. They were also influenced by the anti-war movement. Many activists engaged them in debates. Some veterans started their own peace group, the Vietnam Veterans Against the War. Many burned their discharge papers and medals. At its peak, the VVAW had 25,000 members.

In *France*, just as the second phase of the Tet Offensive unfolded, students started massive actions including occupations in protest of U.S.

Joan Miró's "Mayo 1968" is a tribute to striking students and workers in France 1968.

imperialism and its Southeast Asian war, and against capitalism. They opposed France's consumerism, its traditional institutions and values. In May, Paris witnessed daily student marches, usually culminating in skirmishes between students throwing stones and the police firing tear gas. May 10, the Latin Quarter was filled with clouds of tear gas, Molotov cocktails, exploding automobile gas tanks, cobblestones hurled at the police, students beaten—more than 300 people injured but fortunately no gunfire and no deaths.

Workers and students joined hands as never before, or since. Eleven million workers struck. That was two-thirds the work force, one-fourth the total population. The movement was characterized by its spontaneous and de-centralized wildcat disposition. This created conflict with the Establishment, many trade unions and workers' parties, including the Communist Party.

"The objectives were self-management by workers ("autogestion"), a decentralization of economic and political power and participatory democracy at the grass roots. The great fear was that contemporary capitalism was capable of absorbing any and all critical ideas or movements and bending them to its own advantage. Hence, the need for provocative shock tactics. 'Be realistic: Demand the impossible!' was one of the May movement's slogans," wrote the *NYT* reporter Peter Steinfels, "Paris, May 1968: The revolution that never was". (http://www.nytimes.com/2008/05/11/world/europe/11iht-paris.4.12777919.html

The movement laid a basis for possible revolution. It created the largest general strike ever attempted in France, and the first nationwide wildcat general strike. Among strikers were state television and radio workers. At the height of its fervor, it brought the entire economy to a virtual halt. The protests reached such a point that political leaders feared civil war or revolution. The national government momentarily ceased functioning when President Charles de Gaulle secretly left France for a few hours. On the morning of May 29, de Gaulle postponed the meeting of the Council of Ministers and secretly removed his personal papers from Élysée Palace. He told his son-in-law Alain de Boissieu, "I do not want to give them a chance to attack the Elysée. It would be regrettable if blood were shed in my personal defense. I have decided to leave: nobody attacks an empty palace," wrote Mattei Dogan, "*How Civil War Was Avoided in France*", International Political Science Review, 1984.

France's president went to visit his military leader stationed in Baden-Baden. General Jacques Massu persuaded de Gaulle to return to France. His wife gave the family jewels for safekeeping to their son, who stayed in Baden. The de Gaulles' considered Germany as a possible refuge.

In these last days of May, an agreement was reached between the capitalists, the government, and trade unions that the minimum wage would be raised, working hours cut, retirement age reduced, and the right to organize would be universal.

After a month of anti-capitalist, anti-war, pre-revolutionary struggle, the French Communist Party and union leaders under its influence called on students and workers to accept the bourgeois government compromise so that capitalism could continue. This was treachery in the eyes of revolutionaries. Nevertheless, for many people the May movement represented the possibility of liberation, while for others, including socialists and some communists, it represented the danger of anarchy. Lenin had been forgotten.

"May 68" had an impact on French society that resounds today. The protests spurred an artistic movement, with songs, imaginative graffiti, posters, and slogans. It is considered a cultural, social and moral turning point in the history of the country.

PRAGUE SPRING

1968 was also a difficult year for Yugoslavia and Warsaw Pact countries. Students in Belgrade went on a seven-day strike in June demanding social justice, and protested censorship and high unemployment. President Josip Tito offered some reforms. There were no jail sentences or violence.

Warsaw Pact governments, however, were more than skeptical when Czechoslovakia President Alexander Dubcek made some reforms in what became known as the Prague Spring, or Socialism with a Human Face, itself an anti-communist insult.

The Prague Spring is the term used for the period January 5 to August 21, 1968 when the government of Czechoslovakia sought to extend citizen rights and political participation, and distance the country somewhat from Moscow. Farmers were also allowed to set up cooperatives and direct their production without orders from the central government. Trade unions were given greater bargaining rights. Dubcek assured Warsaw Pact countries that Czechoslovakia would remain in it and that the others had nothing to worry about regarding national reforms. The West, of course, had an standing interest in fomenting pro-capitalist disturbances.

On August 20-21, 250,000 Soviet troops and 2000 tanks entered Czechoslovakia. Most of the soldiers and tanks were Soviet—their numbers soon doubled—but a handful of other Warsaw Pact countries made a contribution. Romania did not collaborate and criticized the attack. Albania, influenced by the Chinese, angrily withdrew from the Warsaw Pact, calling it "social-imperialism."

Dubcek called upon the people not to resist but some did. The minor rebellion was quickly put down with the loss of 82 Czechs and Slavs, and 700 seriously or lightly injured. The attack caused upwards of 300,000 to migrate, most to the West where they were well received.

Dubcek was taken to Moscow but was soon returned to office on the condition that he abolish the reforms, which he did. Nevertheless, he was removed from the government and Communist party in April 1969. Once removed, he took a job in the Forestry Service.

The intervention became known as the Leonid "Brezhnev Doctrine"—meaning that any Warsaw Pact country attempting a shift to capitalism would meet similar consequences.

Tlatelolco massacre in Mexico City, October 2, 1968, resulted in the murder of 300 to 400 students and other civilians by military and police. The massacre began at a demonstration at the Plaza de las Tres Culturas in the Tlatelolco section. More than 1,300 people were arrested. The United States supported the massacre, because the Olympic Games had to go on and protestors were dismissed as communists and anarchists.

The massacre was part of the "Mexican Dirty War"—government violence to suppress political opposition (still ongoing). University and high school students opposed police and military repression on their campuses, and demanded that money being spent for hosting the upcoming Olympic Games be used instead for education and social welfare.

Mexican security forces and the CIA spread the lie that students had fired upon 5000 soldiers and police first. The defenders of law and order then "returned" the fire from the ground and from two helicopters, and they continued shooting people throughout the night. Many of the killed and wounded had nothing to do with the protests.

Under President Vicente Fox, government documentation was released, in 2002, proving that the presidential guard opened fire. The Pentagon had helped one of their favorite presidents, Gustavo Diaz Ordaz, put down many student protests during 1968. The U.S. army sent military radios, weapons, ammunition, and riot control training material to Mexico before and during the crisis. The CIA station in Mexico City produced daily reports concerning developments within the university community. (7)

Other Latin American countries faced similar treatment before and after 1968 by both national Establishments and the United States when people made a shift to the left.

Operation Condor was the most infamous of the programs to eradicate the democratic left as well as insurgents in Latin America in the 1960-80s. Operation Condor was so named, in 1975, after the world's largest carrion bird. The Pentagon and CIA either put totalitarian military regimes in power or backed those already installed, first in: Chile, Argentina, Uruguay, Bolivia, Paraguay, and Brazil; later joined by Peru and Ecuador. The objective was: there would be no more Cubas, and capitalism is holy under U.S. imperialism. In other words: Manifest Destiny.

"Condor was a covert intelligence and operations system that enabled the Latin American military states to hunt down, seize, and execute political opponents across borders. Refugees fleeing military coups and repression in their own countries were 'disappeared' in combined transnational operations. The militaries defied international law and traditions of political sanctuary to carry out their ferocious anticommunist crusade," wrote J. Patrice McSherry. (https://www.globalpolicy.org/component/content/article/168/28173.html See also: https://www.theguardian.com/world/2016/may/26/operation-condor-trial-argentina-court-death-squads)

Estimates vary but the operation caused at least 60,000 murders, thousands more "disappeared" and exiles; and the torturing of thousands. School of the Americans, then located in Panama, was a major United States training center for teaching torture methods. Victims included dissidents and leftists, union organizers and peasant leaders, priests and nuns, students and teachers, intellectuals suspected and actual guerrillas. While Operation Condor ended officially in the 1980s, such tactics are still used against the same sort of people in many parts of Latin America.

The list of murdering and overthrowing governments smelling of true democracy is long. (See chapter 18 for lists.) Suffice it to mention here Chile 1970-3. Socialist Party leader Salvador Allende did not win the 1964 Chilean elections mainly due to CIA subversion. It financed his opponent Eduardo Frei. But they couldn't prevent him from winning the September 1970 election with a plurality. (8)

One month after taking office, right-wing militarists back by the CIA kidnapped and murdered his army commander in chief, René Schneider.

In his three years in office, Allende endeavored to establish a peaceful, gradual path to socialize society. He nationalized some heavy industry, mainly copper mining, and the banks. As done in Cuba, and tried in Guatemala, the state financed education and health care, and helped with housing. Minimum wage and wages generally were raised. He displeased many army officers and businessmen, and, of course, the United States Establishment, especially those with high profit businesses in Chile: Anaconda, Kennecott and ITT. Nevertheless, he refused to arm the workers. (It was correctly regarded by many advisors that with the Chilean military largely in bourgeois hands, arming the workers would be the ideal pretext for an all-out US-managed intervention that would plunge the nation into a major civil war.)

President Richard Nixon gave the CIA an extra $10 million to "unseat Allende". And Secretary of State Henry Kissinger's direct covert action executive branch, 40 Committee, was in overall charge of getting rid of the "pinko". On September 11, 1973, some of the military under General Augusto Pinochet made a quick coup. Some activists fought to prevent a takeover of the government but were killed. Allende shot himself, in order to avoid humiliation.

The Pinochet military junta ruled until 1990.

Allende left a legacy of hope. His farewell address:

> *"Workers of my country, I have faith in Chile and its destiny. Other men will overcome this dark and bitter moment when treason seeks to prevail. Keep in mind that, much sooner than later, great avenues will again be opened through which will pass free men to construct a better society. Long live Chile"! Long live the people! Long live the workers!"*

Greek military junta 1967–1974; Rule of the Colonels was a series of extreme-right-wing military juntas that ruled Greece following the coup d'état led by a group of colonels on April 21, 1967. They were fearful that socialists and communists might win the forthcoming election. During its regime, the junta jailed tens of thousands of Greeks for political reasons and forced thousands into exile, including most of the country's civilian political leadership. Torture became a deliberate, chronic practice by security police and military police.

The dictatorship ended on July 24, 1974 under pressure by the Turkish invasion of Cyprus, establishing the Third Hellenic Republic.

According to testimony before the House Intelligence Committee, the junta contributed financially to Richard Nixon's successful 1968 presidential campaign. Vice President Spiro T. Agnew, who was of Greek descent, angered many Greeks when he visited in 1971 and embraced junta leaders, calling them the country's best leaders since Pericles ruled ancient Athens. The Junta also paid for Watergate defendants to keep quiet, which Nixon thanked them for in his Oval office. (http://www.washingtonpost.com/wp-srv/national/longterm/nixon/103097pappas.htm)

In a November 1999 visit to Greece, President Bill Clinton "acknowledged the U.S. government's support for the widely despised military junta that ruled Greece more than 25 years ago, but he stopped short of apologizing outright for Washington's letting Cold War concerns obscure a moral obligation to oppose a dictatorship". http://articles.latimes.com/1999/nov/21/news/mn-35991

"When the junta took over in 1967 here, the United States allowed its interests in prosecuting the Cold War to prevail over its interests—I should say its obligation—to support democracy, which was, after all, the cause for which we fought the Cold War," Clinton said.

AFGHANISTAN/SOVIET INVOLVEMENT 1978-89

Author interview with Russia's ambassador to Denmark, Mikjail Vanin.

> *"Russia's war in Afghanistan was ideologically and expansionist based. A great mistake! Russia went in without knowing the country's real history and culture. So feudalist was it that it is not possible to be transformed into a socialist society—not in reality, nor according to Marx's analysis.*

> *But Russia did not invade. We were asked by the Afghanistan government several times to come to its aid against a counter-revolutionary patriarchy supported by a foreign power [the United States] which financed and armed terrorism.*
>
> *We paid a terrible price—one that we feel even today. Because of our losses in this conflict, with our own lives and for our economy, internal opposition arose. We lost economic stability. We were nearly ruined by the war, and this influenced the demise of the Soviet Union."*

Afghanistan had always been ruled by regional kings or foreign empires during its 2500 year history until the Communist ascension to power on April 27, 1978. The last foreign empire was Britain. The Afghans fought three wars against its oppression (1839-42, 1878-80, 1919) until their victory on August 8, 1919. The national Musahiban monarchy ruled between 1929 and 1978.

In 1964, King Mohammad Zahir Shah (king 1933-73) introduced the country's first quasi-democratic liberalization with a bicameral legislature, in which one-third of deputies were elected by the people. Political parties were allowed and the Communist-led People's Democratic Party of Afghanistan (PDPA) took root.

The king had appointed his cousin, Mohammad Daoud Khan, prime minister in 1953 until he was forced to resign in 1963. On July 17, 1973, Daoud overthrew the king in a non-violent coup. He made himself president and ruled dictatorially. He introduced a harsh land reform program that pleased few, and repressed any opposition, particularly aimed at the PDPA factions.

On April 27, 1978, Daoud's government came to a violent end in what was called the Saur Revolution (named after the month of the year) when insurgent troops led by the People's Democratic Party of Afghanistan stormed his Kabul palace. Daoud and his brother Naim came out with pistols in hand and were shot dead.

The initial PDPA Revolutionary Council cabinet appeared to be carefully constructed to alternate ranking positions between Khalqis and Parchamis. The former faction sought rapid transition to a socialist revolution, while the Parchamis recognized that neither the material nor subjective conditions were propitious for a rapid transformation.

Parchamis planned for progressive reforms gradually leading to socialism.

Nur Muhammad Taraki (Khalqi) was made Prime Minister, Babrak Karmal (Parchami) became senior Deputy Prime Minister, and Hafizullah Amin (Khalqi) became foreign minister. Their unity was short-lived. In June, a failed Parchami coup led the central committee to give the Khalqist faction total control. In July, Taraki and Amin relieved most of the Parchamis from their government positions. Karmal was exiled to Prague.

The PDPA now tried to implement a socialist agenda. It changed the national flag from traditional Islamic green color to a near-copy of the Soviet red flag, which was an affront to most people in this conservative Islamic country. It prohibited usury, but without this form of credit system, or any alternative, agricultural production fell. Land reform was inefficiently, haphazardly introduced.

Women who wanted gender rights organized the Afghanistan Women's Council (AWC) when the new government began. It grew to 150,000 members. Although it was not under the PDPA, the Communists listened to their demands. The October Decree declared equality of genders. Women had first won the right to vote in 1919 but it was repealed in 1929, again established in 1964. Suffrage continued, and now women could be politicians, workers in most trades, allowed full education with compulsory education up to age 16, decide whom to marry and what to wear.

AWC's leader, Masuma Esmati-Wardak, became the minister of education, in 1991. A survey the group undertook that year found that most of the nation's teachers were women, 22,000, and 190 were university professors. There were 230,000 women students plus 7000 in universities.

All this angered conservatives who considered equality an attack on Islam. The government vigorously suppressed opposition and arrested thousands, executing thousands as well.

Local warlords of various ethnic tribes and religious groupings fought government forces on local levels and a mujahideen (religious strugglers/warriors) grew from that resistance into seven quasi-allied parties, what became known as the Islamic Unity of Afghanistan Mujahideen (1981).

In February 1979, the contentious law and order situation led to a serious diplomatic incident involving Afghanistan, the United States and the Soviet Union when the U.S. ambassador to Afghanistan, Adolph Dubs, was kidnapped by a mysterious group of militants. They are sometimes alleged to have been part of the radical communist faction, *Settam-e-Melli* ("National Oppression"), but are also sometimes described as Islamists. The kidnappers demanded the release of their leader Badruddin Bahes, whom the Afghan government denied holding.

The Afghan security forces tried to negotiate with the kidnappers to no avail. Accompanied by Soviet advisers, security forces surrounded the Kabul Hotel where he was held, and fired on the kidnappers. The ambassador died in a cross fire. The U.S. blamed the security forces for his death, putting more stress on U.S.-Afghan-Soviet relations.

The month before, President James Carter had told National Security Adviser Zbigniew Brzezinski and Secretary of State Cyrus Vance that it was vital to "repair our relationships with Pakistan" in light of the unrest in Iran, and thereby support Afghan opposition.

"The Islamic Revolution in neighboring Iran—also in crucial 1978-79—resulted in the overthrow of the U.S.-supported Pahlavi dynasty at that time under Mohammad Reza Shah Pahlavi. The Iranian Revolution was a violent and widely popular overthrow of a ferocious U.S.-inspired regime installed after the CIA-organized overthrow of the democratically elected government led by Premier Mohammad Mossadegh on August 19, 1953," wrote Gaither Stewart, who witnessed events unfold in Iran. (http://greanvillepost.com/2017/10/07/dr-najib)

Afghanistan was "thoroughly divided, much of it opposed to the Communist revolution. The chief resistance forces were also divided; the U.S.-supported Mujahideen. One might conclude that the Afghan War was a proxy war, between the USSR and the USA—the USA to control these two contiguous countries near the top of the world, Iran and Afghanistan, both bordering the Islamic part of the Soviet Union; the Soviet Union to defend itself from incursions into its Islamic Republics in Central Asia," Stewart wrote.

Robert Gates, former CIA director under Bush #1 and defense secretary under Bush#2 explained U.S. involvement. "The Carter administration turned to CIA ... to counter Soviet and Cuban aggression (sic) in the Third World, particularly beginning in mid-1979," wrote

Bruce Riedel *What We Won: America's Secret War in Afghanistan, 1979–1989*. Brookings Institution Press, 2014, p.98.

In March 1979, "CIA sent several covert action options relating to Afghanistan to the SCC [Special Coordination Committee]" of the U.S. National Security Council. At a March 30 meeting, U.S. Department of Defense representative Walter B. Slocombe "asked if there was value in keeping the Afghan insurgency going, 'sucking the Soviets into a Vietnamese quagmire?'" wrote Robert Gates, *From the Shadows: The Ultimate Insider's Story of Five Presidents and How They Won the Cold War*, Simon & Schuster, 2007. (9)

When asked to clarify this remark, Slocombe explained: "Well, the whole idea was that if the Soviets decided to strike at this tar baby [Afghanistan] we had every interest in making sure that they got stuck," wrote John Bernell White, *The Strategic Mind Of Zbigniew Brzezinski: How A Native Pole Used Afghanistan To Protect His Homeland*, Louisiana State University, 2012.

That same month, an insurrection occurred in and around the town of Herat. It was both a popular uprising and a mutiny of some Afghan army troops against the government. The communist government made its first appeal to Soviet allies for help, but they declined. The insurgents held the city for a week before the regime retook it. Many thousands were killed.

Instability increased markedly and the government was on the brink of collapse. *Confronted with anarchy and imminent revolution, the communist regime in Kabul made frequent pleas to Moscow, requesting military intervention, but still Soviet leaders did not want to get involved.*

Following the Herat uprising, President Taraki contacted Alexei Kosygin, chairman of the USSR Council of Ministers, and asked for practical and technical assistance with men and armament. Foreseeing the negative political repercussions such an action would have for his country, Kosygin rejected all further attempts by Taraki to solicit Soviet military aid in Afghanistan. Taraki then approached Leonid Brezhnev, the general secretary of the Communist Party and head of state. Brezhnev warned Taraki that full Soviet intervention "would only play into the hands of our enemies—both yours and ours". Brezhnev also advised Taraki to ease up on the drastic social reforms and to seek broader support for his regime, according to Paul Grigory, *Lenin's*

Brain and Other Tales from the Secret Soviet Archives. Hoover Press, 2008, p. 121.

Soon thereafter Taraki, returning from Non-Aligned Movement conference in Havana, met in Moscow with Brezhnev, Gromyko and other Soviet officials. Finally on his fourth attempt, Taraki was successful in negotiating some Soviet support: redeployment of two Soviet armed divisions at the Soviet-Afghan border; 500 military and civilian advisers and specialists sent to Afghanistan; and the delivery of Soviet armed equipment sold at 25 percent below the original price. However, the Soviets were not pleased about the developments in Afghanistan, and Brezhnev impressed upon Taraki the need for party unity again. The Soviets continued to refuse Soviet troop intervention within Afghan during Taraki's rule as well as later during Amin's short rule.

"We believe it would be a fatal mistake to commit ground troops...If our troops went in, the situation in your country would not improve. On the contrary, it would get worse. Our troops would have to struggle not only with an external aggressor [the U.S.], but with a significant part of your own people. And the people would never forgive such things." So wisely and tragically predictable spoke Alexei Kosygin.

In May 1979, U.S. officials secretly began meeting with rebel leaders through Pakistani government contacts. A former Pakistani military official claimed that he personally introduced a CIA official to Gulbuddin Hekmatyar that month. Hekmatyar is an Afghan warlord tied to Muslim Brotherhood, and became prime minister twice under future U.S. occupation. (http://nsarchive2.gwu.edu//NSAEBB/NSAEBB57/essay.html)

On July 3, Carter signed a "presidential finding" that "authorized the CIA to spend just over $500,000" on "non-lethal" aid to the mujahideen, which "seemed at the time a small beginning." Brzezinski later claimed that, "We didn't push the Russians to intervene, but we knowingly increased the probability that they would." (http://therealnews.com/t2/story:4716:The-Afghan-war-and-the-'Grand-Chessboard'-Pt2)

Seeing the United States material support for the counter-revolutionaries, the Soviet Union sent 15-20 helicopters in July, plus a detachment of tanks and crews to guard the government in Kabul, and to secure the Bagram and Shindand airfields. Several leading politicians, including Alexei Kosygin and Andrei Gromyko, were still against intervention.

Inter-party rivalry caused President Taraki to be deposed, on September 14, by followers of his now rival Hafizullah Amin, who took over the presidency. Taraki was killed in October.

Soviet leaders were of different minds about this event. No one wished to add to the split in the Afghanistan communist government, and all were worried about their border being challenged by fanatic Islamist anti-communist mujahedeen backed by the U.S. Some leaders tried to stop an armed intervention, but those who saw no alternative won out. Deteriorating internal relations and the worsening rebellion led Brezhnev to deploy the 40th Army—80,000 troops—on December 27, 1979. Arriving in the capital Kabul, they staged a coup. Their previous favorite, President Amin, was killed. Another Soviet loyalist, Babrak Karmal, was brought back from exile as the new chairman of the revolutionary council and chairman of the council of ministers.

It is important to stress that the Soviets waited 20 months after dismissing several official government invitations before they reluctantly sent troops to protect the state. If the tables were turned would the United States hesitate to intervene?

United States war policy makers were delighted with the events in Afghanistan. Not only did the Soviet intervention provide propaganda opportunities, but the Soviets were confronted with what U.S. politicians called "their own Vietnam". Washington sought to make the Soviet task more difficult by destabilizing the communist regime, arming and training its enemies. Working mostly through Pakistan, U.S. operatives provided military equipment and funds to the fundamentalist mujahideen. CIA agents in Pakistan trained these warriors and recruited members. To start with the CIA smuggled in $20 million per year, increasing to an annual peak of $630 million. Saudia Arabia matched this sum. In all, around $7.4 billion tax monies were used just for training. Arms were additional costs. (http://www.academia.edu/2897792/Operation_Cyclone_1979-1989_A_Brief_Analysis_of_the_U.S._Involvement_in_the_Soviet-Afghan_War) (10)

One of the rebel groups was Taliban, young mujahideen jihadist warriors, which the CIA and ISI created. Another beneficiary of U.S. tax payers' earnings was a young wealthy Saudi-born Islamic fanatic, Osama bin Laden, who later formed al-Qaeda to terrorize his learned instructor-mentors.

In January 1980, foreign ministers from 34 nations of the Islamic Conference adopted a resolution demanding "the immediate, urgent and unconditional withdrawal of Soviet troops from Afghanistan." The UN General Assembly passed a similar resolution.

At the same time, China entered into a tri-partite alliance with the U.S. and Pakistan, to sponsor Islamist Afghan armed resistance. Deng Xiaoping, the paramount leader of China, required the removal of "three obstacles" so that Sino-Soviet relations might improve: 1)The massed Soviet Army at the Sino-Soviet border, and in Mongolia; 2) Soviet support of the Vietnamese occupation of Kampuchea; 3) The Soviet occupation of Afghanistan.

President Carter had established diplomatic relations with China, January 1, 1979. China agreed to this once the U.S. no longer recognized two Chinas, the other in Taiwan. One year later, Carter sent Brzezinski to China to solidify a military alliance against fellow but rival communist governments in Afghanistan and the Soviet Union.

The prestigious *Mediterranean Journal of Social Sciences* published an important article about this cross-ideological alliance, "Pak-China-US Triangle vis-à-vis Soviet Union in Afghan War". Excerpt: "For the first time an American representative admitted the possibility of concluding an anti-Soviet military alliance between the USA and the People's Republic of China." (11)

"During [the 1980s], US (CIA), Pakistan's Inter Services Intelligence (ISI), and the Chinese Intelligence services developed a close collaborative relationship based on convergent perceptions of the Soviet Union and exchange of information...From 1979 to 1987 Pakistan received [from the U.S. and China] 12.73 billion dollars. Pakistan served as a meeting place of weapons supply to mujahideen from different countries. The CIA was busy taking weapons and ammunition from China and flying over sensitive areas of Kashmir...throughout the Soviet presence in Afghanistan, the three countries aligned together to get the Red Army out of Kabul... The Indo-Soviet axis tried to balance the game effectively but in vain."

The Soviets and its Afghan government allies now had to face the world's largest Communist-led government allied with world's mightiest anti-communist "democratic" capitalist government in cahoots with anti-democratic, misogynist-patriarchal-jihadist capitalists.

In June 1981, Sultan Ali Keshtmand took over the chairmanship of the council of ministers, and Karmal continued as government chairman. He tried to broaden a base for the PDPA by introducing several reforms, including a general amnesty for those imprisoned during Taraki's and Amin's rule. He also replaced the Khalqist flag with a more traditional one. These policies failed to increase the PDPA's legitimacy in the eyes of most Afghans.

Upon winning the presidency, Ronald Reagan launched The Reagan Doctrine: aiding any and all anti-communist, anti-Soviet resistance the world over. Reagan deployed CIA Special Activities Division paramilitary officers to equip the mujihadeen forces with the highly effective Stinger missiles. According to the 1993 US Air Defense Artillery Yearbook, Stingers accounted for downing 269 of the 451 Soviet aircraft destroyed-figures based on mujihadeen sources. The U.S. supplied perhaps as many of 2000 Stingers.

Although the Soviet-Afghan forces controlled most of the cities, four-fifths of the country was usually under the control of local tribes and Islamic groups. These reactionaries had 4000 bases. During this decade of Cold-Hot war by proxy and directly, the Soviet Union shifted leadership four times: Leonid Brezhnev (October 1964-November 1982); Yuri Andropov (November 1982-February 1984); Konstantin Cherneko (February 1984-March 1985); Mikhail Gorbachev (March 1985-December 25, 1991).

In Afghanistan, Dr. Muhammad Najibullah became the fourth PDPA top leader. At the beginning of PDPA government, Najibullah had been sent to Iran as its ambassador. From there he went to Moscow. Upon his return to Afghanistan, he headed, "the dreaded Khad, the secret police, during which time he personally acquired a reputation for brutality: torture and execution of the opposition was the norm, as it was in Iran (under the Shah, particularly), as in much of the world today. He had the close support—if not control—of the KGB. His Khad was modeled on the Soviet Committee of State Security (KGB)… [which] grew in size to the point it allegedly had 300,000 troops, and was considered effective in the pacification of wide parts of the country," Gaither Stewart wrote. (http://www.greanvillepost.com/2017/10/07/dr-najib/)

Gorbachev tried to mend PDPA internal relationships and its

isolation from most of the people. In May 1986, he encouraged Karmal to place Najibullah as head of the party, and in November as chairman of the government. Karmal was allowed to come to Moscow for retirement.

"As subsequent history would show, Najibullah's approach [the Parcham faction] to resolving the civil war in Afghanistan was quite different from that of the PDPA [Khalq] faction... However, for the observer today, Najibullah's more political National Reconciliation policy (which failed) between the government and the Mujahideen opposition and the clergy is a key to understanding not only contemporary Afghanistan but also Afghan-Soviet relations in general and the withdrawal of Soviet troops ordered by Soviet leader Mikhail Gorbachev in 1989," Stewart wrote.

"Things had begun changing with the arrival of Mikhail Gorbachev to power...Though Soviet-controlled Afghanistan was a dangerous place to be, one of Gorbachev's gravest mistakes was to pull his troops out...leaving Najibullah and his government to face the growing firepower of the Mujahideen ... and the threat of U.S. intervention. The then President Najibullah understood this quite well and did all in his power to convince Soviet authorities to leave their troops in place."

Gorbachev called the occupation of Afghanistan a "bleeding wound". The last Soviet forces left in February 1989, but warfare continued until 1992.

During the Afghan-Soviet part of the war, 620,000 Soviet troops served—14,453 were killed; 53,753 were wounded or injured; 415,932 fell sick; about 100 went missing.

At the end, Afghanistan fatalities amounted to around 1.5 million (mujahideen, government soldiers and noncombatants), and 3 million maimed or wounded, mainly noncombatants.

A Russian daily newspaper, "Russian Beyond" ("Russkaya Semoyorka") wrote in 2017 that the war had cost $2-$3 billion annually. That would mean $18 to $27 billion, a cost the newspaper staff contends was unjustified.

"The Afghan conflict created the 'forgotten and betrayed soldier.' This image was atypical in Russian tradition. The Afghan conflict had undermined the morale of the Russian Army, and young men began to dodge the draft. The war inspired horror, and scary legends were spread about it. They sent soldiers there as punishment for misdeeds, and hazing flourished, which became the scourge of the modern army. At this time, the military profession ceased to be attractive. The 'echo of Afghanistan' remains loud to this day." (https://www.rbth.com/international/2017/01/12/7-things-you-probably-didnt-know-about-the-soviet-war-in-afghanistan_678758)

REAGAN-GORBACHEV AND THE END OF THE SOVIET UNION

Ronald Reagan was born in Tampico, a small Illinois town, in 1911. His father worked as a salesman in a store; his mother as a housewife. They were Irish-Scottish-English immigrants, some of whose families had been tenant farmers.

Reagan started his career as a radio sports announcer, then as a B screen actor in Hollywood B films. He worked for big capitalism as an advertizing voice for General Electric before entering politics on the side of Barry Goldwater for president. He held his first political job as governor of California (1967-75), and then as president of the United States (January 1981-January 1989). During his years as a Hollywood actor and union member, Reagan was an FBI informer.

From the start, Reagan set his sights on crushing the Berlin Wall and the Soviet Union. One way of doing this was by doubling the defense budget to $253 billion, in order to provoke the Soviet government into escalating its defense budget to keep abreast with new U.S. weapon technology. The U.S. budget did not include moneys for wars, such as the *contra* war against Nicaragua. Reagan also allowed secret plans to be formulated so that his government could rule secretly.

Mikhail Gorbachev was also born in a small town, Privolnoye, in 1931, to peasant Ukrainian-Russian parents. His father was a combine harvester on a collective farm where his mother also worked. Gorbachev took a law degree, and quickly rose in the Communist party. In 1979, he was on the Politburo. On March 11, 1985 he was made General Secretary; on May 25, he became Chairman of the Supreme Soviet of the South Union.

In contrast to Reagan, Gorbachev started his government with a vision to democratize society, and to eliminate nuclear weapons and therewith prevent a nuclear world war. Gorbachev introduced a troika of slogans in a campaign to reform a faltering Soviet system. He called for glasnost (openness) in public discussion, perestroika (restructuring) in the economy and political system, and *novoye mneniya* (new thinking) in foreign policy.

Gorbachev's most positive intention was to abolish nuclear armaments and to diminish the cold-hot war blowing from the West. On April 8, 1985 he suspended deployment of SS-20 missiles in Europe. In September, he proposed to Reagan a reduction by half of their nuclear arsenals.

REAGAN-IRAN I

Twenty minutes after Ronald Reagan was inaugurated, Iran's Ayatollah Khomeini government released 52 U.S. hostages held since November 4, 1979. This raised suspicions of foul play. (12)

The 2500-year continuous Persian monarchy had come to end on February 1, 1979 after the successful anti-Shah movement brought victory to Khomeini Islamists. The Shah had fled to the U.S. while the CIA network tried to subvert the new government with its spies and money. This led hundreds of students to invade the U.S. embassy and seize diplomats, marines, CIA officers, and a handful of US American civilians as hostages. Khomeini supported their cause.

President Jimmy Carter ordered a complete embargo of Iranian oil, and stronger economic embargoes followed. On April 8, 1980 Carter severed diplomatic relations with Iran after negotiations for the hostages' release failed. Later that month, Carter authorized a top-secret mission, Operation Eagle Claw, to free the hostages, but it failed. Over the months that followed, Carter's chances for reelection diminished no matter how he tried to resolve the dilemma. The American media's sensationalist, right-leaning obsessive coverage of the embassy situation fomented jingoist hysteria ("Day XYZ of America Held Hostage!" blared many television stations.) Reagan won the November 1980 election, in part, because he may have made a deal with Iran.

GLASNOST-PERESTROIKA

By increasing local, regional and republican controls, allowing for greater media reportage, reducing civil service-bureaucracy and executive branch corruption, Gorbachev sought to make the country's management transparent, thus circumventing the narrow circle of apparatchiks who exercised extensive-excessive control over society.

The media began exposing problems previously unreported: poor housing, food shortages, alcoholism, widespread pollution, creeping mortality rates, the second-rate position of women, as well as the history of state crimes against the population. However, this caused more disillusionment and more curiosity about U.S./European cultures and politics.

Perestroika allowed ministries more independent actions, and permitted enterprises self-financing and some market-like reforms. The goal of perestroika, however, was not to end central planning but rather to make socialism work more efficiently to better meet the needs of the citizenry, a sort of mild NEP for the 1980s.

In July 1987, the state passed the Law on State Enterprise, which freed state institutions to determine output levels based on demand from other official entities and consumers. Enterprises had to fulfill state orders, but they could dispose of the remaining output as they saw fit.

The Law on Cooperatives, enacted in May 1988, was more radical. For the first time since Vladimir Lenin's New Economic Policy was abolished in 1928, the law permitted private ownership of businesses in the services and manufacturing. Cooperative restaurants, shops, and manufacturers became part of the Soviet scene.

Gorbachev's perestroika eliminated the monopoly that the Ministry of Foreign Trade had held on trade operations. It permitted industrial and agricultural government branches to conduct foreign trade, as well as regional and local organizations.

The most significant and potentially dangerous of Gorbachev's reforms in the foreign economic sector allowed foreigners to invest in the Soviet Union in the form of joint ventures, at first limiting the foreign part to 49% ownership and later without limitations of ownership.

REAGAN- IRAN II-NICARAGUA

The *Iran–Contra affair* (aka *Irangate, Contragate*) occurred in conjunction with Lebanese Islamic extremists kidnapping 30 U.S. and other Western citizens between 1982 and 1992.

"U.S. officials believed that the Iranian-backed Hezbollah was behind most of the kidnappings and the Reagan administration devised a covert plan. [By 1984] Iran was desperately running out of military supplies in its [U.S.-instigated] war with Iraq, but Congress had banned the sale of American arms to countries like Iran that sponsored terrorism. Reagan was advised that a bargain could be struck—secret arms sales to Iran, hostages back to the U.S.," reported the Public Broadcasting Service, "Terrorists attacks on Americans, 1979-1988." (http://www.pbs.org/wgbh/pages/frontline/shows/target/etc/cron.html)

"In August 1985, the first consignment of arms to Iran was sent—100 anti-tank missiles provided by Israel; another 408 were sent the following month. As a result of the deal," five U.S. hostages and other nationalities were eventually released.

With the money Iran paid for the arms, Reagan's secret state funneled it to the *contras* fighting to overthrow the Sandinista government in Nicaragua. (Many *contras* were ex-guardsmen of the Nicaraguan National Guard and other right-wing figures who had fought for Nicaragua's ex-dictator Somoza). The Congress had, quite unusually, passed an arms embargo against the *contras* (Boland Amendment) due to their systematic brutality and wanton murder, which the majority of U.S. citizens opposed, and many did so loudly on the streets.

In the same period, the International Court of Justice found the U.S. guilty of war crimes against Nicaragua in its 1986 finding: *The Republic of Nicaragua v. The United States of America.*

The court ruled in favor of Nicaragua and ordered the United States to pay reparations. The court held that the U.S. had violated international law by supporting the *contras*, and by mining Nicaragua's harbors. The U.S. refused to participate in the proceedings, and blocked enforcement of the judgment by the UN Security Council, thereby preventing any compensation. For Reagan, the murderous *contras* were "*modeled after our Founding Fathers*". (9)

This was the first time an international court had found a country guilty of such war crimes. But this was just one of many thousands committed against Latin Americans since the U.S. congress had passed the "Monroe Doctrine", in 1823. Nicaragua had been subjected to 12 such U.S. military "Manifest Destiny" interventions.

The Somoza family dictators had ruled for four decades in the 20th century before a popular liberation army, the Sandinistas, defeated them and took power on July 19, 1979. President Franklin D. Roosevelt had said of Anastasio Somoza, the first in the dynasty: "*he may be a son-of-a-bitch, but he's our son-of-a-bitch.*"

GORBACHEV DISARMAMENT

Gorbachev's efforts to prevent a possible nuclear war brought Reagan to the Geneva summit in November 1985. There was no final agreement about how much to reduce nuclear weapons but a tone was established that a nuclear war cannot be won and must never be fought. This was an advance from the 1960s days of "Dr. Strangelove" cowboys riding the H bomb to Armageddon, a la Stanley Kubrik's 1964 film dealing with the Cuban Missile Crisis.

The Geneva summit was followed up by the Reykjavik Summit. Gorbachev again met Reagan, this time in Iceland, October 11-12, 1986. The talks collapsed at the last minute, but they brought about the Intermediate-Range Nuclear Forces Treaty (INF) between the countries on December 8, 1987.

The Soviets proposed to eliminate 50% of all strategic arms, including ICBMs, and agreed not to include British or French weapons in the count, on the condition of a U.S. pledge not to implement strategic defenses (SDI) for the next ten years. Reagan argued for the right to deploy strategic defenses, viewing SDI research ("star wars") as inviolable. *Gorbachev suggested eliminating all nuclear weapons within a decade.*

The INF Treaty compromise eliminated all nuclear and conventional missiles and launchers with short ranges of 500–1,000 kilometers and intermediate-ranges of 1,000–5,500 km. The treaty did not cover sea-launched missiles. By May 1991, 2,692 missiles were eliminated—846 U.S. and 1,846 Soviet. Each country was permitted to render inoperative and retain 15 missiles and launchers. There followed 10 years of on-site verification inspections.

REAGAN ESTABLISHES A SECRET GOVERNMENT

Reporter Alfonso Chardy wrote one of the few stories published exposing plans for an extensive and secret, anti-democratic government set up by Reagan's executive team. The article, "Reagan's Aides and the 'Secret' Government" ran, surprisingly, in the conservative Miami Herald, on July 5, 1987. Chardy, a native of Mexico, won a Pulitzer Prize in 1987 for disclosing Oliver North's role in the Iran-Contra affairs. (https://ratical.org/ratville/JFK/ReaganAidesAndSG.html)

Here are excerpts from this important and forgotten work:

"Some of President Reagan's top advisers have operated a virtual parallel government outside the traditional Cabinet departments and agencies almost from the day Reagan took office, congressional investigators and administration officials have concluded.

"Investigators believe that the advisers' activities extended well beyond the secret arms sales to Iran and aid to the contras now under investigation. Lt. Col. North, for example, helped draw up a controversial plan to suspend the Constitution in the event of a national crisis, such as nuclear war, violent and widespread internal dissent or national opposition to a U.S. military invasion abroad."

"In a secret assessment of the activities, the lead counsel for the Senate Iran-contra committee called it a 'secret government-within-a-government.' The arrangement permitted Reagan administration officials to claim that they were not involved in controversial or illegal activities, the officials said. 'It was the ultimate plausible deniability,' said a well-briefed official."

"The heart of the secret structure from 1983 to 1986 was North's office in the Old Executive Office Building adjacent to the White House, investigators believe. North's influence within the secret structure was so great, the sources said, that he was able to have the orbits of sophisticated surveillance satellites altered to follow Soviet ships around the world, call for the launching of high-flying spy aircraft on secret missions over Cuba and Nicaragua and become involved in sensitive domestic activities."

"Others in the structure included some of Reagan's closest friends and advisers, including former national security adviser William Clark, the late CIA Director William Casey and Attorney General Edwin Meese, officials and investigators said [who also] said the Iran deal was just one of the group's initiatives."

"This is the part of the story that reveals the whole secret government-within-a-government, operated from the [Executive Office Building] by a Lt. Col., with its own army, air force, diplomatic agents, intelligence operatives and appropriations

> *capacity," [Senate committee chief counsel Arthur] Limon wrote in the memo, parts of which were shared with* The Herald."
>
> *"Officials say the genesis may have been an October 1980 decision by Casey, Reagan's campaign manager and a former officer in the World War II precursor of the CIA, to create an 'October Surprise Group' to monitor Jimmy Carter's feverish negotiations with Iran for the release of 52 American hostages." (12)*

Another part of the secret government was North's plan for FEMA. North worked in collaboration with the Federal Emergency Management Agency director Louis Guiffrida on a contingency plan to suspend the Constitution during an external or internal crisis (uprising for example), and turn executive power over to FEMA's 17 hand-picked leaders. The plan resembled a thesis Guiffrida had written, in 1970, at the Army War College in Pennsylvania, in which he advocated martial law in case of a national uprising by black militants. At least 21 million "American Negroes" would be rounded up and transferred to "assembly centers or relocation camps", reported Chardy.

> *"Congressional sources familiar with national disaster procedures said they believe Reagan did sign an executive order in 1984 that revised national military mobilization measures to deal with civilians in case of nuclear war or other crisis."*

Despite these totalitarian illegalities no one was punished. Reagan was judged by congressional committee investigators for a "lax managerial style and aloofness from policy detail." Lt. Col. North was sentenced to a three-year *suspended* jail term, which was later vacated. Mass detention plans of thousands or millions of indignant citizens protesting racism or aggressive foreign wars—such as REX84 (Readiness Exercise 1984) and Garden Plot (the new army action), which Ronald Ridenhour exposed (Counter Spy, 1975)—were never repealed or exist under other code names.

"Lt. Col. Oliver North, Elliott Abrams and other U.S. officials lied repeatedly as they sought to give credence to the absurd notion that Nicaragua, an impoverished country of three million, with no navy or air force to speak of, posed a serious threat to the security of the United

States. The anti-Sandinista propaganda offensive included oft-repeated allegations of Nicaraguan complicity with Khomeini's Iranian ironic charge given that North and the CIA were secretly supplying weapons to Iran at the time. Such deliberate falsifications were part of a protracted disinformation campaign designed to manufacture a 'Nicaraguan threat,'" wrote Martin A. Lee and Norman Solomon. *Unreliable Sources: a guide to detecting bias in news media*, Lyle Stuart, 1990. (http://www.thirdworldtraveler.com/Norman_Solomon/Disinformation_USNS.html)

New York Times news editor Bill Kovach: "We've been dealing with... an administration that freely states-and stated early-that literal truth was not a concern," wrote Lee and Solomon.

THE END OF THE WARSAW PACT AND THE SOVIET UNION

Gorbachev's original goal of reforming the Soviet Union with the Communist Party still in partial control failed. By allowing citizens to criticize the Soviet system, it inadvertently released long-suppressed political, social and economic tensions, and national sentiments in the republic states that wanted to assert their independence, and undermined the authority of the Soviet central-government. It was an historic case of too little too late.

One feature common to most of these developments was popular civil resistance campaigns opposing one-party rule. Romania was the only country where the overthrow of its Communist regime occurred violently.

The illegal and popular Solidarnosc/Solidary union, led by Lech Walesa, won its legalization in April, 1989. In August, a Solidarity-led coalition of parliamentary forces took over the government. Walesa was elected president in November 1990. The CIA had been funding Solidarity for several years, for a total of at least $10 million. (13)

Reformists in Hungary took to the streets in 1988 and 1989. On June 27, 1989, the foreign ministers of Austria and Hungary cut through their borders' wire fence with bolt cutters. This led to the flight of East Germans through Hungary to Austria and beyond. Hungarian reformists won state power in October 1989. A multi-party system was legalized in March 1990. East Germany, Bulgaria, Romania and Czechoslovakia followed suit.

After several weeks of civil unrest, the East German government announced on November 9, 1989 that all GDR citizens could visit West

Germany and West Berlin. Crowds of East Germans crossed or climbed onto the wall. Over the next few weeks, euphoric people and souvenir hunters chipped away pieces of the wall. The governments later removed what was left. The end of the wall paved the way for German reunification, which formally took place on October 3, 1990.

According to Western figures, before the wall's erection 3.5 million East Germans had circumvented emigration restrictions and crossed over the border into West Berlin and beyond. Between 1961 and 1989 only about 5,000 people attempted emigration over the wall with a death toll ranging from 136 to 200. East Germany maintains that 98 people were killed trying to escape.

The new freedoms arising from Gorbachev's democratization and decentralization led to civil unrest in several of the constituent republics (Azerbaijan, Georgia, and Uzbekistan) and to outright attempts to achieve independence in others (Lithuania). While Gorbachev used military force to suppress bloody interethnic strife in several of the Central Asian republics in 1989–90, he introduced mechanisms that provided for the lawful secession of republics.

In 1990, Gorbachev accelerated the transfer of power from the party to elected governmental institutions. On March 15, the Congress of People's Deputies elected him to the newly created post of president of the USSR with extensive executive powers. At the same time, the Congress abolished the Communist Party's constitutionally guaranteed monopoly of political power, thus paving the way for the legalization of other political parties.

Gorbachev was awarded the Nobel Peace Prize, in 1990, for his "leading role in the peace process which today characterizes important parts of the international community."

A year later, still trying to avert the dissolution of the Soviet Union, Gorbachev set up a referendum for all the republics in March 17, 1991—to preserve the USSR as "a renewed federation of equal sovereign republics in which the rights and freedom of an individual of any nationality will be fully guaranteed."

Six republics boycotted it: the three Baltic republics plus Moldavia, Georgia and Armenia. But nine republics voted. Russians voted 77.8 % for preserving the union. The other eight republics voted at least 70% for. But soon events took a turn for the worst.

On July 1, 1991 the Warsaw Pact ceased to exist. Gorbachev's power radically diminished.

Some hard-line members of government tried to take control of the country. A Soviet coup d'état attempt, also known as the *August Coup*, lasted two days, August 19-21. The State Committee on the State of Emergency coup leaders opposed his reform program and the new union treaty he had negotiated, which decentralized much of the central government's power to the republics. The leader was Gennady Yanayev, the vice-president Gorbachev had appointed the year before.

The coup was opposed by an effective campaign of civil resistance led by the new President of Russia, Boris Yeltsin, elected in the first popular vote for the presidency on June 12, 1991. Yeltsin had been both an ally and critic of Gorbachev. Although the coup collapsed and Gorbachev returned to government, the event destabilized the Soviet Union and contributed to its demise.

Gorbachev was hated by many Russian Communists for making too many concessions to the Yankees, and many non-Communists disliked him as well, but he was appreciated by many Westerners who understood the need for world peace and thought Gorbachev did his best for that. To this day, many people remain confused about Gorbachev's naiveté about the way Washington really operates.

On Christmas day 1991, Gorbachev called his friend President George H.W. Bush.

> **M.G.:** Let me say that in about two hours I will speak on Moscow TV and will make a short statement about my decision…I would like to reaffirm to you that I greatly value what we did working together with you, first as vice president and then as president of the United States. I hope that all leaders of the commonwealth and, above all, Russia understand what kind of assets we have accrued between the leaders of our two countries. I hope they understand their responsibility to preserve and expand this important source of capital.
>
> The debate in our union on what kind of state to create took a different track from what I thought right. But let me say that I will use my political authority and role to make sure that this new commonwealth will be effective.

> **G.B.:** Mikhail, let me say first how grateful I am for this call... We will stay involved, particularly with the Russian republic, whose enormous problems could get worse this winter. I am delighted you won't plan to hide in the woods and that you will be active politically. I have total confidence that will benefit the new commonwealth.

The Soviet Union was dissolved the next day, and eleven Soviet republics became independent: Armenia, Azerbaijan, Belarus, Georgia, Kazakhstan, Kyrgyzstan, Moldova, Tajikistan, Turkmenistan, Ukraine and Uzbekistan. The Baltic states—Estonia, Latvia and Lithuania—regained their independence.

The rest of the Soviet Union became Russia. Albania and Yugoslavia ceased being communist states (1990-1992). U.S./NATO split Yugoslavia into five states: Bosnia and Herzegovina, Croatia, Macedonia, Slovenia and the Federal Republic of Yugoslavia. (14)

Notes:

1. http://www.nytimes.com/1993/06/08/opinion/cia-funny-businesses.html "C.I.A. Funny Businesses"

   Here is a 2012 listing of about 500 proprietaries. Today there are probably fewer. Some of them shown here no longer exist. https://cryptome.org/2012/10/cia-proprietaries-agents.htm

   See also: https://deeppoliticsforum.com/forums/showthread.php?1063-List-of-known-CIA-front-companies#.WennvmiCzcs , and Victor Marchetti & John D. Marks *The CIA & The Cult of Intelligence* (Alfred A. Knopf, 1974).

   Here is a guide to how to find items on the CIA's own website. Although proprietaries as such do not appear, there is material on the two airlines mentioned herein. https://www.muckrock.com/news/archives/2017/sep/22/crest-search-guide/ Here is one link: https://www.cia.gov/news-information/featured-story-archive/earthquake-mcgoons-final-flight.html

2. See: Bernard Fall's book *Hell in a Very Small Place: The Siege of Dien Bien Phu*, J.B. Lippincott, 1967; and Jules Roy's *The Battle of Dienbienphu*, Carroll & Graf, 1997. https://en.wikipedia.org/wiki/Battle_of_Dien_Bien_Phu

3. "I am convinced that the French could not win the war because the internal political situation in Vietnam, weak and confused, badly weakened their military position. I have never talked or corresponded with a person knowledgeable in Indochinese affairs who did not agree that had elections been held as of the time of the fighting, possibly 80 per cent of the population would have voted for the Communist Ho Chi Minh as their leader rather than Chief of State Bao Dai. Indeed, the lack of leadership and drive on the part of Bao Dai was a factor in the feeling prevalent among Vietnamese that they had nothing to fight for." Dwight D. Eisenhower *Mandate for Change* (Doubleday, 1963).

4. http://www.nytimes.com/1993/06/08/opinion/cia-funny-businesses.html. http://www.nytimes.com/1972/12/17/archives/drug-feared-sent-in-bodies-of-gis-court-told-that-smugglers-used.html https://forum.davidicke.com/showthread.php?t=262504 See also: http://humansarefree.com/2015/02/overwhelming-evidence-that-cia-is.html

5. http://www.latimes.com/news/la-na-vietnam6aug06-story.html "Civilian Killings Went Unpunished" by Nick Turse and Deborah Nelson. See also Douglas Valentine 1990 book *The Phoenix Program: America's Use of Terror in Vietnam*, (Open Road), and Jules Roy's *The Battle of Dienbienphu*. Valentine's book is based on extensive interviews with Phoenix operatives. The CIA at first allowed these interviews but changed its mind and tried unsuccessfully to suppress the book.

6. Guenter Lewy is a political scientist whose 1978 book, *America in Vietnam*, is considered a classic by the mass media. His research is well respected but his view is antagonistic to the anti-war and peace movements.

7. See Kevin Sullivan, "Mexico to Seek Genocide Charges Against Officials in 1968 Massacre", *Washington Post*, January 14, 2005.

8. See William Blum, *Rogue State: A guide to the world's only superpower*, Zed Nooks, 2001; his *The CIA: a forgotten history*, Zed Books, 1986; and Phil Agee's *CIA Diary: Inside the Company*, Penguin Books, 1975–among a plethora of excellent accounts about CIA-U.S. military diabolic actions the world over.

9. That was also Gates "value" in his involvement in the Iran-Contra Affair. The scandal was based on President Ronald Reagan illegal sale of weapons to Iran, which was under his own presidential and the Congress arms embargo for holding U.S. hostages, and then giving the weapons to Nicaraguan counter-revolutionaries, which was also illegal due to an unprecedented congressional arms embargo for anti-communists. But these contras were highly unpopular not only in Nicaragua but in the United States for their systematic torturing and murdering of any Nicaraguans not directly connected to them. But Gates boss, Reagan, called them the "*Moral equivalent to our Founding Fathers.*" Gates was forced to retire as CIA director, in 1993, due to this scandal.

10. See U.S. government documents of its role in Afghanistan war (1978-92) at National Security Archives. http://nsarchive2.gwu.edu//NSAEBB/NSAEBB57/us.html. According to author William Malley, *The Afghanistan Wars* (Palgrave MacMillian, 2002), the CIA provided between 500 and 2000 FIM-92 stingers to its proxy warriors. Each stinger costs $38,000, so that would be between $19 and $76 million. But other accounts contend that 900 stingers were unaccounted for at the end of the war. The U.S. offered to buy back 300 missiles at $183,300 each. It collected most of those, but 600 more went unaccounted for. If the Yankees bought back, say, 200 that would have cost $36 million.

11. "Pak-China-US Triangle vis-à-vis Soviet Union in Afghan War" Mediterranean Journal of Social Sciences MCSER Publishing, Rome-Italy, September 2014. By Dr. Manzoor Khan Afridi Head of Department of Politics and International Relations, International Islamic

University Islamabad-Pakistan; Musab Yousufi M.Phil Scholar, International Islamic University Islamabad-Pakistan; M.Phil Scholar, International Islamic University Islamabad-Pakistan. http://www.mcser.org/journal/index.php/mjss/article/viewFile/3965/3881

12. The "October Surprise" conspiracy is boosted by the quick release of hostages. According to the allegation Reagan's presidential campaign people, led by Richard Allen, conspired with Iran to delay the release until after the election to thwart President Carter from pulling off an "October surprise" that would have freed the hostages and thereby improve his chances for reelection. Once Reagan became president, he rewarded Iran by supplying it with weapons in its war against U.S.'s ally, Iraq. Reagan would also unblock Iranian monetary assets in U.S. banks. (https://en.wikipedia.org/wiki/October_Surprise_conspiracy_theory)

    Former Iranian President Abulhassan Banisadr, and former naval intelligence officer and National Security Council member Gary Sick stand by this story. See Sick's book, *October Surprise: America's Hostages in Iran and the Election of Ronald Reagan*, Random House, 1991.

13. "Looking to the Future: Essays on International Law" Michael Reisman, Yale Law School.

14. Renamed Serbia and Montenegro after the U.S. and NATO invaded and broke up what remained of Yugoslavia in 2006. Serbia was then further split with the breakaway of Kosovo in 2008. Czechoslovakia had dissolved, in 1992, splitting peacefully into the Czech Republic and Slovakia. Communism was soon abandoned in Cambodia, Ethiopia, South Yemen and Mongolia–which, however, democratically re-elected a Communist government that ran the country until 1996.

Part III: RUSSIA AT THE CROSSROADS—PUTIN'S ERA

These final chapters concern the new Russia with a capitalist economy post socialist-oriented Soviet Union. In 1992, the new President Boris Yeltsin started a crash program to rid society of all vestiges of socialism and introduce a crude capitalist economy for the interests of a few Russians and U.S. /EU capitalists and their politicians. Chapters fourteen through seventeen concern Vladimir Putin's leadership for sovereignty with some governmental controls over limitless capitalism, coupled with defending the nation against aggression.

Chapter eighteen shows how the United States Military Empire acts to limit the sovereignty of everybody else, and recently created the fake Russiagate *campaign to make Putin appear as the demon that must be eliminated even if it means a major war. Chapter nineteen offers some ideas for a future.*

CHAPTER 13

The 1990s: Betrayal of Russian Sovereignty with U.S. Intervention

BORIS YELTSIN WAS born in a small village, Butka, part of the Talitsky district, in Sverdlovsk, Russia, on February 1, 1931. His parents were peasants, whose land was collectivized a year after his birth. They moved to Kazan where his father found work on a construction site.

As a lad, Boris learned construction trades. From 1955 to 1963, Boris worked as a foreman at different construction sites. In 1963, he became chief engineer, and in 1965 head of the Sverdlovsk House-Building Combine. Yeltsin joined the Communist Party in March 1961, and the party appointed him head of construction in 1968. Yeltsin made the Central Committee in March 1981, and four years later rose to the Politburo.

In March 1990, Yeltsin was elected to the Congress of People's Deputies of Russia, and soon elected chairman of the Presidium of the Supreme Soviet of the Russian Soviet Federative Socialist Republic (RSFSR). Gorbachev had personally pleaded with the Russian deputies not to select Yeltsin. The power struggle was, partly, between leaders of the Soviet Union and the RSFSR structures. On June 12, in an attempt to gain more power, the RSFSR Congress adopted a declaration of sovereignty. A month later, Yeltsin resigned from the CPSU.

Following the attempted coup against Soviet leader Gorbachev in August 1991, Yeltsin, now Russia's president, banned Communist Party activities on Russian soil, on November 6. At the end of December, the SU no longer existed and Yeltsin could begin the counter-revolution against socialism and communist vision in all seriousness, but not without abundant help from the United States.

Among the many reforms Yeltsin promulgated was cutting out most of the aid the Soviet Union had given to many countries and not only those in the union or other allies, but also several poor countries especially African ones. I was living in Cuba at the time and I saw and personally felt how much Soviet comradeship had meant.

Fidel Castro announced the "Special Period in Peacetime". Fewer ships docked at our harbors since Russia stopped most trade with Cuba. In those years (1990-2), I was often sailing on Cuban ships as a volunteer merchant marine, as I mention in the foreword. I was gathering experiences and material for my next book, *Cuba at Sea*. It never got published in Cuba. In fact, the publishing house I worked for, *Editorial José Martí*, was closed down later in the decade. I had two books in Spanish ready to be published by this house and another Cuban publishing house, both translations of books published in English. They didn't make it either. The government had to cut publishing by 90%, only the most critically important works were printed. (1)

During the "special period", which lasted the decade, we lost weight. My teeth had been white and soon turned brown. Thousands of people lost partial eyesight from malnutrition. No one starved to death, as so many did/do in some Latin American countries and elsewhere, but we often went to bed hungry. Many social programs had to be cut back but not free education and health care, albeit there was much less medicine since some had come from the Soviet Union, or was paid for in precious few dollars the government had and at high prices from Europe because of the Yankee blockade. Oil and gasoline became scarce since most had come from Russia for Cuban sugar, which also suffered in loss of production. Light bulbs, for instance, could hardly ever be found in stores so that when they went out in homes candles were used or bulbs were stolen from work places, which also became darker. In fact, there was much less of everything except solidarity among the people. We helped each out more, we exchanged items, and we complained less about government bureaucracy, in part, because there was more flexibility. We struggled to hang on to what socialism had been achieved, even though the economy was opened to some of capitalism's marketing mechanism, which today are taking over all too much.

RUSSIAN ECONOMY

President Yeltsin implemented economic shock therapy: price liberalization and nationwide privatization. Unlike Gorbachev's reforms, which sought to expand democracy in the socialist system, the new regime aimed to completely dismantle socialism. In discussions about this transition, Yeltsin's advisers debated issues of speed and sequencing.

On January 2, 1992, Yeltsin, acting as his own prime minister, ordered the liberalization of foreign trade, prices and currency. At the same time, Yeltsin followed a policy of "macroeconomic stabilization", a harsh austerity regime designed to control inflation. Due to the total economic shift, a majority of national property and wealth fell into the hands of a small number of oligarchs. The millionaire-billionaire oligarchs likened themselves to 19th century robber barons. Rather than creating new enterprises, Yeltsin's democratization led to international monopolies hijacking the former Soviet markets, arbitraging the huge difference between old domestic prices for Russian commodities and the prevailing world market prices.

On December 12, 1993, a Russian Federation Constitution was approved by 54.5% of those voting, which was 55% of those eligible. About 33 million people wanted this Constitution while 25 million either preferred the 1978 RSFSR Constitution or something else. (http://www.mid.ru/en/foreign_policy/official_documents//asset_publisher/CptICkB6BZ29/content/id/571508)

The new Constitution guaranteed private property rights and a market economy: "In the Russian Federation the integrity of economic space, free flow of goods, services and financial resources, support of competition, and the freedom of economic activity shall be guaranteed." Article 8.

Civil liberties are also granted—freedom of speech and press, censorship shall be banned, rights of assembly and peaceable protest are guaranteed. Article 29.

The world's largest financial educational website, Investopedia, is based in New York and Canada, and is Establishment oriented. Its January 21, 2016 article, "The Russian Economy since the Collapse of the Soviet Union" by Matthew Johnston reveals how ruinous Yeltsin's capitalism was for the people all the while the U.S. government encouraged and financially supported this ruin. (http://www.investopedia.com/articles/investing/012116/russian-economy-collapse-soviet-union.asp)

"The privatization reforms would see 70% of the economy privatized by the middle of 1994 and in the run-up to the 1996 presidential election, Yeltsin initiated a 'loans-for-shares' program that transferred ownership of some natural resource enterprises to some powerful businessmen in exchange for loans to help with the government budget. These so-called 'oligarchs' would use some of their newly acquired wealth to help finance Yeltsin's re-election campaign," in 1996.

Russians saw their disposable incomes rapidly decline, and national capital was leaving the country en masse, $150 billion in six years. Real GDP growth declined 4.9% by 1998.

YELTSIN-CLINTON

Russia's foreign policy now reversed to align with U.S. imperialism. A major step was to withdraw completely from Afghanistan.

According to Russian journalist-film documentarian Andrey Karaulov, the main trigger for President Muhammad Najibullah losing power in Afghanistan was Russia's refusal to sell oil products to Afghanistan. The Yeltsin government did not want to support communists or former communists, which effectively triggered an embargo. In April, Najibullah and his government fell to the mujahideen, which replaced Najibullah with a new and contentious governing council. (https://en.wikipedia.org/wiki/Soviet%E2%80%93Afghan_War)

Dr. Najib found refuge in the UN compound where he lived during the next four years of civil war between several contending political-ethnic-disparate-Muslim groupings. Taliban controlled much of the territory and finally seized state power on September 27, 1996. One of its first acts was to grab Najibullah from his UN refuge, castrate him, then drag him behind a car over Kabul streets before shooting him. They then hung his body, and that of his brother, from a traffic post.

The United States had won the long "Cold War" conflict against Russia and the other Soviet Republics, for the time being, and would now assure that their man ruled Russia as the U.S. saw fit. Meddling with the economy and politics, including election fixing, was now the empire's strategy.

Both Presidents George Bush and Bill Clinton embraced the wild alcoholic as their perfect post- Soviet Union leader. The first of 18 meetings during Yeltsin-Clinton presidencies took place in Vancouver

April 3-4, 1993, as a serious internal struggle over politics and economics was unfolding inside the Kremlin. Here are excerpts from Clinton's talk at a news conference in Vancouver.

> *"The heroic deeds of Boris Yeltsin and the Russian people launched their reforms toward democracy and market economies and defended them valiantly during the dark days of August of 1991. Now it is the self-interest and the high duty of all the world's democracies to stand by Russia's democratic reforms in their new hour of challenge."*
>
> *"The emergence of a newly productive and prosperous Russia could add untold billions in new growth to the global economy. That would mean new jobs and new investment opportunities for Americans and our allies around the world. We are investing today not only in the future of Russia but in the future of America as well."*
>
> *"Mr. President, our Nation will not stand on the sidelines when it comes to democracy in Russia. We know where we stand. We are with Russian democracy. We are with Russian reforms. We are with Russian markets. We support freedom of conscience and speech and religion. We support respect for ethnic minorities. We actively support reform and reformers and you in Russia."*
>
> *"I discussed with President Yeltsin the initiatives totaling $1.6 billion intended to bolster political and economic reforms in Russia... We will invest in the growth of Russia's private sector through two funds to accelerate privatization and to lend to new small private businesses. We will resume grain sales to Russia and extend $700 million in loans for Russia to purchase American grain. We will launch a pilot project to help provide housing and retraining for the Russian military officers as they move into jobs in the civilian economy."*

The U.S. Congress with broad, bipartisan majority approved the program in September fully cognizant of the Russian Constitutional crisis underway.

CONSTITUTIONAL CRISIS 1993

This initial $2.7 billion in U.S. "gifts" and loans was not viewed propitiously by large numbers of ordinary people and many political activists, not only Communists. The Yeltsin-U.S. economic shock treatment forebode disaster. President Clinton's friendship was seen for what it was by many, encroachment upon Russia's sovereignty.

Just days after the first Clinton-Yeltsin meeting, on April 25, a referendum was held to fortify Yeltsin's direction. Two of the four questions on the referendum were most relevant: 1) yes or no confidence vote for Yeltsin as President—yes 60%; no 40% of the 64% who voted; 2) should there be early elections for parliament—yes 69%; no 31%.

Tensions grew between Yeltsin and most members of the parliament. The constitutional crisis reached a head on September 21, 1993 when Yeltsin arbitrarily dissolved the legislature. The parliament asserted that the president had no legal authority to do so, and then impeached Yeltsin.

The parliament cited Article 121 of the Constitution as amended 1989-93:

> *"The powers of the President of Russian Federation cannot be used to change the national and state organization of the Russian Federation, to dissolve or to interfere with the functioning of any elected organs of state power. In this case, his powers cease immediately."*

The parliament then proclaimed former Soviet General and Vice President Alexander Rutskoy as acting president. His vice-president would be the chairman of the Supreme Soviet of Russia, Ruslan Khasbulatov, a former supporter of Yeltsin. They served from September 22 to October 4.

For days, police, soldiers and civilians demonstrated and collided on the street from various viewpoints. On October 3, pro-Yeltsin demonstrators removed police cordons around the parliament, took over the mayor's offices and tried to storm the Ostankino television center.

Former general Rutskoy appealed to his officer colleagues. Most of the army initially declared neutrality. Some stated their intention to back the parliament, but most generals did not want to take their chances with a Rutskoy-Khasbulatov regime. On the morning of October 4, under Yeltsin's orders, generals instructed soldiers to storm the Supreme Soviet building. By noon, troops entered the White House and occupied it, floor by floor. They arrested the leaders of the legal resistance.

The "second October Revolution", as some called it, entailed the deadliest street fighting in Moscow since 1917. According to government estimates, 187 people were killed and 437 wounded, while non-governmental sources put the death toll as high as 2,000. Many of the death occurred when Yeltsin ordered the parliament bombed, killing many legislators.

The West's political leaders and their mass media all but applauded the death toll as necessary for "democracy" to prevail. U.S., EU, NATO leaders gushed forth with support and pleasure. Even the small but most loyal vassal state, Denmark (where the author lives) heralded Yeltsin's victory. Its foreign minister, Niels Helvig Pedersen, called Yeltsin "our hope. He stands as a guarantee for democratic development."

Upon victory, Yeltsin repeated his announcement of a constitutional referendum, and new legislative elections for December. Yeltsin claimed that by dissolving the Russian parliament he was clearing the tracks for a rapid transition to a functioning market economy. With this pledge, *he received strong backing from the leading powers of the West.* Yeltsin's relationships with Western powers, particularly the United States, made him unpopular with many Russians. But Yeltsin had control over television and pro-parliamentary views were censored.

In December 1993, a new Constitution was adapted on a referendum and new Duma elections took place. This Constitution gave the president more power, including the ability to appoint high-ranking officials. It also divided the parliament into two houses: the State Duma became the lower chamber and the Federation Council was established as an upper chamber. In 1994, the new Duma pardoned those who defied Yeltsin's attack and they were released from jail.

YELTSIN-U.S. MEETINGS OF MINDS

U.S. government Office of the Historian wrote: "Clinton was strongly inclined not only to like Yeltsin but also to support his policies, in particular, his commitment to Russian democracy. During the seven years both were in office, 'Bill and Boris' met eighteen times, nearly as often as their predecessors had met throughout the entire Cold War." (https://history.state.gov/milestones/1993-2000/clinton-yeltsin)

This is a partial list of official meetings, U.S. government moneys given to Yeltsin's government, and U.S.-Russia reaching agreement to bring Russia into NATO. (https://en.wikipedia.org/wiki/Russia%E2%80%93United_States_relations, and sources from mainstream media, book authors, and U.S. government documents.)

- **1992:** Russian President Yeltsin visits the U.S. on January 26. He and Bush set up the United States-Russia Joint Commission on P.O.W./M.I.A.'s. Its mission is to discover what happened to POWs and those missing in action during the Cold War, as well as planes shot down, missing submarines. The committee had access to classified archives from the FBI and the KGB.
- **1992:** Russia attends the Washington Summit on June 16. The United States and Russia sign an Agreement Concerning Cooperation in the Exploration and Use of Outer Space for Peaceful Purposes on June 17.
- **1993:** Bush and Yeltsin sign the START II treaty in Moscow on January 3.
- **1993:** First summit meeting between U.S. President Bill Clinton and Yeltsin on April 4, in Vancouver, Canada.
- **1994:** Presidents Clinton and Yeltsin sign the Kremlin accords on January 14 in Moscow. Russia is to dismantle its nuclear weapons in the Ukraine
- **1994:** First joint U.S.-Russia Space Shuttle mission on February 3.
- **1994:** The United States and Russia move to end the practice of aiming their strategic nuclear missiles at each other on May 30.
- **1994:** Russia joins the Partnership for Peace program on June 22. A NATO program aimed at creating trust with other states in Europe and the former Soviet Union; 21 states are members.
- **1995:** Russia joins the NATO-led IFOR—a one-year peace enforcement force in Bosnia—on December 20.
- **1996:** Clinton and Yeltsin attend the Summit of the Peacemakers in Egypt to condemn terrorist attacks in Israel and to declare their support for the Middle East peace process on March 14.
- **1997:** Russia joins the NATO-led Euro-Atlantic Partnership Council to cooperate on political and security issues on January 1.

- **1997:** Clinton and Yeltsin hold another summit on European Security in Helsinki, Finland, on March 21. They reach some economic agreements, but there is disagreement on NATO expansion.
- **1997:** Russia attends the NATO summit in Paris, France, on May 27.
- **1997:** The NATO-Russia Founding Act provides the formal basis of bilateral cooperation between the U.S., Russia and NATO is signed on May 27. Allows participation in NATO decision making; Russia agrees to drop opposition to NATO expansion in Central Europe.
- **1997:** Russia joins the G8 at 23rd summit in Denver, Colorado, on June 20 to June 22.
- **1998:** Clinton and Yeltsin agree to exchange information on missile-launchings and to remove 50 metric tons of plutonium from their nuclear weapons stocks in a summit in Moscow September 1-2.
- **1999:** March: Operation Allied Force: NATO bombing of Yugoslavia to force it out of Kosovo. Moscow condemned it as a breach of international law and a challenge to Russia's status in the Balkans. Nevertheless, on June 12 Yeltsin's government joined NATO-led KFOR peacekeeping force following the Kosovo War.
- **1999:** Clinton and Yeltsin meet at an Organization for Security Cooperation in Europe Summit Meeting in Istanbul, Turkey November 18–19 to discuss arms control, Chechnya and events in Europe. Clinton remarks that the international community does not dispute Russia's right to defend its territorial integrity and to fight terrorism.

The only real difference on foreign policy between Yeltsin and Clinton was over U.S. wars in Iraq and Yugoslavia. Yeltsin thought Clinton ought to be more "conciliatory" and not "dictate terms". Yeltsin could also foresee that NATO forces might get too close to Russia itself. (http://articles.latimes.com/1993-01-26/news/mn-2013_1_united-states)

NATO intervened in the Bosnian War between Croats—led by pro-Nazis—Bosnians and Serbs in Bosnia-Herzegovina. The internal war—

April 1992-December 1995—was brutal on all sides. The UN gave NATO the green light for a "humanitarian" operation so NATO bombed the Serbs August-September 1995.

Serbian President Slobodan Milosevic (1989-97; and Yugoslav president 1997-2000) was viewed as the culprit. He was the last truly socialist leader in Europe—he founded the Socialist Party of Serbia. He ended the one-party system. His government was a democratically elected coalition with the farmers' party. The West wanted him out and sought to divide Yugoslavia, eventually successfully into separate five states.

The Kosovo Liberation Army (KLA), known terrorists and drug dealers as so listed by the United States, sought to "liberate" Kosovo where the majority were Albanians. NATO again flexed its muscles, this time without UN backing, and bombed Serbia 78 days consecutively March-June 1999, in another "humanitarian intervention". The CIA financed and armed the terrorist KLA. They killed between 5,000 and 18,000 Serbs in those 78 days; wounded 15,000; destroyed 25,000 homes, dozens of schools and churches. And they arrested Milosevic for genocide, crimes against humanity, mass killings and deportations.

They refused to let the man, who had a weak heart, see a cardiologist. Instead guards gave him a pill without his knowledge and he died of a "heart attack", March 11, 2006. Ten years later, March 24, 2016, *the International Criminal Tribunal court on Yugoslavia (ICTY) found Milosevic not guilty of the accused crimes. But its exoneration was buried on page 1,303 of a 2,590-page verdict.* (https://www.globalresearch.ca/slobodan-milosevic-the-killing-of-an-innocent-man/5541534)

The Western media, and some politicians, had called Milosevic a Hitler just like they do Putin. Kosovo today, regarded by many as a "gangster state," boasts one of America's largest bases in the world, Camp Bondsteel.

ECONOMY II

Seeing Clinton buttering up to Yeltsin helped many Western capitalists invest in the new Russian economy. U.S.-owned Otis Elevator, for example, formed four joint ventures, investing an initial $50 million in 1990-2. Foreign capitalists got the golden opportunity to buy into the new economy with little risk and great profit yields.

U.S. agribusiness also got richer exporting food to the previously self-sufficient food producing country, because 80% of Russian farms went bankrupt between 1991 and 1998.

The *Harvard Business Review*, May-June 1994 issue, reported: "The climate for international joint ventures has never been better...Russia has a cheap and highly educated workforce, inexpensive land, and abundant natural resources. According to a study [by Siberian-born Vladimir] Kvint conducted of joint ventures attempted between 1989 and 1993, between 35% and 38% of those consummated are already profitable or well on the way. That's the highest success rate in the world for new businesses." (https://hbr.org/1994/05/the-russian-investment-dilemma)

"As the figurehead of liberal reform in the turbulent political environment of post-Soviet Russia, President Yeltsin was often the focus of Clinton's policy initiatives...Clinton also lobbied for even larger multilateral aid through the G7, nearly doubling the sum previously agreed by George Bush and his partners to a total of $43 billion, while setting only vague conditions for implementation," wrote mainstream international journalists and filmmaker Frederick Bernas, June 4, 2011. http://www.frederickbernas.com/2011/06/clinton-russia.html

This became the real *russiagate.*

"The reforms of the 1990s were mainly the work of [Yeltsin] advisers...Fearing that the population might soon have a change of heart and turn its back on reform, Yegor Gaidar and Anatoly Chubais, the chief Russian architects of the process, decided to accelerate it, selling off state resources and enterprises at little or no charge. Not long into the process, ownership of some of Russia's most valuable resources was auctioned off by oligarch-owned banks...the bank auctioneers rigged the process and in almost every case ended up as the successful bidders. This was how [Mikhail] Khodorkovsky got a 78 percent share of ownership in Yukos, worth about $5 billion, for a mere $310 million, and how Boris Berezovsky got Sibneft, another oil giant, worth $3 billion, for about $100 million...Since the state was very weak, these 'new Russians' paid little or no taxes on their purchases," wrote author Marshall Goldman, Harvard professor of economics and associate director of Russian Studies. (Khodorkovsky was worth $15 billion in 2003 and considered to be the wealthiest Russian. He served 10 years in prison for fraud from 2003-13 once Putin took some control over the economy.)

1996 ELECTIONS

The Yeltsin era was marked by widespread corruption. As a result of that and his careless rush to capitalism with persistent low oil and commodity prices, Russia suffered inflation, economic collapse, and enormous political and social problems, which also affected former USSR republics. At the end of the Soviet Union, 20% of the population lived in poverty (World Bank). By 1996, average income had fallen by 50% and the poverty level had reached 40% of the population. *The average length of life had fallen from 69 to 64 years of age in just five years.*

Many of Yeltsin's initial supporters now criticized his leadership, and Vice President Alexander Rutskoy even denounced the reforms as "economic genocide".

By the beginning of 1996, there were eleven candidates for presidential elections scheduled for June 16. Polls showed Yeltsin with only 8% of potential votes while the Communist candidate, Gennady Zyuganov, was leading all candidates with 21% polled.

U.S. President Bill Clinton had to bail his capitalist politician friend out of this democratic mess. What better way than with money for his campaign, loans from IMF to bolster the failing economy, and good old fashioned CIA "black arts" to control the media and to subvert opponent campaigns.

Authors David M Kotz, professor of economics at the University of Massachusetts Amherst, and Fred Weir, Canadian journalist and Moscow correspondent for Christian Science Monitor, wrote the book, *Russia's Path from Gorbachev to Putin: The Demise of the Soviet System and the New Russia*, (Rooutledge, 2007) in which they state that Yeltsin used "black arts" to win.

Russia's electoral law limited campaign spending to $3 million per candidate. The Communist Party did not have the financial resources to overspend the limit. However, estimates of the funds spent by the Yeltsin campaign range from $700 million to $2 billion. A huge amount of money was raised by oligarchs and other business interests. An even larger sum was made available indirectly by the West. Urged by the U.S., the International Monetary Fund granted a $10.2 billion loan in February, which enabled the government to spend huge sums to pay back wages and pensions to millions of Russians, with some overdue checks arriving shortly before the June election.

William Blum has documented that just since WWII the United States has perverted/subverted elections in 30 countries, some of them several times—Chile, Bolivia, Panama, Nicaragua, Italy. This illegal, anti-democratic intervention includes: giving money to favored candidates, false media propaganda, controlling media, advertising, gathering information about opponent candidates and subverting their campaigns —remember Watergate.

We are not talking here about the 20 violent coups made or attempted against sitting governments, or untold scores of assassinations of government and civic leaders—those are other categories which the CIA has performed in its illustrious career for democracy.

Here is an excerpt from Blum's book, *Rogue State*, on U.S government-capitalist "perverting elections" in Russia's 1996 election—remember the Italian 1948 election.

> *"For four months (March-June), a group of veteran American political consultants worked secretly in Moscow in support of Boris Yeltsin's presidential campaign. Although the Americans were working independently, President Clinton's political guru, Dick Morris, acted as their middleman to the administration, and Clinton himself told Yeltsin in March that he wanted to 'make sure everything the United States did would have a positive impact' on the Russian electoral campaign.*
>
> *"Boris Yeltsin was being counted on to run with the globalized-free market ball and it was imperative that he cross the goal line."*
>
> *"The Americans emphasized sophisticated methods of message development, polling, focus groups, crowd staging, direct-mailing, etc., urged more systematic domination of the Communists. Most of all they encouraged the Yeltsin campaign to 'go negative' against the Communists, painting frightening pictures of what the Communists would do if they took power, including much civic upheaval and violence, and, of course, a return to the worst of Stalinism. With a virtual media blackout against them, the Communists were extremely hard pressed to respond to the attacks."*

In the first round of voting, Yeltsin edged the Communists by 35% to 32%. About 75 million people voted; a 70% turnout. The second round between the two leading contenders was decisive for the candidate with the most money and greater media coverage. About the same numbers of people voted. Yeltsin got 54% and Zyuganov 40%.

"Democracy" won, crowed *Time* magazine, July 15, 1996. Yeltsin graced (or disgraced) the publication's cover.

Projection, according to Merriam-Webster dictionary, means, "the attribution of one's own ideas, feelings, or attitudes to other people or to objects; *especially*: the externalization of blame, guilt, or responsibility as a defense against anxiety."

That is exactly what the Clintons, President Bill and President-to-be Hillary fell into when, in 2016, the female imperial warrior lost what she assumed was a shoe-in presidential election campaign. She and hubby knew that they had done the dirty deed of subverting the Russian elections, in 1996, and envisioned reciprocity—chickens coming home to roost two decades later. Their allegation of "Russian interference", "Russian hacking" was reinforced by their Deep State ally, which fabricated the whole lie—to be discussed in chapter 17.

ISLAMIST TERROR THREAT TO RUSSIA

In addition to economic chaos, the use of totalitarian methods to stifle political opposition and the majority will—debilitating the lives of much of the people—the Yeltsin regime was confronted by Islamist terrorism, which grew out of the Afghanistan war backed by the U.S..

Many Islamists who fought the Communist regime in Afghanistan, such as Osama bin Laden's al Qaeda, had come from other Muslim-led countries. At the end of the war, most returned to their country of origin or went elsewhere to continue spreading Jihad, one of those areas was Chechnya, a small semi-autonomous region of the Russian Federation with 1.2 million people. Chechen Islamist guerrilla commander Shamil Basayev, for example, had insurgents under his command from several Arab countries, among those were fundamentalists who had been armed and trained by the U.S. in Pakistan and Afghanistan.

Moscow feared politicized religious identity could produce demands for separate and small Islamic states, just as earlier political demands from ethnic groups led to secessionist movements, and would lead to more violent conflicts. In December 1994, Yeltsin ordered a military intervention of Chechnya in an attempt to restore Moscow's control over the republic, which was splitting. The First Chechnya War ended with a peace treaty, August 1996, and Russian troops were withdrawn.

Casualties were large: tens of thousands of civilians killed, at least 3000 secessionist fighters and from 5,700 to 14,000 Russian soldiers.

The main conflict in foreign affairs between the Yeltsin and Clinton regimes was over secession of Chechnya. Unusual for the United States, it did not get involved in this conflict directly, no troops, no drones, no violence from the CIA. U.S. ambivalence toward the Russo-Chechen conflict arose from a greater strategic interest to support the new Russian government, and score billions for its capitalist investors in Russia. (2)

Dagestan is also a small autonomous region within the Russian Federation. Its three million inhabitants have been a heterogeneous people of several dozen ethnic groups. Upon the conclusion of Communist rule in Afghanistan, however, some Sufi and Wahhabi Muslims advocating medievalist sharia laws—rule by scriptures according to Imams wherein males dominate females—demanded religious, political and economic concessions with the use of weapons.

In spring 1999 local authorities engaged in a standoff with Wahhabi villages in Dagestan, where the inhabitants had amassed weapons. In August 1999, Chechen forces led by Shamil Basayev invaded neighboring Dagestan to support Wahhabis, providing a trigger for a new war between Moscow and Chechnya. Later, Basayev was an organizer of the seizure of 850 hostages in a Moscow theater in October 2002, in which 130 died and 40 of the 50 Chechen terrorist separatists also died.

A Swedish photographer, Jens Olof Lasthein, held a photo exhibition in Copenhagen, in 2017 on "Caucasian borderlands". Someone he photographed, an elder man from Dagestan, said: "Things were better in the old days, in Soviet Times." He said most "everyone being friends—when we didn't care about nationality or religion, when we didn't have to worry about borders and conflict zones."

As terror spread to Dagestan, the Second Chechnya War broke out in October 1999. When it ended in February 2000 between 25,000 and 100,000 civilians had been killed, as well as 14-16,000 separatists, and 3,500 Russian soldiers. Guerrilla warfare continued sporadically for years.

Photograph by Swedish photographer Jens Olof Lasthein

Acts of terror, and politically and commercially motivated assassinations were a fact of life inside Russia in the 1990s, too. By 1999, apartment building bombings in Moscow and Volgodonsk brought political violence to a new level.

ENTER PUTIN

Vladimir Putin started a political life in Saint Petersburg in 1991 as an international affairs advisor for the Mayor's office. Throughout the 1990s, he held several positions in local government. On March 26, 1997, President Yeltsin rewarded this disciplined and efficient worker by making him deputy chief of his presidential staff. In July 1998, Yeltsin appointed Putin Director of the Federal Security Service (FSB), the primary intelligence and security organization of the Russian Federation and the KGB successor. He held that position until August 9, 1999 when Yeltsin made him one of three first deputy prime ministers, and on the same day appointed him acting prime minister. The State Duma then approved that appointment, its fifth in 18 months.

Virtually unknown to the general public few expected Putin to last longer than his predecessors. He was initially regarded as a Yeltsin loyalist, whose main opponents campaigned to replace the ailing president with someone other than Putin. His law-and-order image and his unrelenting approach to the Second Chechen War against the unrecognized Chechen Republic of Ichkeria raised Putin's popularity and allowed him to overtake all rivals.

Not associated with any party, Putin pledged his support to the newly formed Unity Party. It won the second largest percentage of the popular vote (23.3%) in the December 1999 Duma elections.

On December 31, 1999, Yeltsin unexpectedly resigned. According to the Constitution of Russia, Putin became Acting President of the Russian Federation. He won early presidential elections on March 26, 2000 on the first round with 53% of the vote, and was inaugurated on May 7.

When Yeltsin suddenly resigned from office, Clinton praised his counterpart for helping to achieve "genuine progress" in U.S.-Russian relations. "Of course, we have also had our differences," Clinton observed, "but the starting point for our relationship has always been how Russia and America can work together to advance our common interests."

Those common interests were well described by Mortimer Zuckerman, an Establishment member of the Council on Foreign Relations and owner of US News & World Reports as, "the largest giveaway of a nation's wealth in history"—so quoted in F.W. Engdahl's 2018 book, "Manifest Destiny: Democracy as Cognitive Dissonance. Former KGB generals were bribed by "The Enterprise", set up by some of 800 CIA officials fired by President Jimmy Carter to loot the entire gold reserves of the Russian National Bank during Yeltsin's years. They were placed in CIA-controlled Swiss banks and off shore bank havens.

Notes:

1. When it became clear that my book couldn't come out, I waited several years before finishing it. Socialist Resistance (London) published it May 2008. I had it translated into Spanish Cuba en Altamar by Omar Pérez López, one of Che's sons. It never got published in Cuba. You can find it here in English: http://resistancebooks.org/product/cuba-at-sea/

   This is something I wrote about Omar. https://dissidentvoice.org/2011/04/che%E2%80%99s-poet-son-omar/

2. The small secessionist Ichkeria movement lost both uprisings and by 2000 many of its leaders went into exile in Poland and England. In October 2007, one leader, Dokka Umarov gave himself the noble Arabic title of Emir. He took public responsibility for organizing several suicide terror attacks, the gravest in 2010 and 2011. The former, at the Moscow Metro killed 40 people and injured 100 at random; the latter, at Moscow's Domodedovo International Airport killed 37 and injured 173 people at random.

   One month after the Emir self-appointment, another leading Chechen secessionist, Akhmed Zakayev declared himself Prime Minister in exile, in London. Russia sought his return on charges of terrorism, which Zakayev denied. Nevertheless, he declared Jihad and encouraged foreign Islamists to fight beside his Chechen separatists.

In the two Chechnya wars several thousand came from other Arabic countries to fight for Chechnya's secession.

A March 2003 referendum established the post of President of the Chechen Republic, an autonomous republic within the Russian Federation. Four parties were formed. Akhmat Kadyrov, an Islamic scholar (Mufti) won the October 5, election with 80% of the vote, although Western sources and secessionists disputed its authenticity. The West suspected Kadyrov, because President Putin had appointed him, in July 2000, as interim head of administering the government. Islamist militants murdered him on May 4, 2004.

Akhmed Zakayev was allowed to return to Chechnya. He won the November 2007 elections, and served as prime minister until August 2009.

While the U.S. government did not get directly involved, the mass media clearly sided with the secessionists and the U.S.'s right-wing. The Guardian published a piece about this by John Laughland, "The Chechen's American Friends", on September 8, 2004. John Laughland is a trustee of the British Helsinki Human Rights Group.

https://www.theguardian.com/world/2004/sep/08/usa.russia

"There have been numerous editorials encouraging us to understand - to quote the Sunday Times - the 'underlying causes' of Chechen terrorism (usually Russian authoritarianism), while the widespread use of the word 'rebels' to describe people who shoot children shows a surprising indulgence in the face of extreme brutality."

The main fount of Chechen independence terrorists came from the American Committee for Peace in Chechnya (ACPC). "The list of the self-styled 'distinguished Americans', who are its members is a roll call of the most prominent neoconservatives who so enthusiastically support the 'war on terror': Richard Perle, the notorious Pentagon adviser; Elliott Abrams of Iran-Contra fame;...Frank Gaffney of the militarist Centre for Security Policy; Bruce Jackson, former US military intelligence officer and one-time vice-president of Lockheed Martin, now president of the US Committee on Nato; Michael Ledeen of the American Enterprise Institute, a former admirer of Italian fascism and now a leading proponent of regime change in Iran; and R James Woolsey, the former CIA director who is one of the leading cheerleaders behind George Bush's plans to re-model the Muslim world along pro-US lines."

Former FBI agent and its chief counsel in Minneapolis, Coleen Rowley confirmed United States support for Chechnya terrorists, in a consortium news article, April 19, 2013, "Chechen Terrorists and the Neo-cons".

CHAPTER 14
President Putin's First Terms

"CHINA AND RUSSIA—these are two nations with whom we have super relations, the best in years," Secretary of State General Colin Powell told print journalists in Washington DC, on May 26, 2004.

"When I was Chairman at the end of the Cold War and I was testifying one day, I said, well, you know, the Soviet Union is gone, the Warsaw Pact is gone, you know, I'm running out of enemies. And it was a whimsical way of saying that I have to redesign the Army and the whole Armed Forces of the United States because everything we had been focused on for 30, 40 years was going away. And I said I'm down to Kim Il-Sung and Castro."

"Nobody worries about conflict between the United States and Russia now, or the United States and China. There's a caution that I have to put in here because Taiwan is an issue, but, you know, we're not – we're working with them peacefully to solve regional problems. We're working with Russia and China to improve trading relations and economic relations. We have security interests in Asia that we talk to the Chinese about. We don't want to see any conflict in Asia. We don't want to see any conflict in the world that can be avoided. And working with people that used to be considered adversaries of ours, or competitors of ours, is a fundamental difference over the last 10 or 12 years." (https://2001-2009.state.gov/secretary/former/powell/remarks/32872.htm)

No doubt Colin Powell had watched as President Bill Clinton and President Vladimir Putin embraced shortly after the latter took the reins of power as president. In June 2000, Clinton came to Putin in Moscow and they signed two agreements to decrease war possibilities—destroying many tons of plutonium and sharing an early warning radar system in

Jette Salling's paraphrase art of peace dove rising to the sun.

Moscow. They disagreed, however, on Clinton's proposal to modify the 1972 ABM treaty that would allow the U.S. to build a missile defense system, a missile shield as it became known, as that would give the U.S. the ability for a first strike without much fear of commensurate retaliation.

In Putin's first state of the nation address, in July, he announced plans to reverse the increase in poverty and falling living standards. He probably did not think that that would upset the United States but he was not experienced enough yet. Putin continued trying to please his counterparts by pardoning Edmond Pope, a spy for the Defense Intelligence Agency. Pope had been sentenced to 20 years in prison just eight months before for buying and smuggling classified military equipment out of Russia. Pope maintained he was innocent and had been framed. Regardless of who was most truthful, the fact that he was sent home should have been a positive sign.

The Russian government repudiated Marxism-Leninism, emphasizing capitalism with some government controls and cooperation with the West. Once George Bush captured the presidency, Putin met with him several times, and they described themselves as friends. At their first meeting, June 16, 2001, held in Slovenia, Bush said: "I looked him in the eye and got a sense of his soul. I could trust him." Putin said about Bush: "He's easy to talk to, sincere even sentimental."

Putin said the two countries "are not enemies", and there is no need to "expand NATO. We could be fully good allies." Putin even theorized about NATO bringing Russia into it to relieve any tensions and war plans, just as he had theoretically proposed to Clinton during his last visit to Moscow as president, June 6, 2000.

Putin told Oliver Stone, *The Putin Interviews*. Skyhorse Publishing, 2017. Page 40:

> *"I told him—half-seriously/half as a joke—'probably Russia should think about joining NATO'. And his response was, 'Why not? I think that's possible.' But when we saw the reaction of his team, we understood that they were somewhat bewildered or even frightened by this idea."* (See more of Stone-Putin interviews further down.)

That's for certain. President Clinton's team—just like later with President Bush's team from the PNAC (Project for a New American Century)—realized that would mean the loss of trillions of dollars in profits for the military-industrial complex, and ever-heightening salaries for tens of thousands of military and intelligence officers.

Unlike Yeltsin, Putin understood the need to integrate with the whole world. He strengthened ties with China by signing the Treaty of Good-Neighborliness and Friendly Cooperation, and building the Trans-Siberian oil pipeline to assist China's energy needs. He traveled to Cuba and embraced Fidel. After Angela Merkel was elected Chancellor, November 2005, they began a close and frequent exchange over telephone and in person. Putin learned German fluently, and Merkel was brought up in East Germany with both languages.

On the day of the terror attacks in New York and elsewhere, Putin and his wife attended their Russian Orthodox Church to light a candle for those killed and injured, and they prayed for them. In Moscow, women who spoke no English were filmed sobbing in front of a makeshift tribute on a sidewalk. Television and radio stations went silent to commemorate the dead.

President Putin put Russian troops on alert in response to the attacks. He held emergency meetings with security officials planning a tough response to these "barbaric acts". (*New York Times*, September 12, 2001). He told National Security Advisor Condoleezza Rice that all pre-existing hostility between the two countries would be put aside while the U.S. dealt with the tragedy.

Powell was obviously pleased with President Vladimir Putin for offering Russian aid to his President George Bush's war against Afghanistan, and to himself as secretary of state.

The Establishment Brookings Institute President, retired four-star Marine General John R. Allen, praised the Russian president for his support. The U.S. assumed Putin would be like Yeltsin.

"When Russian President Vladimir Putin picked up the phone to express his sympathy to President Bush in the aftermath of September 11 and then followed up by providing concrete assistance to the campaign in Afghanistan and quickly acquiescing to U.S. plans to establish bases in central Asia, Washington policymakers and analysts concluded Putin had made a strategic, even historic, choice to align Russia's foreign policy with that of the United States," reported Fiona Hill, June 1, 2002. (https://www.brookings.edu/articles/putin-and-bush-in-common-cause-russias-view-of-the-terrorist-threat-after-september-11/)

> *"From the beginning of his presidency...Putin pushed the idea of a concerted campaign against terrorism with American and European leaders. He was one of the first to raise the alarm about terrorist training camps in Afghanistan and to warn of linkages between these camps, well-financed terrorist networks, and Islamic militant groups operating in Europe and Eurasia. Russia also actively supported the Northern Alliance in its struggle with the Taliban in Afghanistan. In December 2000, Moscow joined Washington in supporting*

United Nations sanctions against the Taliban [and wanted] sanctions against Pakistan for aiding the Taliban."

Putin, in fact, sent arms supplies to the U.S. Northern Alliance ally. He arranged for one of Russia's few close allies, the former Soviet Republic Kyrgyzstan, to let the U.S. military use one of its bases as a spy center and launching pad for flights to and from Afghanistan. The Yankees were there until June 2014. They had moved 5.3 million servicemen (some more than once) in and out of Afghanistan in 136,000 flights.

Two other former Soviet republics assisted. Uzbekistan allowed the U.S. to use military bases, which stationed 1,500 troops there until 2005. Russia had a military division in Tajikistan, and it allowed the U.S. military to use it, in order to supply weapons and other cargo to its forces in Afghanistan. The U.S. trained some Tajikistan troops.

"The terrorist attacks also came at a time when Putin was trying to improve Russia's relationship with the United States. After a rocky start with the Bush administration—marked by spy scandals and a dispute over U.S. intentions to build a missile defense shield and withdraw from the 1972 Anti-Ballistic Missile Treaty—Putin had worked hard to build a personal affinity with Bush, remove the sense of confrontation, underscore that the Cold War was finally over, and find some mechanism for transcending differences. After September 11, it seemed that the war against terrorism could be just that mechanism. Russia and the United States had finally made common cause," reported Brookings' Fiona Hill. (From 2006 to 2009, Hill served as national intelligence officer for Russia and Eurasia at The National Intelligence Council.)

Despite Russia opening its arms, literally, to the arch enemy, the enemy had not really changed its attitude regardless of the "cordial" personal exchange between the two presidents.

On December 13, 2001, President George W. Bush gave Russia the required 6-month notice of U.S. intent to withdraw from the Anti-Ballistic Missile Treaty so that the Yankees could pursue development of the National Missile Defense (NMD), which was already under way in violation of treaty obligations. Without the ABM treaty, a new U.S. arms race was reinitiated.

OLIVER STONE ON PUTIN

Sixteen years later, Oliver Stone's said that his question-and-answer film on President Vladimir Putin (*Interviews with Putin*) shows that, "Mr. Putin is one of the most important leaders in the world and in so far as the United States has declared him an enemy—a great enemy—I think it's very important we hear what he has to say." http://www.smh.com.au/entertainment/movies/director-oliver-stone-on-his-new-film-subject-russian-president-vladimir-putin-20170422-gvq7mu.html

Stone had made four trips to Moscow between July 2015 and February 2017, interviewing the president 12 times. I saw the film and thoroughly read the book. I'll be citing from it quite a lot. Stone shows the man for himself, the president of the world's largest country, who drove Stone through Moscow streets in his own car, a president who can show this American one of Russia's war rooms, and live images of Russian operations in Syria—a man, as President Bush said of him, whose word you can trust.

This excellent portrait motivated me to take on my own project herein. I identify with Stone's statement on page 101: "I am not pro-Russian. I am pro-peace. It's very important to me, in my lifetime I would like to see peace and I'm scared right now. I'm worried for the world, because I'm worried about my country's attitude towards peace. And it doesn't seem to understand the stakes that it has raised. That's the point I'm trying to make in my documentary here."

The sentence before this quote, Stone said, "I am not anti-American". It is fair to say that I am anti-American if that means that I know that its economic-political rulers do, in fact, "understand the stakes that [they] have raised," and they don't care. They do not die in the wars they dictate. They pay others to do their dirty work while they make more profits, buy more manors and future trips to Mars. They are Americans obsessed with the American Dream to rule the world.

I thought that President Putin would have understood that, but it took him several years before he finally stood his ground and demonstrated that enough's enough, no more encroachments. In the first years of his presidency he tried hard to make an alliance with the U.S. Yet even after the Second Chechnya war, CIA operatives agitated for terrorist attacks against pro-Russian forces. And Putin knew it. He told Stone (pg. 33-4):

"Al Qaeda is not the result of our activities. It's the result of the activities of our American friends. It all started during the Soviet war in Afghanistan. When the American intelligence officers provided support to different streaks of Islamic fundamentalism, helping them to fight the Soviet troops in Afghanistan. So it was the Americans who nurtured both Al Qaeda and bin Laden. But it all spun out of control and it always does. So they're to blame."

"We assumed that the Cold War was over, that we had transparent relations with the United States, with the whole world, and we certainly counted on support. But instead we witnessed the American intelligence services support terrorists. And even when we confirmed that, when we demonstrated that Al Qaeda fighters were fighting in the Caucasus, we still saw the intelligence services of the United States continue to support these fighters.

"There was one episode. I told President Bush about that, and he said, 'Do you have any concrete data [which] specifically does what specifically?' And I told him, 'Yes, I do have such data,' and I showed him, and I even named those persons of the American intelligence services who were working in the Caucasus, including in Baku...they also provided technical support, they helped transfer fighters from one place to another."

Bush told Putin, "I'll sort this all out." This was in 2004-5, and Putin had to wait a long time. Finally, "the CIA sent us a letter. The response was quite peculiar. 'We support all the political forces, including the opposition forces, and we're going to continue to do that." (https://www.reuters.com/article/us-russia-chechnya-cia/russias-chechen-chief-blames-cia-for-violence-idUSTRE58N5S120090924)

When Putin spoke to *The Moscow Times* about this, he said Russian intelligence had intercepted calls between separatists in the North Caucasus and the U.S. intelligence based in the former Soviet Republic Azerbaijan during the early 2000s, proving that Washington was helping the insurgents.

Putin said that President Bush promised to "kick the ass" (a favorite Bush expression) of the intelligence officers in question. But after the CIA letter came to Russia's intelligence service, Federal Security Service (FSB), where Putin had been director, no more was heard from Kick Ass Bush. (https://themoscowtimes.com/articles/putin-accuses-us-of-supporting-separatists-in-russias-north-caucasus-46103)

Putin also told Stone (p.30), rather reluctantly, that he thought it was wrong of the U.S. "to impose on other nations and peoples [their] own standards and models… Democracy cannot be imported from outside, it can only be born within society…I think it would be senseless and damaging if the Soviet Union itself was to impose on other peoples and other nations their rules of conduct."

After reading Stone's book, I interviewed Russia's ambassador to Denmark (June 27, 2017). I wanted to know what a compatriot thought of Putin's attempts to side with this historic enemy.

INTERVIEW WITH RUSSIAN AMBASSADOR MIKHAIL VANIN

Author: President Putin began his presidency by reaching out to President Bush, just as had Yeltsin and Gorbachev. Didn't Putin realize that the U.S. takes the finger offered and demands the hand?

M. V.: *Since the Russia Federation was created, Russia has been injured by terrorism we hadn't before experienced, a terrorism based on fanaticism, on extremist Islamism, and some of them are close to our country and some inside it. That is why when George Bush asked for our help in fighting terrorism that had caused September 11, 2001 President Vladimir Putin came to his aid.*

President Putin wanted new and good relations with the United States, as well as seeking to prevent more violent fundamentalism from Afghanistan extending into Russia. So, we offered whatever surveillance we could, any information, and the use of our territory for U.S. aircraft. But our American friends don't understand those things. They accepted our help but didn't respond in kind.

Author: Putin had been in the KGB and the FSB, and yet he wanted to come into NATO, one of the key arms of U.S. domination?

M.V.: *Maybe if Russia were in NATO, it could curb its expansionism, temper its warring. This shows that the President wanted 'normal' relations, hoping to spend less for military on all sides, helping world peace.*

Well, he knows better now. The U.S. withdrew from the ABM agreement, escalated armaments. The U.S., its deep state, forced President Putin to become a realist. Read his 2007 Munich speech.

As an ambassador in Europe, I ask its leaders to see this [threat to world peace] about the U.S., and to count on their own authority—less weapons, better life. We have a low military budget compared to the U.S., more social welfare and less poverty. But they don't listen."

ECONOMIC REFORMS ACTUALLY HELP ORDINARY PEOPLE

At the end of the Soviet Union, only 1.5% of the people lived under the poverty line, according to World Bank statistics. However, one-fourth the GDP was based on the defense sector. When Yeltsin took over, he cut back on defense and fired most of that work force, which was one in five workers. (The U.S. had one in 16 workers in the defense/weapons sector at that time.) Yeltsin did not find viable substitutes. Half his people went to bed hungry.

Putin changed all that, and that is his biggest sin.

When President Putin called the new rich oligarchs to the bargaining table, he made it clear that while he encouraged profit-making, the need to fortify Russia as a sovereign nation came first. He knew that a country can only ensure its sovereignty if it secures a good economy, a good rate of growth, a minimal amount of inflation, and an economically secure people. Therefore, he insisted that the rich pay adequate taxes and wages, and stop stealing.

"While the 1998 financial crisis had immediate negative effects and severely damaged Russia's financial credibility…it created conditions that allowed Russia to achieve rapid economic expansion throughout most of the next decade. A significantly depreciated ruble helped stimulate domestic production leading to a spurt of economic growth [with] real growth reaching 8.3% in 2000 and approximately 5% in 2001," wrote Matthew Johnston, January 21, 2016, for Investopedia. (https://www.investopedia.com/articles/investing/012116/russian-economy-collapse-soviet-union.asp)

"The coincidence of Putin's succession to power in 1999 with the reversal of economic fortunes gained the new president significant popularity, and he made it his goal to avoid the economic chaos of the previous decade and move the country towards long-term growth and stability. Between 2000 and the end of 2002, Putin enacted a number of economic reforms including simplifying the tax system and reducing a number of tax rates. He also brought about the simplification of business registration and licensing requirements, and the privatization of agricultural land.

"Putin confiscated Russia's largest and most successful company, the Yukos oil company. This event signaled the beginning of a wave of takeovers of private companies by the state. Between 2004 and 2006, the Russian government renationalized a number of companies in what were considered to be 'strategic' sectors of the economy. An estimate by the OECD claims that the government's share of total equity market capitalization sat at 20% by mid-2003 and had increased to 30% by early 2006," Johnston wrote.

In the first four years of Putin's policies, poverty fell to 17.6% and fell further to 13.2% in 2007, the same level as in the United States. By 2004, average income had doubled. Between 2000 and 2008, real GDP growth grew an average of 6.7% annually, and real average income grew 11% annually. Industrial production increased by 125% between 2000 and 2008 and regained pre-Soviet collapse level. Gross domestic production increased from $764 billion in 2007 to $2.1 trillion in 2014.

There were more poor people during the first years of the economic crisis (from 2008), but in 2015 the amount of people living in poverty fell back to 13%. In 2010, the average length of life had risen again to 69 years from 64 years a decade ago.

Putin told Stone that he had not sought to stop privatization, "I just wanted to make it more equitable." By making private property and profit "more fair", Russia paid off its debt to the International Monetary Fund. While the U.S. national debt is nearly $20 trillion or 102% of the GDP; Russia's is $150 billion or 12% of its GDP. And Russia is paying 83% of Chechen's government budget.

"It is not just about Chechnya. Out of 85 constituent entities across Russia, there are [only] 10 which bring in more money than they spend."

Putin had brought stability to the economy, to the country—that is why Wall Street, The Establishment, the Deep State hate him.

PUTIN THE MAN

Vladimir Putin was born October 7, 1952, in Leningrad, of a working class family. Two children died before he was born, one in the 28-month long Siege of Leningrad.

"We lived simply—cabbage soup, cutlets, pancakes, but on Sundays and holidays my Mom would bake very delicious stuffed buns [pirozhki] with cabbage, meat and rice, and curd tarts [vatrushki]," President Vladimir Putin says, as published on an official website: http://eng.putin.kremlin.ru/bio

His mother was a factory worker and a warden. His father had been a conscript in the Soviet Navy, serving in the submarine fleet, and later in the regular army. After the war, he worked in factories as a security guard, foreman, and engineer. He had graduated from vocational college.

After the war, the Putin family moved into a room in a communal apartment [kommunalka], in a typical St Petersburg dwelling house on Baskov Lane. Vladimir Putin recalls, "It was a building with a well-liked yard. Fifth floor. No elevator."

In his early youth, Putin told Stone, "I lived in freedom and I spent much time in the courtyard and the streets. And certainly I was not always as disciplined as some would have liked me to be."

"It became clear that street smarts were not enough, so I began doing sports." At age 12, Vladimir began to practice sambo, a Soviet form of martial art, and judo. His mother did not approve of his decision to do judo. "Every time I went to a practice session, she would grumble, 'He's off to his fights again.'" Things changed after Vladimir's coach visited his home and told his parents about what he did and what he achieved.

Sports, however "was not enough for maintaining my status, so to speak, for very long. I realized that I also needed to study well," Putin says. In 1970, he became a law student at Leningrad State University, earning his degree in 1975. In the late 1970s and early 1980s, Putin studied at a KGB School. Putin was assigned to work in the state security agencies. "My perception of the KGB was based on the idealistic stories I heard about intelligence."

Vladimir met Lyudmila Shkrebneva. She worked as a flight attendant on domestic airlines. They got married on July 28, 1983.

In 1985, before their departure for Germany, Vladimir and Lyudmila welcomed their first daughter, Maria. Their second daughter, Katerina, was born in 1986, in Dresden.

In 1985-1990, Vladimir Putin worked in East Germany at the local intelligence office in Dresden. Over the course of his service, he was promoted to the rank of lieutenant colonel and to the position of senior assistant to the head of the department.

After returning to Leningrad in 1990, Putin became an assistant to the rector of Leningrad State University in charge of international relations. In 1996, he and his family moved to Moscow, where his political career began. In 1997, he earned a candidature degree in economics.

In his presidential 2000 inauguration speech he said, "We have common aims, we want our Russia to be a free, prosperous, flourishing, strong and civilized country, a country that its citizens are proud of and that is respected internationally."

"I consider it to be my sacred duty to unify the people of Russia, to rally citizens around clear aims and tasks, and to remember every day and every minute that we have one Motherland, one people and one future."

"Is Putin Incorruptible?" is an insightful article about the man Putin, written from an unusual angle by Sharon Tennison, founder of Center for Citizen Initiatives (1983), which seeks to "bring about a constructive relationship with the Soviet Union" (and since with Russia). (www.CCISF.org)

Tennison is also a member of Rotary Club in Palo Alto, California—a business, executive fraternity with a service orientation. She wants to help capitalism grow and to be more people friendly.

The article appeared on a website oriented to bringing *The Guardian* back to its purported origins: https://off-guardian.org/2017/04/15/is-putin-incorruptible/

"I don't pretend to be an expert, just a program developer in the USSR and Russia for the past 30 years. But during this time, I've have had far more direct, on-ground contact with Russians of all stripes across 11 time zones than any of the Western reporters or for that matter any of Washington's officials.

I met Putin years before he ever dreamed of being president of Russia, as did many of us working in St.Petersburg during the 1990s. Since all of the slander started, I've become nearly obsessed with understanding his character. I think I've read every major speech he has given (including the full texts of his annual hours-long telephone 'talk-in' with Russian citizens). I've been trying to ascertain whether he has changed for the worse since being elevated to the presidency, or whether he is a straight character cast into a role he never anticipated—and is using sheer wits to try to do the best he can to deal with Washington under extremely difficult circumstances. If the latter is the case, and I think it is, he should get high marks for his performance over the past 14 years. It's not by accident that Forbes declared him the most Powerful Leader of 2013, replacing Obama who was given the title for 2012. The following is my one personal experience with Putin.

The year was 1992…the place was St.Petersburg. For years I had been creating programs to open up relations between the two countries…A new program possibility emerged in my head. Since I expected it might require a signature from the Marienskii City Hall, an appointment was made. My friend Volodya Shestakov and I showed up at a side door entrance to the Marienskii building. We found ourselves in a small, dull brown office, facing a rather trim nondescript man in a brown suit…After scanning the proposal I provided he began asking intelligent questions. After each of my answers, he asked the next relevant question.

I became aware that this interviewer was different from other Soviet bureaucrats who always seemed to fall into chummy conversations with foreigners with hopes of obtaining bribes in exchange for the Americans' requests. CCI stood on the principle that we would never, never give bribes. This bureaucrat was open, inquiring, and impersonal in demeanor. After more than an hour of careful questions and answers, he quietly explained that he had tried hard to determine if the proposal was legal, then said that unfortunately at the time it was not. A few good words about the proposal were uttered. That was all. He simply and kindly showed us to the door. Out on the sidewalk, I said to my colleague, 'Volodya, this is the first time we have ever dealt with a Soviet bureaucrat who didn't ask us for a trip to the US or something valuable!' I remember looking at his business card in the sunlight—it read Vladimir Vladimirovich Putin.

December 31, 1999: *With no warning, at the turn of the year, President Boris Yeltsin made the announcement to the world that from the next day forward he was vacating his office and leaving Russia in the hands of an unknown Vladimir Putin. On hearing the news, I thought surely not the Putin I remembered—he could never lead Russia. The next day a NYT article included a photo. Yes, it was the same Putin I'd met years ago! I was shocked and dismayed, telling friends, 'This is a disaster for Russia, I've spent time with this guy, he is too introverted and too* *intelligent—he will never be able to relate to Russia's masses.' Further, I lamented: 'For Russia to get up off of its knees, two things must happen: 1) The arrogant young oligarchs have to be removed by force from the Kremlin, and 2) A way must be found to remove the regional bosses (governors) from their fiefdoms across Russia's 89 regions'. It was clear to me that the man in the brown suit would never have the instincts or guts to tackle Russia's overriding twin challenges.*

February 2000: *Almost immediately Putin began putting Russia's oligarchs on edge. In February a question about the oligarchs came up; he clarified with a question and his answer: 'What should be the relationship with the so-called oligarchs? The same as anyone else. The same as the owner of a small bakery or a shoe repair shop' This was the first signal that the tycoons would no longer be able to flaunt government regulations or count on special access in the Kremlin. It also made the West's capitalists nervous. After all, these oligarchs were wealthy untouchable businessmen--good capitalists, never mind that they got their enterprises illegally and were putting their profits in offshore banks.*

Four months later Putin called a meeting with the oligarchs and gave them his deal: They could keep their illegally-gained wealth-producing Soviet enterprises and they would not be nationalized ...if taxes were paid on their revenues and if they personally stayed out of politics. This was the first of Putin's 'elegant solutions' to the near impossible challenges facing the new Russia. But the deal also put Putin in crosshairs with US media and officials who then began to champion the oligarchs, particularly Mikhail Khodorkovsky. The latter became highly political, didn't pay taxes, and prior to being apprehended and jailed was in the process of selling a major portion of Russia's largest private oil company, Yukos Oil, to Exxon Mobil. Unfortunately, to U.S. media and governing structures, Khodorkovsky became a martyr (and remains so up to today).

March 2000: *I arrived in St.Petersburg. A Russian friend (a psychologist) since 1983 came for our usual visit. My first question was, 'Lena what do you think about your new president?' She laughed and retorted, 'Volodya! I went to school with him!' She began to describe Putin as a quiet youngster, poor, fond of martial arts, who stood up for kids being bullied on the playgrounds. She remembered him as a patriotic youth who applied for the KGB prematurely after graduating secondary school (they sent him away and told him to get an education).*

Year 2001: *Jack Gosnell (former US Counsel General) explained his relationship with Putin when the latter was deputy mayor of St.Petersburg. The two of them worked closely to create joint ventures and other ways to promote relations between the two countries. Jack related that Putin was always straight up, courteous and helpful. When Putin's wife, Ludmila, was in a severe auto accident, Jack took the liberty (before informing Putin) to arrange hospitalization and airline travel for her to get medical care in Finland. When Jack told Putin, he reported that the latter was overcome by the generous offer, but ended saying that he couldn't accept this favor, that Ludmila would have to recover in a Russian hospital. She did—although medical care in Russia was abominably bad in the 1990s.*

From 2001 up to today, I've watched the negative U.S. media mounting against Putin ... even accusations of assassinations, poisonings, and comparing him to Hitler. No one yet has come up with any concrete evidence for these allegations. During this time, I've traveled throughout Russia several times every year, and have watched the country slowly change under Putin's watch. Taxes were lowered, inflation lessened, and laws slowly put in place. Schools and hospitals began improving. Small businesses were growing, agriculture was showing improvement, and stores were becoming stocked with food.

Highways were being laid across the country, new rails and modern trains appeared even in far out places, and the banking industry was becoming dependable. Russia was beginning to look like a decent country -- certainly not where Russians hoped it to be long term, but improving incrementally for the first time in their memories.

My 2013/14 Trips to Russia: *In addition to St.Petersburg and Moscow, in September I traveled out to the Ural Mountains, spent time in Ekaterinburg, Chelyabinsk and Perm. We traveled between cities via autos and rail—the fields and forests look healthy, small towns sport new paint and construction. Today's Russians look like Americans (we get the same clothing from China). Old concrete Khrushchev block houses are giving way to new multi-story private residential complexes which are lovely. High-rise business centers, fine hotels and great restaurants are now common place—and ordinary Russians frequent these places. Two and three story private homes rim these Russian cities far from Moscow.*

We visited new museums, municipal buildings and huge super markets. Streets are in good repair, highways are new and well marked now, service stations look like those dotting American highways. In January I went to Novosibirsk out in Siberia where similar new architecture was noted. Streets were kept navigable with constant snowplowing, modern lighting kept the city bright all night, lots of new traffic lights…It is astounding to me how much progress Russia has made in the past 14 years since an unknown man with no experience walked into Russia's presidency and took over a country that was flat on its belly.

Based on my earlier experience with him, and the experiences of trusted people, including U.S. officials who have worked closely with him over a period of years, Putin most likely is a straight, reliable and exceptionally inventive man. He is obviously a long-term thinker and planner and has proven to be an excellent analyst and strategist. He is a leader who can quietly work toward his goals under mounds of accusations and myths that have been steadily leveled at him since he became Russia's second president.

So why do our leaders and media demean and demonize Putin and Russia? Could it be that we project on to Putin the sins of ourselves and our leaders? Could it be that we accuse Russia of 'reconstituting the USSR'—because of what we do to remain the world's 'hegemon'? Could it be that we project warmongering off on Russia, because of what we have done over the past several administrations?"

What irritates the war-makers most about Vladimir Putin is that they can't beguile him into committing irrational actions that they could use as a pretext for "humanitarian operations" with the aim of overthrowing his regime.

Oliver Stone also got to the core of Putin's character that allows him to meet the war-makers challenges.

OS: "We're in 2000 now. This is a dark time—the Chechen War is going on. It looks very bad and the oligarchs…privatization is everywhere. You push back…There was the greatest struggle it seems to me—one of the darkest times of your life…Did you wake up at four in the morning? Did you ever sleep?"

VP: "No, I never woke up at 4 a.m. I went to sleep at midnight and I woke up at seven or so. I always slept for six to seven hours."

OS: "Very disciplined. No nightmares?"

VP: "No…I think that's thanks to sport and to military service as well...If you're not disciplined then you will not have enough strength to address the current issues. Let alone the strategic ones. You always have to keep fit."

OS: "Your theory of life they say is summed up in the philosophy of Judo?"

VP: "Yes, more or less. The main idea—the flexible way, as it were—that's the main idea of Judo. You must be flexible. Sometimes you can give way to others, if that is the way leading to victory."

(*The Putin Interviews*, pages 17, 18, 23)

MUNICH SPEECH

President Vladimir Putin watched carefully as his "partners", as he likes to call the obstreperous Yankees, negate peace-making measures—withdraw from ABM treaty, invade and decimate Iraq, stoke the fire in Caucasus, expand NATO with former Russian allies. Oliver Stone told him that some Americans, himself included, are frustrated that Russia doesn't come out more with public relations, with explanations, and he seemed pleased that in the February 10, 2007 Munich speech, Putin did make a "statement that there was indeed a new attitude in Russia."

But Putin interpreted his speech in other terms: "I didn't want to say that the policy would be different. I was just saying that I thought it was unacceptable what the United States was doing. And I said we saw what was happening and that we had to take measures. I was saying that we would not let ourselves be dragged to the slaughter house and applaud that at the same time."

President Vladimir Putin speech shows a keen grasp of history, and clarity about international issues, something anathema to American education, mass media and politicians. Excerpts: https://en.wikisource.org/wiki/Speech_and_the_Following_Discussion_at_the_Munich_Conference_on_Security_Policy

"It is well known that international security comprises much more than issues relating to military and political stability. It involves the stability of the global economy, overcoming poverty, economic security and developing a dialogue between civilizations.

"This universal, indivisible character of security is expressed as the basic principle that 'security for one is security for all'. As Franklin D.

Roosevelt said during the first few days that the Second World War was breaking out, 'When peace has been broken anywhere, the peace of all countries everywhere is in danger.'"

Putin refers to the unipolar world the U.S. wishes as a contradiction to security and democracy.

"What is a unipolar world? However one might embellish this term, at the end of the day it refers to one type of situation, namely one centre of authority, one centre of force, one centre of decision-making. It is a world in which there is one master, one sovereign. And at the end of the day this is pernicious not only for all those within this system, but also for the sovereign itself because it destroys itself from within.

"And this certainly has nothing in common with democracy, because, as you know, democracy is the power of the majority in light of the interests and opinions of the minority.

"Incidentally, Russia—we are constantly being taught about democracy. But for some reason those who teach us do not want to learn themselves."

"We are seeing a greater and greater disdain for the basic principles of international law. And independent legal norms are, as a matter of fact, coming increasingly closer to one state's legal system. One state and, of course, first and foremost the United States, has overstepped its national borders in every way. This is visible in the economic, political, cultural and educational policies it imposes on other nations. Well, who likes this? Who is happy about this?

"In international relations we increasingly see the desire to resolve a given question according to so-called issues of political expediency, based on the current political climate.

"And of course this is extremely dangerous. It results in the fact that no one feels safe. I want to emphasize this – no one feels safe! Because no one can feel that international law is like a stone wall that will protect them. Of course such a policy stimulates an arms race."

"But do we have the means to counter these threats? Certainly we do. It is sufficient to look at recent history. Did not our country have a peaceful transition to democracy? Indeed, we witnessed a peaceful transformation of the Soviet regime—a peaceful transformation! And what a regime! With what a number of weapons, including nuclear

weapons! Why should we start bombing and shooting now at every available opportunity? Is it the case when without the threat of mutual destruction we do not have enough political culture, respect for democratic values and for the law?

"I am convinced that the only mechanism that can make decisions about using military force as a last resort is the Charter of the United Nations."

"The potential danger of the destabilization of international relations is connected with obvious stagnation in the disarmament issue.

"Russia supports the renewal of dialogue on this important question.

"It is important to conserve the international legal framework relating to weapons destruction and therefore ensure continuity in the process of reducing nuclear weapons.

"Together with the United States of America we agreed to reduce our nuclear strategic missile capabilities to up to 1700-2000 nuclear warheads by 31 December 2012. Russia intends to strictly fulfill the obligations it has taken on. We hope that our partners will also act in a transparent way and will refrain from laying aside a couple of hundred superfluous nuclear warheads for a rainy day ....Russia strictly adheres to and intends to further adhere to the Treaty on the Non-Proliferation of Nuclear Weapons as well as the multilateral supervision regime for missile technologies. The principles incorporated in these documents are universal ones."

"In Russia's opinion, the militarization of outer space could have unpredictable consequences for the international community, and provoke nothing less than the beginning of a nuclear era. And we have come forward more than once with initiatives designed to prevent the use of weapons in outer space. Today I would like to tell you that we have prepared a project for an agreement on the prevention of deploying weapons in outer space...Let's work on this together.

"Plans to expand certain elements of the anti-missile defense system to Europe cannot help but disturb us. Who needs the next step of what would be, in this case, an inevitable arms race? I deeply doubt that Europeans themselves do."

"Simultaneously the so-called flexible frontline American bases with up to five thousand men in each. It turns out that NATO has put its frontline forces on our borders, and we continue to strictly fulfill the treaty

obligations and do not react to these actions at all...And what happened to the assurances our western partners made after the dissolution of the Warsaw Pact? Where are those declarations today? No one even remembers them. But I will allow myself to remind this audience what was said...NATO General Secretary Mr Woerner in Brussels, on 17 May, 1990, said: 'The fact that we are ready not to place a NATO army outside of German territory gives the Soviet Union a firm security guarantee'. Where are these guarantees?"

"And let's say things as they are—one hand distributes charitable help and the other hand not only preserves economic backwardness but also reaps the profits thereof. The increasing social tension in depressed regions inevitably results in the growth of radicalism, extremism, feeds terrorism and local conflicts. And if all this happens in, shall we say, a region such as the Middle East where there is increasingly the sense that the world at large is unfair then there is the risk of global destabilization. It is obvious that the world's leading countries should see this threat. And that they should therefore build a more democratic, fairer system of global economic relations, a system that would give everyone the chance and the possibility to develop."

Concurrent with the Munich speech, President Putin declared that the INF Treaty no longer served Russia's interests. It had been signed by Gorbachev and Reagan and implemented with massive reductions of such weapons.

On February 14, 2007, General Yuri Baluyevsky, Chief of General Staff of the Armed Forces, said that Russia could pull out of the INF, and that the decision would depend on the United States' actions with its proposed Ground-Based Midcourse Defense missile defense system at Russia's border in Poland and the Czech Republic. The U.S. made a slight adjustment by placing one in Romania instead of Czechoslovakia but did place one in Poland.

The Russians did not pull out of the treaty!

Four months after the Munich speech, President Bush and his former president father invited him to go fishing. The elder Bush, 83, was at the helm in nearby salt water when Putin caught a sea bass, the only one to make a catch. Although it was large enough to eat, Putin tossed it back to live.

Putin's fish with Bush clapping—all three presidents on a two-day visit at Bush home in Kennebunkport, Maine.

GEORGIA

"The director of the CIA, James Woolsey, flew to Georgia yesterday to collect the body of a murdered American identified as a diplomat but widely believed to have been an intelligence agent.

"The visit, and the publicity accorded it by US officials, suggests a desire by Washington to stake out a clear presence in a region once Moscow's exclusive preserve but now among the most volatile bits of the fragmented Soviet empire," wrote Andrew Higgins, on August 10, 1993, for *The Independent*. (http://www.independent.co.uk/news/world/envoy-death-reveals-us-role-in-georgia suspected-cia-agent-was-part-of-washington-policy-to-1460369.html)

"There was no official word on reports that the dead American, Fred Woodruff, 45, was a CIA agent sent to strengthen personal security arrangements for the Georgian leader, Eduard Shevardnadze, the former Soviet foreign minister. Woodruff was described after the murder as a 'regional-affairs officer' on temporary assignment.

"In Washington, though, a State Department spokesman effectively confirmed reports that the Clinton administration had decided to play a more active role in former Soviet republics. This new strategy, as detailed by the Washington Post, would have the United States act as a mediator in regions such as Georgia, where Mr. Shevardnadze has spent the past year trying to crush a separatist rebellion in the Black Sea region of Abkhazia.

"But sections of the Russian military and more nationalistic politicians see more sinister motives and accuse the US of trespassing on Moscow's turf and harboring imperial ambitions of its own."

"Woodruff died while travelling by car on Sunday night with Mr. Shevardnadze's security chief and two other Georgians. Details remain murky but most reports say he was killed by a single bullet to the head. No one else was hurt."

Two years before this, Georgia declared its independence from Soviet Union/Russia. In January 1991, ethnic Ossetians in the small autonomous region of South Ossetia fought for their independence from Georgia. The conflict ended in June 1992. Many Georgian people (30% of the population) fled to other parts, and the Ossetia people held independent territory. There were more armed disputes in 2004 and 2008. Today, there are 53,000 people in South Ossetia.

In another autonomous region of Georgia, Abkhazia, a war of independence broke out in August 1992 and ended a year later with the death of or flight of 60% of the population. Of the original 525,000 people, only 250,000 remained. Nearly half the population was Georgian. Five thousand Abkhazians and ca. 4000 Georgian troops were killed. The Abkhazia people won their independence albeit Georgia, the U.S. and its European allies did not recognize their independence.

The killing of CIA's man coincided with these struggles.

The Caucasus area is immense with mountain ranges and oil and mineral reserves in various places. The U.S./West wanted to use Georgia for a crude oil pipeline. This is a major cause for warring in many parts of the world—either against the country, which has the desired natural resources (Iraq, Libya), or a country that could transport oil/gas riches through a pipeline (Afghanistan, Syria).

Although Georgia has no significant oil or gas reserves, its territory now hosts part of the Baku–Tbilisi–Ceyhan pipeline supplying oil to Europe. An agreement was reached in 1998 by the Georgian President Eduard Shevardnadze, leaders of Kazakhstand, Uzbekistan and Turkey, and witnessed by a gleeful U.S. Secretary of Energy Bill Richardson.

The agreement was put into effect the next year by the governments of Georgia, Turkey and Azerbaijan. Construction companies from the U.K., Greece and Turkey were under the main contractor, Bechtel, the largest construction and civil engineering company in the U.S.

Eleven energy companies own the pipeline, only one in the area—Azerbaijan with 25%; the UK with 30%; three U.S. companies with 14%; Norway, 8.7%; Turkey, 6.5%; Japan, 6%; France and Italy, 5% each. Georgia owns nothing. It cost $4 billion to build.

Russia, Iran and the Persian Gulf countries were against the pipeline construction, which circumvents both Russia and Iran. Because it has decreased Western dependence on Middle Eastern oil, the pipeline has been a major factor in the United States' support for Georgia.

Shevardnadze ruled by nepotism and rampant corruption. In 2003, massive protests, the Rose Revolution, forced him to resign in November 2003. Mikjail Saakashvili became president in January 2004.

The 1,768 kilometer-long pipeline was opened in May 2005, and the first oil was pumped from the Baku end to Ceyhan, May 28, 2006. The crude oil pipeline pumps from the Azeri–Chirag–Gunashli oil field in the Caspian Sea to the Mediterranean Sea. The Caspian Sea lays on top of one of the world's largest oil and gas funds.

During the NATO summit in Bucharest, in April 2008, President Bush lobbied for offering a Membership Action Plan (MAP) to Georgia and Ukraine, a path to full NATO membership. Germany and France said that offering them MAP would be "an unnecessary offence" to Russia. NATO stated that Ukraine and Georgia would become members of the alliance anyway. President Vladimir Putin said that expansion of NATO to Russia's borders "would be taken in Russia as a direct threat to the security of our country". Thus the road to another war was laid.

The five-day Georgia war took place August 7-12, 2008.

Georgian, Russian, and Ossetia troops had been stationed in South Ossetia since the 1991-2 war. Most of the Ossetians, as well as Abkhazians, had Soviet passports, and many had or were obtaining Russian passports.

Oliver Stone asked Putin about his and Russia's involvement with the Georgian conflict. As is usual in his responses to contemporary international problems he gave the necessary background to understand the present.

"After the first World War, after the so-called October Socialist Revolution (sic)—back then Georgia declared that it wanted to be an independent state. And Ossetia declared it wanted to be part of Russia. And back then, in 1921, Georgian troops undertook two punitive actions against these factions...We had to gain the trust of the people if Georgians wanted to preserve the territorial integrity of their country."

"Many times I told Saakashvili, if he wanted to restore the territorial integrity, he had to be very cautious with regards to the population of Abkhazia and South Ossetia. I told him we're willing to help you, and moreover I think George [Bush] can confirm that. I told him that he had to avoid potential aggression because if he were to launch hostilities...there were people living in adjacent regions in the Russian Federation who couldn't have stayed outside that conflict...there is North Ossetia, as a constituent entity of the Russian Federation. And the same people live in both [regions]...Russia would not have been able to stay outside that conflict. Our American partners were telling us, 'Yes, we understand it.' It all led to the war which was started by Saakashvili."

Saakashvili sent troops against Ossetians: "They destroyed the peacekeeper space—Russian peacekeepers. During the first strike, 10 or 15 people died. The strike performed by the Georgian troops with multiple rocket launcher systems, and people simply didn't have time to get out of their barracks. And afterward, Georgia performed a large-scale military assault...Mr. Saakashvili publicly announced that he ordered his troops to commence that action." (*The Putin Interviews*, pages 51-2, 184-7)

About 1,000 to 1,200 military, police and civilians on all sides were killed, and 2000 or more wounded. 135,000 people fled inside Georgia or to Russia. By year's end, 25-30% had not returned.

On August 12, Russia halts firing, and agrees to temporary cease fire.

On August 13, President Bush offers Georgia $1 billion in "humanitarian aid" as Congress passed a resolution defending Georgia's "right to territorial integrity". The U.S. had helped transport 2,000 Georgian troops fighting beside it against the nation of Iraq so that they could fight against South Ossetia and Abkhazia.

On August 15, France President Nicolas Sarkozy brokers a permanent cease fire between Georgia and Russia.

On August 26th, Russia withdraws its troops from Georgia and officially recognizes South Ossetia and Abkhazia as independent sovereign states.

On December 2, the European Union decides for the "first time in its history" to "intervene actively in a serious armed conflict" to establish the facts. The Independent International Fact-Finding Mission on the Conflict in Georgia (IIFFMCG) was formed.

In September 2009, *the IIFFMCG issued a 44-page report. The immediate cause of the conflict lay in Georgia's hands.* http://news.bbc.co.uk/2/shared/bsp/hi/pdfs/30_09_09_iiffmgc_report.pdf

"On the night of 7 to 8 August 2008, a sustained Georgian artillery attack struck the town of Tskhinvali. Other movements of the Georgian armed forces targeting Tskhinvali and the surrounding areas were under way, and soon the fighting involved Russian, South Ossetian and Abkhaz military units and armed elements. It did not take long, however, before the Georgian advance into South Ossetia was stopped." (page 10)

"The shelling of Tskhinvali by the Georgian armed forces during the night of 7 to 8 August 2008 marked the beginning of the large-scale armed conflict in Georgia, yet it was only the culminating point of a long period of increasing tensions, provocations and incidents. Indeed, the conflict has deep roots in the history of the region, in peoples' national traditions and aspirations as well as in age-old perceptions or rather misperceptions of each other, which were never mended and sometimes exploited."

While the EU commission made no analysis about the role of the United States, an important member of the U.S. Establishment, Paul J. Saunders, executive director of the Nixon Center and associate publisher of the National Interest, did. He was a State Department political appointee from 2003 to 2005. This is part of his piece in the "US News & World Reports". (https://www.usnews.com/news/articles/2008/08/12/the-united-states-shares-the-blame-for-the-russia-georgia-crisis)

"War became unavoidable in the Caucasus when Georgian President Mikheil Saakashvili sent the country's military to 'liberate' the autonomous region of South Ossetia from its Moscow-back country's military to 'liberate' the autonomous region of South Ossetia from its Moscow-backed local

authorities. While Georgia and Russia bear principal responsibility for a conflict that both have been courting for years, the United States also shares the blame. And now American interests will suffer, not only in Georgia and the former Soviet Union but around the world."

"America contributed to the war in Georgia in two important ways. First, together with its European allies, *Washington established two precedents: use of force without approval of the United Nations Security Council and the division of a sovereign nation without U.N. consent.* Both precedents emerged out of Kosovo's quest for independence from Serbia, which led in 1999 to U.S.-directed NATO airstrikes against Serbia to drive Serbian military and police forces out of its Kosovo province. The Clinton administration and NATO conducted the strikes—both in Kosovo and in Serbia proper, where the attacks targeted not only security units but also civilian infrastructure, like power stations—over Russia's strong opposition in the Security Council. Russia today is repeating NATO's 1999 justification of its action in arguing that Georgia conducted ethnic cleansing and genocide in South Ossetia and that Moscow was obliged to respond because of its role as a peacekeeper.

"More recently, in 2007 and 2008, the United States and some European governments endorsed Kosovo's desire for independence, despite the fact that it remained a part of Serbia, and recognized it earlier this year.

"The U.S. also provided hundreds of millions of dollars in foreign aid, and essentially ignored Saakashvili's growing authoritarianism. More important, the United States provided extensive military aid and training for Georgian troops. Some have argued that this help increased Georgian leaders' confidence that military action in South Ossetia could succeed."

"Secretary of State Condoleezza Rice added fuel to this fire on July 10 when appearing beside Saakashvili in Tbilisi, she said, 'Mr. President, we always fight for our friends,'" and she spoke of beginning the process of "bringing Georgia into NATO by offering a membership action plan".

Another U.S. Establishment and geopolitical pundit, Russian-born Vladislav Zubok, wrote that Putin was a reluctant player in this conflict. See, "Russia, the U.S. and the Backstory Behind the Breakdown". (https://

wilsonquarterly.com/quarterly/the-post-obama-world/russia-the-u-s-and-the-backstory-behind-the-breakdown/)

"Vladimir Putin is now taken in the West for a thuggish strongman, yet he tried to build a special partnership with the United States after 9/11. Only gradually, as his biographers document, did he decide that a defiance of and resistance to the superior American power was inevitable. Putin came to regard American economic interests in Russia and neighboring countries as a danger. He gave up on the Russian liberal dream of deeper integration with the West and began to build an authoritarian crony-state capitalism—the only system that he believed could give him control over Russia's 'sovereignty' and resources, and make him a 'free actor' autonomous from Washington's pressures. In regional affairs, Putin began to build an 'Eurasian' integration project to balance off the advancing Western institutions, NATO and the EU, where Russia was not likely to become a member and could not have a say."

The key direct warring player was President Saakashvili. He is also known for rampant corruption and abuse of power. In 2013, the new Georgian President Giorgi Margvelashvili accused him of such, of illegally breaking up demonstrations, of sending forces to raid a TV station, and of illegally pressuring the judiciary. Rather than face charges, he fled to the Ukraine where he energetically supported the neo-fascistic Euromaidan movement.

On May 30, 2015 the coup president, Petro Poroshenko, appointed him governor of Odessa Oblast province even though he spoke Ukrainian poorly, but was granted Ukrainian citizenship. Georgia stripped him of his Georgian citizenship since by law one cannot hold dual citizenship.

On November 7, 2016, Saakashvili resigned as governor blaming Poroshenko for enabling corruption in Odessa. On July 26, 2017 he was stripped of Ukrainian citizenship while in the United States. Although Ukraine's government declared that if he returned, he would be extradited to Georgia to face criminal charges, Saakashvili forced his way with supporters across a frontier border between Poland and Ukraine in September 2017.

The next day, Saakashvili held a press conference in the western city of Lviv. Despite being stateless, he said he would oppose Poroshenko in the 2018 elections. Although Poroshenko's government had said he would be extradited to Georgia, by November he was still in the Ukraine and claimed to be looking forward to winning elections. Polls showed him with 2% of potential voters and Poroshenko with 11%. Saakashvili started a new party, "Movement of New Forces", a right-wing grouping against Poroshenko's right-wing grouping.

PUTIN-MEDVEDEV-RUSSIA 2008-13

After two terms as president, Putin could not be a candidate in the March 2008 elections. United Russia Party chose Dmitry Medvedev as its candidate. He won with 71% of the vote. The Communist Party candidate Gennady Zyuganov came in second place with 18%. A liberal third party got 9.5%. Medvedev had been Putin's first deputy prime minister, and as president he appointed Putin to that post.

November 2008: Parliament votes overwhelmingly in favor of a bill that would extend the next president's term of office from four to six years.

July 2009: President Medvedev on his first official visit to the U.S. makes a deal with President Barack Obama to reduce nuclear weapons stockpiles.

September 2009: Russia welcomes U.S. decision to shelve missile bases in Poland and the Czech Republic.

April 2010: President Medvedev signs a new strategic arms agreement with U.S. committing both sides to cut arsenals of deployed nuclear warheads by about 30 percent.

June 2010: Presidents Medvedev and Obama meet again in Washington. Obama says the U.S. will back Russia's accession to the World Trade Organization. In 2012, Russia formally joins the World Trade Organization after 18 years of negotiations.

July 2010: A customs union between Russia, Belarus and Kazakhstan comes into force. The Customs Code generally applies to all member states of the Eurasian Economic Union. In 2015, Armenia and Kyrgyzstan joined.

March 2012: Vladimir Putin wins presidential elections with 64%. Communist Party leader Zyuganov again came in second, with 17%. This is his fifth try. Opponents take to the streets of several major cities to protest the election; hundreds are arrested. Opposition parties, including the C.P., accuse the government of electoral fraud, including disallowing equal access to publicity during electoral campaigns.

A March 5 article in *The Guardian*, "Russian Elections: does the data suggest Putin won through fraud?" says the allegation of fraud was inconclusive. https://www.theguardian.com/news/datablog/2012/mar/05/russia-putin-voter-fraud-statistics)

Why would Putin's government fix elections when all the polls, those conducted by private companies both nationally and internationally, consistently show that the majority—over 50%—of the population, the majority of voters want this man as their president?

CHAPTER 15
Russia Averts War Against Syria, Iran

SYRIAN PATRIOTS FOUGHT Nazis and French Vichy governments, and won their independence from France in 1946. Following several unstable governments—some elected, some coup regimes—stability was established in November 1970 when one branch of the pan-Arab Ba'ath Party, led by military officer Hafez-al-Assad, took power. The Baath Party was formed in 1963, combining socialism, secular ideology, French civil law and authoritarian political rule.

During Hafez-al-Assad's reign society's economy developed but he was brutal to any opposition be it from Sunni Muslim Brotherhood, Syrian Shiites or Lebanese. Nevertheless, relations between the U.S. and Syria improved from the mid-1950s when the CIA overthrew the elected leader, Shukri-al-Quwatli because he would not cooperate completely with the Dulles brother' schemes to dominate Syrian oil. This was followed by two unsuccessful attempted coups, and failed efforts to assassinate military officers the CIA had hired the Muslim Brotherhood to perform.

The Dulles brothers and President Eisenhower rejected the Soviet proposal to keep the Middle East out of the Cold War—*let Arabs rule Arabs* was the Soviet motto. The U.S. preferred to split Middle Eastern powers, backing Saudi Arabia and other Gulf States, in order to determine the affairs of not only Syria but also Iran, Iraq, Jordan and Egypt at a time when their leaders sought to rule their own country from a nationalist perspective.

Syria's Baath Party was similar to Iraq's Baath Party led by Saddam Hussein, but the Assad government assisted the U.S. in its first war against Iraq. Syria did not send soldiers or war equipment but allowed U.S. war planes to

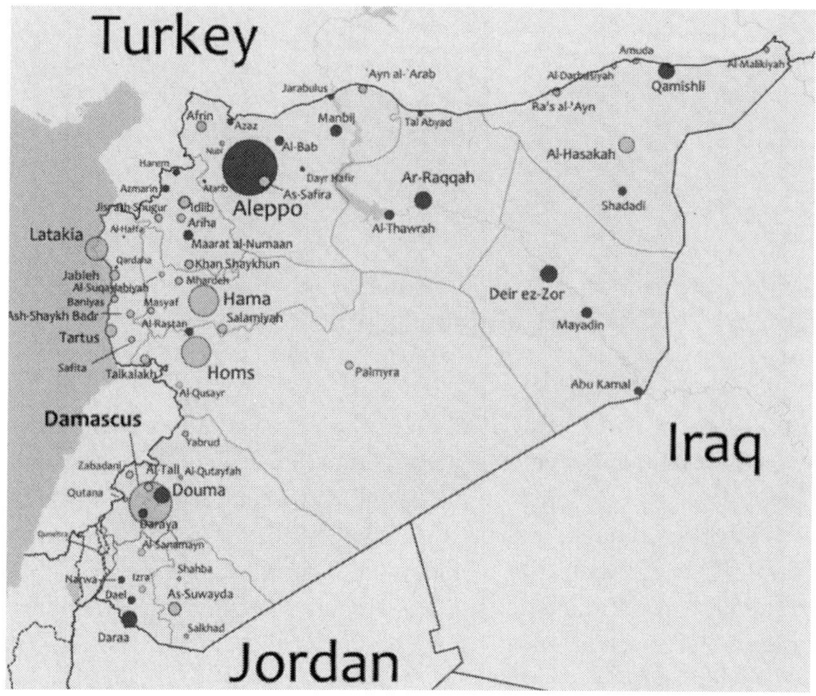

use its airspace, and the government assisted the U.S. "counter-terrorism" program. This angered many Syrians, who saw Hussein as a brother-comrade.

Part of the reason for the Syrian government backing the war against Iraq was that the two Baath parties were at odds over regional power, and the Syrian government was made up mainly of minority Alawi Shiite Muslims aligned with the Shiites in Iran. Hussein was Sunni Muslim but there were also Shiites and Sunni Kurds in his government.

The last census that included religious adherence was taken in 1960: 88% Muslim. Of them, 74% Sunnis; 14% Shias, and most of them were Alawis and Ismailis (followers of specific Imans). There are few Alawis in the world; most are in Syria, some in Turkey and Lebanon. Christians of the Eastern Orthodox make up nearly 8%. Three percent are Druze, a Unitarian community combing many religions and philosophies. There are or were a few thousand Jews.

Hafez-al-Assad died in June 2000 and elections were held the next month. The only candidate, his son Bashar-al-Assad, won with 99.7%

of the vote. While he is also a minority Alawi, most of his government and army are Sunni, and he married a Sunni woman. There was no outright discrimination against religions and Christians felt safe with him. Once the 2001 civil war began some Sunnis chased and killed Christians, and people of other religions.

In his early years, President Bashar Assad was friendly with the U.S. and even allowed his prisons to be used for CIA's "ghost detainees" between 2001 and 2003. Syrian-born Canadian Maher Arar was one "detainee". The CIA suspected him as a "pro-terrorist". They abductted him in New York and sent him to Syria, where he was interrogated and tortured. Luckily he was released and returned to Canada. He sued and the Canadian court found he had been tortured and was not a terrorist. The Canadian government apologized but neither the U.S. nor Syria admitted any wrong-doing.

Several other "ghost detainee" cases in Syria were exposed, principally by Stephen Grey. (1)

Former CIA agent Robert Baer described the policy. "If you want them to be tortured, you send them to Syria. If you want someone to disappear—never to see them again—you send them to Egypt". (https://www.theguardian.com/world/2011/aug/31/extraordinary-rendition-backstory)

I can't think of a more appropriate and interested source to explain why the U.S. decided to turn on Assad than the son of Robert F. Kennedy (RFK), Robert F. Kennedy, Jr. He sought to understand what motivated the Palestinian-Jordanian immigrant Sirhan Sirhan to shoot his father, and he wrote a soul-searching essay, "Why the Arabs don't want us in Syria". (2)

> *"America's unsavory record of violent interventions in Syria—little known to the American people yet well-known to Syrians, sowed fertile ground for the violent jihadism that now complicates any effective response by our government to address the challenge of ISIL,"*
>
> *"To understand this dynamic, we need to look at history from the Syrians' perspective and particularly the seeds of the current conflict. Long before our 2003 occupation of Iraq triggered the Sunni uprising that has now morphed into the*

Islamic State the CIA had nurtured violent jihadism as a Cold War weapon and freighted U.S./Syrian relationships with toxic baggage."

Robert Kennedy Jr. did his homework well when he wrote that the reason for the U.S. to side with the Sunni protestors and terrorists had nothing to do with a "humanitarian operation" but, again, oil, and geo-politics.

In 2000, Qatar proposed to construct a $10 billion, 1,500 kilometer pipeline through Saudi Arabia, Jordan, Syria and Turkey. This would have "linked Qatar directly to European energy markets via distribution terminals in Turkey...giving the Sunni kingdoms of the Persian Gulf decisive domination of world natural gas markets."

Qatar hosts two huge U.S. military bases and its Mideast central command. The Qatar pipeline would also have benefited the Saudi Sunni monarchy by giving it a foothold in Shia-dominated Syria so Assad was not pleased with the idea. Russia was also an ally, and it would have lost European energy markets, its largest customer, to the geo-political and economic advantage of U.S./NATO/EU. Assad rejected the proposal clearly in the interest of the country.

Russia proposed an "Islamic pipeline" running from Iran's side of the gas field through Syria to the ports of Lebanon, which would make Iran stronger. So, Israel was also against that.

"Secret cables and reports by the U.S., Saudi and Israeli intelligence agencies indicate that the moment Assad rejected the Qatari pipeline, military and intelligence planners quickly arrived at the consensus that fomenting a Sunni uprising in Syria to overthrow the uncooperative Bashar Assad was a feasible path to achieving the shared objective of completing the Qatar/Turkey gas link," wrote Bobby Kennedy, Jr.

"In 2009, according to WikiLeaks, soon after Bashar Assad rejected the Qatar pipeline, the CIA began funding opposition groups in Syria," *well before the Arab Spring began.*

ARAB SPRING IN SYRIA

The United States did not intervene on the side of democracy-seeking protestors where the Arab Spring broke out. On December 17, 2010 unarmed peaceful demonstrators protested against the Tunisian dictator

Ben Ali regime after Mohamed Bouazizi self-immolation in protest to police brutality and corruption. This inspired Egyptians to join on January 25, 2011. (3)

In the weeks of uproar in these two countries around two thousand unarmed demonstrators were killed by police and soldiers, and several thousands were wounded. The long-time dictators Ali and Egypt's Hosni Mubarak were good friends with U.S. governments so no aid came to the protestors. Nor did the U.S. lift a finger in Yemen or Bahrain where the movement spread. In fact, Bahrain called in Saudi armed forces to mow down peaceful protestors without any meaningful outcry from Western "democracies". But it was different when protests began in Libya and Syria.

Hasan Ali Akleh set himself on fire, on January 28, 2011, in a small northeastern Syrian city, Al-Hasakah. It was said he did so in protest against the Assad government. Handfuls of people publically called for reforms in a few Syrian towns in February; some called for Assad's ouster.

For weeks there was not much violence nor any killings but many arrests. It is difficult for me to know who fired the first shots writing as I do from Denmark and Spain and not having ever stepped foot inside Syria. Nevertheless, from the many sources I have read, it seems clear that the first killings were made by Syrian security forces in mid-March in Daraa.

The first Daraa demonstration, on March 15, 2011, led by Kurds protested police torture of students who had painted anti-government graffiti. They sought civil liberty reforms and Assad's ouster. In fact, Assad responded by granting them nationality, and on April 21 he repealed the dreaded 1963 emergency law that readily allowed the suspension of constitutional rights.

Unlike in Tunisia and Egypt, some protestors began shooting at police early on, and later at soldiers. One of the few mass media reporters, whose reportage is usually reliable, is Robert Fisk—this is not an endorsement for every word he has written, but he has been a correspondent in the Middle East for 40 years and speaks Arabic. His August 31, 2017 piece in *The Independent*, "When did protest against the Assad government turn to war in Syria," is worth reading, as is the author he writes about, Nikolas van Dam. (4)

Van Dam is a scholar, professor, author and former Dutch diplomat in several Middle Eastern countries, including Syria. He is fluent in Arabic and knew Syria so well that "even members of the Baath party would reportedly turn to pages [of his first book on Syria] to understand the history of their institution and the nature of the regime for which they worked," wrote Fisk.

His new book is "perhaps the only one so far published about the conflict that attempts to set out coldly what the opposition as well as the Assad government did wrong." Van Dam "notes how early the 'peaceful' opposition turned to violence once the crisis began."

> *"On the Syrian border with north-eastern Lebanon, inside Lebanese territory but in sight of the plain of Homs in the spring of 2011, I listened to a fierce gun battle being fought only a few hundred meters across the frontier—at a time when only the Syrian army and the security police were supposed to be using weapons against unarmed demonstrators. A week later, an Al Jazeera camera crew—working for the Qatar-funded channel whose ruling family would soon fund the Nusra-al Qaeda fighters in Syria, as even its royal family acknowledged—asked to meet me in Beirut. They showed me footage also taken near the north-eastern border of Lebanon. Their tape clearly showed armed men shooting at Syrian troops. Al Jazeera, adhering to the 'soldiers-shoot-down-unarmed-demonstrators' story, had refused to air their film. They had resigned. Later, Syrian state television itself showed—all too real—film of armed men among the crowds of protestors in Dera'a. Van Dam dismisses reports that these men were government 'provocateurs'."*

Van Dam "does not dispute the Assad government's killing of the innocent—though he suggests this came about through the inherent and untamed brutality of the regime's security apparatus rather than a policy decision by Bashar al-Assad himself." "'Bad mistakes' had been made there. But such 'discoveries' were useless. Within months, the public's demand for 'reforms' had turned into an uprising determined to overthrow a regime that then resorted to all out-war against its enemies. Early reports of a massacre of Syrian troops by armed men at Jisr al-Chagour, dismissed by government opponents as the killing of army deserters by the regime, were, Van Dam concludes, true. The soldiers were murdered by those whom we would soon call 'rebels,'" wrote Fisk.

Soon, the Syrian National Council was formed, which included the banned Islamic Syrian Muslim Brotherhood, some Kurdish factions (Sunnis), and some tribal figures. Some Sunni soldiers defected and formed the Free Syrian Army on July 29, 2011, and the civil war really began. Over the years to come, hundreds of opponent groups formed and many fought one another. On July 5, 2012, Wikileaks began publishing the "Syrian Files", a collection of 2.5 million emails from Syrian political figures, ministries, and corporations, dating from August 2006 to 2012. They show how the CIA was involved from the beginning.

From the outset, the U.S. with the UK and France joined Qatar, Saudi Arabia and Turkey to assure a "regime change". The U.S. provided $6 million to the British TV channel, Barada, to produce propaganda for Assad's ouster. A Wikileaks whistle blower leaked Saudi intelligence documents showing that the government was arming, training and financing radical jihadist Sunni fighters in both Syria and Iraq from 2012. Qatar pitched in with $3 billion to build the terrorist insurgency.

In September 2013, Obama told U.S. Senators that the CIA had trained just 50 "insurgents". In fact, Special Activities Division teams were deployed to train 10,000 in Jordan and Turkey, and most were jihadists. Wikileaks reported that the U.S. government has been covertly funding the Syrian opposition since 2006. Obama also spent $500 million that we know of for, what he called, the "moderate" opposition. Much of that got into the hands of what Obama said were his terrorist enemies since these groups generally dominated the fighting.

Bobby Kennedy, Jr. comes in again.

> *"As predicted, Assad's overreaction to the foreign-made crisis— dropping barrel bombs onto Sunni strongholds and killing civilians — polarized Syria's Shiite/Sunni divide and allowed U.S. policymakers to sell Americans the idea that the pipeline struggle was a humanitarian war. When Sunni soldiers of the Syrian Army began defecting in 2013, the western coalition armed their "Free Syrian Army" to further destabilize Syria."*

[The "barrel bombs" charge, like Assad's use of CW on his own people, has been shown to be a Western propaganda fabrication by Prof. Tim Anderson and other experts in the Syria conflict. See NATO's Dirty War in Syria, http://21stcenturywire.com/2016/06/25/interview-with-prof-tim-anderson-natos-dirty-war-on-syria/] He then cites an extremely revealing U.S. Defense Intelligence Agency report about what was happening in Syria and who was siding with whom.

> *"2012 Defense Intelligence Agency document: West will facilitate rise of Islamic State 'in order to isolate the Syrian regime'"*

This is the headline of the released document to Judicial Watch on May 19, 2015: https://levantreport.com/2015/05/27/the-dia-gives-an-official-response-to-levantreport-com-article-alleging-the-west-backed-islamic-state/

This is the DIA original report: http://www.judicialwatch.org/wp-content/uploads/2015/05/Pg.-291-Pgs.-287-293-JW-v-DOD-and-State-14-812-DOD-Release-2015-04-10-final-version11.pdf?V=1

I use Brad Hoff citations of the pdf document.

"On Monday, May 18, the conservative government watchdog group Judicial Watch published a selection of formerly classified documents obtained from the U.S. Department of Defense and State Department through a federal lawsuit.

"While initial mainstream media reporting is focused on the White House's handling of the Benghazi consulate attack, a much 'bigger picture' admission and confirmation is contained in one of the Defense Intelligence Agency documents circulated in 2012: that an 'Islamic State' is desired in Eastern Syria to effect the West's policies in the region.

"Astoundingly, the newly declassified report states that for 'THE WEST, GULF COUNTRIES, AND TURKEY [WHO] SUPPORT THE [SYRIAN] OPPOSITION... THERE IS THE POSSIBILITY OF ESTABLISHING A DECLARED OR UNDECLARED SALAFIST PRINCIPALITY IN EASTERN SYRIA (HASAKA AND DER ZOR), AND THIS IS EXACTLY WHAT THE SUPPORTING POWERS TO THE OPPOSITION WANT, IN ORDER TO ISOLATE THE SYRIAN REGIME...'

"The DIA report, formerly classified "SECRET//NOFORN" and dated

August 12, 2012, was circulated widely among various government agencies, including CENTCOM, the CIA, FBI, DHS, NGA, State Dept., and many others.

"The document shows that as early as 2012, U.S. intelligence predicted the rise of the Islamic State in Iraq and the Levant (ISIL or ISIS), but instead of clearly delineating the group as an enemy, the report envisions the terror group as a U.S. strategic asset."

"Forensic evidence...as well as recent admissions of high-level officials involved...have since proven the State Department and CIA's material support of ISIS terrorists on the Syrian battlefield going back to at least 2012 and 2013..."

The newly released DIA report makes the following summary points concerning "ISI" (in 2012 "Islamic State in Iraq,") and the soon to emerge ISIS:

- *Al-Qaeda drives the opposition in Syria*
- *The West identifies with the opposition*
- *The establishment of a nascent Islamic State became a reality only with the rise of the Syrian insurgency (there is no mention of U.S. troop withdrawal from Iraq as a catalyst for Islamic State's rise, which is the contention of innumerable politicians and pundits; see section 4.D. below)*
- *The establishment of a "Salafist Principality" in Eastern Syria is "exactly" what the external powers supporting the opposition want (identified as "the West, Gulf Countries, and Turkey") in order to weaken the Assad government*
- *"Safe havens" are suggested in areas conquered by Islamic insurgents along the lines of the Libyan model (which translates to so-called no-fly zones as a first act of 'humanitarian war'; see 7.B.)*
- *Iraq is identified with "Shia expansion" (8.C)*
- *A Sunni "Islamic State" could be devastating to "unifying Iraq" and could lead to "the renewing facilitation of terrorist elements from all over the Arab world entering into Iraqi Arena."*

[The DIA Report's "General Situation"]

A. INTERNALLY, EVENTS ARE TAKING A CLEAR SECTARIAN DIRECTION.

B.THE SALAFIST THE MUSLIM BROTHERHOOD, AND AQI [Al

Qaeda] ARE THE MAJOR FORCES DRIVING THE INSURGENCY IN SYRIA.

C.THE WEST, GULF COUNTRIES, AND TURKEY SUPPORT THE OPPOSITION; WHILE RUSSIA, CHINA AND IRAN SUPPORT THE REGIME.

...

3.Al QAEDA – IRAQ (AQI):...

3.B. AQI SUPPORTED THE SYRIAN OPPOSITION FROM THE BEGINNING, BOTH IDEOLOGICALLY AND THROUGH THE MEDIA...

...

4.D. THERE WAS A REGRESSION OF AQI IN THE WESTERN PROVINCES OF IRAQ DURING THE YEARS OF 2009 AND 2010; HOWEVER, AFTER THE RISE OF THE INSURGENCY IN SYRIA, THE RELIGIOUS AND TRIBAL POWERS IN THE REGIONS BEGAN TO SYMPATHIZE WITH THE SECTARIAN UPRISING. THIS (SYMPATHY) APPEARED IN FRIDAY PRAYER SERMONS, WHICH CALLED FOR VOLUNTEERS TO SUPPORT THE SUNNI'S IN SYRIA.

...

7. THE FUTURE ASSUMPTIONS OF THE CRISIS:

7.A. THE REGIME WILL SURVIVE AND HAVE CONTROL OVER SYRIAN TERRITORY.

7.B. DEVELOPMENT OF THE CURRENT EVENTS INTO PROXY WAR: ...OPPOSITION FORCES ARE TRYING TO CONTROL THE EASTERN AREAS (HASAKA AND DER ZOR), ADJACENT TO THE WESTERN IRAQI PROVINCES (MOSUL AND ANBAR), IN ADDITION TO NEIGHBORING TURKISH BORDERS. ***WESTERN COUNTRIES, THE GULF STATES AND TURKEY ARE SUPPORTING THESE EFFORTS.*** *THIS HYPOTHESIS IS MOST LIKELY IN ACCORDANCE WITH THE DATA FROM RECENT EVENTS,* ***WHICH WILL HELP PREPARE SAFE HAVENS UNDER INTERNATIONAL SHELTERING, SIMILAR TO WHAT TRANSPIRED IN LIBYA WHEN BENGHAZI WAS CHOSEN AS THE COMMAND CENTER OF THE TEMPORARY GOVERNMENT.***

...

8.C. ***IF THE SITUATION UNRAVELS THERE IS THE POSSIBILITY OF*** *ESTABLISHING A DECLARED OR UNDECLARED SALAFIST PRINCIPALITY IN EASTERN SYRIA (****HASAKA AND DER ZOR****),*

AND THIS IS EXACTLY WHAT THE SUPPORTING POWERS TO THE OPPOSITION WANT, IN ORDER TO ISOLATE THE SYRIAN REGIME, WHICH IS CONSIDERED THE STRATEGIC DEPTH OF THE SHIA EXPANSION (IRAQ AND IRAN)

*8.D.1. ...**ISI COULD ALSO DECLARE AN ISLAMIC STATE THROUGH ITS UNION WITH OTHER TERRORIST ORGANIZATIONS IN IRAQ AND SYRIA**, WHICH WILL CREATE GRAVE DANGER IN REGARDS TO UNIFYING IRAQ AND THE PROTECTION OF ITS TERRITORY.*

The last point (8.D.1) was written two years before the actual Islamic State (ISIS Caliphate) was formed by Salafist/Wahhabists. Salafist is a reactionary Sunni sect with three factions and is the same as or connected to Saudi Arabia's Wahhabism. These fundamentalists were established in 1932 and have ruled S.A. since. "Coincidentally", the regions IS occupied were the proposed Qatari pipeline route. Qatar, S.A., Turkey were among IS customers for the oil they controlled.

In 2014, the Sunni jihadists began to frighten most Westerns (and probably most people in the world) when they severed people's heads before cameras and drove a million refugees into Europe.

One of Bobby Kennedy, Jr. sources is Tim Clemente. He chaired the FBI's Joint Terrorism Task Force (2004-2008), and was liaison in Iraq between the FBI, the U.S. military and Iraq National Police. He told Kennedy:

"We made the same mistake when we trained the mujahideen in Afghanistan. The moment the Russians left, our supposed friends started smashing antiquities, enslaving women, severing body parts and shooting at us."

Kennedy says that Arabs know what's going down: "The evidence of U.S. involvement is so abundant that they conclude that our role in fostering the Islamic State must have been deliberate. In fact, many of the Islamic fighters and their commanders are ideological and organizational successors to the jihadists that the CIA has been nurturing for more than 30 years from Syria and Egypt to Afghanistan and Iraq."

"Prior to the American invasion, there was no Al Qaeda in Saddam Hussein's Iraq. President George W. Bush destroyed Saddam's secularist government, and his viceroy, Paul Bremer, in a monumental act of mismanagement, effectively created the Sunni Army, now named the

Islamic State. Bremer elevated the Shiites to power and banned Saddam's ruling Ba'ath Party, laying off some 700,000 mostly Sunni, government and party officials from ministers to schoolteachers. He then disbanded the 380,000-man army, which was 80 percent Sunni."

Kennedy concludes:

> *"It's time for Americans to turn America away from this new imperialism and back to the path of idealism and democracy. We should let the Arabs govern Arabia."*

That is just what Russia is saying and the Soviets before. Does that make Kennedy a Putin lackey?

What most people in the West don't know or don't want to know is that most Syrians, including those under the brutal force of the terrorists, do not support "the opposition".

In a rare admission by an Establishment institution, the British polling organization ORB International, an affiliate of WIN/Gallup International reports how Syrians inside Syria feel. Oddly enough, ORB works with U.S. and UK governments. Nevertheless, it repeatedly finds that *most Syrians throughout Syria oppose ISIS by about 80% as they also blame the U.S. for ISIS.*

1. **82% agree "IS [Islamic State] is US and foreign made group."**
2. **79% agree "Foreign fighters made war worse."**
3. **70% agree "Oppose division of country."**
4. **65% agree "Syrians can live together again."**
5. **64% agree "Diplomatic solution possible."**
6. **57% agree "Situation is worsening."**
7. **51% agree "Political solution best answer."**
8. **49% agree "Oppose US coalition air strikes."**
9. **22% agree "IS is a positive influence."**
10. **21% agree "Prefer life now than under Assad."**

The below link to ORB's poll no longer appears on the internet, interestingly enough, but here is *The Guardian* article: https://off-guardian.org/2015/12/19/western-poll-assad-supported-by-most-syrians/ Missing Link: https://www.orb-international.com/perch/resources/syriadata.pdf

GAS ATTACK FOP

The ORB poll was taken after the alleged Assad-directed Sarin gas attack, August 21, 2013, yet most mass media ignored the poll and/or did not give it any significance. The lie of Assad's gas attack took priority and remains so as of this writing four and one-half years later despite the fact that the truth has been discovered and sparsely reported.

"Syrian activists reported that Assad forces struck Jobar, Zamalka, 'Ain Tirma, and Hazzah in the Eastern Ghouta region with chemical weapons. Activists at the Syrian Revolutionary Command Council said that at least 635 were killed in a nerve gas attack. Unverified videos uploaded showed the victims, many of who were convulsing, as well as several dozen bodies lined up. Other sources reported a figure of 213 in a poisonous gas attack. The SNC chief said that the overall death toll stood at an estimated 1300, as only a fraction of the bodies could be collected and many died within their own homes," reported Israel National News. All western mass media blamed Assad. (http://www.israelnationalnews.com/News/News.aspx/171141#.UhSh70C0Pdc)

There are several things wrong with this report:

1. "Syrian activists" sounds harmless but these activists spoken about are armed and killing any who support the government.
2. The Syrian Revolutionary Command Council was not formed until a year later, on August 3, 2014. 72 "rebel factions", secular and Islamists formed the council and agreed to work together to overthrow the government and its army. The council fell apart in late 2015.
3. Before the formation of SRCC, many of these groups were fighting with al Qaeda and its Syrian part al-Nusar.
4. SNC is not defined but it was the Syrian National Council, which was formed two days after the alleged gas episode in Istanbul. The SNC was the exiled wing of the patriarchal Muslim Brotherhood.

Another problem with this story is that the attack did not come from Assad forces. I'll come back to that a bit further down, but first here is what was known at the time:

1. Surface-to-surface rockets (perhaps eight) were fired in the area.

2. Doctors without Borders could confirm that hundreds, and perhaps as many as 3,600 persons, had "neurotoxic symptoms". Hundreds died.

The UN requested permission to investigate and President Assad agreed. The team of chemical investigators did not ascertain who was responsible but by examining the debris and impact area where rockets struck, they found "sufficient evidence" to "calculate azimuths, or angular measurements", that allow their trajectories to be determined "with a sufficient degree of accuracy".

"On the basis of the evidence obtained during the investigation of the Ghouta incident, the conclusion is that chemical weapons have been used in the ongoing conflict between the parties in the Syrian Arab Republic, also against civilians, including children, on a relatively large scale," wrote the report by chief U.N. investigator Ake Sellstrom of Sweden. "In particular, the environmental, chemical and medical samples we have collected provide clear and convincing evidence that surface-to-surface rockets containing the nerve agent sarin were used," it said.

Syria and Russia said the militant opposition was responsible.

The fact that many people died or suffered painful wounds gave hawks the chance to invade Assad military forces. However, most unusual not all U.S. allies were so anxious for yet another war, nor were several members on the UN Security Council. U.K. PM David Cameron was willing but lo and behold, the Parliament majority said no dice. Even U.S. Congress wasn't ready.

Then Putin came up with a way out. He convinced President Assad to let all of his chemical weapons be destroyed. Obama accepted the "compromise". On September 27, the UN Security Council adopted resolution 2118 requiring, "Syria to assume responsibility for and follow a timeline for the destruction of its chemical weapons and its chemical weapon production facilities."

The Organization for the Prohibition of Chemical Weapons announced, on June 23, 2014, that "The last declared chemical weapons were shipped out of Syria for destruction. The destruction of the most dangerous chemical weapons was performed at sea aboard the *Cape Ray*, a vessel of the United States Maritime Administration's Ready Reserve Force, crewed with U.S. civilian merchant mariners. The actual destruction operations, performed by a team of U.S. Army civilians and contractors, destroyed 600 metric tons of chemical agents in 42 days." https://en.wikipedia.org/wiki/Destruction_of_Syria%27s_chemical_weapons

In Oliver Stone's February 20, 2016 interview with Putin, he asked:

"How close were we to war in Syria when you negotiated with Assad and the Americans to take chemical weapons out of Syria?"

VP: "I think we were quite close. There was a great danger of a war erupting and I believe that back then President Obama made the right decision. And he and I managed to agree on coordinated actions. As a matter of fact, he distinguished himself as a leader—as the Americans like to say—and thanks to these concerted actions we've managed to avoid an escalation of the conflict."

OS: "So it seems to be a very tense presidency you have."

VP: "And when was it simple? Times are always difficult. We simply have to thank God for giving us an opportunity to serve our country."

OS: "Well you've had a lot of opportunities and you've done an incredible job of maintaining your cool under this enormous pressure. And I think many—maybe millions of people—owe their lives, without knowing it, to your intervention." (*Interviews with Putin*, Skyhorse, 2017, pg. 146-7).

Three months before this rocket attack, UN's Independent Commission of Inquiry on Syria member Carla Del Ponte told media that testimony gathered from casualties and medical staff indicated that the nerve gas sarin was being used by "rebel fighters." (http://www.independent.co.uk/news/world/middle-east/uns-carla-del-ponte-says-there-is-evidence-rebels-may-have-used-sarin-in-syria-8604920.html)

"A United Nations inquiry into human rights abuses in Syria has found evidence that rebel forces may have used chemical weapons, its lead investigator has revealed," wrote the newspaper.

"'Our investigators have been in neighboring countries interviewing victims, doctors and field hospitals and, according to their report of last week which I have seen, there are strong, concrete suspicions but not yet incontrovertible proof of the use of sarin gas, from the way the victims were treated." "'This was used on the part of the opposition, the rebels, not by the government authorities,'" Del Ponte said in an interview broadcast on Swiss-Italian television on Sunday.

Nothing definitive was determined by the UN largely due to U.S.'s negation that their rebels could have done such acts. But muckraking Seymour Hersh's nose itched.

When the *London Review of Books* still published this daring truth-seeking journalist, it ran his piece, "Whose sarin?" on December 19, 2013.

> *"Barack Obama did not tell the whole story this autumn when he tried to make the case that Bashar al-Assad was responsible for the chemical weapons attack near Damascus on 21 August. In some instances, he omitted important intelligence, and in others he presented assumptions as facts. Most significant, he failed to acknowledge something known to the US intelligence community: that the Syrian army is not the only party in the country's civil war with access to sarin, the nerve agent that a UN study concluded—without assessing responsibility—had been used in the rocket attack."* (https://www.lrb.co.uk/v35/n24/seymour-m-hersh/whose-sarin)
>
> *"In the months before the attack, the American intelligence agencies produced a series of highly classified reports, culminating in a formal Operations Order—a planning document that precedes a ground invasion—citing evidence that the al-Nusra Front,* ***a jihadi group affiliated with al-Qaida, had mastered the mechanics of creating sarin and was capable of manufacturing it in quantity.*** *When the attack occurred al-Nusra should have been a suspect, but the administration cherry-picked intelligence to justify a strike against Assad."*[my emphasis]

By April 17, 2014, when Hersh's next story on the matter was published, he had found out the whole truth, "The Red Line and the Rat Line." (https://www.lrb.co.uk/v36/n08/seymour-m-hersh/the-red-line-and-the-rat-line)

Hersh reported that British intelligence had obtained a sample of the sarin used and analyzed it at a defense laboratory in Wiltshire. *The gas used "didn't match the batches known to exist in the Syrian army's chemical weapons arsenal. The message that the case against Syria wouldn't hold up was quickly relayed to the US joint chiefs of staff."*

Not all military brass wanted a wider war in the Middle East, which they conveyed to Obama. That, coupled with the fact that Assad was willing to give all his chemical weapons, turned the tide.

A former senior U.S. intelligence officer told Hersh: "We knew there were some in the Turkish government, who believed they could get Assad's nuts in a vice by dabbling with a sarin attack inside Syria—and forcing Obama to make good on his red line threat."

Hersh writes that the U.S. Joint Chiefs of Staff, "*also knew that the Obama administration's public claims that only the Syrian army had access to sarin were wrong. The American and British intelligence communities had been aware since the spring of 2013 that some rebel units in Syria were developing chemical weapons. On 20 June analysts for the US Defense Intelligence Agency issued a highly classified five-page 'talking points' briefing for the DIA's deputy director, David Shedd, which stated that al-Nusra maintained a sarin production cell: its program, the paper said, was 'the most advanced sarin plot since al-Qaida's pre-9/11 effort'.*"

"*(According to a Defense Department consultant, US intelligence has long known that al-Qaida experimented with chemical weapons, and has a video of one of its gas experiments with dogs.) The DIA paper went on: 'Previous IC [intelligence community] focus had been almost entirely on Syrian CW [chemical weapons] stockpiles; now we see ANF attempting to make its own CW … Al-Nusrah Front's relative freedom of operation within Syria leads us to assess the group's CW aspirations will be difficult to disrupt in the future.' The paper drew on classified intelligence from numerous agencies: 'Turkey and Saudi-based chemical facilitators,' it said, 'were attempting to obtain sarin precursors in bulk, tens of kilograms, likely for the anticipated large scale production effort in Syria.'*

Obama's 2012 Red Line threat to Syria about using chemical warfare is yet another double speak hypocrisy. How do these terrorists get to be moral judges? The U.S. admitted dropping 7.5 million liters of Agent Orange over 1.8 million hectares of Vietnam, Cambodia and Laos killing and injuring millions, including their own soldiers. There was napalm, depleted uranium, and a long list of chemical-biological warfare that the U.S. used in that unprovoked war plus in many other aggressive wars, not the least in North Korea, and Cuba as well (recall chapters 6, 11, 12).

ISLAMIC STATE FORMS IN SYRIA AND IRAQ

When the United States of America decided it was destined to bring democracy and liberty to the enslaved people of Iraq, and in the process killed untold numbers of people, destroyed much of their cultural and religious heritage, banned the Baath party and the army, pit Shiites against Sunni, it left an internal power vacuum that the terrorist al Qaeda organization decided to fill. Having never been allowed to exist during Saddam Hussein's government, it sent members from outside Iraq to recruit unemployed and banned people by U.S warlords. They initiated an even more sectarian and terrorist organization known by its Arabic acronym Daesh, or Islamic State of Iraq and the Levant.

Wahhabi and Salafi fundamentalists saw their duty as forcing the world's Muslims to abide by jihadist militancy and sharia law—men dominate women, who must not show their heads or bodies, rule by a patriarch who is omnipotent, and other strict rules. Their fighters grew to 30-50,000 by 2014-5. Already in April 2013 many went over to eastern Syria from western Iraq where they took Palmyra, and later into the northwest and seized Syria's largest city, 7000-year old Aleppo. In June 2014, they took over Iraq's second largest city, Mosul.

Turkey helped them in northern Syria, as did Saudi Arabia and Qatar. Saudis hold to the same jingoist faith that encouraged IS to kill all "infidels" and destroy their cultural and religious heritage. Infidels include Christian, Shiites, Jews, and certainly atheists and true democrats. Nevertheless, U.S. Deep State appreciates their anti-Syrian government and anti-Russian government policies so they assist them.

Sometimes the CIA helps Daesh, sometimes they act as though they fight them since that is the American way. Since the President of the United States must hate them for some of their "anti" principles, Barak Obama put the CIA in charge of operations at an official $1 billion a year (later cut back 20% by Congress in a gesture of appearing rational) to fight both the terrible Bashar al-Assad government and Daesh in a balancing act for justice. The CIA used some funds to facilitate arms to their "moderate" warring allies—the Free Syrian Army, Islamic Mujahedeen Army and other "rebel" groupings—from Libya, which it had recently liberated from the very terrible dictator Gaddafi. It helped that their good freedom-loving allies in Saudi Arabia and Qatar, and the infidel Zionist State of Israel, helped out. Naturally, their brother-in-arms, the former Imperial Colonizer of much of the world, the United Kingdom, was as always eager to help in a good cause—not to mention the freest of all libertarian nations, H.C. Andersen's swan country. (5)

On September 17, 2014, the U.S. congress voted to authorize additional funds to train Syrian "rebels", which also would be sent somehow to the Syrian "health activists", the "White Helmets", who operated in the major IS city of Aleppo—where no one can enter or leave or work without approval of the rabid protectors of Islam. Of course, the brave medical workers who can treat patients hit by poisonous gasses without wearing any protection should be given the Nobel Peace Prize so that they sit at the same peace table with Nobel Peace President Barak Obama.

One of the tactics Daesh uses to convince infidels that they have Allah on their side is to behead them. To show that they do not hold to favorites, they behead and otherwise murder many Sunni Muslims including Syrian soldiers since they make up the large majority of the government's army. They also behead Shiites, Christians, and Japanese with Buddha on their side.

When they beheaded US American free lance journalist, James Foley, on August 19, 2014, in Aleppo, and showed the video tape to the world, U.S. media stopped sending reporters to the field. Instead they used "news" from their favorite Syrian "activists", the White Helmets.

The mass media used such copy to "glorify the armed groups and agitate for more forceful Western military intervention against Syrian President Bashar al-Assad", so wrote Rania Khalek—albeit there were no reports from anywhere that the evil president had beheaded anybody. (https://fair.org/home/in-syria-western-media-cheer-al-qaeda/)

Khalek is a rare breed for today's media workers. She is of Lebanese background, albeit an atheist, and a U.S. natural citizen. Most rare of all, she actually goes to the war zones, and she calls the shots as she sees them. Her January 4, 2017 article in the unique Fairness and Accuracy in Reporting medium begins:

"The Syrian government—a dictatorship known for imprisoning, torturing and disappearing dissidents—is easy to vilify. And over the last five years of Syria's civil war, it has committed its share of atrocities. But there is more than one side to every story, and US media coverage has mainly reflected one side—that of the rebels—without regard for accuracy or basic context.

As the Syrian government recaptured East Aleppo from rebels in recent weeks, media outlets from across the political spectrum became rebel mouthpieces, unquestioningly relaying rebel claims while omitting crucial details about who the rebels were."

Khalek goes on to report how the "rebels" are really those dreadful Daesh terrorists who behead people, even US American journalists. So why is it that the US media supports them and their "media activists", the "White Helmets"? Could it be that the highest priority is as house organ for The Establishment and its Deep State, and not their own editorial workers?

Why is it that in government-held areas where Khalek worked as an independent journalist, she learned that the vast majority support the government, despite that fact that many "were sharply critical of the Assad regime"? Because, she says, they don't appreciate the brutality and religious fundamentalism of Assad's enemies, whom the U.S. supports. Indeed, these terrorists destroy hospitals, schools, courts and imprison and torture any critics.

U.S. STARTS BOMBING SYRIA

Logic in politics, especially geopolitics is most complicated, especially for working people with little time to do research. It is also confusing to fathom for this politically experienced author. Someone far more knowledgeable about how and why it is so complicated, former CIA official and author John Stockwell, explains simply:

> *"It is the function of the CIA to keep the world unstable, and to propagandize and teach the American people to hate, so we will let the Establishment spend any amount of money on arms."*

On September 22, 2014, the United States, Bahrain, Jordan, Qatar, Saudi Arabia, and the United Arab Emirates began to attack, officially, the Islamic State of Iraq and the Levant forces inside Syria—the Khorasans in west Aleppo, and al-Nusra around Raqqa. Now remember each and every one of those countries had ties with those they began to fight. The Middle Eastern states were buying oil in the territory IS had confiscated, and they did all this against the will of the Syrian government and against sovereign law and right to decide who "helps" and who doesn't.

Turkey confused the situation all the more as it hates its fellow religious Sunni Kurds, because they are not Turks and want equal rights inside Turkey, so they bomb them both inside Turkey and in northern Syria. The U.S. sides with the Syrian Democratic Forces led by Kurds who work alongside some Sunni Arabic opponents to Assad. The U.S. is also with Turkey as it is in NATO. Yet Turkey is also is a major trading partner with Russia.

When it is said that the U.S. sides with the "moderate" rebels, one should say some U.S. military forces do. But the CIA sides with one and all at any given time and place. This has been going on for years but first made the mass media (as far as I can tell) on March 17, 2016 when the "Los Angeles Times" published the article, "In Syria, militias armed by the Pentagon fight those armed by the CIA" by W. J. Hennigan, Brian Bennett and Nabih Bulos.

"Syrian militias armed by different parts of the U.S. war machine have begun to fight each other on the plains between the besieged city of Aleppo and the Turkish border." (http://beta.latimes.com/world/middleeast/la-fg-cia-pentagon-isis-20160327-story.html)

"The fighting has intensified over the last two months, as CIA-armed units and Pentagon-armed ones have repeatedly shot at each other while maneuvering through contested territory...In mid-February, a CIA-armed militia called Fursan al Haq, or Knights of Righteousness, was run out of the town of Marea, about 20 miles north of Aleppo, by Pentagon-backed Syrian Democratic Forces moving in from Kurdish-controlled areas to the east."

"Last year, the Pentagon helped create a new military coalition, the Syrian Democratic Forces. The goal was to arm the group and prepare it to take territory away from the Islamic State in eastern Syria and to provide information for U.S. airstrikes. The U.S. backing for a heavily Kurdish armed force has been a point of tension with the Turkish government, which has a long history of crushing Kurdish rebellions and doesn't want to see Kurdish units control more of its southern border.

"The CIA, meanwhile, has its own operations center inside Turkey from which it has been directing aid to rebel [read: terrorist] groups in Syria, providing them with TOW antitank missiles from Saudi Arabian weapons stockpiles."

PUTIN SAVES IRAN AND THE WORLD FROM WAR

President Putin had his hands full with the Ukraine and Syrian situations but he had to stop the Yankees from invading Iran too.

The United States began assisting Shah Mohammad Reza Pahlavi to create conditions for nuclear energy plants in the mid-1950s. This was after the CIA, and UK's MI6, overthrew the democratically elected government of Prime Minister Mohammad Mosaddeq, in 1953, and returned its favorite brutal dictator to power.

Efforts to create conditions for nuclear power plants were sluggish and when the 1979 revolution took place the U.S. backed out. In the 1990s, France, Argentina and Russia assisted the project while U.S. neo-cons accused Iran of secretly enriching uranium for nuclear bombs. Iran was leery of the West—having recently been the brunt of the U.S.-backed Iraqi war—and did not cooperate with the International Atomic Energy Agency (IAEA). It had signed the Non-Proliferation Treaty. But in the first decade of 2000, IAEA reported several times that it was possible that a nuclear weaponry program was taking place. The U.S. and other Western countries punished Iran with economic sanctions. Iran's first nuclear power plant (Bushehr I reactor) opened September 12, 2011 with Russian aid. U.S. hawks and Israel called for military action. Because of that and the war in Syria, Russia could not sit tight. World war was in the offing.

The new Iranian president Hassan Rouhani agreed to meet with P5+1 in October 2013. The permanent members of the UN Security Council (U.S., Russia, China, France, and UK) plus Germany, which has many petrochemical firms working in Iran, constitute P5+1. In July 2015, the EU as a whole joined in an agreement brokered by Russia with Iran. It called for:

1. The current stockpile of low enriched uranium to be reduced by 98 percent, most likely by shipping much of it to Russia.
2. Iran agreed to transform its deeply buried plant at Fordo into a center for science research. Another uranium plant, Natanz, is to be cut back rather than shut down. Some 5,000 centrifuges for enriching uranium will remain spinning there, about half the current number.

3. Iran agreed to limit enrichment to 3.7 percent and to cap its stockpile of low-enriched uranium at 300 kilograms for 15 years. That is considered insufficient for a bomb rush.
4. Iran was constructing a nuclear reactor at Arak that would have used natural uranium to produce Pu-239, which can fuel bombs. It will rebuild the reactor so it could not produce weapons-grade plutonium. The reactor's spent fuel, which could also be used to produce a bomb, will be shipped out, probably to Russia. Iran will not build any more heavy water reactors for 15 years.

The fact that President Putin had influenced Iran's president to make this agreement was a major achievement for a bit of peace. Roland Oliphant wrote from Moscow:

"Mr. Obama praised Vladimir Putin for his role in the agreement and said there could now be an 'opening' for further detente in the worst crisis in American-Russian relations since the Cold War.

Speaking shortly after a historic agreement to curb Iran's nuclear program was signed in Vienna, Mr Obama said that there was now an opportunity for a 'serious conversation' with Mr. Putin about the fate of Bashar Assad, the embattled Syrian president." (http://www.telegraph.co.uk/news/worldnews/barackobama/11740700/Barack-Obama-praises-Putin-for-help-clinching-Iran-deal.html)

*"Mr. Obama said Mr. Putin's cooperation had 'surprised' him. "Russia was a help on this. I'll be honest with you. I was not sure given the strong differences we are having with Russia right now around Ukraine, whether this would sustain itself. Putin and the Russian government compartmentalized on this in a way that surprised me,' he told [*The New York Times*]."*

"'We would have not achieved this agreement had it not been for Russia's willingness to stick with us and the other P5-Plus members in insisting on a strong deal.'"

"Russia worked hard to achieve a nuclear deal and Vladimir Putin praised the agreement achieved on Tuesday, saying that the 'world heaved a sigh of relief' and promising that 'Russia will do everything' to implement it."

A month later, however, the Nobel Peace Prize winner thought he had to put on his gorilla uniform. On August 5, Obama spoke defensively-aggressively about Syria at the American University.

"As commander-in-chief, I have not shied away from using force when necessary. I have ordered tens of thousands of young Americans into combat... [and have] ordered military actions in seven countries."

Writing in "The Intercept", Glenn Greenwald explained, "What he means is that he has ordered bombs dropped, and he has extinguished the lives of thousands of innocent people, in seven different countries, all of which just so happen to be predominantly Muslim."

"The list includes one country where he twice escalated a war that was being waged when he was inaugurated (Afghanistan), another where he withdrew troops to great fanfare only to then order a new bombing campaign (Iraq), two countries where he converted very rare bombings into a constant stream of American violence featuring cluster bombs and 'signature strikes' (Pakistan and Yemen), one country where he continued the policy of bombing at will (Somalia), and one country where he started a brand new war *even in the face of Congressional rejection of his authorization to do so*, leaving it in tragic shambles (Libya). That doesn't count the aggression by allies that he sanctioned and supported (in Gaza), nor the proxy wars he enabled (the current Saudi devastation of Yemen), nor the whole new front of cyber attacks he has launched nor the multiple despots he had propped up, nor the clandestine bombings that he still has not confirmed (Philippines)." Glenn Greenwald glenn.greenwald@theintercept.comt@ggreenwald

RUSSIA FORCED TO COME INTO THE WAR

President Assad had long asked Putin to help him militarily. Until September 2015, Assad's only aid came from Hezbollah and Iran. Hezbollah sent some troops; Iran sent only arms. About two thousand Hezbollah volunteers from Lebanon were killed by both al-Nusra and their hated Zionist Israeli-comrades-in-arms. Israel bombed Hezbollah near Palmyra and Iranian arms depots.

Vladimir Putin was reluctant, just as had been Leonid Brezhnev with the Communist government of Afghanistan. But by summer 2015, Putin was afraid that the U.S. and its terrorist state allies in the Middle East, along with NATO-Turkey, all alongside Daesh and other jihadists would topple the Syrian government and a disastrous situation as in Libya would take place. Russia would be even more surrounded by enemies. So, President Putin finally relented and came to the rescue with military might, especially from the air. It was the first time since the Cold War that Russia used military action outside the borders of its former Soviet Union.

Two years later, *Washington Post* associate editor David Ignatius [a well-known Deep State mouthpiece and war hawk] wrote as the war seemed to be coming to an end: "CIA analysts began to speak that summer [2015] about a 'catastrophic success'—in which the rebels would topple Assad without creating a strong, moderate government. In a June 2015 column, I quoted a U.S. intelligence official saying, 'Based on current trend lines, it is time to start thinking about a post-Assad Syria.' Russian President Vladimir Putin was warily observing the same trend, especially after an urgent visit to Moscow in July that year by Maj. Gen. Qasem Soleimani, commander of Iran's Quds Force and Assad's regional patron.

"Putin got the message: He intervened militarily in September 2015, decisively changing the balance of the Syrian war." (https://www.washingtonpost.com/opinions/what-the-demise-of-the-cias-anti-assad-program-means/2017/07/20/f6467240-6d87-11e7-b9e2-2056e768a7e5_story.html?utm_term=.f3a9b6dc7a05

Just two months after entering the war, on November 24, a Russian aircraft was shot down. Two Russian Su-24 jets had just bombed two groups fighting the Syrian government when a Turkish jet fired air-to-air missiles and downed one plane. As the navigator and pilot parachuted they were shot at by Turkmen living in Syria. Turkey had armed and trained several thousands in the Syrian Turkmen Brigades. The pilot was killed; the navigator escaped. Then a Russian helicopter flying to the rescue was shot at and the pilot killed.

Since Russia had begun its air campaign, it and the U.S. had exchanged information about where and when their aircraft were attacking. Putin said that the U.S. military, "which leads the coalition that Turkey belongs to, knew about the location and time of our planes' flights, and we were hit exactly there and at that time". (http://www.bbc.com/news/world-middle-east-34912581)

Interestingly, BBC reported that these Turkmen brigades "work with other opposition armed groups in the northern Latakia countryside, including the [Free Syrian Army], *the al-Qaeda affiliated Nusra Front and the Islamist Ahrar al-Sham.*"

Russia remained patient. It did not do what the United States always does: kick ass. No, Putin froze the work underway on a gas pipeline from Russia to Turkey and into Europe, and his government advised Russian tourists to avoid Turkish resorts, a huge business for the Turks.

President Tayvip Erdogan was influenced by this economic loss, too many refugees flooding into Turkey from Syria, and the increased regional insecurity that reached inside Turkey. He could foresee that Russia was determined to prevent the fall of his arch rival, Assad. Erdogan might be completely out in the cold once his terrorists were defeated. The West was criticizing him somewhat over refugees. So, in June, 2016, he apologized for the shootings and asked to come into trade again with Russia. Putin accepted. (https://www.reuters.com/article/us-russia-turkey-jet/kremlin-says-turkey-apologized-for-shooting-down-russian-jet-idUSKCN0ZD1PR)

It was only a month later that internal divisions broke out into an attempted coup, which Erdogan forces put down with brutal aftereffects. This convinced Erdogan to subtly scale down support for terrorism in Syria and he told Putin he would cooperate with the Syrian situation.

Meanwhile the U.S. wasn't nearly as effective in the civil war as was Russia. In early 2016, Russian aircraft were making 70-120 airstrikes daily while the illegal U.S. coalition was making but two to five. Russia and Syria, along with its invited allies Hezbollah and Iran were abiding by both national and international law in their joint efforts to crush terrorism against the state. They bombed and otherwise fought all armed opposition. Of course, their bombings also killed innocent civilians. It was the U.S. and its coalition that was in the country illegally, but they did not see this logically.

"John Kerry condemns Russia's 'repeated aggression' in Syria and Ukraine", ran *The Guardian* February 13, 2016 headline. (https://www.theguardian.com/us-news/2016/feb/13/john-kerry-condemns-russias-repeated-aggression-in-syria-and-ukraine

During his speech at the Munich Security Council, Secretary of State Kerry had the gall to tell Russia which armed groups it could fight and which not.

"To date, the vast majority, in our opinion, of Russia's attacks have been against legitimate opposition groups [sic] and to adhere to the agreement it made, we think it is critical that Russia's targeting change," Kerry said. Kerry added that the only way to end the Syrian conflict and ultimately defeat the Islamic State group is a political transition that removes Assad from power.

Some of these "legitimate" opposition groups, including the Turkman, protected oil routes from IS territory into Turkey. Putin spoke to Oliver Stone about this (The Putin Interviews pages 135-6). He said he even showed aerial photos of the routes and the "rebel" patrols at a G20 meeting—"there are thousands of trucks going through that route. It looks as if it were a living pipeline."

In the same period when Obama was condemning Russia and Syria for killing "legitimate rebels" and innocent civilians, the U.S. was bombing civilians. On July 20, 2016, it was reported that the U.S. had killed at least 73 civilians, mostly women and children, near an IS location. https://www.theguardian.com/world/2016/jul/20/us-airstrike-allegedly-kills-56-civilians-in-northern-syria

Hillary Clinton—running to follow in Obama's footsteps as a female warring president—was accusing Trump of nearly being a peacenik because he preferred to hold his hand out to the big bear. She was calling for a "no fly zone" over her Syria. If Russia did not acquiesce, she would shoot down its planes. World War Three with atomic bombs was not a problem for this macho lady.

U.S. DIRECT ATTACKS ON SYRIAN GOVERNMENT

Then, on September 17, just weeks before election day the U.S. killed Syrian troops.

"Russia and Syria asserted that 62 were killed and about 100 others were injured. Although the Central Command statement did not mention casualties, a senior administration official said the United States had 'relayed our regret' through Russia 'for the unintentional loss of life of Syrian forces fighting ISIL,'" wrote *The Washington Post*. (https://www.washingtonpost.com/world/middle_east/russia-and-syria-blame-us-led-coalition-for-deadly-strike-on-syrian-troops/2016/09/17/8dabf5d6-7d03-11e6-8064-c1ddc8a724bb_story.html?utm_term=.8c985540c780)

"The U.S. Central Command acknowledged the strike, in eastern Syria's Deir al-Zour province, saying it was 'halted immediately' when U.S. forces were informed by Russia 'that it was possible the personnel and vehicles targeted were part of the Syrian military.' Central Command said the intended target had been Islamic State forces in the area."

Peace doves struggles against eagles collage by Jette Salling

"It marked the first time the United States has engaged the Syrian military since it began targeting the Islamic State in Syria and Iraq two years ago. The strike also came at a particularly sensitive time in U.S. and Russian efforts to forge a cease-fire in Syria's civil war."

"The Syrian military said in a statement that its troops had been surrounded by militant fighters and that the U.S. strike 'paved the way for ISIS terrorists to attack' a nearby hilltop."

Danish planes had been in this attack so the Danish daily, "Politikan", was granted an interview with President Assad, September 23. Assad said there was no way it was a mistake. "Four aircraft attacked for almost an entire hour…on the Syrian soldiers' position…There were no terrorists near them"…"Then, after the attack, IS troops arrived and attacked our troops."

On October 9, the Danish Defense Ministry admitted that during coalition bombings it had been co-responsible for killing 70 civilians. Danish international studies researchers maintained the figure was much higher. The NGO Airwars, which keeps statistics on such things, reported the coalition had dropped 54,611 bombs and killed 1,642 civilians.

Then, as if out of the blue, the unexpected occurred in the world's military empire. The ill-read, non-political, fantasy world reality showman, and richest-in-his-own-right capitalist won the presidential election. Donald Trump is a caricature of—as Hillary Clinton called half of US Americans who voted for him—the "irredeemable" "basket of deplorables".

The Ku Klux Klan celebrated, the gun lobby was ecstatic, Wall Street was leery, Zionists were uncertain. Obama-Clinton Democrats and their stunt man Bernie Sanders were appalled, liberal feminists were indignant, African-Americans were shocked, Mexican-Americans and Mexicans were scared, and European Establishment-U.S. partners were perplexed—what now.

Denmark, for example, decided to call back its F-16s in Syria and Iraq. I had predicted this could be one of potentially positive reactions from European vassal state leaders as they would for the first time since World War II feel real distrust of a U.S. president—IF he stayed his no war course.

Following Trump's inauguration on January 20, 2017, his cabinet appointments went mainly to rich guys and military brass. The one clearly wise choice, in the context of preventing a world war, was former Army Lt. General Michael Flynn as his national security advisor. Another possible sane candidate was the former CEO of the world's largest oil concern ExxonMobil Rex Tillerson as Secretary of State. Neither Flynn nor Tillerson were die-heart enemies of Russia as were most Republicans and Democratic careerists such as the Clintons. But Flynn made the mistake of actually talking to Russia's ambassador in secret and somehow that was a no no, which made Trump look like a lackey of Putin and that could only be redressed by letting the rational Flynn leave office. And so it goes on. Trump had blinked, and was on the road to appease his tormentors by making more concessions. (See chapter 17.)

The military-industrial complex President Eisenhower warned about, of which he was a part, had deepened its power. This complot and its Deep State went into full swing against any Trump peacemaking. God forbid that the weapons industry's profit growth would fall, and Deep State and military budgets decline. So something had to happen to stop the madman from limiting profits.

After he showed weakness with Flynn, they convinced Trump that in order to make America Great Again he had to raise the war budget by a colossal $80 billion at official figures, for starters. Now something had to happen in Syria so that Trump would truly show American greatness.

"Witnesses and activists say warplanes attacked Khan Sheikhoun, about 50km (30 miles) south of the city of Idlib, early on 4 April, when many people were asleep." Reported BBC. (http://www.bbc.com/news/world-middle-east-39500947)

Who are "activists" in a town run by terrorist al-Qaeda? But BBC, as other UK and United States mass media, concentrated on describing the town as run by the legitimate "rebels" alongside these "activist" and "opposition" categories. The article does mention once that "al-Qaeda linked jihadists" were there but chose not to term them "terrorists." These "rebels" were quoted as saying that 89 people were killed (33 children and 18 women) and 541 injured.

BBC continued: "Hundreds suffered symptoms consistent with reaction to a nerve agent after what the opposition and Western powers said was a Syrian government air strike on the area.

"Syrian President Bashar al-Assad said the incident was fabricated, while his ally Russia said an air strike hit a rebel depot full of chemical munitions," and struck "a large terrorist ammunition depot" on the town's outskirts."

These "rebels" have their own media and BBC sees fit to use their words and photographs without qualms. "Hussein Kayal, a photographer for the pro-opposition Edlib Media Center (EMC), was reported as saying that he was awoken by the sound of an explosion..."

I could not see what Kayal reported nor did the link to his photographs work for some reason.

BBC continues: "Opposition activists said government warplanes dropped bombs containing chemicals." And then we see Reuters photos of "activists" around these dead and dying people not wearing any protective clothing or masks. Was Reuters actually present? I doubt that. Were they "activist" or "pro-opposition" photographs that Reuters put its name to? We can't know.

So, I checked to see what reliable reporter Sy Hersh would write. This time in the German medium *Die Welt*. The June 25 headline read:

"Trump's Red Line" (https://www.welt.de/politik/ausland/article165905578/Trump-s-Red-Line.html)

"On April 6, United States President Donald Trump authorized an early morning Tomahawk missile strike on Shayrat Air Base in central Syria in retaliation for what he said was a deadly nerve agent attack carried out by the Syrian government two days earlier in the rebel-held town of Khan Sheikhoun. Trump issued the order despite having been warned by the U.S. intelligence community that it had found no evidence that the Syrians had used a chemical weapon.

"The available intelligence made clear that the Syrians had targeted a jihadist meeting site on April 4 using a Russian-supplied guided bomb equipped with conventional explosives. Details of the attack, including information on its so-called high-value targets, had been provided by the Russians days in advance to American and allied military officials in Doha, whose mission is to coordinate all U.S., allied, Syrian and Russian Air Force operations in the region.

"Some American military and intelligence officials were especially distressed by the president's determination to ignore the evidence. 'None of this makes any sense,' one officer told colleagues upon learning of the decision to bomb. 'We KNOW that there was no chemical attack ... the Russians are furious. Claiming we have the real intel and know the truth ... I guess it didn't matter whether we elected Clinton or Trump.'"

"Within hours of the April 4 bombing, the world's media was saturated with photographs and videos from Khan Sheikhoun. Pictures of dead and dying victims, allegedly suffering from the symptoms of nerve gas poisoning, were uploaded to social media by local activists, including the *White Helmets, a first responder group known for its close association with the Syrian opposition.*" [My emphasis]

"I was told that the Russians passed the [Syrian jet flight plan] directly to the CIA," Hersh wrote. He said that a U.S. intelligence officer told him, that the Russians "were playing the game right."

Hersh quotes this senior adviser to the U.S. intelligence community, who had been in the Defense Department and the CIA: "The rebels control the population by controlling the distribution of goods that people need to live – food, water, cooking oil, propane gas, fertilizers for growing their crops, and insecticides to protect the crops."

"The basement was used as storage for rockets, weapons and ammunition, as well as products that could be distributed for free to the community, among them medicines and *chlorine-based decontaminants for cleansing the bodies of the dead before burial."*

"The Russian bomb, which it gave to the Syrians to drop on this site, was" 'not a chemical weapons strike,' the adviser said. 'That's a fairy tale.'" He added that if sarin were involved everyone handling victims "would be wearing Hazmat protective clothing in case of a leak.'"

"A Bomb Damage Assessment (BDA) by the U.S. military later determined that the heat and force of the 500-pound Syrian bomb triggered a series of secondary explosions that could have generated a huge toxic cloud that began to spread over the town, formed by the release of the fertilizers, disinfectants and other goods stored in the basement, its effect magnified by the dense morning air, which trapped the fumes close to the ground."

The senior adviser said, "The strike itself killed up to four jihadist leaders, and an unknown number of drivers and security aides. There is no confirmed count of the number of civilians killed by the poisonous gases that were released by the secondary explosions..."

Doctors Without Borders 100 kilometers away treated patients with constricted pupils, muscle spasms and other symptoms consistent with sarin gas but the fact that they smelled of bleach suggests that the conventional bomb triggered secondary explosions from chlorine stored by the terrorists, Hersh reported his source as saying. The veteran intelligence officer continued:

"'*What doesn't occur to most Americans is if there had been a Syrian nerve gas attack authorized by Bashar, the Russians would be 10 times as upset as anyone in the West. Russia's strategy against ISIS, which involves getting American cooperation, would have been destroyed and Bashar would be responsible for pissing off Russia, with unknown consequences for him. Bashar would do that? When he's on the verge of winning the war? Are you kidding me?'"* [my emphasis]

Nevertheless, Hersh wrote: "Despite military intelligence to the contrary, and his own knowledge of the mass media's constant use of 'false news,' Trump believed that Syria-Russia used chemical weapons, or so he said." Quoting Trump:

"That attack on children yesterday had a big impact on me. Big impact ... It's very, very possible ... that my attitude toward Syria and Assad has changed very much."

Hersh's intelligence source told him.

"'The CIA also told them [Trump's team] that there was no residual delivery for sarin at Sheyrat [the airfield from which the Syrian SU-24 bombers had taken off on April 4] and Assad had no motive to commit political suicide.' Everyone involved, except perhaps the president, also understood that a highly skilled United Nations team had spent more than a year in the aftermath of an alleged sarin attack in 2013 by Syria, removing what was said to be all chemical weapons from a dozen Syrian chemical weapons depots."

But Trump's "human nature" is to react emotionally. As the intelligence advisor told Hersh:

"'*Everyone close to him knows his proclivity for acting precipitously when he does not know the facts. He doesn't read anything and has no real historical knowledge*. He wants verbal briefings and photographs. He's a risk-taker. He can accept the consequences of a bad decision in the business world; he will just lose money. But in our world, lives will be lost and there will be long-term damage to our national security if he guesses wrong. *He was told we did not have evidence of Syrian involvement and yet Trump says: 'Do it.'"'*

"The attack on the airfield did minimal damage, the intelligence officer said, and almost no casualties as the 'enemy' had been forewarned. But it had the 'gorilla' effect so Trump could beat his breast.

And despite what one would think is a war-weary American public, Hersh wrote:

"*The next few days were his most successful as president. America rallied around its commander in chief, as it always does in times of war.* Trump, who had campaigned as someone who advocated making peace with Assad, was bombing Syria 11 weeks after taking office, and was hailed for doing so by Republicans, Democrats and the media alike."

Hersh concluded with his source's words: "'*The Salafists and jihadists got everything they wanted out of their hyped-up Syrian nerve gas ploy,*' he told me, referring to the flare up of tensions between Syria, Russia and America."

Die Welt wrote that Hersh had "exposed the My Lai Massacre in Vietnam in 1968. He uncovered the abuses at Abu Ghraib prison in Iraq and many other stories about war and politics." He is a real reporter, and as such blacklisted by most mass media.

Hersh had first offered this piece to his latest of publishers, London Review of Books (LBR), after U.S. mass media blacklisted him. LBR fact-checked and accepted the article, even paid for it, and then refused to publish. Hersh says he was told that they were afraid that critics would contend they were pro-Syrian, pro-Russian.

The year before, however, LRB had published his piece, "Military to Military", in which he reported that the chairman of the Joint Chiefs of Staff, General Martin Dempsey, had forecast that the fall of Assad's regime would lead to chaos and a takeover of Syria by jihad extremists, which would end up like Libya has and that was not in the American interest.

SANITY IN THE HOUSE OF REPRESENTATIVES

The sarin gas fake news story killed the only sane congressional member's bill to stop the U.S. government-military from supporting the very terrorists in Syria who do use chemical weapons against their own people.

Tulsi Gabbard from Hawaii is quite an exceptional politician, one willing to learn and change her mind. She started at 21 in the Hawaii legislature, then joined the U.S. Army and was sent to Iraq in a medical unit, in 2004. She earned the rank of major and was a volunteer soldier to Kuwait in 2008-9. Gabbard took in the reality she saw that "regime change" wars do more damage than good. She began opposing such wars: Iraq, Libya and Syria. She said not only do they harm the people of those countries but they cause refugee crises that the West does not want.

Gabbard became the first Samoan American and first Hindu to win a seat in the U.S. House of Representatives (2013). On January 4, 2017 she introduced bill H.R. 258 to prohibit the use of U.S. government funds to provide assistance to Al Qaeda, Jabhat Fateh al-Sham, and ISIS and those countries supporting those organizations.

Announcing the legislation, she said: "If you or I gave money, weapons or support to al-Qaeda or ISIS, we would be thrown in jail. Yet the U.S.

government has been violating this law for years, quietly supporting allies and partners of al-Qaeda, ISIL ... and other terrorist groups with money, weapons and intelligence support, in their fight to overthrow the Syrian government." (https://www.npr.org/2016/12/10/505079126/hawaii-congresswoman-tulsi-gabbard-introduces-bill-to-halt-u-s-arms-supplies-to)

Besides the fake sarin gas matter, another drawback for Gabbard's bill was the White Helmets.

WHITE HELMETS

When Hersh's key source spoke of the "White Helmets" as having a "close association with the Syrian opposition", and in the same sitting spoke of fake news, it doesn't take too much imagination to think that this Hollywood winning "activist" group is a fake news group that the mass media just loves. There has been, however, one major flaw. The charlatans finally went too far and got exposed, even by CNN. On November 25, 2016, CNN published this story.

"It's a familiar scene: Syria Civil Defense, also known as the 'White Helmets,' rushing to rescue a man covered in rubble, but unlike thousands of other videos from Aleppo, this one is staged.

"The short video—a take on the Mannequin Challenge—was created by the Revolutionary Forces of Syria (RFS), an opposition media group, to draw attention to the crisis amid a renewed aerial assault on the besieged city."

"This video and the related posts were recorded by RFS media with Syria Civil Defense volunteers, who hoped to create a connection between the horror of Syria and the outside world using the viral 'Mannequin challenge.' 'This was an error of judgment, and we apologize on behalf of the volunteers involved,' the statement read."(http://edition.cnn.com/2016/11/24/middleeast/mannequin-challenge-white-helmets-syria/index.html

The White Helmets, however, did not just make one "error of judgment".

Vanessa Beeley, an independent English journalist, writes mainly for http://21stcenturywire.com/

She wrote the following about her August 2016 trip to Syria: "I re-entered Syria as an independent writer and photographer and extended

my visa to three weeks in total which enabled me to visit many areas, including Aleppo. My primary reason for being in Syria was to complement my research into the multi-million NATO and Gulf State funded, terrorist-linked White Helmets, created in 2013 by a British ex military and intelligence officer, James Le Mesurier. As part of this research, I met with the REAL Syria Civil Defense, established in 1953 and a member of the ICDO [International Civil Defence Organization] and recorded their testimony against the White Helmets." (https://thewallwillfall.org/about/)

Here is an excerpt from her Syrian series: "The White Helmets receive funding from the U.K. Foreign Office, curiously through the Conflict, Stability and Security Fund (CSSF) for non-humanitarian aid. According to a statement made by the Foreign and Commonwealth Office, "the total value of funds committed between June 2013 and the end of the current financial year [31 March 2016] is £19.7m. At the end of September 2016, U.K. Foreign Secretary Boris Johnson pledged a further £ 32 million." (http://21stcenturywire.com/2017/10/09/white-helmets-state-sanctioned-terrorism-hollywood-poster-boys-war/)

The Obama regime also donated $23 million for the White Helmets "humanitarian" work inside war zones dominated by terrorists groups. Other allies were not to be outdone: Germany and Holland ($4.5 million each), Denmark ($3.2 million), and Japan (undisclosed sum). As is usually the case with "black ops", the White Helmets probably also receive many additional (but undisclosed) millions and general assistance from other Gulf states like Qatar and the Saudis, as well as the CIA.

In one White Helmets promotional they advertise for the CIA-NATO funded Free Syrian Army, which Beeley shows. The FSA was absorbed into the ranks of the Nusra Front, whose weapons capability far outstripped the FSA armory.

"The leader of the White Helmets, Raed Saleh," Beeley writes, "was deported from Dulles Airport in the U.S. in April [16] 2016. No real explanation was ever given for this decision. Mark Toner of the U.S. State Department fielded questions from media during a press briefing, but did admit to funding the group to the tune of $23 million, as well as suggest that Raed Saleh might have 'extremist connections.' Raed Saleh was then allowed back into the U.S. in September 2016 and spoke at the UN Headquarters in New York with the Dutch Mission. Saleh was involved in closed sessions with Syrian activists and former Secretary of State John Kerry, as noted by *The New York Times* [By Anne Barnard September 30, 2016].

"In leaked conversations, Raed Saleh and another Syrian 'regime change' activist and blogger, Marcell Shehwaro, lobbied hard for U.S. military intervention to bring about their desired regime change. The White Helmets' penchant for political statements and lobbying, calls into question their claims of being an apolitical, humanitarian-centric organization."

BREAST-BEATING TRUMP HITS AGAIN

When U.S. warships launched 59 Tomahawk cruise missiles at the Syrian airfield in April, it was the first time the U.S. had directly attacked the Assad regime. And Trump did it again on June 18.

"A U.S. warplane shot down a Syrian army jet on Sunday in the southern Raqqa countryside, with Washington saying the jet had dropped bombs near U.S.-backed forces and Damascus saying the plane was downed while flying a mission against Islamic State militants." (https://www.reuters.com/article/us-mideast-crisis-syria-usa/u-s-warplane-downs-syrian-army-jet-in-raqqa-province-idUSKBN1990XI)

The downing of the Syrian fighter marked the first time in this century that a U.S. warplane has shot down a plane of another country. The last instance took place in 1999 during the U.S.-NATO war against Serbia, when a U. S. jet shot down a Serbian MiG.

The U.S. complained that the Syrian jet had attacked its favorite Syrian Democratic Forces. The Syrian Army said it was advancing in destroying Daesh terrorists, and had seized back many villages and oil fields under their control. The U.S. was competing for these territories by encouraging the SDF and other "rebels" to take land for post-war negotiations in what it hopes could be a split up of Syria a la Yugoslavia.

Two days after downing the Syrian jet, a U.S. warplane shot down a drone fired against terrorists in southeast Syria by Trump's most hated country, Iran.

President Putin said: enough is enough!

Henceforth, the Russian Defense Ministry announced, "Russia is halting cooperation with its US counterparts in the framework of the Memorandum on the Prevention of Incidents and Ensuring Air Safety in Syria following the coalition's downing of a Syrian warplane." (http://www.greanvillepost.com/2017/06/19/us-recklessly-and-lawlessly-shoots-down-syrian-plane-russia-says-enough-is-enough/)

"In the areas of combat missions of Russian air fleet in Syrian skies, any airborne objects, including aircraft and unmanned vehicles of the international coalition, located to the west of the Euphrates River, will be tracked by Russian ground and air defense forces as air targets," the Russian Ministry of Defense stated.

Downing the military jet within Syrian airspace "cynically" violates the sovereignty of the Syrian Arab Republic, Russian military said. The actions of the US Air Force are in fact "*military aggression*" against Syria, the statement adds.

The ministry emphasized that Russian warplanes were on a mission in Syrian airspace during the U.S.-led coalition's attack on the Syrian Su-22, while the coalition failed to use the communication line to prevent an incident. (https://www.rt.com/news/393028-syria-russia-us-plane/)

In other words, next time you do it, we retaliate. The gravity of the event was underscored by Australia grounding its planes that had been flying over Syria.

Meanwhile, NATO held a ceremony in the former Soviet Baltic republic of Latvia to mark what it said was the full deployment of a 4,500-strong "deterrent force" on Russia's border. The Pentagon had recently deployed B-2 stealth bombers and other aircraft as well as Army units to the region for "exercises." Russia countered with a buildup of its own on its western border.

In September, Russia flexed muscle. This is "The Saker" September 22 report, "Russian special forces repel a US-planned attack in Syria, denounce the USA and issue a stark warning".

"Something rather unprecedented just happened in Syria: US backed 'good terrorist' forces attempted a surprise attack against Syrian government forces stationed to the north and northeast of the city of Hama. What makes this attack unique is that it took place inside a so-called 'de-escalation zone' and that it appears that one of the key goals of the attack was to encircle in a pincer-movement and subsequently capture a platoon of Russian military police officers deployed to monitor and enforce the special status of this zone.

"The Russian military police forces, composed mainly of soldiers from the Caucasus region, fought against a much larger enemy force and had to call for assistance. For the first time, at least officially, Russian special operations forces were deployed to rescue and extract their comrades. At the same time, the Russians sent in a number of close air support aircraft who reportedly killed several hundred 'good' terrorists and beat back the attack."

"(Russian sources speak of the destruction of 850 fighters, 11 tanks, three infantry fighting vehicles, 46 armed pickup trucks, five mortars, 20 freighter trucks and 38 ammo supply points; you can see photos of the destroyed personnel and equipment here)". http://thesaker.is/

"What also makes this event unique is the official reaction of the Russians to this event."

Head of the Main Operations Department at Russia's General Staff Colonel General Sergei Rudskoi declared that: "*Despite agreements signed in Astana on September 15, gunmen of Jabhat al-Nusra and joining them units that don't want to comply with the cessation of hostilities terms, launched a large-scale offensive against positions of government troops north and northeast of Hama in Idlib de-escalation zone from 8 am on September 19(...) According to available data, the offensive was initiated by American intelligence services to stop a successful advance of government troops east of Deir ez-Zor.*"

Russian Defense Ministry's spokesman, Major General Igor Konashenkov declared that:

"*Russia unequivocally told the commanders of US forces in Al Udeid Airbase (Qatar) that it will not tolerate any shelling from the areas where the SDF are stationed (...) Fire from positions in regions [controlled by the SDF] will be suppressed by all means necessary."* http://www.greanvillepost.com/2017/09/22/russian-special-forces-repel-a-us-planned-attack-in-syria-denounce-the-usa-and-issue-a-stark-warning/ and https://colonelcassad.livejournal.com/3693287.html

Russia's reply to terrorism impacted, so much so that on November 22, a summit meeting was held in Sochi, a summer resort by the Black Sea in Russia. Here is much of the text that the world's best contemporary diplomat, President Vladimir Putin, achieved—an agreement between Russia and the arch enemies President of Iran Hassan Rouhani and President of Turkey, Recep Tavyip Erdogan:

"The Presidents expressed satisfaction with the current level of tripartite coordination on maintaining and strengthening the ceasefire regime in Syria, of which Iran, Russia and Turkey are guarantors.

The Heads of state noted that, following several years of international efforts to defeat...terrorist groups in Syria, over the 11 months since the establishment of the ceasefire regime on December 29, 2016, a breakthrough had been made in bringing closer the elimination of ISIL, Nusra Front and all other terrorist organizations as designated by the UNSC and agreed that Iran, Russia and Turkey will continue cooperation for their ultimate defeat.

The Presidents emphasized that the creation of the de-escalation areas established in Astana process in Syria have been quite efficient and greatly helped to reduce violence, alleviate the humanitarian suffering, curb the flow of refugees, and start working to provide conditions for the safe return of refugees and internally displaced persons.

The Presidents decided that Iran, Russia and Turkey would continue their coordinated efforts to ensure that the progress in reduction of violence is irreversible. They agreed to assist the Syrians in restoring unity of the country, and achieving a political solution of the crisis through an inclusive, free, fair and transparent Syrian-led and Syrian-owned process leading to a constitution enjoying the support of the Syrian people and free and fair elections with the participation of all eligible Syrians under appropriate UN supervision.

The Heads of state reaffirmed their strong commitment to sovereignty, independence, unity and territorial integrity of The Syrian Arab Republic and emphasized that under no circumstances the creation of the above-mentioned de-escalation areas and at political initiative to solve the Syrian

crisis undermine the sovereignty, independence, unity and territorial integrity of The Syrian Arab Republic.

The Presidents expressed their support for a broad intra-Syrian dialogue involving representatives of all segments of Syrian society.

The Presidents called on the representatives of The Government of The Syrian Arab Republic and the opposition that are committed to the sovereignty, independence, unity, territorial integrity and non-fractional character of the Syrian state to participate constructively in the Syrian national dialogue congress in Sochi in near future. They agreed to actively contribute to the success of the Congress. Iran, Russia and Turkey will consult and agree on participants of the Congress.

The Presidents underscored the need for rapid, safe and unhindered humanitarian access and emphasized the need for the Syrian parties to take confidence-building measures, including the release of detainees/abductees and the handover of the bodies as well as identification of missing persons to create better condition for political process and lasting ceasefire. They called upon members of the international community to support the process of de-escalation and stabilization in Syria, inter alia, by sending additional aid to the Syrian people, facilitating the humanitarian mine action, preserving historical heritage, and restoring basic infrastructure assets, including social and economic facilities.

The Presidents expressed the hope that the progress in resolving Syrian crisis achieved through cooperation of Iran, Russia and Turkey would have a positive effect on the overall situation in the region, and reduce the risk of ethnic and sectarian divide." (http://en.kremlin.ru/supplement/5256)

Pepe Escobar, writing in *Asian Times*, on November 24, was both encouraged by this agreement and skeptical about how the United States would react to its loss.

"The Pentagon, which is in Syria without a UN resolution (Russia and Iran were invited by Damascus)" shows no evidence of having plans "to relinquish military bases set up in territory recaptured by the US-supported Syrian Democratic Forces (SDF), contiguous to Syrian oil and gas fields. Defense Secretary James Mattis insists US forces will remain in Syria to 'prevent the appearance of ISIS 2.0.' For Damascus, that's a red line." (http://www.atimes.com/article/syria-war-sochi-peace/)

"The Sochi summit was choreographed to the millimeter. Previously, Putin held detailed phone calls with both Trump and Saudi King Salman (not MBS); the emir of Qatar; Egypt's Sisi; and Israel's Netanyahu. Parallel to a meeting of Syria-Russia military top brass, Syrian President Bashar al-Assad dropped in; a non-surprise surprise Sochi visit to tell Putin in person that without Russia's military campaign Syria would not have survived as a sovereign state.

"The facts on the ground are stark; the Syrian Arab Army (SAA)—fully expanded, retrained, re-equipped and re-motivated—recaptured Aleppo, Palmyra, Deir Ezzor and almost the whole southeast; borders with both Iraq and Lebanon are open and secured; cease-fires are in effect in over 2,500 towns; Turkey desisted from years of...supporting 'moderate rebels' and is now part of the solution; ISIS/Daesh is on the run, now no more than a minor rural/desert insurgency."

"With Sochi in mind, a further joker in the pack is how a Trump-Putin possible entente will be regarded by the Pentagon, the CIA and Capitol Hill—which will always refuse the notion of a Putin-led peace process and no 'Assad must go' to boot.

"Most of what lies ahead hinges on who will control Syria's oil and gas fields. It's Pipelineistan all over again; all wars are energy wars. Damascus simply won't accept an energy bonanza for the US-supported SDF, actually led by the YPG.

"And neither would Russia. Apart from Moscow holding on to a strategic eastern Mediterranean base, eventually Gazprom wants to be an investment partner/operator in a newly feasible Iran-Iraq-Syria gas pipeline, whose main customer will be the EU. Beyond Sochi, the real—Pipelineistan—war has only just begun."

The 4th media outlet wrote in that vein as well.

"True, the Islamic State (IS) is routed but the United States intends to maintain large military presence in Syria...The American military will maintain a presence in northern Syria—where the Americans have trained and assisted the Syrian Democratic Forces (SDF) against the IS and establish new local governance, apart from the Assad government, in those areas...

"US-supported forces also hold territories east of the Euphrates River in Syria's southeast, as well as along the borders of Israel and Jordan in the southwest. There is no reason to believe that the legitimate Syrian government could establish control over these areas as long as the US-led coalition is there." (https://www.strategic-culture.org/news/2017/11/24/us-military-stay-syria-even-after-islamic-state-defeat.html)

That statement came in November but just two months later, Turkey feels sassy enough to tell the U.S. to get the hell out of "its" party of Syria where the U.S. backs the SDF. Turkey had begun bombing their captured territory and were using the U.S. backed FSA, now under Turkey control, to attack the Kurds on the ground.

A January 27, 2018 headline read: "Turkey tells USA to leave Manbij immediately".

"As Turkish and allied militant forces from the so-called Free Syrian Army (FSA) advance further upon Kurdish positions in northern Syria, Turkey has called upon the United States to vacate its military bases in the Syrian district of Manbij." Speaking to reporters on Saturday, Turkish foreign minister Melet Cavusoglu said that Ankara is calling upon the US, its official ally in NATO, to cease any and all support to Syrian Kurdish forces and militias." (https://www.almasdarnews.com/article/turkey-tells-usa-leave-manbij-immediately/)

US National Security Adviser Herbert Raymond McMaster about the ongoing Turkish invasion of Syrian soil is reported "to have promised during the talk that the US would no longer provide weapons to the YPG[SDF] militias, while both agreed to increase coordination and clear up "misunderstandings" regarding Syria.

"While both Turkey and the United States are in violation of international law by entering Syria with military forces without permission by Damascus or a UN mandate, both countries have vastly different interests in the country.

"The United States has for years supplied weapons and training to Kurdish militias in northern Syria, causing concerns that they seek an eventual secession of Kurdish-occupied lands from Syria. Turkey on the other hand, having supported so-called moderate rebel groups such as the FSA since at least 2015, actively seeks to prevent the existence of a YPG-controlled area to its southern border, as it sees the Syrian Kurdish units as an affiliate of the banned Kurdistan Workers' Party, which is active within Turkey."

At this point, it seems that Assad and Putin are letting the two ally-rivals fight it out without direct intervention. As of now, the Syrian government controls about two-thirds of Syria but its enemies seek to split Syria up even if a full scale war ends, for now at least.

According to *The Washington Post*'s David Ignatius, while the CIA program ultimately failed in its objective of removing Assad from power, it was hardly "bootless". "The program pumped many hundreds of millions of dollars to many dozens of militia groups. One knowledgeable official estimates that the CIA-backed fighters may have killed or wounded 100,000 Syrian soldiers and their allies over the past four years." (https://www.washingtonpost.com/opinions/what-the-demise-of-the-cias-anti-assad-program-means/2017/07/20/f6467240-6d87-11e7-b9e2-2056e768a7e5_story.html?utm_term=.5451feb8e1b1

Russia—with Iran and Hezbollah and Syria's loyal majority—had saved Syria so far from falling into Yankee hands, but can the torn country be reunited with the U.S. frothing?

There were 23 million Syrians in 2001 before the civil war. About half a million have been killed; perhaps four million wounded. UN High Commissioner for Refugees says 6.6 million are internally displaced; 4.8 four million have fled to neighboring countries (especially Turkey); and one million seek asylum in Europe. Within the six year period of war life expectancy fell from 76 to 56 years.

How can anyone conclude that "the war against/for terrorism", and the "war for democracy", the "humanitarian operation" has benefited the people of Syria?

Notes:

1. *New Statesman*, "America's Gulag," May 17, 2004; CBS 60 minutes, January 21, 2004.

2. "Why the Arabs don't want us in Syria" was published February 23, 2016: https://www.politico.eu/article/why-the-arabs-dont-want-us-in-syria-mideast-conflict-oil-intervention/

   RFK was shot several times on June 5, 1968 at the Ambassador Hotel in Los Angeles. He had just won the California Democratic Party primary for the presidency. Sirhan was captured after the shooting, in which five other persons were wounded. He pled guilty but the judge demanded a full trial. Sirhan was born in Jerusalem of a Christian Greek Orthodox family and hated Israel. He saw the Kennedys as his enemies for their support of the occupiers. Sirhan was found guilty and sentenced to be executed. The decision was later changed to life imprisonment. A second defense lawyer, Laurence Teetey claimed that Sirhan might have been hypnotized, a method that the CIA is known to use. A later defense team asserted that two guns had been fired, as in the assassination of John F. Kennedy. During Robert Kennedy's presidential campaign he proposed that if elected he would reopen his brother's murder.

3. See my piece, "A Marxist Analysis: Arab Uproar." http://www.thiscantbehappening.net/node/428

4. *Destroying a Nation: The Civil War in Syria* (I.B. Tauris, June 2017). http://www.independent.co.uk/voices/syria-civil-war-rebellion-isis-assad-western-intervention-arms-a7921526.html

5. See my piece on why Gaddafi had to go. https://dissidentvoice.org/2011/05/libya-fact-sheet/

CHAPTER 16
Ukraine: The Last Straw

THERE ARE TWO parts where Russia is exposed: Its Kazakhstan border, and there is no threat there; its western border where Europe is strong. Any European invasion has historically been, and will be from this part just as it was for Hitler's Nazis. If Russia controls these buffer states, any aggressor that wishes to invade must first break through this barrier. That would be difficult and give Russians time to prepare to repel an attack. (Abe Iskandar)

The Nazi invasion and occupation of the Ukraine started June 22, 1941 and lasted nearly three years. The Ukrainian Auxiliary Police was created by Heinrich Himmler immediately upon the invasion. It was made up of ca. 5000 nationalists in the Ukrainian People's Militia. They were a major force under German Nazi leadership of the extermination of about 900,000 of the 1.5 million Ukrainians Jews. This included the Babi Yar massacre, and the Lviv pogroms inside Poland.

Between 10 and 13 million other Ukrainians were killed, about half civilians and half soldiers on both sides. Another 2.2 to 2.5 million Ukrainians were sent to Germany as slave laborers. At the end of the war only 27.4 million of the 41.7 million remained. That is 35% of the population, greater than all the deaths of Germans, Italians, Frenchmen, Brits and its entire Commonwealth, plus US Americans combined. http://mfa.gov.ua/en/article/open/id/2503

The Ukrainian Auxiliary Police grew to 40,000. In all, maybe 200,000 Ukrainians joined various police units on the Nazi side, some were guards at the death camps, such as Ivan the Terrible and others were in the Nazi-led governing bureaucracy. The nationalist Ukrainian Auxiliary Army (UPA) grew out of the police. About 10,000 well trained

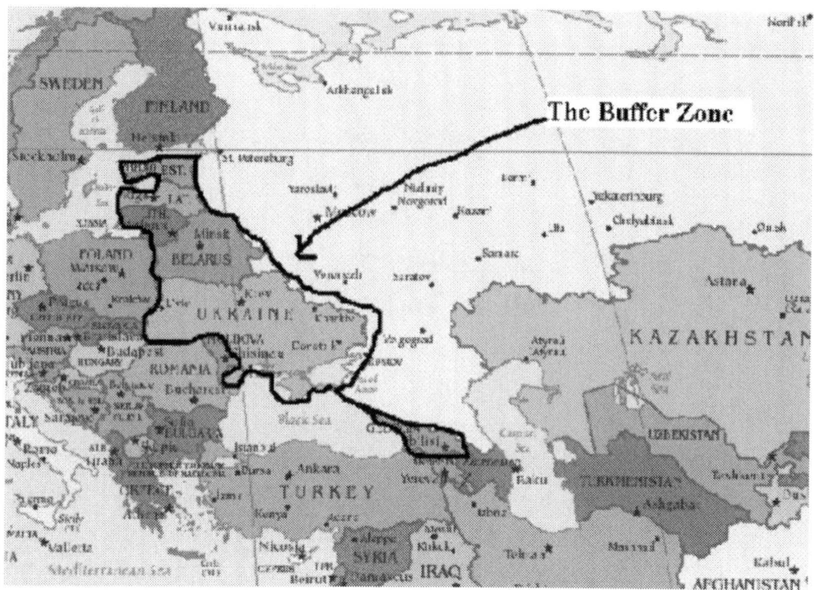

and armed policemen initiated this partisan army that fought for the Nazis against the Soviets, and later on also against the Nazis.

Statistics vary but several million Ukrainians fought on the Soviet side, far more than did on the German side. Hundreds of thousands of Soviet soldiers were killed, and nearly one million captured, the majority killed or otherwise died in captivity. Tens of thousands of schools and hospitals were destroyed; 720 entire towns and cities, and 28,000 villages demolished.

Ukraine was also used to cross into Russia before the Nazis by Imperial Germany and Napoleonic France. So naturally Russia is alert and concerned that any self-declared enemy of its government, that is, the United States, would do it again.

Foreign Affairs writer and political science professor John Mearsheimer wrote, "The United States and its European allies share most of the responsibility for the [current Ukrainian] crisis," published by the Establishment "Council of Foreign Affairs". (https://www.foreignaffairs.com/articles/russia-fsu/2014-08-18/why-ukraine-crisis-west-s-fault)

Mearsheimer is not just an academic but a West Point graduate and Air Force officer (1965-75).

Another professor (Yale) and Ukrainian expert, Timony Snyder, spoke about this crisis and U.S. responsibility to the German Parliament on June 22, 2017.

"As you will all know, the American frontier empire was built largely by slave labor. As we don't always remember, it was precisely that model of frontier colonialism, of a frontier empire built by slave labor that was admired by Adolf Hitler. When Adolf Hitler spoke about the United States, it was generally, before the war at least, with admiration. And it was a question for Hitler: who will the racial inferiors be? Who will the slaves be in the German Eastern Empire?

"And the answer that he gave, both in *Mein Kampf*, and in the second book, and in practice in the invasion of 1941, the answer was: the Ukrainians. The Ukrainians were to be at the center of a project of colonization and enslavement. The Ukrainians were to be treated as Afrikaner, as Neger, the word was very often used, as those of you who read German documents from the war will know, by analogy with the United States.

"The idea was to create a slavery-driven, exterminatory [*Vernichtungskrieg*] regime in Eastern Europe with the center in Ukraine." (https://www.kyivpost.com/article/opinion/op-ed/timothy-snyder-germany-must-past-atrocities-ukraine.html)

Thousands of pro-Nazi Ukrainians marched with torches and Nazi insignias in Kiev on October 14, 2017 to commemorate the 75th anniversary of the Ukraine Insurgent Army and one of its principal founders, Stepan Bandera. This Waffen SS Nazi collaborator was co-responsible for murdering thousands of people, mostly Jews. These demonstrators included organizations that led the February 2014 coup and formed a coalition government—the Svoboda (Social National) party and the Right Sector; and the Azov Battalion, which is a principal fighting force against Russian-Ukrainians in the east.

Viktor Yushchenko, Ukraine's president 2005-10, was a Bush fan and wanted in NATO. Just before leaving office, he officially "rehabilitated" the fascist Bandera and named him "Hero of Ukraine". Yushchenko even had his image honored on a postage stamp as a true nationalist.

The Simon Wiesenthal Center and other Jewish organizations have condemned the glorification of Bandera in Ukraine.

Retired journalist and novelist Gaither Stewart, who knows Russia and speaks its language, wrote a recent article about Bandera, "The most hated man who ever lived".

"To his memory are dedicated streets, squares, monuments in Ukraine, especially in his native West Ukraine. Today, Nazis of all nationalities pay homage to his memory"..."he is revered as a patriotic freedom-fighter, a martyr who led the struggle for independence from the Soviet Union." (http://www.greanvillepost.com/2017/12/30/the-most-hated-man-who-ever-lived/)

In Bandera's lifetime however, "The Russia-hating, West Ukrainian Nazi was hated by literally everybody. His political opponents within the Ukrainian independence movement hated him, as did many of his own allies and followers. Jews and ethnic Russians hated him for his crimes against them. Even his German Nazi masters considered him despicable because he was a traitor and murderer of his own people. The masses of displaced Ukrainians living in West Germany after World War II hated him for his crimes against his own people. Elements of the post-war German government and many of Germany's American occupiers hated him... even those he served. Poles hated him for his crimes against

Andrig Parubiy commemorating the Ukrainian WWII Nazi leader Stepan Bandera

the Polish people. Russians hated him in a special way because Bandera, in his German SS uniform, was responsible for the elimination of hundreds of thousands of Russians, soldiers, prisoners of war and civilians alike. Today his figure is hated by nearly all Russians because of everything he stood for. Ukrainian immigrants in Russia hate him and dislike being called Banderites simply because they are Ukrainian."

"But those terrible Russians were right again. For the vast majority of Russians today, the term *Banderovtsy* or Banderite is even worse than Liberal applied to that small minority who worship Western things, yearn for America, the European Union and NATO and detest Putin and Russian nationalists."

In 2014, the Bandera loving Svoboda (Social-National) party was part of the coup government coalition under the U.S.-hand-picked interim Prime Minister Fatherland Party leader Arseniy Yatsenyuk. Svoboda has had between three and six three high-level cabinet posts of the 20-25. Its co-leader, Andrig Parubiy, was made National Security and Defense Counsel Chief. Since April 2016, he has been chairman of the parliament. The symbol of the Social-National Party is a modified Nazi Wolfsangel, which stands for "unleash the beast in man with our wolf's hook".

Svoboda's other co-leader, Oleh Tyahnyna, sought unsuccessfully to ban the use of Russian. He was in the parliament until October 2014 when he fell short of the limited number of votes but his party continued in the coalition government. He is infamous for speaking at the gravesite of a commander of the fascistic UPA in the summer of 2004, in which he said: "*we're not afraid and we should not be afraid. They [UPA] took their automatic guns on their necks and went into the woods, and fought against the Muscovites, Germans, Jews and other scum who wanted to take away our Ukrainian state.*"

An expert on the Svoboda party and the Ukrainian-Russian conflict is the Finn lawyer, author and journalist Jon Hellevig. He has worked in a Russian law firm for two decades. He writes:

> *"From 1998 to 2004, Parubiy led the Patriot of Ukraine, a paramilitary organization of the Social-National Party. The Patriot of Ukraine also admitted to its overt racist and neo-Nazi political beliefs and its specialization in promoting political*

violence as a means to an end (alas, the end, which has been achieved). It constituted a paramilitary wing of the Social-National Assembly of Ukraine (S.N.A.), an assemblage of neo-Nazi organizations and other radical violent groups affiliated with the Svoboda party.

"In his role as the commandant of Euromaidan from December 2013 to February 2014, Parubiy was the leader of the military wing of the coup that brought down the democratically elected President Yanukovich and subjected the parliament to a reign of terror. In this capacity, he brought into the Maidan all the neo-Nazi storm battalions that he had fostered under the S.N.A. umbrella. (1)

"Independent evidence strongly points to the fact that it was precisely Parubiy, who was directly in charge of the Maidan snipers. In this role, he was tasked with the brutal repression that swept the country after the Maidan coup. He organized and coordinated the National Guard and other ultra-right, neo-fascist and neo-Nazi storm battalions like the Azov Battalion, which unleashed the terror in Eastern Ukraine. This would also imply that he condoned the Odessa and Mariupol massacres." (https://www.globalresearch.ca/meet-andriy-parubiy-the-former-neo-nazi-leader-turned-speaker-of-ukraines-parliament/5520502)

The EU foreign affairs chief, Catherine Ashton, sent an investigator on the February 20, 2014 sniper killings of demonstrators on both sides and police. Estonian Foreign Minister Urmas Paet reported to her by telephone on February 26. The call got leaked. The culprits were not government people under President Viktor Yanukovych, which Ashton had assumed, but rather the coup coalition. Paet said he interviewed insiders, including Petro Porshenko, who would soon become president. Excerpts: https://www.youtube.com/watch?v=ZEgJ0oo3OA8 and Eric Zuess' story. Paet said:

"...what was quite disturbing, the same oligarch [Poroshenko—and so when he became President he already knew this] told that well, all the evidence shows that the people who were killed

by snipers, from both sides, among policemen and people from the streets, [this will shock Ashton, who had just said that Yanukovych had masterminded the killings] that they were the same snipers, killing people from both sides" [so Poroshenko himself knows that his regime is based on a false-flag U.S.-controlled coup d'etat against his predecessor]. (http://www.greanvillepost.com/2017/11/18/participants-in-2014-ukrainian-coup-confess/)

"...so that yes, whew, my impression in this is sad, that there is, well, no trust, that there was the sense that there was those politicians who will return now to the coalition, well, people from Maidan [the anti-Yanukovych demonstrators] and from civilian society [non-governmental leaders in Ukraine], they say they know everybody who will be in your [whatever the Maidaners install as constituting the new] government, and all these guys have dirty past" [f.e., even the Maidan leaders know that everyone who stands even a chance to be installed into the new government has a "dirty past"] (http://www.fort-russ.com/2015/02/the-paet-ashton-transcript.html).

"So that and then she [Dr. Olga Bolgomets] also showed me some photos, she said that as medical doctor, she can, you know, say that it's the same handwriting, the same type of bullets, and it's really disturbing that now the new coalition that they don't want to investigate, what exactly happened; so that now there is stronger and stronger understanding that behind the snipers, it was not Yanukovych, but it was somebody from the new coalition."

About 88 people were murdered on February 19-20, at least 50 by sniper fire at the Independence Square. The Euromaidan demonstrators opposed President Yanukovych's decision to suspend the immediate signing of an association agreement with the EU. Yanukovych sought to hold together a trade relationship with Russia and did not wish to make an exclusive choice, which the West demanded, although President Putin did not so demand.

Russia had offered to buy $15 billion of government bonds and cut gas prices to keep Ukraine in the Commonwealth of Independent States. After the breakup of the Soviet Union, the CIS Free Trade Zone Agreement was signed by Russia, Belarus and Ukraine on December 8, 1991. By 2011, members were Russia, Ukraine, Belarus, Kazakhstan, Kyrgyzstan, Tajikistan, Moldova and Armenia. Once the coup occurred, Russia and Ukraine continued some of the trade. Since December 2015, there has been little trade and Ukraine does not participate in CIS meetings. Nevertheless, Russia continued to supply gas without payment. (2)

Anti-government demonstrations had begun in Kiev on November 21, 2013. About 130 people, including 18 policemen, were killed at these demonstrations between November and February 22.

The day before the February 21 coup, Yanukovych was forced to make concessions to the opposition to end the bloodshed, including calling for early elections. An agreement was reached with Oleh Tyahnybok, Arsenly Yatsenyuk and popular heavyweight world champion boxer Vitaly Klitschko. It was witnessed by the foreign ministers of Germany and Poland, and a French foreign ministry department director. The Russian representative present refused to sign. The pact immediately fell apart as the right-wing tasted victory. Why wait for elections?

The democratically elected president left Kiev the next day to attend a conference in Kharkov. Upon leaving the city, coup leaders seized his administration building and his residence. His prosecutor general was shot, one of his security officers was wounded, and the president's motorcade was shot at. President Yanukovych was literally chased out of the country.

Fortunately for Yanukovych he was close to Russia and escaped there before neo-Nazis and or the CIA murdered him, as these forces have done so many times. (See Chapter 18 for a partial list.)

Despite the leaked telephone conversation between Ashton and Paet, the West continuing claiming that the snipers on February 19-20 were under Yanukovych's orders. The real murderers, in fact, surfaced on November 15, 2017. Three Georgians came forth in Italy to give their story to the newspaper *Il Giornale*, and to the popular TV station Mediaset Matrix TV Chanel 5. Eric Zuesse was the first in the English-language media to discover this and make it available to English language audiences. He sent it to many alternative media and mass media. As of this writing, no English mass medium had picked it up. (http://www.greanvillepost.com/2017/11/18/participants-in-2014-ukrainian-coup-confess/)

Excerpts from TV 5: ***"The version of snipers on the Kiev massacre: «Opposition orders»"*** November 15, 2017 head. (This is a machine and poor translation from the Italian. My Emphasis)

"Everyone started shooting two or three shots at a time. It went on for fifteen, twenty minutes. We had no choice. We had been ordered to shoot both on the police and on the demonstrators, without making a difference."

"I was totally amazed", wrote the unnamed reporter. "So the Georgian Alexander Revazishvilli recalls the tragic shooting of February 20, 2014 in Kiev when a group of mysterious snipers opened fire on crowds and policemen slaughtering over 80 people. That massacre horrified the world and changed the destinies of Ukraine forcing the pro-Russian President Viktor Yanukovich to flee, accusing him of organizing the shooting. But the massacre also changed the destinies of Europe and our country, triggering the crisis that will lead to sanctions against Putin's Russia. Sanctions turned out to be a boomerang for the Italian economy."

"The confessions of Revazishvilli and two other Georgians—collected by the writer in the documentary «*Ukraine, the hidden truths*» aired tonight at 11.30 on Matrix, Canale 5—reveal a different and disconcerting truth. The truth of a massacre hatched and implemented by the same opposition that accused Yanukovych and his Russian allies. Revazishvilli and his two comrades—met and interviewed in the documentary—are a former member of the security services of former Georgian President Mikhail Saakashvili and two former militants of his own party. Engaged in Tbilisi by Mamuka Mamulashvili, military adviser to Saakashvili, they are asked to support—along with other Georgian and Lithuanian volunteers—the demonstrations underway in Kiev in exchange for a final fee of 5,000 dollars each. Equipped with false passports they arrive in Ukraine to coordinate demonstrations and provoke the Ukrainian police, initially without the use of weapons. The weapons enter the scene on 18 February and are distributed to various groups of Georgians and Lithuanians by Mamulashvili and other Ukrainian opposition leaders."

[Recall that Saakashvili fled to the Ukraine to avoid a court case for criminal corruption.]

"In each bag there were three or four weapons, there were Makarov pistols, Akm machine guns, carabines And then there were packs of cartridges," Revazishvilli told the reporter.

"The next day Mamulashvili and the leaders of the protest explain to the volunteers that they will have to face a police assault on the building of the Conservatory and the Ukraine hotel. In that case—it is explained—*we must shoot the square and sow chaos.*" "But one of the protagonists confesses [writes the reporter] to having received another explanation, much more exhaustive:"

"'When Mamulashvili arrived I [said] things are getting complicated, we have to start shooting—he replied we can not [wait for] the early presidential elections. *But who should we shoot? I asked him. He replied that the who and where did not matter [we] had to shoot somewhere to sow chaos.*"

"'*You could hear screams*"', "Alexander confesses" '*There were dead and wounded. My first and only thought was to leave quickly before they noticed me. Otherwise they would have torn me apart. Someone was already shouting that there were snipers*"'.

"Four years later," the reporter explains, "Alexander and his two companions say they have not yet received the slightest reward and have decided for this reason to tell the truth about who used them and abandoned them."

"'*At that moment I did not realize, I was not ready, then I understood. We have been used. Used and wedged*"'.

Admittedly, it seems odd that these hired killers were not paid. Five thousand dollars each is not much money when the stakes for the United States and NATO are so high. Nevertheless, it is convincing evidence considering that they came forth, and two of them are seen on television. One wonders what happened to them afterward!

Two key leaders of the bloody coup who organized it on the ground and handled the snipers were the Right Sector's founder Dmitriy Yarosh (also a Bandera fan), and Svoboda's Andriy Parubiy.

Zuesse's article about leaders of these para-militaries explains that, "Dmitriy Yarosh is the founder and head of one of Ukraine's two racist-fascist, or nazi, parties, Right Sector. He is officially the #2 Ukrainian national-security official, working directly under Andreiy Paribuiy, who heads Ukraine's other nazi party (the party that used to call itself Ukraine's "Social Nationalist Party," after Hitler's National Socialist Party, but which the CIA renamed "Svoboda," meaning "Freedom," so as to make it more acceptable to US Americans). (http://rinf.com/

Photo of possible sniper published in the Italian newspaper.

alt-news/breaking-news/meet-ukraines-master-mass-murderer-dmitriy-yarosh/)

"However, Yarosh has turned out to be Ukraine's actual leader…His nominal boss, Paribuiy, had been appointed by Arseniy Yatsenyuk, who was chosen on February 4th (18 days prior to the coup) to be Ukraine's new leader, by Victoria Nuland, who was appointed by Hillary Clinton and John Kerry, who were appointed by Barack Obama (the actual ruler of the new Ukraine).

"As Yarosh said this past [March 13, 2014] in an interview with *Newsweek*, he has 'been training paramilitary troops for almost 25 years,' and his 'divisions are constantly growing all over Ukraine, but over 10,000 people for sure.'"

In the *Newsweek* interview, "Dmitry Yarosh, The Man Who Claims Victory in the Ukrainian Revolution, Speaks," by Anna Nemtsova, she simply held the microphone before this self-declared fascist-racist and let him speak to a captive audience.

On May 2, the Yarosh-led Right Sector and Svobada fascists killed 46 Ukrainian supporters of President Yanukovych in Odessa. Many were burned alive in a trade union building after fascists threw Molotov cocktails inside and fired upon the mainly unarmed workers. Only two attackers were killed. (https://www.youtube.com/watch?v=H4dJRnI-X8Q)

Just after the coup, Dmitry Yarosh was granted an audience with Israel's ambassador to Ukraine, Reuven Din El, as published on March 7 by the United States Zionist newspaper *Forward.*

"Israel's ambassador in Kiev, Reuven Din El, opened a hotline with a Ukrainian ultra-nationalist movement to 'prevent provocations.'

"The agreement came at the end of a meeting held last week between Din El and Dmitry Yarosh, the leader of the Right Sector paramilitary group, which participated in the overthrow of the government of President Viktor Yanukovych."

At the meeting, "Yarosh stressed that Right Sector will oppose all [racist] phenomena, especially anti-Semitism, with all legitimate means," the embassy wrote on its website. "The parties agreed to establish a 'hotline' to prevent provocations and coordinate on issues as they arise," it said.

"Last month [Yarosh] told the *Ukrainian Pravda* newspaper that his outfit shares many beliefs with the xenophobic Svoboda party and cooperates with it, but rejects the xenophobia displayed by Svoboda members and leaders.

"'We have a lot of common positions on ideological issues, but there are big differences. For example, I do not understand racist elements and I do not adopt them,' he said."

"Svoboda lawmakers have regularly used the pejorative 'zhyd,' which is equivalent to 'kike,' to describe Jews. In response to protests from Jewish leaders, Svoboda argued 'zhyd' was a correct and neutral, albeit archaic term.

"Svoboda's leader, Oleh Tyahnybok, has in the past referred to a 'Moscow-Jewish mafia' which he said ruled Ukraine. Din El and Tyahnybok spoke in March 2013 in a meeting which the Israeli foreign ministry said was not coordinated with Jerusalem." (https://forward.com/news/breaking-news/194014/israel-envoy-meets-with-ukraine-anti-semite-dmitry/#ixzz3HZolhwc8)

Right Sector co-leader, Alekandr Muzychko, is another anti-Semite coup leader infamous among Jews for having pledged to fight, "Communists, Jews and Russians as long as blood flows in my veins."

Russian courts charged him for murdering more than 20 Russian soldiers under his captivity in the First Chechen War. He was killed in Kiev on March 24, 2014—maybe it was revenge.

Under the watch of Yarosh and his allies, neo-Nazism has since exploded across Ukraine, with mass marches of torch-bearing fascists filling the streets of Kiev and monuments to pogrom Nazi collaborators sprouting up around the country. "Ukraine has more statues 4 killers of Jews than any other country," the anti-Nazi activist and Holocaust historian Efraim Zuroff lamented on Twitter.

"Understandably, all of this has caused alarm within the Jewish community. Ukrainian Rabbi Moshe Reuven Azman has called on Kyiv's Jews to flee. 'I told my congregation to leave the city center or the city all together and if possible the country too,' he recently told the Israeli paper, Maariv. 'I don't want to tempt fate but there are constant warnings concerning intentions to attack Jewish institutions.'" (https://globalnews.ca/news/1194100/blind-eye-turned-to-influence-of-far-right-in-ukrainian-crisis-critics/)

U.S. Senator John McCain, center, speaks as Democratic senator from the state of Connecticut, Chris Murphy, second left, and Opposition leader Oleh Tyahnybok, right, stand around him during a Pro-European Union rally in Independence Square in Kiev, Ukraine, Sunday, Dec. 15, 2013. AP

Nevertheless, for Israel and its American Anti-Defamation League it is more important to work with Ukrainian anti-Semites against Russia. The ADL refused to support a congressional bill that would have prevented the U.S. from supplying arms, training and all support to these neo-Nazi groups. (https://www.alternet.org/world/how-israel-lobby-protected-ukrainian-neo-nazis)

Many of these "democratic" coup makers are not only anti-Semitic but also anti-black racists.

"Some of the neo-Nazis President Obama helped put in power in Ukraine carried Confederate flags. U.S. society has been moving rightward for decades—and pulling much of Europe with it," wrote civil rights African-American Ajamu Baraka, Green Party's last vice-president candidate. (https://blackagendareport.com/story-charlottesville-was-written-blood-ukraine)

With so much evidence of how the "regime change" of President Yanukovych was an illegal and bloody coup led by neo-Nazi street hooligans, the overthrow cannot be perceived as a "democratic revolution". However the U.S. not only supported the coup with money,

Charity Lady Victoria Nuland passing out bread to the poor Ukrainian Maidan demonstrators, December 11, 2014.

it picked its government leaders. They included several Sovboda cabinet members, among them the deputy Prime Minister Oleksandr Sych, and the key killer leader Andrig Parubly. (3)

On December 13, 2013, Victoria Nuland, assistant secretary of state for European and Eurasian affairs, told the US-Ukrainian Foundation that since 1991 the United States has spent $5 billion to teach Ukrainians "democratic skills". (https://www.youtube.com/watch?v=U2fYcHLouXY)

Two days before she and the U.S. ambassador to Ukraine Goeffrey Pyatt demonstrated against the elected Yanukovych government. They joined anti-government protestors calling for his overthrow at Independence Square. The Charity Lady handed food to them. (https://www.cbsnews.com/news/us-victoria-nuland-wades-into-ukraine-turmoil-over-yanukovich/)

Try to imagine that Russia acted for "regime change" of the U.S.-supported Canadian government; gave lots of money for the violent opposition; and even sent top government coup makers to demonstrate in the capital where they handed out bread!

A leaked taped telephone conversation between Nuland and Pyatt proves how the U.S. got what it paid for. On February 4, three weeks before the coup, Nuland told Pyatt who should sit in the coup government, and they then arranged for that to happen.

When Ambassador Pyatt suggests that the heavyweight champion boxer Wladimir Klitschko [Klitsch] is the most popular candidate for prime minister, Nuland corrects him and states that the more politically savvy "Fatherland" party leader Arseniy Yatsenyuk [Yats] should be prime minister. She also thinks that the fascist Svoboda leader Oleh Tyahnybok should be in the government but more on the outside ring. Here are excerpts from the conversation.

Nuland: "I don't think Klitsch should go into government. I don't think it's necessary. I don't think it's a good idea."

Pyatt: "yeah...I mean I guess. You think...what...in terms of him not going into the government, just let him sort of stay out and do his political homework and stuff. I'm just thinking in terms of the process moving ahead, we want to keep the moderate democrats together. The problem is going to be Tyahnybok and his guys [that is, the fascists]. I'm sure that's what Yanukoyvch is calculating on all this."

Nuland: "I think Yats is the guy who's got the economic experience, the governing experience. What he needs is Klitsch and Tyahnybok on the outside and he needs to be talking to them four times a week...I think with Klitsch going in at that level working for Yats, it's not going to work."

Nuland: "My understanding is that the big three [Yatsenyuk, Klitsch and Tyahnybok] were going in to their own meeting and that Yats was going to offer in that context a three plus one conversation with you."

Pyatt: "That's what he proposed but knowing the dynamic that's been with them where Klitsch has been top dog; he's going to take a while to show up at a meeting, he's probably talking to his guys at this point so I think you reaching out to him will help with the personality management among the three and gives us a chance to move fast on all this stuff and put us behind it before they all sit down and he explains why he doesn't like it."

Nuland: "...when I talked to Jeff Feltman [U.S. diplomat in UN] this morning, he had a new name for the UN guy ...Robert Serry – he's now gotten both Serry [Dutch diplomat in UN] and Ban ki Moon [U.S.'s South Korean choice for UN General Secretary until 2016] to agree that Serry could come in Monday or Tuesday... so that would be great I think to help glue this thing and have the UN help glue it and you know fuck the EU. (https://www.youtube.com/watch?v=MSxaa-67yGM)

The Guardian reported February 6 that State Department's spokeswoman "Jen Psaki said that Nuland, 'has been in contact with her EU counterparts and of course has apologized for these reported comments'" about fucking the EU. The fact that she picked a so-called sovereign state's next government leaders was not relevant enough to discuss or apologize for. (https://www.theguardian.com/world/2014/feb/06/us-ukraine-russia-eu-victoria-nuland)

Moreover, the true criminal here is the Russians because they leaked the dictators' phone conversation. This is the same pretext—leaking phone calls and emails—that gave the excuse for "Russiagate". The problem is not world war but the "possibility" that the Russkies tape and leak—not even hack—what the Yankees say and do to subvert democracy and world peace.

As *The Guardian* wrote, "At the State Department, Psaki said that if the Russians were responsible for listening to, recording and posting a private diplomatic telephone conversation, it would be '*a new low in Russian tradecraft*'. As if the United States has never conducted "lows" in its own "tradecraft". Pressed on whether the call was authentic, Psaki said: "'I didn't say it was inauthentic.'"

The hand-picked leaders announced their new government on February 27. The pattern of "democratic" "humanitarian" "regime change" had long been established as the worn-torn countries of Afghanistan, Iraq and Libya can attest. The pattern includes "free elections" after the U.S government decides who is to be in their proxy government. So, on May 25, with Eastern Ukraine and Crimea in uproar against this coup, the U.S. got their billionaire chocolate king Petro Poroshenko elected with only part of the country voting.

But even before the election, U.S. government favorites could begin plundering. Human rights activist and union lawyer Dan Kovalik's timely book, *The Plot to Scapegoat Russia* (Skyhorse, 2017), contains a wealth of information about how the United States' "expands as Russia contracts: broken promises and humiliation."

Kovalik points out (p. 127) that Vice-President Joe Biden's son, Hunter, was appointed to the board of directors of Burisma, a major Ukrainian natural gas company right after the coup. His investments in Ukraine and his ties to the U.S. government helped out.

"Joe Biden has been the White House's go-to guy during the Ukraine crisis, touring former Soviet republics and reassuring their concerned leaders," writes the National Journal's Marina Koren. "And now, he's not the only Biden involved in the region." (http://www.bbc.com/news/blogs-echochambers-27403003)

Koren "says that by appointing Hunter Biden head of its legal affairs unit, 'Burisma is turning to US talent—and money and name recognition—for protection against Russia'".

Again U.S. Ambassador Pyatt was helpful. He arranged for the British government to drop freezing $23 million of Burisma's accounts in London banks while the company was under investigation for money laundering. The Bidens continued their plundering under the new president.

Michael Collins wrote on June 9, 2014: "Two diplomatic messages from the *WikiLeaks Public Library on U.S. Diplomacy* indicate that newly elected President of Ukraine, Petro Poroshenko was an agent for United States State Department. A confidential message from the U.S. Embassy in Kiev on April 29, 2006 mentions the newly elected Ukraine president twice." (https://www.globalresearch.ca/president-petro-poroshenko-our-ukraine-insider-for-the-u-s-state-department/5386891). (Collins is a mainstream and alternative media journalist. He won the George Orwell Prize in 2005 for his book, *The Likes of Us: A Biography of the White Working Class.*)

"Secretary of State Hillary Clinton met with the current president in 2009 when he served as Ukraine Foreign Minister. The content of the meeting was described in a confidential message from the U.S. Embassy in Kiev on December 18, 2009," concerning "'pathways to NATO membership'".

After neo-Nazi militarists led Ukrainian troops into fighting Eastern Ukrainians and burning people alive, Poroshensko needed better PR than he was getting. He hired the Great Dane politician, former States Minister Anders Fogh Rassmussen, who had just left the United States' post as NATO chief. In Denmark, Rassmussen was known for convincing much of the population that there were no classes and that the unions had fulfilled their role. He was also known for the Big Lie that Saddam Hussein had Weapons of Mass Destruction despite the fact that the military intelligence department (FET) had reported to him that Hussein did not posses any. This was the main reason why his government declared war on Iraq, the only country to actually declare war.

Major Frank Grevil was on the team that gathered and communicated the intelligence so he knew that the prime minister was lying to the public. Despite the fact that both men were members of the same conservative party (Venstre), Grevil had a conscience. He disclosed the true facts in February 2004. Daniel Ellsberg came to Denmark for his defense. Grevil was sentenced to six months in prison for revealing military secrets while Rasmussen continued as prime minister for a second term (2001-9) and then his buddy President George Bush got him the secretary general post at NATO where he oversaw wars until 2014. He then started a consultant PR firm, Rasmussen Global, and Poroshenko hired him in 2016 to reshape his brutal image.

Rasmussen formed "The Friends of Ukraine Group with other former European politicians who have "kick ass" portfolios. (I use the term "kick ass" not only because it is a favorite Bush expression for murdering and overthrowing government leaders who don't do his bidding but also because it is the title of a Danish play, "Let's Kick Ass", about Rasmussen catering to Bush.)

See here how Rasmuusen's group assists Poroshenko's "humanitarian" soldiers and mercenaries. (https://rasmussenglobal.com/the-ukraine-initiative/friends-of-ukraine)

When Poroshenko became president, *Forbes* wrote of him as the country's "chocolate tycoon" worth $1.3 billion. Two years later when the Panama Papers were exposed, it was revealed that Poroshenko's money was being managed by Mossack Fonseca in tax shelters on the British Virgin Islands. At the same time that the coup president was hiding his sweet profits, he asked the Ukrainian Supreme Court to declare that the unseating of President Viktor Yanukovych was an unconstitutional coup. He was apparently worried that the extreme right would do the same to him.

"Ukraine's Pres. Poroshenko Says Overthrow of Yanukovych Was a Coup", headlined Eric Zuesse's June 22, 2015 article. (http://www.washingtonsblog.com/2015/06/ukraines-pres-poroshenko-says-overthrow-of-yanukovych-was-a-coup.html)

This is the document in Ukrainian, and not posted in English. Again the U.S. mass media did not see fit to pick this up. (http://ccu.gov.ua/doccatalog/document?id=276628)

"I ask the court to acknowledge that the law 'on the removal of the presidential title from Viktor Yanukovych' as unconstitutional," Zuess cites. I cannot find any results on the internet.

THE CRIMEA

Ukraine has 42.4 million people: 78% Ukrainian; 17% Russian; 5% other nationalities. Russians are the majority on the Crimea, 68% of the 2.3 million population, 16% is Ukrainian, 10% Crimea Tatars. All their languages are official, but the coup-makers sought to ban Russian.

Crimea is a peninsula of 27,000 square kilometers connected to the Ukraine and three kilometers from Russia, which began building a bridge across this Kerch Strait in May 2015. Approximately 200 bombs from the World War II era were found in the area during pre-construction clearance.

In 1783, the Russian Empire took Crimea as the result of Russo-Turkish War (1768–1774). Following the Russian Revolution, Crimea became an autonomous republic within the Russian Soviet Federative Socialist Republic in the USSR, in 1921-2. In 1954, it was transferred to the Ukrainian SSR by Nikita Khrushchev in a gesture of symbolic solidarity.

With the collapse of the Soviet Union, Ukraine became an independent state, and most of the peninsula was reorganized as the Autonomous Republic of Crimea. The city of Sevastopol retained its special status within Ukraine. The 1997 Partition Treaty on the Status and Conditions of the Black Sea Fleet (former Soviet Black Sea Fleet) allowed Russia to continue basing its fleet in Crimea. Most of the Ukrainian Naval Forces and Russian's Black Sea Fleet were headquartered in Sevastopol. Ukraine extended Russia's lease of the naval facilities under the 2010 Kharkiv Pact in exchange for discounted natural gas.

Black Sea Fleet ships are in two other Russian locations. In all, the fleet has 25,000 sailors and marines, 45 warships and six submarines. The location is vital for the defense of Russia.

Russia had not had plans to get involved in Crimea until the coup-makers takeover. At that point, President Putin saw that "the time to act against Ukraine and the West had arrived," wrote political scientist John Mearsheimer in "Foreign Affairs". "The task proved relatively easy, thanks to the thousands of Russian troops already stationed at a naval base…"

"Washington may not like Moscow's position, but it should understand the logic behind it. This is Geopolitics 101: great powers are always sensitive to potential threats near their home territory. After all, the United States does not tolerate distant great powers deploying military forces anywhere in the Western Hemisphere, much less on its borders," wrote John Mearsheimer. (https://www.foreignaffairs.com/articles/russia-fsu/2014-08-18/why-ukraine-crisis-west-s-fault)

Russia sent only six helicopters and two boats with about 500 "little green men" or "polite police" to keep order, as Russian Admiral Igor Kasatonov confirmed. At a press conference on December 17, 2015, Putin recognized this assistance as Spetsnaz special police force.

Russia did not "invade" the Crimea, as the West claims. Upwards to 25,000 military personnel were already there. They would not allow Ukraine to let NATO take over.

When Russia's Black Sea Fleet sailors and marines surrounded the Ukrainian Navy base its leader, first deputy commander Sergei Yeliseyev, defected to the Russians. He was followed by many officers and men. The Russians later released most of the Ukrainian ships but kept two new corvettes. They did not integrate them into their fleet but held them so they could not be used against the people in Donbass. (https://www.reuters.com/article/us-mideast-crisis-syria-russia-fighters/dying-for-a-paycheck-the-russian-civilians-fighting-in-syria-idUSKBN1EF0RI)

It must be taken into account that at this time, Hilliary Clinton addressed one of those fundraisers where she is given hundreds of thousands of dollars for her words of pearls to please the rich. On March 6, *The Guardian* reported that she told them:

"Putin has said he is protecting ethnic Russians by moving troops into Crimea. Clinton said on Tuesday at a closed fundraising luncheon in Long Beach that Putin's actions were similar to what happened in the Nazi era in Czechoslovakia and Romania.

Quoting her: "'Now if this sounds familiar, it's what Hitler did back in the 30s…'" Hitler kept saying: 'They're not being treated right. I must go and protect my people.' And that's what's gotten everybody so nervous.'" (https://www.theguardian.com/world/2014/mar/06/hillary-clinton-says-vladimir-putins-crimea-occupation-echoes-hitler)

The Russians did not conduct a Holocaust against any people. In all, there were six killings on Crimea between February 23 and March 19 followed by full stability. Two deaths were Crimea Russian civilians, one Crimea Ukrainian civilian, one Russian soldier, one Ukrainian soldier, and one Crimea self-defense soldier. Right Sector militants were suspected in the murders of soldiers and one was detained. The Russian military and police did not kill anyone that is known.

On February 23, the day coup-makers issued an arrest warrant for the legitimate President Yanukovych, pro-Russian Crimeans seized government buildings at Crimea's capital in Simferopol.

On March 11, the parliament declares Crimea's independence from Ukraine, following a vote of 78 in favor and 22 against secession.

March 16 referendum results of 1,274,096 voters (83% of potential): 1,233,002 for integration into Russian Federation (96.8%); 32,000 for remaining in Ukraine (2.5%). (https://www.rt.com/news/crimea-referendum-results-official-250/)

There were no charges of rigged voting. Although it was not observed by Westerners, many politicians claimed the Russians forced the vote with arms. No locals made such claims.

March 17, Crimea parliament recognizes the results and applies to become an independent state within the Russian Federation.

March 18, President Vladimir Putin Russia accepts the application, and recognizes the prime minister, Sergey Aksyonov, and parliament. Ten other states recognize Crimea as part of the Russian Federation, while Ukraine continues to claim Crimea as an integral part of its territory, supported by most foreign governments and United Nations General Assembly Resolution 68/262.

Associated Press' Moscow reporter Vladimir Isachenkov wrote: "With a sweep of his pen, President Vladimir Putin added Crimea to the map of Russia on Tuesday, describing the move as correcting a past injustice and responding to what he called Western encroachment upon Russia's vital interests. While his actions were met with cheers in Crimea and Russia, Ukraine's new government called Putin a threat to the whole world and U.S. Vice President Joe Biden warned that the U.S. and Europe will impose further sanctions against Moscow."

Take note of the phrase, "his actions were met with cheers in Crimea". Now isn't that what the U.S. would say about their war to breakaway Kosovo from Yugoslavia, and what the U.K. would say about Falklands (Malvinas)?

The Mexican people were not cheering, however, when the United States invaded their country (April 25, 1846), and 22 months later annexed half of it—now Texas, Oklahoma, Kansas, Colorado, Nevada, Utah, Wyoming, Arizona, New Mexico and California. American Manifest Destiny!

The United States and the European Union immediately announced asset freezes and other sanctions against Russian and Ukrainian officials involved in the Crimean crisis. The Group of Eight world powers suspended Russia's participation in the elite club. They claimed Russia invaded and annexed Crimea.

Incidentally, one year after the "illegal" referendum, "The radical, pro-Putin Forbes magazine [as Kovalik ironically relates in his book, page 128, quoting Establishment *Forbes*] wrote: "The US and European Union may want to save Crimeans from themselves. But the Crimeans are happy right where they are. One year after the annexation of the Ukrainian peninsula in the Black Sea, poll after poll shows that the locals there—be they Ukrainians, ethnic Russians or Tatars are mostly all in agreement: life with Russia is better than life with Ukraine." (https://www.forbes.com/forbes/welcome/?toURL=https://www.forbes.com/sites/kenrapoza/2015/03/20/one-year-after-russia-annexed-crimea-locals-prefer-moscow-to-kiev/&refURL=https://www.google.dk/&referrer=https://www.google.dk/)

Kovalik concludes: "It is not clear to me how Russia's actions regarding Crimea, especially as they ended up being welcomed by the Crimeans, is any cause for Americans to believe that Russia is somehow a threat to humanity."

DONBASS OBLAST

The Donbass Oblast (region) in Eastern Ukraine borders Russia. It contains 4.4% of the land mass and has ten percent of the Ukrainian population, 4.5 million people. Ukrainians make up 57% and Russians 38%. But the Russians language is the main tongue for 75% of the people; Ukrainian for 24%. Most people there have a long history with Russia. The area was called Stalino Oblast (after Stalin) between the 1920s and until 1961.

When coup-makers tried to ban the Russian language and sought to shun Russia for EU and NATO, many Donbass people sought independence; many also desired to become part of Russia. The coup-makers started a war on April 6, and the next day separatists seized the Donetsk Oblast administration building and declared independence.

On May 11, the two main cities, Donetsk and Luhansk, held a referendum. According to their figures, there was a 75% turn-out in Donetsk and 81% in Luhansk. 89% of Donetsk voters were for independence opposed to 10% for remaining in Ukraine. In Luhansk it was 96% for and 4% against. These figures are not confirmed by any other source, and no country recognized the referendum. Russia said it "respected" the referendum.

The self-declared Donetsk People's Republic (DPR) and Luhansk People's Republic (LPR) asked to be admitted to the Russian Federation but the government rejected the proposal.

On September 5, 2014, representatives of Ukraine, the Russian Federation, the Donetsk People's Republic, and the Luhansk People's

Republic signed the Minsk Protocol, an agreement of 12 points to halt the war. They resembled Ukrainian President's Poroshenko's 15-point peace plan of June 20.

The agreement was signed after extensive talks under the auspices of the Organization for Security and Co-operation in Europe (OSCE). The agreement, which followed previous attempts to stop the fighting in the Donbass, called for an immediate ceasefire, but it failed to stop the fighting.

By November 15, 2017, there had been 10 truces. At that time, the UN High Commission of Human Rights reported there had been 10,303 killings: 2,821 civilians (most against the coup); 3,880 Ukrainian military and volunteer mercenaries; 3.600-4,000 separatist fighters. Among the civilians killed were 298 passengers and crew of the downed Malaysian Airlines Flight, 11 Russians journalists and one Italian reporter. (4)

The U.S. State Department claims that Russia has heavy weapons even tanks on Ukrainian territory, and that between 400 and 500 Russian soldiers had been killed by November 2017. While the Russian Federation admits some Russians have joined the independence movement they do so as volunteers. It would seem obvious that if Russia really intended to aid the separatists with its military, it could easily win the war. But fake news sometimes gets disclosed.

The German federal TV channel of Zweiten Deutschen Fernsehens (ZDF) aired a photograph that purports to show Russian military presence in eastern Ukraine, a claim that Moscow denied. Timing of this claim "incidentally" occurred on the same day leaders of Russia, Germany, France and Ukraine were meeting in Minsk in an effort to broker another ceasefire.

The German media watch group, Open Committee, lodged a complaint of the "news" segment with the photo caption, "*Russian armored vehicles moved through Isvarino in the Luhansk region, February 12, 2015*," citing "*Ukrainian army spokesman Andrei Lysenko.*" There is one glaring problem with the photograph in question: it shows Russian tanks in South Ossetia, not Ukraine.

On February 11, 2015, high-ranking U.S. Senator Jim Inhofe —a man whose corruption and servilism to the corporate Deep State stands out even in that political body—presented to members of Congress what he said were photos of Russian tanks operating in eastern Ukraine.

"*Putin keeps saying 'we don't have any Russians in there with the separatists, it's not us, we're not doing it.' Look, here they are. These are the pictures we brought back with us.*" After showing the photographs, Inhofe presented grisly photos of dead Ukrainian civilians.

Inhofe said the things that are happening in Ukraine are just as bad as what is happening "*in ISIS, in Syria, and other places.*"

The same day Inhofe was forced to retract his allegations and issue an apology: "[T]*he Ukrainian parliament members who gave us these photos in print form as if it came directly from a camera really did themselves a disservice," Inhofe said in a statement. "We felt confident to release these photos because the images match the reporting of what is going on in the region. I was furious to learn one of the photos provided now appears to be falsified from an AP photo taken in 2008.*"

On February 14, the *NYT* reported that Inhofe had been given the false photos at a meeting with many Ukrainian military officers present, alongside three members of the Parliament and former Pentagon official, Phillip Karper. The *NYT* wrote:

"While there appears to be much more compelling evidence of Russian military involvement in Ukraine, *this is also not the first time that Ukraine's government has presented photographic evidence that was later revealed to be false*. In fact, one of the images showing Russian tanks in South Ossetia in 2008 that was provided to Mr. Inhofe was posted on the website of Ukraine's foreign ministry on Aug. 1 as supposed proof that 'a long convoy of armored vehicles and several KAMAZ with armed men crossed Ukrainian-Russian border' one day earlier," [my emphasis] (https://www.nytimes.com/2015/02/14/world/europe/sifting-ukrainian-fact-from-ukrainian-fiction.html)

Veteran journalist John Pilger was an important source for me during my anti-Vietnam war activism, as he was for many. He knows firsthand about media lying. Pilger explains in his October 27, 2016 piece, "Inside the Invisible Government: War, Propaganda, Clinton and Trump":

"The American journalist, Edward Bernays, is often described as the man who invented modern propaganda. The nephew of Sigmund Freud, the pioneer of psycho-analysis, it was Bernays who coined the term 'public relations' as a euphemism for spin and its deceptions."

"Bernays' influence extended far beyond advertising. His greatest success was his role in convincing the American public to join the slaughter of the First World War. The secret, he said, was 'engineering the consent' of people in order to 'control and regiment [them] according to our will without their knowing about it'.

"He described this as 'the true ruling power in our society' and called it an 'invisible government'.

"Today, the invisible government has never been more powerful and less understood. In my career as a journalist and film-maker, I have never known propaganda to insinuate our lives as it does now and to go unchallenged."

"Propaganda is most effective when our consent is engineered by those with a fine education—Oxford, Cambridge, Harvard, Columbia—and with careers on the BBC, The Guardian, The New York Times, *the* Washington Post. *These organizations are known as the liberal media. They present themselves as enlightened, progressive tribunes of the moral zeitgeist. They are anti-racist, pro-feminist and pro-LGBT.*

And they love war."

"All have misrepresented events in Ukraine as a malign act by Russia when, in fact, the coup in Ukraine in 2014 was the work of the United States, aided by Germany and Nato.

"This inversion of reality is so pervasive that Washington's military intimidation of Russia is not news; it is suppressed behind a smear and scare campaign of the kind I grew up with during the first cold war. Once again, the Ruskies are coming to get us, led by another Stalin, whom The Economist depicts as the devil.

"The suppression of the truth about Ukraine is one of the most complete news blackouts I can remember. The fascists who engineered the coup in Kiev are the same breed that backed the Nazi invasion of the Soviet Union in 1941. Of all the scares about the rise of fascist anti-Semitism in Europe, no leader ever mentions the fascists in Ukraine - except Vladimir Putin, but he does not count." (http://johnpilger.com/articles/inside-the-invisible-government-war-propaganda-clinton-trump)

As I was finishing the first draft of this manuscript in Spain, in January-February 2018, I coincidentally met a Russian-Ukrainian doctor who lives with his second family here. He told me that in recent weeks the Ukrainian government had stepped up its war against the entire population of

Donbass by cutting off all facilities it controls, from water to gas and electricity. He could no longer call his mother and other family members living in Donbass because mobile connections were dead. "If it weren't for Russian supplies coming to our region everyone would probably die," he said worriedly.

US-NATO BUILDUP

The United States and NATO had already made political-economic-military inroads into several Soviet Union republics in addition to Eastern Europe but now with the "Russian invasion" of Crimea and Donbass, no holds bar took over.

The legendary Herman Kahn, a key researcher at the military think tank Rand Corporation and model for Stanley Kubrick's "*Dr. Strangelove*, had carved out a scenario about how the good guys could run a society after an atomic war. His followers at Rand showed the government that it needed to update its military might around Russia because the renewed enemy could easily overtake the Baltic States, despite the NATO pact that all 29 members would come to each member's aid if attacked. This absurdity led the U.S. to demand that each NATO country had to use 2% of its gross national product for military outlays. One after another began buying the record expensive F-35 bomber-jets capable of carrying nuclear missiles.

Thousands of U.S. and NATO troops maneuvered closer to Russian borders from the Baltic States, Poland, Romania and Bulgaria. The U.S. increased its military expenditures in Europe nearly four times over, from $800 million to $3.4 billion. Troops increased to 100,000, plus more non-combat ready military personnel.

NATO Response Force upgraded its High Readiness Joint Task Force to deploy anywhere in the world within 48 hours. NATO had no mission once the Soviet Union disappeared, but the lucrative military-industrial complex reshaped its defensive origins to offensive warriors—the so-called "Readiness Action Plan". The out-going modern Danish Viking NATO Secretary General Rasmussen called the plan his "lightning spearhead force" ready for nuclear blitzkrieg, as though it was all a video game to see how many enemy targets can be eradicated.

Dr. Paul Craig Roberts explains why the U.S. will not cease its drive to dominate Russia and China.

In 1981, President Reagan appointed him to the Treasury Department as assistant secretary for economic policy, and he became a leading policy maker; and later a consultant for the Department of Defense. Roberts was an economics professor at several universities; a writer and editor for several mainstream media, including the *Wall Street Journal*, and now for alternative media. See his website here: https://www.paulcraigroberts.org/.

"The [Paul] Wolfowitz doctrine is the basis of US policy toward Russia. The doctrine regards any power sufficiently strong to remain independent of Washington's influence to be 'hostile.'"

The doctrine was formed in 1992 under the Bush I regime and applies to China as well.

"Our first objective is to prevent the re-emergence of a new rival, either on the territory of the former Soviet Union or elsewhere...[this] new regional defense strategy [] requires that we endeavor to prevent any hostile power from dominating a region whose resources would, under consolidated control, be sufficient to generate global power." "The Wolfowitz doctrine justifies Washington's dominance of all regions. It is consistent with the neoconservative ideology of the US as the 'indispensable' and 'exceptional' country entitled to world hegemony.

"Russia and China are in the way of US world hegemony. Unless the Wolfowitz doctrine is abandoned, nuclear war is the likely outcome." (http://dissidentvoice.org/2014/05/washington-intends-russias-demise/#more-54002).

Veterans Intelligence Professionals For Sanity (VIPS) was formed by dozens of former secret service officials and government-military intelligence officers in 2003, just as the U.S. was preparing to invade Iraq. Ray McGovern, former Army infantry/intelligence officer and CIA analyst, took the initiative. Mike Gravel, a former senator and top secret control officer, is one of a score on the steering committee. Another is Scott Ritter, a Marine major and later UN weapons inspector in Iraq, who warned against military action since Iraq had no WMD.

VIPS April 28, 2014 communiqué on Ukraine:

"We the undersigned are veteran intelligence, military, and law enforcement officers. Taken together, our years of service to our country total nearly 200 years. Unlike many experts and advisers who base their

arguments on abstract notions about the international scene, our insights are drawn from a depth of hands-on experience inside the U.S . government—here and abroad."

"We are particularly concerned over what appears to be a largely unfocused yet virulent mood among members of Congress and the mainstream media to 'do something' about Russia—a sentiment that is both ill-advised and quite the reverse of what this nation should be doing to nurture a constructive and ultimately beneficial relationship with Moscow and the rest of Europe."

"To put it in stark terms, Russian engagement with Ukraine—a country that is on Moscow's doorstep and which is, in part, ethnically Russian—does not threaten vital U.S. interests; nor does it threaten any U.S. allies. Washington's response should be a measured one, based on the actual risks versus possible gains. Sanctions should be employed with considerable restraint, as their effectiveness is questionable and they frequently serve only to harden adversarial positions. Significant military moves, whether unilateral or in conjunction with NATO, should be avoided as they can be seen as provocative while providing no solution to existing disagreements."

"Today, Russia is capable of protecting its interests in the areas it calls its 'near frontier.' It will not accept the incorporation of Ukraine into NATO. Attempts to force that issue will not make Europe more secure; rather, it will increase the danger of war.

"There is an important step you can take, Mr. President. We recommend that you ask NATO to formally rescind the following part of the declaration agreed to by the NATO heads of state in Bucharest on April 3, 2008: 'NATO welcomes Ukraine's and Georgia's Euro-Atlantic aspirations for membership in NATO. We agreed today that these countries will become members of NATO.'"

Other Establishment militarists and political policy makers also have had enough of the apocalyptic jingoists. Former Clinton Secretary of State William J. Perry is one. "The New York Review of Books" reviewer Jerry Brown wrote about his 2016 book, *My Journey at the Nuclear Brink.*

Brown says he knows of no "person who understands the science and politics of modern weaponry" better than Perry. He cites him:

"Today, the danger of some sort of a nuclear catastrophe is greater than it was during the Cold War and most people are blissfully unaware of this danger." He also tells us that the nuclear danger is "growing greater every year" and that even a single nuclear detonation "could destroy our way of life." (http://www.nybooks.com/articles/2016/07/14/a-stark-nuclear-warning/)

Perry was part of CIA Director Allen Dulles team during the Cuban Missile Crisis, and says it was luck and Vasili Akrhipov that "avoided a nuclear confrontation."

Perry also opposes NATO expansionism. He was the only Clinton cabinet member to oppose incorporating the Eastern Europeans countries, which NATO had earlier promised. He knows, however, that armaments and the nuclear threat is good for business, including for his former employer, Sylvania.

In this connection, reviewer Brown cites another former Establishment policy maker, Cold War liberal hawk George Kennan. On May 2, 1998, Kennan told "The New York Times":

"I think [NATO expansion] is the beginning of a new cold war. I think the Russians will gradually react quite adversely and it will affect their policies. I think it is a tragic mistake. There was no reason for this whatsoever. No one was threatening anybody else. This expansion would make the Founding Fathers of this country turn over in their graves."

PRESIDENT PUTIN SPEAKS ABOUT EXCEPTIONALISM

President Vladimir Putin addressed the Russian Federal Assembly on March 18, 2014:

"The USA prefers to follow the rule of the strongest and not international law. They are convinced that they have been chosen and they are exceptional, that they are allowed to shape the destiny of the world, that it is only them that can be right. They act as they please. Here and there they use force against sovereign states, set up coalitions in accordance with the principle: who is not with us is against us."

Putin is obviously one of those "against us". Ronald Reagan's former Special Assistant to the Director of Central Intelligence and Vice

Chairman of the CIA's National Intelligence Council, Henry E. Meyer, wrote about "How to Solve the Putin Problem":

"Russian President Vladimir Putin is a serious threat to world peace." (http://www.americanthinker.com/2014/08/how_to_solve_the_putin_problem.html#ixzz520gIlizl)

"If Putin is too stubborn to acknowledge that his career is over, and the only way to get him out of the Kremlin is feet-first, with a bullet hole in the back of his head—that would also be okay with us. Nor would we object to a bit of poetic justice.... For instance, if the next time Putin's flying back to Moscow from yet another visit with his good friends in Cuba, or Venezuela, or Iran, his airplane gets blasted out of the sky by some murky para-military group that somehow, inexplicably, got its hands on a surface-to-air missile."

This "threat to world peace" escaped at least five assassination attempts, as he told Oliver Stone (5)

Here are more of Putin's "threat to world peace" thoughts as recorded by Oliver Stone:

VP: *As to Crimea, I'd like to ask you, what is democracy? Democracy is a policy which is based on the will of the people...*

OS: *"...the United States would say that you have violated international law..."*

VP: *...I'd like to emphasize that in the course of the Kosovo crisis, the International Court of Justice considered very cautiously this situation and the ICJ arrived at a conclusion saying that when the issue of self-determination of a nation is concerned, in accordance with Point Two of the United Nations charter...the concerns of the central authorities of this or that country on this matter are not required...I was always wondering if Kosovars were allowed to do it, why is that not allowed to Russians, Ukrainians, Tatars, and Crimeans?"*

Stone asks about the possibility of a U.S. seizure of the Russian base at the Crimea, a desire that many coup-makers have, or perhaps building a NATO military base.

VP: *"Those consequences would have been very grave, because, well this base per-se doesn't mean anything — no significance, but if they had* *tried to station either ABM systems or offensive systems in those territories, that would no doubt have aggravated this situation in the whole of Europe. Incidentally, that is what is happening in Eastern European countries."*

"What we're concerned about is the practice of how decisions are made [in NATO]." "When a country becomes a member of NATO, bilateral talks are held on this country and it's quite easy to deal with this country on a bilateral basis, including on the placement of weapons systems that are threatening to our security. Once a country becomes a member of NATO, it is hard to resist the pressure of such a large presence as the United States, and any weapons systems can be stationed in this country all of a sudden. An ABM system, new military bases, and if need be, new offensive systems. And what are we supposed to do in that case?...And the situation becomes more tense. And who needs that, and why?"

My reply to President Putin's "who needs this" would be the same as President Eisenhower: the military-industrial complex. Putin's point here is a key reason why the majority of Swedes and Finns do not want to join NATO despite pressure from their governments.

Putin continues:

In April 2014, "NATO cut off all contact with us in the framework of the Russian-NATO council," [Putin told Stone. In 2015, NATO] *"carried out at least 70 exercises within the close proximity of Russian borders, and that certainly draws our attention...* [in 2015] *"we adopted a new national security strategy...This is about building conditions for co-operation on security in the areas which we believe are the most challenging, the most menacing to us and to our neighbors."*

"...the current level of the defense industry of the United States are so high that it gives them grounds to believe that they will be able to make such a breakthrough that no one is going to be able to catch up with them. Just right now...there are ongoing discussions at the International Committee of Armaments Control. This committee was established within the United Nations back in the 1950s and it's still working, still functional. This international committee is working in Russia [also China] *and has brought up the issue of preventing the militarization of outer space. Unfortunately, our American partners have blocked this proposal. What does that tell us?"*

"They [U.S. European allies] *are trying to create an image of a common threat—an outside threat. And such a threat is such that they can only protect themselves by pulling themselves around the United States." "The*

philosophy of American foreign policy in this region consists of and I'm absolutely sure about that, the need to prevent, by all means necessary, Ukraine cooperating with Russia. Because this rapprochement is perceived as a threat...I think it was based on this ideology and not about seeking freedom for the Ukrainian people. That was the basis for the actions of our partners in the United States and Europe. Supporting radical nationalist elements in the Ukraine to create a split—a fissure—in relations between Russia and Ukraine. But if Russia starts responding to that, then it's very easy to demonize Russia, to accuse it of all the deadly sins and to draw allies, because a visible adversary emerges. So in this sense those who were behind it have accomplished their goals and they did that impeccably."

"Unlike many partners of ours, we never interfere within the domestic affairs of other countries. That is one of the principles we stick to in our work."

2017-2018

If Ukraine and its Western allies refuse to reach a political settlement; Ukraine's use of military force including the use of war planes and tanks; coupled with NATO's encroachment up to Russian borders; the flight to Russia of 2.5 million Ukrainian refugees mainly from Donbass; and internal Russian political pressure, may force President Putin to reconsider his decision to not accept Donbass as part of the Russian Federation.

Gaither Stewart wrote on November 23, 2017:

"As an example of the internal pressure on Putin, Dmitry Novikov, First Deputy Chairman of the State Duma (the Parliament) Committee for International Affairs (Communist Party faction), declared the need to recognize the People's Democratic Republic of Donetsk and the People's Republic of Luhansk (East Ukraine or Novorossiya).

"'*We favor recognizing the Luhansk and Donetsk people's republics. The lack of such recognition leads to the fact that politicians in Luhansk are beginning to speak about the possibility of reintegration into Ukraine,*'" he said threateningly at a recent press conference in Moscow. Novikov stressed that Russia must deal with its problems '*without external interference*'. He pointed out that an attempt is being made to destabilize the situation in Russia with the aim of inspiring a color revolution that would lead to the disintegration of the country. [The U.S. neoliberal vision of future Russia.] '*Russia must defend itself*,' the MP stressed." (http://www.greanvillepost.com/2017/11/25/berlin-moscow-moscow-berlin/)

Not all of U.S. European allies are blinded by U.S./NATO/EU false propaganda.

On April 6, 2016, the Dutch rejected the EU-Ukraine Association Agreement, in a referendum: Thirty-two percent voted. Of those 61% rejected accepting the Ukraine in EU, while 38.1% voted for. This is mainly indicative of discontent with the EU and disenchantment with the Ukrainian rapprochement movement.

On April 7, BBC reported that the low voting percentage was valid: "Prime Minister Mark Rutte said the government might have to reconsider the deal, although the vote is not binding."

"The result creates a headache for the Dutch government, as the Dutch parliament approved the EU association agreement with Ukraine last year. All the other 27 EU member states have already ratified the deal." (http://www.bbc.com/news/world-europe-35976086)

Maybe German Chancellor Angela Merkel will listen too, if the rising German right-wing doesn't take over. On September 11, 2017, it was reported that Merkel thought Putin was reasonable.

"German Chancellor Angela Merkel has expressed support for President Vladimir Putin's proposal to deploy a UN peacekeeping contingent to the Eastern Ukraine to protect the OSCE monitoring mission there.

"Merkel '*generally welcomed Putin's initiative*' during a phone conversation with the Russian president, the German government's press service said in a statement. The two leaders also agreed on the extension of the UN mission's mandate.

"Chancellor Merkel added that the peacekeeping mission should not be limited only to the contact line separating Kiev's forces from the Donbass rebels, but that they should be empowered to accompany members of the Organization for Security and Cooperation in Europe monitoring mission to every region in which they operate.

"Putin '*reacted positively*' to Merkel's suggestions and said Moscow would consider removing these restrictions from the text of the resolution that Russia submitted to the UN Security Council, a statement from the Kremlin said." [This happened.]

"The representatives of the self-proclaimed People's Republics of Donetsk and Luhansk have previously expressed their readiness and willingness for dialog on the issue. The proposal was also welcomed by the OSCE Secretariat and its current chair, Austria.

"Ukraine, however, has been reluctant to support the initiative. Ukrainian officials said Kiev would never agree to coordinate the details of the mission with the self-proclaimed republics as it would mean their '*legalization.*' It also emphasized that it does not want to see any Russian, CSTO [Collective Security Treaty Organization] or CIS [Commonwealth of Independent States] troops among the peacekeepers." https://www.rt.com/news/402966-putin-merkel-peacekeepers-ukraine/

The Ukrainian government is as adamant as the Israeli government so long as the United States "permanent war doctrine" holds. No dialogue. Shoot first. Maybe ask questions later.

This policy even comes down to song.

Yuliya Olegovna Samoylova (on cover), Russian singer and composer, is well known for, "Flame is Burning". Ukraine banned her for three years for having sung in the Crimea in 2015. The Ukrainian government prevented her from taking part in the 2017 Eurovision Song Contest.

"It is very funny to look at all this, because I do not understand what they saw in me—such a small girl" (and confined in a wheelchair since childhood), she told Russia's First Channel.

"They saw some kind of threat. I am not actually upset. I continue to practice. I think somehow that everything is going to change." Samoylova performed instead in Sevastopol, Crimea, on the day of the Eurovision semi-final. Her song is a Russian wish for peace and love.

FLAME IS BURNING

Day and night and all I do is dreaming
Pacing sick and staring at the ceiling
I wish I had the answers
I wish I had the courage to know
Everybody is talking about the reasons
All I wanna do is find the feeling
I wanna feel the power

I wanna go to places I don't know
If there's a light then we have to keep dreaming
If there's a heart then we must keep believing inside
Ohh
After the night there's a light
And in the darkest time a flame is burning
It shines so bright
Deep in the night love is alight
And in the dark a flame is burning
A flame is burning
All my life I'm searching for the meaning
Now I've learned to seeing is believing
I wish I knew where light is
I wish I had the courage to go
If there's a light then we have to keep dreaming
If there's a heart then we must keep believing inside
After the night there's a light
And in the darkest time a flame is burning
It shines so bright
Deep in the night love is alight
And in the dark a flame is burning
An open window for love
And let the wind blow into the hearts
And we're never apart and you'll know
After the night there is a light
And in the darkest time a flame is burning
It shines so bright
Deep in the night love is alight
And in the dark a flame is burning
A flame is burning
A flame is burning
(Songwriters: Leonid Gutkin / Netta Nimrodi / Arie Burshtein)

Notes:

1. S.N.A. Social-National Assembly–neo-Nazi and other radical violent groups in Svobada
   Euromaidan is a acronym for demonstrations for Europe (EU) at the Maidan (Independence Square), officially called Maidan Nezalezhnosti. These protests begn on November 21, 2013 and were mainly led by pro-fascists organizations such as Svobada.

2. The U.S.-dominated IMF approved a $15.1 billion loan for Ukraine in 2010 and then suspended it after providing only $3 billion because the new Yanokovych government would not adopt its usual extreme austerity measures to cut social needs–wages and pensions, and increase gas prices. The new loan offered and taken by the coup government has the same austerity conditions.

   This history started with the 2004 elections (at least), which occurred over three voting terms: October 31, November 21 and December 26. Yankovych was prime minister and member of the Party of Regions. The other main candidate of 26 in the running was independent Viktor Yushchenko. The former was seen as more pro-Russian, the latter as more pro-West. The corrupt and criminal pro-U.S. Georgian President Saakasvili also supported Yushchenko. No one achieved a majority vote on October 31, so there was a run-off, which Yankovych supposedly won but he was widely charged with having rigged the election. Major protests occurred, including civil disobedience. This became the "Orange Revolution". The Supreme Court called for a new election, which Yushchenko won with 52% against Yankovych with 44%.

   In the January 17, 2010 election, the main candidates were again Yankovych and Fatherland Party's Yulia Tymoshenko. She had been an Orange Revolution leader and a former prime minister. With no majority, the February 7 run-off went to Yankovych with 49%; and 45.5% for Tymoshenko. This election was not contested, although Tymoshenko refused to recognize her opponent as president. She was convicted of embezzlement and abuse of power on October 11, 2011 and sentenced to seven years in prison. Her Western and Ukrainian supporters considered the criminal charges to be false for political reasons. The coup makers got her released from prison on February 22, 2014. She is now the parliament's Fatherland party faction leader.

3. National Endowment for Democracy billions funded the so-called "Orange Revolution" and another 64 projects. A capitalist associate, George Soros "Open Society" "charities" added his economic support.

   On May 25, 2014, Soros told CNN, "I set up a foundation in Ukraine before Ukraine became independent from Russia. And the foundation has been functioning ever since and played an important part in events now." http://transcripts.cnn.com/TRANSCRIPTS/1405/25/fzgps.01.html.

   Another big time donor is the billionaire owner of the eBay auction site and the online publication "Intercept".

   See Huffington Post's article on how American taxpayer monies fund the coup government and right-wing political parties. http://www.huffingtonpost.com/2014/03/07/us-foreign-aid-ukraine_n_4914682.html

4. The MH17 was shot down by a missile. As of this writing there is no verification of who did it or why. Russia maintains it was the Ukrainian military, while Ukraine says it was either Russia or "their" Ukrainian rebels. Some independent observers believe it could have been Ukrainian separatist fighters who mistook the flight for a Ukrainian military invading aircraft.

5. Stone's book, *The Putin Interviews*, Skyhorse, 2017, first edition, page 5. See also pages 68-9, 17-6, 155, 117, 121, 124 for subsequent remarks made in interviews conducted on July 4, 2015, February 19, 2016 and May 10-11, 2016.

CHAPTER 17
Russiagate

SHOOT-FROM-THE-HIP DONALD TRUMP scared the military-industrial complex and its Deep State from the start of his presidential campaign against its star candidate Hillary Clinton.

The Establishment became worried that he might just implement some of his more outlandish "peacenik" sloganeering. Furthermore, his wealth did not come from the war industry as did the Clintons. These lawyers go way back as promoters of that part of the Establishment when they were partners in the Rose Law firm. In later years they've made a fortune from speeches that titillate big capital. In 2014-5, they scored $25 million, and many millions since.

Trump, however, is not a capitalist servant but a real capitalist. The main difference is he earned his profits from building construction mostly unrelated to globalization and its war needs. He also proposed an economy based on nationalistic-isolationists premises, less taxes for the rich surely but not so much war. Well, as we saw with Syria and North Korea he is relenting. Nevertheless once his inter-class enemies launched the notion that he stood with Putin in a conspiracy to steal the election from superstar Hillary, there was no letting up on him.

In May 2017, Robert Mueller, FBI director 2001-2013, was appointed by Deputy Attorney General Rod Rosenstein as special counsel to oversee an investigation into the alleged Russian intervention in the 2016 presidential election. This developed following a report by three of the 17 intelligence agencies, which "concluded with high confidence that the Russian government engaged in electoral interference". A January 2017 assessment by the Office of the Director of National Intelligence (ODNI) stated that Russian leadership preferred Donald

Trump over Hillary Clinton, and that President Vladimir Putin personally ordered an "influence campaign" to harm Clinton's electoral chances and "undermine public faith in the US democratic process." (https://motherboard.vice.com/en_us/article/4xa5g9/all-signs-point-to-russia-being-behind-the-dnc-hack)

It is not possible for any author of a book that will come out in some months to foresee how all this speculation will end. Maybe there will be an impeachment. Maybe when you read this book Trump will no longer be president. Maybe the Deep State will have invaded Russia to get at the demon Putin, just like it has done in so many other lands (see next chapter). But if they do try to depose President Putin they will not succeed. They will, however, bring death of many millions of us.

As events and non-events proceed in a whirlwind of ever-mounting absurdity all I can do with this chapter is point out some of the lies they have told us, which probably most of you already know—how it has been proven that Putin (Russia) did not hack the Democratic National Committee emails; or bring about so much confusion amongst the chronically ill informed US American citizenry that many voted for "the wrong man"; nor was it Putin who endangered the nation by writing or releasing Secretary of State Hillary Clinton's emails. As Trump said, she should go to jail for that one.

HYSTERIA AND REALITY

The Real News Network producer Aaron Maté interviewed *The Guardian* (UK) reporter Luke Harding about his premise that Trump and Putin are in a conspiracy, and that Putin got him elected president. Harding wrote a book about this subject, *Collusion: Secret Meetings—Dirty Money, and how Russia Helped Donald Trump Win* (Vintage, November 2017).

This 28-minute interview-debate, December 23, 2017, is revealing in two senses: a) Harding is a commentator not a reporter; b) He did not offer one piece of evidence, not one fact of any "collusion". When Maté confronted Harding about his unsubstantiated claims, he repeated the phrases "look at the whole context" and we need to be "improvisational".

I choose this interview as representative of how shallow and scandalous the adherents to Russiagate are. (http://therealnews.com/t2/story:20761:Debate:-Where's-the-'Collusion

I think the polite and calm Maté was even soft on Harding by not bringing forth for his comment why the mass media is being exposed, or exposing itself, for advertising this fake news story.

Take the notorious CNN for instance.

On June 26, 2017, three prominent journalists, including the executive editor in charge of an investigative unit, were forced to resign after publication of an unfounded Russiagate story. It was retracted and an apology offered to the key person named, Anthony Scaramucci, an ally of President Donald Trump.

CNN was too embarrassed to meet the press. Instead, it sent a note: "On June 22, 2017, CNN.com published a story connecting Anthony Scaramucci with investigations into the Russia Direct Investment Fund. The story did not meet CNN's editorial standards".

Thomas Frank, who wrote the story, Eric Lichtblau, an editor in the unit, and Lex Haris, who oversaw the unit, left CNN. Their resignations were accepted. (http://money.cnn.com/2017/06/26/media/cnn-announcement-retracted-article/index.html)

The same week that CNN was having this credibility crisis, another one cropped up. CNN also admitted this one but took it on the hoof.

"CNN says a clandestine video of one of the network's producers criticizing its coverage of President Trump is legitimate, further fraying an already strained relationship between the news network and the White House. The video taken by Project Veritas, the political group founded by the conservative provocateur James O'Keefe, shows a CNN producer from its medical coverage team commenting pointedly about the network's coverage of the alleged ties between Trump and Russia. When asked by an unrevealed videographer why CNN has been aggressive in covering the story, the producer, John Bonifield, replied: 'Because it's ratings, '" wrote *USA Today*. (https://www.usatoday.com/story/money/2017/06/27/cnn-shrugs-off-veritas-video-trump-lashes-out-network/432423001/)

The conservative activist James O'Keefe founded Project Veritas in 2010 "to investigate and expose corruption, dishonesty, self-dealing, waste, fraud and other misconduct."

CNN producer Bonifield did not know he was being videotaped during several sessions with a Veritas reporter. Among other statements he made about the Russiagate unending story were:

"I mean, it's mostly bullshit right now." "It's a business...All the nice cutesy little ethics that used to get talked about in journalism school... that's adorable. That's adorable. This is a business."

"Just to give you some context," Bonifield explained, referring to what CNN CEO Jeff Zucker said in an internal meeting regarding President Trump's pulling out of the international climate agreement: *"he said, good job everybody covering the climate accords, but we're done with that, let's get back to Russia."* [my emphasis]

CNN decided not to fire Bonifield, maintaining that he offered his own opinion not the company's.

Another misreporting that got retracted came from *The New York Times* after it reported that all 17 U.S. intelligence agencies agreed that the evidence showed that Russia hacked the DNC mails. The former Director of National Intelligence James Clapper told the Senate Judiciary subcommittee on May 8, 2016, that the January 6, 2016 intelligence report was investigated by "the two dozen or so analysts" who were "hand-picked" for the task. The Senate committee should have asked with what objective were they "hand-picked".

Remember that Clapper flat out lied to the U.S. Congress, on March 12, 2013, about his agency spying on US Americans. He claimed: "No, sir" and "not wittingly" to a question about whether the National Security Agency was collecting "any type of data at all" on millions of Americans.

About three months after this claim, documents leaked by former NSA contractor Edward Snowden revealed Clapper answered untruthfully, and that the NSA was collecting domestic call records in bulk, along with internet communications.

After Snowden proved Clapper to be a liar, he admitted it and apologized. Nevertheless, Clapper was not tried for this criminal offense and even remained NSA director for the next five years.

Why wouldn't such a Deep State liar "hand-pick" other spooks to lie regarding Putin and Russia "hacking"? We all know that Ronald Reagan's key Iran-Contragate man, Colonel Oliver North, lied about that operation. He even got convicted for it. And we know, as former CIA officer Phil Agee and many other former CIA agents have testified, that it has always been a CIA principle to lie. And not only lie as in "plausible denial", but to spread fake news in phony articles and editorials planted in willing collaborating newspapers. (See Agee's, *Inside the Company: CIA Diary*, Penguin, 1975)

On June 29, 2016, the NYT corrected its June 25 piece for having "referred incorrectly to the source of an intelligence assessment that said Russia orchestrated hacking attacks during last year's presidential elections. The assessment was made by four intelligence agencies—the Office of the Director of National Intelligence, the Central Intelligence Agency, the Federal Bureau of Investigation and the National Security Agency. The assessment was not approved by all 17 organizations in the American intelligence community."

The mass medium focusing most on so-called Trump-Putin ties, and the fantasy of Russian hacking, is the *Washington Post*.

Glenn Greenwald wrote: "Several of the most humiliating of these episodes have come from the Washington Post. On December 30 [2016], the paper published a blockbuster, frightening scoop that immediately and predictably went viral and generated massive traffic. Russian hackers, the paper claimed based on anonymous sources, had hacked into the 'U.S. electricity grid' through a Vermont utility." (https://theintercept.com/2017/06/27/cnn-journalists-resign-latest-example-of-media-recklessness-on-the-russia-threat)

"That, in turn, led MSNBC journalists, and various Democratic officials, to instantly sound the alarm that Putin was trying to deny Americans heat during the winter:

"Literally every facet of that story turned out to be false. First, the utility company—which the Post *had not bothered to contact—issued a denial, pointing out that malware was found on one laptop that was not connected either to the Vermont grid or the broader U.S. electricity grid. That forced the Post to change the story to hype the still-alarmist claim that this malware 'showed the risk' posed by Russia to the U.S. electric grid, along with a correction at the top repudiating the story's central claim.*

"But then it turned out that even this limited malware was not connected to Russian hackers at all and, indeed, may not have been a malicious code of any kind. Those revelations forced the Post to publish a new article days later entirely repudiating the original story. 'Russian

government hackers do not appear to have targeted Vermont utility, say people close to investigation.'"

"Embarrassments of this sort are literally too numerous to count when it comes to hyped, viral U.S. media stories over the last year about the Russia Threat. Less than a month before its electric grid farce, the Post published a blockbuster story—largely based on a blacklist issued by a brand new, entirely anonymous group—featuring the shocking assertion that stories planted or promoted by Russia's 'disinformation campaign' were viewed more than 213 million times.

"That story fell apart almost immediately. The McCarthyite blacklist of Russia disinformation outlets on which it relied contained numerous mainstream sites. The article was widely denounced. And the Post, two weeks later, appended a lengthy editor's note at the top:

By Craig Timberg November 24, 2016

Editor's Note: The Washington Post on Nov. 24 published a story on the work of four sets of researchers who have examined what they say are Russian propaganda efforts to undermine American democracy and interests. One of them was PropOrNot, a group that insists on public anonymity, which issued a report identifying more than 200 websites that, in its view, wittingly or unwittingly published or echoed Russian propaganda. A number of those sites have objected to being included on PropOrNot's list, and some of the sites, as well as others not on the list, have publicly challenged the group's methodology and conclusions. The Post, which did not name any of the sites, does not itself vouch for the validity of PropOrNot's findings regarding any individual media outlet, nor did the article purport to do so. Since publication of The Post's story, PropOrNot has removed some sites from its list.

The flood of "fake news" this election season got support from a sophisticated Russian

Glenn Greenwald gives many more examples. This one is at the heart of the Russiagate scare plot.

"Perhaps the most significant Russia falsehood came from CrowdStrike, the firm hired by the DNC to investigate the hack of its email servers. Again in the same time period — December 2016 — the firm issued a new report accusing Russian hackers of nefarious activities involving the Ukrainian army, which numerous outlets, including (of course) the Washington Post, uncritically hyped:

"'A cyber security firm has uncovered strong proof of the tie between the group that hacked the Democratic National Committee and Russia's military intelligence arm — the primary agency behind the Kremlin's interference in the 2016 election,'" the Post claimed.

"'The firm CrowdStrike linked malware used in the DNC intrusion to malware used to hack and track an Android phone app used by the Ukrainian army in its battle against pro-Russia separatists in eastern Ukraine from late 2014 through 2016.'"

"Yet that story also fell apart. In March, the firm 'revised and retracted statements it used to buttress claims of Russian hacking during last year's American presidential election campaign' after several experts questioned its claims, and 'CrowdStrike walked back key parts of its Ukraine report.'"

Incidentally, before proceeding further, let us keep in mind that all evidence about the DNC "hack" points that it was not a hack, but an insider "leak". The data was copied and stolen, probably on a flash drive. To understand politics, it is always relevant to know where the money is and who owns the mass media. What is the context of *Washington Post* Russia bashing and the ownership of the formerly respected medium for its righteous exposes, especially "Watergate", the first "gate"?

Billionaire Jeff Bezos —currrently rated as the single richest man in the world (except perhaps for the Gulf despots), bought the paper in August 2013 for a mere $250 million in cash. He has since surpassed Bill Gates (sometimes) as the world's richest person, worth $100 billion as of January 2018. He got rich by founding Amazon, the world's largest online retailer. He is its CEO and owns 17% shares (worth $84 billion). Bezos also owns $3 billion in Google shares—all this according to Wikipedia. What Wikipedia does not tell us is that he is in partnership with the bloody CIA, which is THE agency behind bashing Trump and demonizing Putin's Russia.

"The intelligence community is about to get the equivalent of an adrenaline shot to the chest. This summer, a $600 million computing cloud developed by Amazon Web Services for the Central Intelligence Agency over the past year will begin servicing all 17 agencies that make up the intelligence community," wrote Frank Konkel in *The Atlantic*, July 17, 2014. (https://www.theatlantic.com/technology/archive/2014/07/the-details-about-the-cias-deal-with-amazon/374632/)

"The vision was first outlined in the Intelligence Community Information Technology Enterprise plan championed by Director of National Intelligence James Clapper and IC Chief Information Officer Al Tarasiuk almost three years ago. Cloud computing is one of the core components of the strategy to help the IC discover, access and share critical information in an era of seemingly infinite data."

"Snowden was able to access and download classified information intelligence officials said he shouldn't have been able to access," wrote Konkel.

So the Amazon boss is helping the 17 intelligence agencies prevent the public from ever more learning about agency secrets.

"In early 2013, after weighing bids from Amazon Web Services, IBM and an unnamed third vendor, the CIA awarded a contract to AWS worth up to $600 million over a period of up to 10 years," Konkel continued.

IMB appealed the decision, won on the first round and then lost. Now why is it that the CIA prefers Amazon's Bezos over the much older Establishment partner IBM? Not because, I'm certain, it had been a Hitler partner.

The Deep State, I suspect, prefers Amazon because it owns most of online book sales, has big influence on Google, and bought the Capitol Hill-based daily *Washington Post* at the same time the CIA deal was being made. The newspaper doesn't mention its financial connections to the CIA when its stories claim that the CIA's key target, Russia, is behind all evils. We must also remember that the Post has long had close ties with the government, the Dulles brothers, and the CIA just as has *The New York Times*. One of the two Watergate muckrakers was Carl Bernstein. He told us all about that in 1977.http://www.carlbernstein.com/magazine_cia_and_media.php

In sum: The CIA gets Amazon and the *Post*—this gigantic information and fake news octopus, and its advanced IT technology all at once. And if this book ever gets published and distributed, it will be on Amazon—unless!

"WHOSE BRIGHT IDEA WAS RUSSIAGATE?"

Paul Craig Roberts, the former Reagan appointee introduced earlier, knows more about how the Establishment works than most. Here is his take.

"The answer to the question in the title of this article is that Russiagate was created by CIA director John Brennan. The CIA started what is called Russiagate in order to prevent Trump from being able to normalize relations with Russia. The CIA and the military/security complex need an enemy in order to justify their huge budgets and unaccountable power. Russia has been assigned that role. The Democrats joined in as a way of attacking Trump. They hoped to have him tarnished as cooperating with Russia to steal the presidential election from Hillary and to have him impeached. I don't think the Democrats have considered the consequence of further worsening the relations between the US and Russia.

"Public Russia bashing pre-dates Trump. It has been going on privately in neoconservative circles for years, but appeared publicly during the Obama regime when Russia blocked Washington's plans to invade Syria and to bomb Iran.

"Russia bashing became more intense when Washington's coup in Ukraine failed to deliver Crimea. Washington had intended for the new Ukrainian regime to evict the Russians from their naval base on the Black Sea. This goal was frustrated when Crimea voted to rejoin Russia.

"The neoconservative ideology of US world hegemony requires the principal goal of US foreign policy to be to prevent the rise of other countries that can serve as a restraint on US unilateralism. This is the main basis for the hostility of US foreign policy toward Russia, and of course there also are the material interests of the military/security complex.

"Russia bashing is much larger than merely Russiagate. The danger lies in Washington convincing Russia that Washington is planning a surprise attack on Russia. With US and NATO bases on Russia's borders, efforts to arm Ukraine and to include Ukraine and Georgia in NATO provide more evidence that Washington is surrounding Russia for attack. There is nothing more reckless and irresponsible than convincing a nuclear power that you are going to attack." (https://www.paulcraigroberts.org/2017/10/03/whose-bright-idea-russiagate/)

The Deep State and its mass media, therefore, need to have Putin be so evil and omnipresent with his subversion. They need the demonic fury so that enough US Americans, and European vassals, will accept a U.S.-imposed "regime change" in Russia.

Some of the UK/USA mass media has even linked Putin to causing

Brexit, because he wants the EU to fall apart. Putin is also behind Jeremy Corbyn, because he is against war and might become the Prime Minister if not maligned enough. The struggle for independence in Spain's Catalonia is also Putin's doing, again to break up Europe. You know, the "cold-eye former K.G.B. lieutenant colonel", as the *NYT* calls this "authoritarian" ruler. (https://www.nytimes.com/2017/09/12/opinion/putin-russia-mikhail-khodorkovsky.html)

I wonder, as does William Blum in his Anti-Imperialist Report 151, why the newspaper that prints all the news worth printing doesn't refer to former President George H.W. Bush as the "cold-eye former CIA Director". It was during his watch that CIA assets Luis Posada Carriles and Orlando Bosch exploded Cuba's passenger airline Flight 455 and murdered all aboard. Both are considered heroes among Miami *gusanos*—Cuban exile "worms" whom have murdered and sabotaged to overthrow the Cuban government under CIA control. Although Posada Carriles was on the FBI terrorist list he lived free in Miami until his death on May 23, 2018. (See my book *Backfire* and chapter six herein.)

Putin even sends Russian made Nordic trolls into US American society, infiltrating social media and the black liberation movement. William Blum writes about them.

"Russian Internet trolls are trying to stir up even more controversy over National Football League players crouching on one knee ("taking a "knee") during the national anthem, said Sen. James Lankford (R-Okla.), warning that the United States should expect such divisive efforts to escalate in the next election."

"'*We watched even this weekend,*' Lankford said, '*the Russians and their troll farms, and their Internet folks, start hash-tagging out 'take a knee' and also hash-tagging out 'Boycott NFL'.*" The Russians' goal, he said, was '*to try to raise the noise level in America to try to make a big issue, an even bigger issue as they're trying to just push divisiveness in the country. We've continued to be able to see that. We will see that again in our election time.*'" [my emphasis]

"Russia 'causing divisiveness' is a common theme of American politicians and media. Never explained is WHY? What does Russia have to gain by Americans being divided? Do they think the Russians are so juvenile? Or are the Americans the childish ones?

"CNN on October 12 claimed that Russia uses YouTube, Tumblr

and the Pokemon Go mobile game 'to exploit racial tensions and sow discord among Americans,' while the *Washington Post* (October 12) reported that 'content generated by Russian operatives was not aimed only at influencing the election. Many of the posts and ads intended to divide Americans over hot-button issues such as immigration or race.'"

"Imagine … the American public being divided over immigration and race … How could that be possible without Russian trolls?" (https://williamblum.org/aer/read/152)

Margaret Kimberly writes about Russian trolls, too, "Russiagate Targets Black People".

"There is no last refuge for the scoundrels' intent on stoking cold and possibly hot war against Russia. Neo-cons in both parties and the corporate media have all spent years demonizing Russia's president even as they commit and abet horrific crimes against humanity at home and abroad. Every charge leveled against Vladimir Putin is a sinister projection of the American rap sheet. That is just one reason the so-called Russiagate story won't be allowed to die." (https://www.blackagendareport.com/freedom-rider-russiagate-targets-black-people)

"The latest and most shameful charge is that Russia has targeted black Americans in an effort to 'sow division' in the United States via social media. We are told that the Russian government spent a grand total of $100,000 to undermine the election and American society. Twitter and Facebook posts on issues ranging from the second amendment to police murder are now said to be tools of Russian espionage.

"The cynical plot kills several birds with one stone. Democrats can explain away their dismal electoral failures. Democrats and Republicans make the case for imperialism. Now a phony concern for the plight of black Americans will be the rationale for targeting not only the Russian government, but all leftists in this country. From the Propornot campaign to changes in search engine algorithms, leftists and even progressive Democrats are being censored. That attack is committed under the guise of fighting Vladimir Putin and the effort is completely bipartisan.

"Black people must not defend the system which oppresses them."

"There is no American democracy left to undermine anyway. America is not a democracy and nothing proves it like the police killing three people every day or the fact that one million black people are held behind bars in this country."

"Black people were not chattel slaves in Russia and didn't create a financial powerhouse through unpaid labor in that country as they did here in the United States."

"It would be an insult to the legacy of the liberation movement if black people allow themselves to become dupes for the bipartisan neo-cons. Division is the direct result of the racist American project and there should be no confusion about that fact. All the criminality is committed right here by this government. There is no need to look abroad for perpetrators."

It turns out that U.S. Army Intelligence has been using its own trolls probably for a long time but just now allows the public to see that they are requesting to do such.

On January 11, 2018, RT broadcast a story about this the day after the U.S. Army officially requested permission to introduce cyber trolls.

"The US Army wants a new intelligence tool able to understand social media posts in languages including Russian, Arabic and French. It must also be able to answer on its own—just like those pesky 'Kremlin bots' we hear about," said RT.

"According to former MI5 officer Annie Machon, the Pentagon could be attempting to use the allegations of 'Russian troll farms' to justify and deflect attention away from the fact that US military intelligence has been engaged in exactly this kind of activity for years."

"'*The most obvious interpretation would be that this is a pushback against the allegations that have been made consistently for the last 18 months about so-called Russian troll farms influencing elections across the West, and it's interesting to see the languages they are advertising for are the languages of Iran, and of course North Korea and Russia, so that would be a giveaway about which countries they want to be targeting,*" Machon told RT.

"'*Having said that, the timing to me is interesting, because for sure the West has been running these so-called troll farms against other countries as well for a long time, so are they just trying to expand their operations by developing this new software? Or are they trying to disingenuously suggest to people that actually they haven't done it before and only the Big Bad Russians, or the Big Bad Chinese, have run troll farms.*'" (https://www.rt.com/usa/415609-us-army-ai-language-bot/)

This is part of the Army's submission:

"A. Capability to translate foreign language content (message text, voice, images, etc.) from the social media environment into English. Required languages are Arabic, French, Pashtu, Farsi, Urdu, Russian, and Korean.

"B. Identify specific audiences through reading and understanding of colloquial phrasing, spelling variations, social media brevity codes, and emojis." (https://www.fbo.gov/index?s=opportunity&mode=form&id=f393b9220232ea7a1be97a47f0afc429&tab=core&_cview=0)

WHAT'S WRONG WITH TALKING TO PUTIN?

Anti-Communist Republican President Ronald Reagan appointed Jack Matlock as his ambassador to the Soviet Union in its last Gorbachev years—April 1987 to August 1991 when Matlock retired after having been reappointed by the first George Bush. Matlock had also been a diplomat in Moscow during the Cuban Missile Crisis. He speaks Russian and admires its literature, especially Dostoyevsky. That should have put Reagan and Bush on alert.

The following is on Matlock's website, "Contacts with Russian Embassy". Published on March 4, 2017, I checked publication results on January 10, 2018. There were less than 300 and not one mass medium picked up this formidable Establishment man's words of wisdom.

"Our press seems to be in a feeding frenzy regarding contacts that President Trump's supporters had with Russian Ambassador Sergei Kislyak and with other Russian diplomats. The assumption seems to be that there was something sinister about these contacts, just because they were with Russian diplomats. [After 35 years] working to open up the Soviet Union and to make communication between our diplomats and ordinary citizens a normal practice, *I find the attitude of much of our political establishment and of some of our once respected media outlets quite incomprehensible. What in the world is wrong with consulting a foreign embassy about ways to improve relations? Anyone who aspires to advise an American president should do just that.* [my emphasis] (http://jackmatlock.com/2017/03/contacts-with-russian-embassy/)

Yesterday I received four rather curious questions from Mariana Rambaldi of Univision Digital. I reproduce below the questions and the answers I have given.

Question 1: Seeing the case of Michael Flynn, that has to resign after it emerged that he spoke with the Russian ambassador about sanctions against Russia before Trump took office, and now Jeff Sessions is in a similar situation. Why is it so toxic to talk with Sergey Kislyak?

Answer: Ambassador Kislyak is a distinguished and very able diplomat. Anyone interested in improving relations with Russia and avoiding another nuclear arms race—which is a vital interest of the United States—should discuss current issues with him and members of his staff. To consider him "toxic" is ridiculous…[I] see nothing wrong with his contact with Ambassador Kislyak so long as it was authorized by the president-elect. Certainly, Ambassador Kislyak did nothing wrong.

Question 2: According to your experience, are Russians ambassadors under the sight of the Russian intelligence or do they work together?

Answer: This is a strange question. Intelligence operations are normal at most embassies in the world. In the case of the United States, ambassadors must be informed of intelligence operations within the countries to which they are accredited and can veto operations that they consider unwise or too risky, or contrary to policy…During the Cold War, at least, we sometimes used Soviet intelligence officers to get messages direct to the Soviet leadership. For example, during the Cuban missile crisis, President Kennedy used a "channel" through the KGB resident in Washington to work out the understanding under which Soviet nuclear missiles were withdrawn from Cuba.

Question 3: How common (and ethical) is that a person related with a presidential campaign in the US has contact with the Russian embassy?

Answer: Why are you singling out the Russian embassy? *If you want to understand the policy of another country, you need to consult that country's representatives. It is quite common for foreign diplomats to cultivate candidates and their staffs.* That is part of their job. If Americans plan to advise the president on policy issues, they would be wise to maintain contact with the foreign embassy in question to understand that country's attitude toward the issues involved. Certainly, both Democrats and Republicans would contact Soviet Ambassador Dobrynin during the Cold War and discuss the issues with him. As the person in charge of our embassy in Moscow during several political campaigns, I would often set up meetings of candidates and their staffs with Soviet officials. Such contacts are certainly ethical so long as they do not involve disclosure of classified information or attempts to negotiate specific issues. In fact, I would say that any person who presumes to advise an incoming president on vital policy issues needs to understand the approach of the country in question and therefore is remiss if he or she does not consult with the embassy in question."

[Regarding Attorney General Sessions speaking with Kislyak] "I believe it is wrong to assume that such conversations are somehow suspect. *When I was ambassador to the USSR and Gorbachev finally allowed competitive elections, we in the U.S. embassy talked to everyone. I made a special point to keep personal relations with Boris Yeltsin when he in effect led the opposition. That was not to help get him elected (we favored Gorbachev), but to understand his tactics and policies and to make sure he understood ours.*

The whole brou-ha-ha over contacts with Russian diplomats has taken on all the earmarks of a witch hunt. President Trump is right to make that charge. If there was any violation of U.S. law by any of his supporters—for example disclosure of classified information to unauthorized persons—then the Department of Justice should seek an indictment and if they obtain one, prosecute the case. Until then, there should be no public accusations. Also, I have been taught that in a democracy with the rule of law, the accused are entitled to a presumption of innocence until convicted. *But we have leaks that imply that any conversation with a Russian embassy official is suspect. That is the attitude of a police state, and leaking such allegations violates every normal rule regarding FBI investigations.* President Trump is right to be upset, though it is not helpful for him to lash out at the media in general.

Finding a way to improve relations with Russia is in the vital interest of the United States. Nuclear weapons constitute an existential threat to our nation, and indeed to humanity. *We are on the brink of another nuclear arms race which would be not only dangerous in itself, but would make cooperation with Russia on many other important issues virtually impossible. Those who are trying to find a way to improve relations with Russia should be praised, not scapegoated."*

The witch-hunt against Putin and Trump, as this Republican diplomat describes, reminds me of the early years of the U.S. war against Vietnam when all of us who protested were accused of being communists. In fact, even anti-communist celebrities were so dubbed. One example was Steve Allen—radio and TV personality, comedian, actor, author, musician. Like all good Democratic Party leading figures, he was anti-communist. Allen was also against nuclear arms escalation and warring against a people who had done no harm to his America so he spoke out. But every time he began a speech, he would say (from memory): "I am not now nor have I ever been a communist!"

I guess it has gotten to the point that if one does not want a war against Putin's Russia, one has to begin by stating: "I am not now nor have ever been a fan of Putin! In fact, I find him despicable…"

WHO REVEALED THE DNC EMAILS?

Former DNC chairwoman Donna Brazile wrote a book about the emails and how Hillary Clinton rigged the primaries so that Bernie Sanders could not win.

In her book, *Hacks: The Inside Story of the Break-ins and Breakdowns that Put Donald Trump in the White House*, Brazile "reveals collusion and bad smell complicity. She insists, however, that there was nothing 'criminal' in it, though it 'compromised the party's integrity'. 'If the fight had been fair, one campaign would not have control of the party before the voters had decided which one they wanted to lead,'" quotes Binoy Kampmark from Brazile's book. (https://dissidentvoice.org/2017/11/why-wikileaks-was-right-rigging-the-democratic-way/)

"Right around the time of the convention, the leaked emails revealed Hillary's campaign was grabbing money from the state parties for its own purposes, leaving the states with very little to support down-ballot races."

The implication is that had the party apparatus been fair and not favored Clinton, Sanders may well have won the primary. Some polls indicated that he could have beaten Trump in the election campaign. Here are the emails leaked to Wikileaks: https://wikileaks.org/dnc-emails/

Nobody in this *Russiagate* witch hunt is suggesting that President Vladimir Putin intervened inside the Democratic Party apparatus to fix the primary. The question for the Establishment is not the conspiracy against Sanders but the matter of who let the cat out of the bag.

The November 14, 2017 *Washington's Blog* story, "How to Instantly Prove (or disprove) Russian Hacking of U.S. Elections" maintains that NSA knows who and how and won't tell. (http://www.washingtonsblog.com/2017/11/70011.html)

"It's newsworthy that CIA head Mike Pompeo recently met with Bill Binney—who designed the NSA's electronic surveillance system—about potential proof that the DNC emails were leaked rather than hacked." William Binney is also a mathematician and Russia-specialist.

"It's also noteworthy that the usual suspects—Neocon warmongers such as Max Boot—have tried to discredit both Binney and Pompeo. But there's a huge part of the story that the entire mainstream media is missing …Specifically, Binney says that the NSA has long had in its computers information which can prove exactly who hacked the DNC … or instead prove that the DNC emails were leaked by a Democratic insider.

"Remember—by way of background—that the NSA basically spies on everyone in America … and stores the data long-term. After the story of Pompeo's meeting with Binney broke, Binney told *Washington's Blog*:

'Here's what they would have from the programs you list [i.e. NSA's Fairview, Stormbrew and Blarney spying programs, which Edward Snowden revealed] plus hundreds if not thousands of trace route programs embedded in switches in the US and around the world.

First, from deep packet inspection, they would have the originator and ultimate recipient (IP) of the packets plus packet series 32 bit number identifier and all the housekeeping data showing the network segments/path and time to go though the network. And, of course, the number of packet bits. With this they would know to where and when the data passed.

From the data collection, they would have all the data as it existed in the server taken from. That's why I originally said ***if the FBI wanted Hillary's email, all they have to do is ask NSA for them****.*

All this is done by the Narus collection equipment in real time at line rates (620 mbps [mega bits per second,] for the STA-6400 and 10 gbps [giga bits per second] for the Insight equipment).'"

Edward Snowden message July 25, 2016:

"Even if the attackers try to obfuscate origin, #KEYSCORE makes following ex-filtrated data easy. I did this personally against Chinese ops."

"Binney told us," wrote *Washington's Blog*, '*Snowden's right and the MSM is clueless.*'"

'You can tell from the network log who is going into a site. I used that on networks that I had. I looked to see who came into my LAN, where they went, how long they stayed and what they did while in my network... ***If it were the Russians, NSA would have a trace route to them and not equivocate*** *on who did it. It's like using "Trace Route" to map the path of all the packets on the network. In the program Treasuremap NSA has hundreds of trace route programs embedded in switches in Europe and hundreds more around the world. So, this set-up should have detected where the packets went and when they went there.'"*

"Wikileaks is (and has been) a cast iron target for NSA/GCHQ/etc for a number of years there should be no excuse for them missing data going to anyone associated with Wikileaks...Which suggests they don't have proof and just want to war monger the US public into a second cold war with the Russians. ***After all, there's lots and lots of money in that for the military-industrial-intelligence-governmental complex of incestuous relationships,'"*** Binney concludes.

An unusually objective piece in the mass media weekly magazine, *Newsweek*, by Jeff Stein, October 13, 2016, substantiates much of the above information.

"Credentialed skeptics abound here, too, about the origin of the attacks. Former NSA executive William Binney maintains that U.S. officials 'know how many people [beyond the Russians] could have done this but they aren't telling us anything. All they're doing is promoting another cold war.'" "Binney, who quit the NSA in 2001 rather than participate in the agency's domestic data collection program, even compared allegations about Russian hacks to previous U.S. fabrications of intelligence to justify the invasion of Iraq in 2003 and the bombing of North Vietnam in 1964.

"'This is a big mistake, another WMD or Tonkin Gulf affair that's being created until they have absolute proof' of Russian complicity in the DNC hacks," he charged during a *Newsweek* interview.

If Obama officials 'have the evidence now' of who hacked the DNC, he charged. 'So let's see it, guys,'" Binney told *Newsweek*.

The Establishment newsmagazine also interviewed another insider, James Matthews, a 35-year CIA veteran who served in Moscow. He told the magazine that the Russians didn't need to hack Hillary Clinton's private email servers when she was Secretary of State.

"'They collected them via SIGNT'—signals intelligence, or electronic eavesdropping—'***when Hillary and company sent them unencrypted.***' For the *Spetsvaz*, Russia's version of the NSA, he says, 'it was like finding gold without once swinging a pickaxe.'" [my emphasis]

"And it left no trace. *Investigators found no 'direct evidence' that Clinton's email account had been 'successfully hacked,'* FBI Director James B. Comey testified, which 'both private experts and federal investigators immediately understood' to mean that 'it very likely had been breached, but the intruders were far too skilled to leave evidence of their work,' according to David Sanger, the *New York Times* cyber expert.

"If U.S. intelligence officials are to be believed, Putin has escalated the battle by feeding Wikileaks purloined Clinton campaign emails. But they've offered no definitive proof of a link between the two," concludes *Newsweek*. (http://www.newsweek.com/russian-hacking-whodunnit-509505)

A score of other former intelligence officers in Veterans Intelligence Professionals for Sanity also know that the Russians didn't hack into DNC mails. In a memo to President Trump, the group, which includes Binney and other NSA specialists, cites forensic studies to challenge that claim. See: https://consortiumnews.com/2017/07/24/intel-vets-challenge-russia-hack-evidence/

WHISTLE BLOWER SUSPECT KILLED

Seth Conrad Rich was a data programmer for the Democratic National Committee. He was fatally shot in the rough Bloomingdale neighborhood of Washington, D.C., on July 10, 2016. His murder was still unsolved as of this writing. Many believe he could have been the whistle blower to Wikileaks, which offered $20,000 for information about his suspicious murder. Police said they believed he was a victim of an attempted robbery.

Police have no witnesses and no solid motivation. He had several bruises and two .22 bullets in the back. Nothing was taken other than a turkey.

Joe Lauria—former reporter for *Wall Street Journal*, Boston Globe, *Sunday Times of London*, and author of *How I Lost by Hillary Clinton* (OR books, June 2017)—wrote a serious piece about the possibility that Rich was the leaker, "A New Twist in Seth Rich Murder Case". (https://consortiumnews.com/2017/08/08/a-new-twist-in-seth-rich-murder-case/)

Lauria links to a 6.40 minute telephone conversation Sy Hersh had with Ed Butowsky about *Russiagate* "hacking" of DNC, which Hersh says is "bullshit," an "American disinformation", "Brennan operation", just as Paul Craig Roberts contends. John Brennan was Obama's last CIA director (March 2013 to January 2017). Hersh does not believe, however, that is why Rich was murdered, rather that hoodlums did it.

I am sorry that the Hersh phone conversation was tapped and released without his knowledge and approval, but it is in the public interest, so I use it as well.

Hersh says: "'All I know is that he [Rich] offered a sample, an extensive sample, I'm sure dozens of emails, and said 'I want money.' Later, WikiLeaks did get the password, he had a DropBox, a protected DropBox," he said. They got access to the DropBox," wrote Cassandra Fairbanks for: https://bigleaguepolitics.com/audio-seymour-hersh-states-seth-rich-wikileaks-source/

Hersh also states that Rich had concerns about something happening to him, and he "shared this DropBox with a couple of friends, so that 'if anything happens to me it's not going to solve your problems,'" he added. "WikiLeaks got access before he was killed.'"

Ed Butowsky is a wealthy Republican who offered to finance an investigation into Seth Rich murder. Here are other key points in the talk.

(1) Obama's intelligence chiefs fabricated Russiagate to get Hillary Clinton elected

(2) The NSA and CIA briefed the press on Russiagate and "run" the mainstream media, and they "all fucking lie about" Trump.

(3) Regardless of how Wikileaks got the emails, "*the democrats themselves wrote this shit.*"

Assange is so hated by Clinton that she wanted to "drone" him. This is what Wikileaks leaked:

Clinton's State Department was getting pressure from President Obama and his White House inner circle, as well as heads of state internationally, to try and cutoff Assange's delivery of the cables and if that effort failed, then to forge a strategy to minimize the administration's public embarrassment over the contents of the cables. Hence, Clinton's early morning November meeting of State's top brass who floated various proposals to stop, slow or spin the Wikileaks contamination. That is when a frustrated Clinton, sources said, at some point blurted out a controversial query.

"Can't we just drone this guy?" Clinton openly inquired, offering a simple remedy to silence Assange and smother Wikileaks via a planned military drone strike, according to State Department sources. The statement drew laughter from the room which quickly died off when the Secretary kept talking in a terse manner, sources said. Clinton said Assange, after all, was a relatively soft target, "walking around" freely and thumbing his nose without any fear of reprisals from the United States.

John Pilger interviewed Assange in the Ecuadorian embassy in London in November 2016. (https://www.fairobserver.com/region/europe/wikileaks julian-assange-latest-news-headlines-34055/)

Pilger: What's the significance of the FBI's intervention in these last days of the US election campaign, in the case against Hillary Clinton?

Assange: If you look at the history of the FBI, it has become effectively America's political police. The FBI demonstrated this by taking down the former head of the CIA [General David Petraeus] over classified information given to his mistress. Almost no-one is untouchable. The FBI is always trying to demonstrate that no-one can resist us. But Hillary Clinton very conspicuously resisted the FBI's investigation, so there's anger within the FBI because it made the FBI look weak. We've [WikiLeaks] published about 33,000 of Clinton's emails when she was secretary of state. They come from a batch of just over 60,000 emails, [of which] Clinton has kept about half—30,000—to herself, and we've published about half.

Then there are the Podesta emails we've been publishing. [John] Podesta is Hillary Clinton's primary campaign manager, so there's a thread that runs through all these emails; there are quite a lot of pay-for-play, as they call it, giving access in exchange for money to states, individuals and corporations. [These emails are] combined with the cover up of the Hillary Clinton emails when she was secretary of state, [which] has led to an environment where the pressure on the FBI increases.

Pilger: The Clinton campaign has said that Russia is behind all of this, that Russia has manipulated the campaign and is the source for WikiLeaks and its emails.

Assange: The Clinton camp has been able to project that kind of neo-McCarthy hysteria: that Russia is responsible for everything. Hilary Clinton stated multiple times, falsely, that 17 US intelligence agencies had assessed that Russia was the source of our publications. That is false; ***we can say that the Russian government is not the source***. [my emphasis]

WikiLeaks has been publishing for 10 years, and in those 10 years, we have published 10 million documents, several thousand individual publications, several thousand different sources, and *we have never got it wrong*."

Pilger: There is the accusation that WikiLeaks is in league with the Russians. Some people say, "Well, why doesn't WikiLeaks investigate and publish emails on Russia"?

Assange: We have published about 800,000 documents of various kinds that relate to Russia. Most of those are critical; and a great many books have come out of our publications about Russia, most of which are critical. Our [Russia] documents have gone on to be used in quite a number of court cases: refugee cases of people fleeing some kind of claimed political persecution in Russia, which they use our documents to back up.

Just after Trump won, his team said that those who claim Russians hacked the DNC to help Trump get elected, "are the same people that said Saddam Hussein [had] weapons of mass destruction."

On January 3, 2017: Trump tweeted twice: "Julian Assange said, 'a 14 year-old could have hacked Podesta'—"Why was DNC so careless? Also said, Russians did not give him the info!"

Tweet 2: "Julian Assange on U.S. media coverage: 'It's very dishonest #Hannity "More dishonest than anyone knows."

NORTH KOREA, TRUMP, PUTIN

As if backing terrorists in Syria á la Libya, encouraging a semi-fascist coup in Ukraine, creating a completely false fairy tale about Putin interference in the 2016 election, in order to get his puppet elected, were not enough they had to make North Korea an enemy once again.

"The growing North Korean menace also reflects the chronic failure of multilateral counter-proliferation efforts and, in particular, the longstanding refusal of acknowledged nuclear-armed states such as the US and Britain to honor a legal commitment to reduce and eventually eliminate their arsenals;" wrote Simon Tisdall, September 5, 2017, "How the nuclear-armed nations brought the North Korean crisis on themselves." (https://www.theguardian.com/world/2017/sep/05/nuclear-armed-nations-brought-the-north-korea-crisis-on-themselves)

"In other words, the past and present leaders of the US, Russia, China, France and the UK, whose governments signed but have not fulfilled the terms of the 1970 nuclear non-proliferation treaty (NPT), have to some degree brought the North Korea crisis on themselves. Kim Jong-un's recklessness and bad faith is a product of their own.

"The NPT, signed by 191 countries, is probably the most successful arms control treaty ever. When conceived in 1968, at the height of the cold war, the mass proliferation of nuclear weapons was considered a real possibility. Since its inception and prior to North Korea, only India, Pakistan and Israel are known to have joined the nuclear 'club' in almost half a century."

It is totally acceptable that those three countries, especially Israel, rejected the big powers demand but not North Korea, which, in fact, did sign on in 1985. North Korea and the U.S. made the "Framework Agreement" in 1994. North Korea promised it would not conduct a nuclear energy program in exchange for obtaining two light-water nuclear reactors from the U.S., which also agreed to recognize its existence, officially end the war, and lift it from its terrorism list.

North Korea kept its bargain. The U.S. did not—the same scenario we have seen with the Soviet Union (since Russia), and hundreds more agreements the U.S. signs and ignores.

We must remember that not only did the U.S. refuse to recognize the North Korean government neither did South Korea or Japan, under orders. In the Korean War nearly one-third of the Koreans in the north were murdered by the crazy generals MacArthur and LeMay. MacArthur was so crazy he planned to invade China with the nuclear bomb. (Chapter 11).

In 2000, President Bush II made matters worse by declaring North Korea part of his "Axis of Evil", a "rogue regime against which the US should be prepared to use force". That sounds all too familiar to Koreans. So, in 2002, they began building what became their first bomb in 2006. By 2017, they had tested six. Koreans know they can't win a war against the greatest military power in history, but they are determined to at least let it know that it too would be damaged if it warred on them.

South Korea and Japan considered acquiring nuclear weapons, while the new U.S. president prepared to scrap the landmark deal with Iran that assured it wouldn't have a nuclear bomb. Trump then warned "rocket man" that he would unleash "fire, fury and frankly power, the likes of which this world has never seen before."

North Korea borders on both China and Russia, two of few countries that have extensive trade relations with it. They all feel the threat from Pentagon-Langley-White House, and Russia and China leaders seek to calm President Kim Jong-un down. In September 2017, they told him they had to make some sanctions against his country, hoping he would realize that his rhetoric is too provocative, no matter how understandable it may be, and hoping also to calm the other "rocket man" down.

At the 9th summit of the five BRICS countries, China President Xi Jinping encouraged them all (China and Russia plus Brazil, India and South Africa) to take on a more proactive role in mediating geopolitical disputes. Their combined populations of 3.6 billon account for 41% of the world; combined GDP of $16.6 trillion is 22% of the gross world product. They could have more clout.

China and Russia cut back half its petroleum products to North Korea, ended its textile imports, stopped hiring more of its workers, and applied a few other restrictions. But that wasn't enough for the Yankees. You offer a hand, they take your arm. They demanded that Putin stop all oil and gas exports. President Putin refused to comply. Like other peace-minded Russians (f.ex. Yuri Gagarin and Vasili Arkhipov), he stated to do so would hurt ordinary people by disrupting hospitals and other necessary facilities and needs. Instead Putin offered his skills to mediate between presidents Kim Jong-un and Donald Trump. Guess what the United States Establishment's reply was.

PUTIN SPEAKS

Despite all the evidence to the contrary abut Russian "hacking" and intrusion in U.S. society, the Congress imposed sanctions against Russia for its "interference", "its" war in Syria, and "taking" Crimea. Trump felt the need to sign these sanctions into law, August 2017, which means he cannot end the sanctions without Congressional approval. The U.S. also imposed a travel ban on some Russians, embargoed export of all weaponry and some technology, especially related to energy, and demanded that EU countries follow suit by prohibiting energy deals with Russia or "face the consequences"—the same attitude it has had with countries trading with Cuba. Several EU countries objected especially Germany, Austria and France, and EU President Jean Claude Juncker. They don't want to be treated like "America's backyard".

President Putin responded by kicking out 755 U.S. diplomats, many of whom were CIA officials in grandmother nightgowns, and stopped importing some EU food stuff. Trump then closed three Russian consulates, and required RT television station broadcasting in English in the U.S. to register as a foreign agent. Russia did the same to U.S. media networks and required them to reveal how they are financed.

Oliver Stone: "Russia has been accused of enormous treachery now…It makes it impossible to correct relations with Russia. Very difficult for Mr. Trump if indeed he intends to do so, to reset relations."

VP: "*…any talk about our influencing the outcome of the election in the United States, all these are lies. But we see that this campaign of manipulating the information has a number of goals. First, they are trying to undermine the legitimacy of President Trump. Second, they are trying to create conditions that preclude us from normalizing our relations with the U.S. Third, they want to create additional weapons to wage an internal political war. And the Russia-US relations in this context are a mere instrument, a weapon in the internal political fight in the U.S.*"

"*You see, it's internal politicking inside the United States and we do not want to get mired in that…They are only going to use our refutations in order to continue this war using new instruments. We know all their tricks.*" (The Putin Interviews pg. 213-4)

On Ukraine 2014, Putin says: "*We did everything to achieve a political settlement. But they had to give support to this unconstitutional seizure of power. I still wonder why they had to do that. Incidentally, that was a first step to further destabilization of the country.*"

OS: "You have to tell this story; you have to somehow get your raw intelligence into the system."

VP: "*You see, that's quite impossible, because this point of view that we present is ignored by the whole media. And if it's ignored, not on equal footing with the other perspectives, then almost no one hears it. So a narrative is being constructed of some evil Russia…*"

OS: "—I wouldn't give up on that, I wouldn't give up. You have to fight back. And you're doing a great job but more, better."

VP: "*I'll bear that in mind, but I think this critique is justified.*" (pg. 243-4)

A young Russian supporter of President Putin who has his own blog, Pavel Shipilin, gives Westerners a good picture of how the president is viewed by most of his countrymen. These are excerpts from his May 28, 2017 piece, "Russia Won't Be Treaded On—That's The Problem":

"Whatever they say, Russia is no longer a monster behind an iron curtain. Our image changed, while Western propagandists still see themselves as cold war soldiers, but the opposite effect…"

"Things have gone so far that they can't be changed without revolutions."

"To Europeans, Russia's resistance to the new world order often looks like the desperation of a knight who stands alone on the battlefield against the enemy. To the surprise of the spectators, he begins to win because he is a skillful fighter who knows how to use a sword."

"The main mistake of global players is…accusing us either of nonexistent sins or of things they are guilty of themselves. As a result, the number of Russian allies among their populations is slowly growing. It's clear to many people that these are prewar times. The enemy will have to say it like it is: we don't like Russia because it dares to put spokes in the wheels of our main goal, which is the total power of transnational corporations. Propaganda clichés about democracy are out-of-date."

"There will not be a global war because the movers and shakers want to live, not to sacrifice themselves for their companies. They will try to exhaust us with local conflicts in border-states, which we will be trying to avoid.

"I wish we would remain standing for at least twenty years, until Europeans grew into a revolt: against their corrupt presidents, against a powerless EU that was imposed on them instead of sovereignty, against the real landlords of the continent. Perhaps everything will be all right in the end." (http://russia-insider.com/en/politics/west-stupidly-preparing-previous-cold-war/ri14641; http://www.fort-russ.com/2016/07/pavel-shipilin-fifa-is-next.html)

The bear is tired of being pecked by the eagle. Russia is preparing for what hopefully is not the inevitable. I have cited many U.S. Establishment diplomatic, military and intelligence voices throughout this writing indicating that the military-industrial-deep state complex has gone berserk in its spiraling grab after endless profits made from war."'Russian business should be prepared to switch to production to military needs at any time', said Vladimir Putin on Wednesday. The Russian president was speaking at a conference of military leaders in Sochi," wrote *The Independent*, November 22, 2017 http://www.independent.co.uk/news/world/europe/vladimir-putin-russia-business-war-production-sochi-military-talks-a8069951.html

"'The ability of our economy to increase military production and services at a given time is one of the most important aspects of military security,'" Mr. Putin said. "'To this end, all strategic, and simply large-scale enterprise should be ready, regardless of ownership.'"

The day before, Putin said, "Our army and navy need to have the very best equipment — better than foreign equivalents," "The Independent" quoted him. "'If we want to win, we have to be better.'"

Despite this emphasis on military preparations, the next two year forecast cut backs military expenditures from 3.3 percent to 2.8 percent of the GDP. But that seems to frighten the West anyway, according to *The Independent*, and the West increases its military funding.

"Though that budget remains less than 30 per cent of the combined Nato budget in Europe, many countries are increasing their military spending in response to the 'The Russian Threat'. Nato military command has also been restructured—it says in response to Russian cyber and military threats."

But what Vladimir Putin would rather do than build up a military defense is to play piano and sing "Blueberry Hill" with other Fat Cats, his American partners as he refers to them. See him play and sing: https://www.youtube.com/watch?v=IV4IjHz2yIo .

CHAPTER 18
United States of America Military Empire

SUBJECTS
U.S. Wars & Military Interventions
Overthrowing Governments (bombings, assassinations, suppress movements, pervert elections)
Military Budgets
Armaments
Global Weapons Industry
Military Bases
Military Pollution
CIA Torture/Drugs

Onward, Christian soldiers, marching as to war,
With the cross of Jesus going on before.
Christ, the royal Master, leads against the foe;
Forward into battle see His banners go!

REFRAIN:
Onward, Christian soldiers, marching as to war,
With the cross of Jesus going on before.

At the sign of triumph Satan's host doth flee;
On then, Christian soldiers, on to victory!
Hell's foundations quiver at the shout of praise;
Brothers, lift your voices, loud your anthems raise.
Like a mighty army moves the church of God;
Brothers, we are treading where the saints have trod.

We are not divided, all one body we,
One in hope and doctrine, one in charity...
Onward then, ye people, join our happy throng,
Blend with ours your voices in the triumph song.
Glory, laud, and honor unto Christ the King,
This through countless ages men and angels sing.

I WAS BROUGHT UP in a split family, back and forth—mother submissive to religion, father agnostic loyalist soldier for America the Great, grandmother "ignorance is bliss" advocate. Onward Christian Soldiers fit in with their understanding of the American Dream. My father had been in Asia during the Second World War and decided to make the Army and then the Air Force his career.

We were stationed in Recife, Brazil when President Getúlio Vargas shot himself, on August 24, 1954. In a suicide note, the "father of the poor", as many called Vargas, wrote that he sought to "protect the national interests" against U.S. wishes. He had been elected president twice (1930s and 1950s), and seized power as dictator (1937-45). His politics were anti-communist and nationalist.

When my father came home the day Vargas killed himself he was livid. I recall him cussing the president for being ungrateful to the United States which had helped Brazil so much. Apparently President Vargas thought that the U.S. dictated too much. A decade later, on April 1, 1964, the U.S. fully backed a military coup—which President Kennedy had approved in 1962 as a possibility—with warships against the democratically elected Joao Goulart, who had infuriated national generals and capitalists, and their United States counterparts for initiating FDR-type reforms. The military ruled repressively until 1985.

Our family returned from Brazil in 1955 and the next year I joined the Air Force to fight "commies." I was a senior in High School when my father and I listened to radio news about Russia invading Hungary. My father had to sign permission for me to join as I was just 17. Soon, I was off to Lackland Texas Air Force base for training to fight the Communists: Onward Christian soldier was I marching as to war with the cross of Jesus going on before.

Unfortunately for my father, I began to wake up when I was stationed in Japan, about which I referred to in chapter four. Upon discharge, in

1960, I attended college in Los Angeles and soon joined the new free speech student movement followed by anti-war and anti-racism activism.

The second to last time I saw my father we attended a baseball game. At the beginning, the national anthem Star Spangled Banner was played. I refused to stand up to spite its jingoism and racism—"the land of the free", which when written, in 1814, meant only whites. My father never forgave me for that, and in 1968 after a short last visit he sent me a two-line letter "divorcing" me. My name was banned from his house and there was no communication for the next 27 years when he died.

STAR SPANGLED BANNER
O say can you see, by the dawn's early light,
What so proudly we hail'd at the twilight's last gleaming, Whose broad stripes and bright stars through the perilous fight
O'er the ramparts we watch'd were so gallantly streaming? And the rocket's red glare, the bomb bursting in air,
Gave proof through the night that our flag was still there,
O say does that star-spangled banner yet wave
O'er the land of the free and the home of the brave?

On the shore dimly seen through the mists of the deep
Where the foe's haughty host in dread silence reposes,
What is that which the breeze, o'er the towering steep,
As it fitfully blows, half conceals, half discloses?
Now it catches the gleam of the morning's first beam,
In full glory reflected now shines in the stream,
'Tis the star-spangled banner - O long may it wave
O'er the land of the free and the home of the brave!

And where is that band who so vauntingly swore,
That the havoc of war and the battle's confusion
A home and a Country should leave us no more?
Their blood has wash'd out their foul footstep's pollution.
No refuge could save the hireling and slave
From the terror of flight or the gloom of the grave,
And the star-spangled banner in triumph doth wave
O'er the land of the free and the home of the brave.

O thus be it ever when freemen shall stand
Between their lov'd home and the war's desolation!
Blest with vict'ry and peace may the heav'n rescued land Praise the power that hath made and preserv'd us a nation! Then conquer we must, when our cause it is just,
And this be our motto - "In God is our trust,"
And the star-spangled banner in triumph shall wave
O'er the land of the free and the home of the brave.

What follows is a long summary of U.S. aggression which could easily be an encyclopedia, and explains why father-son parted ways.

U.S. WARS AND MILITARY INTERVENTIONS

Two centuries+ of existence. Two centuries+ of nearly constant wars with sporadic periods of not invading others. For a generation now the United States has forced upon the world the Permanent War Age. The goal is simple: world domination! The American Dream fulfilled.

Most U.S. white Americans believe they are the best, the strongest, the bravest, owners of the Land of Opportunity. If war is necessary (profitable) to maintain that predominance, so be it—although since the 2008 capital-created economic crisis, there are some cracks in that wall.

Granted, there have been wars ever since the idea of private property took root. Wars stem from the first sedentary "civilizations" about 14,000 years ago in Eastern Mediterranean and Mesopotamia. Wars really got going, though, when empires were forged, the first being Akkadia 4400 years ago.

While emperors sought territorial expansion and control over socio-political entities, modern imperialism concentrates on economic domination without a permanent military presence, until a military intervention is deemed necessary to put down domestic unrest or other foreign influence.

For the last generation since the fall of state socialism in the Soviet Union and Eastern Europe, the U.S. has stood as the world's sole superpower. The so-called Cold War ended then but wars continue. The militarization of the world marches hand in hand with globalization extending even into outer space. The United States gets away with its aggressive wars by simply declaring them necessary to stop terrorism, especially in oil rich Middle East excepting its terrorist friends in Israel and Saudi Arabia/Gulf States.

This self-righteous excuse for warring is rationalized by the propitious attacks on September 11, 2001. No matter that almost all of those allegedly identified terrorists were Saudi Arabians—none were from Afghanistan or Iraq—the Pentagon and Langley warriors unleashed patriotic murder and torture in Afghanistan and Iraq, soon extending to other Middle Eastern and African countries where challengers lurk, and the use of Cuban territory at Guantánamo naval base for torture.

"The War-On-Terror" script was written just a year before. It is aimed at grabbing all oil and gas fuel and other raw materials anywhere it can. The business warlord promoters, who wrote the script "to promote American global leadership", had founded the right-wing think tank, Project for a New American Century (PNAC), in 1997. In September 2000, the PNAC published its imperial report, "Rebuilding America's Defenses: Strategies, Forces, and Resources for a New Century". [http://templatelab.com/rebuilding-americas-defenses/] They knew it would be unpopular so they predicted that, in order for it to be accepted by sufficient numbers, a tragedy on the scale of Pearl Harbor would have to occur.

Lo and behold! September 11, 2001 was the best of days for the militarists, the weapons, oil, finance, and construction industries. And it fortified the new "service" branch of professional paramilitary mercenaries into a large international killing industry. Now that the stage was set, the Permanent War Age had to be sold. We good humans must be fearful of the terrorists, and thus we passively or actively support the wars the various U.S. governments render us, which also means we must accept their terror laws, the demise of civil and labor rights we fought for and won.

> *"When a state is committed to such policies, it must somehow find a way to divert the population, to keep them from seeing what's happening around them. There are not many ways to do this. The standard ones are to inspire fear of terrible enemies about to overwhelm us, and awe for our grand leaders who rescue us from disaster in the nick of time," so asserted Noam Chomsky even before 9/11, in his book,* What Uncle Sam Really Wants *(Odonian Press, 1992).*

The September 13, 2001 edition of the *Philadelphia Inquirer* spoke to those fears aroused on 9/11 with the headline: "Give War a Chance," a vile mockery of our "give peace a chance" vision.

George Bush declared "War On Terror", on October 7. He granted military forces unlimited money, weapons and resources. The CIA got *ten times* the previous amount of money for bribes and payments to mercenaries and torturers. "Preventative" war was approved with new weapons of mass destruction weapons including nuclear and bacteriological weapons.

PNAC spokesmen took up many important posts in the Bush regime—Donald Rumsfeld, Paul Wolfowitz, William Kristol, Elliott Abrahams, John Bolton, Richard Perle, John Ashcroft. Richard Cheney, Halliburton's former CEO, took the decisive reins as vice-president. They succeeded in ramming through the Patriotic Act. People can now be arrested and detained indefinitely without a judge's approval or even a trial. A police state is in place.

Ten days after the terror attacks in New York and Pentagon, former NATO Commander, U.S. General Wesley Clark, said that the Bush regime had plans to invade several of 40 countries it listed as "rogue states". Top of the list were: Afghanistan, Iraq, Libya, Syria, Lebanon, Somalia, Sudan and Iran. What they had in common was oil—or as in the case of Afghanistan, access to oil—and banks not under the multinational corporation control of the Banking International Settlement (BIS) rules that benefit private capital interests. One of the empire's fears, for example, was that Saddam Hussein had agreed with France President Jacques Chirac to switch from dollars to Euros in oil trading. Six months later oil dollar-rich Bush invaded Iraq.

Despite initial hesitancy from several European governments, the Bush regime succeeded in drawing nearly all of Europe, including most Social Democrats and Socialists, into its wars. NATO's constitution had been limited to defense but was remade to allow for aggressive warring in any area of the world.

The big lie of 9/11 worked. It was the answer to Secretary of State Collin Powell's worry that the U.S. had no more enemies. With the terror attack, the United States Military Empire concocted its next enemy: Muslim terrorists. The fact that the destroyed buildings in New York could not have collapsed the way the government told us, the fact that a huge passenger aircraft could not have made only such a small hole in the Pentagon was simply to be denied as "conspiracy buff stuff". But how is it that the entire defense system fell asleep that day? There is hard and soft evidence that proves the United States government lied to us about that day, and there is ample material to point a finger at the same government, and its comrade-in-arms Zionist Israel, as at least complicit in the whole bloody nightmare.

While the Bush government was held down to two wars at a time, the Barak Obama regime stepped up the ante with seven: adding Pakistan, Yemen, Uganda, Somalia and Libya. Syrian terrorist fundamentalists also received (receive) U.S. and allied political and material support.

I excerpt parts of just one article to spark reader interest to search further into the true meaning of 9/11 to "legitimize" U.S. government's permanent war euphoria. I could choose Dr. Paul Craig Roberts, "9/11 After 13 Years".

His credentials within the Establishment make his judgments about what happened and why on September 11 all the more worthy of taking seriously. See his website here: https://www.paulcraigroberts.org/. The article is here: http://dissidentvoice.org/2014/09/911-after-13-years/#more-55657.

"The tragedy of September 11, 2001, goes far beyond the deaths of those who died in the towers and the deaths of fire fighters and first responders who succumbed to illnesses caused by inhalation of toxic dust. For thirteen years a new generation of Americans has been born into the 9/11 myth that has been used to create the American warfare/police state.

"The corrupt Bush and Obama regimes used 9/11 to kill, maim, dispossess and displace millions of Muslims in seven countries, none of whom had anything whatsoever to do with 9/11.

"A generation of Americans has been born into distain and distrust of Muslims.

"A generation of Americans has been born into a police state in which privacy and constitutional protections no longer exist.

"A generation of Americans has been born into continuous warfare while needs of citizens go unmet.

"A generation of Americans has been born into a society in which truth is replaced with the endless repetition of falsehoods.

"According to the official story, on September 11, 2001, the vaunted National Security State of the World's Only Superpower was defeated by a few young Saudi Arabians armed only with box cutters. The American National Security State proved to be totally helpless and was dealt the greatest humiliation ever inflicted on any country claiming to be a power.

"That day no aspect of the National Security State worked. Everything failed.

"The US Air Force for the first time in its history could not get interceptor jet fighters into the air.

"The National Security Council failed.

"All sixteen US intelligence agencies failed as did those of America's NATO and Israeli allies.

"Air Traffic Control failed.

"Airport Security failed four times at the same moment on the same day. The probability of such a failure is zero."

"Watching the twin towers and WTC 7 come down, it was obvious to me that the buildings were not falling down as a result of structural damage. When it became clear that the White House had blocked an independent investigation of the only three steel skyscrapers in world history to collapse as a result of low temperature office fires, it was apparent that there was a cover up."

"Osama bin Laden, a CIA asset dying of renal failure, was blamed despite his explicit denial. For the next ten years Osama bin Laden was the bogyman that provided the excuse for Washington to kill countless numbers of Muslims. Then suddenly on May 2, 2011, Obama claimed that US Navy SEALs had killed bin Laden in Pakistan. Eyewitnesses on the scene contradicted the White House's story. Osama bin Laden became the only human in history to survive renal failure for ten years. There was no dialysis machine in what was said to be bin Laden's hideaway. The numerous obituaries of bin Laden's death in December 2001 went down the memory hole. And the SEAL team died a few weeks later in a mysterious helicopter crash in Afghanistan. The thousands of sailors on the aircraft carrier from which bin Laden was said to have been dumped into the Indian Ocean wrote home that no such burial took place."

"The 9/11 lie has persisted for 13 years. Millions of Muslims have paid

for this lie with their lives, the destruction of their families, and with their dislocation. Most Americans remain comfortable with the fact that their government has destroyed in whole or part seven countries based on a lie Washington told to cover up an inside job that launched the crazed neoconservatives' drive for Washington's World Empire."

The Bush regime invaded the nearly defenceless Afghanistan government and beat it to surrender within two months. Taleban went underground but did not pick up their weapons again for a long time. CIA assets within the U.S. military backed Northern Alliance of several war lords and fundamentalist Islamists started the insurgency. CIA sponsored murders of top leaders of the Noorzai and Ishaqzai tribes forced surviving leaders to Pakistan where they prepared for counter-attacks. It was a war the CIA/Pentagon/ Bush government begged for.

Douglas Valentine is perhaps the only writer who was lucky enough to interview many of the CIA murderers from the Phoenix project and live to write about it. He has continued to trace CIA crimes. He cites from Anand Gopal's book (*No Good Men Among the Living*), who also is unique in that he lived with Taleban groups who allowed him to interview them perhaps because he could speak their language and they felt he would report their point of view objectively.

"The American public is largely unaware that the Taliban laid down its arms after the American invasion in 2001, and that the Afghan people took up arms only after CIA installed [Gul Agha] Sherzai in Kabul. In league with the Karzai brothers, Sherzai supplied the CIA with a network of informants that targeted their business rivals, not the Taliban [who had smashed the opium trade when in power]...As a result of Sherzai's friendly tips, the CIA methodically tortured and killed Afghanistan's most revered leaders in a series of Phoenix-style [Vietnam War murder strategy] raids that radicalized the Afghan people." (1)

Gopal's book won the 2015 Ridenhour Prize for demonstrating "why the United States' emphasis on counterterrorism at the expense of nation-building and reconciliation inadvertently led to the Taliban's resurgence after 2001." His 2010 article, "America's Secret Afghan Prisons" run by the Joint Special Operations Command (a body of all the military branches) is also a must read. (http://www.webcitation.org/query?url=http%3A%2F%2Fwww.thenation.com%2Fdoc%2F20100215%2Fgopal_audio&date=2010-02-17)

These two books written by on-the-scene US American citizens seeking the truth should be enough information and evidence to put all U.S. military careerists and CIA professional murderers behind bars or, better yet, picking cotton. Some of the torture committed by these patriots has been exposed, such as the torture chambers at Guantánamo and Abu Ghraib, Iraq, and their Rendition, Detention and Interrogation (RDI) program. This proxy torturing "program" takes captured persons the CIA wants tortured by others than themselves and "renders" them to allies in the Middle East and Eastern Europe where their friends do the dirty deed. Ironically, Syria and Iraq were such rendition places before the U.S. decided to get rid of Saddam and try to do the same with Assad.

Despite the fact that some of these crimes have been exposed, it hasn't stopped them from continuing to use the most painful and "inhumane" methods to torture and kill people. Valentine tells us here one of the reasons why they can get away with it:

"*American's militant leaders used 9/11 to recruit and motivate a new generation of special operations forces…to invade private homes at midnight on snatch and snuff missions. Nowhere, in any Establishment media outlet, is it ever mentioned that our political and military leaders did this because they wanted to seize Afghanistan and use it to establish a colony in a strategic location near Russia and China*" [and Iran]. (*The CIA as Organized Crime*, p. 97)

"*In Afghanistan, CIA officers manage the drug trade from their hammocks in the shade. Opium production has soared since they purchased the government in 2001. They watch in amusement as addiction rates soar among young people whose parents have been killed and whose minds have been damaged by 15 years of US aggression. They don't care that the drugs reach America's inner cities. CIA officers have an accommodation with the protected Afghan warlords who convert opium into heroin and sell it to the Russian mob. It's no different than cops working with the Mafia in America; it's accommodation with an enemy that ensures the political security of the ruling class.*"

"Afghanistan is a means to get at Russia, similar to how Nixon played the China Card in Vietnam."

"The Afghan people hate the Americans more and more, year after year. And that makes the CIA happy, in so far as it spells protracted war and increased profits for its sponsors in the arms industry. Afghan anger means more resistance...a neat pretext for the eternal military occupation of a disposable nation strategically located near Russia and China.

"The Taleban will never surrender and, for the CIA, that means victory in Afghanistan. But it also means spiritual defeat for America, as it descends ever further into the black hole of self-deception, militarism, and covert operations." (pages 125-8)

Valentine's chapter, "How the CIA Commandeered the Drug Enforcement Administration" is a must read to see how the CIA—from the early days of the Vietnam War, Iran-Contragate, and into the current wars in the Middle East—has dealt big time with drugs. Drugs bring in unaccountable income while it keeps a lot of people from rebelling, and it makes lots of problems for the leaders and states that the CIA wants to destroy. They use drugs in U.S. ghettos to keep black people from organizing rebellions, too.

"In 1976, Congresswoman Bella Abzug submitted questions to [President] Ford's CIA director, George H.W. Bush, about the CIA's role in international drug trafficking. Bush's response was to cite a 1954 agreement with the Justice Department that gave the CIA the right to block prosecution and keep its crimes secret in the name of national security. In its final report, the Abzug Committee wryly noted: 'It was ironic that the CIA should be given responsibility of narcotic intelligence, particularly since they are supporting the prime movers.'" (page 197). (https://www.bibliotecapleyades.net/sociopolitica/sociopol_cia33.htm https://www.muckrock.com/news/archives/2017/may/25/abzugs-distrust/)

Besides Russia, we see the same mechanism working with the other two bordering nations to Afghanistan, China and Iran. It is in CIA interests to spread drug addiction, AIDs disease through dirty needles, and chaos—geopolitics for American World Domination. Bush regime promoters called it, Project for the New American Century (PNAC).

Caleb Maupin's article, "Why is the USA in Afghanistan? An Answer to the Big Question", is helpful to understand the policy.

"US operations in Afghanistan have almost always been related to Russia. At the time of the Russian Revolution, Central Asia was dominated by the British Empire. The British had largely de-forested Afghanistan, and had already introduced the scourge of heroin. The Bolsheviks happily embraced the government of Habbibula Khan, the Emir of Afghanistan who had stood up to the British, and kept the country neutral in the First World War. In 1919 the Afghan ambassador told Lenin, 'I proffer you a friendly hand and hope that you will help the whole of the East to free itself from the yoke of European imperialism'". (http://www.greanvillepost.com/2017/09/25/why-is-the-usa-in-afghanistan-an-answer-to-the-big-question/)

Keeping Afghanistan unstable is certainly causing lots of problems for Russia, and its ally governments in Central Asia face a growing problem of Wahabbi extremism. The internal conflict in Chechnya had to do with "CIA strategy of Islamic terrorism and heroin in Afghanistan" where the "USA and Saudi Arabia had already been supporting Islamic Extremists," sell heroin and commit acts of terrorism intended to harm the Soviet government, wrote Maupin.

Statistics on how much heroin and HIV infection there was in the Soviet Union before 1990 is hard to nail down. Reading through several sources, my conclusion is that there was very little until the latter years of the Soviet Union engagement in the war in Afghanistan. While the Communist-led government did what it could to wipe out the poppy plant, some remained and got turned into heroin and some Soviet troops used it. I found a figure of 100 known cases of AIDS in Russia in 1989, but it is not definitive.

With the CIA now in control of much of the heroin traffic—Afghanistan now produces over 90% of the world's heroin—more comes directly in to Russia, and former Republics of Tajikistan, Kyrgyzstan, and Kazakhstan, plus Chechnya.

Ninety thousand Russians died of overdoses of the 1.5 million known heroin addicts as of 2015. There are another five to six million users of other drugs. Perhaps as many as one million people have AIDS due to intravenous drug use with dirty needles and unsafe sex.

The U.S.'s president in Afghanistan, Hamid Karzai, has learned that his former master is not interested in shaping a better society for his people. On April 19, 2017, he told the U.S. military-connected Voice of America, of all places:

"'After it [the U.S.] dropped the bomb on Afghanistan, it did not eliminate Daesh,' Karzai said, referring to last week's 'mother of all bombs [MOAB]' attack against Islamic State."

"'I consider Daesh their tool,' Karzai told VOA's Afghan service in an exclusive interview in Kabul, using the Arabic acronym for IS. 'I do not differentiate at all between Daesh and America.'"(https://www.voanews.com/a/former-afghan-president-hamid-karzai-callms-islamic-state-tool-us/3817463.html)

Karzai said that the U.S. is not sincere in bringing peace in the country. "'A conference was recently convened in Moscow. Why didn't America participate in it?' Karzai asked. 'Why did it ask the Afghan government to send a low-level delegation to the conference?'"

In this VOA interview, Karzai dismissed criticism of Moscow's ties with the Taliban. Karzai has become closer to Russia since leaving office. He a 2015 visit to Moscow to meet President Putin, he said that he supported the "annexation of Crimea".

Karzai speaks of having cordial relations with President Putin whom, he said is trying to negotiate for peace in Afghanistan, and that he talks with Taliban leaders about moving towards peace. But the U.S. doesn't wish to hear any of that.

Heroin politics works in Iran too, so well that a 2006 estimate contended that eight percent of Iranians are addicted, and every year another 130,000 or more become so.

"Iran's revolutionary guards are constantly working to stop narcotics from flowing over the Afghan border. The poppy fields of Afghanistan… have destroyed the lives of literally millions of Iranians," wrote Maupin.

The British Empire invaded China twice in the 19th century (Opium Wars) to force governments to allow the poppy seed for commercial profit purposes. The UK with the Yankees, Japan, Russia and four other allies intervened during the 1899-1901 Boxer Rebellion. The Boxers, whom Mark Twain called "patriots" and wished them "success", rose up against foreign imperialism, with its Christian chauvinist missionaries and heroin. Boxers lynched drug dealers, and sought to promote traditional Chinese culture. When the Qing imperial court, led by Empress Dowager Cixi, joined them, 60,000 troops and 54 ships from eight invading countries warred against them. They were able to topple the rebels and the government and occupied much of China for a year or more—murdering, raping and plundering wantonly.

"The 20th century in China has largely been a story of struggling to break free from foreign domination, drug addiction, and poverty, and restore itself as global power," wrote Maupin."

"The Chinese government works relentlessly to make sure that heroin is never imported into the country. The majority of those who receive the death penalty in China are somehow related to drug smuggling."

Mao is credited with having eradicated heroin and most opium. Today there is little of either but some opium poppy grows in a few northwest provinces but is not exported.

China's historically Islamic region, Xianjing, has been the site of anti-government terrorism in recent decades. Not surprisingly, this region also borders Afghanistan. Some of China's Islamic Uiygir minority have sworn allegiance to IS and gone to Syria to fight the Baathist government.

"These three Eurasian countries serve as bastions of stability, and more than that, they are competitors with Wall Street. Russia sells oil and natural gas on the international markets. Every barrel of oil sold by Russia, is a barrel of oil that could have been sold by a US or British oil company. Iran is also an oil exporter, and it has recently joined the natural gas trade.

"While China does not have very much domestic oil, it is starting to innovate natural gas extraction, and it produces steel, copper, and aluminum more than any other country on earth. Cell phones produced by Huwai, the state controlled telecommunications manufacturer, are sold across the world. A stable China is also a competitor," Maupin explains.

The permanent war in Afghanistan has other advantages as well. There is the incentive of a gas pipeline that perks U.S. interest in controlling Afghanistan. Craig Murray, former British Ambassador to Uzbekistan, said it succinctly:

"Almost everything you see about Afghanistan is a cover for the fact that the actual motive is the pipeline they wish to build over Afghanistan to bring out Uzbek and Turkmen natural gas which together is valued at up to $10 trillion." For telling this truth he was denied a U.S. visa. (2)

Furthermore, in 2010, it was discovered that Afghanistan has several rare earth minerals, but they have not yet been tapped. All the more evidence that the key reason for the U.S. war and occupation of the country is mainly to subvert and, hopefully, overthrow the stable governments of its neighbors: Russia, Iran China. The oil pipeline and minerals are there for future exploitation once the three countries fall under U.S. military-political domination, so they hope.

How long can the U.S. hang onto Afghanistan and harass its neighbors who are not submissive to the Military Empire? If the chief prosecutor of the International Criminal Court, Fatou Bensouda, gets her way the aggressor would be put on trial, at least, for war crimes it commits there.

"The chief prosecutor of the international criminal court is seeking approval to investigate allegations of war crimes in Afghanistan, including possible torture by US forces and the CIA.

"If authorized, the investigation would also look at crimes allegedly committed by armed opposition groups, such as the Taliban, and Afghan government forces." (https://www.theguardian.com/world/2017/nov/03/war-crimes-prosecutor-seeks-investigation-into-afghan-conflict-icc-us-force-cia-taliban)

This is unprecedented for the ICC. Since its founding, in 2002, it has tried or sought to try 39 individuals, all Africans, and never a state. The chances are, however, it won't succeed, in part because the goliath will not present itself before any court nor honor their decisions.

Bill Clinton signed the Rome treaty that established the ICC, but his successor George W Bush renounced the signature, arguing that Americans would be unfairly prosecuted for political reasons.

Although the US is not a member of the court, "Americans could still potentially face prosecution if they commit crimes within its jurisdiction in a country that is a member, such as Afghanistan, and are not prosecuted at home," The Guardian reporters concluded.

President George Bush, and seven of his leading cohorts, were, in fact, symbolically tried for war crimes and convicted in a Malaysian War Crimes Commission trial in May 2012. Retired Prime Minister Mahathir Mohamad took this initiative.

The prosecutor was international law professor Frances Boyle, a lawyer who represents many indigenous and oppressed peoples both in courts of law and International People's Tribunals, such as this one. He is also an activist against wars and for human rights and self-determination.

This was the first conviction of its kind in the world. Transcripts were sent to the United Nations and Security Council.

To be able to understand how the U.S. got the way it is today—the world's dominating war power—we must look at its two hundred year history.

MILITARY IMPERIAL HISTORY

We have earlier been introduced to "high class muscle-man for Big Business", General Smedley Butler. My research discovered many more sources about the Military Empire: U.S. government and military departments, the Congress, historians, journalists, and former empire warriors. Many researchers have written formidable books on the subject, some of them are in my bibliography. Listing names and figures is boring reading but bear with me because these facts are startling.

The first war began even before the United States gained nationhood. While still a British colony, white European colonists warred against indigenous "Indians", in order to take over the lands that they simply used. Formal warring began in 1775 with the declared Chickamauga War. The "Indian wars" lasted for a century. Estimates are that before Europeans came there were between two and seven million natives. The 1900 census reported 250,000 survivors incarcerated on "reservations".

This war, and those to come against Latin Americans, was part of "Manifest Destiny", ordained to "expand territory", "to extend and enhance political, social and economic influences".

The "Monroe Doctrine" legalized: Hands off America's backyard, Latin America. After World War II, and especially after September 11, 2001, Manifest Destiny extended to the entire globe.

War was waged in 1798-1800 against France over its colonies in the Caribbean. Then it was Britain's turn in 1812, in which both sides contested territory. The United States stole half of Mexico in 1846-8—Texas, California, New Mexico, Colorado, Utah, Nevada and Wyoming.

Of the thousands of times that U.S. military force has been deployed, many countries have been subjected several times. Cuba has been attacked 12 times since 1814; Nicaragua 12 times since 1853; Panama on 13 occasions since 1856. Although Latin America has been the most targeted, China has been attacked 30 times from 1843 "gunboat diplomacy" to 1999 when the U.S. bombed its embassy in Yugoslavia.

Between 1869 and 1897, *the U.S. sent war ships with orders to intervene in Latin American harbors 5,980 times—one ship every two days over three decades*. Hundreds of these landings resulted in the murders of local workers on strike and insurgents against repressive local governments. (3)

In a 2008 report to Congress, 330 military interventions were detailed: 167 interventions from 1798 to 1941, plus 163 interventions from 1945 to 2008. Since then wars against or within Pakistan, Libya, Somalia, Yemen and Uganda must be added, totaling 335. All these wars were/are aggressive. Both world wars in the 20th century are not included since they were defensive wars. (4)

After World War Two, the United States economy was booming and its territory unscathed unlike all of Europe, China, Korea and Japan. Its tycoons and politicians seized the perfect opportunity to strive for world domination. State Department chief for national security planning, George Kennan, expressed this succinctly in the secret Policy Planning Study of 1948:

> *"...We have about 50% of the world's wealth but only 6.3% of its population. This disparity is particularly great between ourselves and the peoples of Asia. In this situation, we cannot fail to be the object of envy and resentment. Our real task in the coming period is to devise a pattern of relationships which will permit us to maintain this position of disparity without positive detriment to our national security. To do so, we will have to dispense with all sentimentality and day-dreaming; and our attention will have to be concentrated everywhere on our immediate national objectives. We need not deceive ourselves that we can afford today the luxury of altruism and world-benefaction."*
>
> *"In the face of this situation [Asiatic problems among the peoples themselves, overpopulation, lack of food, and Moscow's luring influence. Ed. note] we would be better off to dispense*

> *now with a number of the concepts which have underlined our thinking with regard to the Far East. We should dispense with the aspiration to 'be liked' or to be regarded as the repository of a high-minded international altruism. We should stop putting ourselves in the position of being our brothers' keeper and refrain from offering moral and ideological advice. We should cease to talk about vague and—for the Far East—unreal objectives such as human rights, the raising of the living standards, and democratization. The day is not far off when we are going to have to deal in straight power concepts. The less we are then hampered by idealistic slogans, the better."* (5)

Kennan was considered to be "liberal" just as were John Kennedy, Bill Clinton and Barak Obama.

U.S. military bases on foreign soil were used 200 times between 1945 and 1991 to intervene in third world countries. Millions were killed during the alleged Cold War period. (6)

Several analysts add to the above aggressions the use of military power as successful threats to force governments to do what the U.S. demands without the use of bullets. This has happened at least 218 times just between January 1946 and January 1976. (7)

The U.S. has conducted violent military interventions/wars 535 times—combining direct military attacks and lesser military interventions—between 1798 and the present; 368 of these attacks occurred since World War 11 (8) in 60 countries. (9)

Of these invaded countries *the U.S. bombarded 30 nations* between the Second World War and 2000. (10). Since 2000 add: Afghanistan, Pakistan, Yemen, Uganda and Syria for *35 nations*.

"How many September 11 has the United States caused in other nations since WWII," asked James Lucas, "Deaths in other Nations since WWII due to US Interventions". (http://www.countercurrents.org/lucas240407.htm)

Lucas' extensive report estimated the number of human beings that the United States has killed in 37 nations at 20-30 million. That is around 10,000 times the numbers of people killed on 9/11.

To that must be added those killed in non-regular warfare, covert warfare. In 1987, 13 former officials of the CIA, military and other intelligence agencies formed a group to expose these crimes, the Association of Responsible Dissidence. Former CIA official and Colonel Phil Roettinger was chosen as its leader. These experienced killers surmised that their agencies of death had killed six million people since WWII. (http://www.informationclearinghouse.info/article4068.htm) (11)

In 1975 and 1976, Senator Frank Church's Committee found that the CIA had committed 900 large and 3,000 lesser covert and violent operations. (12) John Stockwell, one of the CIA officers who became a whistle-blower, said, in 1990, that the CIA had completed 3,000 large and 10,000 lesser covert operations during its existence. (11)

It is commonly believed that for every person killed in warfare another 10 are wounded. So, *the United States is guilty for having murdered upwards to 36 million people and wounding 360 million just since WWII; and those figures are a decade old.*

These wars and covert actions also produce lots of refugees. In June 2017, the United Nations Refugee Agency (UNHCR) reported that there were more people "forcibly displaced" worldwide than since WWII—65.6 million. That translates to *20 people being forced to flee their homes every minute.* (http://www.unhcr.org/figures-at-a-glance.html)

Before the state of permanent war, there were "only" 19.8 million. Most refugees and stateless persons flee wars, and most of the wars are either started by or inflamed by the U.S.

The Chairman of the United States Joint Chiefs of Staff, General Martin Dempsey (2011-15), knew first-hand when he said, "I will personally attest to the fact that [the world is] more dangerous than it has ever been." The next day, he warned: "There is no foreseeable peace dividend. The security environment is more dangerous and more uncertain." (http://foreignpolicy.com/2013/02/26/most-dangerous-world-ever/)

A major direct cause of human flights is bombing them. In 2016, the U.S. bombed seven countries with 26,171 bombs, and that is just the figure the military releases. Moreover, the United States is not officially at war with anyone. Read John Rachel's "A Nation of Relentless Savagery". (https://dissidentvoice.org/2017/11/a-nation-of-relentless-savagery/#more-73563)

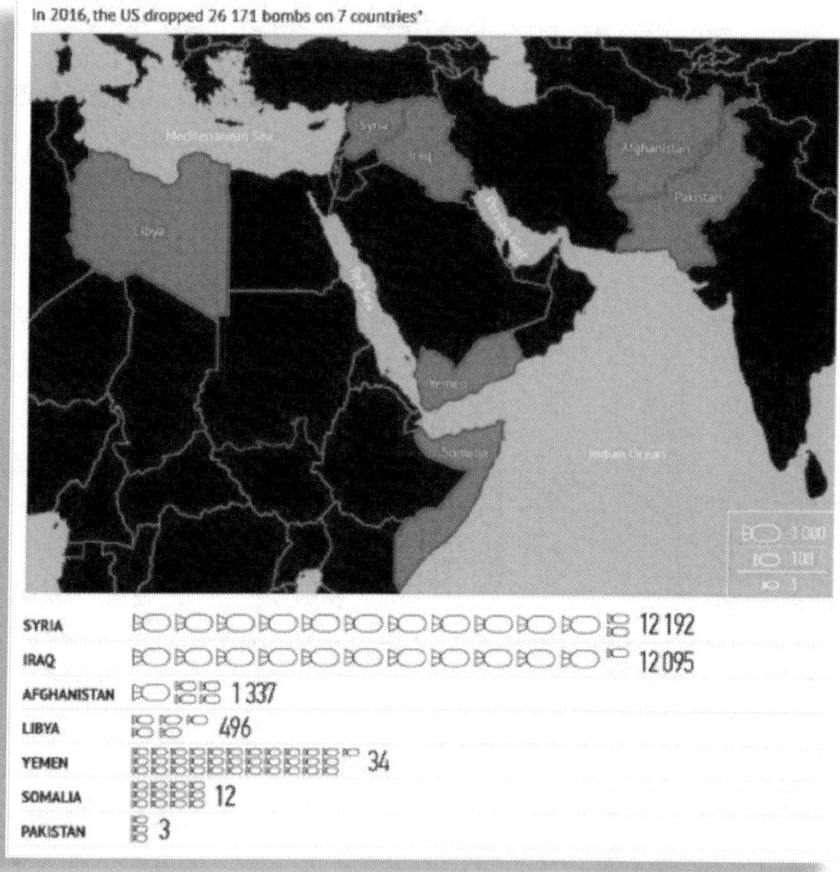

LIBYA

Let us see what was really at stake in one of these "rogue state" countries that required excising.

Libya was Africa's largest exporter of oil, 1.7 million tons a day, which quickly was reduced to 300-400,000 tons due to US-NATO bombing in 2011.

Libya had exported 80% of its oil: Italy (32%), Germany (14%), France and China (10% each), and U.S. (5%). While Gaddafi had turned much of oil sales towards the West, inviting in many of the major oil companies for great profits (BP, EXXON Mobil, Shell, Total), he did not join U.S. wars against Afghanistan and Iraq as did the oil rich Gulf

States. Nor did he sign on with AFRICOM, a pact oriented towards U.S. economic and military benefit in Africa, which is also aimed at prohibiting China from Africa's natural resources.

Libyans had the highest standard of living on the entire African continent, and no poverty. With just 20% of the extracted oil used nationally there was plenty of money to afford education and health care for the entire population without individual payment. There were schools, libraries, hospitals enough for all. Youths studying abroad had their education paid for by the state. *Each newlywed couple received $50,000 from state coffers to start a family.* And there was plenty left over for wealth to the Muammar Gaddafi clan. (13)

However, Gaddafi was preparing to launch a gold dinar for oil trade with all of Africa and other interested countries. France President Nickola Sarkozi called this, "a threat for financial security of mankind". Much of France's wealth—more than any other colonial-imperialist power—comes from exploiting Africa. There is evidence from Gaddafi defectors (especially Nouri Mesmari, who was under French protection) that France started preparing a Benghazi-based rebellion against Gaddafi in November 2010, in order to stop his plans to switch from the dollar to a new gold currency. U.S. politician, Rep. Dennis Kucinich confirmed this. (14)

Central Bank of Libya was 100% owned by the state and was outside BIS banking control. The state could finance its own projects and do so without interest rates, thereby reducing the costs of dealing with private banks by half. Libya's central bank had 144 tons of gold in its vaults, which it could use to start the gold dinar. BRIC countries China, Russia, India, and Iran are also stocking great sums of gold rather than relying only on dollars.

The Central Bank used $33 billion, without interest rates, to build the Great Man-Made River of 4,000 kilometers with three parallel pipelines running oil, gas and water. This supplies 70% of the people (4.5 of its 6 million) with clean drinking and irrigation water, and provides adequate crops for the people. This allowed Libya to be a competitive exporter of vegetables with Israel and Egypt.

The Central Bank also financed Africa's first communication satellite with $300 million of the $377 million cost. It started up for all Africa, on December 26, 2007, thus saving African nations an annual fee of

$500 million previously pocketed by Europe (mostly France) for use of its satellites. This means much less cost for telephones and other communication systems for all Africans.

But there had always been internal opposition to Gaddafi, and on February 15, 2011 protestors demonstrated in Benghazi, an area of many Islamists and clan lords. At first, they were peaceful but already on February 18, two policemen were killed by protestors, and 50 black African workers, mostly from Chad, were executed; 15 of them lynched at the courthouse in Bayda. From then on, the opposition became guerrilla fighters and the government responded with firepower.

The opposition included former Gaddafi ministers. They set up a central bank in Benghazi to replace Libya's central bank there even before they had set up a government. It was immediately recognized by Paris' stock exchange and other Westerners. This is the first time in history that rebels had set up a bank before having a government.

Key western powers decided that Gaddafi was no longer reliable and France, along with the UK, took the lead to overthrow him. In early March 2011, Gaddafi threatened to throw western oil companies out of Libya. On March 17, UN Resolution 1973 called for a no-fly zone strategy but not a regime shift. Ten states voted for, but it was not backed by key powers: China, Russia, Brazil, India and Germany, although they cowardly abstained from voting.

Of the 28 NATO countries then, only 14 were involved in the Libyan war campaign and only six of those (including Denmark) took part in the air war, which soon escalated far beyond a "no-fly" strategy to bomb and strafe any target. The Gaddafi forces did not use any aircraft once the Triumvirate—U.S., NATO and the European Union—invaded.

China had 50 major economic projects going in Libya with $18 billion investment. Before the invasion, there were 30,000 Chinese working on these projects. They had to leave and much of China's investment was destroyed.

Human Rights Watch (which some call an imperialist-oriented NGO) reported that there *had not been a civilian bloodbath by Gaddafi as claimed*. In Misurata, for example, with 400,000 people (second largest city) after two months of war only 257 people including combatants were killed. Of 949 wounded, only 22 (3%) were women. (*Boston Globe*, April 14, 2011)

Nevertheless, the West accused Gaddafi of murdering "innocent civilians". What he did was to threaten those with arms if they did not surrender them. They were not "innocent civilians" but armed insurrectionists. Every government fights armed insurrections.

After seven months of Western bombing and material support to fundamentalist Islamists, including al Qaeda, the Gaddafi forces fell apart. He was captured and painfully murdered on October 20, which inspired the sadist Hillary Clinton to laughingly quip: "We came. We saw. He died."

What the U.S.-NATO-EU hoped to achieve was to replace the half-reliable partner Gaddafi with a neo-liberal government that would do their bidding: sign in on AFRICOM, kick China out, reverse the central bank to a BIS private enterprise, continue using dollars, and have the new leaders join in their permanent war age throughout the Middle East and Africa.

What the Triumvirate achieved is: 20-40,000 dead people; a destroyed country in which human smuggling is normal; armed struggles in which the Islamic State and al Qaeda are a part; and three Islamist fundamentalist factions vying for power—one Western recognized "government" and two rival self-declared governments.

U.S. GREATEST THREAT TO WORLD PEACE

"The United States is the greatest threat to world peace. That's the finding of an end-of-the- year, WIN/Gallup International survey of people in 65 countries," wrote the *New York Post*, January 5, 2014. (http://nypost.com/2014/01/05/us-is-the-greatest-threat-to-world-peace-poll/)

"Of the 66,000 people polled, just under a quarter named Uncle Sam as the greatest threat to world peace. Other menaces didn't even come close: 8 percent named Pakistan, putting that country in second place, while 6 percent named China. A mere 4 percent found Iran threatening — which tied it with Israel."

What the NYP *did not tell was that only 2% of the 67,806 polls believed that Russia was the greatest threat. Also most relevant is that of the 4,556 Americans asked, Russia was still down the list at 3% while the USA tied with North Korea for third place at 13%.* Iran was first with 20% and Afghanistan second at 14%. China was seen by 5% as the greatest threat.

WIN/Gallup has not dared redo this poll, but a February-May 2017 PEW Research Center poll of 41,953 people in 38 countries came to essentially the same conclusion about attitudes towards the U.S. but with a different approach. The question was not put forth as "greatest threat" but "a major threat". This resulted in 35% viewing the U.S. as a major threat, with Russia and China close.

OVERTHROWING GOVERNMENTS

The US American writer who has written most about his country's violent aggression is beyond a doubt William Blum, another former governmental civil servant. I pass on Blum's Anti-Imperialist Report #149, March 7, 2017, his February 2013 list of "Overthrowing other people's governments"; the "Bombing List"; "Assassination list" of foreign leaders; "U.S. attempts to suppress populist or nationalist movements"; plus his book *Rogue State* "Perverting election" list. (https://williamblum.org/aer/read/149)

Unless otherwise indicated the text below is Blum's words. His research is impeccable.

Just since the end of World War 2, the United States has:

- ***Attempted to overthrow more than 50 foreign governments, most of which were democratically-elected.***
- ***Dropped bombs on the people of more than 30 countries.***
- ***Attempted to assassinate more than 50 foreign leaders.***
- ***Attempted to suppress a populist or nationalist movement in 20 countries.***
- ***Grossly interfered in democratic elections in at least 30 countries.***
- ***Though not as easy to quantify, has also led the world in torture; not only the torture performed directly by Americans upon foreigners, but providing torture equipment, torture manuals, lists of people to be tortured, and in-person guidance by American instructors.***

Where does the United States get the nerve to moralize about Russia? (15)

Here is the list of United States overthrowing, or attempting to overthrow a foreign government since the Second World War: (* indicates success.) ouster of a government)

- China 1949 to early 1960s
- Albania 1949-53
- East Germany 1950s
- Iran 1953 *
- Guatemala 1954 *
- Costa Rica mid-1950s
- Syria 1956-7
- Egypt 1957
- Indonesia 1957-8
- British Guiana 1953-64 *
- Iraq 1963 *
- North Vietnam 1945-73
- Cambodia 1955-70 *
- Laos 1958 *, 1959 *, 1960 *
- Ecuador 1960-63 *
- Congo 1960 *
- France 1965
- Brazil 1962-64 *
- Dominican Republic 1963 *
- Cuba 1959 to present
- Bolivia 1964 *
- Indonesia 1965 *
- Ghana 1966 *
- Chile 1964-73 *
- Greece 1967 *
- Costa Rica 1970-71
- Bolivia 1971 *
- Australia 1973-75 *
- Angola 1975, 1980s
- Zaire 1975
- Portugal 1974-76 *
- Jamaica 1976-80 *
- Seychelles 1979-81
- Chad 1981-82 *
- Grenada 1983 *
- South Yemen 1982-84
- Suriname 1982-84
- Fiji 1987 *
- Libya 1980s
- Nicaragua 1981-90 *
- Panama 1989 *
- Bulgaria 1990 *
- Albania 1991 *
- Iraq 1991
- Afghanistan 1980s *
- Somalia 1993
- Yugoslavia 1999-2000 *
- Ecuador 2000 *
- Afghanistan 2001 *
- Venezuela 2002 *
- Iraq 2003 *
- Haiti 2004 *
- Somalia 2007 to present
- Honduras 2009
- Libya 2011 *
- Syria 2012
- Ukraine 2014 *

Q: *Why will there never be a coup d'état in Washington?*
A: *Because there's no American embassy there.*

I insert a couple comments to add to Blum's list. The Honduras coup occurred without U.S. direct military intervention. But in a May 13-18 2009 speech, Secretary of State Hillary Clinton mentioned Bush's insufficiency in dealing with the new "rogue states" in Latin America.

And she warned about Russian, Chinese and Iranian growing influence. Clinton also blamed Bush, in effect, for Hugo Chavez ascendancy in Venezuela, Evo Morales in Bolivia, and Daniel Ortega in Nicaragua. Honduran General Romeo Vasquez was among Clinton's devout listeners. Less than two months after Clinton's speech, he led a coup d'état against the popularly elected president Manuel Zelaya. The coup government was immediately declared legal and supported by Clinton and her president, Obama, which all of Latin America, except the rich and their militarists, opposed.

Three years afterward, June 2012, another progressive president—former Catholic Bishop Fernando Lugo—was ousted from office by a "congressional coup d'état". Practically all of Latin America, including conservative Colombia and Chile, denounced the coup. Paraguay's new government was expelled from cooperative unions such as Mercosur. As in the case with Honduras, no matter how much denunciation there may be as long as the world's policeman backs totalitarianism so be it.

THE BOMBING LIST:

- Korea and China 1950-53 (Korean War)
- Guatemala 1954
- Indonesia 1958
- Cuba 1959-1961
- Guatemala 1960
- Congo 1964
- Laos 1964-73
- Vietnam 1961-73
- Cambodia 1969-70
- Guatemala 1967-69
- Grenada 1983
- Lebanon 1983, 1984 (both Lebanese and Syrian targets)
- Libya 1986
- El Salvador 1980s
- Nicaragua 1980s
- Iran 1987
- Panama 1989
- Iraq 1991 (Persian Gulf War)
- Kuwait 1991
- Somalia 1993
- Bosnia 1994, 1995
- Sudan 1998
- Afghanistan 1998
- Yugoslavia 1999
- Yemen 2002
- Iraq 1991-2003 (US/UK on regular basis)
- Iraq 2003-2015
- Afghanistan 2001-2015
- Pakistan 2007-2015
- Somalia 2007-8, 2011
- Yemen 2009, 2011
- Libya 2011, 2015
- Syria 2014-2017

List of prominent foreign individuals whose assassination (or planning for same) the United States has been involved in since the end of the Second World War.

The list does not include several assassinations in various parts of the world carried out by anti-Castro Cubans employed by the CIA and headquartered in the United States. [Cuba's security asserts that the CIA and its civilian terrorists have had over 636 murder plots against Fidel.]

- 1949: Kim Koo, Korean opposition leader
- 1950s: CIA/Neo-Nazi hit list of more than 200 political figures in West Germany to be "put out of the way" in the event of a Soviet invasion
- 1950s: Chou En-lai, Prime minister of China, several attempts on his life
- 1950s, 1962: Sukarno, President of Indonesia
- 1951: Kim Il Sung, Premier of North Korea
- 1953: Mohammed Mossadegh, Prime Minister of Iran
- 1950s (mid): Claro M. Recto, Philippines opposition leader
- 1955: Jawaharlal Nehru, Prime Minister of India
- 1957: Gamal Abdul Nasser, President of Egypt
- 1959, 1963, 1969: Norodom Sihanouk, leader of Cambodia
- 1960: Brig. Gen. Abdul Karim Kassem, leader of Iraq
- 1950s-70s: José Figueres, President of Costa Rica, two attempts on his life
- 1961: Francois "Papa Doc" Duvalier, leader of Haiti
- 1961: Patrice Lumumba, Prime Minister of the Congo (Zaire)
- 1961: Gen. Rafael Trujillo, leader of Dominican Republic
- 1963: Ngo Dinh Diem, President of South Vietnam
- 1960s-70s: Fidel Castro, Cuba
- 1960s: Raúl Castro, Cuba
- 1965: Francisco Caamaño, Dominican Republic opposition leader
- 1965-6: Charles de Gaulle, President of France
- 1967: Che Guevara, Cuban leader
- 1970: Salvador Allende, President of Chile
- 1970: Gen. Rene Schneider, Commander-in-Chief of Army, Chile
- 1970s, 1981: General Omar Torrijos, leader of Panama
- 1972: General Manuel Noriega, Chief of Panama Intelligence

- 1975: Mobutu Sese Seko, President of Zaire
- 1976: Michael Manley, Prime Minister of Jamaica
- 1980-1986: Muammar Qaddafi, leader of Libya, several plots and attempts upon his life
- 1982: Ayatollah Khomeini, leader of Iran
- 1983: Gen. Ahmed Dlimi, Moroccan Army commander
- 1983: Miguel d'Escoto, Foreign Minister of Nicaragua
- 1984: The nine comandantes of the Sandinista National Directorate
- 1985: Sheikh Mohammed Hussein Fadlallah, Lebanese Shiite leader (80 people killed in the attempt)
- 1991: Saddam Hussein, leader of Iraq
- 1993: Mohamed Farah Aideed, prominent clan leader of Somalia
- 1998, 2001-12: Osama bin Laden, leading Islamic militant
- 1999: Slobodan Milosevic, President of Yugoslavia
- 2002: Gulbuddin Hekmatyar, Afghan Islamic leader and warlord
- 2003: Saddam Hussein and his two sons
- 2011: Muammar Qaddafi, leader of Libya

In addition to Blum's list above, Ewen MacAskill reported in *The Guardian*, on May 5, 2017, that the North Korean government believes the CIA tried to kill its leader, Kim Jong-nu with "the use of biochemical substances including radioactive substance and nano poisonous substance". Lethal results from these poisons do not take place for six to twelve months. (https://www.theguardian.com/us-news/2017/may/05/cia-long-history-kill-leaders-around-the-world-north-korea)

"The US has developed much more sophisticated methods than polonium in a tea pot, especially in the fields of electronic and cyber warfare [referring to the charge that Russian intelligence poisoned dissident Alexander Litvinenko with polonium hidden in a teapot]. A leaked document obtained by WikiLeaks and released earlier this year showed the CIA in October 2014 looking at hacking into car control systems. That ability could potentially allow an agent to stage a car crash," MacAskill wrote.

Blum lists President Charles de Gaulle as a CIA target. Despite being a Western ally, he had dared to pull France's military out of NATO, in order to "regain full sovereignty over French territory." De Gaulle also sought to release Algeria as a colony, all of which angered France's right-wing generals as well as Langley and Pentagon. There were two coup attempts, and murder attempts on his life. In one 1962 attempt, two of his motorcycle body guards were murdered.

See the October 20, 2015 article by David Talbot, founder of "Salon", and a CIA biographer. (https://whowhatwhy.org/2015/10/20/jfk-assassination-plot-mirrored-in-1961-france-part-1/)

"JFK was suddenly besieged with howls of outrage from a major ally, accusing his own security services of seditious activity."

"It was a stinging embarrassment for the new American president, who was scheduled to fly to Paris for a state visit the following month. To add to the insult, the coup had been triggered by de Gaulle's efforts to bring French colonial rule in Algeria to an end—a goal that JFK himself had ardently championed.

"The CIA's support for the coup was one more defiant display of contempt—a back of the hand aimed not only at de Gaulle but at Kennedy.

"JFK took pains to assure Paris that he strongly supported de Gaulle's presidency, phoning Hervé Alphand, the French ambassador in Washington, to directly communicate these assurances. But, according to Alphand, Kennedy's disavowal of official US involvement in the coup came with a disturbing addendum—the American president could not vouch for his own intelligence agency. *Kennedy told Alphand that 'the CIA is such a vast and poorly controlled machine that the most unlikely maneuvers might be true.'"*

The June 15, 2015 edition of *The Guardian* also reported that, at least, the CIA "was asked to help kill the French president in 1965." (https://www.theguardian.com/world/2015/jun/16/general-de-gaulle-cia-assassination-plot-1975)

In 1975 and 1976, Senator Frank Church's Committee *United States Senate Select Committee to Study Governmental Operations with Respect to Intelligence Activities* published fourteen reports on the formation of U.S. intelligence agencies, their operations, and the abuses of law and power that they had committed, together with recommendations for reform, some of which were allegedly put in place. Among the matters investigated were attempts to assassinate foreign leaders, including Patrice Lumumba of the Congo, Rafael Trujillo of the Dominican Republic, the Diem brothers of Vietnam, Gen. René Schneider of Chile, and the CIA and President John F. Kennedy's plan to use the Mafia to kill Fidel Castro of Cuba.

Back to William Blum!
United States attempts to suppress a populist or national movement since WWII. (* = Successful)

- China – 1945-49
- France – 1947 *
- Italy – 1947-1970s *
- Greece – 1947-49 *
- Philippines – 1945-53 *
- Korea – 1945-53 *
- Haiti – 1959 *
- Laos – 1957-73
- Vietnam – 1961-73
- Thailand – 1965-73 *
- Peru – 1965 *
- Dominican Republic – 1965 *
- Uruguay – 1969-72 *
- South Africa – 1960s-1980s
- East Timor – 1975-1999 *
- Philippines – 1970s-1990s *
- El Salvador – 1980-92 *
- Colombia – 1990s to early 2000s *
- Peru – 1997 *
- Iraq – 2003 to present *

Rogue State: A Guide to the World's Only Superpower.
Chapter 18: Perverting Elections. 29 countries; many of them with several attempts and successes

- Italy 1948-1970s
- Philippines 1950s
- Lebanon 1950s
- British Guiana/Guyana 1953-64
- Indonesia 1955
- Vietnam 1955
- Japan 1958-70s
- Nepal 1959
- Laos 1960
- Brazil 1962-4
- Dominican Republic 1962
- Guatemala 1963
- Chile 1964, 1970
- Bolivia 1966, 2002
- Portugal 1974-5
- Australia 1974-5
- Jamaica 1976
- Panama 1984, 1989
- Nicaragua 1984, 1990, 2001
- Haiti 1987-8
- Bulgaria 1990-1
- Albania 1991-2
- Russia 1996 (See also my chapter 13)
- Mongolia 1996
- Bosnia 1998
- Slovakia 2002
- El Salvador 2004
- Afghanistan 2004
- Palestine 2005-6

MILITARY BUDGETS

Inspired by President Donald Trumps' "make America great again", the United States Senate overwhelmingly approved a new spending plan, allocating another $80 billion to the military for 2018. Bernie Sanders pledged to make public universities free in his 2016 campaign. This plan would have cost the federal government $47 billion annually, $33 billion left over for more wars.

The official U.S. military budget is $700 billion. That's really only part of the budget for Fiscal Year 2018, which is more than the next nine countries combined. China is second at $216 billion. China is nearly as large as the United States and has nearly four times the population. Russia comes in third in military expenditures at $70 billion, but it plans to cut back by at least 5% or more.

At the official figure, 5% of the world's population is spending 37% of the world's military expenditures, according to SIPRI (Stockholm International Peace Research Institute) figures. The world's total military spending is listed at $1.69 trillion.

However, the real military/war costs to US American taxpayers is at least $1.1 trillion, which would be 66% of the world's total IF all the other countries statistics are reported correctly, which could be dubious. $1.1 trillion is one-fourth the U.S. federal budget.

Hundreds of billions of dollars in "defense" spending aren't counted in the Pentagon/defense budget. One has to find these "extra" costs in other parts of the national budget. Current wars, for example, are not included in the defense budget. Here is how William Hartung of the Center for International Policy figures the true costs. (https://warisboring.com/the-trillion-dollar-military-budget/)

Starting with Pentagon's base defense budget=$575 billion, add "other defense"=$8 billion; current wars=$64.6 billion; modernize 6,800 nuclear warheads=$20 billion; military aid to 140 countries=$7 billion; supporting war veterans=$186 billion (three times what it was before the U.S. invaded Afghanistan, in 2001); military retirement=$80; DoD share of the annual national debt interest payment $100 billion (total is $500 billion). Then add 16 intelligence agencies plus the Office of Director of National Intelligence=$70 billion. The final blow to our pocket books is the mega-agency of 22 entities called "Homeland" Security=$50 billion, which would not have been "necessary" had the U.S. not invaded Afghanistan, then Iraq, then...

Besides the waste of waging wars against people, there is departmental-bureaucratic waste. There are no transparent audits so we don't know how much of the money was spent, where it was spent, or whose pockets went home bulging. Moreover, the government knows this and protects the thieves and waste mongers.

"The department's budget is awash in waste, as you might expect from the only major federal agency that has never passed an audit. For example, last year a report by the Defense Business Board, a Pentagon advisory panel, found that the Department of Defense could save $125 billion over five years just by trimming excess bureaucracy. And a new study by the Pentagon's Inspector General indicates that the department has ignored hundreds of recommendations that could have saved it more than $33.6 billion," wrote Hartung.

The Inspector General also disclosed that "Army and Defense Finance and Accounting Service Indianapolis personnel did not adequately support $2.8 trillion in third quarter adjustments and $6.5 trillion in yearend adjustments made to Army General Fund data during FY 2015 financial statement compilation." These "adjustments" had been made prior to unacceptable reports, but were still failing to explain where the money had gone. (https://solari.com/blog/dod-and-hud-missing-money-supporting-documentation/)

"We are concerned with the accuracy and reliability of the Department's estimation process. Without a reliable process to review all expenditures and identify the full extent of improper payments, the Department will not be able to improve internal controls aimed at reducing improper payments." (http://www.dodig.mil/pubs/documents/DODIG-2016-113.pdf)

Interestingly when one clicks on the above cited dod document the page can no longer be found but read solari's reports and interviews for the figures and quotations. (https://solari.com/00archive/web/solarireports/2017/unsupported_adjustments/Unsupported_Adjustments_Report_Final_3.pdf)

We must add to the U.S. military funds those of its allies and NATO. The 29-member military alliance uses $275 million for its civil budget and $1.5 billion for military expenses. Add to that the military budgets of allies such as Saudi Arabia, $65 billion; France, $58 billion; UK, $53 billion; Japan, $48, South Korea $38 billion, plus a score more states.

Compare South Korea and its U.S. warlord expenditures to North Korea at $10 billion.

All 29-NATO states are vowed to come to each others' defense if Russia, China or North Korea were to invade, as the mass media scenario shrills to us. Such a scenario is ludicrous.

"The U.S., bounded by two oceans and two weak neighbors, has never been really invaded. Strategically, it is practically an island. In fact not since the war of 1812—more than 200 years ago— the country has not seen an actual foreign army on its soil," wrote Ted Rall, "Military Spending is the Biggest Scam in American Politics," May 31, 2017. (https://www.counterpunch.org/2017/05/31/military-spending-is-the-biggest-scam-in-american-politics/)

Pearl Harbor was a raid not an invasion as was the September 11, 2001 terror attack.

In contrast to the United States, Russia is surrounded with problematic conflicts, which the U.S. loves to create and exacerbate.

"Russia has twice as much territory to defend against: NATO/U.S. missiles to their west in Europe, a southern border full of radical Islamists in unstable countries like Kyrgyzstan and Uzbekistan, Afghanistan a stone's throw away," Rall added.

ARMAMENTS

So much financing for military/war has to produce something, besides dead bodies that have to be buried or rot, and wounded bodies that have to be treated. It produces military jobs for men, and now with gender equality in many countries jobs for women murderers and torturers as well. It also produces civilian jobs in the weapons industry, perhaps two million in the U.S.

CURRENT TROOP (2016) FIGURES INTERNATIONAL INSTITUTE FOR STRATEGIC STUDIES					
COUNTRY	ACTIVE MILIARY	RESERVE	PARAMILITARY	TOTAL PER 1000 CAPITA	TOTAL
China	2.183.000	510.000	660.000	3.530.000	2.4
Russia	831.000	2.000.000	659.000	3.490.000	24.5
USA	1.347.000	865.000	14.850	2.227.200	6.9

SIDE BY SIDE COMPARISON OF RUSSIAN AND U.S. MILITARY	
RUSSIAN ARMY (2016) • 15,398 main battle tanks • 31,298 armored fighting vehicles • 5,972 self-propelled guns • 4,625 towed artillery • 3,793 multiple-launch rocket systems • 334 tactical ballistic missile systems	U.S. ARMY (2016) • 8,848 main battle tanks • 41,062 armored fighting vehicles • 1,934 self-propelled guns • 1,299 towed artillery • 1,331 multiple-launch rocket systems • 340 tactical ballistic missile systems
RUSSIAN NAVY (2016) Total naval strength: 352 ships • 1 aircraft carriers • 1 battlecruisers • 3 cruisers • 15 destroyers • 4 frigates • 81 corvettes • 60 submarines	US NAVY (2016) Total naval strength: 415 ships • 19 aircraft carriers • 22 cruisers • 62 destroyers • 6 frigates • 0 corvettes • 75 submarines
RUSSIAN AIR FORCE (2016) • 173 bombers • 873 fighters/interceptors • 476 attack aircraft • 1,124 transports • 1,237 helicopters • 478 attack helicopters	US AIR FORCE (2016) • 159 bombers • 2,308 fighters/interceptors • 319 attack aircraft • 5,739 transports • 6,084 helicopters • 957 attack helicopters
NUCLEAR WARHEADS • 2500 ready / 8000 (2015) (Wikipedia+ sources)	NUCLEAR WARHEADS • 1900 ready / 4760 (2015) (Wikipedia+ sources)

Add to the U.S. side, 300 French, 215 UK, and 80 Israeli nuclear warheads. One can also consider that Russia could be aided by the 260 Chinese nuclear warheads.

The U.S. Federation of Science (FAS) 2017 figure for NATO's three nuclear countries is 7,315 of which 2,200 are ready to launch. Russia has 7,000 of which 1,950 are ready. China with 270, Israel 80, Pakistan 120-130, India 110-120. FAS estimates are that North Korea might have enough "fissile material to potentially produce 10 to 20 nuclear warheads".

The Treaty of Non-Proliferation of Nuclear Weapons (NTP) is a 1970 UN voluntary resolution, which Israel, Pakistan and India ignored.

On July 7, 2017, the UN General Assembly voted for a legally binding accord—122 for, 1 against (Netherlands) and 69 abstentions. If ratified it would comprehensively prohibit nuclear weapons, with the goal of leading towards their total elimination.

In order to come into effect, ratification by at least 50 countries is required. For those nations that are party to it, the treaty prohibits the development, testing, production, stockpiling, stationing, transfer, use and threat of use of nuclear weapons, as well as assistance and encouragement to the prohibited activities.

Guess who abstained—all the nuclear weapons states and all NATO states (except Netherlands). After the vote, NATO banned member states from ratifying the treaty.

GLOBAL WEAPONS INDUSTRY

Sales of arms and military services by the largest arms-producing and military services companies, totaled $370.7 billion, in 2015, according to data on the international arms industry released by SIPRI. The overall 2017 total is perhaps $500 billion.

Companies based in the United States continue to dominate the Top 100 with total arms sales amounting to $209.7 billion for 2015. (https://www.sipri.org/media/press-release/2016/global-arms-industry-usa-remains-dominant)

Of the top ten weapons manufacturers, seven are U.S. owned. Their take in 2015 was a combined $145 billion, and they employed 750,000 workers: Lockheed Martin ($36.5 billion); Boeing ($28); Raytheon ($23); Northrop Grumman ($20); General Dynamics ($19); United Technologies ($9.5); L3 Technologies ($8.8). Their combined *profits* are over $20 billion, the lion share of all U.S. weapons companies at around $35 billion.

The closest countries in weapons sales are: South Korea at $35 billion; Russia at $30 billion; France at $21.4 billion. Britain sold $12 billion and two-thirds of those sales went to Middle Eastern countries including the largest terrorist states Saudi Arabia and Israel. $10.4 billion of UK weapons sales come from countries judged by its own Foreign Office to be "human rights priority countries", and have "the worst or greatest number of human rights violations," as reported by Britain's Foreign & Commonwealth Office.

China is a new kid on the block. Beginning just two to three years ago, it has made deals to sell aircraft, armored vehicles, guns and boats to Myanmar, and last year some radar, anti-ship missiles and other weapons to Indonesia. This year, China made a $277 million deal with Malaysia for patrol vessels, and 28 tanks to Thailand for $147 million. China also gave 3000 assault rifles to the Philippines at a value of $3.3 million. (http://www.scmp.com/news/china/diplomacy-defence/article/2114172/weapons-sales-making-china-big-gun-southeast-asia)

MILITARY BASES

"The Coalition Against Foreign Military Bases" is a new campaign focused on closing all U.S. military bases abroad. "This campaign strikes at the foundation of US empire, confronting its militarism, corporatism and imperialism," wrote Kevin Zeese and Margaret Flowers, "New Campaign: Close all US Military Bases on Foreign Soil," July 29, 2017. https://popularresistance.org/new-campaign-close-all-us-military-bases-on-foreign-soil/

The new coalition held its first conference on January 12-14, 2018 at the University of Baltimore. Three dozen organizations participated, including veteran anti-war activists and young ones, former Deep State people in VIPS, and victims from foreign countries. (http://noforeignbases.org/ http://thepeacereport.com/learned-conference-u-s-foreign-military-bases/ http://noforeignbases.org/wp-content/uploads/2018/01/Conference-Program.pdf)

Among its reports and actions was a call for demonstrating to return the Guantánamo naval base and surrounding territory stolen by the U.S. to its rightful owners, the Cuban people.

Zeese and Flowers article cites Chalmers Johnson's, "America Empire of Bases".

> *"As distinct from other peoples, most Americans do not recognize—or do not want to recognize—that the United States dominates the world through its military power. Due to government secrecy, our citizens are often ignorant of the fact that our garrisons encircle the planet. This vast network of American bases on every continent except Antarctica actually constitutes a new form of empire...*
>
> *Our military deploys well over half a million soldiers, spies, technicians, teachers, dependents, and civilian contractors in other nations."*

> *"The Pentagon currently owns or rents 702 overseas bases in about 130 countries and has another 6,000 bases in the United States and its territories...[It] employs an additional 44,446 locally hired foreigners. The Pentagon claims that these bases contain 44,870 barracks, hangars, hospitals, and other buildings, which it owns, and that it leases 4,844 more."*

That was 14 years ago. Today, the estimated number of bases is at least 800 and up to 1000, or 95% of all foreign military bases in the world. In addition, it now has 19 naval air carriers (another 15 planned), "each as part of a Carrier Strike Group, composed of roughly 7,500 personnel, and a carrier air wing of 65 to 70 aircraft — each of which can be considered a floating military base," according to DoD base structure report. It reports on 4,800 worldwide sites (not all are bases) with 562,000 facilities, valued at $585 billion. (https://www.acq.osd.mil/eie/Downloads/BSI/Base%20Structure%20Report%20FY15.pdf)

The Department of Defense states there are still 40,000 U.S. troops at 179 military bases in Germany; over 50,000 at 109 bases in Japan; 28-40,000 troops at 85 bases in South Korea. In July, 2017, it was reported that the U.S. had created ten new military bases in Syria, which Turkey angrily exposed, and the Syria government and Russia protested.

Several governments besides Syria oppose having U.S. military bases and personnel on their soil, but the U.S. ignores their wishes and legal rights and just moves in. Cuba is an example regarding the U.S. torture-center military base at Guantanamo. Okinawa and Diego Garcia are others.

In addition to U.S. worldwide military bases and warehouse facilities, NATO has 30 military bases of its own, primarily in Western Europe.

The Department of Defense admits to 4,154 military bases in all 50 U.S. states, plus 114 on its territories, and 587 overseas bases (2015). See page 28. (https://www.acq.osd.mil/eie/Downloads/BSI/Base%20Structure%20Report%20FY15.pdf)

Some sources, such as Canadian geographer and Professor Jules Dufour, report 6000 bases and military warehouses in 63 countries. (https://www.globalresearch.ca/the-worldwide-network-of-us-military-bases/5564)

"These facilities include a total of 845,441 different buildings and equipments...According to J. Gelman, who examined 2005 official Pentagon data, the US is thought to own a total of 737 bases in foreign lands. Adding to the bases inside U.S. territory, the total land area occupied by US military bases domestically within the US and internationally is of the order of 2,202,735 hectares, which makes the Pentagon one of the largest landowners worldwide."

Today, the U.S. has military bases where it never had before the fall of European socialist states, including in several sovereign states earlier under the Soviet Union, but also in Iraq and Afghanistan, even in Australia. It has doubled its number of bases in Colombia to eight. It operates military war games with previous enemies in Viet Nam and Cambodia.

The Establishment even realizes that it has too many bases.

"By its own estimates, the DoD is operating with 21 percent excess capacity in all its facilities. If nothing is done, that will increase to 22 percent by 2019. "Trump Wants to Rebuild the Military, But Budget Would Close Bases", CNN Politics, May 30, 2017.

"Unfortunately, Congress won't allow DoD to close bases. The Bi-Partisan Budget Act of 2013 blocked future military base closings. Few elected officials are willing to risk losing local jobs caused by base closures in their states. Instead, the Pentagon will need to reduce the number of soldiers so it can afford the benefits of bases," wrote *The Wall Street Journal,* August 1, 2013, "Pentagon Lays Out Way to Slash Spending."

One base that they especially don't want to close is the School of the Americas (SOS).

TORTURE SCHOOL OF THE AMERICAS

"U.S. Army intelligence manuals used to train Latin American military officers at an Army school from 1982 to 1991 advocated executions, torture, blackmail and other forms of coercion against insurgents, Pentagon documents released yesterday show," reported Diana Priest, *The Washington Post*, on September 21, 1996. (https://www.washingtonpost.com/archive/politics/1996/09/21/us-instructed-latins-on-executions-torture/f7d86816-5ab3-4ef0-9df6-f430c209392f/?utm_term=.46d638a7ecf3

"Used in courses at the U.S. Army's School of the Americas, the manual says that to recruit and control informants, counterintelligence agents could use 'fear, payment of bounties for enemy dead, beatings, false imprisonment, executions and the use of truth serum,' according to a secret Defense Department summary of the manuals compiled during a 1992 investigation of the instructional material and also released yesterday. A summary of the investigation and four pages of brief, translated excerpts from the seven Spanish-language manuals were released."

The Army School of the Americas was first located in Panama just after WWII but was moved in 1984 to Fort Benning, Georgia. Panama President Jorge Illueca shut it down, declaring it to be "the biggest base for destabilization in Latin America." By 2017, it had trained 80,000 military and police officers from Latin America and the U.S.

The "Washington Post" article continued: "Its graduates have included some of the region's most notorious human rights abusers, among them Roberto D'Aubuisson [who ordered the assassination of Archbishop Oscar Romero, in 1980], the leader of El Salvador's right-wing death squads; 19 Salvadoran soldiers linked to the 1989 assassination of six Jesuit priests; Gen. Manuel Antonio Noriega, the deposed Panamanian strongman; six Peruvian officers linked to killings of students and a professor; and Col. Julio Roberto Alpirez, a Guatemalan officer implicated in the death of an American innkeeper living in Guatemala and to the death of a leftist guerrilla married to an American lawyer.

"The material was based, in part, on training instructions used in the 1960s by the Army's Foreign Intelligence Assistance Program, entitled 'Project X'. The 1992 investigation also found the manual was distributed to thousands of military officers from 11 South and Central American countries, including Guatemala, El Salvador, Honduras and Panama, where the U.S. military was heavily involved in counterinsurgency.

"On several occasions it uses the words 'neutralization' or 'neutralizing,' which were commonly used at the time as euphemisms for execution or destruction, a Pentagon official said.

"The manual on 'Terrorism and the Urban Guerrilla' says that 'another function of the CI [counter-intelligence] agents is recommending CI targets for neutralizing. The CI targets can include personalities, installations, organizations, documents and materials . . . the personality targets prove to be valuable sources of intelligence. Some examples of these targets are governmental officials, political leaders, and members of the infrastructure,'" Diana Priest reported.

On August 9, 1983, theology of liberation priest Father Roy Bourgeois and two other human rights activists, Father Larry Rosebaugh and Linda Ventimiglia, entered the Georgia torture base disguised as officers. Once inside, they climbed a tree close to where El Salvadoran soldiers were quartered and played a tape of Archbishop Romero's last sermon. His March 23, 1980 speech prompted El Salvador military intelligence officer D'Aubuisson and SOS 1972 student to order his murder. A sniper bullet to the heart ended the life of the Father of Peace the next day as he held mass.

"I would like to make a special appeal to the members of the army and specifically to the ranks of the National Guard, the police and the military. Brothers, each one of you is one of us. We are the same people. The peasants you kill are your own brothers and sisters. When you hear the voice of a man commanding you to kill, remember instead the voice of God: THOU SHALL NOT KILL!"

"It was a sacred moment," Bourgeois later recalled. "Those soldiers coming out of the barracks, looking into the sky, not being able to see us, hearing the words of this prophet." (16)

Military Police threatened to shoot the three up the tree and trained their weapons on them. Finally, MPs climbed 20 meters up the tree and dragged them down. They were hit on the head and body, stripped of their clothes, dogs barking and snapping. In jail, Father Roy went on a two-month long hunger strike. They spent 18 months in prison.

Bourgeois and associates founded the School of the Americas Watch: http://www.soaw.org/border/

"SOA Watch is a nonviolent grassroots movement working to close the SOA / WHINSEC and similar centers that train state actors such as military, law enforcement and border patrol. We strive to expose, denounce, and end US militarization, oppressive US policies and other forms of state violence in the Americas. We act in solidarity with organizations and movements working for justice and peace throughout the Americas.

We Demand:

- An end to US economic, military and political intervention in Latin America
- Demilitarization and divestment of the borders
- An end to the racist systems of oppression that criminalize and kill migrants, refugees and communities of color
- Respect, dignity, justice and the right to self-determination of communities
- An end to Plan Mérida and the Alliance for Prosperity"

These brave and determined humans have protested in creative ways in front of the torturer military base. Hundreds of people passed some of their lives in prison—weeks, months, even years, often in solitary confinement—for civilly disobeying the authorities abusing their power to murder and torture, to incarcerate and silence the voices of ordinary decent human beings who take the perilous step to exercise the very basic democratic right and duty to say NO to injustice, to say NO to aggressive murder, torture, racial/ethnic "cleansing".

They have held hundreds of protests and an annual picket before the base since the November 1989 murders of six Jesuit priests, their housekeeper and her daughter at the Central American University in El Salvador in which graduates of the School of the Americas were involved.

In 2001, long and hard besieged by activist determination and adverse attention, the School of the Americas changed its name to the Western Hemisphere Institute for Security Cooperation (WHINSEC). It claimed that it no longer teaches how to torture. How are we to believe that? The name, *School of the Assassins* (aka School of the Americas) stuck in the tongues and hearts of millions of victims and good people, empathizing with their pain, demanding an end to it all.

I am proud to have participated with these people, flying to the fort from Denmark, on November 13, 2013. (http://ronridenour.com/articles/2013/1126--rr.htm)

"Diego Lopez, Guatemala. Presente!

Francisca Chavez, El Salvador. Presente!

We tearfully placed the man and the baby's little wooden crosses into the cyclone fence, one of three barbed-wired steal barriers separating thousands of peace-makers from the war-makers at Fort Benning, Georgia.

School of the Americas (SOA) Watch Vigil, the 24th since1990, drew me from Denmark, my friend James Smith from Ensenada, Mexico, and upwards to 3000 others from across the United States, Canada, and Latin American countries to protest in front of this key US Army combat-counter-insurgency training base."

"SOA victims include: 200,000 Guatemalans, mostly Mayans, murdered during three US-backed dictator regimes (15of 27 military cabinet members were trained at SOA); nearly 100,000 Colombians killed and six million displaced by 10,000 troops (and others) trained in Georgia; 18 high-ranking Mexican army graduates have played key roles in civilian-targeted warfare against indigenous communities, and drug gangs have obtained training and military weaponry from SOA because many deserted from Mexico's military; 400 resistance movement Hondurans have been murdered by troops under the leadership of SOA graduates also responsible for the coup against President Manuel Zelaya, in 2009; and hundreds of thousands other Latin Americans have been murdered by graduates of SOA."

Demonstrators before SOS showing names of people on crosses who SOS graduates have murdered

*"Our batteries recharged and our hearts morally revitalized, we left the scene of the crime ready to oppose other crimes against humanity. Roy Bourgeois says: '**It has always been about solidarity...to accompany, and to make another's struggle for justice and equality your struggle**'."*

As we drove our legs before the wired torture base, each of us carried a cross with the name of one of the murdered person. My spiritually connected brother was Felix Rolando Murillo López, murdered on September 17, 2001 in Honduras. *Presente camarada!*

RUSSIA, CHINA MILITARY BASES

Russia, in contrast, has no School of the Americas and only 16 military bases abroad in 10 countries, most in former Soviet republics. There are about 50,000 military personnel in six countries. I could not find the numbers in the other four countries.

1. Armenia, 102nd military base and 3624th airbase with between 3,214-5,000 personnel
2. Belarus radar and communication center, and 61st fighter airbase, 1,500 personnel
3. Georgia 2 bases in Abkhazia and South Ossetia, 8,000 personnel
4. Kazakhstan radar station, anti-ballistic missile testing range and a space launch facility, unknown number of personnel
5. Kyrgyzstan Kant air base & 338th naval communication center with torpedo testing range, unknown number of personnel
6. Moldova facility in Transnistria separatist region with 1,500 peacekeepers
7. Syria naval facility in Tartus and Khmeimin air base, unknown number of personnel
8. Tajikistan 201st military base with 7,500 personnel
9. Ukraine Black Sea Fleet in Sevastopol Crimea with 26,000 military personnel
10. Vietnam naval resupply facility at Cam Ranh Base, unknown personnel

China has only ONE military base beyond its borders. It is called a "logistical support" facility in the small African country of Djibouti, not far from where the U.S. has a base. Besides the U.S., France and Japan also have military bases on this east African nation of 942,000 people.

"'You would have to characterize it as a military base,' Marine Gen. Thomas Waldhauser, chief of US Africa Command, told reporters in Washington this week. 'It's a first for them. They've never had an overseas base.'" (http://nordic.businessinsider.com/chinese-base-in-djibouti-near-camp-lemmonnier-africa-us-concern-2017-3?r=US&IR=T) [author emphasis]

China only has one other overseas port base and that is a commercial one at Hambontota in Sri Lanka. Two others are in construction in Myanmar and Pakistan. None of them have military missions per se. Djibouti, for instance, is at the Horn of Africa where there have been a lot of pirate raids, because much of the world's shipping passes by.

By contrast again, the U.S. has 4000 military personnel at Lemonnier, in Djibouti, its largest permanent base on the continent where it plans bases and military personnel in each nation.

China is developing military installations on a few islands close to its land. They are to be mainly unsinkable aircraft carriers, an answer to the "pivot to Asia" challenge introduced by Barak Obama. China has one of four underway, a 10,000-tonne destroyer. U.S. has several ships encircling China.

MILITARY POLLUTION

According to the 2005 *CIA World Factbook*, if it were a country the DoD would rank 34th in the world in average daily oil use, coming in just behind Iraq and just ahead of Sweden.

"'The US Department of Defense is one of the world's worst polluters. Its footprint dwarfs that of any corporation: 4,127 installations spread across 19 million acres [7.69 million hectares] of American soil'. Maureen Sullivan, who heads the Pentagon's environmental programs, says her office contends with 39,000 contaminated sites."

"'Almost every military site in this country is seriously contaminated,' said John D Dingell, a soon-to-retire Michigan congressman, who served in the Second World War," wrote Newsweek. (http://www.newsweek.com/2014/07/25/us-department-defence-one-worlds-biggest-polluters-259456.html)

Yet nearly all environmentalists groups, NGOs and grass roots, ignore the military and their wars when condemning and protesting environment pollution and climate change. When I worked as a volunteer activist for Greenpeace in Copenhagen for two years not long ago, I tried to bring this to their attention. I was waved aside. A few admitted, though, that if they took up this major cause of crimes against Mother Earth, they'd lose most of their donations. And the media follows suit.

"Last week, mainstream media outlets gave minimal attention to the news that the U.S. Naval station in Virginia Beach had spilled an estimated 94,000 gallons [355,828 liters] of jet fuel into a nearby waterway, less than a mile from the Atlantic Ocean. While the incident was by no means as catastrophic as some other pipeline spills, it underscores an important yet little-known fact—that the U.S. Department of Defense is both the nation's and the world's largest polluter," wrote Whitney Webb, on May 15, 2017. (http://www.mintpressnews.com/u-s-military-is-worlds-largest-polluter-hundreds-of-bases-gravely-contaminated/227776/)

"Producing more hazardous waste than the five largest U.S. chemical companies combined, the U.S. Department of Defense has left its toxic legacy throughout the world in the form of depleted uranium, oil, jet fuel, pesticides, defoliants like Agent Orange and lead, among others."

Whitney Webb continued, "In addition, the U.S., which has conducted more nuclear weapons tests than all other nations combined, is also responsible for the massive amount of radiation that continues to contaminate many islands in the Pacific Ocean. The Marshall Islands, where the U.S. dropped more than sixty nuclear weapons between 1946 and 1958, are a particularly notable example. Inhabitants of Marshall Islands and nearby Guam continue to experience an exceedingly high rate of cancer."

"The American Southwest was also the site of numerous nuclear weapons tests that contaminated large swaths of land. Navajo Indian reservations have been polluted by long-abandoned uranium mines where nuclear material was obtained by U.S. military contractors."

Dr. Sohbet Karbuz, an energy expert formerly with the International Energy Agency in Paris, wrote twelve years ago that: "The US Department of Defense is the largest oil consuming government body in the US and in the world," and "the biggest purchaser of oil in the world," using "93% of all government oil consumption…[and is] the single largest consumer of petroleum in the US." (http://www.resilience.org/stories/2006-02-26/us-military-oil-consumption/)

"According to the US Defense Energy Support Center Fact Book in

Fiscal Year 2004, the US military fuel consumption increased to 144 million barrels [395,000 barrels per day]. This is about 40 million barrels more than the average peacetime military usage."

Those figures do not include what pollution comes from warring.

"*The Army calculated that it would burn 40 million gallons [151.4 million liters] of fuel in three weeks of combat in Iraq, an amount equivalent to the gasoline consumed by all Allied armies combined during the four years of World War I,*" told American Petroleum Institute President and CEO Red Cavaney to a USAF banquet in Arlington, Virginia, July 15, 2004.

In a March 2008 study conducted by Oil Change International, authors Nikki Reisch and Steve Kretzmann maintained that in the first five years of the war against Iraq: "The war is responsible for at least 141 million metric tons of carbon dioxide equivalent (MMTCO2e)... To put this in perspective: CO2 released by the war to date equals the emissions from putting 25 million more cars on the road in the US this year. If the war was ranked as a country in terms of emissions, it would emit more CO2 each year than 139 of the world's nations do annually...the war each year emits more than 60% of all countries." (http://priceofoil.org/2008/03/01/a-climate-of-war/)

U.S. military action has resulted in the desertification of 90 percent of Iraqi territory, crippling the country's agricultural industry and forcing it to import more than 80 percent of its food. "The U.S. use of depleted uranium in Iraq during the Gulf War also caused a massive environmental burden for Iraqis. In addition, the U.S. military's policy of using open-air burn pits to dispose of waste from the 2003 invasion has caused a surge in cancer among U.S. servicemen and Iraqi civilians alike." (http://www.mintpressnews.com/u-s-military-is-worlds-largest-polluter-hundreds-of-bases-gravely-contaminated/227776/)

CIA TORTURE/DRUGS

Project *MK Ultra*, also called the *CIA mind control program* is the code name given to a drug program of experiments on human subjects. These experiments were/are intended to identify and develop drugs and procedures for use in interrogations and torture, in order to weaken the individual to force confessions through mind control. Organized through the CIA's Scientific Intelligence Division, the project coordinated with the Special Operations Division of the U.S. Army's Chemical Corps. They used LSD, chemicals, hypnosis, sensory deprivation, isolation, and other forms of torture on U.S. and Canadian citizens. Some were captives, but others were not and were given drugs without their knowledge. (17)

The CIA worked out of Fort Detrick, a U.S. Army Medical Command installation located in Frederick, Maryland. Fort Detrick was the center for biological weapons program from 1943 to 1969. *MK Ultra* continued elsewhere until 1973, officially. In addition to its own center, the CIA had research conducted at 80 institutions, including 44 colleges and universities, as well as 185 private front operations in hospitals, prisons, and pharmaceutical companies.

Project *MK Ultra* was first brought to public attention in 1975 by the Church Committee of the U.S. Congress, and a Gerald Ford commission to cursorily investigate CIA activities within the United States. Investigative efforts were hampered by the fact that CIA Director Richard Helms ordered all *MK Ultra* files destroyed in 1973, oft-repeated CIA tactic to thwart oversight and democracy. The Church Committee and Rockefeller Commission investigations had to rely principally on sworn testimony of direct participants and on the relatively small number of documents that survived Helms' destruction order.

The extent of damage to human guinea pigs is not known but at least one was murdered, or simply died of the drugs he was given without his knowledge. Frank Olson was an army biochemist and biological weapons researcher, who was given LSD without his knowledge in November 1953. He allegedly jumped out of a hotel room to his death, which was conveniently ruled a suicide.

The CIA's own internal investigation concluded that the head of *MK Ultra*, CIA chemist Sidney Gottlieb, had conducted the LSD experiment with Olson's prior knowledge, although it admitted Olson and other experimenters were told after ingestion. Gottlieb, incidentally, later provided the CIA with drugs to murder Patrice Lumumba and Fidel Castro.

The Olson family disputes the official version of events. They maintain that Frank Olson was murdered because he was viewed as a security risk. Olson had expressed moral disapproval over biological warfare research, assassination materials used by the CIA, and collaboration with former Nazi scientists (Operation Paperclip). He quit his position as acting chief of the Special Operations Division at Detrick, and tried to resign from the CIA.

Forensic evidence later found conflicted with the official version of events. When Olson's body was exhumed cranial injuries indicated that he had been knocked unconscious before he exited the window. The medical examiner termed Olson's death a "homicide". In 1975, Olson's family received a $750,000 settlement from the U.S. government and formal apologies from President Gerald Ford and CIA Director William Colby. Their apologies were limited to "informed consent issues" concerning Olson's ingestion of LSD. No one went to prison for murder. On November 28, 2012, the Olson family filed suit against the U.S. federal government for the wrongful death of Frank Olson. (18)

"The sons of a Cold War scientist who plunged to his death in 1953 several days after unwittingly taking LSD in a CIA mind-control experiment sued the government Wednesday. They claimed the CIA murdered their father...pushing him from a 13th-story window of a hotel - not, as the CIA says, that he jumped to his death," Associated Press wrote, November 28, 2012.

On July 23, 2013, federal judge James Boasberg dismissed the case for being too old and because the family had already accepted a financial settlement. Incidentally, the judge also sits on the Foreign Intelligence Surveillance Court.

Another side effect of the *MK Ultra* project was the dying admission of its chief scientist. Gottlieb said the program was useless.

Nevertheless, *MK Ultra*-type experiments may not have been abandoned, according to some former CIA officials and CIA expert observers. There is little reason to believe it does not continue today under a different set of acronyms, stated Victor Marchetti who spent fourteen years in the CIA. He has told various interviewers that the CIA routinely conducts disinformation campaigns and that CIA mind control research continues. In a 1977 interview, Marchetti specifically called the CIA claim that MKUltra was abandoned a "cover story". http://www.skepticfiles.org/socialis/marcheti.htm

Marchetti wrote one of the early ex-CIA whistle-blower books, *The CIA and the Cult of Intelligence*, Knopf, 1974.

In the skeptic files interview, Marchetti explained that the CIA is a systematic liar and censor.

"The basic reason for secrecy is not to keep the enemy from knowing what you're doing. He knows what you're doing because he's the target of it, and he's not stupid. The reason for the CIA to hide behind secrecy is to keep the public, and in particular the American public, from knowing what they're doing. This is done so that the President can deny that we were responsible for sabotaging some place over in Lebanon where a lot of people were killed.

"So that the President can deny period! Here is a good example: President Eisenhower denied we were involved in attempts to overthrow the Indonesian government in 1958 until the CIA guys got caught and the Indonesians produced them. He looked like a fool. So did the N.Y. Times and everybody else who believed him. That is the real reason for secrecy.

"There is a second reason for secrecy. That is that if the public doesn't know what you are doing you can lie to them because they don't know what the truth is. This is a very bad part of the CIA because this is where you get not only propaganda on the American people but actually disinformation, which is to say lies and falsehoods, peddled to the American public as the truth and which they accept as gospel. That's wrong. It's not only wrong, it's a lie and it allows the government and those certain elements of the government that can hide behind secrecy to get away with things that nobody knows about. If you carefully analyze all of these issues...this is always what is at the heart of it: That the CIA lied about it, or that the CIA misrepresented something, or the White House did it, because the CIA and the White House work hand in glove. The CIA is not a power unto itself... [rather] the inner circle of government, the inner circle of the establishment in general. The CIA is doing what these people want done so these people are appreciative and protective of them, and they in turn make suggestions or even go off on their own sometimes and operate deep cover for the CIA. So it develops into a self-feeding circle."

Another former member of the Establishment, Peter Dale Scott, once a diplomat for the Canadian government, is also a poet, professor, and political scientist who came over to the people's side. He has written

US-led soldiers protecting poppy fields

many important books and articles about the military states (US/NATO). One of them, *Drugs, Oil and War: The United States in Afghanistan, Colombia and Indochina* (Rowman & Littlefields, 2003) shows how, "Drug networks are important factors in the politics of every continent. The United States returns repeatedly to the posture of fighting wars in areas of petroleum reserves with the aid of drug-trafficking allies—drug proxies—with which it has a penchant to become involved."

It looks like this amoral mentality—the CIA omnipotence mentality—dominates United States politics and culture. They kill and or torture whomever they want; buy or steal any nation they want; and make entertainment out of it, warping the minds of most of its own citizens and Europeans to believe that the U.S. actually protects them against some greater evil. But there are those who see an end to this apparently endless power.

One of them is Dr. Chandra Muzaffar, president of the International Movement for a Just World (JUST). He wrote, "China and Russia: The Bilateral Relationship That Matters," July 24, 2017. (https://www.globalresearch.ca/china-and-russia-the-bilateral-relationship-that-matters/5600737)

"The US's pursuit of its hegemonic agenda in the vicinity of China and Russia has undoubtedly brought the two states closer together. Chinese and Russian leaders are only too aware that there are concerted moves by the intelligence apparatus in the US and elsewhere to drive a wedge between China and Russia. If anything it has increased their determination to remain united."

One cannot conclude that by China and Russia becoming more potent than the United States that our problems of war and violence will end. But it might just curb the insatiable US American desire for constant warring. When key sectors of the populations of the U.S. and Europe finally get tired of it all, maybe, just maybe they will rise up and crush the war machine!

A global empire has emerged.
An empire which encourages greed to grow and
selfishness to spread is a threat to humanity. It
undermines the spiritual and moral basis of
civilization. It would be a tragedy if such an empire becomes the
inheritance of our children.
This is why, all of us, wherever we are, and whoever we
are, must do all we can to help create a just world. This
is the duty and responsibility of every human being.
See JUST here: http://www.just-international.org

Notes:

1. See pages 92, 97-9, 125-6 of Douglas Valentine's book, *The CIA as Organized Crime: How illegal operations corrupt American and the world.* Clarity Press, 2017. See also: *No Good Men Among the Living* by Anand Gopal, Metropolitan Books, 2013.

2. See "How a Torture Protest Killed a Career," Consortium News, October 26, 2009; "U.S. Denies Entry to former British Ambassador Craig Murray," Global Research, September 12, 2016.

3. William Appleman Williams, *Empire as a Way of Life.* Oxford University Press, 1980.

4. History US Military Overt and Covert Global Interventions (http://www.brianwilson.com/history-us-military-overt-and-covert-global-interventions/)

   Congressional Research Service (CRS). (February 2, 2009). *Instances of Use of United States Armed Forces Abroad, 1798-2008.* Washington D.C.: CRS Report to Congress.

5. Secret memorandum written on February 24, 1948 for Secretary of State George Marshall. It is called PPS/23 (Policy Planning Staff): 'Review of Current Trends: U.S. Foreign Policy'. My excerpts are taken from part VII: Far East. This memo was printed by the magazine, Foreign Relations of the United States, 1948, Volume 1, 509-529.

6. J. Gerson, and B. Birchard, eds., The Sun Never Sets. South End Press, Boston, 1991.

7. B. M. Blechman, and S.S. Kaplan, *Force Without War: U.S. Armed Forces as a Political Instrument*, Appendix B. Wash., D.C.: The Brookings Institution, 1978.

8. See: Congressional Research Service, Gerson's and Barnaby's essays, Blechman and Collins, J.M. (1991). *America's Small Wars: Lessons for the Future.*

9. Fred Barnaby, *The Gaia peace Atlas.* New York; Doubleday, 1988. Plus later interventions cited elsewhere.

10. William Blum *Rogue State.* Common Courage Press, 2000, pp. 92-95, and his anti-imperialist report #149.

11. J. Prados (1996). *President's secret wars: CIA and pentagon covert operations from World War 11 through the Persian Gulf.* Chicago, 1996. See also, John Stockwell, *The Praetorian Guard: The U.S. role in the new world order.* South End Press, Cambridge, Ma., 1991. "The CIA and the Gulf War" – a speech by John Stockwell; February 20, 1991, Santa Cruz, Ca.

    One can see 345 of these wars and military interventions on the website: http://www.endusmilitariasm.org/forceandinterventions.htm. See also: http://en.wikipedia.org/wiki/Timeline_of¬_United_States_military_operations

12. http://en.wikipedia.org/wiki/Church_Committee

13. Peter Dale Scott, "T*he Libyan War, American Power and the Decline of the Petrodollar System*" ; "*Bombing of Libya – punishment for Gaddafi for his attempt to refuse US dollar*" as cited by Ellen Brown in "*Libya: All About Oil, or All About Banking*." For this and other points made here see also: Petras, James, "*Euro-US War on Libya: Official Lies and Misconceptions of Critics*".

14. Franco Bechis, "French plans to topple Gaddafi on track since last November. http://www.voltairenet.org/article169069.html

15. Russia has intervened in other countries a handful of times but they have either been part of the old Soviet Union (Hungary and Czechoslovakia) or the new Russian Federation (Chechnya and Dagestan) or, in the case of Georgia, separatist movements in South Ossetia and Abkhazia seeking independence. Georgia is also right up at Russia's border and had the U.S. achieved a NATO base there it would have clearly been a security risk.

16. Read the marvelous story of Father Roy Bourgeois and the Movement to Close the School of Americas, *Disturbing the Peace* by James Hodge and Linda Cooper , Orbis Books, Maryknoll, 2004.

17. See Advisory on Human Radiation Experiments, July 5, 1994, National Security Archives. http://www.nytimes.com/packages/pdf/national/13inmate_ProjectMKULTRA.pdf , congressional hearings. "New York Times", August 4, 1977, "80 Institutions Used in C.I.A. Mind Studies: Admiral Turner Tells Senators of Behavior Control Research Bars Drug Testing Now".

18. H. P. Albarelli *A Terrible Mistake: The Murder of Frank Olson and the CIA's Secret Cold War Experiments*. Trine Day, 2009

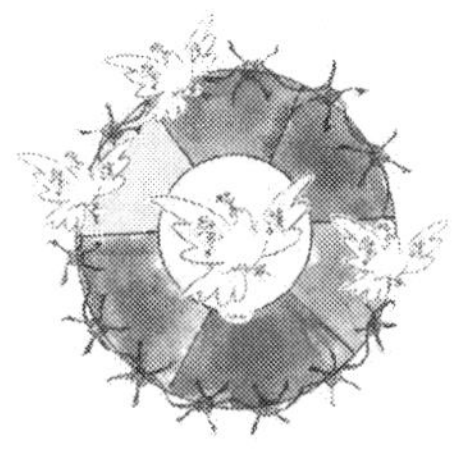

CHAPTER 19
American Exceptionalism

AMERICAN EXCEPTIONALISM IS an ideology in itself. It holds that "America" is unique among all countries for being a "land of opportunities". Americans are unique among all peoples for their ideals of democracy, liberty, personal freedom, individualism— that everyone who works hard regardless of roots or class can become rich and even become a president—everyone who is white and male, that is. That last caveat was the "exception to the rule" of American Exceptionalism until the 20th century when, first women and later black people could officially be equal, and could occupy the White House built by African slaves. (1)

French political scientist and historian Alexis de Tocqueville was the first writer to describe the country as "exceptional" in his book, *Democracy in America* (1835).

American Exceptionalism embraces *Manifest Destiny*—the belief that it is Americans' destiny to expand their "exceptional" qualities first throughout the Americas, in mid-19th century, and later to the whole world—spreading the good word with sword and movies. Many believe Americans are chosen by God to civilize the world, to bring the world its democracy. The first war fought with "god on its side" was against Mexico (chapter 18).

This superior view of America's place in the world was already codified in 1823 with the Monroe Doctrine, named after President James Monroe's foreign policy. First it warned Europe that Latin America was to come under United States doctrine while Europe could keep its other colonies.

Abraham Lincoln stated in the Gettysburg address (1863) that Americans have a duty to ensure that "government of the people, by

Jette Salling paraphrase of B. Helles a new beginning

the people, for the people, shall not perish from the earth." This got interpreted to mean it is Americans' mission to extend their superiority over other nations.

Many presidents took up the term American Exceptionalism in their wars, among them: Ulysses Grant, Theodore Roosevelt, Dwight Eisenhower, John F. Kennedy and Ronald Reagan.

While American Exceptionalism does not apply only to one religion or ethnic group (in later years blacks could be included), it is akin to what many Jews believe of themselves as being God's "chosen people", entitled to the Palestinian "promised land…of milk and honey" at the expense of the Arab peoples. U.S. manifest destiny promoters accept this postulate as it aids their drive for Middle Eastern oil—so much so that for the only time in history, it looked the other way when another state attacked it. The survivors of the *USS Liberty* know this first hand after Israel bombed their ship for hours and killed 34 American sailors. (http://www.whatreallyhappened.com/WRHARTICLES/ussliberty.html)

The actual phrase American Exceptionalism may have originated in the Soviet regime of Joseph Stalin. He condemned many American Communists, including some leaders, who suggested that the U.S. was impervious to communist ideals, that American workers were "exceptional" because there were no rigid class distinctions, and they would not embrace a socialist revolution. With minor exceptions few workers have, in fact, embraced the classic Marxist concepts of the need for class struggle and socialist revolution.

Why is that? Colleague Gaither Stewart writes in "The Greanville Post", October 2, 2017:

"In a great dialectic the survival needs of the bourgeoisie generate the resistance that can ultimately crush it—the resistance that according to Marxist theory will crush it someday. These days, there for everyone to see, for everyone to feel, is the spreading sense of unease marking its successive economic-financial crises point to the eventual demise of bourgeois, bandit capitalism.

So why has it not already happened, one must wonder? Why hasn't it collapsed long ago? Though the bourgeoisie—capitalist class— is small and the proletariat wage earners an overwhelming majority, why don't the exploited classes rebel and rebel, revolt and revolt, again and again? Why not? The reason is clear: the exploited classes are not only victims. They are also accomplices—half victim, half accomplice. The historical paradox! The ruling class counts on this dichotomy to maintain the system. Divide and rule. Meritocracy. Rewards for obedience. Two cars and bigger houses for staying in line. A system based on money, domination, pervasive indoctrination of Orwellian proportions, and fear. Religion too, and FEAR. Fear of fear. Fear of change. Fear, fear, fear. A fearful people is an obedient people." (http://www.greanvillepost.com/2017/10/02/definitions-the-bourgeoisie/)

I agree with Stewart and add that the U.S. capitalist class can afford to give a bit more to many of its homeland exploited as the capitalists exploit workers in "third world" countries all the more. They create false consciousness through the divide and conquer rule, and by instilling fear.

American Exceptionalism works best on Americans when they convince themselves to believe the ruler's lies thereby maintaining their ignorance. They feel safe by refusing to see the truth, by accepting the rules for fear of losing their jobs, fear of being outcast by friends and family, fear of being jailed or even killed if they decide to seek the truth and then act upon it. That is what stands behind a lot of America's racist and genocidal violence perpetrated by the white working class clothed in overalls or military uniforms under the orders of the ruling elite.

My editor, Patrice Greanville, a onetime academic and lifelong media and social critic, with a multicultural background in Europe and Latin America, has also found American Exceptionalism a compelling phenomenon. In correspondence with me, he offers some thoughts on why so many Americans may have come to believe they are superior to other peoples and all other countries. The below is excerpted from a monograph in preparation:

> *American exceptionalism is one of those peculiarities that make the U.S. such an exasperating enigma to so many people around the world. Exceptionalism, per se, is just one form of chauvinism, itself an offshoot of tribalism, a recognition that humans are (and feel) divided by real or imagined differences, and that many tend to feel superior to others.*
>
> *Just about every country under the sun today—big and small, old and young— is chauvinist in some way. Bolivia and Chile, I know for a fact, are chauvinist, and so is Brazil and France, of course, and Britain, and Italy—as anyone attending an international soccer match can attest—is in a class by itself. Russia, naturally, to some extent, shares this trait, too, and even China and India, both ancient, foundational civilisations noted for their inner balance and firm identities, also show instances of national vanity. The Germans even had a national anthem once proclaiming to be "uber alles"—it doesn't get more explicit than that. Little Togo is probably chauvinist in its own peculiar way. So "exceptionalism" is not that rare at all.*
>
> *But, there are degrees of chauvinism among nations, like differences in temperament, in narcissism, and these differences can have serious consequences. In that sense—as shown by recent polls—US chauvinism is very pervasive. It's chauvinism on steroids—insistent, intrusive, obnoxious, and even devious.*

And these are just what we might call its "mundane" characteristics, where it most resembles other cases of acute national self-approval. The problem is that narcissism at the national level is no less toxic a personality disorder than at the individual level. And when this trait defines the character of a reality-averse, often petulant jejune superpower, US exceptionalism really becomes a threat to everything alive on the face of this planet. How did this monstruous deformation come to occupy the center of US political life, to be seen as a "foundational belief" with many of the accoutrements of a de facto *religion? I say religion because religions are not supposed to be questioned in their logic or factuality.*

A closer look at US exceptionalism begins to give the game away. It finds its claims false or undistinguished and its uses malignant: The ideal mask for modern US imperialism, immunising it, at least in the eyes of the vastly disinformed home populace, against any and all possible charges of impure intent and wanton criminality. But the exceptionalist myth, an organism comprised of subsidiary mythologies, goes even further: wrapped in its customary sanctimoniousness, it grants the ruling plutocrats unlimited access to the blood, muscle and treasure of most ordinary Americans, while also proclaiming with the audacity of a shameless mountebank the right of the United States to be acknowledged as the world's natural leader, the "indispensable nation" under God.

Casual observers might think the rise of exceptionalism was largely spontaneous: a nation of immigrants—the losers fleeing Europe's brutal class wars—showing, rather compulsively, their eternal gratitude to the new land of opportunity. But they would be mistaken. Nothing with real power consequences is ever that accidental or left to chance in America, especially when it has been found by the ruling orders to be an extremely useful tool in the management of their subject population. To paraphrase media analyst pioneer Alex Carey, the American system of pseudo democracy saw in exceptionalism's multifaceted manifestations another terrific instrument to "take the risk out of democracy," something the Founding Fathers themselves had been keenly interested in and maneuvered to implement. (They mostly succeeded.). In a way, the immigrants' naive vision of America gave the expansionist wing of the US ruling class, the folks who had embraced Manifest Destiny with a passion, and already stolen half of Mexico by mid 19th century, a shot in the arm, the ultimate seal of approval.

John Gerassi, a noted Latin Americanist and political scientist had little trouble puncturing the conceits of US exceptionalism, and by extension its devilish spawn, US foreign policy, a criminal enterprise, with rare lapses, almost from inception. Speaking about Manifest Destiny, something Bolivar and Marti also warned us about, he states:

"That has been our policy in Latin America. It began in recognizable manner in 1823 with President Monroe's declaration warning nonhemisphere nations to stay out of the American continent. Because of its rhetoric, America's liberal historians interpreted the Monroe Doctrine as a generous, even altruistic declaration on the part of the United States to protect its weaker neighbors to the south. To those neighbors, however, that doctrine asserted America's ambitions: it said, in effect, Europeans stay out of Latin America because it belongs to the United States. A liberal, but not an American, Salvador de Madariaga, once explained its hold on Americans:

'I only know two things about the Monroe Doctrine: one is that no American I have met knows what it is; the other is that no American I have met will consent to its being tampered with. That being so, I conclude that the Monroe Doctrine is not a doctrine but a dogma, for such are the two features by which you can tell a dogma. But when I look closer into it, I find that it is not one dogma, but two, to wit: the dogma of the infallibility of the American President and the dogma of the immaculate conception of American foreign policy.'" (*Violence, Revolution, and Structural Change in Latin America, https://www.greanvillepost.com/2018/02/21/violence-revolution-and-structural-change-in-latin-america/*).

As promulgated by its national identity myth, America is good, was born good, and can only do good. We have an obligation to share our good with other nations. It follows that if the immaculate conception defines our highly moral foreign policy, our similarly excellent economic system—capitalism—or "free enterprise" if you like—could and must define "americanness", what to be an American, a truly free individual, really means, not to mention the onetime much envied "American Way of Life."

For only in the US to be against capitalism is also to be "un-American", a suspect in patriotic virtue, an illogical and absurd construct that no one seems to notice, let alone oppose, due to the sheer enforced ubiquity of the concept due to nonstop propaganda legitimating it. In Italy, Germany, Mexico, France, or even England, where capitalism first matured, the idea of calling, say, a British communist "anti-British" or an Italian socialist "anti-Italian", would sound odd if not downright laughable. But not here. How come?

Built on a tissue of mostly transparent lies that few rational minds would have difficulty uncovering, the exceptionalist myth is enormously resilient. Cursory inspection reveals layer upon layer of self-flattering claims and assumptions (many riddled with contradictions), while thick hypocrisy lubricates every nook and cranny of the mendacious edifice, making the whole a well-integrated, smoothly functioning imperialist ideology ideally tailored to a population that believes itself to inhabit a democracy. As the author points out at the beginning of this chapter, US exceptionalism is no run-of-the-mill hyper-nationalism as we observe in other nations; it is a full-blown catechism informing and enabling many aspects of the US governmental apparatus. Indeed, the "American Way of Life" never had a deeper meaning than in this essential aspect of its existence. For—to the misery of the world—the US ruling class has learned to use this ideology adroitly for conquest and subversion abroad and pacification at home.

Empires, however, especially compulsory hegemonists like the U.S., do not do well in holy matrimony with genuine democracies. One tends to exclude and cancel the other. In the U.S., with a very weak or pretend democracy, this organic tension does not really exist, although the task of keeping appearances is becoming increasingly challenging to all the main parties involved. The fact is that Americans now live in a violent, lawless empire, not a regular nation, the US homeland merely serving as the outward carapace for the business of the transnational capitalist hegemon, whose sole object is to advance and defend the interests of the global plutocracy, of which the US branch is (still) the undisputed leader.

This is of course a fraud of colossal proportions, especially for trusting souls stuck on Civics 101, but one which the propaganda system is still managing to keep afloat. Fractures on the bubble's wall are finally starting to appear. As certified now even by Ivy League political scientists, the US is only a make-believe democracy. With the core unit of capitalism, the corporation, as the dominant social engine, the whole nation's dynamic issues from a hierarchic tyranny.

An article by investigative historian Eric Zuesse confirms this heretical finding:

"A study, to appear in the Fall 2014 issue of the academic journal Perspectives on Politics, finds that the U.S. is no democracy, but instead an oligarchy, meaning profoundly corrupt, so that the answer to the study's opening question, 'Who governs? Who really rules?' in this country, is:

"Despite the seemingly strong empirical support in previous studies for theories of majoritarian democracy, our analyses suggest that majorities of the American public actually have little influence over the policies our government adopts. Americans do enjoy many features central to [formal, not ubstantive] democratic governance, such as regular elections, freedom of speech and association, and a widespread (if still contested) franchise. But, they go on to say,

"America's claims to being a democratic society are seriously threatened" by the findings in this, the first-ever comprehensive scientific study of the subject, which shows that there is instead "'the nearly total failure of 'median voter' and other Majoritarian Electoral Democracy theories [of America]. When the preferences of economic elites and the stands of organized interest groups are controlled for, the preferences of the average American appear to have only a minuscule, near-zero, statistically non-significant impact upon public policy."

To put it short: The United States is no democracy, but actually an oligarchy. The authors of this historically important study are Martin Gilens and Benjamin I. Page, and their article is titled 'Testing Theories of American Politics.' The authors clarify that the data available are probably under-representing the actual extent of control of the U.S. by the super-rich." (*See "US Is an Oligarchy Not a Democracy, says Scientific Study", by Eric Zuesse, Common Dreams, April 14, 2014 (https://www.commondreams.org/views/2014/04/14/us-oligarchy-not-democracy-says-scientific-study*).

While Gilens and Page document the long known fact that the super rich are no friends of democracy, they are coy in naming capitalism as the system that makes the rise of tycoons inevitable.

But enormous wealth concentration has other highly toxic effects in America. The grotesque inequality and non-existence of actual governing power by the masses at home has been the hidden counterpart to the brutal imperialistic regime abroad implemented by the native elites, something to which hundreds of millions of people in scores of nations, large and small, can attest. In this manner, protected by its "exceptionalist" propaganda endowing it with axiomatic, unerring, moral superiority, and (as tirelessly proclaimed by its ruling class) charged with the "sacred duty" to carry "freedom and democracy" to all corners of the planet, the US has been able to lead a sordid double life for almost 200 years: arguably mostly Dr Jekyll at home, murderous meddlesome Mr Hyde across the globe.

Some readers no doubt will argue at this point that it was capitalism that gave America the distinction of being the first nation to spawn a large, affluent middle class, with many of its members living as well or better than their social superiors in the old world.

While this is true in the narrow sense, the phenomenon was largely a historical accident not inherent in capitalism. It was war spending—a form of military Keynesianism—that rescued America from a still debilitating Great Depression. The timing of modern era's European wars to divide the world's "colonial spoils", also serendipitous, presented America with extremely fortunate opportunities to develop its industrial might and political clout. Indeed except for self-inflicted wounds such as the Civil War the U.S. has enjoyed uninterrupted peace in its own homeland for over three centuries thanks to its exquisite geostrategic location, making it a virtual island continent flanked by two gigantic oceans and two weak powers, one an easy target for land grabs, Mexico, the other—Canada—a satellite of a declining empire almost from inception. Thus, by 1945 America stood as the sole world superpower with both its population and industrial infrastructure virtually intact, and in a state of readiness to flood the world with its cornucopia of goods, all of which allowed labor to negotiate better terms and capitalists to grant them, thereby laying the groundwork for the age of affluence that characterised the "golden years" of US capitalism.

Add to this the infusion of cheap labor for many generations via mass immigration due to the deplorable European and other old world class systems, coupled with another great accident, having the best topsoil in the world, and you get the makings of a veritable miracle in US agriculture: the most productive, even without its high quotient of early mechanization.

Thus, when we compare Russian/Soviet and U.S. agricultural output, the "fix was in", so to speak. Besides being poor, in turmoil, with its underdeveloped infrastruture in shambles for a long time due to war wounds, and encircled by enemies, Russians had to contend with one of the hardest lands to cultivate, a lot of it permafrost. Yes, the USSR/Russia territory is big, 11 time zones, but a lot of that is essentially not very fertile. This advantage which was paraded as a triumph of capitalism over socialism was again, when examined, based on serendipity, an accident of nature. Virtually all the conceits of the "indispensable nation" to justify its sociopathic imperialist trajectory are grounded in bunk. No wonder that historical truth is persona non grata in America.

It should be clear by now that the main purpose of cultivating the exceptionalist myth is to bolster the fortunes of the global capitalist elites, with the Americans in the vanguard, primus inter pares. This prompts a final question: Can we envision a strong, capitalist America, not needing its claims to exceptionalism? Yes we can, but that nation would also be inherently diseased, riddled with incurable sociopathies, and ultimately unviable. The short answer to this is because capitalism itself is a highly unstable, inherently amoral, self-liquidating system. As it grows old, passing from its competitive phase to monopoly, and from a deficient democracy to plutocratic imperialism, it generates more and more contradictions that eventually make it insufferable to everything living under its dominion. Capitalism is a terminal condition. It cannot be fixed. (Excerpted from Understanding US Exceptionalism, a monograph in preparation, P. Greanville, 2018).

What the Yankees have always been good at is deception, especially among whites by enlarging their colorless ego through nearly all the mass media, entertainment and cultural forms. The land of opportunity, and many others, is there for the taking…for whites. If there is not enough backing within the population or among international ally vassals for yet another aggressive war then creating conditions for the wanted war can be accommodated. There are many examples:

1. "Remember the Maine" was the slogan media mogul William Randolph Hearst used to whip up war fury against Spain, in order to take effective control of Cuba by preventing Cubans from winning their anti-colonial liberation war alone. (chapter three)
2. President Lyndon Johnson did the military-industrial complex the favor of reversing JFK's initiation of ending the war against Vietnam by fabricating a Vietnamese attack on the *USS Maddox* in the Gulf of Tonkin. He convinced Congress with this lie to grant him a war without naming it as one. The Gulf of Tonkin Resolution granted the presidency the use of all "necessary" force, which ended in the murder of millions of human beings. (chapter 12)
3. The lie that led to the totally superfluous atomic bombing of Hiroshima and Nagasaki. (chapter 12)
4. The many lies about the terror attack on September 11, 2001, in which some "chickens did come home to roost", and lay the basis for invasions in the Middle East and North Africa.

The chicken roosting simile I associate with morality. Many of the terrorist victims were co-responsible for America's many wars and oppressive domination of other peoples, a moral issue I take up in an agonizing essay. (https://www.ronridenour.com/articles/2002/0101--rr.htm)

I do not know for certain if elements in the U.S. government were co-responsible for the attacks on that day but I do know that there was no defense against these attacks since it seems the entire military apparatus was on an exercise. The training dealt with how to combat such terror attacks. If there were only 19 terrorists directly involved, it seems more than odd that they would choose that propitious day without inside knowledge; also odd that 15 of them were from Saudi Arabia, whose diplomats and bin Laden family members were let free to fly away when no one else could.

It is also odd that Israeli intelligence agents were seen applauding the Twin Towers explosions. Five Israelis were arrested and detained for 71 days. FBI counterintelligence concluded at least two worked for Israeli intelligence, but they were let go, deported to Israel.

Dylan Avery and Jason Bermas made the documentary film *Loose*

Change that is used widely by the 9/11 Truth movement. The film asserts that Flight 77 could not have accounted for the damage at the Pentagon, that the Twin Tower fires were insufficient to cause their collapse, and that cell phone calls from the hijacked airplanes would have been impossible at the time.

How can it be that thousands of architect and engineer professionals demand a new investigation into the cause of the attacks? Michael Moore's *Fahrenheit 9/11* is a powerful documentary about this. Many Hollywood stars and even a former Minnesota governor, Jesse Ventura, speak about the government lies and the need for an independent, honest investigation. (http://911truth.org/achievements/events-campaigns-to-expose-911-truth/)

HAROLD PINTER 2005 NOBEL LITERATURE PRIZE SPEECH

While it is not Pinter's intent to make the chicken-roosting judgment that I do, his poignant speech in acceptance of the Nobel Prize for Literature shows some of the reasons why some seek revenge.

"...the majority of politicians...are interested not in truth but in power and in the maintenance of that power. To maintain that power it is essential that people remain in ignorance, that they live in ignorance of the truth, even the truth of their own lives. What surrounds us therefore is a vast tapestry of lies, upon which we feed.

As every single person here knows, the justification for the invasion of Iraq was that Saddam Hussein possessed a highly dangerous body of weapons of mass destruction, some of which could be fired in 45 minutes, bringing about appalling devastation. We were assured that was true. It was not true. We were told that Iraq had a relationship with Al Quaeda and shared responsibility for the atrocity in New York of September 11th 2001. We were assured that this was true. It was not true. We were told that Iraq threatened the security of the world. We were assured it was true. It was not true.

The truth is something entirely different. The truth is to do with how the United States understands its role in the world and how it chooses to embody it."

"The United States supported and in many cases engendered every right wing military dictatorship in the world after the end of the Second World War. I refer to Indonesia, Greece, Uruguay, Brazil, Paraguay, Haiti, Turkey, the Philippines, Guatemala, El Salvador, and, of course, Chile.

The horror the United States inflicted upon Chile in 1973 can never be purged and can never be forgiven.

Hundreds of thousands of deaths took place throughout these countries. Did they take place? And are they in all cases attributable to US foreign policy? The answer is yes they did take place and they are attributable to American foreign policy. But you wouldn't know it.

It never happened. Nothing ever happened. Even while it was happening it wasn't happening. It didn't matter. It was of no interest. The crimes of the United States have been systematic, constant, vicious, remorseless, but very few people have actually talked about them. You have to hand it to America. It has exercised a quite clinical manipulation of power worldwide while masquerading as a force for universal good. It's a brilliant, even witty, highly successful act of hypnosis.

I put to you that the United States is without doubt the greatest show on the road. Brutal, indifferent, scornful and ruthless it may be but it is also very clever. As a salesman it is out on its own and its most saleable commodity is self love. It's a winner. Listen to all American presidents on television say the words, 'the American people', as in the sentence, 'I say to the American people it is time to pray and to defend the rights of the American people and I ask the American people to trust their president in the action he is about to take on behalf of the American people'

It's a scintillating stratagem. Language is actually employed to keep thought at bay. The words 'the American people' provide a truly voluptuous cushion of reassurance. You don't need to think. Just lie back on the cushion. The cushion may be suffocating your intelligence and your critical faculties but it's very comfortable. This does not apply of course to the 40 million people living below the poverty line and the 2 million men and women imprisoned in the vast gulag of prisons, which extends across the US.

The United States no longer bothers about low intensity conflict. It no longer sees any point in being reticent or even devious. It puts its cards on the table without fear or favor. It quite simply doesn't give a damn about the United Nations, international law or critical dissent, which it regards as impotent and irrelevant. It also has its own bleating little lamb tagging behind it on a lead, the pathetic and supine Great Britain."

"Its official declared policy is now defined as 'full spectrum dominance'. That is not my term, it is theirs. 'Full spectrum dominance' means control of land, sea, air and space and all attendant resources."

"What has happened to our moral sensibility? Did we ever have any? What do these words mean? Do they refer to a term very rarely employed these days—conscience? A conscience to do not only with our own acts but to do with our shared responsibility in the acts of others? Is all this dead?" (https://www.nobelprize.org/nobel_prizes/literature/laureates/2005/pinter-lecture-e.html)

John Rohn Hall calls American Exceptionalism "the illusion of choice." "Sleeping through the American Dream, still believing the lies, counting on the lies, clinging to the lies like their lives depend upon it. Empire's Misinformation Machine knows the drill. Well learned from blood brother Adolph: 'If you tell a big enough lie and tell it frequently enough, it will be believed.'" (https://dissidentvoice.org/2017/08/empires-day-of-reckoning/)

BARAK OBAMA THE WORST PRESIDENT

President Barack Obama used the term American Exceptionalism more than any other president—perhaps to "compensate" for the racist riff-raff hatred against him because of his skin color.

A *Washington Post* May 28, 2014 headline read: "Obama's New Patriotism: How Obama has used his presidency to redefine 'American Exceptionalism'".

Greg Jaffe wrote: "No American president has talked about American Exceptionalism more often and in more varied ways than Obama. As an Illinois state legislator, young U.S. senator and presidential candidate, he spoke about it most frequently through the prism of his own remarkable story. His father had grown up in Kenya herding goats. His wife carried 'blood of slaves and slave owners,' he noted during his first presidential campaign. He had brothers and sisters, nieces and nephews of every race and many religions, scattered across continents."

"In Libya, many of his top advisers, including his defense secretary, urged him not to use the U.S. military to protect citizens from attacks by forces loyal to dictator Moammar Gaddafi. The United States didn't need another war in a country of only peripheral interest. Obama overruled them, citing America's 'indispensable' role." (http://www.washingtonpost.com/sf/national/2015/06/03/obama-and-american-exceptionalism/?utm_term=.56ee66d9c6f7)

Obama used the al Qaeda lie that they knew Gaddafi would "massacre" them in a day. His (and Hillary Clinton) war on Gaddafi is what they call preemptive war, something Zionists have used against Arab countries at will.

Eight months before the *Washington Post* article, in September 2013, Obama was about to war on Syria, because of another terrorist lie that the government had used sarin gas to kill people. (chapter 15). President Putin warned him about using "American Exceptionalism" to commit a military invasion that could easily lead to a world war. Despite the "New York Times" alliance with the war-machine it wisely published his opinion piece and on a special day, September 11 (2013): "A Plea for Caution" by Vladimir V. Putin.

> *"Recent events surrounding Syria have prompted me to speak directly to the American people and their political leaders. It is important to do so at a time of insufficient communication between our societies. Relations between us have passed through different stages. We stood against each other during the cold war. But we were also allies once, and defeated the Nazis together. The universal international organization—the United Nations—was then established to prevent such devastation from ever happening again."*

With a prayer for peace the man most demonized by U.S. politicians and their media concluded:

> *"My working and personal relationship with President Obama is marked by growing trust. I appreciate this. I carefully studied his address to the nation on Tuesday. And I would rather disagree with a case he made on American exceptionalism, stating that the United States' policy is 'what makes America different. It's what makes us exceptional.' It is extremely dangerous to encourage people to see themselves as exceptional, whatever the motivation. There are big countries and small countries, rich and poor, those with long democratic traditions and those still finding their way to democracy. Their policies differ, too. We are all different, but when we ask for the Lord's*

> *blessings, we must not forget that God created us equal."* (http://www.nytimes.com/2013/09/12/opinion/putin-plea-for-caution-from-russia-on-syria.html?_r=0)

John Pilger is not nearly as diplomatic as President Putin in his description of Obama's embrace of American Exceptionalism. Excerpts from his piece, "The Issue is not Trump, It is US:"

"One of the persistent strands in American political life is a cultish extremism that approaches fascism. This was given expression and reinforced during the two terms of Barack Obama. 'I believe in American Exceptionalism with every fiber of my being,' said Obama, who expanded America's favorite military pastime, bombing, and death squads ('special operations') as no other president has done since the Cold War. (https://www.counterpunch.org/2017/01/17/the-issue-is-not-trump-it-is-us/)

"According to a Council on Foreign Relations survey, in 2016 alone Obama dropped 26,171 bombs. That is 72 bombs every day. He bombed the poorest people on earth, in Afghanistan, Libya, Yemen, Somalia, Syria, Iraq, Pakistan.

"Every Tuesday—reported *The New York Times*—he personally selected those who would be murdered by mostly hellfire missiles fired from drones. Weddings, funerals, shepherds were attacked, along with those attempting to collect the body parts festooning the "terrorist target". A leading Republican senator, Lindsey Graham, estimated, approvingly, that Obama's drones killed 4,700 people. 'Sometimes you hit innocent people and I hate that,' he said, 'but we've taken out some very senior members of Al Qaeda.'"

"Under Obama, the US has extended secret 'special forces' operations to 138 countries or 70 per cent of the world's population. The first African-American president launched what amounted to a full-scale invasion of Africa. Reminiscent of the Scramble for Africa in the late 19th century, the US African Command (Africom) has built a network of supplicants among collaborative African regimes eager for American bribes and armaments...It is as if Africa's proud history of liberation, from Patrice Lumumba to Nelson Mandela, is consigned to oblivion by a new master's black colonial elite whose 'historic mission', warned Frantz Fanon...is the promotion of 'a capitalism rampant though camouflaged'".

I also wrote my take on Obama's significance. In my view he is the worst U.S. president ever because he was the greatest hope especially for African-Americans, other people of color, and white liberals/ progressives. They kept hoping for years without protesting his wars and plundering for the rich. Some even rationalized his wars. See https://dissidentvoice.org/2013/03/obama-the-worst-us-president-ever/

"He is THE president for US corporations. With his black Kenyan roots he can walk into Africa's rich parlors and black White houses and communicate with these butchers better than any of the capitalist class' other presidents, all white.

"Obama is worse than them because he betrays all his black 'brothers and sisters' in the US, all except a few rich and opportunistic ones. He was THE hope; he would improve their lot, and that of the poor, the working people. He has done nothing. Instead, he takes from them to give to the rich, the worst criminals on Wall Street, the war arms industry, the oil and mineral industries."

Another element in American Exceptionalism is the phenomenon of American citizens' shooting wars against their own people. There were "only 290" mass shooting murder incidents (four or more killings) in Obama's last year while Trump's first year was the deadliest of all—345; one every nine of ten days. Americans commit more mass shooting murders than any other country: one-third of them. October 1 was the biggest single citizen murder day in U.S. history when a 64-year old wealthy man killed 58 persons and wounded 500 at an outdoor concert in Las Vegas.

LULLABY

Little war child, where are you going?
East or west?
Where in the world do you believe you can find a friend?
Little war child, what suits you best:
A worn carpet?
A plywood coffin?
A life jacket?
Little war child, where will you die:
Where the bombs fall
Or in the open sea?

Little war child, where do you want to go?
Choose yourself. Just we
Shall never see you again
(By Henrik Nordbrandt, a Danish poet, winner of Nordic Council's 2000 Literature Prize. Translated by this author with his permission)

WHAT TO DO

John Pilger concluded his article with the most pressing question of the century? "...when will a genuine movement of opposition arise? Angry, eloquent, all-for-one-and-one-for all. Until real politics return to people's lives, the enemy is not Trump, it is ourselves!"

Harold Pinter is in step: "I believe that despite the enormous odds which exist, unflinching, unswerving, fierce intellectual determination, as citizens, to define the realtruth of our lives and our societies is a crucial obligation which devolves upon us all. It is in fact mandatory.

"If such a determination is not embodied in our political vision we have no hope of restoring what is so nearly lost to us - the dignity of man," Harold Pinter concluded his speech.

Canadian professor Michel Chossudovsky addresses the issues Pilger and Pinter raise, in his January 9, 2018 article, "The Empire's 'Lefty Intellectuals' Call for Regime Change. The Role of 'Progressives' and the Antiwar Movement" (https://www.globalresearch.ca/the-empires-lefty-intellectuals-call-for-regime-change-the-role-of-progressives-and-the-antiwar-movement/5625333)

"What is now unfolding in both North America and Western Europe is fake social activism, controlled and funded by the corporate establishment. This manipulated process precludes the formation of ***a real mass movement against war, racism and social injustice****.*

The anti-war movement is dead. The war on Syria is tagged as 'a civil war'.

The war on Yemen is also portrayed as a civil war. While the bombing is by Saudi Arabia, the insidious role of the US is downplayed or casually ignored. 'The US is not directly involved so there is no need for us to wage an anti-war campaign'. (paraphrase)

War and neoliberalism are no longer at the forefront of civil society activism. Funded by corporate charities, via a network of non-governmental organizations, social activism tends to be piecemeal. There is no integrated anti-globalization anti-war movement. The economic crisis is not seen as having a relationship to US led wars.

In turn, dissent has become compartmentalized. Separate 'issue oriented' protest movements..."

"What is required is ***the development of a broad-based grassroots network*** *which seeks to disable patterns of authority and decision making pertaining to war.*

This network would be established at all levels in society, towns and villages, work places, parishes*. Trade unions, farmers' organizations, professional associations, business associations, student unions, veterans associations, church groups would be called upon to integrate the antiwar organizational structure. Of crucial importance, this movement should extend into the Armed Forces as a means to breaking the legitimacy of war among service men and women.*

The first task would be to disable war propaganda through an effective campaign against media disinformation*.*

The corporate media would be directly challenged, leading to boycotts of major news outlets, which are responsible for channeling disinformation into the news chain. This endeavor would require a parallel process at the grass roots level, of sensitizing and educating fellow citizens on the nature of the war and the global crisis, as well as effectively 'spreading the word' through advanced networking, through alternative media outlets on the internet, etc. In recent developments, the independent online media has been the target of manipulation and censorship, precisely with a view to undermining anti-war activism on the internet.

The creation of such a movement, which forcefully challenges the legitimacy of the structures of political authority, is no easy task. ***It would require a degree of solidarity, unity and commitment unparalleled in World history****. It would require breaking down political and ideological barriers within society and* ***acting with a single voice****. It would also require eventually unseating the war criminals, and indicting them for war crimes.*

America's hegemonic project in the post 9/11 era is the 'Globalization of War' whereby the U.S.-NATO military machine—coupled with covert intelligence operations, economic sanctions and the thrust of 'regime change'—is deployed in all major regions of the world. The threat of pre-

emptive nuclear war is also used to black-mail countries into submission.

This 'Long War against Humanity' is carried out at the height of the most serious economic crisis in modern history.

It is intimately related to a process of global financial restructuring, which has resulted in the collapse of national economies and the impoverishment of large sectors of the World population.

The ultimate objective is World conquest under the cloak of 'human rights' and 'Western democracy'.

Gabriel Rockhill wrote an excellent article about that published on December 13, 2017, entitled, "The U.S. is not a Democracy; it never was". After analyzing why that is the case, which this book also deals with, he offers a bit of hope that we can do something about that.

"Rather than blindly believing in a golden age of democracy in order to remain at all costs within the gilded cage of an ideology produced specifically for us by the well-paid spin-doctors of a plutocratic oligarchy, we should unlock the gates of history and meticulously scrutinize the founding and evolution of the American imperial republic. This will not only allow us to take leave of its jingoist and self-congratulatory origin myths, but it will also provide us with the opportunity to resuscitate and reactivate so much of what they have sought to obliterate.

"In particular, *there is a radical America just below the surface of these nationalist narratives, an America in which the population autonomously organizes itself in indigenous and ecological activism, black radical resistance, anti-capitalist mobilization, anti-patriarchal struggles...*It is this America that the corporate republic has sought to eradicate, while simultaneously investing in an expansive public relations campaign to cover over its crimes with the fig leaf of 'democracy'..." (https://www.counterpunch.org/2017/12/13/the-u-s-is-not-a-democracy-it-never-was/) [my emphasis]

Gareth Porter offered a proposal in line with this simmering radical America at the *NoWar2016* conference: "How We Could End the Permanent War State". It is posted on *World Beyond War* run by anti-war activist and writer David Swanson. (http://worldbeyondwar.org/end-permanent-war-state/)

World Beyond War endeavors to be "a global nonviolent movement to end war and establish a just and sustainable peace". It has chapters in several cities of the world. Porter wrote:

"I want to present a vision of something that has not been discussed seriously in many, many years: a national strategy to mobilize a very large segment of the population of this country to participate in a movement to force the retreat of the permanent war state."

"I suggest that it is time for a newly invigorated national movement to come together around a concrete strategy for accomplishing the goal of ending the permanent war state by taking away its means of intervening in foreign conflicts.

"The following are the four key elements that we would need to include in such a strategy:

(1) A clear, concrete vision of what eliminating the permanent war state would mean in practice to provide a meaningful target for people to support.
(2) A new and compelling way of educating and mobilizing people to action against the permanent war state.
(3) A strategy for reaching specific segments of society on the issue.
(4) A plan for bringing political pressure to bear with the aim of ending the permanent war state within ten years."

"So we should update General Smedley Butler's memorable slogan from the 1930s, 'War is a Racket' to reflect the fact that the benefits that now accrue to the national security establishment make those of war profiteers in the 1930s seem like child's play. I suggest the slogan such as 'permanent war is a racket' or the 'the war state is a racket'".

The Real News covered this conference and videos are presented of the various talks and panels. (http://worldbeyondwar.org/nowar2016/)

One of many groups participating at this unique conference was "Voices for Creative Non-Violence" (http://vcnv.org/). Among its many activities is advocating Peace with Russia, in which they make study trips to the country. (http://vcnv.org/category/u-s-russia-tensions/)

My friend William Hathaway has ideas worth implementing too. His book, Radical Peace is a favorite of mine. (http://media.trineday.com/radicalpeace/ 2010).

I quote here from his article, "Sedition, Subversion, Sabotage: A Long-War Strategy For The Left."

"Despite its recurring crises, this system is still too strong, too adaptable, and has too many supporters in all classes for it to be overthrown any time soon. We're probably not going to be the ones to create a new society." (https://popularresistance.org/sedition-subversion-sabotage-a-long-war-strategy-for-the-left/) (A must website for all activists. Look up his piece for more details.)

"But we can now lay the groundwork for that, first by exposing the hoax that liberal reforms will lead to basic changes. People need to see that the purpose of liberalism is to defuse discontent with promises of the future and thus prevent mass opposition from coalescing. It diverts potentially revolutionary energy into superficial dead ends. Bernie Sanders' 'long game' campaign is really only a game similar to that of his reformist predecessor, Dennis Kucinich, designed to keep us in the 'big tent' of the Democratic Party. Capitalism, although resilient, is willing to change only in ways that shore it up, so before anything truly different can be built, we have to bring it down.

"What we are experiencing now is the long war the ruling elite is fighting to maintain its grip on the world." To bring it down, Hathaway suggests "the path out...will include conflict and strife. Insisting on only peaceful tactics and ruling out armed self defense against a ruling elite that has repeatedly slaughtered millions of people is naïve, actually a way of preventing basic change. The pacifist idealism so prevalent among the petty-bourgeoisie conceals their class interest: no revolution, just reform. But until capitalism and its military are collapsing, it would be suicidal to attack them directly with force.

"What we can do now as radicals is to weaken capitalism and build organizations that will pass our knowledge and experience on to future generations. If we do that well enough, our great grandchildren (not really so far away) can lead a revolution. If we don't do it, our descendants will remain corporate chattel.

"Our generational assignment—should we decide to accept it—is sedition, subversion, sabotage: a program on which socialists and anarchists can work together."

One sign of the few encouraging ones we have today is the many Establishment policy makers: civil servants, ambassadors, militarists and cloak and dagger murderers who have come over to the people's side. I have come across scores of them, and used many of their words herein. Everyone knows of Chelsea Manning and Edward Snowden. Among the covert types are the Veteran Intelligence Professionals for Sanity. Some of the war-intelligence professionals have admitted big sins, such as E. Howard Hunt confessing to having been privy to the murder of President Kennedy by his own "comrades". The government-the military-industrial complex-deep state-mass media do not listen to them, however, nor does it seem does the much-alienated American Working Class.

Ernesto "Che" Guevara's 1965 essay, "Socialism and Man in Cuba," is one of my favorite works regarding alienation, morality and creating the new revolutionary person and society.

"Work under all forms of exploitative economies—all those predating an economy based upon collective ownership and decision-making—results in alienation of the individual and producers. Liberating us from this exploitation and its associates—oppression and repression—is a principal task of any post-capitalist economy, starting with socialism. Work, in the new economy, will be based on basic human needs and moral incentives, not materialism/consumerism," Che wrote.

"The alienated human specimen is tied to society as a whole by an invisible umbilical cord: the law of value. This law acts upon all aspects of one's life, shaping its course and destiny."

"That is why it is very important to choose the right instrument for mobilizing the masses. ***Basically, this instrument must be moral in character, without neglecting, however, a correct use of the material incentive—especially of a social character."***

"Those who play by the rules of the game are showered with honors—such honors as a monkey might get for performing pirouettes. The condition is that one does not try to escape from the invisible cage."

"In these circumstances one must have a large dose of humanity, a large dose of a sense of justice and truth in order to avoid dogmatic extremes, cold scholasticism, or an isolation from the masses. We must strive every day so that this love of living humanity is transformed into actual deeds, into acts that serve as examples, as a moving force." "We socialists are freer because we are more fulfilled; we are more fulfilled because we are freer."

We don't need to wait until capitalism is abolished before we begin implementing some of Che's ideas about post-capitalism. For instance, there are firms owned by and worked by workers in the United States, some taking lead from the Spanish Mondragon Corporation. There are over 250 such companies in various countries run by about 75,000 workers. This type of production relationship could be enhanced with a perspective of making a socialist transition of society. (https://www.mondragon-corporation.com/en/)

Chris Wright's "The Necessity of a Moral Revolution" seems to suggest something similar.

"We're embarking on a revolutionary era, an era that promises to be more radical even than the 1930s." (https://www.counterpunch.org/2017/08/08/the-necessity-of-a-moral-revolution/)

"The core of the protracted revolution, of course, is to create new institutions, ultimately new relations of production. Every revolution is essentially a matter of changing social structures; the goal of transforming ideologies makes sense only as facilitating institutional change. Nevertheless, to spread new ways of thinking, new values, can indeed serve as an effective midwife of revolution, and thus is a task worth undertaking.

"The fundamental moral transition that has to occur (in order, for example, to save humanity from collective suicide) is from a kind of nefarious egoism to a beneficent communism. This is the ideological core of the coming social changes, this shift from individualistic greed—'Gain wealth, forgetting all but self'—to collective solidarity. We have to stop seeing the world through the distorted lens of the private capitalist self, the self whose raison d'¬être is to accumulate private property, private experiences, private resentments, finally private neuroses, and instead see the world as what it is, a vast community stretching through time and space. Such a change of vision might facilitate the necessary institutional changes—which themselves, later, will naturally engender and instill this communist-type vision."

Randy Shields is one of those pesky radicals who tells it just like he feels it, and these excerpts from his piece, "When I Started Hating America", fit the topic here to my taste.

"I thought of McGovern recently because I was trying to pin down when I first started hating America. I've been a little tired of all these Osama and Anwar al-come-lately's and the glory they get for hating America when many of us have toiled unpaid and unknown—hating America for decades." (https://dissidentvoice.org/2012/07/when-i-started-hating-america/)

"McGovern got land-slided in 1972 and the American working class has been land-sliding the world ever since in proud ignorance, cowardly violence, and infinite obedience. So I say, contra Carl Sandberg: the people, no, hail no, for god sakes, no. I know as a Marxist I'm supposed to promote working class solidarity but I'm never really feeling the love. The union guys I work with don't know anything about May Day, Big Bill Haywood or surplus value but they're idiot savants when it comes to fantasy football, Philly strip clubs, and the most Eden-like places to blow away defenseless animals."

"It's hard to relate to something as alienated and shut down as the American working class..." but then Randy sees a way out:

"I was very excited about what Julius Levin was saying about the socialist industrial union form of government: a government based on industry instead of an anachronism like territory, a government of nurses, farmers, machinists, secretaries, plumbers, etc., democratically elected at every level—local, regional and national—from all workplaces with no union reps making any more money than the average worker. This all-industrial council of workers would replace the nonproductive pampered professional politicians called Congress. In short, industrial unionism would make Jefferson's citizen-legislators real—ALL the citizens: Blacks, women, un-propertied White males, everybody. Capitalism's Supreme Court weather vanes would be sent packing and the Whitey House would be turned into a museum honoring working class heroes."

Despite Randy's, and my own, despair about the American Working Class maybe its belief in American Exceptionalism is diminishing a bit. Polls indicate that the majority does not want more war; at least the feeling is there if not the action. NBC's July 2017 poll determined that 76% of the Americans fear a major war while most oppose making one. That was 10% over the same poll half-a-year earlier. The July poll found that 62% believed the U.S. should consider its allies' interests even if it meant making compromises; 59% over 35% believe diplomacy rather than military means should be used to resolve conflicts with so-called enemies. This is something old fashioned American Exceptionalism would not tolerate.

Who are the big threats to the United States that could result in war? Fortunately, the major threat was not Russia. In contrast to the Establishment Russia bashing, only 18% feared Russia most. The biggest threat comes from Trump's main enemy at that time, North Korea, with 41%. North Korea surpasses even the real terrorists, ISIS, which the U.S. helped create—which 28% most fear. (https://www.nbcnews.com/politics/national-security/nbc-news-poll-american-fears-war-grow-n783801)

The major problem we in "the real left" face is how to turn these well meaning people into revolutionaries or, at the very least, into a fighting force that could effectively stop the war machine. I've presented some activist-radical thinkers' ideas. I add to this discussion with a view that is largely ignored or rejected by "the real left". We need to include in our movements still-in-the-making two key points: a) an open discussion, a running dialogue both within the movements and presented to those we wish to mobilize and organize just what type of society we wish to create; b) see and admit our own flaws, and endeavor to overcome our own illusions.

I have spent nearly six decades primarily as a radical-revolutionary, anti-war, anti-racist activist; secondly as a journalist and propagandist writer. Unlike most of my kind in the West, I was also an activist in a socialist society, Cuba for eight years, and have spent a couple years in other Latin American countries striving to become socialist. I have learned that these governments did not want their people to decide how to run the fields and factories, not to mention the governments. I have learned that most people do not like that about these governments and, as surely can be seen by all who look, most Cubans wish to embrace capitalism today—although they wish to keep the social welfare that they have achieved. But that social welfare can also be achieved in a capitalist system.

I have learned that solidarity workers and socialist-communist parties in the West that stand side by side with these countries do not wish to hear about their serious mistakes, the authoritarian power structures, the unwillingness to turn over the reins of power to the workers. I don't see how we can convince our own workers in capitalist states to risk their lives fighting against the barons' bayonets if we can't convince them that what we stand for is a better life for all, not only materially but spiritually and one in which they will make the key decisions. Only in that way, can we begin to eliminate the alienation about which Marx and Che speak.

We need to look reality in the face, all reality, and tell it like it is, not to malign but to improve, to project a world in which we stop fooling ourselves and our people. No more self-denials; no more illusions. At least one advantage to dropping illusions is that we won't become disillusioned. We don't abide by so many other illusions. Let us not abide our own!

At age 93, former French diplomat Stéphane Hessel wrote the pamphlet *Indignez-vous!* (*Time for Outrage*). Within three months it sold 600,000 copies—the most sold book in France.

This call for uprising both reflected and anticipated the spirit of student demonstrations in France, Britain and the U.S. Occupy Wall Street movement, as it did the wave of revolt challenging dictatorships in the Middle East.

After fighting against fascism in WWII, Hessel was involved along with Eleanor Roosevelt in drafting the United Nations Universal Declaration of Human Rights. His voice was always on the side of the oppressed, the exploited. Here is a key extract, one that we must adhere to today.

"The motivation that underlay the Resistance was outrage. We, the veterans of the Resistance movements and fighting forces of Free France, call on the younger generations to revive and carry forward the tradition of the Resistance and its ideas.

"We say to you: take over, keep going, get angry! Those in positions of political responsibility, economic power and intellectual authority, in fact our whole society, must not give up or let ourselves be overwhelmed by the current international dictatorship of the financial markets, which is such a threat to peace and democracy. I want you, each and every one of you, to have a reason to be outraged. This is precious. When something outrages you, as Nazism did me that is when you become a militant, strong and engaged. You join the movement of history, and the great current of history continues to flow only thanks to each and every one of us."

THE END

Stéphane Hessel's indignation uproar interpreted by Jette Salling

NOTES

(1) Throughout I have mainly used U.S., United States and US American instead of "America" and "Americans" because I wish to make the point, as do many Latin Americans that "America" applies to both continents and to all its inhabitants. The term was given to both continents by European rulers who chose the Italian explorer Amerigo Vespucci for "America". I use the term "Americans" in this chapter to fit their own sense of self in the context of "American Exceptionalism".

AFTERWORD

Waiting for Apocalypse

WAITING AND WAITING! Waiting for the end of the world! Waiting for Godot! Although, unlike in Samuel Beckett's Theater of the Absurd play, in which Godot never arrives, the mad men and mad women leaders of U.S., France and UK (and Israel) are bringing us their bombs.

April 13, 2018: I am waiting for them to drop their death machines any minute. Paul Craig Roberts writes today:

"The criminally insane governments of the US, UK, and France are sending a flotilla of missile ships, submarines, and an aircraft carrier to attack Syria in the face of Russian warnings…There are no protests from European governments. There are no protesters in the streets of European and US cities." (https://www.paulcraigroberts.org/2018/04/12/ten-days-end-world/)

After reading about the possible apocalypse this morning, I was at my doctor's office for hypertension. He told me that by taking medicine I could live a year longer than otherwise, statistically speaking. I asked why live longer in such an absurd world? He shrugged.

On the way home to my writing machine, six unassociated people of varying ages boarded the bus at one stop. Five of them had plugs in their ears attached to cords connected to "smart" mobile telephones. These zombies joined three other passengers on the bus with similar apparatuses plugged into their heads. No one spoke or looked out the windows. I wondered why they all seemed out of touch with their environment. Perhaps they too were waiting—waiting for something unknown to me. They do not want to be in the present I'm sure. They do not want to hear about wars, and God forbid the thought that they should do something about it. They are in silent fellowship with millions and millions of Western runners, cyclists, walkers all escaping the present with plugs in their ears.

(I just learned from the Internet that there is an absurd Google video game called "Soldier of Failure: Operation Zombie"! To make the unbelievable more believable the Centers for Disease Control and Prevention published an article, on May 18, 2011, *Preparedness 101: Zombie Apocalypse,* providing tips on preparing to survive a zombie invasion," according to Wikipedia.

"The article does not claim an outbreak is likely or imminent, but states: 'That's right, I said z-o-m-b-i-e a-p-o-c-a-l-y-p-s-e. You may laugh now, but when it happens you'll be happy you read this...' The government-run CDC goes on to summarize cultural references to a zombie apocalypse. It uses these to underscore the value of laying in water, food, medical supplies, and other necessities in preparation for any and all potential disasters, be they hurricanes, earthquakes, tornadoes, floods, or hordes of ravenous brain-devouring undead.'"

"The CDC also published a graphic novel, Zombie Pandemic, alongside a series of related articles." (*What the hell is going on?*)

As I sit before my computer to add to my book what the West's latest threats for world war could mean, Samuel Beckett's play, Waiting for Godot (written in 1949) popped up. Irish-born Beckett was among many Paris-based writers who formed the Theater of the Absurd school of thought and verse. Also in this school was English playwright Harold Pinter, whom I quoted from his Nobel Prize for Literature speech in my last chapter—"*what has happened to our moral sensibility*"?

Another of my favorite cultural existentialist artists/instructors is the contemporary Danish filmmaker Lars van Trier. At the end of his 2011 film "Melancholia", his character Justine speaks as the earth is about to be demolished. I deem her closing words as prophetic for what the very rich and powerful, and the indifferent mean to humanity and the planet:

> *"Life is only on Earth; and not for Long. The earth is evil. We don't need to grieve for it...Life on earth is evil."*

Beckett's two main characters, the philosophical Vladimir and Estragon engage in existential discussions while awaiting Godot—one being: why live in this absurd world. Another existential theme is "civilization's" invention of slavery and racism. There is also the possible allegory to the Cold War in the figures of Pozzo and Lucky (master and slave).

Must there be such "inhuman" behavior amongst humanity? Should we not all struggle against these evils, otherwise accept being a part of them when we do nothing? Isn't it a fundamental existential value and necessity of life that we not make war, especially not for the mere profit in it, the desire to dominate other nations—which is clearly what the current permanent wars that the U.S. promulgates since the September 11, 2001 terror attack are all about?

At the end of Beckett's play, Vladimir and Estragon agree to hang themselves if Godot does not appear. And that is what Western warmongers want Vladimir to do: commit suicide when they come with their phallus-laden missiles. Moreover, now with gender equality not all the missiles are phalluses. There is also pussy war power from Golda Meir-Margaret Thatcher-Madeleine Albright-Hillary Clinton-Theresa May. Even the falsely viewed "peaceful" Danes have had a woman prime minister warrior. Helle Thorning Schmidt (2011-15) was a shoulder-to-shoulder war-maker.

However, another Dane, Soeren Kirkegaard (1813-50) is thought to be the philosophic creator of existential thinking, which influenced Theater of Absurd writers. He highlighted the need for individuals to take responsibility for their personal choices and commitments. One could not hide behind "those were the times", or "our government did it" clichés. Kirkegaard also meant that there is inherent meaning in the universe, a universal ethic, but humans are incapable of finding it due to some undefined limitation.

I wrote about this in my agonizing essay, "The Guilty Innocent, 9/11" http://ronridenour.com/articles/2002/0101--rr.htm.

Existentialist writer Albert Camus also took up these themes in his classic 1942 essay, Myth of Sisyphus. Camus' conclusion is my own, one not clear for Kirkegaard: the realization of the absurd is not suicide but is to revolt. You become a human being when you say "no" to the evil-doers.

Yet today we who think and feel as Camus witness people's apathy more than revolt. Today, most humans cling to the cliché: "our government told us so"—and as such we lunge deeper into the abyss.

A FEW HARROWING WAR-MAKING FACTS: MARCH-MAY 2018

March 4: Former Russian Military Intelligence Officer and double agent Sergei Skripal and his daughter Yulia were victims of a poison attack in Salisbury, England. They were hospitalized and survived. Skripal had given secret Russian information to UK's MI6 during the 1990s and 2000s. Russia's intelligence agency FSB arrested him in 2010 for high treason. He was tried and sentenced to a rather mild prison term of 13 years. (Chelsea Manning was sentenced to life for lesser "crimes"). Skripal was quickly released in a swap of prisoners between the U.S. and Russia, and Skripal settled in England. Whatever he knew of any use was clearly given to the U.S. and UK intelligence agencies eight years ago.

UK Prime Minister Theresa May and Foreign Minister Boris Johnson immediately claimed that Russia, and Putin personally, stood behind this attempted murder. Leading scientific experts at Defence Science and Technology Laboratory at Porton Down denied that the poison came directly from Russia as they had previously claimed. Nevertheless, the UK government continued to claim that Russia and Putin were responsible. They called the alleged poison Novichok ("Newcomer" in English). According to UK leaders it only came from Russia.

Without having evidence of guilt, 29 countries (22 EU states) expelled 150 Russian diplomats. Six EU states refused to comply: Greece, Cyprus, Portugal, Slovenia, Austria and Bulgaria. They said they needed evidence of guilt.

Trump needed no such confirmation. He merely said that he believes Theresa May. He then expelled 60 Russian diplomats and added more sanctions against leading Russians close to President Putin.

These politicians and the mass media did not ask the basic question one must ask: What is to be gained by such a crime? Why would a nation's leader order a chemical attack against people living in another country? Not only is Sergei Skripal no longer any threat to Russia but Putin was in a presidential re-election campaign. He and the world knew that he would be reelected. Surely, Putin must have known that if he ordered or allowed an official Russian agency to attempt such an act the "international community" would retaliate, and the crime would haunt him internally as well.

Other pertinent questions not asked: is it not possible for other countries to make this alleged Novichok poison, or something resembling it, or steal it from Russia? Why did the UK not make samples available to Russia as the (admittedly highly compromised by the US) Organization for the Prohibition of Chemical Weapons (OPCW) rules require—all countries which claim being attacked by another country must provide evidence?

March 18: Vladimir Putin was reelected with 77% of the vote—67.5% of the potential voting population, 107 million people. That means a greater number voted than in the United States for the past many decades, and a greater majority for the winning candidate. In "democratic"

Denmark where I live, the ruling party and its candidate NEVER get a majority of voters.

In December 2017, the West's major polling firm, Gallup, found that 80% of the Russian population of 144 million people approved of Putin's leadership. When did a U.S. president or a UK prime minister ever receive such popular backing?

The West cannot tolerate a sovereign leader to rule Russia. The West preferred opposition liberal activist Aleksei Navalny ("liberal" in the Russian context sense, which is upside down, actually meaning rightwing and pro-US free marketism, rather logical for Navalny a widely despised and presumed CIA asset). In September 2013, he ran for mayor of Moscow. He came in second with 27% of the vote. Navalny received two suspended sentences for embezzlement, for which Russia's Central Electoral Commission barred him from running for the presidency in December 2017.

The more that the West maligns Putin, the more the vast majority of Russians support him and his policies: not surrendering Russian support to Syria, not allowing NATO and its neo-Nazi Ukranian government to take over the Crimean naval base, and for Putin's policies of state controls over gouging capitalism, and for his policy of collecting taxes from the rich.

James Petras explained it in his piece, "Why the UK, the EU and the US Gang-up on Russia:

"Russia's historic recovery under President Putin and its gradual international influence shattered US pretense to rule over a unipolar world. Russia's recovery and control of its economic resources lessened US dominance, especially of its oil and gas fields. As Russia consolidated its sovereignty and advanced economically, socially, politically and militarily, the West increased its hostility in an effort to roll-back Russia to the Dark Ages of the 1990s.

The US launched numerous coups and military intervention and fraudulent elections to surround and isolate Russia. The Ukraine, Iraq, Syria, Libya, Yemen and Russian allies in Central Asia were targeted. NATO military bases proliferated.

Russia's economy was targeted: sanctions were directed at its imports and exports. President Putin was subject to a virulent Western media propaganda campaign. US NGO's funded opposition parties and politicians.

The US-EU rollback campaign failed."

"Russia is not a threat to the West: it is recovering its sovereignty in order to further a multi-polar world. President Putin is not an 'aggressor,' but he refuses to allow Russia to return to vassalage.

President Putin is immensely popular in Russia and hated by the US precisely because he is the opposite of Yeltsin. He has created a flourishing economy; he resists sanctions and defends Russia's borders and allies." (https://dissidentvoice.org/2018/03/why-the-uk-the-eu-and-the-us-gang-up-on-russia/#more-77972)

Petras' prediction is more optimistic than many other real left pundits:

"In a word, the UK, the EU and the US are ganging-up on Russia, for diverse historic and contemporary reasons. The UK exploitation of the anti-Russian conspiracy is a temporary ploy to join the gang but will not change its inevitable global decline and the break-up of the UK.

Russia will remain a global power. It will continue under the leadership of President Putin .The Western powers will divide and bugger their neighbors—and decide it is their better judgment to accept and work within a multi-polar world."

The Western colonialists and modern imperialist war chiefs know that President Putin is not a warmonger. They know he is not interested in a world war or using nuclear weapons. So they figure that they can just shoot a bunch of missiles here and there without risking a nuclear world war.

Mike Whitney, a columnist published in many leading progressive websites wrote, the West's "assumption is that eventually, and with enough pressure, Putin will throw in the towel. But this is another miscalculation. Putin is not in Syria because he wants to be nor is he there because he values his friendship with Syrian President Bashar al Assad. That's not it at all. Putin is in Syria because he has no choice. Russia's national security is at stake. If Washington's strategy of deploying terrorists to topple Assad succeeds, then the same ploy will be attempted in Iran and Russia. Putin knows this, just like he knows that the scourge of foreign-backed terrorism can decimate entire regions like Chechnya. He knows that it's better for him to kill these extremists in Aleppo [now in Douma] than it will be in Moscow. So he can't back down, that's not an option." (https://www.counterpunch.org/2016/11/01/how-putin-derailed-the-west/)

March 30: President Donald Trump told a cheering Ohio audience: "But just think of it: We spent, as of three months ago, $7 trillion—not billion, not million—$7 trillion, with a 'T'—nobody ever heard of the word 'trillion' until 10 years ago. We spent $7 trillion in the Middle East. We'd build a school; they'd blow it up. We'd build it again; they'd blow it up. We'd build it again; hasn't been blown up yet, but it will be.

"But if we want a school in Ohio to fix the windows, you can't get the money. If you want a school in Pennsylvania or Iowa to get federal money, you can't get the money. We spent $7 trillion in the Middle East. And you know what we have for it? Nothing." (https://www.whitehouse.gov/briefings-statements/remarks-president-trump-infrastructure-initiative/)

The day before, ABC reported that Trump said, "We're coming out of Syria very soon. Let other people take care of it now, very soon. Very soon, we're coming out."

Former Alaska Governor Sarah Palin agreed with Trump about getting out. She said in an interview with Breitbart News Tonight: "Why in the world we would be willing to sacrifice even one of our sons or daughters who will be sent over [to Syria]?"

"We should have learned our lesson with Iraq and Afghanistan." "I hate to say it, but a lot of the talk that's enthusiastic about war, unfortunately, comes from people with strong ties to defense contractors and have strong ties to those who ultimately can make money on the operations. So often you got to follow the money and that leads you to what the root is of some of these arguments." (https://soundcloud.com/breitbart/breitbart-news-tonight-sarah-palin-april-10-2018)

But Palin is no longer politically powerful and Trump is not his own man. He caved in to pressure to appoint "Vietnam war revisionists" to key government and military posts. These hawk revisionists mean that they could have won the war against Vietnam-Cambodia-Laos had the military been given free reign to kill all. But the politicians (even Republicans Nixon and Kissinger) did not let them do what they did to the Koreans in the 1950s—bomb them all. The PNAC (Project for a New American Century) agenda, the Neocon manifesto, was adopted by President George W. Bush. (See chapter 18). These hawks have convinced Trump to hold off on getting out of Syria. After all, there is lots of oil there, and they won't allow Putin to prevent their desired victory in Syria. The U.S. has 10 military bases and 2,000 troops in northwest Syria by Turkey's border. They fight alongside between 30-45,000 Kurds and Arabs in the YPG-led Syrian Democratic Forces. The Kurdish YPG (Peoples Protection Units) is Turkey's enemy. NATO-member Turkey began fighting it in January 2018 as it warned the U.S. to get out of the way, which it obliged partially.

To convince Trump to back down on his desire to get out of Syria, the "revisionists" needed a false flag attack such as the PNAC report maintained—in order to realize its vision of global domination a tragedy, such as the attack on Pear Harbor, would be necessary.

One of the key authors of this PNAC declaration of global-domination-or-else is John Bolton, whom Trump named as his National Security Advisor in April. At the same time, he named former CIA director Mike Pompeo as his Secretary of State. Trump had earlier named Marine general James Mattis as his secretary of defense—all want Russia under U.S. domination.

April 7: Douma, Syria, White Helmets report that the Syrian armed forces dropped a chemical bomb (chlorine) on civilians in Douma. The White Helmets, also (mistakenly) known as Syrian Civil Defense, sent videos to the eager mass media allegedly showing anguished victims of a chemical attack. They stated that there was widespread suffocation in the area, which led to 42 deaths. But as the "volunteers" were assisting the alleged victims they forgot to put on gas masks or protective suits themselves. We see on TV and You Tube these "volunteers" using hoses spewing forth running water to rinse faces, bodies and clothing with their bare hands.

It is not a matter that the so-called NGO doesn't have enough money for such protection since the foreign ministries of the U.S.—through its Agency for International Development, which was created to cover the fact that the CIA is behind it—pay the White Helmets, an outfit developed as a propaganda tool in imperial hybrid wars. Western states and NGOs alongside Gulf State monarchies have given them over $123 million that we know of. (See chapter 15). White Helmets was founded in March 2013 by British official killer mercenary James Le Mesurier, who trained originally as a British military intelligence officer. He trains White Helmets who are embedded with various al-Qaeda groups. It has been caught doctoring film footage, using children as props, and watching al-Qaeda execute children. (https://www.mintpressnews.com/james-le-mesurier-british-ex-military-mercenary-founded-white-helmets/230320/)

How reliable can such an organization be? Its claim of the "chemical attack" was "collaborated" by Jaish al-Islamal, the then controlling terrorist organization in the Eastern Ghouta area. It had been connected to the al-Qaeda group Jabhat a-Nusra in Syrian. Jaish al-Islamal is backed by the U.S., Saudi Arabia, Qatar and Israel. Again, its PR organ is the White Helmets.

Another USAID-funded group, the Syrian American Medical Society (SAMS), reported the same as the White Helmets. SAMS is a lobby group for "regime change" in Syria. In 2015, it received $5.8 million from USAID. SAMS executive director, David Lillie, and its director of operations, Tony Kronfli were USAID staffers. (https://www.truthdig.com/articles/how-the-syrian-american-medical-society-is-selling-regime-change-and-driving-the-u-s-to-war/)

Why did the mass media not ask common sense questions? Why would Assad forces commit such a brutal crime when they were clearly winning the war? Why were only civilians injured or killed allegedly? Why would Assad commit such a horrendous act when he knew that the White Helmets were there and had modern camera and communication equipment paid for by his enemies?

And why do the mass media and Western politicians never refer to the excellent exposes of Seymour Hersh that previous sarin gas attacks blamed on Bashar Assad were false? Why do they not refer to the June 20, 2013 report of the U.S. Defense Department's Defense Intelligence Agency that terrorists fighting the Syria government have sarin production cells?

The British secret services use reports on the conflicts in Iraq and Syria by the independent IHS Markit Conflict Monitor analysis firm. IHS is a subsidiary of Jane security company. IHS delivered a report in November 2016, which the New York Times wrote about on November 21: "ISIS used chemical arms at least 52 times in Syria and Iraq, report says," by Eric Schmitt.

"The Islamic State has used chemical weapons, including chlorine and sulfur mustard agents, at least 52 times on the battlefield in Syria and Iraq since it swept to power in 2014, according to a new independent analysis.

"More than one-third of those chemical attacks have come in and around Mosul, the Islamic State stronghold in northern Iraq, according to the assessment by the IHS Conflict Monitor, a London-based intelligence collection and analysis service.

"The IHS conclusions, which are based on local news reports, social media and Islamic State propaganda, mark the broadest compilation of chemical attacks in the conflict. American and Iraqi military officials have expressed growing alarm over the prospect of additional chemical attacks as the allies press to regain both Mosul and Raqqa, the Islamic State capital in Syria."

"Chlorine is commercially available as an industrial chemical and has been used occasionally by bomb makers from Sunni militant groups in Iraq for about a decade. But it is not known how the Islamic State would have obtained sulfur mustard, the officials said."

"Mosul was at the center of the Islamic State's chemical weapons production," [Columb Strack, senior analyst and head of HIS] said. "But most of the equipment and experts were probably evacuated to Syria in the weeks and months leading up to the Mosul offensive, along with convoys of other senior members and their families."

IHS report stated "the most likely CBR threat emanating from Mosul is posed by the use of chlorine and mustard agents, and to a much lesser extent, the use of a radiological dispersal device (RDD), or 'dirty bomb', by which radiological materials are scattered using conventional explosives." (http://news.ihsmarkit.com/press-release/aerospace-defense-security/islamic-state-used-chemical-weapons-least-19-times-around-m)

Not even John F. Kennedy's nephew's writings impress them. Robert Kennedy Jr. maintains that the U.S. supports the Sunnis, and their terrorists, because of oil and geo-politics, and that is why they fight Assad, because in 2009 he rejected their wish to build a gas link through his country. (See Kennedy's, "Why the Arabs don't want us in Syria". https://www.politico.eu/article/why-the-arabs-dont-want-us-in-syria-mideast-conflict-oil-intervention/)

The day after the alleged chlorine attack, the Syrian Army reported that it had full control of the area. Russian military police are also present. Incomprehensibly to me Russia agreed with the terrorist group—the last remaining opposition group in Eastern Ghouta—that its fighters could abandon Douma and head for another opposition-held area in northern Syria. The agreement includes a ceasefire and the evacuation of fighters and civilians from the area. Russia is to be the key force in Douma and not Assad's forces.

Once in the area, the Russian Reconciliation Center spoke with medical workers in Douma, who reported that they had not received any patients with signs of chemical poisoning, but rather trauma from smoke inhalation caused by a fire in a building. Neither did the Syrian Arab Red Crescent Society, a humanitarian non-profit organization with headquarters in nearby Damascus, find any chemical damage. The society was founded in 1942. It is in the International Committee of Red Cross since 1946 and part of the International Federation recognized by the ICRC.

The Russian Reconciliation Center spokespersons also said that no traces of chemical agents were found in the area where the alleged attack had taken place. It added that videos spread by the "White Helmets" were "fake," aimed to derail the Syrian ceasefire.

AP wrote that "medics from Douma's hospital…said a group of people toting video cameras entered the hospital, shouting that its patients had been struck with chemical weapons and causing panic." The medics had no such knowledge.

"Russian Foreign Minister Sergei Lavrov has stressed that Moscow sought for a just investigation into the incident, and reiterated that Russian military specialists did not find any traces of a chemical attack at site. He has also recalled that last year the White Helmets also worked without any protective clothes at the alleged site of a sarin gas attack". (https://sputniknews.com/middleeast/201804091063367847-white-helmets-chemical-attack-syria/)

The Russian Foreign Minister also said that he had evidence that an unnamed foreign intelligence had staged the scenario. (See following link: https://www.independent.co.uk/news/world/middle-east/syria-chemical-attack-latest-news-staged-secret-services-russia-foreign-minister-lavrov-a8302586.html)

Minister Lavrov's statement was followed up by Russia's Defense Ministry's spokesperson General Igor Konashenkov statement that Britain was "directly involved in the provocation", as reported by AP, taken from https://www.independent.ie/world-news/syria-chemical-attack-staged-by-uk-claims-russia-36804236.html .

Nevertheless, Secretary of Defense Jim Mattis said he was "confident" that Assad had used chlorine and would not "rule out" that sarin was also released by Assad forces. While there was no scientific evidence, there was enough "reliable information" based on eyewitnesses and videos.

The U.S. State Department also claimed it had proof that the Syrian government was the perpetrator of a chemical attack in Douma, but refused to make the evidence public, as it is "classified."

In characteristic overkill, Trump called on Russia to stop supporting "the animal" Assad. He said that one is judged by the friends one keeps. Real reporters should have asked Trump what about his friends: Saudis committing genocide in Yemen, while it and several other Gulf States support al Qaeda and IS; and what about the Saudis' hated-friends in Israel conducting their own genocide against Palestinians.

Not only did the Establishment not wait for the OPCW to investigate but also many liberal-left people fell for the lie without any proof. As Trump planned to attack, Amy Goodman agreed on her April 9 program "Democracy Now" that Assad had made a chemical attack. Her guest was Intercept director Glenn Greenwald. To his shame, he joined the choir, stating there was "overwhelming evidence" that Assad dropped chemical weapons on civilians, committing a "war crime". Goodman didn't bother to ask Greenwald what Assad could have expected to achieve from such an act. Neither she nor Greenwald, though, supported bombing Syria.

(Greenwald subsequently downgraded the term "overwhelming evidence" that Assad did this alleged deed to "likely".)

In contrast to the "progressive" and Establishment media, Paul Craig Roberts is willing to "bet my life" that there was "no chemical attack by Syria". (www.greanvillepost.com/2018/04/10/on-the-threshold-of-war/)

"The goal of these absolutely unsubstantiated lies is to protect the terrorists and the irreconcilable radical opposition that has rejected a political settlement, as well as to justify the possible use of force by external actors."

The Independent newspaper reporter Robert Fisk reminded us that Theresa May needed a distraction to "to step out of the Brexit ditch", referring to the Skripal poisoning about Russia. Fisk's main point, though, was about the hypocrisy of both the UK and especially the U.S. during the Iran-Iraq war when they acquiesced and even backed Saddam Hussein's use of chemical weapons against Iranian troops and Kurds.

"Funny how we forget this now…Talk about the 'normalization' of chemical warfare – this was it!... For the precursors for the Iraqi gas came largely from the United States – one from New Jersey – and US military personnel later visited the battlefront without making any comments about the chemicals which were sold to the Iraqi regime, of course, for 'agricultural' purposes. That's how to deal with insects, is it not?...Of the thousands of Iranians who were asphyxiated, a few survivors were even sent to British hospitals for treatment. I travelled with others on a military train through the desert to Tehran…" (https://www.independent.co.uk/voices/theresa-may-syria-war-uk-chemical-weapons-attack-iran-iraq-thatcher-russia-a8300881.html)

Fisk did not bring up the incalculable amount of chemical-biological weapons that the U.S. systematically used in several recent wars from Vietnam-Cambodia-Laos to Afghanistan and Iraq. Why didn't Russia or other nations drop bombs on the United States' "animal" presidents' countries? According to U.S. reasoning, any nation would have had such "right". The U.S. feels safe, though: no one would dare since it would wipe them off the face of the earth, to use Trump language.

April 14, early morning: Damascus and Homs, Syria. 59 Tomahawk Cruise missiles are launched from two U.S. warship and B-1 bombers. A French frigate and a UK destroyer are nearby. Over a 50 minute period, 103 missiles reportedly hit three targets in Damascus and Homs, 160 kilometers from the capital city. The West claimed their missiles hit a laboratory, and two warehouses where chemical weapons were (supposedly) made and stored. A command post in Homs was also allegedly hit and some military facilities in Damascus as well. Damascus had recaptured Homs in 2014 from the U.S.-backed Free Syrian Army that controlled it for three years. Syrian forces allowed the FSA to leave the area. FSA later joined al-Qaeda.

The Syrian state news agency said the "tripartite aggression" began at 03:55am Damascus time and included approximately 110 missiles fired at targets inside Syria. It is unclear if any military bases were damaged, but Russian units were definitely not targeted.

While the U.S. claimed their missiles met no interference, Syrian news reported that Syrian air defense brought down the majority of the missiles, and confirmed that some hit a research facility, which it said contained scientific labs and an educational centre. Other missiles targeting a military installation near Homs were intercepted and exploded, injuring three civilians, the only civilian casualties from the strikes. Apparently no one was killed.

Trump tweeter followed the raids: "A perfectly executed strike last night. Thank you to France and the United Kingdom for their wisdom and the power of their fine Military. Could not have had a better result. Mission Accomplished!"

Trump's "*mission accomplished*" remarks resemble President George W Bush's infamous speech on board the USS Abraham Lincoln aircraft carrier, in 2003, when he declared the end of combat operations in Iraq in front of a banner stating "*Mission Accomplished*." The U.S. maintains a military presence in torn Iraq today.

Once Again, Russian President Vladimir Putin maintained restraint. Neither he nor Assad responded violently. Both condemned the airstrikes. Putin described them as "*aggression against a sovereign state which is at the forefront of the fight against terrorism.*" Putin stressed that the multi-national strikes were not sanctioned by the UN Security Council, and were carried out "*in violation of the UN Charter and principles of international law*." He added that the current escalation of the Syrian crisis has "*a devastating impact on the whole system of international relations.*" (https://www.rt.com/news/424111-putin-us-strikes-syria-violation/)

As Russia called an emergency meeting of the UN Security Council that evening to discuss the aggressive actions of the U.S. and its allies, the OPCW team readied to begin its investigation work in Douma despite the tri-party warmakers efforts to prevent that. Nevertheless, they succeeded in preventing the UN from officially recognizing its findings. Yet Secretary-General Antonio Guterres personally called for such.

I watched the two hour-long-session. The Russian Federation tabled a resolution that was defeated: 3 for (Russia, China and Bolivia), 8 against, 4 abstentions. No other resolution was presented.

Here are a few of the most important points:

1) UN Secretary-General Guterres called the situation in the Middle East "chaos"; Syria "represents the most serious threat" to the world; "the Cold War is back"; there should have been no military action until the OPCW made its investigation and report, and the UN decide what to do.
2) UN Special Envoy to Syria Staffan de Mistura pointed out that the U.S. is in violation of all international law, including the UN charter by bombing and by occupying one-third of Syrian territory illegally. The elephant's Cold War philosophy is "our way or the highway".

If the three invaders knew that the laboratory and the warehouses they obliterated contained chemical weapons did they not imagine that by exploding the buildings the chemicals would have spread and killed many people? And why did that not happen?

These three states have supported the terrorists all these years, and it is they who have used chemical weapons. By attacking the sovereign state government only incites the terrorists to continue using chemical weapons, because they know their Western allies will shift the blame on the Syrian government.

3) U.S. ambassador to UN Nikki Haley threatened a new attack if Syria were to use chemical weapons "again". "We are locked and loaded".
4) Russia's UN ambassador Vasily Nebenzya condemned the attack as a colonialist, hooligan action in violation of all international laws. They distort international law and engage in hypocrisy.
5) UK envoy Karen Pierce expressed joy that her armed forces attacked targets in Homs.
6) Bolivia's ambassador Sacha Llorenti delivered a passionate speech attacking Western colonialists for violating all laws, including the rule of law. They do not advance democracy and freedom rather "expansion of their own power and domination". They spend untold sums of money to finance the terrorists not only in Syria but in Yemen, in Israel..."

After the defeat of Russia's resolution, Ambassador Nebenzya told the troika attackers that they conducted "diplomacy of the absurd".

April 14 after the bombing and before the UN Security Council: Foreign Minister Lavrov said: "The substance used on Sergei Skripal was an agent called BZ, according to a Swiss lab". "The toxin was never produced in Russia, but was in service in the US, UK, and other NATO states."

The Skripals "were poisoned with an incapacitating toxin known as 3-Quinuclidinyl benzilate or BZ, Russian Foreign Minister Sergey Lavrov said, citing the results of the examination conducted by a Swiss chemical lab that worked with the samples that London handed over to(OPCW)." (https://www.rt.com/news/424149-skripal-poisoning-bz lavrov/?utm_source=browser&utm_medium=push_notifications&utm_campaign=push_notifications)

Minister Lavrov referred to the Spiez Laboratory, which is part of the Switzerland's Federal Office for Civil Protection, whose vision is: "a world without weapons of mass destruction", namely nuclear and bio-chemical weapons.

April 15: None of the four laboratories OPCW used to analyze the poison taken from environmental and blood samples are allowed to speak publically about their reports, but according to Dr. Andrea Galli, an "insider with access to the Swiss-lab has confirmed...the results cited by Lavrov."

Galli, a Swiss investigator for Swiss East Affairs, published an article today about this on the prestigious modern diplomacy website entitled, "Swiss Governmental Lab identifies the Substance used on the Skripal case as linked to the NATO?" (https://moderndiplomacy.eu/2018/04/15/swiss-governmental-lab-identifies-the-substance-used-on-the-skripal-case-as-being-linked-to-the-nato/)

I saw it and fortunately downloaded it, because when I looked for it again on the web a few minutes later it was gone. Here are pertinent excerpts. "According to the report of the Swiss Lab the poison found at Salisbury by OPCW investigators looking into the Skripal affair, there are traces of the toxic agent 3-Quinuclidinyl Benzilate and traces of A-234 – one of the nerve agents of the novichok group – in its original form and in a concentration that would have killed the Skripals, not explaining the clinical picture of the Skripals. However, the presence of 3-Quinuclidinyl Benzilate explains the clinical picture of the Skripals.

3-Quinuclidinyl Benzilate was developed and weaponized in the 1960s as a new chemical agent for battlefield use as a psychochemical and assigned the NATO code Agent BZ.

Agent BZ is a NATO nerve-poisoning agent and a nonlethal chemical weapon that can render the enemy too irritable to fight but have unpredictable effects. While nonfatal, agent BZ causes a wide array of potentially incapacitating symptoms in its victims: soldiers can become disoriented or even experience hallucinations, according to a U.S. Army manual from 1963 that can be obtained through the Freedom of Information Act."

While the piece inexplicably and quickly disappeared from the modern diplomacy website, reddit still had the title posted (as of April 17), but when one clicks on it Error 404 appears. (https://www.reddit.com/r/ukpolitics/comments/8chovb/swiss_governmental_lab_identifies_the_substance/)

moderndiplomacy

Error 404!

The page you requested does not exist or has moved.

"The page you requested does not exist or has moved."

Subsequently I could determine that powerful authorities forced the removal of the article. Interestingly, the April 12 OPCW brief report for public consumption does not contain this information. In the "OPCW Issues Report on Technical Assistance Requested by the United Kingdom", the pertinent sentence is here: "The results of the analysis by the OPCW designated laboratories of environmental and biomedical samples collected by the OPCW team confirm the findings of the United Kingdom relating to the identity of the toxic chemical that was used in Salisbury and severely injured three people." (https://www.opcw.org/news/article/opcw-issues-report-on-technical-assistance-requested-by-the-united-kingdom/)

No more. Nothing about whether the poison was novichok or if so could it have had other elements such as the NATO-produced BZ, as the Russian government contends and about which Dr. Andrea Galli wrote. I called OPCW public affairs office (31-704163242) and had the following exchange with "Jamie", surname not provided.

I asked about the OPCW executive summary report brief finding.

"Jamie" would not answer my question. He merely said: "This is protected information. Our full report only goes to the 192 member states".

Question: "Does this mean that Russia's statement that BZ was an element was correct or not?"

"No comment".

We went around this a bit and then he asked why I kept asking him. I answered:

"Because I am concerned about what the facts are and so should you be, because what really happened could either be an excuse to start a world war or be confirmation that there is no excuse at all to war, and that is clearly related to what did or did not happen in Douma, Syria on April 7."

"No comment."

Among the many contradictions revolving around this poisoning, OPCW reported just half-a-year ago, on October 11, 2017, that Russia had completely destroyed all of its chemical weapons. https://www.opcw.org/news/article/opcw-marks-completion-of-destruction-of-russian-chemical-weapons-stockpile/ (See also footnote 1)

April 27: North and South Korea leaders Kim Jong Un and Moon Jae-in clasp hands at the line of military demarcation between the separated parts of what was once the nation of Korea. The two signed a treaty, the Panmunjom Declaration for Peace, Prosperity and Unification of the Korean Peninsula, which commits the two to a nuclear free peninsula, and to formally end the Korean War, something that the U.S. had forbidden all these years since 1953.

Untold millions of people throughout the world were relieved. UN Secretary General Antonio Guterres saluted the "courage and leadership commitment." One piece of good news, at least in one area of the world where war may be averted! True to character, though, the U.S. government viewed this event as something it had arranged by threatening to war against North Korea if it didn't give up its nuclear weapons. Not something that the U.S. exactly demands of Israel. The North Korean government replied that the U.S. was trying to undermine the sovereign efforts taken by both parts of Korea to end the conflict despite the perpetual war interests of the U.S.

April 29-30: In the night of April 29-30, Israel attacked Syrian military installations at Hama and Aleppo close to the airport with

Bunker Buster bombs probably dropped from aircraft. They killed between 16 and 38 people, mostly military personnel from Syria, Iran and Iraq, wounded scores more and destroyed several surface-to-surface missiles. The impact was measured at a 2.6 earthquake magnitude.

The Israeli Zionist Haaretz newspaper/online reported (May 7):

"President Trump spoke on Sunday [April 29] with Prime Minister Benjamin Netanyahu, according to a White House readout. It said they 'discussed the continuing threats and challenges facing the Middle East region, especially the problems posed by the Iranian regime's destabilizing activities.' The call took place just hours before Netanyahu met for the first time with Trump's new Secretary of State, Mike Pompeo, who is visiting the Middle East.

"Earlier Sunday, Defense Minister Avigdor Lieberman said Israel will maintain freedom of operation in Syria.

"'We have no intention to attack Russia or to interfere in domestic Syrian issues,' Lieberman said at the annual Jerusalem Post conference. 'But if somebody thinks that it is possible to launch missiles or to attack Israel or even our aircraft, no doubt we will respond and we will respond very forcefully.'" (https://www.haaretz.com/middle-east-news/syria/explosions-reported-in-assad-army-base-north-of-homs-syria-1.6035801)

Lieberman has said Israel would not accept limitations from Russia or any other country on its "actions" in Syria. "We will maintain total freedom of action. We will not accept any limitation when it comes to the defense of our ... interests," Lieberman told the Hebrew-language Walla news website. (http://www.presstv.com/Detail/2018/04/30/560136/Israel-minister-Lieberman-Syria-Iran)

"The remarks came less than a month after a strike on an air force compound in Syria that is under exclusive Iranian control – a strike attributed by Syria, Iran, and Russia to Israel. Several members of Iran's Revolutionary Guard Corps were killed in the strike." "At Sunday's conference, Lieberman said that Israel has three problems: 'Iran, Iran, Iran.'" (https://www.haaretz.com/middle-east-news/syria/explosions-reported-in-assad-army-base-north-of-homs-syria-1.6035801)

It is no coincidence that Trump and Pompeo spoke with Netanyahu within hours of Israel's attack. Nor is it coincidental that Israel then announced that it had struck an Iranian military facility in Syria, April 9, and killed seven Iranian troops, an admission it rarely makes. According to UN figures, Israel has violated Syrian airspace more than 750 times in a four-month period in the second-half of 2017. Yet only one Israel jet has been shot down. Israel blithely thinks it can steal territory from Syria, as it did in 1967 by permanently seizing the Golan Heights, and kill Iranians who were welcomed to Syria by the legitimate government.

Iran is Israel's main target. It wants Iran out of Syria and an end to the 2015 Joint Comprehensive Plan of Action (JCPOA nuclear accord) between Iran, all five permanent members of the UN Security Council (U.S., UK, France, Russia, China) and Germany. The JCPOA lifted international sanctions on Tehran in exchange for Iran curbing its controversial nuclear program.

Following the U.S.-UK-France attack on Syria April 14, Russia declared it would provide Syria with a S-300 missile defense system. Russian officials reportedly warned that it anyone attacked them that would cause "catastrophic consequences". Again, Lieberman brushed that off by boasting: "If anyone shoots at our planes, we will destroy them". https://www.reuters.com/article/us-mideast-crisis-syria-israel/russian-envoy-plays-down-tensions-with-israel-over-syria-strikes-idUSKBN1HW0ZE

The day after Lieberman threatened Russia, the same day of the Trump-Pompeo-Netanyahu-Lieberman talks followed by the Zionists two-hour invasion of Syria, Israel's parliament (Knesset) handed war powers entirely over to the pair of war crazy fanatics. This opens the door for an invasion against any country at any time.

So now little Israel—population 8.5 million—is threatening to war against mighty Russia—145 million, as well as Iran, population 80 million. Israel can only have such stupid audacity because it knows the U.S. (and quite probably some of the EU) will back them. Israel is so cocky it doesn't care that Russia unwillingly but necessarily will be drawn into the Syrian war all the more. That means World War Three.

These events took place just before the U.S. decision to back out of the nuclear accord with Iran, and as the Trump regime sought to find Sunni Arabs from Saudi Arabia, Egypt, the UAE, and perhaps Qatar to enter the Syrian conflict directly. Pompeo had spoken with Saudi Arabia's warring monarchy before coming to Israel.

May 8: **Trump withdraws from JCPOA**

"The Iranian regime is the leading state sponsor of terror. It exports dangerous missiles, fuels conflicts across the Middle East, and supports terrorist proxies and militias such as Hezbollah, Hamas, the Taliban and Al Qaeda."

"The fact is, this was a horrible, one-sided deal that should have never, ever been made. It didn't bring calm, it didn't bring peace, and it never will. Today's action sends a critical message: the US no longer makes empty threats. When I make promises, I keep them," Trump bombasted.

Trump pulled the U.S. from the accord despite the International Atomic Energy Agency (IAEA) confirming Tehran's compliance with the deal on numerous occasions. It has constant camera surveillance, and has inspected for 3000 hours in 11 visits, and each time has concluded that Iran is complying with the terms of the accord to "full satisfaction of the requirement."

"A few minutes past two in Washington, the president of the United States adopted the 'Netanyahu Doctrine' wholesale and made it official American policy", wrote the Zionist newspaper Haaretz, "Trump Tells World to Drop Dead as Netanyahu Dictates His Nixing of Iran Deal"

"Israel Will 'Eliminate' Assad if He Continues to Let Iran Operate From Syria, Minister Warns"

The Trump adopted **"Netanyahu Doctrine"** calls for and states as fact:

- *Terminating United States participation in the JCPOA, as it failed to protect America's national security interests.*
- *The JCPOA enriched the Iranian regime and enabled its malign behavior, while at best delaying its ability to pursue nuclear weapons and allowing it to preserve nuclear research and development.*
- *The President has directed his Administration to immediately begin the process of re-imposing sanctions related to the JCPOA.*
- *The re-imposed sanctions will target critical sectors of Iran's economy, such as its energy, petrochemical, and financial sectors.*
- ***Those doing business in Iran will be provided a period of time to allow them to wind down operations in or business involving Iran.***

[Trump demands that his own allies especially in Europe cease all trade for their benefit with Iran, just as his predecessors did with sanctions against trading with Cuba by punishing all governments and firms that dealt with it]

- ***Those who fail to wind down such activities with Iran by the end of the period will risk severe consequences.***
- *United States government believes its withdrawal from the JCPOA*

will pressure the Iranian regime to alter its course of "malign activities and ensure that Iranian bad acts are no longer rewarded. As a result, both Iran and its regional proxies will be put on notice. As importantly, this step will help ensure global funds stop flowing towards illicit terrorist and nuclear activities."

Neither the Trump nor Netanyahu governments thought it necessary to prove how the Iranian government is aiding terrorism. Of course they make no mention of their own terrorism, amply documented, and direct U.S. aid to terrorists in Syria, not to mention Saudi Arabia's fast alliance with al Qaeda and IS groups in Yemen, and Syria.

The *New York Times* news analysis reporter David Sanger wrote:

"The problem of the Iranian nuclear accord was not, primarily, about nuclear weapons. It was that the deal legitimized and normalized the clerical Iranian government, reopening it to the world economy with oil revenue that financed its adventures (sic) in Syria and Iraq, and support of terror groups…As one senior European official said, Mr. Trump and his Middle East allies are betting they can cut Iran's economic lifeline and thus 'break the regime' by dismantling the deal. In theory, that could free Iran to produce as much nuclear material as it wants—what it was doing five years ago, when the world feared it was headed toward a bomb." (https://www.nytimes.com/2018/05/08/us/politics/trump-iran-nuclear-deal-news-analysis-.html?action=click&module=Intentional&pgtype=Article)

Iran's moderate president, Hassan Rouhani, said: "This is a psychological war." He said he believed the agreement could survive IF the other partners agree.

President Rouhani reminded the world that the, "*U.S. never complies with its agreements, and has "been aggressive towards the great people of Iran and our region from the [1953] coup against the legitimate government of [Mohammad] Mosaddegh government and their meddling in the affairs of the last regime, support for Saddam [Hussein during Iran-Iraq war] and downing our passenger plane by a US vessel and their actions in Afghanistan, in Yemen,"* he said.

"*But the Iranian president warned that he has instructed the country's atomic energy agency to prepare to restart enrichment of uranium at an industrial level in a few weeks' time should the deal collapses completely"* (https://www.theguardian.com/world/live/2018/may/08/iran-nuclear-deal-donald-trump-latest-live-updates)

Iran has three options:

1) continue complying with the deal with all the other partners, if they are willing to defy the United States;
2) if Iran drops the deal on its own, or because others pull out, it could then rebuild its nuclear energy capacity to include nuclear weaponry;
3) or be without the deal and without nuclear weaponry—which is what North Korea decided not to do for its sovereign interest, something the South Korean government has respected and thus is making peace.

It isn't just Netanyahu and Lieberman who want this war it is the whole Zionist establishment with minor objections, and most of the Israeli Jews. They accept that they should have the atomic bomb, albeit illegally, and that no one else in the Middle East shall have it. They accept that they illegally occupy Syria's Golan Heights and colonize Palestine. Israel violates international law with impunity and engages in war crimes and crimes against humanity. Its attacks on Lebanon, Gaza, Syria, and Yemen (by proxy) will now escalate to direct confrontation with Iran. Israel hopes Trump will provide all needed military cover even at risk of WWIII.

In these two days, I have read several mass media newspapers from the U.S., UK, Israel and three dailies in Denmark, heard several Danish radio and TV broadcasts about these developments. I have not heard, seen or read any mention that Israel is a terrorist state, that it has nuclear bombs, or any of the other crimes mentioned in the foregoing paragraph.

What is reported is that *Netanyahu had called for Trump to "fix it or nix it"*. So Trump nixed it and Netanyahu applauded "his courageous leadership." "Israel fully supports President Trump's bold decision today to reject the disastrous nuclear deal with the terrorist regime in Tehran."

Israel Minister of Defense Lieberman met with armed forces minutes after Trump signed the declaration of withdrawal. And suddenly Israel reports "irregular activity of Iranian forces in Syria" and deployed air defenses in the northern part of the country according to the Israel Defense Forces (IDF), which released a statement:

"Following the identification of irregular activity of Iranian forces in Syria, the IDF has decided to change the civilian protection instructions in the Golan Heights and instructs local authorities to unlock and ready shelters in the area. The Israeli public should remain attentive to IDF instructions that will be given if necessary.

Additionally, defense systems have been deployed and IDF troops are on high alert for an attack. The IDF is prepared for various scenarios and warns that any aggression against Israel will be met with a severe response."

That same day Trump adopted the "Netanyahu Doctrine," in the evening Israel bombed an alleged arms depot at el-Kiswah near the capital city of Damascus. "Nine fighters belonging to the Iranian Revolutionary Guard Corps or pro-Iranian Shiite militias have been killed" Rami Abd el-Rahman, director of the Britain-based Syrian Observatory for Human Rights, told AFP.

"The state-run Syrian News agency quoted medical sources as saying two civilians were killed." (https://www.haaretz.com/israel-news/syria-blames-israel-for-strike-near-damascus-target-was-iranian-missiles-aimed-at-israel-1.6071960)

The same night and following day Israel's mass media prepared the people for a war with Iran.

"WHAT AN ISRAEL-IRAN WAR COULD LOOK LIKE"

"The prospects of a war breaking out are thus high, certainly high enough to consider how such a war might play out and the ramifications of such a deadly conflict.

"If such a war breaks out, it will signal the end of the era ushered in by the Yom Kippur war in 1973 and formalized in the peace treaty with Egypt, the most powerful enemy state in the Middle East at the time, that spelled the end of the wars between Arab states and Israel." (https://www.jpost.com/Opinion/What-an-Israel-Iran-war-could-look-like-554743)

POTENTIALLY POSITIVE ASPECTS OF PULLING OUT OF THE NUCLEAR DEAL

United Nations general secretary Antonio Guterres called the Trump withdrawal "deeply worrisome", and called on the remaining partners to continue the accord.

EU president Donald Tusk promised a "united European approach" to Trump's decision.

France, Germany, and the UK "regret" the U.S. decision to leave the JCPOA. The nuclear non-proliferation regime is at stake. EU leaders will tackle this at the summit in Sofia in the near future.

France President Emmanuel Macron, Germany's Angela Merkel and Britain's Theresa May all traveled to Washington to speak with Trump about maintaining the JCPOA.

In late April, Macron offered Trump a new deal in which the United States and Europe would tackle the outstanding concerns about Iran beyond its nuclear program. Macron spent three days in the U.S. trying to save the deal. Trump preferred to go with Saudi Arabian and Israeli lust for war against Iran.

Now is a chance Europeans could choose to recapture their sovereignty. They could:

1) continue the nuclear deal with Iran, Russia and China;
2) refuse to comply with the secondary sanctions Trump superimposes on their commercial trade with Iran;
3) they could increase their trade with the East, including Russia and China.

Nevertheless, the mass media in Denmark offers no such discussion, and the people are told they should expect to lose up to one billion dollars by not trading with Iran, mostly in medicines and foodstuffs. While the main capitalist association expressed sorrow over this loss, it did not present any doubt that it would not comply.

Europe as a whole stands to lose $400 billion in trade (new technology, infrastructure, foodstuff, medicine, autos and planes for energy resources mainly) if it follows Trump's global orders to boycott Iran. But if it doesn't Trump could put a crimp in Europe's annual $19 trillion international trade with the U.S. However, such a turn of events would also cripple the U.S. economy, and crush it entirely if both Russia and especially China followed suit.

Whether Europeans find the courage to defy the U.S. directly or not, the Yankees current jingoism could well weaken Europeans' comfort for dependency. And if the key governments do continue the accord without the United States, it could open a crack.

RUSSIA MUST BE MORE RESOLVED

Paul Craig Roberts hopes that Russia will react more decisively than it has in Syria, with Israel, and the West. He recommends Russia to *"turn her back, but not her eyes, on the West, stop responding to false charges, evict all Western embassies and every other kind of presence including Western investment, and focus on relations with China and the East. Russia's attempt to pursue mutual interests with the West only results in more orchestrated incidents. The Russian government's failure to complete the liberation of Syria has given Washington Syrian territory from which to renew the conflict. The failure to accept Luhansk and Donetsk into Russia has provided Washington with the opportunity to arm and train the Ukrainian army and renew the assault on the Russian populations of Ukraine. Washington has gained many proxies for its wars against Russia and intends to use them to wear down Russia. Israel has demanded that Washington renew the attacks on Iran, and Trump is complying. Russia faces simultaneous attacks on Syria, Iran, and the Donetsk and Luhansk Republics, along with troubles in former Central Asian republics of the Soviet Union and intensified accusations from Washington and NATO."* (https://www.paulcraigroberts.org/2018/03/24/washington-declared-hegemony-war/)

"Nothing is more dangerous to the world than Russia's self-delusion about 'Western partners'. Russia only has Western enemies. These enemies intend to remove the constraint that Russia (and China) place on Washington's unilateralism. The various incidents staged by the West, such as the Skripal poisoning, Syrian use of chemical weapons, Malaysian airliner, and false charges, such as Russian invasion of Ukraine, are part of the West's determined intent to isolate Russia, deny her any influence, and prepare the insouciant Western populations for conflict with Russia."

"There is only one Western foreign policy and it is Washington's. Washington's 'diplomacy' consists only of lies and force. It was a reasonable decision for Russia to attempt diplomatic engagement with the West on the basis of facts, evidence, and law, but it has been to no avail. For Russia to continue on this failed course is risky, not only to Russia but to the entire world."

"How the Russian government could ignore the clearly stated US hegemony [agenda] in the 1992 Wolfowitz Doctrine is a mystery. The Wolfowitz doctrine states that the US's primary goal is 'to prevent the re-emergence of a new rival, either on the territory of the former Soviet

Union or elsewhere, that poses a threat on the order of that posed formerly by the Soviet Union.' The doctrine stresses that 'this is a dominant consideration underlying the new regional defense strategy and requires that we endeavor to prevent any hostile power from dominating a region whose resources would, under consolidated control, be sufficient to general global power.' In the Middle East and Southwest Asia, Washington's 'overall objective is to remain the predominant outside power in the region and preserve US and Western access to the region's oil.'

"By 'threat' Wolfowitz does not mean a military threat. By 'threat' he means a multi-polar world that constrains Washington's unilateralism. The doctrine states that the US will permit no alternative to US unilateralism. The doctrine is a statement that Washington intends hegemony over the entire world. There has been no repudiation of this doctrine. Indeed, we see its implementation in the long list of false accusations and demonization of Russia and her leader and in the false charges against Syria, Iraq, Afghanistan, Libya, Somalia, Yemen, Venezuela, China, Iran, and North Korea.

"If Russia wants to be part of the West, Russia should realize that the price is the same loss of sovereignty that characterizes Washington's European vassal states."

A key Putin advisor, Vladislav Surkov, seems to agree with Roberts' main point. He wrote, "The Solitude of a Half-Blood", for the Russian Global Affairs magazine, on April 9. Interestingly the U.S. Congress-funded, CIA-backed Radio Free Europe/Radio Liberty published the article.

Surkov wrote: "'Russia's epic journey toward the West' is over, marking an end to its 'repeated fruitless attempts to become a part of Western civilization' over four centuries." (https://www.rferl.org/a/putin-adviser-surkov-says-russia-abandoning-hopes-integrating-with-west-loneliness-isolation-/29155700.html)

The Yankee medium continued: Surkov "attributed Russia's fascination with joining the West to 'excessive enthusiasm' by Russia's elite. But he said that fervor was now all but gone."

"In the article, he describes Russia as a kind of 'mixed breed' culture that incorporates elements of both the East and the West, like 'someone born of a mixed marriage.'

Russia "'is everyone's relative, but nobody's family. Treated by foreigners like one of their own, an outcast among his own people. He understands everyone and is understood by no one. A half-blood, a half-breed, a strange one.'"

"'It's going to be tough,' he said, but Russia faces a long journey 'through the thorns to the stars'".

CONCLUSION

Theatre of the Absurd presents us with the current gobbledygook about Assad releasing poisons when there is absolutely nothing to be gained from it; the same hogwash about dropping chemicals on civilians in Douma. Equally absurd is the "democratic" Western culture of mass communication. Clearly the mass media means that human existence has no meaning or purpose other than for the elite to gouge endless profits by exploiting people and the planet using endless weaponry. All real communication is broken. Logic, rationality, true debate is eradicated. Irrational, illogical, macho speech takes over, from the White House to Downing Street, from *The New York Times / Washington Post* to *The Guardian* and throughout Western institutions. (Now with gender equality, war-makers must invent a "macho" term for their female counterparts.)

Where are the true cultural workers, the absurdists, the existentialists today?

There are no more Harold Pinters, wrote John Pilger:

"A few years ago, Terry Eagleton, then professor of English literature at Manchester University, reckoned that 'for the first time in two centuries, there is no eminent British poet, playwright or novelist prepared to question the foundations of the western way of life'.

"No Shelley speaks for the poor, no Blake for utopian dreams, no Byron damns the corruption of the ruling class, no Thomas Carlyle and John Ruskin reveal the moral disaster of capitalism. William Morris, Oscar Wilde, HG Wells, George Bernard Shaw have no equivalents today. Harold Pinter was the last to raise his voice. Among today's insistent voices of consumer-feminism, none echoes Virginia Woolf, who described 'the arts of dominating other people... of ruling, of killing, of acquiring land and capital'". (http://johnpilger.com/articles/this-week-the-issue-is-not-trump-it-is-ourselves-)

In a similar vein, another Pilger article, "Inside the Invisible Government: War, Propaganda, Clinton & Trump", explains:

"Propaganda is most effective when our consent is engineered by those with a fine education—Oxford, Cambridge, Harvard, Columbia—and with careers on the BBC, the Guardian, *the* New York Times, *the* Washington Post.

"These organizations are known as the liberal media. They present themselves as enlightened, progressive tribunes of the moral zeitgeist. They are anti-racist, pro-feminist and pro-LGBT. And they love war." (http://johnpilger.com/articles/inside-the-invisible-government-war-propaganda-clinton-trump)

The mass media in Denmark, which I know directly, is no better than that of the UK and the U.S. One difference between Denmark's war making and that of its twin big brothers is that its warring takes on a minor scale, and the public doesn't even acknowledge these crimes against humanity.

North Europe's largest commercial collection of posters is located in Copenhagen's center. Poster Land estimates that the store has 30,000 posters for sale, yet they have only one advocating peace in the world, the iconoclastic John Lennon "Imagine" song with "Peace" under the title.

I asked a young attendant why that was, why there were no war protest posters as there were in the 60s-70s. Denmark was then more than not anti-war and it is now more than not pro-war, engaging in all of the United States' wars-for-profit and domination, and whipping up fear and hatred against the Russians. Isn't it time for a protest, even resistance culture?

The young man pondered before replying.

"It is too difficult to know what is right and wrong with these wars."

But there is more information available to the public than ever before, not so much the mass media but the social media, the Internet, the myriad of websites, I replied.

"Yes, but what can one trust, who can one trust? It is impossible to see through all the information and disinformation. We don't see what we can do about it all." He spoke as if his confusion was universal among the Danish youth, who, in fact, do not protest the wars—so why have posters about it, one could easily conclude.

When I came home, I thought of the piece I wrote a week before the 2016 U.S. election day:

"Trump wants NATO to be less aggressive, less expensive. He wants to curtail US's funding 70% of its lavish budget, and no war against Russia or China. He opposes the corporate proposals for more international trade deals: TTIP, TPP, CETA …

"OK, we can't count on what he says. He lies just as does Hillary Clinton. And if he did win, he might well surround himself with a cabinet and advisors who would be pro-war, just like those Obama embraced from Bush and Bill Clinton's time. Nevertheless, if he does win, the European Establishment and many misguided European citizens could well become disenchanted with the United States because of this scary buffoon, and because behind him are tens of millions of scary voters many of whom support more guns and violence, more racism, sexism and plain old hatred.

"With Trump in the big saddle, Europeans might begin to look for the reasons behind all this bigotry—the fact that contemporary racism is ingrained in an America founded on genocide, slavery and military interventions and wars. Europeans might also seek their own solutions to their issues rather than being captive and dependent upon a United States policeman-of-the world regime." http://ronridenour.com/articles/2016/1031--rr.htm

Well, Trump did surround himself with Dr. Strangeloves, but Europeans still have a chance. This is what P.C. Roberts says about that in another roar for world peace: "What Can Be Done".

"It is up to Europe whether or not the Earth dies in nuclear Armageddon." (https://www.paulcraigroberts.org/2018/04/30/can-done-paul-craig-roberts/)

"European governments do not realize their potential to save the world from Washington's aggression, because the western Europeans are accustomed to being Washington's vassal states since the end of World War 2, and the eastern and central Europeans have accepted Washington's vassalage since the collapse of the Soviet Union. Vassalage pays well if all the costs are not counted.

"By joining NATO, the eastern and central Europeans permitted Washington to move US military presence to Russia's borders. This military presence on Russia's borders gave Washington undue confidence that Russia also could be coerced into a vassal state existence. Despite the dire fate of the two finest armies ever assembled—Napoleon's Grand Army and that of Germany's Wehrmacht—Washington hasn't learned that the two rules of warfare are: (1) Don't march on Russia. (2) Don't march on Russia.

"Because of Europe's subservience to Washington, Washington is unlikely to learn this lesson before Washington marches on Russia.'"

[Elsewhere in this piece, Roberts writes: "In Europe, as in World War 1, the US did not enter the (Second World War) until the last year when the Wehrmacht had already been broken and defeated by the Soviet Red Army. The Normandy invasion faced scant opposition as (nearly, ed.) all German forces were on the Russian front.]

"There are no benefits to Europe of being in NATO. Europeans are not threatened by Russian aggression, but they are threatened by Washington's aggression against Russia. If the American neoconservatives and their Israeli allies succeed in provoking a war, all of Europe would be destroyed. Forever.

"What do Europeans get for the extreme penalties imposed on them as Washington's vassals? They get nothing but the threat of Armageddon. A small handful of European 'leaders' get enormous subsidies from Washington for enabling Washington's illegal agendas. Just take a look at Tony Blair's enormous fortune, which is not the normal reward for a British prime minister.

"Europeans, including the 'leaders', have much more to gain from being connected to the Russia/China Silk Road project. It is the East that is rising, not the West. The Silk Road would connect Europe to the rising East. Russia has undeveloped territory full of resources—Siberia—that is larger than the United States. On a purchasing power parity basis, China is already the world's largest economy. Militarily the Russian/Chinese alliance is much more than a match for Washington."

[China is building nearly 1000 kilometers of the New Silk Road through Iran and is its largest trading partner with over $20 billion involved in 26 projects. Russia is also a major trading partner developing energy sources.]

"Europe must take the lead, especially the central Europeans. These are peoples who were liberated from the Nazis by the Russians and who have in the 21st century experienced far more aggression from Washington's pursuit of its hegemony than they have experienced from Moscow.

If Europe breaks away from Washington's control, there is hope for life. If not, we are as good as dead."

THE END

Postscript:

The book's illustrator and my companion Jette Salling finally convinced me at the last minute to add this afterthought. While in my old age my attitude towards the human race as a whole has become pessimistic, even misanthropic, I concede that, as our soul mate Leonard Cohen sings: "*There's a crack in everything. That's how the light gets in.*"

Notes:

1. The Chemical Weapons Convention (CWC) is an arms control treaty that outlaws the production, stockpiling, and use of chemical weapons and their precursors. The Organization for the Prohibition of Chemical Weapons (OPCW) is the administrator. The treaty entered into force in 1997. The Chemical Weapons Convention prohibits the large-scale use, development, production, stockpiling and transfer of chemical weapons. Very limited production for research, medical, pharmaceutical or protective purposes is still permitted. The main obligation of member states under the convention is to effect this prohibition, as well as the destruction of all current chemical weapons. All destruction activities must take place under OPCW verification.

   As of April 2016, 192 states had become parties to the CWC and accept its obligations. Israel has not ratified the agreement. In September 2013 Syria acceded to its when agreeing to the destruction of its chemical weapons.

   By 2016, Russia destroyed around 94% of its chemical weapons, planning to completely destroy its remaining stockpile by the end of 2018. On September 27, 2017 Russia announced the destruction of the last batch of chemical weapons, completing the total destruction of its chemical arsenal, ahead of schedule.

   As of January 2018, over 96% of all country declared chemical weapons stockpiles had been destroyed, but the U.S., UK and France still have chemical (and biological and nuclear) weapons. The U.S. says it will destroy its by 2022. https://en.wikipedia.org/wiki/Chemical_Weapons_Convention

   On March 16, 2018, OPCW announced that it had never been notified about Novichok-type nerve agents by any state. But according to Vil S. Mirzayanov, a Russian scientist who defected, the nerve agent does exist, is Russian made and is lethal. "Exactly where, when and by whom these chemicals were made, however, and how and who used them against the Skripals remain unclear, triggering a major international crisis", writes https://theconversation.com/novichok-the-deadly-story-behind-the-nerve-agent-in-sergei-skripal-spy-attack-93562.

   The Conversation website is based in London since 2013 and is supported and funded by UK and Australian universities, the UK ministry of education and the Royal Society.

   However, Anton Utkin, a Russian scientist who worked on the destruction of Russian chemical weapons and was a UN inspector in Iraq, told Russian TV Vesti News that the "Newcomer" is not a poisonous gas, and that the Russian military has never used it. He was interviewed by BBC about this but it then refused to run the interview. SKY TV cancelled its planned interview with him 15 minutes before it was to take place.

BIBLIOGRAPHY

Phil Agee, *Inside the Company: CIA Diary*. Penguin Books, 1975.

William Blum, *The CIA: A Forgotten History*. Zed Books, 1986.
William Blum, *Killing Hope: U.S. Military and CIA Interventions Since World War II*. Common Courage Press, 1987.
William Blum, *Rogue State: A Guide to the World's Only Superpower*. Common Courage Press, 2000.
William Blum, *America's Deadliest Export: Democracy*. Zed Books, 2015.

Noam Chomsky, *What Uncle Sam Really Wants*. Odonian Press, 1986.
Noam Chomsky, *The Culture of Terrorism*. South End Press, 1988.
Noam Chomsky & Edward Herman, *Manufacturing Consent*. Pantheon Books, 1988.
Noam Chomsky, *Deterring Democracy*. Vintage, 1991.
Noam Chomsky, *9-11*. Seven Stories Press, 2001.

Claudia Furiati, *ZR Rifle: The Plot to Kill Kennedy and Castro*, Australia: Ocean Press, 1997. Interviews with Cuban General and chief of intelligence Fabian Escalante Font

Sam & Chuck Giancana, *Double Cross: The Mobster Who Controlled America*. Time Warner Books, 1992.
Anand Gopal, *No Good Men Among the Living*. Metropolitan Books, 2014.

William Hathaway, *Radical Peace: People Refusing War*. Trine Day LLC, 2010.
James Hodges and Linda Cooper, *Disturbing the Peace: Father Roy Bourgeois & Movement to Close the School of the Americas*. Orbis Books, Maryknoll, 2004.

Dan Kovalik, *The Plot to Scapegoat Russia*. Skyhorse Publishing, 2017.

Garry Leech, *Capitalism: A Structural Genocide*. Zed Books, 2012.

Sergo Mikoyan with Svetlana Savranskaya, *The Soviet-Cuba Missile Crisis*. Woodrow Wilson Press-Stanford University Press, 2012.

John Rachel, *The Peace Dividend: The most controversial proposal in the history of the world*. Literary Vagabond Books, 2016.

Douglas Valentine, *The CIA as Organized Crime: How illegal operations corrupt American and the world*. Clarity Press, 2017

ABOUT THE AUTHOR

Uncompromising chronicler and critic of his times, participant and witness, Ron Ridenour is fully the model for what we might call a "people's engagé historian."

Born in the Military Empire, Ron Ridenour rejected the American Dream in 1961, and has since acted as a anti-war, solidarity, and radical activist. He has lived in many countries and worked as a journalist-editor-author-translator for four decades, including for Cuba's Editorial José Martí and Prensa Latina (1988-96). He has published six books about Cuba (*Backfire: The CIA's Biggest Burn* and *Cuba at Sea*), plus *Yankee Sandinistas*, *Sounds of Venezuela*, and *Tamil Nation in Sri Lanka*. His website is: www.ronridenour.com ; email: ronrorama@gmail.com

ABOUT THE ILLUSTRATOR

Jette Salling is a Danish artist. She describes her trajectory as follows:

"My work as a health nurse with both new born and school children and their relations has been to see life begin and be lived. The creative angle follows itself in that pedagogic space...I remember clearly as a small child my favorite place where we lived: a peaceful little corner with my paper, colors and scissors. I am especially fascinated of children's spontaneous strokes before the ruler begins to dominate.

All my life I have been engaged in drawing and painting functions especially water colors. I let the picture take form underway. In this process Goethe's color theory plays a role—his six-colored spheres within a circle: blue/orange, yellow/purple, green/red accentuate light's possibilities.

I am 73 years old and still involved in creativity. These are my first collages/ illustrations for a product that will be seen and read. Cooperating in this way with Ron's book has been exciting."

Made in the USA
Columbia, SC
27 June 2018